ACTING STRATEGI
THINKING CRITICALLY
CONCEPTS, CASES, AND TOOLS FOR BUSINESS STUDENTS

Second Edition

by **Michael J. Merenda, Ph. D.**
University of New Hampshire

cognella® | ACADEMIC PUBLISHING

Bassim Hamadeh, CEO and Publisher
Carrie Montoya, Manager of Revisions and Author Care
Kaela Martin, Project Editor
Abbey Hastings, Associate Production Editor
Miguel Macias, Senior Graphic Designer
Alexa Lucido, Licensing Coordinator
Natalie Piccotti, Director of Marketing
Kassie Graves, Vice President of Editorial
Jamie Giganti, Director of Academic Publishing

ISBN: 978-1-5165-2566-9 (pbk) / 978-1-5165-2567-6 (br) / 978-1-5165-4514-8 (al)

BRIEF TABLE OF CONTENTS

CONTENTS

EXERCISES

PREFACE

Welcome to this second edition of *Acting Strategically, Thinking Strategically: Concepts, Cases, and Tools for Business Students*. The book was developed for the required capstone course in undergraduate and graduate business programs. It is designed to meet AACSB assurance of learning goals and standards. Students will gain a foundation in strategic management and its process, become familiar with various strategy schools, and acquire analytical tools. They will learn to identify the concepts and tools used in strategy analysis, crafting, and execution. They will also learn how to act strategically and think critically by applying concepts and tools to cases, thinking critically exercises, and problem solving. This book is divided into two parts. The eight chapters in Part I provide a foundation in core strategy concepts, strategic schools of thought, analytical tools, and frameworks to help prepare business students to act strategically and think critically. Each chapter contains an opening case and several Thinking Critically exercises. Two types of these exercises are presented: (1) company-specific exercises that emphasize pragmatic real-world challenges, models, or pressing issues and (2) exercises aimed at applying and using strategy concepts as a foil for personal development, managing oneself, and continuous learning. The personal development exercises assume that the strategy concepts and tools used in improving and sustaining organizational performance can be applied to individual continuous learning and self-improvement.

PART I: CHAPTER OVERVIEW

Chapter 1 provides an overview of strategy: its purpose and importance, the basic elements of strategic thinking, criteria for identifying a strategic decision, strategy roots and definitions, types of strategies, open- versus closed-system thinking, emergent versus realized strategy, defining competitive advantage, resource capabilities, business models, as well as a brief overview of five schools of strategic thought (i.e., style, competitive forces, resource-based view, learning, and entrepreneurship schools), the strategic management process model, and what it means to act strategically and think critically. Chapter 2 provides a financial framework for business model evaluation. Several company and stock market ratios and metrics are provided for conducting a strategic financial audit. The formulas, meaning, and rules of thumb for interpreting the ratios are offered. The assumption behind the ratio analysis is that the first step of conducting a case analysis is an assessment of a firm's overall financial health and the effectiveness of its business model. The chapter emphasizes the importance of evidence-based research in case study and student learning by presenting several steps for conducting and analyzing cases. The Thinking Critically exercises in the chapter focus on these steps and offer a framework for students to apply strategy concepts and analytical tools in analyzing and preparing cases. To act strategically and think critically, students need to take an active role—learning by doing. The Socratic method in individual learning, along with applying and actively using strategy concepts, are emphasized. Chapter 3 covers the strategic management process model in greater depth, along with an examination of the style (or design) school of thought, and how to conduct SWOT analysis (strengths, weaknesses, opportunities, and threats), PESTEL (political, economic, social, technical, environmental, and legal) analysis, and a strategic audit at the macro, mezzo, and micro levels of analysis. Chapter 3 also lays out the business case for ethics and corporate social responsibility. It does this by presenting two models of corporate governance: the single-sovereign model, where the firm exists to maximize shareholders returns; and the multiple-sovereign model, where the firm needs to manage and balance the interests of several stakeholders or interested and powerful players that can facilitate or block firm performance. The chapter illustrates how to conduct a stakeholder analysis; it concludes with an overview of the principles of business ethics and sustainable (think "green") business practices.

Chapter 4 focuses on external environmental analysis and strategy crafting through the competitive forces school of strategic thought. This school advances the argument that competitive advantage is earned in the external environment by customer purchasing decisions. The chapter focuses on conducting an external situational analysis through an analysis of Michael Porter's five competitive forces framework (power of customers, power of suppliers, threat of new entrants, threat of substitute products, and competitive intensity of industry rivals) and the PESTEL factors. Industry attractiveness and the firm's position in the industry, its influence on competitive dynamics, and success in exploiting its position (PIE) determines its return on invested capital and ability to create and sustain organizational performance. Among other topics covered are: how to prepare a strategic group map, how to identify industry-driving forces and key success factors, how to assess an industry's exit and entry barriers, industry life cycle analysis and S-curve, experience curves, and customer knowledge.

Chapter 5 covers internal environmental analysis and strategy crafting with a focus on the resource-based school of strategic thought and business-level strategy. This school advances the notion that competitive advantage is earned internally by assessing the firm's ability to develop and nurture heterogeneous tangible and intangible resources. The firm's resource strengths, core capabilities, and distinctive competencies can be nurtured and developed in offering customers a superior (over rivals') value proposition. The chapter shows how to conduct a VIRO (valuable, imitable, rare, and organizational) test, a SPACE (strategic position and competitive action evaluation) analysis, and the Boston Consulting Group's (BCG) product portfolio analysis, as well as how to identify and assess the potential sources of a firm's competitive advantage in the primary and supporting activities within its supply and value chains. Other topics covered in the chapter are the multiple business firm, the conglomerate firm, and benchmarking as a tool for evaluating a firm's products, processes, or strategies.

Chapter 6 focuses on crafting and analyzing corporate-level strategy under varying organizational and environmental contexts. The chapter emphasizes the ongoing challenge strategists confront in maintaining a firm's continuous performance in environments that are in constant flux. Among the topics covered are firm vitality, agility, and adaptability. The chapter shows how to construct a GE/McKinsey spotlight matrix for businesses that operate in several markets. It covers three categories of corporate-level strategies (and several substrategies)—offensive (aggressive growth strategies), maintenance (continue as is or conservative strategies), and defensive (turnaround, harvest, or exit strategies); blue ocean versus red ocean strategies; radically inclusive strategic thinking; exponential growth and accelerated change; advances in telecommunications and information technologies; detablized industry boundaries; and skills for individuals to remain vital and agile.

Chapter 7 covers the strategy implementation, execution, and control steps found in the strategic management conceptual model. The chapter covers the critical role that strategic leaders play in executing strategy and managing organizational change through the learning school of strategic thought. Three kinds of leaders (transactional, charismatic, and transformative) and three types of organizational change (incremental, strategic, and transformative) are discussed, along with strategic intent, the competitive advantage life cycle, and gap analysis. Among the topics covered are: challenges associated with strategy implementation and execution, as well as the importance of properly aligning a firm's new crafted strategies with its vision, mission, goals and objectives, culture. It also focuses on strategic intent organizational structure, customer value creation proposition, and value appropriation proposition. The chapter covers four types of organizational structures and the advantages and disadvantages of each—simple, functional, divisional, and matrix. In addition, Chapter 7 discusses the steps normally associated with managing organizational strategic change and managing high-performance teams. Finally, the chapter identifies what it takes to be a successful CEO in career and in life.

Chapter 8 examines strategy crafting and competitive advantage in the international, entrepreneurial, and social enterprises. It covers going international in the context of Porter's Diamond Model of the competitive advantage of nations. The model looks at four drivers of a nation's competitive advantage: factor conditions (basic roads, natural resources, and higher education, think tanks, advanced information technologies, and telecommunications networks); economic conditions and presence of sophisticated and demanding customers;

related and supporting industries (industry clusters and value chains); and rival strategies and structure. Two other factors contained in the model are chance events and the role local, regional, and national governments play in a nation's competitive advantage. The chapter also examines four archetypical types of strategies for competing across borders: international, multidomestic, global, and transnational. It provides an overview of the advantages and disadvantages of doing business across borders including an assessment of business, political, cultural, and technical opportunities and threats. The second half of the chapter focuses on the entrepreneurship school of strategic thought. The entrepreneurial school is rooted in the "mysteries" of intuition, improvisation, and imagination. It shifts strategic thinking away from precise design, plans, positioning, specialized capabilities, and learning to the creative and visionary mind of the entrepreneur. It assumes that strategy setting and execution require constant creativity guided by inside-the-box, outside-the-box, and where-there-is-no-box-at-all strategic thinking and critical inquiry. Among the topics covered are: the innovator's dilemma, strategy as creative destruction, first-mover advantage, what entrepreneurship is, who the social entrepreneurs are, the not-for-profit organization, how to foster creativity and innovation, choosing the legal form of business ownership, and essential questions for preparing a business plan.

PART II: OPENING CHAPTER AND PART II CASE OVERVIEW

Part II contains eight in-depth strategic management cases. The cases can be assigned for classroom discussion, group work, or take-home exams. All the cases are classroom-tested and contain adequate information for students to apply the strategy concepts and tools found in Part I of the book. Many of the cases build on the Thinking Critically exercises found in Part I and offer instructors the opportunity to use and develop their own thinking critically exercises and questions. Part II contains eight cases all of which can be used for class discussions, group case presentations or individual or group case write-ups, and examinations. The eight cases in Part II include the following:

Case 1. Apple, Inc. 2014 and the Global Smartphone Industry: Despite beating market projections for fiscal first quarter (Q1) results of 2014, Apple, Inc., headquartered in Cupertino, California, disappointed industry analysts and Apple watchers when it reported iPhone sales grew at a 7 percent rate, falling short of Wall Street expectations of a 15 percent increase. Apple's supremacy as the top dog in the fiercely contested high-technology consumer electronics industry, especially in the United States, was under attack. Since 2011, Apple was constantly losing ground to the Android operating system in the battle for smartphone supremacy at home and abroad. Analysts were looking for Tim Cook, Apple's CEO, to quickly act to prevent further market erosion and stem the advances of competitors. *Apple, Inc. 2014 and the Global Smartphone Industry* focuses on the competitive forces school. It highlights Cook's challenges in sustaining Apple's competitive advantage after the death of Apple's founder, Steve Jobs.

Case 2. Half a Century of Supply Chain Management at Walmart: This case looks at the company's sources of competitive advantage in its value chain. Walmart was the world's largest retailer by total sales. Competitors had copied many aspects of Walmart's distribution system, including logistics, IT telecommunications strategy, marketing and merchandising, cross-docking products, eliminating storage time in warehouses, positioning stores around distribution centers, and widespread adoption of electronic data interchange (EDI), RFID, data analytics, as well as global sourcing and collaborative supplier networks. A stock analyst for a large U.S. investment house wanted to determine whether Walmart was still a good investment or if his firm should sell its investment in Walmart based on its recent underperformance and increased competition from online rival Amazon, large grocery chains, and entry of several small-format discount retailers, such as Dollar Tree and Dollar General. The case lends itself to an in-depth VIRO test and internal situational analysis based on the resource-based school.

Case 3. Tesla Motors: Evaluating a Growth Company: Tesla is an interesting entrepreneurial venture case that will attract a great deal of student interest and discussion. The case focuses on Elon Musk, Tesla's CEO and serial entrepreneur, and his company's entry into the premium electric vehicle market. Musk's business model calls for beta-testing his electric vehicle entry with a high-priced roadster (more than $100,000) and then moving down the value chain to middle priced (Model X) and lower priced (Model S) mass-market models. Tesla is burning through cash at an exponential rate. If the company cannot introduce a lower-priced Model S and break even (economies of scale), soon its survivability as a company will be called into question. How much of Tesla's success is dependent on Musk the person and how much of it is dependent on the company's bet that it can change the entrenched business models of traditional automobile manufacturers? Musk is undertaking a risky, large-scale organizational process and product innovation. The case highlights the entrepreneurship school of strategic thought, industry dynamics, stakeholder analysis and value chain analysis, and changing industry dynamics.

Case 4. Volkswagen's Diesel Emissions Control Scandal: This case examines the dark side of management actions that not only violate public trust but also undermine the very fabric of democratic societies. It traces the events and efforts that led VW to evade U.S. carbon emission regulatory standards and the actions undertaken by Mathias Müller, its CEO, to restore profitability and public trust in the company. The September 18, 2015, announcement by the U.S. Environmental Protection Agency (EPA) that VW had cheated emissions testing caused its CEO, Martin Winterkorn, to resign. Winterkorn and Müller denied any involvement in the scandal, blaming it on a few senior engineers. While admitting guilt, the company faced many unanswered questions. Who authorized the cheating, and how high up in the VW hierarchy did knowledge of the cheating go? The case ends with a decision by former chairman Ferdinand Piëch to sell his ownership stake in Porsche Automobile Holdings (PAH), the majority stockholder in Volkswagen AG. Piëch's planned actions could threaten Müller' turnaround strategy. The focus of the case is on business ethics and corporate governance, culture, and change management.

Case 5. Ashokan Center: Fostering Deep Connections: The case chronicles the transition of the Ashokan Center from a public, nonprofit entity under the supervision of the State University of New York at New Paltz to a private, nonprofit, social enterprise dependent on program revenues, grants, and donations. The case focuses on husband-and-wife social entrepreneurs Jay Ungar and Molly Mason, co-founders of the Ashokan Foundation Inc. and Ashokan Center, Inc. Early in 2017, Ungar and Mason and the Center's board faced several challenges. Ungar and Mason were two well-known musicians who had recently taken on the interim management of the Center in response to the sudden departure of its executive director. The Center offered educational and community programming in natural sciences, living history, culture, and music and dance. The case ends with Ungar wondering whether the board's recent actions were radical enough to sustain the Center's financial health and achieve its social and economic missions. The focus of the case is on not-for-profits and social entrepreneurship, corporate governance, and stakeholder analysis.

Case 6. Yahoo!: Are the Parts Greater Than the Sum?: The Yahoo! case is designed to enable students to analyze and assess the problems faced by Yahoo! and its CEO Melissa Mayer. Mayer is under the gun to meet the board's and stockholders' expectations regarding the company's declining sales and profits. In July 2016, Yahoo! announced the sale of its core assets to Verizon for $4.8 billion (all-cash deal). The case describes the events that led to the sale of Yahoo!'s core assets and its management's attempts to revive it before the sale. The case also describes the propositions of activist shareholders to revive Yahoo! There is sufficient information in the case for students to analyze and assess the effectiveness of Mayer's strategic attempts to improve performance, and examine her actions through the lenses of corporate strategy, strategy execution, style, competitive forces, and RBV schools.

Case 7. Xiaomi in China: Struggling with "Cooling" Growth: Xiaomi is a China-based smartphone company founded by Lei Jun in 2010. In a very brief span of five years, it became the leading smartphone company in China, threatening Apple and Samsung as a major industry player. Faced with flattening sales in its home market, however Jun and his company considered expansion into international markets, including gearing up for a launch in the U.S. Was it the most opportune time for the company to venture overseas where behemoths like Apple had a strong presence? Should Xiaomi strengthen its position on its home turf when analysts had started questioning its much-hyped valuation figures? What should be the next course of action for Xiaomi? The case is best suited for international strategy, industry analysis, and corporate strategy.

Case 8. Avon's Turnaround Plans: A Move in the Right Track?: Avon Products Inc., a globally leading beauty products manufacturer and direct seller, had been witnessing many restructuring efforts over the years. Andrea Jung, Avon's CEO, faced declining sales and stiff competition from online and brick-and-mortar industry rivals. In response to declining sales, Jung came up with a multiyear restructuring program but failed to reverse the company's declining sales. In 2012, Jung was made chairman and Sheri McCoy became its new CEO. McCoy is faced with the challenges of improving the performance of Avon, revamping its IT business in Brazil, solving the bribery scandal, and also coming up with a strong strategy to survive in the market. McCoy's efforts to turn Avon around were not well-received by some shareholders who wondered whether her actions would work in the long run. The case focus is on business model evaluation, customer value creation and leading and managing organizational and technological change including e-commerce platforms, industry dynamics, and value chain analyses.

ACTIVE LEARNING RESOURCES FOR STUDENTS AND INSTRUCTORS

The *Acting Strategically, Thinking Critically* second edition comes with several online student active learning resources and faculty resources. These include chapter PowerPoint slides, access to videos that support and supplement chapter opening and Part II cases, Thinking Critically exercises, and chapter concepts, chapter quiz banks, chapter tests, concept and term flash cards, sample syllabi, and case instructor notes for Part II cases. The online resources also include a summary overview of the chapter opening cases and Part II comprehensive cases.

CREDITS

ACKNOWLEDGMENTS

This book has been in the making throughout my academic career. It represents a confluence of several streams of thought and experiences that have nourished and guided my life's work. My students have been the lifeblood that has fueled my learning. To my strategy students: thank you for allowing me into the classroom and for giving me the opportunity to work and learn with you. I am extremely grateful to so many individuals who have helped me throughout the process of writing this book. I would like to thank the Cognella academic team for their encouragement, support, and able assistance: John Remington (Senior Field Acquisitions Editor), Jamie Giganti (Senior Managing Editor), Kaela Martin (Project Editor), Allie Kiekhofer (Associate Production Editor), Rose Tawy (Acquisitions Manager), Brian Fahey (Licensing Specialist), Abbey Hastings, Associate Production Editor, and Faye Delosreyes (Project Editor, Student Online Active Learning Aids). I want to thank my faculty colleagues: Manley Irwin, Art Elkins, Lee Mizusawa, John Ela, and Audrey Ashton-Savage. Lee Irwin has inspired me throughout my academic career. His passion for learning, along with his curious mind, work ethic, and accomplishments have set the example and inspired my writing. I owe my professional career to Art Elkins, my mentor and dissertation chair when I was a PhD student at the University of Massachusetts, Amherst. Art, thank you for guiding and leading me through the doctoral program and for inspiring me to always be curious, to explore, to think, and to enjoy the journey. John Ela used the textbook in his classes and provided valuable insight and suggestions for the second edition, including chapter flow, content, company examples, and student feedback. I am especially grateful to Audrey Ashton-Savage, who skillfully reviewed and edited all the chapters in the first edition. Her encouragement and quick turnaround of chapters were the catalysts that helped make this book possible. Nancy Palmer, my able and diligent administrative assistant, worked selflessly and tirelessly over several years on my draft notes and manuscript, often translating my incomprehensible handwriting. Stephanie Jackman carefully read and edited the second edition chapters and several of the cases included in Part II. Stephanie's editing skills were put to the test with my chapter drafts and the constant changes I made to the text. Stephanie was a joy to work with. I want to acknowledge Mike and Chris, my sons. Their special talents, love of life, and passion have made me more reflective and purposeful in my thinking and actions. I owe so much to my loving wife, Claire. She is the light that guided me throughout the book-writing journey. When I was down, she picked me up, and when I was stuck, she inspired me to move on. This second edition, as with the first edition, has indeed been a new stage in my lifelong educational journey, and she traveled it with me. I am forever indebted to you—thank you.

ACTIVE LEARNING

Throughout the text, when you see this Active Learning icon:

an interactive activity is available to complement your reading.

Your instructor may have customized the selection of activities available for your unique course. Please check with your professor to verify whether your class will access this content through the Cognella Active Learning portal (http://active.cognella.com) or through your home learning management system.

PART 1

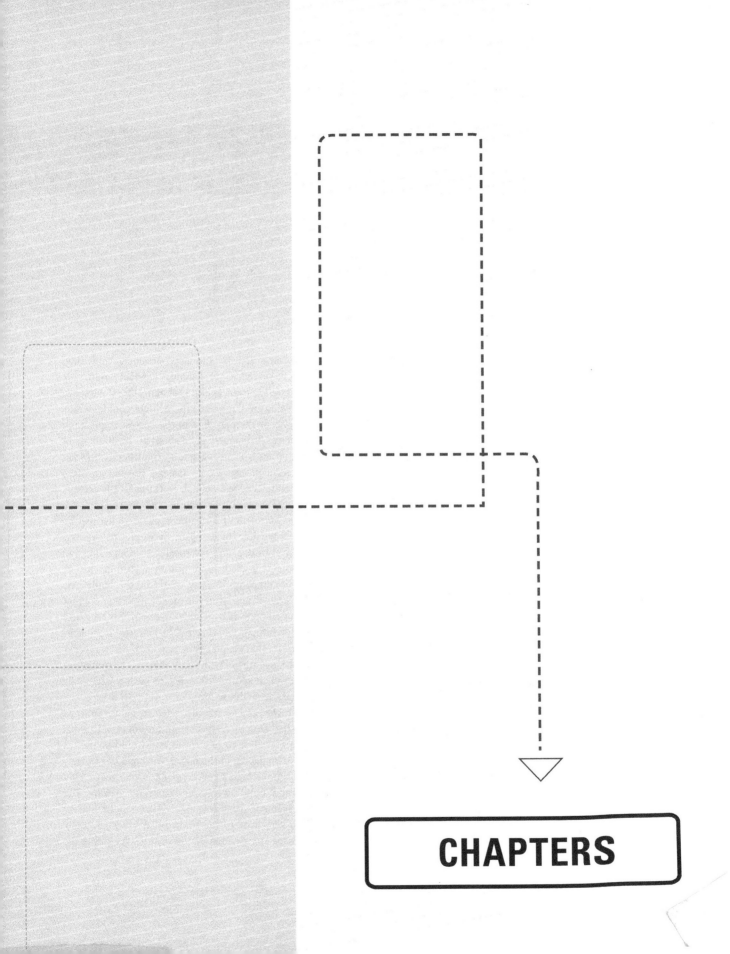

CHAPTERS

CHAPTER 1

STRATEGY CONCEPTS, STRATEGIC THINKING, AND STRATEGIC MANAGEMENT

JIM DONOVAN (A)[1]

Jim Donovan, 37, the new president and chief executive officer of Famous Products, suddenly found himself in the toughest spot of his life. Having just been selected by Omega Corp., a huge conglomerate, to take over as the president of their latest acquisition, Donovan was feeling very good about his position. After growing up on "the wrong side of the tracks," working his way through engineering college, earning an MBA from Harvard Business School, working for 10 years as a management consultant, and for two more years as a successful president of a small company, he felt that he had finally arrived. The company he would manage was known worldwide, had a respectable reputation, and would provide a good opportunity for visibility within the parent company. The pay would be the highest he had ever earned, and while the money itself was not that important (though he'd be able to ensure his wife and four children financial security), he enjoyed the indicator of success that a high salary provided. Jim was eager to manage a company with more than 1,000 employees as the power to accomplish tasks on such a large scale proved very attractive to him.

When Omega had initially selected Donovan, they revealed that Don Bird, the current president of Famous Products, was close to retirement and would be moved upstairs as chairman of the board. Bird had been president of Famous for 22 years and had done reasonably well, steadily building sales and guarding quality. The top management group was highly experienced, closely knit, and very loyal to the company, having held their positions for an extended period of time. As long-term employees, they were not only reported to be good friends of Don Bird, but they also were all in their early 60s and quite proud of the successful record associated with their moderate-sized company. Famous had not, however, grown in profits as rapidly as Omega expected of its operating companies, and Omega's president advised Jim to "grab ahold of Famous and make it take off."

With this challenge ringing in his ears, Jim booked a flight to Milwaukee for his first visit to Famous Products. He had talked briefly with Don Bird to say that he'd be arriving Thursday for half a day and then would be back for good after 10 days at Omega in New York. Bird had been cordial but rather distant on the phone, and Jim wondered how Bird was taking his appointment. "I've only got a few hours here," thought Jim. "I wonder how I should play it ..."

1. INTRODUCTION: QUESTIONS TO THINK ABOUT

- What is a strategic decision?
- What is strategy?
- What is the purpose of strategy, and why is it important?
- What is a business model?
- What are the key elements of strategic thinking?
- What is dynamic strategy?
- How does strategy relate to sustainable competitive advantage?
- What is a strategy school?
- What does the strategic management process entail?
- What is strategic fit? Alignment? Matching?
- What is it to manage oneself?
- Why is it important to think and act like a CEO?

Have you ever wondered what it would be like to be an entrepreneur, president, or CEO of a major company? A Jack Ma, founder and executive chairman of the Alibaba Group; Theo Epstein, president of baseball operations for the Chicago Cubs; or Mary Barra, CEO of General Motors?[2] What were their career paths, and how did they get to be top-tier leadership of successful companies? You are about to embark on a challenging and enriching journey that will take you through the boardrooms and offices of numerous managers empowered with the authority and responsibility for the well-being and health of their respective organizations. In doing this, we ask you to stop and think about what it is you would like to learn and why it is so necessary to study others who have embarked on similar pathways, but usually without the benefit or protection of the classroom. What is it to act like and think like a seasoned CEO or entrepreneur?

The focus of this chapter is introducing the concept of strategy and how it can be applied to the study of organizations and their strategic positioning and management in the 21st century. And, more importantly, how it can apply to your own professional and personal journey throughout your life. By studying strategy concepts and strategy cases, you will begin to develop a richer understanding and appreciation of just what it is like to be a thought leader and seasoned CEO. A strategic manager's primary responsibility is to critically think about and act on the pressing questions and challenges facing the organization. Put simply, do you have an interest in studying or observing the key strategists and decision makers in organizations, as well as why some top managers are consistently recognized as among the best at what they do? Why are some managers the newsmakers and leaders, not only in their own organizations but also in society? Moreover, what exactly is it that these top managers and strategists actually do? What are some of the strategy tools, concepts, and theories available to help them guide and position their organizations for success?

Thinking Critically Exercise 1	JIM DONOVAN (A)

a. Assume you are Jim Donovan. How should Donovan prepare for his first meeting with Don Bird? What questions should he ask Bird? What advice would you give Donovan in anticipation of this initial meeting and his return to Famous 10 days after?
b. Omega is a huge conglomerate. What is a conglomerate? What are some conglomerate strategies? What does Omega's president expect Donovan to do as president of Famous Products?
c. Without knowing why Omega acquired Famous, how should Bird and his managers "play" Donovan's visit? That is, what should they hope to accomplish, and how should they greet Donovan?
d. Donovan, based on his record, appears to be on the fast track to a successful career. What type of career is Donovan pursuing? What are some challenges faced by Donovan as the president of Famous?

1.1 WHY STUDY STRATEGIC MANAGEMENT?

It is evident that, as an area of study, strategic management has come of age. What is more important, however, is that as we advance into the 21st century, strategic management will continue to play a vital role in the competitiveness of organizations, the welfare of society, and the lives of the women and men who make organizational success possible. It is important to study strategy and strategic management because:

- Everyone in the organization needs to play an active, direct, or supporting role in the strategic management of the organization for the organization to be successful
- Understanding what it is to be a more effective and knowledgeable strategic decision maker is important for you personally so that your work performance will be more valued and rewarded accordingly[3]
- Managing strategically better prepares the organization for creating, managing, and exploiting rapidly changing environments
- Managing strategically improves organizational performance

- Managing strategically helps the organization better manage diverse activities that need to be coordinated and focused on for achieving organizational purpose
- Learning to act strategically and think critically can help you in both your career and your life

The study of strategy and strategic management is also important because its primary purpose and focus are on satisfactorily answering the following pressing questions, which all organizations need to ask regularly:

a. What is the overall current financial and strategic health and performance of the organization?
b. What should it be? What might it be?
c. If the financial and strategic health is not what it should or might be, then what strategic actions need to occur to correct the situation?

Failure to recognize and act on these questions in a timely manner puts the organization at serious strategic and financial risk.

1.2 WHY IS IT IMPORTANT TO THINK LIKE A CEO?

The study of strategy is not just about making well-reasoned, thoughtful business decisions. Strategy and strategy concepts can also be applied to managing oneself. Think about the important decisions that you will encounter in your personal life. Decisions about what college you will attend, your major in college, your employment decisions, how you spend your time, and how you allocate your well-earned income all have elements of a strategic decision; that is, what you would like to aspire to in your professional career and in life. Think about the strategic decisions that any business organization constantly faces. History tells us quite a bit about successful businesses and unsuccessful ones. Some of the notable strategic failures include:

- Quaker Oats losing $1.4 billion in Snapple over three years
- Yahoo!'s board turning down a $44.6 billion acquisition offer from Microsoft and then selling to Verizon for less than $6 billion
- Blockbuster passing on buying Netflix, then going bankrupt
- Kodak filing the first patent for a digital camera in 1977 and then filing for bankruptcy in 2012 because it couldn't see past film
- IBM dismissing minicomputers and losing significant revenue
- DEC rejecting PCs, even though it was the first company to introduce minicomputers
- Excite, a search engine, passing on acquiring Google for $250,000
- Decca Records passing on the Beatles because "guitar groups were on their way out"
- Motorola failing to launch a new generation of smartphones, instead leveraging its once highly successful Razr phones. By the time the company released a new line of Razr phones in 2010, Motorola was unable to compete with the Apple iPhone and Android smartphones[4]

Why do businesses (people) make poor decisions? Why do some businesses (people) fail? Businesses or people fail primarily from making poor strategic decisions or choices in life. This could be because of inexperience or incompetence, inability to identify and manage risk, lack of customer focus, inability to handle growth, cash problems, not knowing your business or yourself, and in some cases, just plain "bad luck." All strategic business and life decisions involve risk. Strategic leaders, CEOs, and individuals can lower the risk of a strategic decision by always acting strategically and thinking critically. Unless you do, how can you make good decisions? Employees who think like a CEO advance fast; employees who think and act like a CEO advance even faster. To strategically manage yourself means to act and think like a well-respected, seasoned, and successful

VIDEO 1.1 Tesla CEO Musk Offers Rare Look Inside Model 3 Factory

CEO. Strategy is not just about making and effectively executing critical business, military, or political decisions; it's about making better decisions in business and in life.

2. WHAT IS A STRATEGIC DECISION?

A strategic decision is one that, if not achieved, could seriously affect the long-term viability of the firm. In comparison, a tactical decision affects the day-to-day implementation of actions required to reach the goals of strategy. A strategic decision has at least one of the following characteristics:

- *It involves unusual risk and a high potential for failure.* Think about the risks involved with Elon Musk and his Silicon Valley startup company, Tesla Motors. Starting a new car company from scratch is not often tried in the United States. The last time one was truly successful was about a hundred years ago. Tesla faces some unusual hurdles. Musk not only plans to shift the world over to electric cars through his multibillion dollar startup; he also plans to partner with Panasonic to build advanced lithium-ion batteries at a "gigafactory" in Nevada that could cost as much as $5 billion. He also intends to sell his lithium-ion batteries for use in solar-energy panels. His factory will be larger than the whole of the world's current capacity for manufacturing lithium-ion batteries. There are almost innumerable barriers to the realization of Musk's vision for a sustainable future with electric cars and solar energy. Not the least of these fears are the current low-cost panels and lithium-ion batteries currently being produced in China. He also runs the risk that superior product-technology platforms will make both his lithium-ion batteries and his electric cars obsolete before either venture can achieve economies of scale to lower cost and become profitable.[5]

- *It involves unusual benefits in the event of success.* When Steve Jobs took over Apple Computer Company in 1997, he changed the company name to Apple, Inc. and announced that he was targeting consumers, not just businesses, for his Mac computers and other high-technology products and services. Jobs inspired Apple's consumer products and services including iPhone, iTunes, iTouch, iPad, iStore, iTV, and a host of others. Jobs died in October 2011. At the time of his death, Apple's market capitalization was in the $300 billion market capitalization range (number of common shares outstanding times stock price). Its market capitalization topped $900 billion in November 2017, causing analysts to predict that Apple was on the path of becoming the first trillion dollar company.[6]

- *It involves unusual commitment of critical resources (money, management, physical capacity, and know-how) over long periods of time.* To execute his bold strategies, Musk must commit substantial dollars to factories; professional, technical, and management talent; operating staff; and a wealth of other critical resources. To be successful, Tesla also has to invest in a network of global retail stores and other distribution channels to sell and service its innovative electric cars. The company is unveiling a new network of superchargers—refueling stations that can top off the batteries in its cars in under an hour. So far, Tesla has built a small number of vehicles for the high-end market, but now it wants to go mainstream. To do so, Musk must construct a network of battery-charging stations across the countries where his cars will be sold. In 2013, Tesla sold 23,000 cars. The gigafactory would make enough batteries for 500,000 electric cars by 2020 (it would produce enough batteries annually to store 35 gigawatt hours of electricity, hence the name). Battery companies normally announce factories only after they are funded and a site is selected, and they typically scale up gradually. Not Musk. His commitment to build Tesla Motors, including its gigafactory and physical infrastructure, requires a significant commitment of technical, financial, human, and physical resources.[7]

- *It tends to change the competitive dynamics and nature of industries.* Amazon has transformed several industries as one of the world's most successful e-commerce companies. Under its founder and strategic leader Jeff Bezos, Amazon now rivals Walmart as a discount retail store, Apple as a device maker, and IBM as a data services provider. Bezos's diligence in getting Amazon's strategy right, with his constant focus on monitoring, adjusting, and adapting the company's strategy, has made it the fastest-growing e-commerce company, taking significant market share from rivals. Amazon has also aggressively entered additional markets with a smartphone called Fire, three new Kindle Fire tablets, 8 million square feet of new fulfillment center capacity, and 1,382 newly deployed Kiva robots that roam Amazon's warehouses delivering pallets of products to human workers. Although he does not always get it right the first time or provide short-run profits to Wall Street analysts' satisfaction, Bezos's diligence in monitoring and adjusting Amazon's strategic decisions has transformed the company into an $81.7 billion e-commerce behemoth.[8]

- *It requires leadership at all levels of the organization and ongoing support from everyone in the firm.* General Motors Company's chief executive Mary Barra spent much of her first nine months as CEO bogged down in a scandal over decade-old failures in the company's handling of deadly ignition switch defects. Barra started working for General Motors at the age of 18 as a co-op student in 1980. Nearly 35 years later, in January 2014, she became GM's CEO. During her first year, she issued 84 safety recalls involving more than 30 million cars. Barra now hopes to move past the scandal and GM's decades of weak accountability and profitability, declining U.S. market share, and bankruptcy. A high priority for Barra is changing GM's culture and mindset. Commenting at an investors' meeting, she stated, "I hate the word *culture* … culture is really just how we all behave." She stressed to investors that all GM employees need to behave differently—starting with herself, her top management team, and all GM employees. For GM to be successful, everyone in the company needs to support Barra's plans and vision. Barra was even tough on herself, commenting: "In the past … I was too nice." At a meeting with GM's top 300 executives, Barra explained they could no longer confuse steady progress with winning. She told the executives that GM must do what it takes to be "the world's most valued automotive company," a measure that included customer satisfaction, quality, and financial results. "If you're not in line with this vision," she told the group, "you don't need to be here." The question of how GM will deploy the roughly $39 billion in cash and cash equivalents on its balance sheet to achieve her goals and make it the most valued auto company will require that change and leadership at all levels. Barra's drive to boost profitability will depend on whether she and her top executives change behavior deep in the company's bureaucracy. She noted that GM should be a company where employees go home enthused about a "really cool project" instead of complaining, "I had to go climb Mt. Stupid today to try and get the right thing done."[9]

- *It requires constant monitoring, adjusting, and vigilance to get it right.* It took Gary Hirshberg and Samuel Kaymen (cofounders of Stonyfield Farms, Inc.'s yogurt) and their families nine painful years before the company reached profitability. Gary's wife, Meg Hirshberg, commenting on Stonyfield's road to profitability, wrote:

> We endured countless disasters, mishaps, and near-death experiences. That meant there were countless times we could have rid ourselves of the misery we called a business. Gary and Samuel were overworked and exhausted but determined to persevere. I never had a voice in the decision to carry on, but there were many moments when I was forced to answer the question: Was I in or was I out (in helping the business succeed)?[10]

VIDEO 1.2 Strategy Example: Introduction to busiess strategy

3. WHAT IS STRATEGY?

The word **strategy** and its derivatives (e.g., *strategic, strategically, strategists*) conjure up a lot of different notions, interpretations, and meanings; each of us has our own. A strategic action is distinct from an operational or routine action in that if a strategic action is not achieved, the overall well-being and health of the organization is threatened. If a strategic action is achieved, it provides the organization with the means for improving firm performance.

The word *strategy* is derived from the Greek noun **strategos** (literally interpreted as "the art of the general"). The Greek verb **stratego** means "to plan the destruction of one's enemies through the effective use of resources."[11] These two terms capture the essence of strategy and its enduring value as a key management concept. As a noun, the "art of the general" highlights who is responsible for setting and executing strategy. And the verb *stratego* implies action and forward thinking. "To plan the destruction of one's enemies" lays out the terrain and sets in motion the challenges ahead for the general. Strategy is about the future—to plan and set a direction for an army or an organization. Whether it is to gain political, military, or economic advantage, the essence of good strategy is good management, good leadership, and good execution.

Thinking Critically Exercise 3

WHAT IS A STRATEGIC DECISION?

a. McDonald's announced in April 2015 that it planned to raise wages by more than a dollar per hour and offer employees personal time off for all its U.S. company-owned restaurants. The increase would raise wages for more than 90,000 U.S. employees. Is this a strategic decision or just a salary adjustment? If you consider it a strategic decision, what makes it strategic? If not, why not?

b. In April 2015, General Electric announced that it would be selling or spinning off the bulk of its $500 billion GE Capital business. GE Capital accounted for around half of the company's profits, but it was under pressure from nervous investors who worried about the value of GE's stock. Is this a strategic decision? If so, based on what criteria? How might this decision change GE? How might this decision change the competitive dynamics in the banking and financial services industry? (See http://www.nytimes.com/2015/04/11/business/dealbook/general-electric-to-sell-bulk-of-its-finance-unit.html.)

c. Identify a company that is currently engaged in a major strategic decision or initiative. Identify and explain the characteristics of this strategic decision—that is, what makes it a strategic decision? What's at risk if this decision does not pan out? What's the potential upside to this decision if things do pan out?

In his book *Strategy: A History*, Lawrence Freedman carefully provides an in-depth study of the evolution and development of strategy. Freedman defines strategy as a continuous process for improving organizational performance with no endpoint.[12] In his study, Freedman concludes that strategy is about employing whatever resources are available to achieve the best outcome in situations that are both dynamic and contested. It is about getting more out of a situation than the starting balance of power would suggest. It is the art of creating power.[13]

3.1 FREEDMAN'S THREE BROAD STRATEGY APPROACHES

In *Strategy: A History*,[a] Freedman identifies three broad approaches to strategy that emerged over time. He observes that each strategy approach evolved to help political, military, industrial, and other leaders achieve the best outcome in situations that are dynamic and contested. The approaches he describes are:

I.   ***Strategy as Superior Force Versus Strategy as Guile or Craftiness:*** As seen through the study of Greek classics, confrontations between parties were fought or addressed through strategy as the application of superior force (personified by the heroic Achilles), or guile, the use of seduction (personified by the crafty Odysseus, who conceived the idea of the Trojan horse). Freedman observes that though guile is more seductive because it offers the possibility of cleverness in defeating brute power, he argues that guile alone is overrated, particularly against enemies that are clever as well as strong.

II. ***Strategy as Cunning and Finesse:*** In Sun Tzu's masterful book *The Art of War,* the Chinese general celebrates cunning by arguing that doing the opposite of what your opponent expects ensures victory; and though strategic goals are often best achieved by avoiding the destructive uncertainty of pitched battle, he is quoted as saying, "All men can see these tactics whereby I conquer, but what none can see is the strategy out of which victory is evolved."[b]

Tzu preferred the use of "stratagem and finesse" to defeat an enemy, such as starving one's foe through famine compared to exposing oneself to the risk of battle and "the chance of arms." He forewarned that military should always avoid the destructive uncertainty of pitched battle because depriving or preventing the enemy from using a superior strength or competency in warfare could achieve a winning or superior outcome. Not surprisingly, Sun Tzu's teachings are still used in business schools and military academies today.

III. ***Strategy as Political Negotiation, Bargaining, Military Might, and Science:*** In the late 18th century, largely as a result of the military and political thinking of the Napoleonic wars, strategy became viewed as a way to merge scientific, operational art and the precision of military strategy with the craftiness and skill of a seasoned politician. This concept of strategy is generally considered the main application of business strategy today. As such, strategy became a way of uniting operational art in the military sphere with political objectives. Carl von Clausewitz, the great Prussian general and strategist, described it this way: "War is not merely an act of policy but a true political instrument, a continuation of political intercourse carried on with others."[c]

Freedman concludes in his historical study that strategy is discerning a sensible way to get from one stage (of performance) to the next. With each stage, a new set of problems has to be negotiated before you can move beyond it. He concludes in his masterful book that there is no endpoint when it comes to strategy; strategy is not simply a grander name for a plan. As former professional boxer Mike Tyson painfully discovered: "Everyone has a plan 'til they get punched in the mouth."[d]

---

a   Lawrence Freedman, *Strategy: A History* (New York: Oxford University Press, 2013).
b   "Sun Tzu," Brainy Quotes, http://www.brainyquote.com/quotes/authors/s/sun_tzu.html.
c   "Carl Von Clausewitz," Wikiquote, last modified May 26, 2017, https://en.wikiquote.org/wiki/Carl_von_Clausewitz.
d   Lawrence Freedman, *Strategy: A History* (New York: Oxford University Press, 2013), ix.

Thinking Critically Exercise 4

FREEDMAN'S THREE BROAD STRATEGY APPROACHES

    a. Freedman identifies three broad approaches to strategy. How does the author define or view each strategy approach? Find one business example for each strategy approach. How was the approach used to help improve organizational performance? From a business perspective, is there one approach that is better than another? If so which one? If not, why not?

    b. Find one sports example for each strategy approach. From a sports perspective, is there one approach that is better than another? If so, which one? If not, why not?

    c. Find one political or military example for each strategy approach. From this perspective, is there one approach that is better than another? If so, which one? If not, why not?

Sources: Freedman, Lawrence. "What Is Strategy?" In *Strategy: A History.* New York: Oxford University Press, 2013.; "Why a Strategy Is Not a Plan: Strategies Too Often Fail Because More Is Expected of Them Than They Can Deliver." *The Economist.* November 2, 2013. https://www.economist.com/news/books-and-arts/21588834-strategies-too-often-fail-because-more-expected-them-they-can-deliver-why.; "Sun Tzu: The Art of War." History.com. 2009. http://www.history.com/topics/sun-tzu.

3.2 WHAT CONSTITUTES A GOOD STRATEGY?

Michael Porter defined strategy as what determines corporate performance:

> As a multisport athlete, I was always fascinated with competition and how to win. At Harvard Business School and later at the Harvard Department of Economics, I was drawn to the field of competition and strategy because it tackles perhaps the most basic question in both business management and industrial economics: What determines corporate performance?[14]

Some of the most common observations as to what constitutes a good strategy include:

- Alternative(s) chosen to make a desired future happen, such as achievement of a goal or solution to a problem
- Art and science of planning and marshaling resources for their most efficient and effective use[15]
- A particular set of activities and how they fit together
- A pattern in a stream of decisions[16]
- Creating and sustaining a firm's competitive advantage
- Making choices about what industries to participate in, what products and services to offer, and how to allocate resources[17]
- Positioning an organization for sustainable competitive advantage[18]
- Making choices, trade-offs; it's about deliberately choosing to be different[19]
- An approach for first creating value for customers (value creation) and in turn creating value for the firm (value capture)[20]

Thinking Critically Exercise 5

YOUR FAVORITE COMPANY'S STRATEGY

Do you have a favorite company that you admire for its continued strategic successes? What is the company? Describe the company's strategy in 50 words or less. Explain what it is that you admire about this company.

3.3 WHAT IS THE PURPOSE OF STRATEGY?

We can further understand strategy by how we define it, what its purpose is, and the reasons why so many hours and resources are devoted to getting it right. Good strategy and good execution of strategy drive wealth creation. The primary purpose of strategy is to help strategic managers make informed judgments in anticipation of future success. It is about the decisions, competitive actions, and activities the strategic manager needs to make in the face of uncertain, unpredictable competitive markets. As such, the purpose of strategy is not to eliminate risks in taking strategic actions, but to instead:

- Identify, assess, and understand the nature of risk
- Increase the odds of a favorable outcome
- Help the general manager gain greater control over the firm's external environment than the external environment has over the firm
- Improve organizational performance

4. WHAT IS A BUSINESS MODEL?

VIDEO 1.3 What is a "Business Model"?

Why do entrepreneurs go into business for themselves? Businesses serve a number of economic, social, and political purposes. They drive and sustain economic and social value in society, leading to a higher standard of living and better quality of life for the citizens of a city, state, region, or country. The purpose of a business is to create value of some kind, not just for its owners, but also for customers and others in society. A firm's business model defines and identifies its value creation activities or, in other words, its value proposition. A firm's customers determine whether

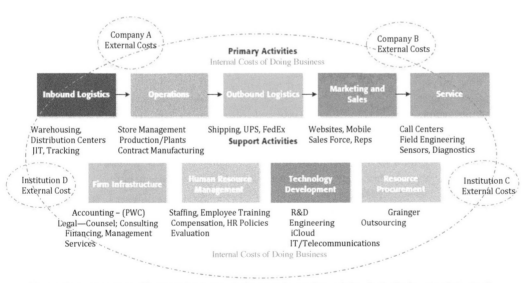

Exhibit 1.1 Value Chain Activities and Internal and External Costs of Doing Business

*Transaction costs cover a wide range of actions and primary and secondary activities in the firm's value chain. A **value chain** is defined as the interlinked value-adding activities that convert inputs into outputs, which in turn add to the firm's top line (revenues) and bottom line (profitability). A value chain shows where and how a firm can create customer value and capture it*

Source: Michael J. Merenda 2018

STRATEGY CONCEPTS, STRATEGIC THINKING, AND STRATEGIC MANAGEMENT   11 a firm's value proposition has value. A **value chain** is defined as the interlinked value-adding activities that convert inputs into outputs, which in turn add to the firm's top line (revenues) and bottom line (profitability). A value chain shows where and how a firm can create customer value and capture it (See Exhibit 1.1: Value Chain Activities and Internal and External Costs of Doing Business).

VIDEO 1.4 The Economics of Uber

4.1 BUSINESS MODEL EFFECTIVENESS AND COMPETITIVE ADVANTAGE

To determine business model effectiveness, examine the firm's profitability and financial health both at a single moment in time and over a longer period (discussed in more detail in Chapter 2). Is the firm's financial performance and health below, equal to, or above the performance and health of its rivals? If the firm's financial health is superior, then there is strong evidence that the firm's customer value proposition is succeeding as it has a superior competitive advantage over its rivals. **Competitive advantage** is when a firm can provide the same value as its competitors at a lower price or charge higher prices by offering greater value through differentiation. Firms employ different business models than their rivals in order to win consumers by providing superior customer value. For example, internet advertising revenues make up the majority of Google's overall revenues and profits. Google's business model and value proposition in the internet advertising e-commerce industry differs from those of Facebook, Amazon, Yahoo, Apple, and others.

Thinking Critically Exercise 6

FINANCIAL SNAPSHOTS

a. Go to your college or university's online databases (or a business publication that reports financial information). Click on a business and economics database link, such as Mergent Online, or a similar service. Find the latest financial information for Starbucks and Dunkin' Brands. Peruse each company's financial statements (income statement and balance sheet or financial highlights) for the past three years. Which company has the superior business model based on its overall financial performance during this three-year time period?

b. Go to your college or university's online databases (or a business publication that reports financial information). Click on a business and economics database link, such as Mergent online, or a similar service. Find the latest financial information for Google, Facebook, and Apple. Peruse each company's financial statements (income statements and balance sheets or financial highlights) for the past three years. Which company has the superior business model based on its overall financial performance during this three-year period? Now what do you think of Yahoo!'s business model and its overall effectiveness?

c. Assume that you received a $10,000 inheritance from a wealthy uncle. The will specifies that you are to buy stock in all three of the following companies: Apple, Inc., Google, Inc., and Facebook. Conduct a brief financial audit for each company. Based on this financial audit, how many shares of each company's stock would you buy, and why? The only restriction in the will is that you need to invest at least 50 percent of the money ($5,000) in one company's shares, and you cannot sell these shares for at least three years.

5. WHAT ARE THE KEY ELEMENTS OF STRATEGIC THINKING?

Strategic thinking is about individuals and organizations trying to make sense of complex, dynamic environments, and relationships.[21] It is reflective and action-oriented, focusing on analyzing, understanding, assessing, and synthesizing information into knowledge.[22] Strategic thinking is a management concept that aids the general manager and students of strategy and management in making informed decisions. It can also have a positive impact on organizations and on one's life. Our definition of strategic thinking includes several elements:

a. **Critical Thinking.** Critical thinking is the art of analyzing and evaluating the thought process with a view toward improving it.[23] The conceptual foundation for critical thinking is **critical theory**. Julia Sloan defines **strategic thinking** as "an intent-driven approach to strategy based on critical theory and supported by a complex cluster of cognitive capabilities that are distinct and different from strategic planning."[24] Critical theory evolved from several different intellectual traditions associated with the meaning of criticism and critique.[25] It was originally derived from the Greek word *kritikos,* meaning "judgment" or "discernment." Critical theory or thinking is based on an epistemological approach to learning. **Epistemology** (referred to as "theory of knowledge") is a branch of philosophy concerned with the nature and scope of knowledge. It questions what knowledge is, how it can be acquired, and the extent to which knowledge is pertinent to any given subject or entity.[26] Critical thinking can be defined as:

> The process of analyzing and assessing thinking with a view to improving it. Critical thinking presupposes knowledge of the most basic structure in thinking (the elements of thought) and the most basic intellectual standards for thinking (universal intellectual standards). The key to the creative side of critical thinking (the actual improving of thought) is in restructuring thinking as a result of analyzing and effectively assessing it.[27]

b. **Mastering Information and Knowledge.** Knowledge is what is understood, known, and generally available to the decision maker. **Knowledge** is the stock of information turned into the know-how used by managers to make decisions with greater certainty.[28] That is, knowledge can reduce uncertainty by identifying and evaluating the nature and degree of risk associated with a strategy or action.[29] Knowledge is tacit and explicit—it is what is already in your head (tacit) and what is written down (explicit). Information turned into useful knowledge is power and can make the difference between an organization's success and failure. **Wisdom** is the creative use of knowledge (See Exhibit 1.2: Data, Information, Knowledge, and Wisdom Pyramid).

c. **Strategic Analysis.** Strategic analysis is a breakdown of the components and elements found in a firm's external and internal environments into understandable, digestible, and workable pieces of information. The input of analysis is data and information. The output is knowledge. Knowledge guides, shapes, and informs the strategic management process. Analysis helps to dissect and map the geographic, temporal, spatial, structural, relational, and behavioral characteristics of the firm's external and internal environments. The goal of strategic analysis is an understanding and assessment of the firm's internal and external environments. Analysis is not a substitute for strategic thinking, but it does help to stimulate, influence, shape, and guide the strategic leader's thinking and actions.

d. **Creativity.** According to Henry Mintzberg, "Strategic thinking, in contrast [to strategic planning], is about **synthesis**. It involves intuition and creativity. The outcome of strategic thinking is an integrated perspective of the enterprise, a not-too-precisely articulated vision of direction ..."[30] **Intuition** is the innate understanding of knowing based on knowledge and experience. **Creativity** is new thought and action—rearranging something that already exists in innovative ways or adopting something completely new. Creativity results in embracing new technologies. Mihaly

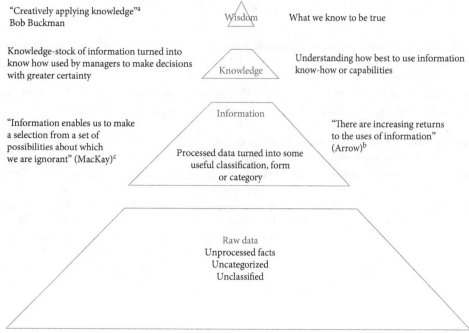

Exhibit 1.2 Data, Information, Knowledge, and Wisdom Pyramid	"Creatively applying knowledge"[a] Bob Buckman	Wisdom — What we know to be true

**Exhibit 1.2
Data,
Information,
Knowledge,
and Wisdom
Pyramid**

"Creatively applying knowledge"[a]
Bob Buckman

Wisdom

What we know to be true

Knowledge-stock of information turned into know how used by managers to make decisions with greater certainty

Knowledge

Understanding how best to use information know-how or capabilities

Information

"Information enables us to make a selection from a set of possibilities about which we are ignorant" (MacKay)[c]

Processed data turned into some useful classification, form or category

"There are increasing returns to the uses of information" (Arrow)[b]

Raw data
Unprocessed facts
Uncategorized
Unclassified

[a]Fulmer, William, F, Case Study: Buckman Laboratories (A) (Harvard Business School Press, 1969)
[b]Kenneth J. Arrow, the limits of organization, (New york, Norton & Company, 1974) 38
[c]D. M. Mackay, *Information, Mechanism and Meaning* (Cambridge, Mass., MIT Press, 1969) 11

Csikszentmihalyi defines **creativity** as "any act, idea, or product that changes an existing domain, or that transforms an existing domain into a new one." He defines **domain** as a set of symbolic rules or procedures.[31] In strategic management, the well-established patterns or behaviors of industry players, along with the conduct and behaviors of firms and their strategic leaders, form the domain in which strategies are crafted, executed, and adapted. Csikszentmihalyi describes a creative person as someone whose thoughts or actions change a domain or establish a new domain. Furthermore, he asserts that a domain cannot be changed without the explicit or implicit consent of a field responsible for it. A **field**, according to Csikszentmihalyi, includes all the individuals who act as gatekeepers to the domain.[32] In strategy, the field of play includes all the individuals who position, influence, and exploit their firms in competitive and dynamic markets. Broadly defined, **technology** is the process by which strategic leaders' creativity transforms labor, capital, materials, and information into new strategies, business models, products or services, processes, and activities aimed at creating customer value. We can view the main elements of acting strategically, thinking critically as an equation:

Strategic Thinking = f (Function) of (a, b, c, and d) = Sense Making

Thinking Critically Exercise 7

YOUR LIFE IN PICTURES

Do you have a mental model of what your ideal "whole" or "big-picture" life would look like in five years, 10 years, and 30 years? Describe in pictures what your life will look like in five years if everything goes according to your social, family, business, and personal aspirations.

6. WHAT IS STRATEGIC MANAGEMENT?

As a discipline, management is classified as a social science. It focuses on the study of behavior of people and the human institutions and organizations they create.[33] Strategic management is the management of the total organization. CEOs or general managers are ultimately responsible for the strategic management of their total organization. Some firms constantly succeed or win because their top managers are good at strategic management and critical thinking. Firms fail for a number of causes, but the biggest reason is poor strategic management—they lack any one or a combination of good management, good leadership, and good execution skills. The study of strategic management is complex. Strategic managers must possess a deep understanding and appreciation of the total organization and the varied and dynamic environmental contexts in which strategic decisions are made and executed. To lead and guide the organization through good and not-so-good times requires the general manager to be forward-thinking and open to change and to have the knowledge, capabilities, and skills necessary to be an effective leader, strategist, and critical thinker. Management scholar Robert Katz defines a skill as "an ability which can be developed, not necessarily inborn, and which is manifested in performance, not merely in potential. So the principal criterion of skillfulness must be effective action under varying conditions of an effective manager."[34] Katz identifies three basic development skills to be an effective administrator (manager):

- *Technical Skills:* An understanding of, and proficiency in, a specific kind of activity, particularly one involving methods, processes, procedures, or techniques. It is easy to identify the technical skills of a data analyst, accountant, musician, and surgeon. For Katz, a technical skill involves specialized knowledge, analytical ability within that specialty, and facility in the use of the tools and techniques of the specific discipline.[35]
- *Human Skills:* These skills primarily focus on working with and relating to people. For Katz, human skills demonstrate an executive's ability to work effectively as a group member and to build cooperative effort within the team he or she leads.[36]
- *Conceptual Skills:* Katz defines conceptual skills as an executive's ability to see the enterprise as a whole. It includes recognizing how the various functions of the organization depend on one another and how changes in any one part affect all the others. It also extends to visualizing the relationship of the individual business to the industry, the community, and the political, social, and economic forces of the nation as a whole.[37]

Bennis and Nanus, two well-known leadership scholars, noted that a business enterprise is not only an economic entity but also a community, possibly the central community of our times.[38] The leader, according to Bennis and Nanus, hopes to unite the people in the organization into a responsible community. They studied successful chief executive officers in 90 businesses and organizations of all types and sizes and found that there seemed to be no obvious pattern for CEO success. The CEOs they studied "were right-brained and left-brained, tall and short, fat and thin, articulate and inarticulate, assertive and retiring, dressed for success and dressed for failure, participative and autocratic."[39] Still, after going over their interviews with the CEOs in further detail and revisiting the CEOs over another two-year time period, they were able to conceptualize four major themes and areas of competencies that all 90 leaders embodied:

- *Attention Through Vision:* Management of attention through vision is the creating focus for a business. All 90 people interviewed had an agenda and unparalleled concern with outcome. Leaders are the most results-oriented people in the world, and results get attention.
- *Meaning Through Commitment:* Leaders have a capacity to relate a compelling image of a desired state of affairs—the kind of image that induces enthusiasm and commitment in others.

- *Trust Through Position:* Trust is the lubrication that makes it possible for organizations to work. Trust implies accountability, predictability, and reliability. As the "glue" that maintains organizational integrity, trust requires knowing where the organization is going and what is right and necessary to get there. It is what sells products and keeps organizations humming.
- *Deployment of Self Through Positive Self-regard:* Positive self-regard consists of three major components—knowledge of one's strengths, the capacity to nurture and develop those strengths, and the ability to discern the fit between one's strengths and weaknesses and the organization's needs.[40]

Other important skills needed to be an effective strategic manager include:

- *Communicative Skills:* Ability to effectively inform, debate, and communicate strategic decisions to and with boards of directors, managers, employees, and other stakeholders.[41]
- *Application Skills:* Ability to demonstrate strategy concept, methodologies, tools, and paradigms that help one's ability to think like a CEO, act strategically, and think critically.[42]

7. HOW ARE STRATEGY AND STRATEGIC MANAGEMENT DYNAMIC?

A **strategic action** is distinct from an operational or routine action in that, if a strategic action is not achieved, the overall well-being and health of the organization is threatened. If a strategic action is achieved, it provides the organization with a **competitive advantage**. The strategic management process is dynamic. The word *dynamics* appears frequently in discussions and writing about strategy, and it is used in two distinct, though equally important, senses. The **dynamics of strategy and performance** concern the "content" of strategy—the initiatives, choices, policies, and decisions adopted in an attempt to improve performance and the results that arise from these managerial behaviors. Secondly, the **dynamic model of the strategy process** is a way of understanding how strategic actions occur. It recognizes that strategic decisions are dynamic—that is, strategy making involves a complex pattern of actions and reactions. It is partially planned and partially unplanned.[43]

Thus, strategy can be viewed as a **deliberate** set of carefully formulated actions and steps with well-defined outcomes or endpoints, or it can be viewed as **emergent or adaptive**, with a set of certain consistent actions or behaviors that form an unintended pattern that was not anticipated in the initial planning phase.[44] For example, though unintended, adopting an emergent strategy might help a business adapt more flexibly to the practicalities of changing market conditions. In a deliberate process, the general manager as strategist operates under a closed-system logic or perspective when making and executing strategy or a strategic plan. In an emergent process, the general manager as strategist assumes an open-system logic or perspective of the firm when making and modifying strategic decisions. A **system** is a set of detailed steps, actions, methods, procedures, and routines created to carry out a specific set of decisions.[45]

7.1 WHAT IS CLOSED- VERSUS OPEN-SYSTEM LOGIC?

Under **closed-system logic,** decisions are analyzed and made within well-defined boundaries that are closed; in other words, they do not interact with the environment or other systems and are not influenced by their surroundings.[46] Under closed-system logic, all decision inputs, outputs, and feedback mechanisms are identified, and strategic decisions maintain a steady, deterministic state despite a changing external environment. Only the components defined within the closed system are significant in the strategic decision-making process.

When an **open-system logic** or perspective is used, general managers make strategic decisions and take continuous strategic actions from a real-world perspective. From this viewpoint, decision boundaries and actions are fluid and open, allowing for constant exchanges of energy, materials, and information within the larger external environment or other systems in which the organization exists.[47] There is an interrelated and interpenetrating nature to strategic decisions and actions. Strategic managers' decisions are not bounded by borders, and they take on different properties—called *emergent properties*—over time. In this sense, strategy formulation and implementation can be viewed as an emergent, adaptive process that requires the ongoing analysis of the external and internal environments, as well as the constant management of information and knowledge used to support and rationalize strategic decisions. As an emergent and adaptive process, initial strategic decisions need to be adjusted and altered with the goal of improved organizational performance. The effective management of this process is important to the organization's long-term survival and success. In terms of process, strategy is viewed as a continual series of decisions and relationships that incrementally move the organization into new areas or ways of doing business; it becomes the ongoing overall management of the organization. Strategies are formed over time, as opposed to being formulated at a point in time from an open-system perspective. Strategic management requires an open-system perspective and consideration of how business actions impact not only internal operations and outcomes (such as costs, sales, and profitability) but also external outcomes—that is, the competitive environment and other social systems in which organizations take part (see Figure 1.1: Open-System Logic).

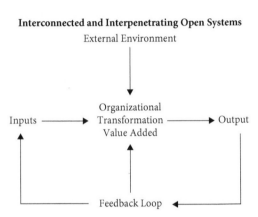

Figure 1.1
Open-System
Logic

7.2 EMERGENT VERSUS DELIBERATE STRATEGY

Henry Mintzberg made a distinction between deliberate strategy and emergent strategy (see Figure 1.2: Deliberate vs. Emergent Strategy).[48] Emergent strategy originates not in the mind of the strategist but in the interaction of the organization with its environment. Mintzberg claims that emergent strategies tend to exhibit a type of convergence in which ideas and actions from multiple sources integrate into a pattern. This is a form of organizational learning; in fact, in this view, organizational learning is one of the core functions of any business enterprise.

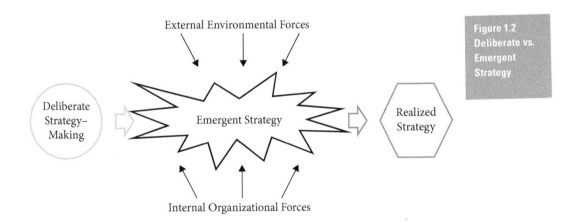

Figure 1.2
Deliberate vs.
Emergent
Strategy

8. WHAT IS STRATEGIC PLANNING?

Strategic planning became prominent in corporations during the 1960s and remains an important aspect of strategic management today. Strategic planning is a process that maps out what future courses of action an organization should take to achieve a desired endpoint. Unlike strategy, there is an endpoint with a plan.[49] A **plan** is something that moves you forward in predetermined steps to a specific desired or planned-for conclusion; strategy, however, does not. A plan specifies the direction, strategies, resources, time frames, responsibilities, and actions needed to achieve a stated endpoint or outcome. A plan may also act as a control mechanism for guiding the implementation of strategy. Strategic planners involve many parties (who conduct research and gather, analyze, and assess data) in order to produce a document that maps out the environment in which the organization is to compete. Strategic planning is also a tool that supports and aids strategic managers in their critical and strategic thinking, as well as strategic management of the organization (see Exhibit 1.3: Three Basic Strategy Concepts: Thinking, Management, and Planning).

Exhibit 1.3 Three Basic Strategy Concepts: Thinking, Management, and Planning

Strategic Thinking: "An intent-driven approach to strategy based on critical theory and supported by a complex cluster of cognitive capabilities that are distinct and different from strategic planning" (Sloan, Julia, *Learning to Think Strategically*, 2nd Ed., Routledge, New York 2014).

Strategic Thinking
Reflective, Interpretive, Knowledge-Driven, Circular, Tacit, Intuitive, Figurative, Conceptual, Rigorous, Metaphoric, Conscience, Sub-conscience, Creative, Innovative Synthesis, Sense-Making Action Focused

Strategic Management is the management of the total organization for competitive advantage. It is the province of an organization's strategic leaders, strategic thinkers and doers acting on behalf of owners and customers.

Strategic Management
Integrative, Across Organizational Units, People and Process Oriented, Action Oriented, Total Organization, Resource Focused, Outcome Driven, Deliberate and Emergent, Open System Logic, Adaptive, Driven by Mental Models

A plan is something that moves you forward in predetermined steps—a strategy doesn't (Freedman, Lawrence, Strategy: A History, Oxford: New York 2013).

Strategic Planning
Deterministic, Future Oriented, Analytical, Formulaic, Numbers Oriented, Scenario Building, Extrapolative, Closed System Logic, Linear, Deliberate, Sequential, Assumptions Driven, Imperfect, End Point Focused

What is Strategy? "It is about employing whatever resources are available to achieve the best outcome in situations that are both dynamic and contested; It is about getting more out of a situation than the starting balance of power would suggest. It is the art of creating power" (Freedman, Lawrence, *Strategy: A History*, Oxford: New York 2013)."

WHAT'S AN OPEN SYSTEM?

Identify and explain which of the following are examples of closed versus open systems. Circle the item(s) that are open systems: nuclear power plant; jet engine; human circulatory system; business organization; business plan; decision-making process; architectural blueprint; gasoline engine; mobile phone; manufacturing plant; ecological system; planet earth; football game.

DELIBERATE AND EMERGENT STRATEGY EXAMPLES

Give one example of a deliberate strategy and one example of an emergent strategy. Why do crafted strategies change over time, and what are some of the driving factors that altered intended or crafted strategies? If we know that crafted strategies change over time, why engage in deliberately crafting strategies?

9. STRATEGIC MANAGEMENT PROCESS MODEL AND STRATEGY ALIGNMENT

Strategic management is as much a philosophy and perspective as it is a well-defined set of activities and actions. The strategic management model can be conceptualized as a seven-step process: Steps 1 and 2 focus on external and internal environmental scanning; Step 3 involves vision and mission; Step 4 deals with goals and objectives; Step 5 emphasizes formulating and making strategy; Step 6 concentrates on strategy implementation and execution; and Step 7 centers on evaluation and strategic control. This process is depicted in Exhibit 1.4: The Strategic Management Conceptual Model. The strategic leader's challenge is to win constantly—that is, to achieve organizational purpose by helping the organization perform at its highest level to continuously deliver customer value. Peter Drucker claimed the most important reason that businesses fail is

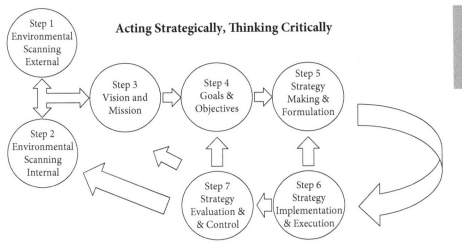

that management did not ask clearly: "What is our business? Who is our customer? What does the customer consider value?" He argues that "an enterprise's purpose begins on the outside with the customer … it is the customer who determines what a business is, what it produces, and whether it will prosper."[50] The purpose of the strategic management process model is to address Drucker's questions.[51]

It is the responsibility of an organization's strategic leaders to oversee the strategic management of the firm. This requires constantly matching and aligning the firm's strategies, resources, actions, and value-creation endeavors to meet customers' wants, desires, and needs. Value is created and achieved through exploiting the firm's intangible and tangible resources, its capabilities, and its distinctive competencies. The firm appropriates value when its customer value-creating activities provide superior revenue and profits (competitive advantage) over its rivals. As such, strategic management is the continuous management of a firm's strategies and resources for competitive advantage. Strategies must be properly aligned and adapted (see Exhibit 1.5: Strategy Alignment). Although strategies are deliberately formed and crafted, external and internal change forces are constantly at work, altering and changing the intended strategies. In reality, intended strategies take on different characteristics as they are constantly adjusted and adapted through the strategic management process. Deliberate and intended strategies seldom mirror or coincide with realized strategies. As such, the strategist's job is to constantly match firm resources with external opportunities and create customer value by exploiting these opportunities. Given that firms operate in dynamic, constantly changing environments, the strategic management process model and strategy alignment require strategic management to be a continuous matching-and-alignment process, rather than a one-time discrete action.

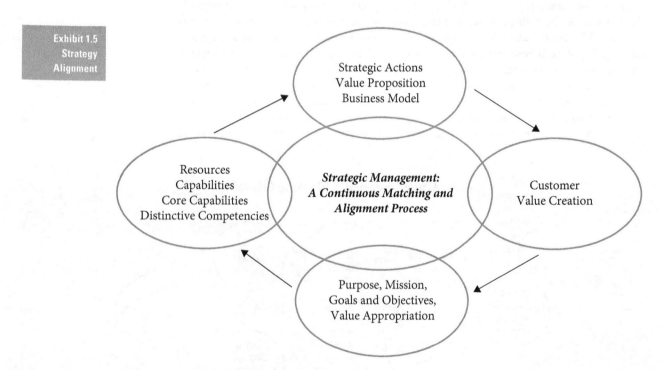

Exhibit 1.5
Strategy
Alignment

10. WHAT IS A STRATEGY SCHOOL?

Strategy schools can help to inform and guide managers' behavior, decision making, and ability to act strategically and think critically. Managers can use strategy schools to help them conceptualize and analyze a firm's external and internal environments. **Strategy schools** offer mental models and normative recommendations or prescriptions for managers' strategic actions, activities, and behaviors (what should be) but are based on positive, descriptive critical inquiry of the real world (what is). A **mental model** is an explanation of someone's thought process about how something works in the real world. It is a representation of the surrounding world, the relationships between its various parts, and a person's intuitive perception about his or her own acts and corresponding consequences. Mental models can help shape behavior and set an approach to solving problems (akin to a personal algorithm) and completing tasks.[52] Jay Wright Forrester defined general mental models as the following: "The image of the world around us, which we carry in our head, is just a model. Nobody in his head imagines all the world, government, or country. He has only selected concepts, and relationships between them, and uses those to represent the real system."[53]

Drucker notes that basic assumptions about reality are the **paradigms** or prevalent general theory of social science. Management is a social science—the study of the behavior of people and human institutions. According to Drucker, assumptions largely determine what the discipline (management and strategy scholars and practitioners) assumes to be reality—what it takes to be true.[54] Assumptions drive management paradigms, mental models, and strategy schools. This textbook covers five of the leading schools of strategic thought: style/design, competitive forces, resource-based view, learning, and entrepreneurial schools (see Figure 1.3: Five Schools of Strategic Thought). The dimensions of the five leading strategy schools can be found in Table 1.1: Schools of Strategic Thought: Basic Assumptions. Although there are many important differences among schools, they are not mutually exclusive but rather intertwined and interdependent.

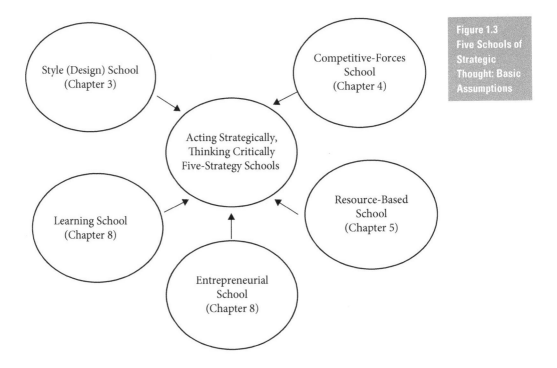

Figure 1.3
Five Schools of Strategic Thought: Basic Assumptions

Table 1.1 Schools of Strategic Thought: Basic Assumptions	Schools	Leading Thinkers	Category	Champion	Intended Message	Realized Message	Analytical Tools
	Style [Design]	Ansoff Drucker Andrews	Prescriptive (Normative)	Case Study Teachers Generalists Harvard Business School	Alignment and Fit Strategy as Intuition Critical Inquiry Evidence– Analytical Design	Strategic Thinking Strategy as Case Study Radically Inclusive Thinking Continuous Improvement	SWOT Case Method Cases Ratio Analysis Stakeholder Analysis PESTEL Analysis Infographics
	Positioning	Porter Sun Tzu "Art of War" Military Strategists	Prescriptive (Normative)	Planners, Consul- tants, Analysts, Economists, Financial Planners	Formal-Analytical Position, Influence, Exploit Strategy as Analysis Evidence Based Critical Inquiry	Calculate, Critical Inquiry, External Situational Analysis Exploit competitive Forces Continuous Improvement	Five Forces Infographics Ratio Analysis S-Curve Experience Curve Strategic Group Map PESTEL Analysis SWOT
	Resource Base View or School	Penrose Hamel, Prahlad Barney	Prescriptive	Organizational Theorists Strategy as Process Sustainable Advantage	Create Value Imitable, Rare, flexible Sustainability Competitive Advantage Evidence Based Critical Inquiry	Adaptability Critical Inquiry Continuous Improvement	(BCG) Product Portfolio Analysis SPACE Analysis Ratio Analysis VIRO Test Value and Supply Chain Analysis SWOT
	Learning	Senge Simon March Life Long- Learners Quinn	Descriptive	People Inclined to Experiment Managing Oneself Problem-Solvers Self-Reflective Thinkers	Continuous Learners Self-Reflection Learn through Experiment Cognitive	Play, Act, Experiment Continuous Learning Continuous Improvement	Problem-Solving Gap Analysis Benchmarking Best Practices GE Spotlight Matrix PEST SPACE Five Forces Ratio Analysis PESTEL
	Entrepreneurial	Schumpeter Timmons Drucker	Descriptive (Positive)	Some Economists Individuals Business Press Entrepreneurship Centers Economic and Community Developers	Envision Creative Visionary Asymmetry Acts Pragmatic	Opportunity Recognition Entrepreneur(s) Parsimonious use of Resources Imagination Creativity Intuition Continuous Improvement	Business Plans Business Proposals Elevator Pitches Business Plan Competitions All analytical tools are available to the entrepreneur Any of the above
	No One Best School	Drucker Combina- tion of All Schools	Descriptive And Prescriptive	Change Leaders Life Long Learners CEOs as Entrepreneurs	Strategy as Change Manage Transitions Organizational Transformation	Strategy is Continuous No End Point in Strategy Crafting and Execution Critical Inquiry	Thinking Critically Thought Provoking Analytical Tools Any of the Above

Sources: Adapted from Vadim Kotelnikov, "Ten Major Strategic Management Schools: A Comparative Analysis," Dimensions of Ten Schools, MIT, Sloan School of Management, Downloaded at: http://1000ventures.com/business_guide/mgmt_inex_stategy_10schools.html; Retrieved 4/15/15

10.1 STYLE (DESIGN) STRATEGY SCHOOL OF THOUGHT

In the 1950s, Andrews, Ansof, Drucker, and others laid the foundation for the style school (also known as the design school) as a conceptual framework and approach for strategy making.[55] The school focuses on the CEO as the person who designs or makes strategy and then forwards it to subordinates for implementation. As such, strategy making is not overly analytical or intuitively difficult to comprehend. Some of the analytical frameworks and decision-making tools and concepts associated with this school are:

- Financial ratio analysis
- Case method
- SWOT template: strengths, weaknesses, opportunities, threats
- PESTEL analysis
- Stakeholder analysis

10.2 COMPETITIVE FORCES STRATEGY SCHOOL

This school (also known as the five forces model, the **industrial organization (IO)** school, and the **positioning** school) is considered to be one of the most dominant conceptual models and analytical tools for strategy making. The school focuses on the attractiveness of a firm's products and services in the industry(s) in which it operates and attempts to address the following question: "What is the market or industry potential for this product or service?" Michael Porter, one of the school's founders and its leading advocate, prescribes structural analysis as a way to answer this question by evaluating industries and competitors.[56] He asserts, "The essence of formulating competitive strategy is relating a company to its external environment."[57] As such, strategy making starts with an analysis of the competitive forces in the external environment. Structural analysis has its roots in classical military strategy and industrial economics. Some of the analytical frameworks and decision-making tools and concepts associated with this school include:

- Company and industry financial ratio analysis
- Industry life-cycle analysis–S-Curve
- Experience curves
- Strategic group map
- Competitive forces analysis
- Entry and exit matrix
- Mobility barriers

10.3 RESOURCE-BASED VIEW (RBV)

The resource-based view (RBV) focuses on an in-depth understanding of the firm's internal tangible and intangible resources, especially a firm's strengths, core capabilities, and distinctive competencies. Advocates of this view assume that firms can deliver and sustain competitive advantage when resources are managed in a way that competitors cannot imitate. Unique or superior resources that are not replicable ultimately become the source of a firm's competitive advantage by erecting competitive barriers for rivals. As such, the RBV takes a decidedly internal view of the firm, one in which people play a critical (if not superior) role compared to other factor inputs and the external environment. Some of the analytical frameworks and decision-making tools and concepts associated with this school are:

- Company and industry financial ratio analysis
- VIRO test (valuable, imitable, rare, organizational)
- Value-chain analysis
- Supply chain analysis
- SPACE analysis
- GE Spotlight analysis
- Product portfolio analysis

10.4 LEARNING SCHOOL

This school of thought largely took shape in the late 1980s and early 1990s—though its conceptual roots are based on the behavioral theory advanced through the seminal organizational research of Simon, Cyert, and March in the 1950s and 1960s.[58] The underlying logic assumes that competitive advantage is built less on controlling resources and commanding people and more on learning. Learning school advocates argue that a firm's competitive landscape is not static with well-defined rules or principles for maximizing behavior but dynamic, constantly changing, hypercompetitive, and unpredictable. These competitive dynamics make it difficult for any firm to sustain its competitive advantage for long. This school operates under the premise that strategists need to create learning organizations that regularly adapt strategies through continuous learning that is retrospective, reflective, and active. Some of the analytical frameworks and decision-making tools and concepts associated with this school include:

- Case method
- Open-system principles
- Socratic method
- Learning disciplines
- Learning by doing
- Experimentation
- Gap Analysis
- Competitive advantage life cycle
- PEST
- VIRO Test

10.5 ENTREPRENEURIAL SCHOOL

The entrepreneurial school argues that strategic managers must be good at both management and innovation. This emphasis on entrepreneurship changes the focus from particular individuals or contexts to the CEO as an entrepreneur and strategic leader. As such, strategic management and entrepreneurship are inseparable concepts. All organizations, no matter their size or context, need to be innovative to sustain performance and survive. Some of the analytical frameworks and decision-making tools and concepts associated with this school are:

- All analytical tools or frameworks found in Chapters 1–8
- Writing a business proposal
- Elevator Pitches–Shark Tank
- Business Plan Competitions and Prizes

11. WHY IS IT ALWAYS IMPORTANT TO ACT STRATEGICALLY AND THINK CRITICALLY?

VIDEO 1.5 How to Think like a CEO and Act like a Leader

We live in exciting and interesting times. Peter Drucker observes that, as we entered the new millennium, the United States transitioned from an industrial-based economy to a knowledge-based economy. He notes, "We should expect radical change in society as well as in business."[59] He continues, "Information will be infinite; the only limiting factor will be our ability to process and interpret information."[60] The knowledge worker will be responsible for productivity improvements by accessing, interpreting, connecting, and translating information into knowledge. The nature of the organization and the nature of competition will be in constant flux. The 21st century will be characterized and driven by disruptive technologies, data analytics, and the rise of knowledge work and knowledge workers.[61] New waves of advanced technologies, the growth in collaborative, distributed, and decentralized networked enterprises will destabilize traditional supply chains, flatten organization hierarchies, disrupt or annihilate industry boundaries, shorten product one-cycles, hasten product obsolesce, and change the nature of work and the way we work. Drucker observes that "success in the knowledge economy comes to those who know themselves—their strengths, their values, and how they perform." He asks, "How will you stay mentally alert and engaged in a career that could span a 50-year working life?"[62]

A recent study conducted by McKinsey Global Institute reported that automation and A.I. (artificial intelligence) have the potential to increase the nation's productivity by .08 to 1.4 percent over the 1.2 percent annual rate.[63] In the 1990s, nonfarm productivity grew 2.2 percent per year. Why is this important to businesses and to you personally? The wealth and welfare of a nation or region are heavily dependent upon the competitiveness of a nation or region's industries. Industry competitiveness is based on its firms' ability to create and sustain competitive advantage. Competitive advantage is achieved through productivity improvements. Productivity improvements are accomplished through constant innovation and advances in technologies. Automation and advances in A.I. present a "double whammy," not only to the enterprise but also to the men and women whose livelihoods depend on them. Automation and A.I. have a significant impact on job creation and job loss, not only for blue-collar workers but also for their white-collar counterparts. The McKinsey study estimated the overall automation potential for each sector of the U.S. economy based on the job-related activities performed. The automation potential (from a low of 27 percent for the educational services sector to a high of 73 percent for the accommodation, food services sector) are graphically displayed in Exhibit 1.6: Automation Ahead. The activity that has the lowest potential for automation across all sectors was managing people, followed by using expertise (decisions, creative tasks), except for retail trade, agriculture, and automation/food service sectors; and interacting with people, except for agriculture, transportation, and accommodation/food services. (Both of the last two categories had less than or equal to 30 percent automation potential.)

How does one stay relevant in an age of dynamic and constant change? To remain significant, individuals must act and think like a strategist and effective CEO; that is, they must act strategically and think critically. Sloan identifies several cognitive capabilities in strategic thinking. Effective strategic thinkers must demonstrate an ability to be popular, reflective, divergent, nonlinear, panoramic, critical, metaphoric, abstract, A-rational, conceptual, intuitive, creative, symbolic, and generative.[64] Maxell, in his book *How Successful People Think,* states, "Strategic thinking can make a positive impact in any area of life."[65] He also identifies five benefits of strategic thinking:

1. Strategic thinking simplifies the difficult.
2. Strategic thinking prompts you to ask the right questions.

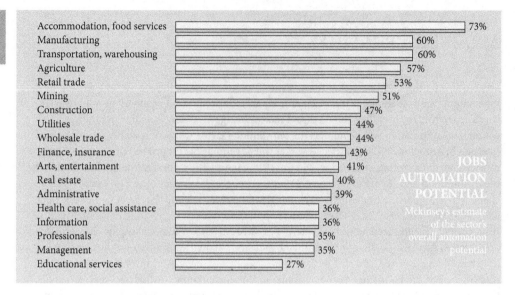

Accommodation, food services	73%
Manufacturing	60%
Transportation, warehousing	60%
Agriculture	57%
Retail trade	53%
Mining	51%
Construction	47%
Utilities	44%
Wholesale trade	44%
Finance, insurance	43%
Arts, entertainment	41%
Real estate	40%
Administrative	39%
Health care, social assistance	36%
Information	36%
Professionals	35%
Management	35%
Educational services	27%

JOBS
AUTOMATION
POTENTIAL
Mckinsey's estimate
of the sector's
overall automation
potential

3. Strategic thinking prompts customization.
4. Strategic thinking prepares you today for an uncertain tomorrow.
5. Strategic thinking reduces the margin of error.[66]

11.1 MANAGING ONESELF

The ability to act strategically and think critically goes hand in hand with the ability to constantly mange oneself. It requires continuous learning and an aptitude to be ready for new opportunities and challenges as they arise. For eminent management scholar and philosopher Peter Drucker, managing oneself starts with asking the right questions:

- *What are my strengths?* Most people, according to Drucker, know what they are not good at, but they do not always know what they are good at. He suggests that one way to better understand what you are good at (what your strengths are) is to a conduct a feedback analysis for a major or significant decision in your like. When you make a key decision or take a crucial action, write down what you expect will happen. Sometime later, compare what you expected would happen with what actually happened. The feedback analysis helps to identify what you are good at doing, what worked, and what did not work. He advises individuals to always try to align themselves where their strengths can produce results.[67]
- *How do I perform? How do I get things done?* How you perform (your strengths and capabilities) are unique to you. To help you determine how you perform, it is important to know how you learn. Do you learn by reading? By listening? Are you a copious note taker? Or do you learn by doing or by practical experience? How you learn reveals a lot about how you acquire, process, and retain knowledge. It also tells you what your strengths are and how you apply them.
- *What are my values? What values do I hold dear?* Personal values are those beliefs that legitimatize your behavior. They are the motivation behind how you use your time. What do you enjoy doing? What are you passionate about? What motivates you? Drucker cautions, "To work in an organization whose value system is unacceptable or incompatible with one's own condemns a person both to frustration and to nonperformance."[68]

- *Where do I belong?* According to Drucker, knowing your strengths, how you perform, and your values will help you figure out where you belong. Are you good with people, or with numbers? Will you do well as an accountant, marketer, human resource specialist, manager, entrepreneur, or CEO?
- *What should I contribute?* Answering this question requires knowing answers to three additional questions: What does the situation require? Given my strengths, my way of performing, and my values, how can I make the greatest contributions to what needs to be done? What results have to be achieved to make a difference?[69]

JIM DONOVAN (B)[70]

Thinking Critically Exercise 10

When Donovan pulled up to Famous Products's headquarters in his rented car, he noticed the neat grounds and immaculate landscaping. To his surprise, Don Bird, dressed in a very conservative blue business suit, black tie, black shoes, and white shirt, met him at the door. He peered at Donovan through old-fashioned steel-rimmed glasses and said, "Welcome to our plant. You're just in time for our usual Thursday morning executive meeting. Would you like to sit in and meet our people?" Donovan, thinking that the meeting would give him a chance to observe the management group in action, readily agreed. He planned to sit back and watch for as long as he could. Donovan was ushered into the most formal meeting room he had ever seen. A long heavy table, with 12 high-backed chairs around it, dominated the dark-paneled room. Seven of the chairs were filled with unsmiling executives in dark suits.

Bird led Donovan to the front of the room, indicated an empty chair to the left of the head of the table, and sat down in the place that was obviously his. Turning to the group, he said, "Gentlemen, I want you to meet Mr. Donovan, but before I turn the meeting over to him, I want you to know that I do not believe he should be here. I do not believe he's qualified, and I will give him no support. Mr. Donovan?"

a. Why do you think Bird took the position he did in introducing Donovan at the board meeting? Do you think that Bird had an obligation to inform Donovan about the board meeting? Why or why not?
b. Now how should Donovan "play it"? What should he say, and how should he respond to Bird's comment and to the rest of Bird's management team?
c. What type of change do you suspect is needed at Famous: incremental, significant, or transformative? Why?
d. What type of leadership style do you believe might fit with the type of change required at Famous?
e. What should Donovan say to Bird after the meeting? To Omega's president when he travels back to New York?

12. REFLECTION

This chapter provided an overview of strategy: its purpose and importance, the basic elements of strategic thinking, criteria for identifying a strategic decision, strategy roots and definitions, types of strategies, open- versus closed-system thinking, emergent versus realized strategy, defining competitive advantage, resource capabilities, business models, as well as a brief overview of five schools of strategic thought (i.e., style, competitive forces, resource-based view, learning, and entrepreneurship schools), the strategic management process model, and what it means to act strategically and think critically. Strategy has been embraced implicitly and explicitly as an important concept throughout the ages. Whether it's military, political, social, business, or personal strategy, it is an essential, if not critical, factor in determining success or failure. Strategy is the glue that ties the firm to its internal and external environments. Knowledge allows this glue to take hold. Leaders create or capitalize on opportunities as they initiate, manage, craft, and implement innovative strategies to exploit opportunities. The strategic leader's challenge is to constantly win—to perform at the highest level.

Strategy is no longer just the domain and responsibility of those residing at the top of an organization. In order to win and improve organizational success, everyone in an organization must be actively involved in the strategic management process by playing either a leading or supporting role. According to Drucker, an organization is really its people—specifically, their knowledge, capabilities, and relationships.[71]

Understanding strategy concepts and what it means to act strategically and think critically is important to organizational and individual success. As we advance into the 21st century, strategic management will continue to play a vital role in the competitiveness of organizations, the welfare of society, and the lives of the women and men who make organizational success possible. Unlike a plan, there is no endpoint to strategy. Strategy is about trying to work out, in a sensible way, how to constantly get from one stage of organizational (or individual) success or performance to the next stage as new challenges arise and circumstances change. Strategy is crafted, implemented, executed, and adapted from an open-system perspective. With each stage, a new set of problems must be negotiated in order to move beyond it. Strategy is not simply a grander name for a plan cast from closed-system logic; rather, strategies emerge and need constant adjustments. Emergent strategies coalesce and converge around new ideas, innovations, and actions from multiple open systems forming consistent patterns. The strategic management process is a form of organizational learning, one of the core functions of any business enterprise. From the perspective of organizational learning, strategists must create learning organizations that regularly launch new strategies based on retrospection, reflection, and sense making. That is, to be successful in dynamic, constantly changing environments and circumstances, strategic managers must act strategically and think critically. They can partially do this through active learning, problem solving, and continuously conducting the strategic management process.

| Thinking Critically Exercise 11 | JIM DONOVAN (C)[72] |

Mind racing and heart pounding, Donovan stalls by smiling broadly at Don Bird and then slowly looks around the room. "*Why don't I smoke a pipe so I could fiddle with it and look wise?*" he thinks ironically to himself. Then, "*Son of a bitch, I'm going to win; I'm going to make sure that the people in this room know that I'm going to lead.*" Folding his arms across his chest and sitting up very straight, Donovan turns to Bird, says, "Thank you, Don," and swivels back towards the others: "I'm delighted to be here this morning, even though some of you probably do not share my enthusiasm. I realize all of you may not be with me. Given the success of Famous Products, it is presumptuous of me to think that you know I'm qualified to lead you; we'll let time tell on that score. In the meantime, I'm looking forward to getting to know all of you well and working with you to make this great company even greater in the future."

Then, determined to not only take charge and establish his leadership but also to show his humanity, Donovan proceeds to tell some nonthreatening facts about himself: he is married, has four kids, is Catholic, and the like. He then concludes by saying, "I hope in the days ahead we become good friends—colleagues—and I will try not to let you down." Then he turns back again to Bird, says, "You lead for a while," and sits back to observe.

What he saw over the next two and a half hours made him feel worse and worse. The meeting seemed to have no point, discussion was superficial and rambling, and only low-level operating details were discussed. Near the end of the meeting, one of the executives, Ed Walker—the only one who appeared to be younger than 60—raises his hand and is called on by Bird. Flushing visibly, and with a voice quivering with emotion, Walker faces Donovan and says, "Jim, I do not understand what kind of a man you are. If you are so good, why didn't you stay with your last company? We don't think we need you; why do you think you can help us?"

Smiling once again, while rapidly thinking to himself, "*He's attacking me, not my qualifications. What kind of a person am I? Am I really pure and doing the right thing? What would General Patton, a great leader, have done now? Oh, hell, you have to be a bit Machiavellian if you're going to be powerful ...*" Donovan readies himself. Taking a deep breath, and looking Walker right in the eye, Donovan says, "Thanks for getting it right out on the table, Ed. It's important that I know how you feel. I hope in the days ahead we get to know each other."

Then the meeting ends. "*That was the most boring, useless meeting I have ever attended,*" thinks Donovan. "*They were right in sacking Bird, and the treasurer is a basket case. Holy Hanna, is this going to be a big headache!*" Just before Donovan leaves that day, Bird takes him aside and says, "Why don't you have a word with Ed Walker?" Musing to himself about great leaders always thinking of the organization's welfare and appreciating Bird's concerns, Donovan finds Walker in his office and reassures him—once again looking him right in the eye—"I see that you're a person who has never uttered a word you didn't believe."

Finally, as hurries to catch his plane, Donovan is stopped by the beer-bellied sales manager. "I'm sorry for the way things went at the meeting, Jim." "Don't feel sorry," replies Donovan, adopting the hearty voice and warm manner key in relating to sales types. "Famous Products is a great company, and I'll see you in 10 days!"

a. Why do you think Walker reacted as he did? What is your assessment of Donovan's actions and responses regarding Bird and Walker? What does this say about Donovan's leadership style and ability to lead Famous?

b. What are some of the strategic and leadership challenges Donovan faces as Famous's new president? How should Donovan play it when he gets back to Omega? What should he report back to Omega's president?

c. Now how should Donovan plan for his return trip to Omega? What should he do, look for, and accomplish in his first weeks on the job? After three or four months on the job? His first year on the job?

d. It certainly appears that Donovan has both strategy-making and strategy-executing challenges ahead of him at Famous. What are the some of the challenges, and what advice would you give him as the president of Famous Products?

e. What type of career development and self-reflection should Donovan engage in as he readies himself for the next step up the corporate ladder? How might Donovan's experience at Famous help you think critically about your career choices and career development?

FREEDMAN'S LEVEL AND TYPES OF STRATEGY

Thinking
Critically
Exercise 12

In his book,[a] Freedman identifies several levels and types of strategy including:

a. *Strategy as Force.* Personified by military strategy and illustrated in some forms as game theory accounting for the rise of asymmetric warfare today. Game theory is a study of strategic decision making. Specifically, it is "the study of mathematical models of conflict and cooperation between intelligent rational decision-makers."[b] Game theory applies to a wide range of behavioral relations

a   Lawrence Freedman, *Strategy: A History* (New York: Oxford University Press, 2013).
b   "Game Theory," Wikipedia, last modified November, 10, 2017. https://en.wikipedia.org/wiki/Game_theory.

and has developed into an umbrella term for the logical side of decision science. Asymmetric warfare describes a conflict in which the resources of two belligerents differ in essence in the struggle, interact, and attempt to exploit each other's characteristic weaknesses. Such struggles often involve strategies and tactics of unconventional warfare with the weaker combatants attempting to employ strategy to offset deficiencies in quantity or quality. The U.S. war on terrorism and its engagement with Al Qaeda and ISIS can best be described as asymmetric warfare where conventional U.S. military doctrine is waged against unconventional strategies and tactics of what would seem to be weaker or inferior terrorists' forces. This is in contrast to symmetric warfare, where two powers have similar military power and resources and rely on tactics that are similar overall, differing only in details and execution.[c]

b. *Strategy from Below.* This strategy examines several forms of political strategy that, according to Freedman, can embody 19th-century professional revolutionaries like Karl Marx who saw himself as the general staff of the downtrodden. A more current example is economist-turned-social activist Muhammad Yunus, who founded Grameen Bank as a way to raise destitute women above poverty. Through Grameen Bank and his social activism, Yunus changed people's mindsets regarding social business and social entrepreneurship, not just for the rich but also for the poor in society. Grameen Bank has given millions of impoverished women the means to make something of themselves.[d]

c. *Strategy from Above.* Strategy from above examines the development of strategy in business, mainly as a late-20th century phenomenon. In this approach, the general manager is accountable for leading, designing, and executing strategy with the main goal of constant improvement in organizational performance.

Sources: Freedman, Lawrence. "What Is Strategy?" In *Strategy: A History.* New York: Oxford University Press, 2013.; "Why a Strategy Is Not a Plan: Strategies Too Often Fail Because More Is Expected of Them Than They Can Deliver." *The Economist.* November 2, 2013. https://www.economist.com/news/books-and-arts/21588834-strategies-too-often-fail-because-more-expected-them-they-can-deliver-why.; "Sun Tzu: The Art of War." History.com. 2009. http://www.history.com/topics/sun-tzu.

---

c   "Asymmetric Warfare," Wikipedia, last modified November 16, 2017, http://en.wikipedia.org/wiki/Asymmetric_warfare.
d   Muhammad Yunus, *Building Social Business* (Philadelphia: Perseus Books Group, 2011), 17–18, 65–66.

FREEDMAN'S LEVELS AND KINDS OF STRATEGY

a. The United States is at war with Al Qaeda and ISIS. What is different about asymmetric warfare versus conventional warfare where superior force is the principle military doctrine (strategy)? How has ISIS used the internet to wage war? How has it utilized the news media? Where is ISIS obtaining its human, financial, and technical resources?

b. Freedman identifies three approaches to strategy. Which of the three approaches exemplifies the tactic used by the United States to fight ISIS? How is the U.S. military using this approach?

c. Can you think of any business examples where a larger company with superior resources fell victim to a much smaller competitor? How did the smaller competitor gain a superior competitive advantage over its much larger rival?

CHAPTER ENDNOTES

1. Cohen, Allan R. and Michael J. Merenda. "Jim Donovan (A)." Durham, NH, 1979.
2. Colvin, Geof. "World's 50 Greatest Leaders." *Fortune* (April 1, 2017).
3. Thompson, Arthur A. *Strategy: Core Concepts and Analytical Approaches*, 3rd ed. Burr Ridge, IL: McGraw-Hill Education, 2014–2015.
4. Power, David. "What Are Examples of Bad Strategic Business Decisions?" Accessed November 29, 2017. http://dssresources.com/faq/index.php?action=artikel&id=318.
5. Korosec, Kristen. "Details Emerge about Tesla's Nevada Gigafactory Deal." *Fortune* (September 5, 2014): http://fortune.com/2014/09/05/details-emerge-about-teslas-nevada-gigafactory-deal/.
6. Bemis, Tom. "Almost Two-Thirds of Apple's $900 Billion Market Cap Came After Steve Jobs Died." Wall Street Journal, November 8, 2017: https://www.thestreet.com/story/14383898/1/almost-two-thirds-of-apple-s-900-billion-market-cap-came-after-steve-jobs-died.html
7. Korosec, Kristen. "Details Emerge about Tesla's Nevada Gigafactory Deal." *Fortune* (September 5, 2014): http://fortune.com/2014/09/05/details-emerge-about-teslas-nevada-gigafactory-deal/.
8. Bensinger, Gregg. "Amazon Fires Up a Smartphone for Shopping." *Wall Street Journal*, June 19, 2014: B5.; Gottfried, Miriam and Dan Gallagher. "Amazon's Smartphone: Where There's Fire, There's Smoke." *Wall Street Journal*, June 19, 2014: C10.; Bensinger, Gregg. "Amazon's Spending Leads to Biggest Quarterly Loss in 14 Years." *Wall Street Journal*, October 23, 2014: https://www.wsj.com/articles/amazons-spending-leads-to-another-loss-1414095239
9. White, Joseph B. "GM Hopes to Shift Gears After Recall." *Wall Street Journal*, September 29, 2014: https://www.wsj.com/articles/gm-to-shift-gears-set-new-goals-1412036113
10. Gitttell, Ross, Matt Magnusson, and Michael Merenda. "Chapter 13, Case: Strategic Mission–Driven Sustainable Business: Stonyfield Yogurt." In *The Sustainable Business Case Book*. Irvington, NY: Flatworld Knowledge, 2013.
11. "Strategos." Wikipedia. Last modified September 10, 2017. https://en.wikipedia.org/wiki/Strategos.
12. Freedman, Lawrence. *Strategy: A History*. New York: Oxford University Press, 2013.
13. Ibid.
14. Jain, Naveen. BrainyQuote. Accessed August 31, 2014. https://www.brainyquote.com/search_results.html?q=jain.
15. Porter, Michael E. "What Is Strategy?" *Harvard Business Review* 74, no. 6 (1996): 61–78.
16. Mintzberg, Henry. *The Rise and Fall of Strategic Planning*. New York: The Free Press, 1994.
17. Porter, Michael E. "What Is Strategy?" *Harvard Business Review* 74, no. 6 (1996): 61–78.
18. Ibid., 61–78.
19. Ibid., 61–78.
20. Michel, Stefan. "Innovation Isn't Worth Much if You Don't Get Paid for It." *Harvard Business Review* (2014): 80.
21. Mintzberg, Henry. *The Rise and Fall of Strategic Planning*. New York: The Free Press, 1994.
22. Ibid.
23. Paul, Richard and Linda Elder. *A Guide for Educators to Critical Thinking Competency Standards*. Tomales CA: Foundation for Critical Thinking, 2005.
24. Sloan, Julia. *Learning to Think Strategically*, 2nd ed. New York: Routledge, 2014.
25. "Critical Theory." *Wikipedia*. Last modified October 31, 2017. https://en.wikipedia.org/wiki/Critical_theory.
26. Ibid.
27. Paul, Richard and Linda Elder. *A Guide for Educators to Critical Thinking Competency Standards*. Tomales CA: Foundation for Critical Thinking, 2005.
28. Arrow, Kenneth J. *The Limits of Organization*. New York: W.W. Norton & Company.
29. Bell, Housel. *Measuring and Managing Knowledge*. New York: McGraw-Hill/Irwin, 2001.
30. Mintzberg, Henry. "The Rise and Fall of Strategic Planning." *Harvard Business Review* (1994): 107–114.
31. Csikszentmihalyi, Mihaly. *Creativity: Flow and Psychology of Discovery and Invention*. New York: Harper Perennial, 1996.
32. Ibid.
33. Drucker, Peter. *Management Challenges for the 21st Century*. Harper Collins, 1999.
34. Katz, Robert L. "Skills of an Effective Administrator." *Harvard Business Review* (1974): https://hbr.org/1974/09/skills-of-an-effective-administrator.
35. Ibid.
36. Ibid.
37. Ibid.
38. Bennis, Warren and Burt Nanus. *Leaders: The Strategies for Taking Charge*. New York: Harper and Row, 1985.
39. Ibid.
40. Barnard, C.I. *The Functions of the Executive*. Cambridge, MA: Harvard University Press, 1968.; *The Functions of the Executive: 30th Anniversary Edition*. Cambridge, MA: Harvard University Press, 1971.
41. Katz, Robert L. "Skills of an Effective Administrator." *Harvard Business Review* (1974).
42. Mauffette-Leenders, Louise A., James A. Erskine, and Michiel R. Leenders. *Learning With Cases*. Ontario Canada: Richard Ivey School of Business, 1997.
43. Porter, Michael E. "Towards a Dynamic Theory of Strategy." *Strategic Management Journal* 12 (1991): 95–117.
44. Mintzberg, Henry and James A. Waters. "Of Strategies, Deliberate and Emergent." *Strategic Management Journal* 6, no. 3 (1985): 257–272.
45. Thompson, J.D. *Organizations in Action*. New York: McGraw Hill, 1967.
46. Ibid.
47. Ibid.
48. Mintzberg, Henry and James A. Waters. "Of Strategies, Deliberate and Emergent." *Strategic Management Journal* 6, no. 3 (1985): 257–272.
49. Freedman, Lawrence. *Strategy: A History*. New York: Oxford University Press, 2013.; Mintzberg, Henry. *The Rise and Fall of Strategic Planning*. New York: The Free Press, 1994.
50. Edersheim, Elizabeth Hass. *The Definitive Drucker*. New York: McGraw-Hill, 2007.
51. Ibid.

52. "Mental Model." Wikipedia. Last modified September 20, 2017. https://en.wikipedia.org/wiki/Mental_model.
53. Forrester, Jay W. AZ Quotes. http://www.azquotes.com/quote/762527.
54. Drucker, Peter F. *Managing in a Time of Great Change.* New York: Penguin Putnam, 1995.
55. Ansoff, H. Igor. "Competitive Strengths and Weaknesses." In *Business Strategy: Selected Readings,* edited by H. Igor Ansoff, 189–190. New York: Penguin Modern Management Readings, 1978.; Ansoff, H. Igor. "Critique of Henry Mintzberg's The Design School: Reconsidering the Basic Premises of Strategic Management." *Strategic Management Journal* 12 (1991): 449–461.
56. Porter, Michael E. *Note on the Structural Analysis of Industry.* Boston, MA: Harvard Business School, 1975.
57. Ibid.
58. Simon, H.A. "A Behavioral Model of Rational Choice." *Quarterly Journal of Economics* (1955): 99–118.; Cyert, R.M. and J.G. March. A *Behavioral Theory of the Firm.* Englewood Cliffs, NJ: Prentice-Hill, 1963.; Mintzberg, H. *Strategy Safari: A Guided Tour Through the Wilds of Strategic Management.* New York: Free Press, 1998.
59. Edersheim, Elizabeth H. *The Definitive Drucker.* New York: McGraw-Hill, 2007.
60. Ibid.
61. Drucker, Peter F. "The Future That Has Already Happened." *Harvard Business Review* (1997): 20.
62. Drucker, Peter F. "Managing Oneself." *Harvard Business Review* (1999): 66.
63. Rapp, Nicholas. "Automation Ahead: Last Byte." *Fortune* (2017): 96.
64. Sloan, Julia. *Learning to Think Strategically,* 2nd ed. New York: Routledge, 2014.
65. Maxell, John C. *How Successful People Think.* New York: Center Street, 2009.
66. Ibid.
67. Drucker, Peter F. "Managing Oneself." *Harvard Business Review* (1999): 66–67.
68. Ibid., 70.
69. Ibid., 70–71.
70. Cohen, Allan R. and Michael J. Merenda. "Jim Donovan (B)." Durham, NH, 1979.
71. Edersheim, Elizabeth H. *The Definitive Drucker.* New York: McGraw-Hill, 2007.
72. Cohen, Allan R. and Michael J. Merenda. "Jim Donovan (C)." Durham, NH, 1979.

CHAPTER 2

CRITICAL INQUIRY, BUSINESS MODEL EVALUATION, AND CASE STUDY

VIDEO 2.1 Joseph's
Gourmet Pasta
- Corporate
Introduction

JOSEPH'S GOURMET PASTA AND SAUCES: AT A CROSSROADS[1]

Joe Faro, founder and CEO of Joseph's Gourmet Pasta and Sauces, Inc. (JGP&S) of Haverhill, Massachusetts, had just come from a meeting with his top management team. It was already a very long day, something that Faro was accustomed to. Sales appeared to be recovering from a decline experienced during the first quarter of 2011, but there was disagreement as to the direction the firm should take and not even the slightest agreement on the cause of the downturn in sales. Faro wanted to come to a decision concerning the future direction of his company and do it reasonably quickly. He did not like the feeling of waiting for others to act and force a decision on him. As he prepared to leave for home, Faro wondered what his next moves should be:

> I want to spend more time with my wife and three kids, but I want to continue with this company. My dad is still working with his bakery, even expanding, slowly. I could go forever, but priorities change. It's been almost two decades at least for the way I run this … . It will run very well up to probably $50 million, but from $50 million to $70 million is where the challenges started to come. My facility is reaching 80–85 percent of current capacity, which is a sweet spot with good margins, but

to expand, I need to be more strategic than operative, not just make next week work ... the strategic piece really suffers.[a]

JOSEPH'S HISTORY

Faro founded Joseph's Gourmet Pasta and Sauces in 1995, shortly after graduating from college with a degree in business. The company initially produced traditional pasta as an extension of Faro's father's bakery business. Faro experienced little success selling this product for the restaurant industry until he met a chef at a restaurant north of Boston. The chef agreed to let Faro try to supply him with lobster-stuffed ravioli. Faro said, "The chef took pity on me. I had been trying to sell pasta to him for several months. I experimented for several days until I felt that I was able to replicate the chef's ravioli." The product was produced and frozen on the unused top floor of the bakery. The chef approved the product and agreed to purchase it from Joseph's. Faro offered a price that was lower than the cost for the chef to produce it himself. The chef was also happy to relieve himself of the tedious task of making the stuffed ravioli. Faro proceeded to sell his stuffed ravioli to a variety of restaurants, from Boston to southern New Hampshire, making the pasta in the morning and delivering it to his customers in the afternoon.

The business grew steadily over the next two decades as he added new customers, restaurants, and an independent food distributor to handle his product. Faro noted that when he could no longer produce enough products to supply his customers, he began searching for ways to automate the production. He traveled to Italy to personally observe the best practices for making and producing pasta. In order to learn how to inject whole chunks of lobster or vegetables into his pastas, he visited Ben and Jerry's manufacturing plants to see how it injects whole chunks of chocolate, fruits, and other ingredients into its ice cream without melting or changing the ice cream's texture. He combined the best production practices and procedures of several other industries to develop his own automated manufacturing processes. In 1997, he hired his former college roommate, Dave Robinson, to help bolster sales. Robinson convinced Faro to expand into both restaurant-chain sales and wholesale clubs such as Costco and BJ's. Sales continued to increase throughout the next two decades. The continued growth caused the company to move, several times, into larger facilities. In the early years, growth was at least 25 percent per year. Joseph's continued to grow by expanding its product line, coverage in geographic area, and the types and numbers of customers served.

In 2006, Faro approached the owner of his largest competitor (La Romagnola, a Florida-based firm) to see if an acquisition was a possibility. The owner, who had recently come to the United States from Germany, proposed a merger instead. Faro, however, felt the owners' management styles were too different to manage together. Two years

---

a   All quotes and comments contained in this case were from a May 2008 interview with Joseph Faro, founder of Joseph's Gourmet Pasta and Sauces, interview by Michael J. Merenda, William Naumes, and Margaret Naumes, University of New Hampshire, Durham, NH, May 2008. © 2015.

later, with La Romagnola facing large losses, the owner approached Faro about selling La Romagnola. After serious negotiations, Faro acquired La Romagnola. The acquisition was primarily to secure distribution in the southeastern region of the United States and to gain access to a large national restaurant chain headquartered in Florida. The acquisition, along with internal organic growth, brought Joseph's sales to more than $34 million by the end of 2009. By the end of 2010, sales and profits had increased to more than $40.8 million and $6.2 million, respectively. Financial results for the years 2006–2010 are presented in Exhibit 2.1: JGP&S Income Statement and Exhibit 2.2: JGP&S Balance Sheet.[b] Faro noted that the company had experienced 52 consecutive growth quarters through the end of 2010. January 2011 was different, however. He explained, "This one month, we were off 14 percent. We will be off about 6 percent for the quarter. The second quarter will be better. We made a decision to pull back. We were doing too many things."

JOSEPH'S SPECIALTY PASTA MARKETS AND INNOVATION

Joseph's produced an expansive line of high-end, frozen stuffed pasta as well as a smaller line of frozen appetizers. The products were frequently tailored to the individual needs of the customers. Although there was a "generic" line of products sold to small restaurants, chains, and wholesale clubs, many of the larger chains had insisted on a look that was unique to their restaurants. Faro had been able to design individual tools to stamp out the pasta shells to make them different for each of these large customers. He won over the customers by inviting them to his plant and demonstrating in a small laboratory how the product would be formed in a large-scale setting. Faro noted, "People ask why we spend so much on a pilot plant that doesn't add to capacity. When we bring in potential customers, they get sold by seeing us produce their product in that lab. We see this as one of the most profitable parts of the company. In the long run, we make more money out of the lab than anywhere else." By 2006, Joseph's had five chefs on staff performing R&D under the direction of Faro and his vice president of culinary and manufacturing operations.

Faro designed the production process to mimic the way chefs made the products by hand. He explained, "We put real pieces of lobster in the ravioli. Actually, we are one of the largest processors of lobster in the country. We have our own processing plant in eastern Canada." Joseph's also employs stuffing consisting of ingredients other than lobster, including several types of cheese, chicken, mushrooms, shrimp, and other food products. The company also produces other forms of pasta shells in addition to ravioli. Joseph's initial market segment of small, local restaurants was served through independent regional food distributors. Faro and Robinson sought out one or two of the best distributors in every region they entered. They believed that though Joseph's had the best product on the market, convincing new restaurants to switch to them from their distributors was difficult. Robinson noted, "Distributors are very loyal to their suppliers, until these suppliers do something seriously wrong." Although Joseph's had secured some suppliers outside of the East, other parts of the country were not well represented, including the West, Southwest, and Northwest.

Large restaurant-chain accounts were developed and serviced by Joseph's in-house sales staff and managed by Robinson and Faro. These accounts were supplied either through the distributors or directly from the company facility. A third segment encompassed large warehouse clubs (including BJ's and Costco) that were typically members-only facilities. A fourth segment, supermarket sales, was abandoned in late 2003, primarily because it had been an expensive division to enter and maintain due to its being a commodity-driven business.

COMPETITION AND INDUSTRY TRENDS

Joseph's main competition was composed of many local pasta makers who had revenues in the $1 million to $3 million range. Most of these competitors produced products manually for local markets. Some competitors

---

b   LOC = line of credit. Source: Joseph's Gourmet Pasta and Sauces, Financial Statements.

had expanded regionally to the $5 million to $7 million range by trying to replicate Joseph's product lines and technologies and by capturing some regional restaurant chains. These competitors, according to Faro, were also still producing manually, with labor costs anywhere from two to four times Joseph's. Joseph's salespeople closely tracked these rivals, regularly sending information back to Faro. Faro believed that though they were competing with Joseph's, they were also helping to spread the word about specialty pastas. He cautioned that these smaller firms were still trying to determine how Joseph's had managed to lower its costs by automating its manufacturing process. Some of Joseph's major customers were pressuring Faro to share his production methods with them, but he refused because he considered this his "magic sauce" and intellectual property. Protecting his technology from being copied by rivals, however, was becoming more and more difficult as Joseph's double-digit growth accelerated. The small companies were lacking in innovation (Faro believed that his company was at least a year ahead of them), but this gap was closing. Faro knew that one of his largest customers (who had asked Faro to provide a second source for Joseph's product) had teamed up with one of the smaller regional rivals to replace a significant amount of Joseph's product for the first quarter of 2011. Although none of the rest of his customers had followed this pattern, he noted that, even with Joseph's cost, some potential customers had expressed concerns about Joseph's being the sole source of his specialty pastas. Faro was being forced by some of the larger restaurant chains and wholesale clubs to lower Joseph's prices so they could increase their profit margins or lower their retail prices.

Joseph's had managed to stay under the radar of big food processing companies, but this changed with the La Romagnola acquisition. Faro noted, "The big food companies now know that we are here, but so far they have not entered our markets." These larger companies dominated the high-volume, lower-priced end of the frozen pasta market. They concentrated on lower-priced, mass-produced, and mass-marketed frozen foods and were unable to successfully enter the higher-quality, higher-priced specialty pasta segment. Faro also saw a change in consumer tastes toward more healthy food options, especially with emerging natural and organic specialty foods.

NATURAL AND ORGANIC FUNCTIONAL FOODS

By 2010, U.S. organic and natural food was a $26.7 billion industry.[c] Natural food and functional food (herbal supplements, vitamin and energy drinks, and dietary remedies) were rapidly expanding from a few specialized health-food stores to becoming a staple on supermarket and retailer shelves, as well as popular menu options in some restaurant chains.[d] Standard and Poor's reported that more and more consumers expected their food and drink, in addition to tasting good, to be low in calories and offer other health benefits as well.[e] In response to this trend, major food companies began to refocus their best product lines and acquire recognized brands to encourage innovation in new areas for growth with higher profit margins. In 2010, the Organic Trade Association (OTA) reported that U.S. organic- and natural-foods sales grew 7.7 percent over 2009 and represented a 4 percent share of the $673 billion U.S. food industry.[f] Beginning in 2002, the North American organic-food industry experienced major structural change. Large food companies who primarily mass-produced and mass-marketed their food products—such as Nestlé, General Mills, Kraft, Dean, Pepsi, Kellogg's, and Cargill—were caught off guard by the rapid growth of the natural and organic markets.[g] In 2010,

c   "US organic industry valued at nearly $29 billion in 2010," *Organic Trade Association*, accessed May 2012, http://www.organicnewsroom.com/2011/04/us_organic_industry_valued_at.html.
d   "Organic Market Analysis," *Organic Trade Association*, accessed May 2012, http://www.ota.com/organic/mt/business.html.
e   Graves, Tom and Easter Y. Kwon. "Foods & Nonalcoholic Beverages: Industry Survey," *Standard & Poor's*, June 9, 2011, http://www.standardandpoors.com.
f   "Organic Market Analysis," *Organic Trade Association*, accessed May 2012, http://www.ota.com/organic/mt/business.html.; "Organic Production," The United States Department of Agriculture, http://www.ers.usda.gov/data/organic.
g   "Organic World: Global Organic Farming Statistics and News," *FiBL*, accessed November 23, 2015, http://www.organic-world.net/index.html.

mass-market retailers (mainstream supermarkets, club/warehouse stores, and mass merchandisers) sold 54 percent of all organic food.[h]

MANAGEMENT TEAM

As Joseph's product lines and sales continue to grow, Faro has maintained all the company's management roles. In 1998, Tom Bean, vice president of administration, was hired as Faro's accountant, and later Faro added other administrative responsibilities as well. Although Faro maintained his charge of production, research and development, and some of the large national sales accounts, he continued to occupy overall control of financial decisions. Both Bean and Robinson became concerned that Faro was not spending enough time and resources developing his management team. Faro agreed that this was a problem after experiencing some difficulty with the La Romagnola acquisition. Faro relied on his management team to keep him in check, stating, "I can find myself fixated on issues; these people are paid to say no and are free to state their concerns." In 2003, Dave Gillen, Joseph's production supervisor, was made vice president of culinary operations and manufacturing; he, along with Bean and Robinson, was paid incentives based on sales and profit goals.

Faro believed that his most productive time period was the early morning when he spent time alone in his office. The founder regularly came in before the rest of his management team, often arriving at 4:30 a.m. However, much to Bean and Robinson's dismay, Faro continued to exercise influence over all parts of the business. Faro explained, "I get the work habits from my father. He was always at the bakery and had his fingers, literally, in everything. We both want to control everything." Although Faro was the majority owner of the company, several family members also held small stakes in the company; however, only Faro's top management team members had been given stock options.

OPTIONS

Faro felt there were still considerable growth opportunities available for his company. After all, Joseph's had been a prime mover, making specialty pasta a main entrée on many restaurant-chain menus, and had successfully penetrated upper-scale, high-end restaurants. As specialty pastas were now offered at many high-end restaurants, providing attractive margins on their menu entrees, Faro no longer considered frozen specialty pasta as just a side dish or appetizer. Accordingly, he and Robinson maintained that many of their best customers saw Joseph's as the leading brand name for specialty pastas. By early 2008, no customer accounted for more than 17 percent of Joseph's sales. Because of this, Faro expected any future acquisitions to further diversify Joseph's customer base.

He did not consider the consumer trend toward low-carbohydrate diets and natural and organic foods as detrimental to company sales. Although Faro also believed that low-carbohydrate diets were more of a fad, he still had concern about the growth in all-natural and organic foods. Correspondingly, he instructed Joseph's R&D group to not only begin working on low-carbohydrate options but also investigate sourcing natural and organic ingredients for its product lines. Faro was also keenly monitoring the recent trend toward gluten-free pastas and other gluten-free food items. Smaller, more innovative food-processing companies were leading the way with gluten-free products. Consequentially, gluten-free food options were beginning to appear on restaurant menus and supermarket shelves. Despite this, both Faro and Robinson maintained that high-end frozen specialty pasta products would continue to experience growth in the company's critical restaurant market. Faro also did not believe that any of Joseph's current rivals posed a serious threat to the company or its markets. He did, however, see potentially serious threats to his company's market with the entry of some of the major food companies. A few of the larger ones and some major investment bankers approached Faro in regard to selling his

---

h   "US organic industry valued at nearly $29 billion in 2010," *Organic Trade Association*, accessed May 2012, http://www.organicnewsroom.com/2011/04/us_organic_industry_valued_at.html.

company. Faro knew that some of his rivals were also engaged in discussion with these potential suitors. He felt that the company was really at a crossroads. Accordingly, Faro outlined several strategic options:

- Aggressively try to grow on their own through internal expansions of the product lines and acquisition. (Faro believed that there were several small companies selling products similar to his, but they were selling to markets where Joseph's was not strong.)
- Take some time to stabilize their current position by building a stronger management team and adopting some better management systems and procedures, and then grow at a reasonable rate while maintaining their strong margins.
- Explore selling the company. Selling would provide some of the private investors and management team with an opportunity to cash out, thus earning a good return on their hard work and investment in the company. It would also provide Joseph's with the needed funds to substantially grow the company and stave off rivals.
- Explore taking on additional private-equity investors with the goal of moving the company public with an IPO (initial public offering). (Joseph's was still regarded as too small to seriously consider this option on its own. Private-equity investors and an IPO would provide Joseph's with the needed funds to substantially grow the company and stay ahead of rivals.)

In Thousands (000)	2006	2007	2008	2009	2010
Net Sales	13125	17730	21593	34688	40841
Cost of Goods Sold	8210	7441	9380	15343	18584
Gross Profit	**4915**	**10289**	**2213**	**19345**	**22257**
Operating Expenses					
Indirect Manu. Expense	—	3638	4395	5623	7128
Selling Exp.	2090	2146	2702	5717	5725
G&S Expense	1449	1595	1983	3502	2858
Total Operating. Expense	**3539**	**7379**	**9080**	**14842**	**15711**
Income From Operations	**1367**	**2910**	**3133**	**4503**	**6546**
Other Income (Expenses)					
Loss on Property Abandon	280	—	—	—	—
Interest Expense	266	461	353	444	359
Interest Income	−45	−49	−35	−40	−23
Total Other Expenses	501	412	318	404	336
Pre Tax Income	**875**	**2498**	**2815**	**4099**	**6210**

Exhibit 2.1 JGP&S Income Statement

Source: Joseph's Gourmet Pasta & Sauces, Financial Statements.

In Thousands ($000)	2006	2007	2008	2009	2010
Current Assets					
Cash	44	30	133	33	695
Accounts Receivable	1350	1180	1978	3054	2725
Inventory	1428	1908	1973	4826	5017
Prepaid Assets	146	342	149	146	333
Total Current Assets	**2968**	**3460**	**4232**	**8059**	**8770**
Property, Plant & Equipment (PP&E)					
Gross PP&E	7100	7693	8807	10127	11622
Accumulated Depreciation	−1184	−1847	−2601	−3480	−4642
Net PP&E	5916	5846	6206	6647	6980
Intangible Assets	233	221	209	198	186
LT Notes Receivable	653	531	458	1604	810
Other LT Assets	886	752	667	1802	996
Total Assets	**9770**	**10058**	**11105**	**16508**	**16746**
Working Capital LOC*	845	1037	0	769	941
Accounts Payable	1597	613	1684	1938	1781
Accrued Expenses	108	313	369	646	601
Total Current Liabilities	**2550**	**1963**	**2053**	**3353**	**3323**
Long-Term (LT) Liabilities					
Long-Term Debt	5349	4729	4090	5812	3830
Deferred Income Taxes	31	58	69	65	113
Total LT Liabilities	5270	4787	4159	5877	3943
Total Liabilities	**7920**	**6750**	**6212**	**9230**	**7266**
Shareholders Equity (SE)					
Common Stock	20	20	25	600	605
Retained Earnings	1830	3288	4868	6678	8875
Total Stockholders' Equity	**1850**	**3308**	**4893**	**7278**	**9480**
Total Liabilities & SE	**9770**	**10058**	**11105**	**16508**	**16746**

Exhibit 2.2 JGP & S Balance Sheet

*LOC = Line of Credit
Source: Joseph's Gourmet Pasta & Sauces, Financial Statements.

Faro believes that he was "almost selfish" in how he managed the company. He admits that he has neither an exit strategy nor diversification strategy, and he is not ready to retire. Although Faro had no personal debt in the company, he did not want to plunge the company into significant debt. He believed that to get this company to $100 million in sales, he needed an additional $15 million to $20 million in debt or equity. Faro reported with concern: "We have seen costs creep up on us. In the past we were able to keep costs and margins the same … do I stay with all my equity tied up in this business or do I sell?"

    a. What is Joseph's strategy? What is Joseph's business model and value proposition? Take a look at Joseph's financials in Exhibits 2.1 and 2.2. Does Joseph's have a below-average, average, or above-average competitive advantage? What standards or assumptions did you use making your assessment of JGP&S's competitive advantage?
    b. Faro is the protagonist or main decision maker in the case. Again, without conducting any in-depth analysis, what is your assessment of Faro's ability to think critically and act strategically? What inferences did you make that allowed you to arrive at this conclusion?

1. INTRODUCTION: QUESTIONS TO THINK ABOUT

"Any road will get you there, if you don't know where you are going!"[2]

- What is a business model?
- What is critical inquiry?
- What is a case?
- Why are cases important as a learning tool?
- How can case study help critical inquiry and strategic thinking?
- What is elegant analytical design?
- What is the student's role in case study?
- What is the instructor's role in case study?
- How does case study help enhance written and oral communicative skills?
- What are the benefits of case study?

This chapter presents, explains, and discusses the science and art of thinking critically, critical inquiry, and case analysis. Cases are commonly used in the study of strategy, strategic management, and decision making. Strategic management is one of the most important courses in a business curriculum. Its aim is to help form an understanding and appreciation of the total organizational context of decision making in varied organizational and environmental contexts through the lens of the general manager. Given this aim, the student's learning through cases is focused on studying general managers and their roles and responsibilities as strategists, strategic managers, and decision makers. Qualities necessary for general managers in their roles as chief strategists include:

- *Conceptual* (big picture): The ability to identify the dynamic, interrelated, and interpenetrating complexity of the organization and the environments in which it functions
- *Technical or Analytical* (breaking down the big picture into meaningful, digestible parts): The ability to make sound and informed judgments based on an analysis of the organization and the environments in which it functions
- *Human or Behavioral* (people skills): The ability to work collaboratively, cooperatively, and productively with others toward a common purpose or outcome
- *Communicative:* The ability to effectively send and receive information

- *Application:* The ability to use conceptual, analytical, behavioral, and communicative skills to effectively manage, engage, and advance an organization[3]

Source: Katz, Robert L. "Skills of an Effective Administrator." *Harvard Business Review* (1974).

2. WHAT IS A BUSINESS MODEL?

A **business model** is an abstract representation of a product, process, function, organization, market, network, or other business activity. For example, architects build tangible or physical scale models as representation of a structure to study aspects of an architectural design or to communicate design ideas to clients, committees, and the general public. Afuah describes a business model as "a set of activities which a firm performs, how it performs them, and when it performs them so as to offer its customers benefits they want and to earn a profit."[4] The process of business-model construction is part of business strategy. At their core, all business models address one basic question: *How will the organization create, deliver, and sustain value to its customers?*[5] Baden-Fuller and Morgan define the business model as "a system that solves the problem of identifying who is (or are) the customer(s), engaging with their needs, delivering satisfaction, and monetizing the value."[6] They identify three main purposes for constructing business models. First, these models can describe different kinds and types of businesses. (Baden-Fuller and Morgan note that this is critical in trying to study organizations analytically.) Second, business models can be shorthand descriptions of how firms operate. (In this role, business models are used to ensure that there is strategic fit across activities.) Third, business models can be employed to depict or describe how the organization will function.[7]

2.1 BUSINESS MODELS AND VALUE CREATION

As mentioned previously in Chapters 1 and 2, a firm's **business model** defines and identifies how it will generate revenues and profits.[8] The business model also provides the economic justification that drives a firm's **value proposition**—the mix of goods and services, price and payment terms, and other amenities offered by the firm to its customers. A firm's customers determine whether its products, services, prices, and other amenities have value. According to Drucker, the main purpose of a business is to "provide value to the customer—to provide something that an independent and knowledgeable outsider who can choose whether or not to buy is willing to get in exchange for his or her purchasing power."[9] As such, a firm's business model details the economics of the firm. **Business economics** in its broadest sense defines how an organization procures, manages, and allocates its resources and capabilities to create a competitive advantage. It includes the value added by the organization and how it decides to compete in its choice of strategy. The business model identifies a firm's cost of doing business or its transaction costs within its value chain. **Transaction costs** cover a wide range of actions and activities in the firm's value chain. A **value chain** is defined as the interlinked value-adding activities that convert inputs into outputs, which in turn add to the firm's top line (revenues) and bottom line (profitability). A value chain shows where and how a firm can create customer value and capture it.

2.2 HOW DO YOU KNOW IF A COMPANY'S BUSINESS MODEL IS WORKING?

The most obvious answer to this question is to look at the firm's profitability and financial health, both at a single moment in time and over a longer period. Is the firm's financial performance and health below, equal to, or above the performance and health of its rivals? If the firm's financial health is superior, then there is strong evidence that the firm's customer value proposition is working and that it possesses a superior competitive advantage over its rivals. **Competitive advantage** is when a firm can provide the same value as its competitors but at a lower price or it can charge higher prices by providing greater value through differentiation. Firms employ business models different from their rivals' in order to win over consumers by providing superior customer value.

YOUR BUSINESS MODEL

Thinking
Critically
Exercise 14

Do you have a personal business model? If so, what is it? How do you create and track value for yourself and others?

2.3 THE FIRST STEP IN EVALUATING BUSINESS MODEL EFFECTIVENESS— FINANCIAL ANALYSIS

Strategic managers do not need to be CPAs, but as leaders of their organization, they must have a firm understanding of their company's financial performance. They also need to know how to read financial statements to assess and interpret the financial health of the organization. The numbers and **data** collected by the organization are transcribed into reports and financial statements. The financial statements provide information to better understand the cost, quality, and price relationships associated with doing business. This **information** is then converted into **knowledge** to make informed decisions. At a minimum, the general manager (responsible for the profit and loss of an organizational entity) must:

- Understand all components of financial statements (e.g., income statement, balance sheet, cash flow).
- Conduct a financial ratio analysis and maintain a working knowledge of the various kinds of ratios: liquidity, turnover or activity, leverage, profitability, and stock market (see Table 2.1: Key Financial Ratios).
- Compare and analyze ratios by contrasting performance against standard company or industry performance metrics (e.g., past financial performance, future expectations or goals, best in class for a particular industry or company). This is particularly important for understanding which rivals are winning (earning above-average profits) and losing (with losses or below-average profits) in the markets in which they compete. If one company is extracting all the industry profits at a single point in time and/or over a longer period, then one can conclude this company has a competitive advantage over its rivals.
- Conduct a vertical analysis: These are common size statements in which all the numbers are reported as a percentage (of total sales for the income statement and of total assets for the balance sheet). For example, the vertical analysis of the balance sheet means every amount on the balance sheet is restated as a percentage of total assets. If inventory is $100,000 and total assets are $400,000, then inventory is presented as 25 percent ($100,000 divided by $400,000).
- Conduct a horizontal analysis or trend analysis: Look at financial performance (expressed as an absolute number or on a percentage basis) over a set time period, using several ratios and financial indicators. For example, what were the compounded average annual sales growth, gross margin growth, and net profit growth for the company over the past five years?

The strategic manager needs to be able to answer the following questions:

- Is the company's business model working?
- Does the company have a competitive advantage?
- Is the company's competitive advantage sustainable?
- Can the company weather financial adversity?

In conducting a financial analysis and audit, the general manager must excel at interpreting, understanding, and using financial information to make informed decisions and take strategic actions. At a minimum, the strategic manager should have a good understanding of the following types of ratios (See Table 2.1: Key Financial Ratios):

- **Liquidity Ratios**: Liquidity ratios measure a firm's short-term solvency. For example, does the firm have adequate short-term cash flow to meet its current and maturing financial obligations and needs? Liquidity ratios usually focus on the current or short-term accounts found in the company's balance sheet (e.g., current assets and current liabilities).
- **Activity or Turnover Ratios**: Activity ratios reflect how well a firm utilizes its resources (e.g., is the firm effectively utilizing its assets?). For example, if inventory is not sold at a reasonable rate, then a firm could have cash needlessly tied up in stagnant or obsolete inventory. Activity ratios reflect movement and are usually calculated by dividing net sales or cost of goods sold by an asset account (e.g., inventory, accounts receivable, property, plants, and equipment).
- **Leverage Ratios**: Leverage ratios measure a firm's long-term solvency or ability to meet lenders and investors' financial requirements. For example, who is financing the firm's assets? Are funds being provided by short-term creditors, long-term creditors (referred to as debt financing), or owners? Leverage ratios keep track of owners' versus non-owners' **claims** on the assets of the business.
- **Profitability Ratios**: Profitability ratios measure how well a business is performing (e.g., its financial health and ability to meet investors' financial expectations). How much income is the business generating relative to total sales, assets utilized, and owners' and non-owners' claims on assets? Are returns on sales, assets, and owners' equity at a level that will attract investors and finance long-term firm growth?
- **Stock Market Ratios**: Stock market ratios measure how investors in publicly traded companies perceive a company's past, present, and future financial performance, as well as its overall attractiveness to current and prospective investors. Among the better-known stock market performance indicators that investors will track are: earnings per share (EPS) (net income/number of "common" shares outstanding); price earnings ratio (PE) (stock price/EPS); dividend yield (dividend declared/stock price); and market capitalization (common shares outstanding multiplied by stock price).

Table 2.1. Key
Financial
Ratios

Key Financial Ratios (Ratios are based on an analysis of the Accounting Equation)

Accounting Equation:

Assets = Claims on Assets
Assets = Liabilities + Owners' Equity
Assets = Non Owners' Claims (Creditors) + Owners' (Stockholders) Claims on Assets
Current Assets + Non Current Assets = Current Liabilities + Non Current Liabilities + Owners' Equity
Owners' Equity = Owners' (Sole proprietors, partners, or stockholders) contributions + Retained Earnings
Retained Earnings = Revenues—Expenses = Net Income—Dividends paid to common stockholders
Assets—Liabilities = Owners' Equity
Assets—Liabilities = Net Worth
Therefore Net Worth = Owners' Equity
Change in Assets = Change in Liabilities + Changes in Owners' Equity (Statement of Cash Flows or Funds Flows)

As a first step financial audit, at a minimum the following ratios should be considered:

1. **LIQUIDITY RATIOS:** Can the organization meet its current and maturing financial obligations? Liquidity ratios usually focus on the current or short-term accounts on the balance sheet (e.g., current assets and current liabilities).

RATIO	CALCULATION	STATEMENT	REPORTED
1. Current Ratio =	$\dfrac{\text{Current Assets}}{\text{Current Liabilities}}$	Balance Sheet	Percentage (%)

Meaning: Compares total dollars in current assets with total dollars in current liabilities. Rule of Thumb: (For a manufacturing concern) 2:1; that is, lenders would prefer to see $2 in current assets for every $1 in current liabilities. For high technology companies and companies that are effective at supply change management a current ratio of less than 2:1 is not unusual.

2. Quick or Acid Test Ratio =	$\dfrac{\text{Current Assets less Current Assets that are not easily Converted into cash (usually Inventory)}}{\text{Current Liabilities}}$	Balance Sheet	Percentage (%)

Meaning: Compares those current assets that are cash or near cash (readily converted into cash) with current liabilities. Rule of Thumb: 1:1; that is, for every $1 in cash or near cash lenders would like to see current liabilities of a $1 or less. For high technology companies and companies that are effective at supply change management a quick ratio of less than less than 1:1 is not unusual.

3. Working Capital =	Current Assets Minus Current Liabilities	Balance Sheet	Dollars

Meaning: Provides a measure of how much greater current assets are (in dollars) current liabilities. Usually the larger the working capital in dollars the more liquid or solvent is the company.

2. **TURNOVER OR ACTIVITY RATIOS:** Is the organization sufficiently utilizing its assets? Activity reflects how well an organization employs or utilizes its resources. For example, is merchandise being moved out of inventory at a reasonable rate or do we have funds needlessly invested in stagnant or slow moving inventory? Activity ratios reflect movement and are usually calculated by dividing total net sales, credit sales or cost of goods sold by an asset account (either short-term or long-term).

4. Inventory Turnover $= \dfrac{\text{Sales (or cost of goods sold)}}{\text{Average (*) Inventory}} =$ Income Statement and Balance Sheet — Times

(*) To calculate an average take beginning inventory plus ending inventory and divide by 2. Remember ending inventory in one year is the beginning inventory for the next year. If only one year's balance sheet is given, then an average cannot be calculated (use total year end inventory).

Meaning: This ratio calculates how many times total inventory, usually finished goods, was replaced during the year. For example, if the inventory rate is 9x (nine times) it means that 9 times during the year finished goods inventory was replaced (restocked). Rule of Thumb: Big-ticket items (cars, airplanes, machinery) have low turnover rates while small ticket items (screws, pens, hamburgers) have high inventory turns. Generally, the quicker inventory is moved out of stock (high inventory rates) the quicker sales can be generated accelerating the company's earning cycle.

5. Days inventory on hand $= \dfrac{\text{Days (365 days)}}{\text{Inventory Turnover}}$ --- Days

Meaning: Calculates how many days on average inventory were held during the year. For example, if finished goods inventory turnover is 9x (9 times) then on average inventory was in stock 40 days (finished goods inventory was replaced every forty days on average).

6. Accounts Receivable (AR) Turnover $= \dfrac{\text{Credit Sales (or Net Total Sales)}}{\text{Average Accounts Receivable}}$ Income Statement and Balance Sheet — Times

7. Collection Period $\dfrac{\text{Days (365 days)}}{\text{AR Turnover}}$ --- Days

Meaning: The longer the collection period the longer it takes to collect accounts receivable. Long collection periods signal customer problems and/or poor credit management or poor credit management or both.

8. Fixed Asset Net Sales   Income Statement   Times
   Turnover   =   --------------------   and
                 Net Fixed Assets   Balance Sheet
                 (Usually defined as long-term
                 total assets less depreciation)

Meaning: Are we generating sufficient sales to warrant an investment in long-term fixed assets, such as plant and equipment? The higher the turnover, the more efficient the firm is in employing fixed assets. For example, if the fixed asset turnover is 9x (nine times) then the company would be generating $9 in revenues for every $1 in fixed assets annually. Higher rates are generally associated with more efficient utilization of fixed assets and higher returns on fixed assets.

3. **LEVERAGE RATIOS:** Who is financing the business or organization? Is it short-term creditors, long-term creditors (referred to as debt financing) or owners (referred to as equity investors)? Leverage compares owner's financial contributions or investment (either direct through capital infusion, or purchase of stock or through income retained in the business) in the assets of the business with the non-owners (debt holders) investment in the assets of the business. Thus, leverage ratios keep track of owners' versus non-owners' claims on the assets of the business.

                 Total Debt (total current   Balance Sheet   Percentage %
                 and non-current liabilities)
9. Debt Ratio = -------------------------
                 Total Assets

Meaning: If the balance sheet reports claims on assets then the debt ratio calculates the portion of assets financed by non-owners (debt holders) compared to the percentage of assets financed by owners. For example, a debt ratio of .40 would indicate that for every $1 owners and non-owners have in claims on assets, creditors have claims of $.40 and owners have claims of $.60. Rule of Thumb: 50%/50% or 1:1. Generally creditors usually do not want to own more than fifty percent of the total claims on assets.

10. Times Interest   Net Income before taxes
    Earned   plus interest expense   Income Statement   Times
                     ----
                     Interest Expense

Meaning: Indicates the number of times interest expense can be covered by earnings. For example, if times interest earned were 5x (5 times), then the company could actually cover five times the interest expense. Creditors like to see high interest expense coverage, usually around a minimum of 2 times.

11. Long-term Debt   Long-Term Liabilities
    to Total Assets = -------------------------   Balance Sheet   Percentage
                     Total Assets

Meaning: Of all creditors' claims on assets what percent is being claimed by long-term creditors?

| 12. | Net Worth = | Total Assets minus Total Liabilities | Balance Sheet | Dollars |

Meaning: Net worth is synonymous with owners or stockholders' equity. Owner or stocker equity represents non-creditors' claims on assets. The higher the net worth, the more confident creditors, as well as current or prospective owners have in current and future company financial performance.

| 13. | Current Liabilities to Net Worth = | $\dfrac{\text{Current Liabilities}}{\text{Net Worth}}$ | Balance Sheet | Percentage |

Meaning: Since net worth reflects owners' claims on assets, then current liabilities to net worth compares short-term non-owner claims on assets with owners' claims on assets. For instance, if current liabilities to net worth is .25, it would indicate that for every $1 owners and non owners have in claims on total assets, short-term creditors have $.25 in claims on assets and owners have $.75 in claims. Rule of thumb is usually $.35 maximum or no more than 35 cents in claims by short-term creditors.

4. **PROFITABILITY RATIOS:** How much income is the organization generating relative to total sales or total assets employed? Is the income sufficient to warrant an investment in this organization? Profitability ratios measure how well the company is performing.

| 14. | Return on Sales (ROS) = | $\dfrac{\text{Net Income}}{\text{Net Sales}}$ | Income Statement | Percentage |

Meaning: Return on sales is a measure of operating efficiency. This ratio reports the percent of net income earned for every dollar in sales generated. For example, a ROS of .07 means that for every dollar in sales $.07 was reported as net income. Conversely, for every dollar in sales, $.93 was reported as expense. Rule of thumb for a manufacture is usually $.05 after tax; consumer goods company around 10 cents on the dollar and 20 to 25 cents on the dollar for established high technology companies.

| 15. | Return on Assets or Investment (ROI) | $=$ | $\dfrac{\text{Net Income before Taxes}}{\text{Total Assets}}$ | Income Statement and Balance Sheet | Percentage |

Meaning: This ratio provides an indication of how much income was generated for each dollar invested in assets. For example, a 15 % ROI means that 15 cents is being return for every dollar in assets. Rule of Thumb: A minimum of 15% ROI. Higher returns are required for higher risk businesses and new ventures. For example, it is not unusual for venture capital investors and investment bankers to expect returns of 40% or higher per year for riskier high technology ventures.

| 16. | Gross Margin (GM) $ = | Net Sales minus Cost of Goods Sold | Income Statement | Dollars |

Meaning: Gross margin dollars provides an indication of operating efficiency or performance. Since cost of goods sold is composed of inventory expense, direct labor expense and overhead expense then operating margin (total dollars available after paying for cost of good sold expenses) must be adequate enough to cover general and administrative expenses, research and development expenses, marketing and sales expense and interest expense. Any dollars remaining after cost of goods sold expenses, operating expenses, and interest expense are covered goes to net income.

17.

$$\text{Gross Margin (GM) \%} = \frac{\text{Gross Margin}}{\text{Net Sales}}$$

Income Statement   Percentage

Rule of thumb: Manufacturing 20–25% gross margins; Consumer goods companies gross margins of 30–35%; High technology companies 50% GM or higher.

18. Return on Equity (ROE)

$$= \frac{\text{Net Income—Preferred Dividends}}{\text{Average Common Shareholder's Equity}}$$

Income Statement and Balance Sheet   Percentage

Meaning: This ratio reports the rate of return common stockholders are receiving on their claims in the assets of the business.

19. Retained Earnings   Net Income minus Dividends or owner's withdrawals   Income Statement   Dollars

Meaning: Retained earnings reflects owners' claims on the assets of the business that were generated from the operations of the business at a moment in time. Note: retained earnings are claims on assets, not dollars or cash retained in the business (although a portion of retained earnings claims could be in cash).

20. DuPont ratio or DuPont analysis:

Calculation (formula): ROE (DuPont formula) = (Net profit / Revenue) x (Revenue / Total assets) x (Total assets / Equity) = Net profit margin x Asset Turnover x Financial leverage.

DuPont ratio or DuPont analysis is used to assess a company's return on equity (profitability), asset turnover (activity or efficiency) and financial leverage. DuPont Corporation developed the method for assessing its operating efficiency, asset use and financial leverage. The DuPont ratio or analysis help it find those parts of its business were underperforming. The higher the ROE, the better. Historically, in the U.S. the average ROE has been around 10% to 12%. The ROE ratio, as do all other ratios, is strongly dependent on the strength of the industry in which the firm competes, how well it is positioned in the industry, and the overall all health of the economies in which the firm competes (Competitive Forces, PESTEL, SPACE, PEST, SWOT analysis). Many firms set an overall goal of a minimum ROE of 15%. The Dupont ratio is often used to assess the performance of the target company is a merger or acquisition negotiation in comparison to the acquiring company's DuPont calculated ROE.

5. STOCK MARKET RATIOS

21. Earnings Per
    Share (EPS)

    $$\text{EPS} = \frac{\text{Net Income—Preferred Stock Dividends}}{\text{Average Number of Common Stockholders Shares Outstanding}}$$

    Income Statement and Balance Sheet — Dollars

Meaning: This ratio measures the number of dollars earned in net income for every common share of stock outstanding.

22. Price Earnings (PE) Ratio

    $$\frac{\text{Common Stock Price}}{\text{Earnings Per Share}}$$

    Times

For example, if a company's stock is trading at $60 a share and its earnings over the last 12 months were $3 per share the company's P/E ratio for the stock is 20 or trading at 20 times earnings.

23. Market Capitalization = Total number of common shares outstanding Multiplied by current market price of common shares. — Dollars

For example if a company's stock is trading on the NYSE at $100 per share and there are 10 million shares outstanding then the company's market capitalization is $10 billion dollars ($100 x 10,000,000 shares).

3. WHAT IS A CASE?

"Knowledge is the beginning of practice; doing is the completion of knowing."[10]

The oldest and most powerful teaching tactic for fostering critical thinking is Socratic teaching, or the Socratic method. The **Socratic-method** approach to case study is based on debate and learning through discovery; that is, asking the right questions and deriving plausible solutions. A **pure** case provides students with a description of a real-life situation including enough intriguing decision points and provocative undercurrents to make a student/student groups want to think and argue about them.[11] A case offers a way to identify and analyze "real-life business problems confronting a business manager at a particular moment."[12] As such, cases provide students with a practical learning laboratory where they can study pragmatic business problems and situations without actually having to leave the classroom. By assuming the role of the general manager, students can practice making strategic decisions and present these decisions to others without fear of making serious career or financial mistakes. Cases allow students to actually learn how to conduct critical inquiry, to strategically think and act, and to assess their own thinking processes.

Strategy cases are usually comprehensive in scope, as they provide detailed descriptions of companies, competitive markets, and administrative and management processes. Through case study, students can assume the roles of CEO, chief strategist, company founder, general manager, functional manager, and others that are key to the strategic-management process.

3.1 CASE PRINCIPLES

Two basic principles apply to case study. First, cases are not designed to prepare you for a specific incident or position you may encounter in your business career. Rather, they are simply vehicles that help you to practice systematic analysis and decision making. Secondly, as in the real world, there are no schooled solutions or answers to the case problems or issues. The case is not to be viewed as a crossword puzzle from *The New York Times*. As in the real world, decision making is not an exact science. There is no "right answer" to a case; only hard work and time will determine whether a particular recommendation is plausible. Just as a piece of music exists only partially when it isn't being sung or played, a case comes to life only when it is being discussed and analyzed in depth by students.

3.2 ACTIVE LEARNING

Case study allows students to take an active role in their learning. Unlike straight lectures, case study fosters dynamic interactive learning environments that facilitate discovery, action, and wisdom. Wisdom cannot be taught; it comes from discovery, reflection, synthesis, and doing. As Robert Frost keenly observes, "Education is hanging around 'til you've caught on."[13] Case study is challenging and time-consuming. Students must be open to learning and maintain the right attitude to successfully approach cases. But why is case study important to the learning process and to future careers? Case study remains significant to student learning because history matters. Cases allow us to learn from others' successes and failures. Cases also provide a tool or vehicle for conducting critical inquiry, studying business processes and decisions, and learning how to strategically think and act. Like strategic decisions in real life, the reality found in case situations is complex and challenging. As such, cases are an effective halfway house between classroom and reality, allowing students to bring a compelling version of reality into the classroom.

4. CRITICAL THINKING, KNOWLEDGE, AND CASE STUDY

As discussed in Chapter 1, critical thinking is the art of analyzing and evaluating thought processes to improve them.[14] The conceptual foundation for critical thinking is critical theory. Critical inquiry questions what knowledge is and how it can be acquired, as well as the extent to which knowledge is pertinent to any given subject or entity.[15] From a business perspective, knowledge is the stock of information that informs decision making. Knowledge aids the strategist in crafting and executing strategy. It also helps to reduce uncertainty in light of complex, unpredictable environments by identifying and evaluating the nature and degree of risk associated with a strategy or action.[16]

Knowledge is power and can spell the difference between an organization or individual's success and failure. Case study is based in critical inquiry; that is, the understanding and/or acquisition of information with the application of knowledge. Critical inquiry through case study helps strategy students synthesize the relevant tacit and explicit knowledge they have acquired in their business programs and elsewhere. As in the real world, critical inquiry and knowledge acquisition instill the confidence and energy for decision makers to act with insight, rigor, and confidence.

Case study, based on critical theory and critical inquiry, is a process for improving thought. It utilizes an epistemological approach to the study of strategy.[17] **Epistemology** is a term first used by the Scottish philosopher James Frederick Ferrier to describe the branch of philosophy concerned with the nature and scope of knowledge; it is also referred to as "**theory of knowledge**."[18] Case study provides students a means to gather and analyze information with the end goal of converting information to knowledge. Case study also helps students use and demonstrate their knowledge to make sound judgments and decisions. When analyzing cases, students better understand and master both thought process and the ability to carry out critical inquiry. As such, case study assists students in identifying the information in the case, specifically what information is useful (facilitates understanding), irrelevant (does not add any value to the decision maker), insignificant (will not lead to understanding), and vital (critical to the matter or issue at hand).[19] General managers understand the importance and value of information in strategic analysis and decision making. Effective managers take the time and effort required to conduct critical inquiry, think at a higher level, and confidently take strategic action. Ineffective managers do not recognize the importance and value of information in conducting critical inquiry and thinking at a high level. Effective strategy making, execution, and monitoring are information-intensive and knowledge-driven processes. A firm's ability to create and sustain a competitive advantage is based on having superior knowledge over rivals. Possessing superior information or knowledge also increases returns to the firm.[20] In sum, case study helps strategy students demonstrate to their instructors their ability and capacity to:

- Demonstrate higher-order thinking skills
- Master business concepts
- Think clearly in complex, ambiguous situations[21]
- Apply analytical tools and frameworks[22]
- Determine useful and vital information from non-useful, non-vital information[23]
- Offer persuasive arguments and recommendations
- Make informed decisions
- Communicate effectively
- Become a lifelong learner
- Act strategically and think critically

VIDEO 2.2 How to Prepare a Business Case Study … and How Not To

5. HOW TO APPROACH A CASE ANALYSIS

"No question is so difficult to answer as that to which the answer is obvious."[24]

Numerous approaches to case study and analysis exist, and each instructor will have her or his own recommended method. Still, there are basic steps to aid you in preparing a case analysis and presentation, which include:

1. Read title, opening, and closing sections of the case
2. Quick review of case subtitles
3. Glance over case exhibits, if included
4. Skim the case
5. Reread the case and make notes in margin; highlight key points
6. Ask the "right" questions
7. Address specific case questions, if assigned
8. Use the case-method approach to think critically and act strategically

Approach a case with an open mind. Cases need to be digested by careful reading and analysis. Do not prejudge a case. Take the time to learn what the case is about and how it should be approached. "A case," according to Ellet, "is a text that refuses to explain itself."[25] It is up to the student to apply meaning to it. To best learn from case study, approach it as a self-guided learning experience that employs critical thinking, analysis, and evidence-based conclusions about a situation. The case method is **heuristic**—a term for self-guided learning that employs analysis to help draw conclusions."[26] To be successful in case study, **think**! Do not just read.[27]

5.1 GENERIC CASE QUESTIONS

Instructors will usually assign discussion questions, exercises, rubrics, or guidelines to help students analyze and prepare cases. In addition to specific assignments, there are some general questions that students need to prepare for class discussion or written assignments:

1. Who is/are the key protagonist(s) and antagonist(s) in the case?
2. What is the case situation? What is the company's strategic health? Financial health?
3. What is the industry like? How attractive is the industry?
4. What is the most pressing critical issue or question facing the company? Why do you think so?
5. What, if anything, should be done to address the pressing critical issue?
6. What options (alternatives) were considered?
7. What options (alternatives) can be accepted or ruled out?
8. What recommendations would you make? Why?
9. How will you communicate and execute your recommendation(s) to senior management?[28]

6. CASE GUIDELINES

The case method entails two separate and distinct parts: (1) a detailed case (situational) analysis and (2) a clear and concise case write-up or presentation. Your instructor is looking for a systematic, rational, and persuasive case analysis—one that leads to sound, well-reasoned, well-analyzed, and professionally presented case recommendations. For class discussion of a case, students should be able to demonstrate a thorough reading of the text and adequate preparation including providing a concise summary of their analysis and recommendation(s). Students should always assume that their instructor has thoroughly read and prepared the case and is quite familiar with the information contained in the case. For written work, your text or narrative should be supported with detailed evidence and supporting exhibits to document and explain how the critical issue was derived and what led to your case recommendation(s). The thrust of your analysis should be on the pressing critical issue(s), alternative selection and analysis, and recommendation(s). It should not be a "description" summary or repeat of the case narrative. Instructors often assign word limits for write-ups or assignment questions. **Word limits** are set to ensure that students focus on useful, significant, and vital information drawn from their situational analysis. With word limits, students will not be able to include all, or even most, of their situational analysis.

6.1 EVALUATING THE QUALITY AND EFFECTIVENESS OF CRITICAL-THINKING SKILLS

The overall quality of one's critical-thinking skills in analyzing a case can be judged by how well a student can communicate the following in arguing a position or making a recommendation:

1. *Relevance:* Does the statement bear on the subject at hand? Statements that do not link up with what the class or case is focused on can actually detract from the learning experience.
2. *Causal Linkage:* Are the logical antecedents or consequences of a particular argument traced out? Statements that push the implications of a fact or idea as far as possible are generally superior.

3. *Responsiveness:* Does the statement react in an important way to what classmates or case protagonists have stated?
4. *Analysis:* Has data from the text, lecture, case, other courses, and personal experience been used, analyzed, and employed to support any assertions made?
5. *Importance:* Does the statement further our understanding of the topic or issue(s) at hand? Is there a connection made with other cases and course concepts?
6. *Clarity:* Is the statement succinct and understandable? Does it align with the subject, or does it wander?

Thinking Critically Exercise 15

WRITTEN WORD LIMITS

It is often said that a written case analysis cannot be adequately presented in fewer than 1,000 words (approximately five pages). Do you agree? What dangers do you face in limiting the number of words in a case analysis? What danger do you face by not limiting the number of words in a case analysis?

6.2 THE STUDENT'S ROLE IN CASE STUDY

Your instructor will not provide "answers" to the case. Given this, the student's role in preparing the case is to:

1. Thoroughly read and understand the case
2. Participate in class discussion
3. Know how to properly analyze and evaluate a case
4. Be an active learner
5. Know how to form and structure critical issues and questions
6. Select and appraise (in a logical and rational manner) creditable alternative(s) to address critical issues and questions
7. Communicate and present recommended courses of action(s) (your option selection)

6.3 THE INSTRUCTOR'S ROLE IN CASE STUDY

Instructors can facilitate student learning through case study when they:

1. Make the assignment and objectives of the case clear
2. Make sure the student is thoroughly prepared for case analysis
3. Play the "devil's advocate" in case discussion
4. Make certain all students have an equal right to participate and ensure all students participate
5. Push students by making them convincingly arrive at and defend their key assumptions, critical questions, and recommendations
6. Are thoroughly prepared for case discussion
7. Facilitate case discussion but do not dominate it
8. Provide constructive criticism and encouragement when warranted
9. Help students learn how to think critically and strategically[29]

7. EVIDENCE, ANALYTICAL DESIGN, AND INFOGRAPHICS

 VIDEO 2.3 Management consulting case study interview with Gil and Lauren

Students should be able to clearly communicate and rigorously support their analyses with carefully crafted and documented **evidence**. Like a lawyer defending his or her client in a court of law, evidence will determine the guilt or innocence of the defendant. Likewise, the prosecutors need to gather, analyze, and skillfully present their evidence, which requires exploratory detective work, critical inquiry, and integrity in how the evidence is gathered and delivered. In providing evidence, the case researcher presents the reasoning behind it and takes whatever action necessary to persuade the receiver of the evidence. Your reputation is on the line to provide the best case for the evidence's acceptance. Students, in presenting the evidence, will oftentimes "dumb it down" by oversimplifying to the point that it weakens the overall quality and integrity of the case analysis. Evidence, analytical design, and documentation are key to student learning through cases. As Edward Tufte so eloquently stated:

> Evidence that bears on questions of any complexity typically involves multiple forms of discourse. Evidence is evidence, whether in words, numbers, images, diagrams, still, or moving. The intellectual tasks remain regardless of the mode of evidence: to understand and to reason about the materials at hand, and to appraise their quality, relevance, and integrity.[30]

Excellent graphical presentation should be judged on the fundamental principles of analytical design. **Information graphics** (or infographics) are graphic visual representations of information—data or knowledge intended to present complex information quickly and clearly. Infographics can improve cognition by utilizing the human visual system's ability to see patterns and trends. The process of creating infographics can be referred to as **data visualization**, **information design**, or **information architecture**.[31] The six principles described in Tufte's book *Beautiful Evidence* are comprised in sections 7.1 to 7.6[32]:

7.1 PRINCIPLE #1: COMPARISONS[33]

VIDEO 2.4 7 Common Types of Infographics

Comparisons show contrasts and differences. The fundamental analytical act in statistical reasoning is to answer the question: *Compared to what?* The **case researcher** in providing graphical evidence must submit well-reasoned analysis and comparisons. For example, in presenting financial ratios, it is essential that the case researcher show comparisons. The reported ratios need to be compared against company expectations or industry standards, such as past financial performance (trend line), future expectations, goals, industry benchmarks or standards, etc.[34]

7.2 PRINCIPLE #2: CAUSALITY

Evidence is examined and displayed to show and "understand causality, mechanism, dynamics, process, or systematic structure."[35] In displaying evidence and making comparisons, the case researcher needs to make inferences, or in other words, determine what the evidence is "saying." The researcher also needs to ask: *What are the sources of differences and variability in the measurements? What is the cause and effect?* For example, if the financial ratio analysis shows that sales have consistently trended downward, the researcher must then investigate and make reasoned inferences for the decline.

7.3 PRINCIPLE #3: MULTIVARIATE ANALYSIS

Multivariate analysis illustrates more than one or two variables. Therefore, depicting the conditions under which a cause-and-effect relationship occurs requires multivariate analysis. Tufte warns against using two-dimensional displays in presenting data because we live in a world that is not flat but multidimensional. He argues, "Strategies of design should make multivariateness routine, nothing out of the ordinary."[36] For example, when presenting financial information, students should display their work in several dimensions, including types of ratios, time period (monthly, quarterly, annually), color, major decisions (product introductions, timing of joint ventures or acquisitions), or exogenous factors (entry of a new competitor). In other words, students need to think beyond one or two dimensions and provide several variables to aid in making comparisons and reasoned inferences about cause and effect.

7.4 PRINCIPLE #4: INTEGRATION OF EVIDENCE

In presenting evidence, case researchers should use all factors available to make their case. This includes words, numbers, images, diagrams, graphics, charts, etc. Distinguishing between different modes of evidence and bringing it together makes for a more believable and convincing case analysis. According to Tufte, "Like good information displays, explanatory investigations, if they are to be honest and genuine, must seek out and present all relevant evidence regardless of form."[37] For example, students, when presenting their financial analysis, should use everything available to them—not just numbers, but charts, tables, written observations, conclusions, etc. as well.

7.5 PRINCIPLE #5: DOCUMENTATION

Thoroughly describe the evidence. Provide a detailed title, indicate the authors and sponsors, document the data sources, show complete measurement scales, and point out relevant issues. Credibility, bias, and responsibility of authorship must be taken into account when accessing evidence. This includes who the authors are, along with dates, sources and references, scales labeled, and details enumerated. According to Tufte, "Thorough documentation is a good sign that a report was constructed with at least care and craft."[38]

7.6 PRINCIPLE #6: CONTENT COUNTS MOST OF ALL

In order to provide credible and believable evidence, the case researcher must deliver quality content and dedicate the time and effort to display it properly. As Tufte notes, analytical presentations ultimately stand and fall depending on the quality, relevance, and integrity of their content.[39] There is no substitute for content-driven critical thinking. Tufte concludes the presentation of the six principles of elegant design with a cautionary note: "Because these six principles are rooted in fundamental cognitive tasks, they are relevant for *producing presentations* and for *consuming presentations*."[40] Tufte illustrates the six principles by analyzing Charles Joseph Minard's figurative map chronicling Napoleon's march on Moscow and the devastating losses the French army experienced in 1812. (See Figure 2.1: Charles Joseph Minard Figurative Map: The Map That Made a Nation Cry.)[41]

Charles Joseph Minard (1781–1870) was a French civil engineer recognized for his significant contribution to information graphics within the field of civil engineering and statistics. Minard was, among other things, especially noted for his representation of numerical data on geographic maps.

Born in Dijon in the Saint Michel parish, Minard was admitted to the prestigious École Polytechnique at age 15 and later studied civil engineering at École Nationale des Ponts et Chaussées. He worked for many years as a civil engineer on the construction of dams, canals, and bridge projects throughout Europe. On November 1, 1830, he was named superintendent of the School of Bridges and Roads, where he continued to serve through 1836. While there, he was awarded the Cross of the Legion of Honor. He then became inspector of the Corps of Bridges until he retired in 1851, after which he dedicated himself to private research.

Minard was a pioneer in the use of graphics in engineering and statistics. He is best known for his cartographic depiction of numerical data on a map of Napoleon's disastrous losses suffered during the Russian campaign of 1812–1813. Modern information scientists claim the illustration may be the best statistical graphic ever crafted. French scientist, physiologist, and chronophotographer Étienne-Jules Marey first called attention to Minard's dramatic portrayal of Napoleon's army in the Russian campaign by stating it "defies the pen of the historian in its brutal eloquence." Minard's famous chart is one of the earliest examples of a flow map. Of the 422,000 men who crossed the Niemen on their way to Moscow in 1812, only 10,000 returned.

As stated earlier, the infamous map (one of the 51 thematic maps Minard created during his lifetime) illustrating Napoleon's army departing the Polish-Russian border was drawn after he retired as inspector general of bridges and roads in 1869. A thick band illustrates the size of his army at specific geographic points during their advance and retreat. It also displays six types of data in two dimensions: the number of Napoleon's troops, the distance traveled, temperature, latitude and longitude, direction of travel, and location relative to specific dates. The numbers of men present are represented by the widths of the colored zones at a rate of 1 millimeter for 10,000 men; these are also written beside the zones. Red designates men moving into Russia; black signals those on retreat. Minard's map also utilizes pie charts to represent the proportion of cattle imported from all around the France countryside for consumption in Paris (1858).

Figure 2.1 Charles Joseph Minard Figurative Map: The Map That Made a Nation Cry

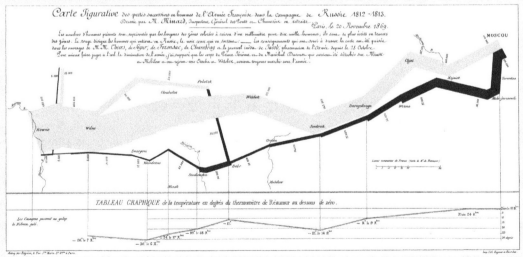

CRITIQUING ANALYTICAL DESIGN BY MEANS OF MINARD'S FIGURATIVE MAP

a. Review Minard's figurative map (go to http://www.masswerk.at/minard/ for the English narrative of Minard's Figurative Map) of Napoleon's march on Moscow and Tufte's six principles of analytical design listed above. Which principles of "elegant analytical design" did Minard use in constructing his map? How did he use them?

b. The figurative map has also been referred to as an excellent example of early infographics. Why do you think some experts consider Minard's map as one of the earliest examples of elegant analytical design and infographics?

BUSINESS ILLUSTRATION OF TUFTE'S DESIGN PRINCIPLES

Go to your college's online index of business databases. Find one article on a publically traded company that graphically illustrates in detail the company's financial, market, or strategic performance using Tufte's design principles. How many of Tufte's principles of elegant design were used in the graphical illustration? Which ones where omitted, if any? Which ones could be added to further enhance the graphical illustration of the company's performance?

8. STEPS IN CASE ANALYSIS

There are seven basic steps in case analysis: (1) Conduct a thorough internal and external situational analysis (use appropriate analytical tools and frameworks); (2) identify the most pressing critical issues or questions confronting the key protagonist in the case, and **clearly state the most pressing central problem** (based on step 1); (3) identify alternatives offered to address or resolve the central problem recognized in step 2; (4) analyze alternatives using your internal and external situational analysis (step 1); (5) offer credible recommendation(s) to address or resolve the central problem (your recommendation comes from one or a combination of your alternatives in step 3); (6) provide a brief statement on how the recommendation is to be implemented (how resources will be allocated); and (7) provide supporting analytical frameworks, tools, or original exhibits.

8.1 INTERNAL AND EXTERNAL SITUATIONAL ANALYSIS

The first step of case analysis consists of a thorough assessment of the organization's external and internal environments. The analysis should show the firm's or general manager's current situation. The situational analysis should demonstrate your understanding of key business, management, and strategy concepts found in this book and in your business studies. In conducting this analysis, you are to select appropriate frameworks and analytical tools. The degree to which you are able to successfully analyze the internal and external environments will reveal your understanding of how to select and apply the appropriate analytical tool. The external task environment consists of those factors that are relevant or potentially relevant in facilitating or hindering a company's strategy and goal achievement. An internal situational assessment aims at providing a detailed analysis of the main characteristics and elements within the organization's

    a. Reread the opening case, *Joseph's Gourmet Pasta and Sauces: At a Crossroads*. Conduct a thorough internal and external situational analysis (use appropriate analytical tools and frameworks).

    b. Identify the most pressing critical issues or questions confronting the key protagonist in the case.

    c. Summarize the company's strategic and financial health by using infographics. Use Tufte's principles of elegant analytical design in constructing your infographic charts, tables, and diagrams. Prepare your infographics as if you would be making a formal presentation to potential investment bankers looking to either invest growth capital in Joseph's or acquire it outright.

internal environment that facilitate or hinder its strategy and goal achievement. A situational analysis of the external environment should lead to an identification of external opportunities and threats as well as any barriers or obstacles to an organization's performance.

8.2 PRESSING ISSUES, QUESTIONS, AND CENTRAL PROBLEM IDENTIFICATION

Identify the most pressing critical issues or questions confronting the key protagonist in the case. Based on the situation analysis, is there a negative gap between existing performance (what is actually happening) and expected performance (what should be happening)? Can the current situation be improved, and if so, how? If the answers to these questions are "yes," then the general manager needs to determine what threats, obstacles, key deficiencies, and pressing questions are hindering performance. That is: *What's the critical issue or central problem?* Based on the situational analysis conducted in step 1, students should be able to conclude whether the firm is at risk (or in a negative situation) or moving forward in a positive direction. To assist in identifying critical issues, students should ask the following questions:

1. What obstacles (threats, weaknesses, key deficiencies) exist that could hinder or prevent the organization from achieving its desired performance (e.g., goals and objectives)?

2. Is management capitalizing on environmental opportunities, its own strengths, and its competencies while staving off or circumventing threats, weaknesses, and deficiencies?

3. Is the organization merely reacting to environmental events or situations (trends), or is it helping to initiate or influence trends in ways that are in its own best interests?

4. Are the current situation and expected performance under control, or are they uncontrollable?

A critical issue does not necessarily have to focus on a negative condition or situation. In other words, the critical issue might center on making an attractive position even more desirable. The critical-issue statement should always be worded in terms of a question that is not easily answered. Examples of critical-issue questions include:

- What actions should the organization adopt in the short term in order to create, maintain, or improve its current performance or situation?

- What actions should the company immediately adopt in order to reverse its current poor strategic and financial performance?
- Is the organization's strategic and financial health so dire that its survival is at stake?
- Are the company's current positive situation and direction defendable, or are they at risk?

Confusion can result when symptoms, certain industry conditions, or phenomena are mistaken for the critical issue(s). **Symptoms** are events or signs that signal something is wrong. For example, poor profitability or a sudden drop in sales are signs that something is astray. The cause of poor profitability or sudden sales decline is the critical issue. An **industry condition** is a characteristic or event that must be considered or addressed by all competitors. For example, an industry that is cyclical in nature presents a condition that all competitors must address. Cyclicality is a condition, not the critical issue; the pressing question is how best to deal with industry cyclicality. In some instances, top management becomes ensnared in what is known as the **success syndrome**. This syndrome is a situation where prior successes are viewed by management as a sufficient proxy for future successes. As a result, management may blindly proceed in action without adequate organizational or environmental observation or analysis.

| Thinking Critically Exercise 19 | JOSEPH'S GOURMET PASTA AND SAUCES, INC.—IDENTIFYING THE MOST PRESSING CRITICAL ISSUE OR CENTRAL QUESTION |

Based your financial assessment and critical inquiry, what is the most pressing critical issue or question facing Joseph's?

8.3 OFFER CREDIBLE ALTERNATIVES

Identify offered alternatives to address or resolve the central problem identified in step 2. The general manager needs to ask: *What actions can be taken to "plausibly" address the issue? Will the action work? Why do I think it will work?* The manager must also formulate or develop credible strategic options. All potential courses of action aimed at the central problem or critical issue resolution must be identified and assessed according to clearly established criteria. Alternative courses of action are "potential solutions" to the critical issue. The eventual selection of a particular alternative or set of alternatives is the recommendation. Strategic managers do not have the luxury of testing alternatives before they are implemented. As a result, due diligence and great care are necessary before the general manager can offer an alternative for consideration. It requires evidence of detailed strategic thinking and critical inquiry. As such, strategic managers must analytically identify and weigh all relevant factors that could have an impact on the viability of an option.

| Thinking Critically Exercise 20 | JOSEPH'S GOURMET PASTA AND SAUCES, INC.—OPTION IDENTIFICATION |

a. Identify Joseph's business model and sources of its competitive advantage.
b. What is the most pressing critical issue or central problem that Faro and his company must address?
c. Identify the most appropriate and viable options that Faro needs to consider in addressing the greatest pressing critical issue or question facing Joseph's that you identified above.

8.4 WEIGH THE PROS AND CONS FOR EACH ALTERNATIVE

Analyze alternatives using your internal and external situational analysis (step 1). What are the pros and cons associated with each alternative? A detailed assessment of options is required. Criteria are measures, either tangible or intangible, used to weigh and assess the desirability of a particular alternative. From the criteria analysis, the most desirable alternatives can be selected and the least desirable eliminated. General **categories of criteria** to be employed in option analysis are:

1. **Appropriateness**: Will the option achieve its intended purpose?
2. **Feasibility**: Are there adequate resources to execute the alternative? If not, can resources be acquired?
3. **Realism**: Does the option align with top management's values, morals, and ethics?
4. **Workability**: Can it gain the necessary commitment from key strategic principals, operating managers, and employees?
5. **Risk**: Does the alternative expose the firm to unreasonable levels of risk?
6. **Values**: Does the alternative significantly change organizational values, purpose, and philosophies?
7. **Timing**: Are alternatives developed to address immediate short-term issues or longer-term ones or both?

8.5 MAKE RECOMMENDATIONS

Offer credible recommendation(s) to address or resolve the central problem (your recommendation comes from one or a combination of your alternatives in step 3). Recommendations are then presented based on the conclusions derived from weighing each alternative against selected criteria. Your analysis may lead you to conclude that existing strategies and actions are appropriate and will achieve the desired results—that is, continue as is with existing strategies and actions. When offering recommendations, also consider a combination of alternatives. If a combination of options is recommended, then treat this as a unique selection that needs to be analyzed separately. Furthermore, the time frame over which a particular recommendation(s) should be implemented must be considered (e.g., short-term, intermediate, and long-term). The definition of short-term (usually less than one year), intermediate (two to three years) and long-term (greater than three years) is contingent upon the nature of the industry and how quickly the critical issue needs to be addressed. This section of your analysis only includes the recommendation(s), no elaboration.

Student recommendation(s) for a critical issue(s) or pressing question(s) contained in a particular case analysis may differ considerably. In fact, the instructor expects recommendations to vary. Although students may offer different recommendations to an identical critical issue, the instructor may accept each student's recommendation. However, the recommendation's acceptability is dependent on how rigorous and thorough a student's analysis is compared to his or her classmates' recommendations. The relevancy of the recommendation to the critical issue or question is equally important. Usually, but not always, the more evidence presented and the more rigorous, thorough, and logical the analysis, the greater the probability that a particular recommendation(s) will be accepted by your instructor. Furthermore, even if two students' recommendations are exactly the same, one student's recommendation may be acceptable while the other's is not. This could be because the unacceptable recommendation:

a. Did not address the right critical issue or question
b. Was not adequately supported or defended
c. Was poorly presented

JOSEPH'S GOURMET PASTA AND SAUCES, INC.—PRO/CON ANALYSIS

Using critical inquiry, what options (alternatives) can be ruled out? Again using your analysis, list at least two pros and three cons associated with each of the remaining options.

JOSEPH'S GOURMET PASTA AND SAUCES, INC.—ACTING STRATEGICALLY AND RECOMMENDATION

Based on your pro/con analysis of each option, what strategic action would you recommend to Faro?

8.6 IMPLEMENTATION AND EXECUTION

Provide a brief statement on how the recommendation is to be applied and which critical resources are to be allocated. A proposed recommendation is useless unless the organization commits to its implementation. When instigating a recommendation, one must consider (at a minimum): Who will be in charge of its implementation? In what time frame? Does the organization need to be restructured, or is the present structure appropriate? How will people be affected by recommendation's implementation (are there too many, not enough, or not the right people)? Will a new motivation or compensation system be necessary? How will we know if the plan is not working? What financial resources are needed? Are new financial resources needed? How will resources, especially financial (if needed) be obtained? Can trends, relationships, or variables in the external environment be exploited, controlled, or influenced in ways that allow the strategist to move the company toward its desired state? In implementing and executing the recommendation, the manager must monitor results and outcomes to assess whether the critical issue has been resolved. Timely and accurate information is needed to determine whether the proposed recommendations are working. The ongoing nature of strategy formulation and execution entails a constant monitoring and appraisal of results. Any variance must be quickly identified and corrected, or new strategies must be identified, evaluated, crafted, and implemented.

VIDEO 2.5 Susan Etlinger: What Do We Do with All This Big Data?

8.7 PROVIDE SUPPORTING ANALYSIS AND EXHIBITS (INTERNAL AND EXTERNAL SITUATIONAL ASSESSMENT)

Students must demonstrate their capacity to offer original or customized exhibits. These exhibits are to be included in a student's case analysis and are integral to presenting solid evidence in support of critical issues, suggested alternatives, alternative analysis, and recommendations. Exhibits should supplement but **not replicate** exhibits contained in the case. Again, your instructor has read the case and wants to see your ability to put your own original exhibits together, use analytical design (see section 7 above: Evidence, Analytical Design, And Infographics), and creatively integrate the information found in the case. Original exhibits can be used to substantiate any statements presented in the case narrative and your write-up of the case. **Students are not to copy exhibits contained in the case.** Students should instead demonstrate their ability to construct original exhibits using case data and other information but avoid using information or references after case publication date. For example, if the latest date referred to in the case is September 30, 2012, then no outside references or information after this date can be employed in the case analysis. Doing so could bias your case recommendations and confuse or lessen the importance of your own critical inquiry, strategic thinking, and presentation.

JOSEPH'S GOURMET PASTA AND SAUCES, INC.—ACTING STRATEGICALLY AND EXECUTION

Thinking Critically Exercise 23

See Table 7.1: Basic Elements of Strategy Implementation, Execution, and Strategic Control in Chapter 7. Strategy implementation and execution require consideration of how your recommendation will be carried out (executed) by the firm. What resources are needed? Who will be responsible for implementing the strategies, and over what time period? Briefly present an implementation strategy to Faro and his management team for carrying out and executing the recommended strategy.

9. CASE RUBRIC AND TIPS FOR ORAL PRESENTATIONS

In assessing the quality of a student's case analysis and presentation abilities (oral and written communication skills) the instructor will usually apply a grading or scoring rubric. The rubric is used to evaluate the quality of the student's work. In the case study, a scoring rubric is used to assess student learning, critical inquiry skills, as well as the depth and quality of the student's strategic thinking and action. The rubric also provides a standard of performance for the student's mastery of concepts and critical thinking skills in relation to his or her peers (fellow students). Students can use the scoring rubric to guide their case analysis and organize their written work or presentations (see Exhibit 2.3: Case Scoring Rubric). The instructor may assign the company case analysis as an individual or group presentation. In some instances, an oral presentation is just as if not more important than a written presentation. This is especially true when assessing the student's ability to present professionally and with integrity. It's not unusual for companies to give job candidates a case study to prepare and present doing an onsite job interview. The company is assessing the candidate's understanding of a particular subject matter, as well as his or her ability to communicate effectively and perform under pressure. Some tips for making an effective oral presentation can be found in Table 2.2: Tips for Making Effective Oral Presentations.

**Exhibit 2.3
Case Scoring
Rubric**

Student Name (Or ID Number) _____ Case _____ Date _____ Grade _____

	Unsatisfactory (F)	Lacks Critical Inquiry (D)	Low Level of Critical Inquiry (C)	High Order Critical Inquiry (B)	Highest Order Critical Inquiry (A)
Central Problem					
Based on the situational analysis what is the most central problem management needs to address?					
Options/Alternatives					
What options should be considered that best address central problem?					
Option Analysis					
Identify at least 2 pros and 2 cons for each option—Use your situational analysis to analyze options–weigh options using criteria					
Recommendation					
Based on the Pro/Con analysis what option(s) best addresses the central problem?					
Implementation					
The Who, What, Why and When for executing the recommendation					
Supporting Exhibits					
Conduct an in-depth internal and external analysis using analytical tools and frameworks					
Presentation Quality					
Documentation, formatting, professional					
Overall Comments Understanding of Course Concepts					

Table 2.2
Tips for
Making
Effective Oral
Presentations

- Know the purpose of the presentation—Is it to persuade, make recommendations, demonstrate competency in a subject matter, educate, other?
- Know your audience—why are they there; what do they want to learn?
- Presentation slides are to support you, not replace you as a presenter
- Be prepared—do your homework
- Check for accuracy—proofread slides, check, check, check
- Be professional—dress properly
- Practice your presentation ahead of time, preferably in the presentation room
- Organize your presentation so that it is logical and easy to follow
- Prepare an agenda slide, tell them what will be covered, cover it and summarize your important conclusions /points
- Be creative, separate your presentation from cookie-cutter presentations
- Makes slides readable (light background, dark text or dark background, light text)
- Do not use annoying bells and whistles—keep slides simple and clear
- If more than one presenter, know your role, assignment
- No throwing other presenters "under the bus"—no interruptions, surprises
- Check your technology—make sure it works
- Stay within time allowed
- Anticipate questions—prepare back-up slides for potential questions
- Make eye contact with audience—do not read from screen
- Know you talking points—never just continuously read from notes or computer screen
- Do not present as if there is a fire in the room—take your time, enunciate, speak clearly, convincingly (avoid boring, monotone speaking)
- Avoid red flags—obvious errors, conclusions that are obvious or too good to be true
- Never argue or criticize a questioner or classmate
- Provide clear evidence, well-supported arguments
- Use tables, graphs, exhibits
- No long paragraphs, or excessive numbers or words—make slides readable
- Show and demonstrate your strategic thinking, critical inquiry
- Close strong—summarize key points
- Have fun, show that you are the expert and have something meaningful to say and offer

Source: Michael J. Merenda 2018

10. REFLECTION

As stated in Chapter 1, to be successful in business and in life, students must think and act like a CEO. They need to be leaders in a knowledge-based society by thinking both critically *and* strategically about their future and the future of the organizations in which they reside. Chapter 2 provides a financial framework for business model evaluation. Several company and stock market ratios and metrics are provided for conducting a strategic financial audit. The formulas, meaning, and rules of thumb for interpreting the ratios are offered. The assumption behind the ratio analysis is that the first step of conducting a case analysis is an assessment of a firm's overall financial health and the effectiveness of its business model. The chapter emphasizes the importance of evidence-based research in case study and student learning by presenting several steps for conducting and analyzing cases. The Thinking Critically exercises in the chapter focus on these steps and offer a framework for students to apply strategy concepts and analytical tools in analyzing and preparing cases. To act strategically and think critically, students need to take an active role—learning by doing. The Socratic method in individual learning, along with applying and actively using strategy concepts, are emphasized. The case method of study provides a framework and methodology for helping students understand how to act like CEOs. The approaches and steps to case analysis presented here are provided as a general checklist aimed at understanding the case situation and making recommendations. It is *not* intended to be exhaustive, either in the questions asked or in the areas covered.

<table>
<tr><td>Thinking Critically Exercise 24</td><td></td></tr>
</table>

SYNTHESIS AND REFLECTIONS

a. What does it mean to be strategic in your thinking and actions? How can strategy schools help you think and act strategically? How have the strategic concepts, analytical tools, and critical-thinking questions and exercises presented in the chapters helped you better understand strategy, thinking critically, and acting strategically?

b. Identify specific conflict situations in your life in which you feel the case method to problem solving could have been used to resolve the discord. Is the case method to problem solving always appropriate for conflict resolution? Identify those situations in which you feel it is not appropriate. Why is it important to always begin a case analysis by clearly identifying a critical issue or central problem?

c. If there is no one schooled solution to a case, how can a case help you make better decisions?

<table>
<tr><td>Thinking Critically Exercise 25</td><td></td></tr>
</table>

IS YAHOO!'S BUSINESS MODEL WORKING?

Yahoo! was founded at Stanford University in January 1994 by two electrical engineering graduate students, Jerry Yang and David Filo, after they created a website named "Jerry and David's Guide to the World Wide Web." The guide was a directory of other websites. In April 1994, Jerry and David's guide was renamed Yahoo! It grew rapidly throughout the 1990s and diversified into a web portal (web portals bring information together from diverse sources in a uniform way), followed by numerous high-profile acquisitions (Maven Networks, RockMelt [a social web browser], Flickr, Tumblr, and others). Maven provided Yahoo! with its internet video players and video advertising tools. Yahoo!'s web products, services, and other offerings include: Yahoo! Search, Yahoo! Mail, Yahoo! Messenger, Yahoo.com (Yahoo!'s homepage), Yahoo! Games, and Yahoo! Music. The Yahoo! homepage provides users with a preview of their mailbox, weather, stock quotes, sports scores, and comics. The company's stock price rose to $118.75 in 2000. After the dot-com bubble burst in 2001, however, it fell to $8.11. In 2008, Yahoo!'s board rejected an acquisition bid from the Microsoft Corporation to buy Yahoo! for $44.6 billion in cash and stock.

On July 16, 2012, former Google executive and Walmart corporate director Marissa Mayer became Yahoo!'s CEO and president at age 37—the youngest CEO of a Fortune 500 company. Mayer was tasked with turning Yahoo! around after several years of declining sales, major management missteps, and a revolving door of Yahoo! CEOs. Key elements of Mayer's transformation strategy included a focus on mobile products and mobile advertising formats, as well as increasing revenue from mobile devices, a platform where Yahoo! was historically weak.

In its 10-K report to the U.S. Securities and Exchange Commission on December 31, 2014, Yahoo! reported that "if we are unable to develop products for mobile devices that users find engaging and that help us grow our mobile revenue, our competitive position, our financial condition, and operating results could be harmed" (see Exhibit 2.4: Yahoo! Summary Income Statement 2007–2014). "In addition, a number of competitors offer products, services, and apps that directly compete for users with our offerings, including e-mail, search, video, social, sports, news, finance, micro-blogging, and messaging." On September 29, 2015, *The Wall Street Journal* reported that Yahoo! intended to sell more than $20 billion worth of stock that it held in Alibaba (China's biggest online commerce company). *The Wall Street Journal* also stated that Mayer "needs to complete the Alibaba spin-off to quell investors, who are growing impatient with her lack of progress reversing the company's struggling online-ad business after more than three years at the helm."[a]

Exhibit 2.4 Yahoo!'s Summary Income Statement 2007–2014

(Thousands)								
Year	2014	2013	2012	2011	2010	2009	2008	2007
Revenues	**4618133**	**4680380**	**4986566**	**4984199**	**6324651**	**7208502**	**6969274**	**5257668**
Cost of revenues	1298314	1349380	1620566	1502650	2627545	3023362	2838758	2096201
Gross profit	3319819	3331000	3366000	3481549	3697106	4185140	4130516	3161467
Total operating expenses	4475191	4090454	4420198	4183858	5552127	4172177	3435103	2053742
Income (loss) from operations	**142942**	**589926**	**566368**	**800341**	**772524**	**12963**	**695413**	**1107725**
Gain from sale of Alibaba Group Shares	—	—	4603322	—	—	—	—	—
Gain on sale of Alibaba Group ADSs	10319437	—	—	—	—	—	—	—
Provision (benefit) for income taxes	4038102	153392	1940043	241767	221523	262717	337263	767816
Net income (loss)	**7532142**	**1376566**	**3950602**	**1062669**	**1244628**	**424298**	**660000**	**1896230**
Net income attributable to Yahoo! Inc.	7521731	1366281	3945479	1048827	1231663	—	—	—
Net income (loss) per share—basic	7.61	1.3	3.31	0.82	0.91	0.31	0.49	1.35
Net income (loss) per share—diluted	7.45	1.26	3.28	0.82	0.9	0.29	0.47	1.28
Number of full time employees	12500	12200	11700	14100	13600	13600	14300	9800

a. Describe Yahoo!'s business model. Based on the financial information found in Exhibit 2.4, does Yahoo! have a competitive advantage? Is its business model working? How do you know if it's working or not?

b. Mayer is planning to spin off Yahoo!'s holdings in Alibaba. The spin-off is projected to provide Yahoo! with pretax capital gains of $20 billion. What should it do with the proceeds? What

---

a   Douglas MacMillan, "Yahoo! Presses Ahead with Alibaba Spinoff." *Wall Street Journal*, September 29, 2015: B1.

portion of the proceeds should she allocate to the turnaround strategy, and how much should be returned to shareholders through dividends?

c. Go to your college or university's online databases (or a business publication that reports financial information). Click on a business and economics database link, such as Mergent online or a similar service. Find the latest financial information for Google, Facebook, and Yahoo! Peruse each company's financial statements (income statements and balance sheets or financial highlights) for the past three years. Which company has the superior business model based on its overall financial performance during this three-year period? Now what do you think of Yahoo!'s business model and its overall effectiveness?

Sources:
http://info.yahoo.com/; https://investor.yahoo.net/sec.cfm; http://files.shareholder.com/downloads/YHOO/789709555x0x826745/b7e0b2eb-68d3-4612-9307-03478b206a37/YahooInc2014AnnualReport.pdf; https://investor.yahoo.net/annuals.cfm; "Altaba Inc (NMS: AABA)." *Mergent Online.* Last modified November 28, 2017. http://www.mergentonline.com.libproxy.unh.edu/companydetail.php?compnumber=87948&pagetype=synopsis.

CHAPTER ENDNOTES

This case was prepared by Michael Merenda, William Naumes, and Margaret Naumes, University of New Hampshire, Durham, New Hampshire. © 2015.

All quotes and comments contained in this case were from a May 2008 interview with Joseph Faro, founder of Joseph's Gourmet Pasta and Sauces. Some of the numbers and dates found in this case have been disguised.

1. Joseph Faro, founder of Joseph's Gourmet Pasta and Sauces, interview by Michael Merenda, William, Naumes and Margaret Naumes, University of New Hampshire, Durham, NH, May 2008. © 2015.
2. "Carroll Lewis." BrainyQuote. Accessed August 31, 2014. http://www.brainyquote.com/quotes/authors/l/lewis_carroll.html.
3. Katz, Robert L. "Skills of an Effective Administrator." *Harvard Business Review* (1974): https://hbr.org/1974/09/skills-of-an-effective-administrator
4. Afuah, Allan. *Business Models: A Strategic Management Approach.* Boston: Irwin/McGraw-Hill, 2004.
5. Baden-Fuller, Charles and Stefan Haefliger. "Business Models and Technological Innovation." *Long Range Planning* 46, no. 6 (2013): 419–426. http://www.sciencedirect.com/science/article/pii/S0024630113000691.
6. Ibid., 16.
7. Ibid.
8. Mauffette-Leenders, Louise A., James A. Erskine, and Michiel R. Leenders. *Learning With Cases.* Ontario, Canada: Richard Ivey School of Business, 1997.
9. Edersheim, Elizabeth Haas. *The Definitive Drucker.* New York: McGraw-Hill, 2007.
10. "Yangming, Wang." *Internet Encyclopedia of Philosophy (IEP).* Accessed August 31, 2014. http://www.iep.utm.edu/wangyang/.
11. Edge, Alfred G. and Denis R. Coleman. *The Guide to Case Analysis and Reporting,* 1st ed. Honolulu, HI: System Logistics, Inc., 1978.
12. Christensen, C. Roland and Abby J. Hansen. *Teaching and the Case Method.* Boston: Harvard Business School Press, 1987.
13. "Robert Frost." BrainyQuote. Accessed August 31, 2014. http://www.brainyquote.com/quotes/quotes/r/robertfros151809.html.
14. "Critical Thinking: Where to Begin." *The Critical Thinking Community.* Accessed May 20, 2015. www.criticalthinking.org/pages/critical-thinking-where-to-begin/796.
15. "Critical Theory, Definition of." Wikipedia. Accessed July 26, 2014. http://en.wikipedia.org/wiki/Critical_theory.
16. Bell, Housel. *Measuring and Managing Knowledge.* New York: McGraw-Hill/Irwin, 2001.
17. "Definition, Critical Inquiry." Wikipedia. Accessed May 20, 2015. http://en.wikipedia.org/wiki/Critical_theory.
18. "Definition, Epistemology." Wikipedia. Accessed May 20, 2015. http://en.wikipedia.org/wiki/Epistemology.
19. Edge, Alfred G. and Denis R. Coleman. *The Guide to Case Analysis and Reporting,* 1st ed. Honolulu, HI: System Logistics, Inc., 1978.
20. Arrow, Kenneth J. *The Limits of Organization.* New York: W.W. Norton & Company, 1974.
21. Edge, Alfred G. and Denis R. Coleman. *The Guide to Case Analysis and Reporting,* 1st ed. Honolulu, HI: System Logistics, Inc., 1978.
22. Ibid.
23. Ibid.
24. "George Bernard Shaw." BrainyQuote. Accessed August 31, 2014. http://www.brainyquote.com/search_results.html?q=George+Bernard+Shaw.
25. Ellet, William. *The Case Study Handbook: How to Read, Discuss, and Write Persuasively About Cases.* Boston: Harvard Business Press, 2007.
26. Ibid.
27. Ibid.
28. Christensen, C. Roland and Abby J. Hansen. *Teaching and the Case Method.* Boston: Harvard Business School Press, 1987.
29. Ibid.
30. Tufte, Edward. *Beautiful Evidence.* Cheshire, CN: Graphics Press, 2006.
31. "Definition, Infographics." Wikipedia. Accessed May 20, 2015. http://en.wikipedia.org/wiki/Infographic.
32. Tufte, Edward. *Beautiful Evidence.* Cheshire, CN: Graphics Press, 2006.
33. Ibid.
34. See: *Hoover's Online, Mergent Online, Standard and Poor's Net Advantage Online.*
35. Ibid., 128.
36. Ibid., 130.
37. Ibid., 131.
38. Ibid., 132.
39. Ibid., 136.
40. Ibid., 137.
41. Ibid., 123–124.

CHAPTER 3

THE STRATEGIC MANAGEMENT CONCEPTUAL MODEL, STYLE STRATEGY SCHOOL, AND BUSINESS ETHICS

TOM BRADY: MANAGING ONESELF—MORE PROBABLE THAN NOT

INTRODUCTION

The NFL's American Football Conference (AFC) championship game on January 17, 2015, between the New England (NE) Patriots (Pats) and the Indianapolis Colts was more than just refs blowing whistles. The morning after the Pats' resounding 45–7 victory, Tom Brady found himself playing in another game, a game that might taint his football identity and legacy. Brady, the multimillion-dollar superstar quarterback and future Hall of Famer, was not accustomed to this kind of limelight, nor to losing; after all, the three-time Super Bowl MVP had amassed accolades and accomplishments unmatched by his NFL brothers. Brady, a "control freak" when it came to managing himself and to properly preparing for football games, suddenly became the center of a highly publicized sports story. Several news reports surfaced alleging that he knowingly played with illegal game balls, a violation of league competition rules. Few people could manage themselves like Brady, whether it was on the playing field or in life. This time, though, the nature of the game and the players had changed, making the stakes much higher than any Super Bowl win. Brady's supporters saw "Deflategate," as it was dubbed in the media, as much ado about nothing—just a lot of hot air; if true, the penalty, at most, should be only a slap on the hand. His detractors saw it as a question of morality, an unfair competitive edge that not only threatened the integrity of the game but also violated trust placed in him for not playing within competition rules. If this was the case, then stiffer penalties should be assessed. Some sports pundits argued for a season-long game suspension and an asterisk beside his name in the NFL record books.

Could the revered quarterback mastermind another late-game comeback, or was this game just the beginning—one with no clock, no league refs, and no NFL rulebook to guide play? This "game" would be played in the NFL club offices, the league office, social media, and the court of public opinion, under vastly different conditions and rules. The stakes were high, not only for Brady but also for all the players in this game. What did Brady know about underinflated footballs, and when did he know it? And did Brady knowingly use underinflated footballs in league games? NFL Commissioner Roger Goodell, the person charged with addressing these questions, hired the high-profile Washington law firm of Weiss, Rifkind, Wharton, & Garrison to conduct the investigation.

DEFLATED GAME BALLS

The start of the second half of the AFC championship game became delayed by more than 10 minutes as Head Referee Walt Anderson and his staff hunted for footballs that met the NFL competition rule because the NFL requires game-day footballs to be filled with air between 12.5 and 13.5 pounds per square inch (psi).

Anderson and his staff were suspicious that the Patriots might have used illegal game balls during the first half of the championship game. The week before the game, the Indianapolis Colts informed the NFL league office that the Patriots were using underinflated footballs during league games. (The Baltimore Ravens, the Patriots' division-round opponent the week before the AFC championship game, may have discussed their own concerns about underinflated footballs with the Colts.)

Brady, during a conference call on a sports radio talk show the morning after the championship game, laughed off the accusations as silly when asked about using underinflated footballs. As the Pats started to prepare for the February 2 Super Bowl, Deflategate became sensationalized news, not only for sports reporters and broadcasters but also for all major networks and media outlets. Could the Patriots be again in violation of league rules? (The Patriots had been found guilty of violating rules in 2007 by illegally videotaping opponents during league games. During that season, the Patriots went undefeated, winning 16 regular-season games and two playoff games before losing to the New York Giants in the Super Bowl.)

As the Deflategate controversy accelerated, the Patriots' owner, Bob Kraft, head coach, Bill Belichick, and quarterback, Brady, went on the offensive. After several days of silence, the NFL announced that it had hired attorney Ted Wells, a former college football player, to investigate whether any member of the Patriots organization intentionally deflated footballs before the AFC championship game. Although the Pats had their legion of loyal fans throughout the NFL, a large number of fans, sports commentators, coaches, team owners, and others disliked them, labeling them "cheaters" and a team that could not be trusted when it came to winning football games. The Patriots ranked second among the NFL's most-hated teams, trailing behind the Dallas Cowboys. This acrimony was particularly hyped leading up to the Super Bowl.

SUPER BOWL WEEK

At several widely anticipated news conferences during Super Bowl week, Brady said that he preferred balls at the lower end of the NFL guidelines. Belichick talked extensively—something highly unusual for the coach—about the science of game-day footballs and the possibility that atmospheric conditions were the cause for deflated balls. Kraft declared that the Patriots, Belichick, and Brady had had nothing to do with underinflated footballs and demanded an apology from the NFL if its investigation failed to find conclusive evidence that the Patriots had tampered with the balls. On February 2, the Pats beat the Seattle Seahawks in the Super Bowl with a thrilling last-minute interception on the goal line by undrafted rookie and free agent Malcolm Butler.

TOM BRADY

Brady played college football for the University of Michigan. He was later selected by the Pats in the sixth round of the 2000 NFL draft. Brady was the 199th pick taken and the seventh quarterback drafted. The celebrated quarterback is fifth on the all-time list for career passing yards and fifth for career touchdown passes. His career postseason record is 21–8; his playoff win total is the highest in NFL history. Brady helped set the record for the longest consecutive win streak in NFL history with 21 straight wins over two seasons (2003–2004). He also set the record for most consecutive playoff wins (10), and in 2007, he led the Patriots to the first undefeated regular season since the institution of the 16-game schedule. Brady has thrown for more passing yards and touchdowns than any quarterback in NFL postseason history, and he has the sixth-highest career passing rate of all time (95.9) among quarterbacks with at least 1,500 career passing attempts.

Brady is considered among the greatest quarterbacks of all time. He and Joe Montana, the former San Francisco star quarterback and Hall of Famer, are the only two players in NFL history to win the NFL's Most Valuable Player and Super Bowl MVP awards multiple times. Brady is the only quarterback to lead his team to six Super Bowls, and he holds the record for the most Super Bowl touchdown passes. He was Associated Press's 2007 Male Athlete of the Year, the first NFL player to be so honored since 1990. After the 2010 season, in a poll of league players, Brady was ranked as the top player in the NFL's Top 100. He also became the first quarterback to throw for 50 or more touchdowns in a season. In 2010, he set the NFL record for consecutive passes without an interception (358) and broke his own record for the highest season touchdown-to-interception ratio (among players who have started a full season) at 9:1. Brady ranked fourth for appearances on *Forbes's* annual Celebrity 100 list. His supermodel wife, Gisele Bundchen, made the *Forbes* cut for 14 straight years.

Brady and Belichick have combined to form one of the most successful quarterback–coach tandems in NFL history, together winning 160 regular-season games, 21 postseason games, and appearing in six Super Bowls—all NFL records.

ROBERT KRAFT AND THE PATS

Kraft purchased the Patriots in 1994 for $172 million. By the start of the 2014 NFL season, the Patriots had amassed more regular-season and playoff wins than any other NFL team since 1994. With its 2014 Super Bowl victory, the Patriots tied the San Francisco 49ers' and Pittsburgh Steelers' record-setting four Super Bowl victories. On-field success was also matched by off-field financial success. Kraft turned the former money-losing Patriots into one of the most successful NFL franchises with a team value of $2.6 billion, only slightly less than the Dallas Cowboys. In 2013, the Patriots' operating income was $147.2 million on revenues of $428 million. (The $428 million did not include Gillette Stadium revenues.) Gillette was opened in 2002 and financed privately by Kraft. The Patriots' win-to-player cost ratio was 154 percent. (The ratio compares the number of wins-per-player payroll relative to the rest of the NFL teams. A ratio of 154 meant that the Patriots achieved 54 percent more victories per dollar of payroll compared to the league average during the 2013 season.) Success on and off the field made Kraft one of the most respected franchise owners in the league, especially by other club owners and the NFL league office. Much to the dislike of some of the other club owners and their fans, however, Kraft and Goodell became close friends. Deflategate severely tested this relationship. Kraft, in an unexpected appearance at a press conference during Super Bowl week, called on the NFL to apologize to the Patriots if the Wells report could not prove the Patriots guilty.

ROGER GOODELL

Goodell, the son of a U.S. senator from New York, was chosen NFL commissioner on August 8, 2006, over four other candidates on the fifth ballot held by league owners. In 2014, Goodell earned a salary of $44 million, a long way from his start in the NFL in 1982 as an intern to NFL Commissioner Pete Rozelle. In 1983, he interned with the New York Jets. In 1987, Goodell was appointed assistant president of the NFL's American Football Conference. In 2001, he became the NFL's executive vice president and chief operating officer. Since becoming commissioner, Goodell was heavily involved with negotiating the collective bargaining agreement (CBA) with the NFL Players Association (NFLPA). Goodell, on several occasions, declared that protecting the integrity of the game and making it safe was his highest priority. In 2014, NFL league revenues hit a record $12 billion.

Goodell's tenure as commissioner was not without controversy. In 2007, after a year of significant scandal involving NFL players, Goodell announced a new NFL personal conduct policy. The policy called for suspensions and fines for players' misconduct both on and off the field. In 2007, Goodell fined the Patriots and Coach Bilichick for attempting to videotape the defensive signals of the New York Jets. (Goodell noted that at the time he had thought about suspending the coach but in the end determined that fining the team and the coach, and stripping them of a draft pick, were more effective than any suspension. In 2013, two political advocacy groups, CREDO and UltraViolet, submitted a petition with more than 100,000 signatures calling on Goodell and the NFL to address its domestic violence problems. The groups' petition came after Baltimore Colts running back Ray Rice was suspended for two games after being accused of assaulting his fiancée (and now wife).

In 2012, in another scandal dubbed "Bountygate," Goodell handed out the harshest penalties in the history of the NFL. He suspended, indefinitely, the New Orleans Saints' defensive coordinator and dispensed a one-year suspension to its head coach. (The suspensions were based on evidence that revealed the Saints' players and coaches were involved in a bounty program where defensive players were paid bonuses for deliberately injuring and knocking opposing players out of games.)

Just before the start of the 2013 season, the NFL reached a tentative $765 million settlement over concussion-related brain injuries among its 18,000 retired players. The NFL agreed to compensate victims, pay for medical exams, and underwrite research. The agreement came after months of court-ordered mediation.

WELLS'S INVESTIGATIVE REPORT

The law firm of Paul Weiss, Rifkind, Wharton, & Garrison, LLP was hired by the NFL to investigate Deflategate. Theodore V. "Ted" Wells Jr. was a prominent criminal attorney in the law firm and the report's lead investigator. Wells earned degrees from Harvard Business School, Harvard Law School, and College of the Holy Cross. Wells and his law firm were best known for defending the likes of I. Lewis Libby, the chief of staff to former Vice President Dick Cheney; Michael Espy, the former agriculture secretary; and Steven A. Cohen, the billionaire Wall Street investor.

On May 6, 2015, after four months of investigation, the much-anticipated Wells report was released. The 243-page document (including a 139-page appendix laced with data behind the science of air in footballs) concluded that team personnel intentionally deflated game-day footballs to gain an unfair advantage in the AFC championship game, violating the NFL's honor code. The Wells report also found that it was more probable than not that Brady was at least generally aware of the inappropriate activities of locker-room attendant Jim McNally and equipment assistant John Jastremski. (Jastremski has been with the team for 14 years. During the past three, he was in charge of preparing game-day footballs.) The Wells report cost the NFL approximately $3.5 million in legal fees.

Wells's Findings Regarding Mcnally and Jastremski

The Wells report noted that McNally and Jastremski deliberately engaged in efforts to circumvent the NFL honor code by deflating game footballs below 12.5 psi prior to the start of the AFC championship game. McNally referred to himself as "The Deflator" and engaged in a series of communications with Jastremski about the inflation levels of game-day footballs. A review of text messages between McNally and Jastremski found that Jastremski had provided needles to McNally to remove air from the footballs. Jastremski had also given McNally cash and "valuable items autographed by Brady the week before the AFC Championship Game."[a]

McNally revealed to Jastremski that he would not go to ESPN … "yet." Because McNally's responsibilities as locker-room attendant did not include inflating or deflating footballs, he violated standard pregame NFL procedure by taking the January 17 game-day balls from the officials' locker room without permission from the game officials. Video showed that McNally took the game balls into a bathroom before the game for a period long enough to deflate them. The Wells report also noted that Jastremski had received a particularly valuable autograph from Brady earlier in the season.

Wells's Findings Regarding Tom Brady

In terms of Brady, the Wells report states, "We also note that there is less direct evidence linking Brady to tampering activities than either McNally or Jastremski. We nevertheless believe, based on the totality of the evidence, that it is more probable than not that Brady was at least generally aware of the inappropriate activities of McNally and Jastremski involving the release of air from Patriots game balls."[b] The report noted that the lack of cooperation by Brady limited investigators' ability to discover relevant evidence.

The evidence regarding the report's conclusions on Brady's general awareness included an "increase in the frequency of telephone and text communications between Brady and Jastremski shortly after suspicions of ball tampering became public on January 19."[c] Brady, in his interviews with Wells investigators, "denied any knowledge of or involvement in any efforts to deflate game balls after the pregame inspection by the game officials."[d] Brady told investigators that "prior to the events surrounding the AFC Championship Game, he did not know McNally's name or anything about McNally's game-day responsibilities, including whether or not McNally had any role relating to game balls or the game officials."[e] The Wells report was critical of Brady's lack of cooperation by his refusal to make available electronic information (including his cellphone) and documents to the Wells investigators. The report also noted that investigators were willing to limit Brady's phone records and information strictly to the investigation and would not take possession of Brady's telephone or other electronic devices. Despite his lack of cooperation in submitting records, Brady did, however, appear for interviews with Wells investigators.

a   Wells, Theodore V., Brad S. Karp, and Lorin L. Reisner. *Investigative Report Concerning Footballs Used During the AFC Championship Game on January 18, 2015*, Paul, Weiss, Rifkind, Wharton, & Garrison LLP, May 6, 2015: 6–7.
b   Ibid., 17.
c   Ibid., 17.
d   Ibid., 19.
e   Ibid., 19.

The Wells report found no evidence that Kraft and Belichick knew about any deflation schemes or the actions of McNally and Jastremski. In addition, Wells reported that he had no idea what Belichick was referring to when the Pats' coach explained at a news conference during Super Bowl week that atmospheric conditions during games could lower the psi of game balls below the minimum 12.5.

THE PENALTY FOR BREAKING THE NFL HONOR CODE

On May 12, 2015, Troy Vincent, the NFL's executive vice president of operations, released a statement regarding the penalties to be served to the Pats and Brady for Deflategate. The statement read that, because of the violation of the "NFL Policy on Integrity of the Game and Enforcement of Competitive Rules," the following actions would be implemented:

- Tom Brady would be suspended for four games without pay. His first game back would be a primetime Sunday night telecast on October 18 against the Colts at Indianapolis. Brady's penalty was the harshest penalty sentenced to a NFL quarterback for violating the integrity of the game and its honor code. If Brady's suspension upon any appeal was upheld, it would cost him $1,882,352 in salary.
- The team would be penalized a first-round draft pick in 2016 and a fourth-round draft pick in 2017 and be fined $1 million.

Immediately following the NFL's announcement, the Pats suspended, indefinitely, McNally and Jastremski. Under the NFL league policy, a player found guilty of tampering with equipment for the first time faced a fine of a maximum $5,512. Kraft released a statement on May 13, 2015, that read: "Today's punishment far exceeded any reasonable expectation. It was based on circumstantial rather than hard or conclusive evidence." Kraft also stated that, "Tom Brady has our unconditional support. Our belief in him has not wavered."

BRADY'S APPEAL

On May 15, Brady filed his appeal of the four-game suspension with the league office. The NFLPA announced that they would fight the NFL and defend Brady. The NFLPA also asked Goodell to remove himself from the appeal, stating that if the Wells report was truly independent of the NFL and Goodell, then the appeal should be heard by a neutral third party. The NFLPA also claimed that Goodell's history of issuing discipline against NFL players rendered him ill-suited to hear Brady's appeal without bias. The NFLPA's collective-bargaining agreement, however, expressly allowed Goodell to act as a hearing officer in appeals of player discipline. NFLPA Councilman Jeffrey Kessler would represent Brady. Kessler was a high-profile rival of the NFL for more than three decades, having won several landmark decisions against the league. Kessler was also behind the efforts that successfully overturned former Baltimore Ravens running back Ray Rice's indefinite suspension. (Rice was originally suspended for two games, but Goodell changed this to indefinitely when a surveillance video appeared of Rice striking his fiancée in an elevator in a New Jersey casino.) Kessler also played a key role in getting Minnesota Vikings running back Adrian Peterson reinstated to play after Peterson was accused of physically abusing his 4-year-old son. (Peterson, remorseful about injuring his son, maintained that he was disciplining him with a "switch" from a tree—the way he himself was disciplined as a child.)

On May 19, Kraft repealed his earlier declaration that he would appeal any NFL penalties if the Wells report was not conclusive in its findings. At the NFL's spring league meetings in San Francisco, Kraft acknowledged that though Pats fans would be disappointed in the team, he would reluctantly accept the penalties assigned by Goodell and discontinue any further dialog regarding the matter. In short, he would not appeal.

On May 22, the NFL rejected the NFLPA's motion for Goodell to recuse himself from Brady's appeal based on a potential conflict of interest. Unless Goodell ruled in favor of Brady's appeal to reverse his four-game suspension, Brady and the NFLPA would have to either accept the suspension or take legal action against the NFL. Brady's appeal was scheduled for June 23. At the appeal, Brady and his legal counsel argued that the quarterback was not notified by the league of the penalty associated with being generally aware of McNally's and Jastremski's actions regarding game-day footballs. Kessler requested that the NFL share some of its attorneys' notes regarding Brady's suspension and his alleged involvement with the deflation of game-day footballs. Kessler also asked to interview Jeffrey Pash, the NFL's executive legal counsel. (Pash co-led the NFL's investigation and coedited the Wells report before it was released.) Goodell and the NFL rejected Kessler's request to interview Nash and for the league to turn over its attorneys' notes from the investigation. In more than 10 hours of testimony, Brady and his legal team provided new evidence to support their claim that the four-game suspension should be reversed because Brady, prior to the appeal hearings and after the four-game suspension was announced, provided the NFL with detailed phone records and text messages regarding his alleged involvement. Brady also offered to accept a lesser penalty.

On July 28, the NFL upheld Brady's four-game suspension. In announcing its decision, the league reported that Brady destroyed his cellphone on or before March 6, the day before being interviewed by Wells. The league based its decision on the evidence provided in the Wells report and presented at the appeal hearing. Goodell concluded that Brady was aware of and supported the actions of McNally and Jastremski. He found that Brady's "deliberate destruction of potentially relevant evidence went beyond a mere failure to cooperate in the investigation and supported a finding that he had sought to hide evidence of his own participation in the underlying scheme to alter the footballs."

On July 29, Brady released a letter in response to Goodell's decision. Brady denied destroying his phone or having had anything to do with tampering the footballs, writing:

> To suggest that I destroyed a phone to avoid giving the NFL information it requested is completely wrong. To try and reconcile the record and fully cooperate with the investigation after I was disciplined in May, we turned over detailed pages of cell phone records and all of the emails that Mr. Wells requested. There is no "smoking gun" and this controversy is manufactured to distract from the fact they have zero evidence of wrongdoing. I authorized the NFLPA to make a settlement offer to the NFL so that we could avoid going to court and put this inconsequential issue behind us as we move forward into this season. The discipline was upheld without any counteroffer. I respect the Commissioner's authority, but he also has to respect the CBA and my rights as a private citizen. I will not allow my unfair discipline to become a precedent for other NFL players without a fight.[f]

NFL MANAGEMENT COUNCIL, PLAINTIFF VS. NFL PLAYERS ASSOCIATION, DEFENDANT

Immediately following Goodell's ruling, the NFL Players Association, on behalf of Tom Brady, took legal action against Roger Goodell and the NFL's Management Council. The NFL won its petition to have the case tried in the U.S. District Court, Southern District of New York.

U.S. District Judge Richard Berman presided over the case. Berman required both Goodell and Brady to go to New York on several occasions to encourage them to settle the case outside of court. Berman announced that he would render his decision in the matter by September 6, just four days prior to the Patriots' opening game

---

f   Bibber, Ryan Van, "Tom Brady Didn't Destroy His Cell Phone, According to Tom Brady," *SB Nation*, July 29, 2015, http://www.sbnation.com/2015/7/29/9066253/tom-brady-cell-phone-deflategate-suspension-nfl-roger-goodell.

against the Pittsburgh Steelers at Gillette Stadium on September 10. The NFL argued that the NFLPA and NFL's collective-bargaining agreement (CBA) gave the commissioner full authority and the right to take disciplinary actions against players and sentence penalties to maintain the integrity of the game. The NFL also argued that the penalties afforded to Brady were justified based on: (1) Brady's failure to cooperate in the investigation, (2) the evidence provided in the Wells report, and (3) penalties awarded by the league in other cases, including a player's violation of the league's policy on steroid use.

On September 3, Judge Berman issued his ruling, lifting Brady's four-game suspension. Berman sharply criticized Goodell and the NFL's actions. He noted it was the league, not Tom Brady, that withheld information. Nor did the league abide by the CBA. Berman cast Brady as the victim of "an arbitrary, capricious, and fundamentally unfair disciplinary process" administered by the NFL. Berman declared that a player must be notified of the policy under which he is being investigated as well as the penalty for violating it. In both cases, Brady was not notified. The league's honor or integrity code of conduct policy was given only to club executives and coaches, not players. Brady was never informed that he would be suspended based on the league's policy for tampering with equipment. Berman concluded that Brady's suspension was the "equivalent of the discipline imposed upon a player who used performance-enhancing drugs." The NFL's action is counter to long-held labor arbitration law that upholds an employee's right to be notified that he violated some standard and the penalties associated with violating it. Furthermore, the NFL did not make Pash available to testify at Brady's appeal hearing and did not provide some of the attorneys' notes as requested by the NFLPA. By withholding information pertaining to the case and denying access to Pash, it was the NFL that failed to cooperate in the investigation, not Brady. These missteps by the NFL and Goodell, according to Berman, added up to Goodell administering his own brand of "industrial justice." Berman wrote that the fundamental fairness of the proceedings apply to Goodell and the NFL, regardless of the authority given to Goodell by the CBA. The CBA agreement does not allow entities (NFL and Goodell) to make up rules as they go, according to Berman.

BRADY'S NEXT STEPS

Although Berman's ruling was overwhelmingly in favor of Brady and the NFLPA, the ruling did not clear Brady's name of the NFL's accusations against him. The Wells report cost the NFL more than $3.5 million. This hefty fee was in addition to the other expenses associated with the investigation. *Sports Illustrated* estimated that the league spent more than $10 million on the Brady case. Immediately following Berman's ruling, Goodell vowed to appeal his decision. He reaffirmed his right to uphold the collective-bargaining agreement and his responsibility to protect the integrity of the game. On September 25, the league filed its petition in federal court to expedite their appeal of Berman's decision and to have Brady serve his suspension during the 2016 NFL season. Was the deflation of footballs, if this was actually the case, just a minor equipment infraction, or was it truly a more serious violation of the league's honor code to protect the integrity of the game? In the end, whose integrity was being violated: Goodell's, Brady's, the Patriots', or the League's?

a. Do you think the fines and penalties levied against the Pats and Brady were fair? What evidence did Wells use to make his case? Why do you think Kraft retracted his decision to fight the NFL and appeal the penalties assigned? For someone who prided himself on self-management and always being in control, how could Brady let himself get involved in Deflategate in the first place?

b. What accounts for the Pats' and Kraft's successes, both on and off the playing field? Do you think the $2.6 billion valuation for the Pats makes sense (after all, this is only a game)? What do you think of Kraft's strategic management of the Pats? What do you think of Coach Belichick's strategic management of the Pats football team and competitiveness? What is business ethics? Why is it so difficult to decide right from wrong in the case of Brady and the Pats regarding the Deflategate controversy?

c. Goodell and the NFL league office decided to appeal Judge Berman's decision to repeal Brady's four-game suspension. What arguments did Berman use in making his ruling? Who has a "stake" in the

NFL's decision to appeal? Place each stakeholder in the stakeholder map (Exhibit 3.6) based on their power, influence, and interests in the NFL's action to appeal Berman's findings. What conclusions can be drawn from the stakeholder map? Should Goodell and the NFL office proceed with the appeal, or should they drop the appeal? Why?

SOURCES

Badenhausen, Kurt. "Tom Brady: By the Numbers." *Forbes*, May 14, 2015. http://www.forbes.com/sites/kurtbadenhausen/2015/05/14/tom-brady-by-the-numbers/.

Bibber, Ryan Van. "Tom Brady Didn't Destroy His Cell Phone, According to Tom Brady." *SB Nation*. July 29, 2015. http://www.sbnation.com/2015/7/29/9066253/tom-brady-cell-phone-deflategate-suspension-nfl-roger-goodell.

Bowers, Rachel G. "Reaction as Swift as Penalties." *Boston Globe*, May 12, 2015: D8.

Branch, John. "Star Probably Knew Footballs Were Doctored, NFL Finds." *New York Times*, May 7, 2015: A1, B12.

Brown, Maury. "With Tom Brady Suspended, Patriots Losing Picks and Fined, How Long Till Roger Goodell Is Fired?" *Forbes*, May 11, 2015. http://www.forbes.com/sites/maurybrown/2015/05/11/with-tom-brady-suspended-patriots-losing-picks-and-fined-how-long-till-roger-goodell-is-fired/.

Brown, Maury. "Robert Kraft Chooses 'La Familia' Over War, While the Emperor of the NFL Has No Clothes." *Forbes, May 20, 2015*. http://www.forbes.com/sites/maurybrown/2015/05/20/robert-kraft-chooses-la-familia-over-war-while-the-emperor-of-the-nfl-has-no-clothes/.

Gasper, Christopher L. "Actually He's Paying for the Sins of Belichick." *Boston Globe*, May 12, 2015: D1, D6.

Glanz, James. "In the End, Science Works Against the Patriots." *New York Times*, May 7, 2015: B12.

Hohler, Bob. "Free to Play: Judge Voids Brady's 4-game Suspension." *Boston Globe*, September 4, 2015: A1, A9.

Macur, Juliet. "Brady's Legacy as One of the Best Takes a Hit." *New York Times*, May 7, 2015: B11, B13.

NFL Communications. "Tom Brady Appeal Decision: Discipline Upheld in Tom Brady's Appeal." July 28, 2015. http://nflcommunications.com/2015/07/28/tom-brady-appeal-decision/.

Orr, Conor. "Roger Goodell Will Hear Tom Brady Suspension Appeal." June 2, 2015. http://www.nfl.com/news/story/0ap3000000495255/article/roger-goodell-will-hear-tom-brady-suspension-appeal.

Powell, Michael. "Now the Pressure Is on Goodell, Poor Roger." *New York Times*, May 7, 2015: B11, B13.

Shaughnessay, Dan. "QB Sacked: NFL Hits Brady and Patriots for Huge Losses." *Boston Globe*, May 12, 2015: D1, D8.

Violin, Ben. "For the NFL, 3 Big Missteps Under the Law." *Boston Globe*, September 4, 2015: A1, A9.

Wells, Theodore V., Brad S. Karp, and Lorin L. Reisner. *Investigative Report Concerning Footballs Used During the AFC Championship Game on January 18, 2015*. Paul, Weiss, Rifkind, Wharton, & Garrison LLP. May 6, 2015: 17.

Young, Shalise Manza. "Owner Kraft Notes Harsh Discipline." *Boston Globe*, May 12, 2015: D1, D8.

1. INTRODUCTION: QUESTIONS TO THINK ABOUT

- What is the strategic management process?
- What is the strategic management conceptual model?
- What does a situational scan of the firm's external environment include?
- What does a situational scan of the firm's internal environment include?
- What is a SWOT analysis?
- What does a strategic audit entail?
- What is a PESTEL analysis?

- What is stakeholder theory?
- What are the levels of corporate social responsibility?
- What are sustainable business decisions?
- What is business ethics?

Strategic thinking is about understanding and making sense of the firm's internal and external environments and taking actions that capitalize on this knowledge. Strategy as practice is about what strategists actually do; that is, how they go about daily making and executing strategy in real life. As a discipline, strategy is considered a social science that focuses on the behavior of people and human institutions.[1] **Paradigms** are what scholars of management assume to be reality or what they take to be true. Paradigms include the intellectual perceptions, models, and widely held beliefs shared by leading scholars, practitioners, scientists, politicians, and others. These intellectual perceptions can coalesce around a model or pattern of how things work in the real world. The strategic management conceptual model and strategy schools of thought are leading paradigms shared by strategy scholars and practitioners. First, this chapter will present the strategic management model, or paradigm, designed to help inform and guide strategic decisions through a seven-step strategy-making and executing process. Second, the style school of strategic thought will be presented. (This school is one of the oldest and most widely used by strategists.) Third, no discussion of strategy is complete without an understanding of the role societal and individual values play in the strategic management of the firm. What is the firm's responsibility to society beyond making profits? Finally, two competing models of the firm, the single-sovereign and multiple-sovereign models, will be presented. This discussion will include business ethics, corporate social responsibility, and sustainable business practices as they pertain to the strategic management of a firm.

2. THE STRATEGIC MANAGEMENT CONCEPTUAL MODEL

The challenge for strategic managers is to improve organizational performance on a continual basis. Critical inquiry, analysis, and strategic thinking and action underlie all aspects of the strategic management conceptual model. The conceptual model, as an open system, is dynamic, not static. It is intended to be a guide and process for strategically managing diverse, complex, and challenging internal and external environments. As a model, it also simplifies the complexity inherent in strategically managing dynamic organizations. Because firms compete in dynamic environments, strategies need to be flexible and adapt to changing environmental conditions and circumstances. As such, strategy encompasses the everyday activities and actions designed to improve organizational performance. Strategies must be formulated, crafted, and adapted over time in ways that reflect the interconnected and interpenetrating dimensions of the firm as an open system.[2] The strategic management conceptual model is an abstract depiction of the steps and activities involved in the total and ongoing management of the organization by strategic leaders. At the broadest level, the model can be viewed as a guide to the steps involved in creating value for the customer and the firm. The strategic management model includes the following: (1) external environmental scan; (2) internal environmental scan; (3) vision and mission; (4) goals and objectives; (5) strategy formulation or strategy making; (6) strategy implementation and execution; and (7) monitor, evaluate, and control. The strategy schools of thought are also included in the strategic management model. Strategy schools include the main strategic thinking, prevailing assumptions, theories, principles, frameworks, and analytical tools used by strategists to craft and execute value-creating strategies (see Exhibit 3.1: Strategic Management Conceptual Model).

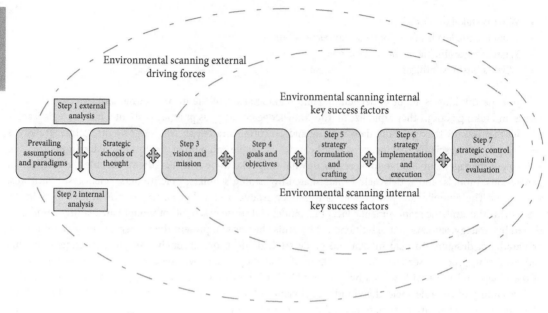

Exhibit 3.1 Strategic Management Conceptual Model

Environmental scanning external driving forces

Environmental scanning internal key success factors

Step 1 external analysis

Step 2 internal analysis

| Prevailing assumptions and paradigms | Strategic schools of thought | Step 3 vision and mission | Step 4 goals and objectives | Step 5 strategy formulation and crafting | Step 6 strategy implementation and execution | Step 7 strategic control monitor evaluation |

Environmental scanning internal key success factors

2.1 STEP 1: ENVIRONMENTAL SCAN—EXTERNAL (OPPORTUNITIES AND THREATS)

This first step in the strategic management model encompasses an analysis and assessment of a firm's external task environment. The **task environment** consists of those external factors that are relevant or potentially relevant in facilitating or hindering a company's goal achievement.[3] The external task environment can be divided into three levels of analysis: macro—contextual, mezzo—industry or market, and micro—organizational or company (see Exhibit 3.2: Environmental Scan: Macro, Mezzo and Micro). A situational analysis of the external environment should lead to an identification of external opportunities and threats, as well as any barriers or obstacles to an organization's performance. Strategic managers need to determine what factors or forces in a firm's macro are relevant or potentially relevant to mezzo or **industry** competitive dynamics and, in turn, a company's strategies and performance. Political, environmental, technical, economic, and legal forces **in the macro** environment drive industry opportunities and threats. In crafting strategies, managers need to first identify, analyze, and assess relevant or potentially relevant macro forces and secondly mezzo or industry forces that drive opportunities and threats. The relevant or potential relevant forces at both levels define a company's task environment.

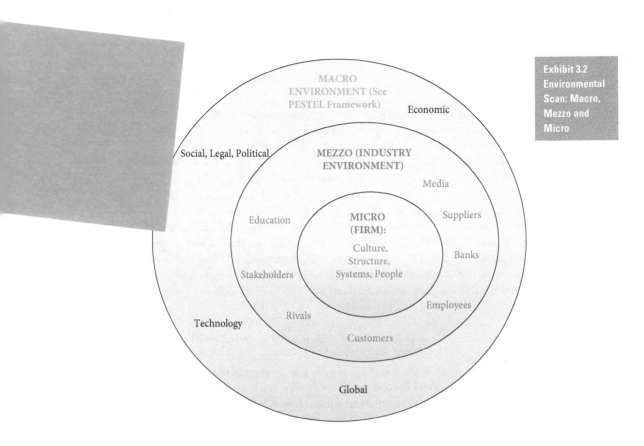

Exhibit 3.2
Environmental
Scan: Macro,
Mezzo and
Micro

Exhibit 3.2 Environmental Scan: Macro, Mezzo and Micro

2.2 STRATEGIC MANAGEMENT MODEL: ACTING STRATEGICALLY, THINKING CRITICALLY

The primary purpose of external environmental scanning is to identify and assess a firm's market opportunities and threats. An **opportunity** is a positive industry trend, condition, or factor that provides an opening in the external environment that an organization can potentially exploit to gain a competitive advantage. A **threat** is an external trend, condition, or factor that can potentially block or destroy an organization's competitive advantage and its ability to create value for customers. A threat, if not staved off or overcome with superior capabilities, can quickly erode or destroy a company's performance. The main objective of an external environmental scan is to determine how best a company can create customer value by identifying and exploiting external opportunities.

The strategist constantly searches for ways to create and sustain a competitive advantage over the firm's rivals. This is accomplished by delivering superior customer value. Only a firm's customers can determine whether a firm has achieved a competitive advantage because the competitive advantage is based on customer purchasing decisions or the amount of money customers are willing to spend on one company's products over another's. **Competitive advantage** is when a firm can provide the same value as its competitors, but at a lower price, or it can charge higher prices by providing greater value through differentiation.

UBER'S CHALLENGES

Founded in 2009, Uber Technologies, Inc. is an American international ride-sharing company headquartered in San Francisco, California. It develops, markets, and operates the mobile app-based transportation network also called Uber. In December 2014, Uber received $1.2 billion in private equity, boosting the company's valuation to more than $40 billion. Ride-sharing service Uber Technologies, Inc. reported that a new round of funding valued it at $41 billion, signaling to the world's top investors that the firm can sustain a breakneck global expansion pace despite fierce challenges from regulators and taxi companies. The $1.2 billion equity will enable the company to expand its workforce, lure new drivers, test a delivery service, and subsidize prices in some of the 250 cities around the world where it operates. The closely held company has raised, to date, eight times as much as its closest ride-sharing rival, Lyft Inc. The funding is a vote of confidence in Travis Kalanick, Uber's co-founder and chief executive, whose brash personality has courted controversy. A recent privacy scandal stirred by one of Kalanick's deputies, however, appears not to have fazed investors focused on Uber's business prospects.[4] In a press conference, Kalanick tried to avoid additional controversy by apologizing for his deputy's statement that Uber stirs up allegations against its critics.[5]

a. Uber is employing a net-centric strategy. The internet is central to Uber's strategies and value proposition. Go to www.uber.com. What is Uber's business model? How has Uber used the internet to monetize its Uber application—that is, creating customer value? Draw a figurative map of Uber's B2B (Uber's connectivity to its drivers) and B2C (Uber's connectivity to customers for payment—those using the app to schedule rides). What are some of the characteristics of the internet that Uber is trying to exploit by creating customer value and appropriating value for Uber's equity investors?

b. What business is Uber in industry-wise? Is Uber's strategy revolutionary or just a natural evolution of the ride-sharing and limousine business? What are some of the external driving forces that Uber's management seems to be exploiting? Do you think that $41 billion is a fair valuation for Uber, especially for such a young start-up venture with zero profits? What's driving this high valuation?

2.3 STEP 2: ENVIRONMENTAL SCAN—INTERNAL (STRENGTHS AND WEAKNESSES)

This step includes an analysis of the company's tangible and intangible resources to determine its strengths, capabilities, core capacities, distinctive competencies, weaknesses, and deficiencies. **Strengths** are organizational resources and capabilities that, when mobilized and used effectively, facilitate goal achievement or the gaining of a competitive advantage. **Capabilities** are based on knowledge and knowing how to act. A capability shows a firm's ability to or expertise in strategically managing internal resources. A core capability is a business activity that a company performs at a consistently high level of competency and is designated by the company as critical to its competitive position in the marketplace. Companies attempt to achieve dominance in a market by focusing on their core capabilities. A **distinctive competence** is a core capability that gives the firm a unique advantage over rivals. Advantage is earned by offering products and services that are more highly valued by a firm's customers than those products and services offered by rivals. A **weakness** is a resource limitation or lack of know-how that can prevent a firm from achieving its goals and gaining or sustaining a competitive advantage. Many companies fail from a shortage or lack of superior or unique strengths and capabilities and/or by having too many weaknesses or deficiencies. Environmental scanning must take advantage of value-creating opportunities while staving off threats. This is partially accomplished by capitalizing on internal strengths and core capabilities while lessening weaknesses and key deficiencies.

2.4 STEP 3: VISION AND MISSION

A **vision statement** captures the long-term direction and purpose for a company. It implies a common thread or unifying theme for a company or organization that remains unchanged over time. As such, a vision usually includes an identification of a company's long-term end values, core purpose, and customer focus. For example, Amazon's vision statement "… is to be Earth's most customer-centric company for four primary customer sets: consumers, sellers, enterprises, and content creators."[6] A vision statement in essence declares **what** the company aspires to be long-term.[7] How a company intends to achieve its vision is usually contained in its **mission statement**.

A **mission** is a short statement of the purpose for a company or organization. The mission statement guides the actions of the organization, exemplifies its overall goal, provides a sense of direction, and guides decision making. It provides "the framework or context within which the company's strategies are crafted and executed." The mission statement broadly specifies a company's goals, objectives, products, services, markets, customers, and technologies.[8] For example, Facebook's mission is to give people the power to share and make the world more open and connected. Google's mission is to organize the world's information and make it universally accessible and useful.[9] Vision and mission statements should identify what is important to the firm and distinguish it from rivals. Vision (long-term orientation) and mission (short-term focus) statements not only act as clear guides for strategy crafting and execution but also elicit a future path and direction.

2.5 STEP 4: GOALS AND OBJECTIVES

VIDEO 3.1 Why the Secret to Success is Setting the Right Goals | John Doerr

Goals are the long-term expected or hoped-for results that, if achieved, will lead to the overall accomplishment of the mission. **Objectives** are the benchmarks or results that are identifiable and measurable milestones on the way toward achieving a firm's short-term mission and longer-term vision. Most senior managers will take the time to develop and articulate appropriate strategic goals for their businesses to illustrate their plans and vision for the company. Strategic objectives should be challenging yet achievable and measurable, and they should reflect a realistic assessment of the firm's performance and business model. Some examples of business goals are:

- To be the leader of next-generation technologies in every industry in which we compete
- To be a fully integrated worldwide marketer of high-quality consumer products
- To be the most innovative company in the world
- To change the world for the better
- To maintain the highest environmental standards in all manufacturing processes
- To have the best athletic footwear on the market
- To be the leader in human resource management

Some examples of business objectives are:

- To grow revenue by 10 percent each year for the next five years
- To increase market share by 10 percent within the next two years

- To lower carbon emissions by 20 percent by 2020
- To achieve an annual return on equity of 15 percent or greater
- To improve labor productivity by 2 percent per year
- To reduced cost per unit by 3 percent per year

2.6 STEP 5: STRATEGY FORMULATION AND CRAFTING

Strategy formulation and crafting is the fifth step in the strategic management process. This step builds on the previous four steps and is aimed at closing **any performance gap** between the firm's present situation (existing strategies and performance—what is) and desired strategies and performance (what should be). Its aim is to move the organization forward toward accomplishing its vision, mission, goals, and objectives (steps 3 and 4). Generally speaking, a firm, depending on the conclusions drawn from the environmental scan (steps 1 and 2) and what it strives to achieve (steps 3 and 4), can choose from a wide array of strategies, actions, and activities. Strategic actions are necessary in three levels of the organization: corporate, business, and functional (see Exhibit 3.3: Strategy Hierarchy). **Corporate** strategy focuses on vision, mission, core purpose, goals, and objectives. This level identifies the specific businesses and markets in which a firm competes. **Business strategies** focus on "how" the firm will compete in each of its businesses or markets identified at the corporate level. The **functional level** focuses on the operational processes, activities, and actions required from each function or operational unit necessary to carry out (implement and execute) corporate- and business-level strategies. Functional strategies also focus on improving operational efficiency and controlling costs within the boundaries set by the organization's corporate- and business-level strategies.[10]

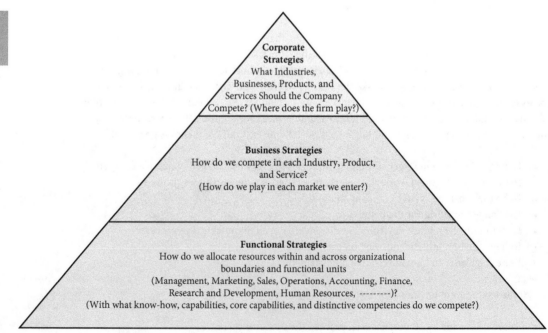

Exhibit 3.3 Strategy Hierarchy

Corporate Strategies
What Industries, Businesses, Products, and Services Should the Company Compete? (Where does the firm play?)

Business Strategies
How do we compete in each Industry, Product, and Service?
(How do we play in each market we enter?)

Functional Strategies
How do we allocate resources within and across organizational boundaries and functional units
(Management, Marketing, Sales, Operations, Accounting, Finance, Research and Development, Human Resources, --------)?
(With what know-how, capabilities, core capabilities, and distinctive competencies do we compete?)

2.7 STEP 6: STRATEGY IMPLEMENTATION AND EXECUTION

Strategy implementation requires consideration of how formulated strategies will be carried out (executed). What resources are needed, who will be responsible for implementing the strategies, and over what time period? Strategy implementation addresses how the organization is to use its resources to achieve a competitive advantage and improve performance. **Resources** provide the firm with the ability and capacity to carry out formulated strategies. Examples of resources are (1) human resources: number, quality, skills, and experience of personnel; (2) physical and material resources: machines, land, buildings; (3) financial resources: money and credit; (4) information resources: pool of knowledge and databases; and (5) intellectual resources: copyrights, designs, and patents.

A firm's culture, principles, and values comprise the main considerations in strategy implementation. Organizational **culture** determines what is acceptable or unacceptable, important or unimportant, right or wrong, workable or unworkable. It encompasses shared explicit and tacit assumptions, beliefs, knowledge, norms, and values, as well as attitudes and behavior in a company. As such, culture can be the best facilitator in effectively executing strategy or facing a major obstacle. Strategic action also needs to be guided by the overall principles and values of the organization. **Principles** capture the fundamental norms, rules, or values that represent what is desirable and positive for an organization or company. Principles guide strategic decisions by helping managers determine what is right or wrong about their decisions and actions.

Values in general are the important and enduring beliefs or ideals shared by the members of an organization regarding what is good or desirable and what is not. Values not only exert major influence on the behavior of an individual but also serve as broad guidelines in all situations. For example, some of Green Mountain Coffee Roasters stated values include:

- We partner for mutual success
- Our boundary-less approach to collaboration creates benefits for all
- We innovate with passion
- With courage and curiosity, we are shaping the future by redefining the customer experience
- We play to win[11]

The general manager's leadership and ability to articulate the formulated strategy with integrity and clarity, given the organization's resources, culture, principles, and values, remains key. Commitment from every individual in the organization is critical to the strategy being executed effectively. As Naveen Jain so eloquently stated, "Success doesn't necessarily come from breakthrough innovation, but from flawless execution. A great strategy alone won't win a game or a battle; the win comes from basic blocking and tackling."[12]

2.8 STEP 7: MONITOR, EVALUATE, AND CONTROL (STRATEGIC CONTROL)

This step assesses whether the formulated strategies (step 5) and implemented strategies (step 6) are working and producing the intended or desired outcomes. Step 7 focuses on an in-depth assessment of the formulated and implemented strategies. Are they the right strategies for the intended results? Were they properly executed and carried out? If the answer to either question is "no," then a return to steps 1 through 6 is required. As stated earlier, there is no endpoint to strategy. Unlike a plan, continuous learning, critical inquiry, strategic thinking, analysis, assessment, and action dynamically drive the strategic management model.

3. STYLE STRATEGY SCHOOL

Andrews, Ansoff, and Drucker primarily laid the foundation for the style school as a conceptual framework and approach for strategy making in the 1950s.[13] This school is also known as the design school, which focuses on the CEO as the chief designer or maker of strategy. Accordingly, the CEO designs strategy and forwards it to subordinates for implementation. Under this school, strategy making is not overly analytical or intuitively difficult to comprehend. The focus of the CEO is on the viability of the firm and not necessarily its people. As such, people assume a passive, less important, secondary role. The Industrial Age, top-down, command-and-control management style dominates strategy making for this school. This is driven by the assumption that only the CEO has access to the prerequisite information for designing strategies. Interest in the school increased with the rise of the large, multinational, centralized organizations that dominated the U.S. economy during the latter part of the nineteenth century and well into the twentieth century. The large, multinational organization, according to design school advocates, was best suited for mass producing standardized products and services for mass markets. It helped to fuel the rapid growth and dominance of the United States as an economic power. The competitive landscape was described as oligopolistic with a "live and let live" prevailing attitude among competing firms. The design school advocates also advanced the notion that strategy making was about matching a firm's internal strengths to external opportunities. Mintzberg notes that the operative term for design school supporters is "capture success" by determining what the firm is good at and matching it with what the world wants and needs.[14] Scholars of this school argue that the primary responsibility of the CEO is to create competitive advantage by identifying and exploiting the firm's capabilities, qualifications, and distinctive competencies.[15] Although in theory the design school approach is not overly analytical or intuitively difficult to comprehend, one of the most dominant and earliest analytical tools coming from this school is SWOT (strength, weaknesses, opportunities, and threats). The SWOT concept model is depicted in Exhibit 3.4.

Strategic Matching or Fit

**Exhibit 3.4
SWOT:
Conceptual
Model**

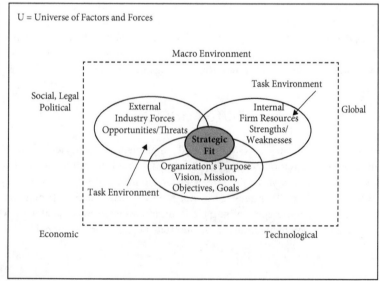

Bob Stiller, Green Mountain's founder and chairman, was a strong advocate for all businesses to help make the world a better place by committing to sustainable practices. Since Stiller's departure from GMCR, maintaining economic performance with a sustainability focus in a highly competitive beverage industry has presented challenges and opportunities for Keurig-GMCR. The company began in Massachusetts in 1992 as the coffee industry's original single-serve brewer and coffee-pod manufacturer. In March 2014, Keurig ceased to be a separate business unit and subsidiary and instead became Keurig Green Mountain. In 2016, Keurig Green Mountain was acquired by an investor group led by private-equity firm JAB Holding Company for nearly $14 billion. In January 2018, Keurig Green Mountain, Inc. and Dr Pepper Snapple Group, Inc. announced that the companies had entered into a definitive merger agreement to create Keurig Dr Pepper, a new challenger company in the beverage space.

Go to Keurig-Green Mountain Coffee Roasters' webpage at www.keuriggreenmountain.com. Click on the menu bar, then select the "Investors" link. Click on "Keurig Kold Investor Presentation." View the presentation.

   a. Based on the presentation, how successful has Green Mountain been under its new management structure?

   b. What is management's new vision and mission for the company given its expanded lines of business?

   c. How has the company performed under its new management team and structure? Would management be "happy" with Green Mountain's company performance and commitment to sustainable business practices? Why or why not?

3.1 SWOT ANALYSIS (STRENGTHS, WEAKNESSES, OPPORTUNITIES, AND THREATS)

 VIDEO 3.2 Business Strategy - SWOT Analysis

A **SWOT analysis** is a structured approach to evaluating the strengths, weaknesses, opportunities, and threats involved in a strategic decision regarding a product, service, process, project, business, or other activity (see Exhibit 3.5: SWOT Analysis Template). A SWOT analysis can be carried out for a new or existing product, service, process, or project. It involves specifying the objective of the business venture or project and identifying the internal and external factors that are favorable or unfavorable to achieving that objective.

Strengths, weaknesses, opportunities, and threats are not the same for every firm. The old adage that "one man's loss is another man's gain" certainly applies when conducting a SWOT analysis (see Exhibit 3.5). An opportunity for one firm may present a significant threat for another. Similarly, a firm's unique or distinctive competency may not necessarily lead to customer-value creation, thus making it a core weakness or deficiency.[16] For example, Kodak's once valuable and unique distinctive competencies in film photography became major weaknesses and severe deficiencies when film photography was eventually displaced by rapid growth in digital photography. Kodak's management dilemma stemmed from its inability to abandon what was once a valuable and highly profitable traditional film business and transition to digital film, which required an entirely different set of distinctive competencies.

Strengths are organizational resources and capabilities that facilitate organizational purpose (goal achievement) by exploiting opportunities or negating threats. Strengths turned into core capabilities and distinctive competencies drive a firm's competitive advantage and performance.

Weaknesses are resource limitations or lack of know-how (capabilities) that can prevent a firm from achieving the organization's purpose—its vision, mission, goals, and objectives. Weaknesses can limit or prevent a firm from creating and sustaining competitive advantage and performance improvements. Strategic managers must determine which weaknesses can be tolerated and which are critical. Managers must also pinpoint severe deficiencies that could block or seriously hinder a firm from achieving organizational purpose. Many companies fail from either a shortage or lack of core capabilities and distinctive competencies, or by having too many core weaknesses and deficiencies.

Exhibit 3.5 **SWOT Analysis** **Template**	SWOT focus: Company, business, function, product, service, other. Specify: _____ Note: SWOT factors may apply to more than one quadrant. See Table 3.1 for Examples of SWOT factors.

Strengths—highlight core capabilities/distinctive competencies

> List and provide qualitative and quantitative support

Weaknesses—highlight key weaknesses or critical shortcomings

> List and provide qualitative and quantitative support

Opportunities—highlight opportunities that best match strengths

> List and provide qualitative and quantitative support

Threats—highlight key obstacles or major external challenges

> List and provide qualitative and quantitative support

Draw Conclusions:
   a. Do strengths/opportunities outweigh weaknesses/threats? Please explain -if so, what action is recommended?
   b. Do weaknesses/threats outweigh strengths/opportunities? Please explain -if so, what action is recommended?
   c. Action recommnded: _____
   _____

Source: Michael J. Merenda (c) 2019

Opportunities are positive industry trends, conditions, or factors that are potentially favorable to a firm's organizational purpose (goal achievement). Because a firm has limited resource strengths, managers need to select only those opportunities that provide the greatest chances for improving firm performance and achieving organizational purpose.

Threats are negative or detrimental industry trends, conditions, or factors that are potentially unfavorable to a firm's organizational purpose and performance. Because a firm has limited resource strengths, managers need to avoid, circumvent, or overcome potentially harmful industry threats. Threats can potentially block or destroy an organization's ability to deliver or create value for customers. As such, threats, if not staved off or overcome with innovative strategies and superior capabilities, can quickly erode or destroy a company's performance and ability to sustain its competitive advantage.

3.2 HOW TO CONDUCT A SWOT ANALYSIS

Step 1: Identify strengths, weaknesses, opportunities, and threats for a business (or product, service, process, or other entity) being evaluated (see Table 3.1: Examples of SWOT Factors).

Step 2: List each SWOT factor in the appropriate quadrant (I–IV) of the SWOT Analysis Template (see Exhibit 3.5: SWOT Analysis Template).[17]

Step 3: Highlight in bold those strengths that are or have the potential to be core capabilities and distinctive competencies.

Step 4: Highlight in bold those opportunities that can be best exploited based on core capabilities and distinctive competencies highlighted in quadrant I.

Step 5: Highlight in bold core weaknesses and deficiencies.

Step 6: Highlight in bold critical threats.

Step 7: A SWOT analysis should conclude with an identification of core capabilities, distinctive competencies, and key deficiencies or obstacles to an organization's performance. Draw conclusions from steps 3 through 6 above based on your responses to the following questions:

a. Do resource strengths (core capabilities and distinctive competencies) and external opportunities outweigh all other cells? If so, it signals high business and industry attractiveness and calls for offensive growth strategies.

b. Do resource strengths and external threats outweigh external opportunities and internal weaknesses? If so, it signals high firm attractiveness and low industry attractiveness and calls for defensive or maintenance strategies (also known as "hold or continue with exiting strategies").

c. Do resource weaknesses and external opportunities outweigh external threats and internal strengths? If so, it signals low business attractiveness and high industry attractiveness and calls for defensive strategies. If the business cannot be righted or turned around, then the recommended action is either to slowly harvest (or come out of) the business by not investing in it or to sell or close the business.

d. Do resource weaknesses and external threats outweigh external opportunities and internal strengths? If so, it signals low business attractiveness and low industry attractiveness and calls for exiting or harvesting the business (see c above).

**Table 3.1
Examples of
SWOT Factors**

Some typical examples of opportunities are:

- Stage of industry life cycle, market volume, demand trends
- Growth in GNP, PPP, strength of economies, standard of living
- Advances in IT, telecommunication technologies, and innovations
- Advances in next-generation technologies, such as nanotechnology and biotechnology
- Basic and advanced factor conditions
- Favorable export tariffs, exchange rates, economics
- Industry profitability, health, and competitiveness
- Strong stock market performance and sources of equity and debt financing
- Industry consolidation, merger and acquisition trends
- Weak industry competitors
- New product and process innovations
- Global market relationships, resources, knowledge
- Emerging and growing markets
- Favorable changes to industry structure and relationships
- Niche target markets
- Market need for new unique price, cost, quality relationships
- Government policies and spending
- Network and collaborative value-chain relationships
- Outsourcing and lean manufacturing
- Favorable transaction-cost relationships
- Asymmetries in information and superior knowledge
- Social and lifestyle trends
- Stock of knowledge, think tanks, universities, brain power
- Wide acceptance of sustainable business practices
- Weather and climate changes

Some typical examples of threats are:

- Stage of industry life cycle, mature or declining markets
- Depressed markets and economies
- Market dominance by powerful competitors
- Fiercely competitive markets and hypercompetition
- Rapid product obsolescence
- Rapid technological infusion and diffusion
- Unfavorable price, cost, quality relationships
- Unexpected or unusual competitive practices and behaviors, especially from foreign competition
- Unfavorable economic conditions at home and abroad
- Poor industry profitability, health, and competitiveness
- Poor stock market performance and limited sources of equity and debt financing
- Industry consolidation, merger and acquisition trends
- Strong industry competitors
- Unfavorable size, scale relationships, and learning-curve economics
- Unfavorable changes to industry structure and relationships
- Government policies and actions
- Unfavorable value-chain relationships
- Asymmetries in information and superior knowledge
- Unfavorable social and lifestyle trends

- Limited or no availability of knowledge workers or access to superior knowledge
- Weather and climate changes
- National security and threats from terrorists

Some typical examples of strengths are:
- Unique business model
- Unique value proposition
- Continuous process innovation
- Continuous product innovation
- Price, cost, quality relationships
- Number and magnitude of core capabilities and distinctive competencies
- Sustainable competitive advantages
- Numerous sources of competitive advantages
- Unique strategies
- People strengths, talents, experience, knowledge
- Resource quality and availability
- Financial health and leverage
- Marketing—reach, distribution, awareness
- Ability to bridge time and space
- Location and geographical advantages
- Culture and values fit
- Good leadership
- Good strategy
- Ethical and moral leadership
- Strategy execution

Some typical examples of weaknesses are:
- Imitable business model
- Value-proposition disadvantages
- Limited or insufficient core capabilities
- None or few distinctive competencies
- Lack of competitive strengths
- Poor reputation, image, brand
- Limited financial resources, inability to weather financial adversity
- Limited product line
- Price, cost, quality relationships
- Known or unavoidable vulnerabilities
- Limited ability to respond to competitive threats
- Insufficient knowledge, unreliable data, lack of critical information
- Limited or insufficient management skills
- Poor processes and systems
- Poor culture and values fit
- Resistance to change
- Inexperience or weak management
- Dysfunctional organizational structures

KEURIG DR PEPPER MERGER: INVESTORS PRESENTATION

On July 9, 2018, Keurig Dr Pepper (NYSE: KDP) announced the successful completion of the merger between Keurig Green Mountain and Dr Pepper Snapple Group. Go to http://investors.keurigdrpepper.com/events-and-presentations. Go to "News and Events" and click on "Events and Presentations." Go to the March 20, 2018 Keurig Dr Pepper Investor Day Audio Webcast and download. View presentation.

a. Why did the two companies merge?
b. Based on this presentation summarize the combined strengths of the merged company and opportunities that the merged companies plan on exploiting.
c. What weaknesses and potential threats might jeopardize the success of the merger?

4. STRATEGIC AUDIT

A **strategic audit** is a useful framework and tool for critically analyzing a company's overall internal strengths and weaknesses and external opportunities and threats. It is frequently used to conduct an annual checkup of a company's overall strategic and financial health. Similar to an annual physical or medical examination for an individual, the strategic audit provides a detailed record of the soundness and effectiveness of a company's strategies and business model. A strategic audit is also appropriate when assessing the merits of a specific strategic decision. In general, a strategic audit is required when the firm is confronted with a change in strategy as a result of:

- Major change or event in the firm's external environment
- Serious crisis or major event in the firm's internal environment
- Strategic decision that involves internal and/or external support from the firm's stockholders, board of directors, regulatory personnel, financial parties, or other stakeholders

4.1 LEVELS OF ANALYSIS IN CONDUCTING A STRATEGIC AUDIT

A strategic audit can be a daunting task for any organization. When conducting a strategic audit, a distinction can be made at three levels of analysis: (a) **macro**—contextual, (b) **mezzo**—transactional, and (c) **micro**—organizational. The macro level consists of "global forces," such as economic trends and developments, demographics, politics, technological trends, and social trends and developments. The mezzo level consists of industry and market forces including: customers, suppliers, supply and demand, distribution channels and customers, competitors, and other stakeholders. The micro level involves factors that address the internal environment of the firm: culture, values, vision, mission, strategies, financial, technical and human resources, processes, products, and services. For example, when competing across international borders, the strategic manager must consider any differences in the macro, mezzo, and micro forces and factors found in a country's institutions, industries, and organizations compared to the manager's home country.

4.2 MACRO—CONTEXTUAL FORCES

VIDEO 3.3 PESTEL
Analysis

Numerous macro factors can influence the competitive dynamics or intensity of a firm's mezzo (industry) environment. These factors can be grouped into several broad categories including: political, environmental, social, technological, economic, and legal—or **PESTEL** (see Figure 3.1: PESTEL Factors).[18] Conducting a PESTEL analysis is useful in identifying and assessing the interplay of macro, mezzo, and micro forces in a firm's strategies and actions. Macro factors can be emergent (new developments), active (directly impactful), or latent (passive or no impact on forces). Macro forces can also facilitate or hinder the demand for a firm's products and services either directly or indirectly, thus impacting a firm's ability to compete and perform.

For example, government subsidiaries, tax credits, and other incentives help drive demand and competition in all-electric vehicles and solar-powered panels. Similarly, the rapid growth and expansion of telecommunication companies and their high-speed networks spurred demand for new products and services. In this case, growth in telecommunication networks complemented demand for e-commerce companies and a host of products and services, including financial services and banking (fintech, mobile banking, bitcoins), content, information services, and consumer goods and services. Growth in these products and services were further aided by increased network bandwidth or capacity and speed. Increased availability, accessibility, and affordability caused an explosion in demand for internet services and products. The emergent and

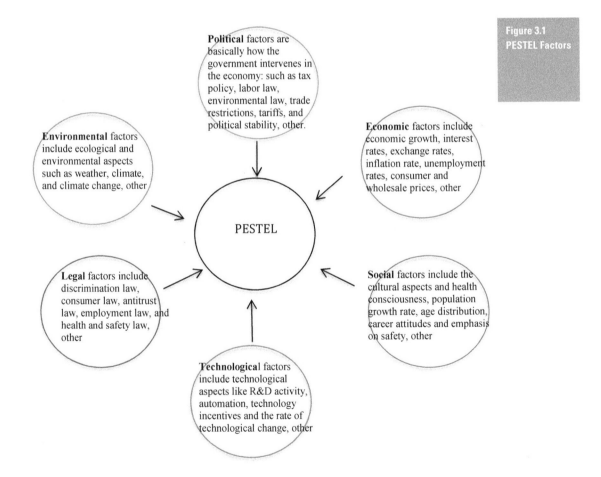

**Figure 3.1
PESTEL Factors**

rapid growth in ecommerce companies—such as Salesforce, Amazon, Alphabet, Uber, Airbnb, Priceline, and a host of others—spurred increased demand for numerous products and services, games, courses, media, news, sporting events, music, photos, and computer services (cloud services, memory, data analytics, and storage). The rapid growth in e-commerce companies, especially Amazon.com, have threatened or stymied demand in traditional brick-and-mortar retail and service companies such as Sears, Barnes & Noble, and other book publishers and media companies. In short, telecommunication services and internet connectivity have complemented demand and spurred growth in numerous industries while threatening the very existence of others.

<table>
<tr><td>**Thinking Critically Exercise 29**</td><td></td></tr>
</table>

DARK POOLS

Several PESTEL forces in high-speed trading have transformed how and where stocks are traded, in turn spurring the rapid growth in private stock exchanges ("dark pools") and high-frequency trading.[19] *Forbes* reports:

> The stock market is fragmented into over 50 individual marketplaces owned and operated by the giants of finance (Credit Suisse, Goldman Sachs, Barclays, Morgan Stanley) and other large securities firms who do not allow unwanted customers to trade there. These "dark pools" are "dark" because they are not transparent to the public, to ordinary traders, or to the media. They get their business in great part from the computers of high frequency trading firms, mainly quant hedge funds like Renaissance.

The rise of high-speed trading brought about new regulatory oversight by the SEC, along with public criticism and outrage over the ethics of several major investment banks and brokerage firms because of their indiscriminate use of dark pools.

a. What are dark pools? What PESTEL factors drove the growth in dark pools?
b. How have dark pools changed the way stocks are bought and sold?

Source: Lewis, Michael. *Flash Boys: A Wall Street Revolt, 224–9*, Contributor: Robert Lenzner. New York: Norton, 2014.; "Dark Pools Fragment the Stock Market into 50 Private Stock Markets." *Forbes*. Accessed June 9, 2015. http://www.forbes.com/sites/robertlenzner/2014/06/27/dark-pools-fragment-the-stock-market-into-50-private-stock-markets/.

4.3 MEZZO—INDUSTRY AND MARKET FORCES

In order for strategists to craft and implement effective strategies, they must first understand what is happening in the markets and industries in which their firms compete. In other words, strategists need to constantly assess the changes taking place within the industry. What industry opportunities are helping rivals? What industry threats are hurting rivals? Changes taking place at the mezzo level can positively or negatively impact a company's strategies and performance. Consequentially, strategists must continually assess external forces and decide how best to respond to these changing industry forces. The way the firm responds to industry forces will determine the viability and sustainability of its business model, value proposition, and competitive advantage.

The strategic audit at the micro level includes assessing a company's strategy alignment, resource strengths, capabilities (know-how), core capabilities, and distinctive competencies. Its focus is on evaluating the overall strategic and financial health of the firm and its prospects for the future. Two subcategories of the strategic audit are the **management audit** and the **financial audit**. Both types are often necessitated by major changes in a firm's strategies or business model, as well as major external or internal events. The purpose of the micro-level audit is to evaluate the strategic health of the firm. Strategic audits are also conducted to evaluate management's effectiveness, especially with regard to the firm's vision, mission, strategic objectives and strategies, and its overall resource strengths. Some of the events that call for a strategic audit are top management changes, mergers and acquisitions, and succession planning. A management audit, depending on the nature of the strategic decisions at hand, focuses on assessing the firm's financial health as well as the capabilities and competencies of its management team at all levels of the organization including corporate, business, and functional (see Table 3.2: Conducting a Strategic Audit—Questions).

A. Macro Level:

Socio-cultural Dimensions. What is the relationship of the organization to norms, values, attitudes, social systems and societal expectations practiced or shared by its citizens and legitimized through its institutions?

Political-legal Dimensions. What is the relationship of the organization to policies, philosophies, laws and regulations as practices by local, state, national, and international governments?

Economic Dimensions. What is the relationship of the organization and the accumulation and allocation of society's scarce resources? How are resources priced and distributed in society? What are the fiscal and monetary policies aimed at protecting society's economic welfare? (See Appendix A)

Technological Dimensions. What are the relationships of the organization to science and its application and diffusion in society?

Global Dimensions. What is the relationship of the organization to international and global competition, the politics and issues that transcend geographic and national boundaries?

B. Mezzo/Industry Level:

Industry Health. What is the relationship of organizational performance to: market demand, size of market, industry profitability, product and industry life cycles and an industry's general well being?

Competition. What is the nature of competition in the industry and how do we compare to major competitors relative to their strategic profile, strategic capability, strengths, weaknesses, degree of vertical and horizontal integration, products and services offered, managerial philosophy?

> **Table 3.2**
> **Conducting a Strategic Audit—Questions**

Industry Structure and Characteristics. How is an organization's competitive position and performance affected by: capital markets, concentration ratios, threat of new industry entrants, threat of substitute products, rivalry among competitors, pricing, segmentation strategies, industry and trade associations, labor unions, environmental issues, employee rights, consumerism, ethics?

Other. What unique technological, political and social trends and factors are germane or unique to our industry?

C. Micro/Company Level:

Observation must also focus on an identification of organizational strengths and weaknesses found in the internal task environment. For observation and analysis, the internal task environment can be viewed in terms of two main components: Top Management and Its Functions and The Organization and Its Functions.

In addition to a strategic audit of the entire firm or organization a management audit is also necessary for proper analysis and assessment as it applies to strategic managers. A management audit focuses on an assessment of: Strategic Managers, Hierarchy of Strategy and Management Functions.

Strategic Managers. Strategic managers are individuals who are instrumental either in the development or implementation of the organization's strategies, goals and objectives and continuous success. Chief Executive Officers (CEO), Chief Operating Officers (COO), Board of Directors, Functional, and Business managers are key strategic managers responsible for the well being and performance of the firm. An audit of the hierarchy of strategy by strategic managers entails observing key strategies, policies, tactics and rules contained in the enterprise, corporate, business and/or functional levels of the organization. Usually, strategic management effectiveness is directly associated with how adept they are in each of the management functions. The functions of management are: Planning, Organizing, Motivating, Controlling, Directing, Staffing, and Leading.

Top Level Management. The administration function within the organization should be held responsible for an assessment of: organization structure (divisional, functional, matrix, conglomerate, multinational); stages of organization life cycles (Entrepreneurial Phase I, Functional Phase II, Multinational Phase III); line/staff relationships; board membership; management succession; employee welfare; public policy issue management; human resource management (its development, growth, planning).

Financial Audit. A strategic audit should help senior level managers answer the following questions: How well is the organization performing? Can it survive financial adversity? What factors would lead to financial adversity? What is top management's attitude toward risk? What funds are available to the organization? From what specific sources? Answers to these and other questions can be obtained through a detailed audit of all financial statements, including: Balance Sheet, Income Statement, and Statement of Changes in Financial Position. Financial results for an organization should be viewed in terms of: past performance (known as trend or horizontal analysis); future performance (referred to as pro forma analysis); industry comparative performance (competitor statement analysis); and statement item comparisons on a percentage basis (known as vertical analysis).

Accounting. In addition to a financial audit, a critique of the finance and accounting function must also be undertaken. Staffing, control systems, reporting mechanisms, budgets, standard operating procedures, and cash flow management are among the items to observe.

Marketing. The market and sales functions in the organization should be held accountable for an assessment of: product quality, depth and breadth; segment analysis; sales growth; market research; channels of distribution; advertising and promotion; new product development, product life cycle analysis (introduction, growth, maturity, decline); industry life cycle analysis; customer service.

Operations/Manufacturing. The operations and manufacturing functions within an organization should be held responsible for an assessment of: plant capacity, production methods; plant layout and design; quality control; operating leverage, production technology (computer aided manufacturing—CAM), robotics; assembly requirements; material control and purchasing.

Engineering and Research and Development. Engineering within a manufacturing firm can be divided at a minimum into Design, Manufacturing Engineering, and Research and Development Departments or components. An assessment of this function would include, at a minimum, an audit of: new product research and design, existing product design and engineering support; methods; design costs; product performance; field service.

Management Information Systems and Technology. A management information system (MIS) provides information that organizations require to manage themselves efficiently and effectively. Management information systems are typically computer systems used for managing the five primary components: 1) Hardware, 2) Software, 3) Data (information for decision-making), 4) Procedures (design, development and documentation), and 5) People (individuals, groups, or organizations). Management information systems are distinct from other information systems because they are used to analyze and facilitate strategic and operational activities.

Human Resources. Human resources are the set of individuals who make up the workforce of an organization. "Human capital" is sometimes used synonymously with human resources, although human capital typically refers to a more narrow view (i.e., the knowledge the individuals embody and can contribute to an organization). The professional discipline and business function that oversees an organization's human resources is called human resource management (HRM, or simply HR).

Other.

4.5 BENEFITS OF THE STRATEGIC AUDIT

- Conducting a strategic audit is vital to the success of a company. Customers, markets, and technologies constantly change. Keeping abreast of and assessing these changes is a crucial step in crafting and implementing strategy. The strategic audit examines the company's position in the market and its chances for success. Changes in markets and customers necessitates a closer look at the exiting company's strategies in order to determine what the type and degree of change (if any) is needed for a firm to continuously improve performance. The audit should address the following questions:

- Are current strategies working as planned?
- What changes, if any, are needed in the way the firm conducts business?
- Does the firm have a competitive advantage?
- Is the competitive advantage sustainable?
- What are the market and financial risks of staying with existing strategies?
- What are the risks involved with changing existing strategies?
- What is the potential of this business?
- What resources are needed to continually perform at a high level?

5. COMPETING MODELS OF THE FIRM: SINGLE-SOVEREIGN AND MULTIPLE-SOVEREIGN MODELS

An organization can be viewed as a collection of resources: financial, physical, technical, managerial, and human. Management must obtain the correct mix of resources and properly allocate these resources for the organization to be effective. Two opposing models of the allocation of resources are the classical economics (or single-sovereign) model and the stakeholder (or multiple-sovereign) model of the firm (the second model is also known as the social responsibility model). The two models have contrasting assumptions about the role of business in society and the role of the strategic manager in allocating resources.

5.1 SINGLE-SOVEREIGN MODEL OF THE FIRM

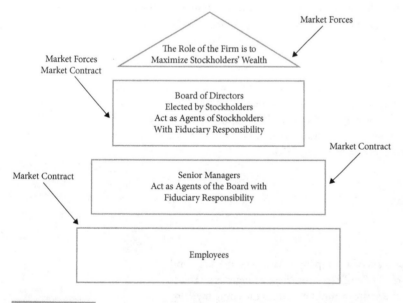

Figure 3.2
Single-Sovereign Model of the Firm

Friedman maintains, "Few trends could so thoroughly undermine the very foundations of our free society as the acceptance by corporate officials of a social responsibility other than to make as much money for their stockholders as possible."[20] Friedman's perspective highlights the classical market contract view of the firm. Market efficiency will decide whether the firm succeeds. A rational manager's goal is to maximize profits for stockholders; to do otherwise is pure and unadulterated socialism. The manager's job, as an agent of the shareholder, is to turn all profits not reinvested into the firm back to shareholders in the form of dividends. The *shareholders'* values and interests will determine how dividends are to be used, not the manager's. Furthermore, if the manager were to engage in social activities, these activities come with a price or added cost to the customer. Friedman argues that the added cost results in higher prices that will make the firm less competitive in the marketplace. Also, higher prices can be viewed as an added tax on the product, and managers do not have the right to set taxes; only elected officials can do so (see Figure 3.2: Single-Sovereign Model of the Firm).[21]

Under the multiple-sovereign (or stakeholder) model, the strategic leader must take into consideration a number of competing influences and interests from multiple stakeholders (those who have an interest or "stake" in how the resources of an organization are obtained, managed, and allocated) in crafting and executing strategy. Advocates of this view argue that the firm is accountable to a number of interests or stakeholders, not just to stockholders. A **stakeholder** is any group or individual who is affected, negatively or positively, by the decisions of the firm and who, accordingly, can have an impact, positively or negatively, on the firm. Thompson holds that "the relationship between an organization and its task environment is essentially of exchange, and unless the organization is judged by those in contact with it as offering something desirable, it will not receive the input necessary for its survival."[22] Stakeholder theory argues that third-party interest groups, civic organizations, individual managers, governmental agencies, etc. present various social concerns and pressures on the organization. Strategic managers must buffer these concerns by protecting the organization's main strategies, actions, and decisions from uncertainty or potential conflict with stakeholders. The degree to which the organization is successful in executing strategy is measured by how well significant stakeholders are satisfied, as shown through their interaction with the organization.[23]

Advocates of the multiple-sovereign model argue that managers need to use discretion and power in a socially acceptable context; that is, firms are surrounded by multiple stakeholders or interest groups, each having some authority on the firm's resources or energies. Stockholders hold no special status in this model. Management, acting as a hub of activity, is entrusted with equitably distributing its energy, corporate rewards, or resources among stakeholders and interest groups. The firm has a market contract to survive by making money as well as a **social contract**.[24] Social contract advocates maintain that the firm gets its right to exist from society. If the firm abuses its rights, its right to exist can and will be taken away. In this regard, the manager is viewed as a "steward" of the interests of not only shareholders but also all stakeholders who are impacted by the firm's actions. Society expects managers of organizations to always act in society's best interest. If the stakeholder perspective is taken, then strategic managers need to identify and understand competing stakeholder interests, values, and potential actions in crafting and executing strategies (see Figure 3.3: Multiple-Sovereign Model of the Firm).

Figure 3.3 Multiple-Sovereign Model of the Firm

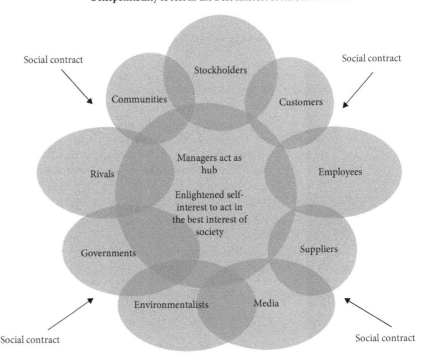

Board of Directors and Managers are Stewards of the Firm's Resources with a Responsibility to Act in the Best Interest of All Stakeholders

The literature on agency theory has grown considerably since the turn of century. Since the mid-1980s, law and economic scholars dominated the study and application of agency theory. These scholars, along with their financial-agency colleagues, considered the corporate board shareholders. This claim ran against stakeholder theory, where board members and managers were not only agents of shareholders but also **stewards** of the organization's resources and responsible to society and all stakeholders. Proponents of stewardship theory hold the position that managers, left on their own, will indeed act as responsible stewards of the assets they control. It is in the strategic manager's (and the firm's) **enlightened self-interest** to protect, develop, and grow the assets of the firm. The enlightened self-interest philosophy in business ethics holds the belief that strategic managers will act to further the interests of others because to do so furthers their own self-interest and the self-interest of the firm. It has often been simply expressed by the belief that an individual, group, or commercial entity will "do well by doing good."

Both agency and stewardship theorists hold the belief that managers function as impartial coordinators who owe allegiance to the firm as an ongoing concern. Still, some agency theorists insist that the stakeholder position has several flaws. First, stakeholder theory underestimates the conflict of interest between management and the firm's wealth-maximizing purpose. Managers have an interest in utilizing profits and cash to reduce bankruptcy and exploit future wealth-generation opportunities. Second, shareholders differ from other stakeholders in two ways. Shareholders assume a residual risk—they receive payment only after all other contracts have been met. Because shareholder wealth depends on the firm's ability to generate profits, shareholder interest closely aligns with the firm's social purpose: to create new wealth. Finally, agency theory advocates argue that stakeholder theory undoes maximizing behavior because it is difficult for managers to maximize performance while balancing the multiple interests of several stakeholders. They argue that the goal of boards of directors and strategic managers should be to maximize shareholder value creation.[25]

6. STAKEHOLDER ANALYSIS

Stakeholder analysis remains a key part of strategy making, crafting, and execution. A stakeholder analysis of strategic actions consists of weighing and balancing all of the competing demands on a firm by each of those who have a claim on it. This reveals the firm's, individual's, or group's stake in the strategic action. Stakeholder analysis attempts to analyze and assess the attitudes and actions of others toward management's strategic decision or action. A stakeholder is any person or organization who can be positively or negatively impacted by, or cause an impact on, the actions of a company. Stakeholders can be divided into three categories: primary, secondary, and key. **Primary** stakeholders are individuals, groups of individuals, and organizational entities that are ultimately affected, either positively or negatively, by an organization's actions. **Secondary** stakeholders are the "intermediaries": people or organizations that are indirectly affected by an organization's actions. **Key** stakeholders are primary or secondary stakeholders who have significant importance or influence on the decisions and actions of managers. The goal of stakeholder analysis is to carefully examine the potential positive or negative impact of a strategic decision on stakeholders to ensure the action is acceptable (see Table 3.3: Types of Stakeholders).[26]

Table 3.3
Types of
Stakeholders

- Company shareholders
- Customers (by distribution channel)
- Company board of directors
- Senior managers (CEO, COO, CFO, VPs, other)
- Full-time employees
- Part-time employees
- Contract employees (outsourced work)
- Vendors and suppliers
- Rivals (by power, threat, relationships)
- Indirect competitors
- Governments (domestic, foreign, national, regional, local)
- Local community members and institutions (schools, religious organizations)
- NGOs (non-governmental organizations)
- Activists
- Scientific community
- Media
- Financial institutions (banks, venture capitalists, creditors)

6.1 STEPS IN STAKEHOLDER ANALYSIS

Step 1: Identify the strategic action (new program initiative or major strategic action) being analyzed from the perspective of stakeholders.

Step 2: List who might have a stake (positive or negative) or interest in the strategic action being analyzed (at this time, do not classify stakeholders as primary, secondary, or key).

Step 3: Map or place each stakeholder in the nine-cell (3x3) matrix representing two dimensions of interest (see Exhibit 3.6: Stakeholder Map). Common dimensions used in prioritizing stakeholders in the matrix are:

- Power (high, medium, low): Power can either have a positive or negative impact on the strategic action
- Influence (high, medium, low): Influence can either have a positive or negative impact on the strategic action
- Interest (strong, medium, weak): Stakeholder interest in the strategic action can either be positive or negative

Step 4: Using a third dimension, such as color or a symbol (e.g., a circle), represent the individual stakeholder power, influence, and interest in the strategic action or decision (for example, use green if the power, influence, and interest are high).

Step 5: Identify how best to manage each grouping of stakeholders (e.g., green, red, yellow).

Step 6: Draw conclusions:

  i.   Green: high priority, be interactive, build collaborative partnerships
  ii. Red: engage, be proactive, keep satisfied
  iii. Yellow: low priority, be reactive, monitor

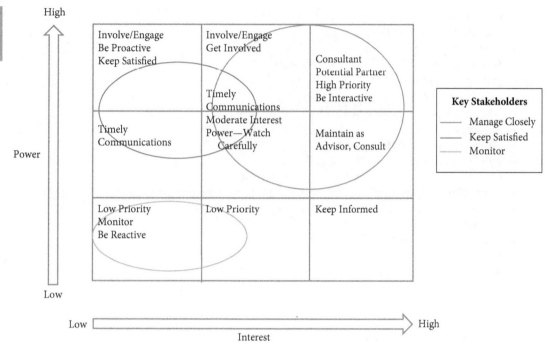

Exhibit 3.6 Stakeholder Map

Thinking Critically Exercise 30

VOLKSWAGEN AG—EVADING CARBON-EMISSIONS TESTING

When Volkswagen AG, the parent company of the Volkswagen brand, disclosed in September 2015 that its top engineers installed software in its diesel-powered cars to bypass emissions-control standards during routine EPA testing, the statement shocked the company. The admission also raised social and governmental concerns about the entire global auto industry's pattern of unethical behaviors and competitive practices. The deadly consequences of several auto manufacturers' failures to disclose vehicle safety defects in a timely fashion added to a host of governmental, regulatory, social, and legal pressures and demands on an already fiercely competitive industry. GM's defective push-button ignition switches, Takata's malfunctioning vehicle airbags, and the sudden and uncontrollable acceleration of Toyotas were just a few subjects of high-profile governmental investigations that resulted in billions of dollars in compensatory damages, governmental penalties, fines, legal costs, and damaged brands.

The increased public and congressional scrutiny came at a time of excess global manufacturing capacity, rising labor costs, and an increased threat of game-changing technological innovations coming from Tesla and others. For example, Google and Apple were developing their own versions of game-changing, next-generation all-electric vehicles. As a result, the traditional competitive forces of the auto industry were falling under attack. The general fear was that Apple and Google, through their technology and software strategies, would extract most of the profits generated by car sales and turn traditional automakers into low-margin car manufacturers.

This was clearly evident in VW's announcement that some of its engineers conspired to bypass U.S. and E.U. emissions standards. The admission resulted in the resignation of its CEO, Martin Winterkorn, and prompted an apology from its U.S. president, Michael Horn, during a contentious U.S. congressional subcommittee investigation. Because of VW's indiscretions, it announced in early October that it would cease selling diesel-powered vehicles in the United States for the foreseeable future as it failed to receive U.S. certification for carbon-emissions standards. Volkswagen also considered temporarily closing its plant in Chattanooga, Tennessee, which accounted for more than one-third of its diesel car output. The company was unclear on how to best rectify the lack of EPA certification for its diesel-powered VWs owned by more than 500,000 U.S. customers. Nor did VW know the most effective way to work with its dealers across the United States. VW's U.S. customers were not only driving vehicles that would have failed U.S. emission standards without the rigged software, but these vehicles were now practically worthless in the resale and trade-in markets as well. Similarly, VW dealers and suppliers were ensnared with an inventory of unsellable cars and components.

VW sold more than 10.8 million diesel-powered vehicles worldwide, with 2.8 and 1.2 million sold in Germany and the U.K. respectively. Among the diesel-powered brands sold under Volkswagen AG were: Volkswagen (largest brand with more than 5 million cars sold in 2014), Audi, Volkswagen commercial vehicles (trucks), Skoda, and SEAT. In testifying to the subcommittee, Horn noted that the cheating scandal may have been prompted by cost pressures at home and in the United States. It may also have been influenced by the difficulty VW engineers experienced in developing a diesel-powered engine that would deliver on its carbon-emissions and miles-per-gallon (MPG) efficiency goals. Although VW refused to issue full refunds to its U.S. customers, it did set aside $7.5 billion to help address the problem. Horn reported that he had also recently learned the cheating was the work of senior engineers Ulrich Hackenberg, Audi's chief engineer; Wolfgang Hatz, a developer of racing engines; and Hienz-Jakob Neussr, head of development for the Volkswagen brand.

VW's leading position as the world's largest automobile company became seriously threatened as a result of its rigged carbon testing. This only added to the company's already high labor costs and issues with labor unions at home and abroad. In 2014, Volkswagen generated $246 billion in revenue and $13.2 billion in net income with 592,586 employees. At that same time, Toyota had $227 billion in revenues and $18.1 billion in net income with 344,109 employees and General Motors had $155.9 billion in revenues and $3.95 billion in net income with 216,000 employees.[a] The scandal caused VW's stock to lose 35 percent of its value in the week following its announcement. Globally, the company's unethical strategies also threated labor markets and local economies. Winterkorn set an annual production goal of 10 million cars by 2018; ironically, he reached this goal in 2014, but at what cost?

In May 2018, the U.S. Justice Department indicted Winterkorn on conspiracy charges. The indictment was one of the most high-profile corporate prosecutions in decades. But in Germany, the former star manager's birthplace and current residence, the news caused little more than a shrug of the shoulders. U.S. environmental officials disclosed in 2015 that the German car maker had been involved in widespread fraud aimed at concealing the toxicity of emissions from the diesel engines equipped in millions of its vehicles. Having since arrested, tried, and sentenced two former Volkswagen employees, U.S. authorities have now set their sights on Winterkorn and five more former executives, arguing that the conspiracy wasn't the work of underlings gone rogue but stemmed all the way from the top. Yet on the morning after an indictment that threatened the man who was once Germany's best-paid executive with up to 25 years in jail and $275,000 in fines, the German government declined to comment, and a spokesman for the justice ministry said Germany wouldn't extradite the 70-year-old German national, making it unlikely that he would stand trial unless he voluntarily left the country.

---

a   Mergent Online at http://www.mergentonline.com.libproxy.unh.edu/competitors.php?compnumber=8830&isprintpage=1&orderby=[1,%22desc%22.

a. What factors do you believe led to VW's unethical strategies regarding carbon-emissions testing? While Winterkorn resigned as VW AG's CEO, Horn denied any knowledge of the unethical practices. Should Horn resign his position as VW's U.S. president? Why or why not?

b. Horn announced that Volkswagen AG set aside $7.5 billion to help address the company's emissions scandal. In addition to the financial costs to VW's bottom line, what are some of other tangible and intangible costs to VW? To customers? Dealers? Suppliers? Employees?

c. Who has a stake in VW's ability to strategically and ethically deal with the current crisis? Using the stakeholder map, identify stakeholders and map each one based on their power, influence, and interest in VW's management's ability to strategically address the current crisis.

d. Codetermination is a practice whereby the employees have a role in the management of a company. The word is a literal translation from the German word *mitbestimmung*. In Germany, labor has a shared responsibility in the management of the company; in fact, Germany's labor unions have seats on VW's board and report to the company's board of directors. How might VW's labor unions respond to the company's emissions standards scandal? What responsibilities, if any, do VW's labor unions have in helping to resolve the crisis in a timely manner?

e. Why do you think the representative from the German government publically stated that Germany wouldn't extradite the 70-year-old German national? What stake and interest does the German government have in U.S. actions to indict VW's former CEO? What other stakeholders might have influenced Germany's government to deny extradition?

Sources:

Bennett, Jeff. "VW Scandal Threatens Suppliers." *Wall Street Journal*, September 28, 2015: B6.;

Clark, Pilita, and Andy Sharman. "Fallout Threatens to Choke Diesel Cars." *Financial Times,* September 23, 2015: 17.;

Ewing, Jack. "As Apple and Google Rethink Cars, Automakers Plan Their Defense." *New York Times,* September 18, 2015: B4.;

Foy, Henry, and James Politi. "Volkswagen Scandal Fuels Fears for Jobs Across Europe." *Financial Times*, October 13, 2015.;

Neil, Dan. "VW Lost its Moral Compass in Quest for Growth." *Wall Street Journal*, September 24, 2015.;

Spector, Mike, and Amy Harder. "VW's U.S. Chief Apologizes, Says Engineers at Fault." *Wall Street Journal*, October 9, 2015: B1, B2.;

Spector, Mike, and William Boston. "VW to Halt New Diesel Sales in U.S." *Wall Street Journal*, October 8, 2015: B1, B2;

Roberts, Adrienne, and Christina Rogers, "U.S. Indicts VW's Former Chief." *Wall Street Journal*, May 4, 2018: B1, B2.

VIDEO 3.4 The Business Benefits of Doing Good | Wendy Woods

7. LEVELS OF CORPORATE SOCIAL RESPONSIBILITY

Carroll provided a practical conceptual framework for capturing the responsibilities of the firm. He argues that managers of business firms have four levels of responsibilities: economic, legal, ethical, and discretionary.[27] Using this framework as a guide, the manager's first level of responsibility is **economic**—that is, generating profits by creating value for customers. As such, the firm has a market contract and must provide goods and services of value to society to remain in business. Secondly, strategic managers have a **legal** responsibility to abide by society's laws (common law and statutory). These include governmental laws, rules and regulations, as well as standards in carrying out their business activities. If laws are abused, the company and managers face criminal and civil sanctions at best, and at worst, the right of the firm to exist (continue) can be revoked. Businesses and managers have a social contract and obligation to abide by society's formal laws. The third level is **ethics**. Strategic managers should always try to follow the generally held beliefs, ethical standards, and values surrounding behavior in society. They have a **moral** responsibility that goes beyond just abiding by society's laws and regulations, as laws and regulations do not always make a distinction between what is legally right and morally right. Finally, **discretionary** responsibilities are purely voluntary obligations a manager might undertake, but only if the first three levels have been met.

Thinking Critically Exercise 31

DUNKIN' BRANDS CORPORATE SOCIAL RESPONSIBILITY STRATEGY, VISION, MISSION, AND GOALS

Go to Dunkin' Brands at http://www.dunkinbrands.com/responsibility. Click on "Social Responsibility Report" (CSR).

    a. Based on the Dunkin' Brands CSR report, what are the Dunkin' Brands CSR strategy, vision, mission, and goals? Would stockholders be "happy" with the Dunkin' management team and company performance regarding its social mission? Why or why not?

8. SUSTAINABLE BUSINESS DECISIONS AND BUSINESS STRATEGY

Sustainable business involves making decisions and taking actions that consider the long-term impact of the business on society and the environment while still maintaining profitability. In crafting and executing a sustainable business strategy, firms can adopt a triple-bottom-line approach to business, where people, planet, and profit are incorporated into their strategies and actions (see Figure 3.4). The triple-bottom-line strategic approach to business is reflected in the organization's vision, mission, values, goals, and objectives. Additionally, its strategies are formed and executed in the context of all the elements and components of the strategic management conceptual model. A sustainable business views the triple bottom line as not only good for society but also beneficial for business. It is in firms' enlightened self-interest to take strategic actions that are good for both the environment and society while also helping to improve the business. This varies from traditional businesses, which are predominantly focused on profits as their measure of success.

The triple-bottom-line approach reflects a proactive and/or interactive strategic approach to ethics, corporate social responsibility, and public policy. In meeting challenges from shareholders and other stakeholders, corporate leaders have several options including:

Sustainable Business Model—Balance People, Profit, Planet Strategic Fit

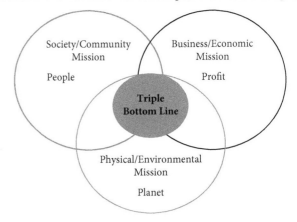

- **Confrontation**. A business may aggressively attack either the message or the messenger; in extreme cases, businesses have felt justified in suing their critics for libel.

Figure 3.4 Triple Bottom Line: Profit, People, Planet

- **Participation**. A business may develop coalitions or partnerships with nongovernmental organizations (NGOs) like McDonald's with the Environmental Defense Fund (EDF) or The Home Depot with the Rainforest Alliance.
- **Anticipation**. A business may adopt management programs to forecast emerging issues and to adjust or change business practices in advance of the passage of stringent laws or regulations.

According to Gittell, Magnusson, and Merenda, "when business is in a **reactive** response mode, it most often engages in confrontation with its adversaries. When it assumes an **interactive** response mode, it participates in dialogues with stakeholders and develops collaborative, ongoing, and open dialogue with them to address or advance the issue or concern at hand. In a **proactive** manner, the strategic leader attempts to anticipate future pressures, issues, or concerns and adjusts its own strategic actions and activities. A reactive stance is usually not strategic and often only delays or heightens the issue at hand, which in turn causes more problems for the organization. An interactive or proactive approach is usually a better strategy, often enhancing the firm's reputation and in some cases providing new and innovative ways of not only addressing the issue but also advancing the organization.[28]

For example, **SC Johnson**, a fifth-generation, privately held family business in the chemical and packaging industries (among others), has a long history of anticipating environmental and consumer issues and in taking a proactive and interactive approach to address them.[29] SC Johnson's CEO, Fisk Johnson, takes great pride in the company's values and "doing the right thing, even when it might hurt business."[30] In fact, the company faced a major ethical decision with its classic brand Saran Wrap. Saran Wrap was acquired from Dow by SC Johnson in 1998 and was highly profitable as it possessed several competitive advantages, including creating an impenetrable barrier to food odor and superior microwave ability.[31] Ultimately, the chemical polyvinylidene chloride (PVDC) gave Saran Wrap its highly profitable competitive advantage. Around the time that Johnson acquired it, the U.S. Food and Drug Administration, environmental groups, and consumers began to express concern over the use of polyvinyl chloride (PVC). PVC is used in a variety of products in numerous industries, including construction, packaging, toys, electronics, health care, fashion, and automotive.[32] When burned in municipal incinerators, PVC releases toxic chemicals into the environment. Some of the company's packaging contained PVC but not Saran Wrap. In 2001, the company implemented a process called "Greenlist" to help it reevaluate its use of PVC. Greenlist became Johnson's most significant innovative step in its ongoing sustainability efforts. Although Saran Wrap did not contain PVCs, the whole packaging category fell under scrutiny, while the difference between PVC and PVDC became increasingly blurred. Concerned that the general public could not discern PVC from PVDC (the latter is nontoxic when burned) Johnson decided to replace the original Saran Wrap with a newly formulated polyethylene product even though the company knew that the new formula would lose its differentiation in the market. As result, Saran Wrap's market share dropped from 18 percent in 2004 to 11 percent by 2015.[33] Johnson did not regret his decision, noting, "Ultimately, however, changing Saran Wraps' formulation was the right thing to do. After all, we call ourselves 'SC Johnson—a family company,' and by doing the right thing we stayed true to our name, both as a company and as a family. And that's something you just can't put a price on."[34]

9. BUSINESS ETHICS

No discussion of strategic management is complete without considering a firm's ethical or moral obligations and responsibilities to its people and the communities in which it operates. Consider the case of Tyco's CEO, Dennis Kozlowski, and its CFO, Mark Swartz. On June 17, 2005, Kozlowski and Swartz were convicted of grand larceny, conspiracy, and fraud. In September 2005, Kozlowski and Swartz received sentences of 8.3 to 25 years at Mid-State Correctional Facility near Utica, New York. State Supreme Court Justice Michael Obus ordered Kozlowski and Swartz to pay a total of $134 million in restitution; in addition, Kozlowski was fined $70 million and Swartz $35 million. The sentences ended a case that exposed the executives' extravagant lifestyles after they pilfered some $600 million from the company, including a $2 million toga birthday party for Kozlowski's wife on a Mediterranean island and an $18 million Manhattan apartment with a $6,000 shower curtain. Kozlowski and Swartz were just two of the more celebrated corporate malfeasance cases decided in the early 2010s. John Regas, former CEO of Adelphia Communications, was sentenced to 15 years (it would have been longer, but he was already 80 and in poor health at the time of his sentencing), and his son, Timothy, the company's chief financial officer, received 20 years after being found guilty of stealing $100 million and hiding $2 billion in corporate debt, thus looting and defrauding shareholders. Other notable sentences went to Andrew Fastow of Enron (10 years), Sam Wakal of ImClone Systems (7 years), Jamie Olis of Dynergy (24 years), and Bernie Ebbers of WorldCom (25 years). These cases proved significant due to the severity of the sentences. Traditionally, corporate malfeasance cases resulted in convictions that amounted to a mere slap on the hand. These individuals received prison sentences similar to those received by hardened criminals. Hubris cost these executives dearly in terms of retribution payments, personal freedom, and integrity.[35]

A study by KRW International examining CEO leadership and character found that CEOs rated high by their employees on moral principles deliver better financial results for their companies compared to CEOs that rated low.[36] Four moral principles or key traits were rated: integrity, responsibility, forgiveness, and compassion. The CEOs were scored on a 100-point scale, where 50 meant the leader displayed the trait about half the time. The gap between the top scorers and lowest scorers persisted across the board. The top scorers were called "virtuoso CEOs," and the lowest scorers were called "self-focused CEOs."[37] The study found that CEOs who scored high for character had an average company return on assets (ROA) of 9.35 percent over a two-year period, compared to an average ROA of 1.93 percent for those companies whose CEOs scored low on character. Fred Kiel, cofounder of KRW, commented, "In addition to outperforming the self-focused CEOs on financial metrics, the virtuoso CEOs received higher employee ratings for vision and strategy, focus, accountability, and executive team character."[38] The *HBR* article elaborated: "Hubris and greed have a way of catching up with people, who then lose the power and wealth they've so fervently pursued … [one's character] isn't something you're born with. You can cultivate it and continue to hone it as you lead, act, and decide."[39]

Questions of whether organizations have ethical and moral obligations that go beyond the law are not only timely but also critically important in crafting and executing strategy, and in understanding one's own moral fabric and values. Business ethics and the role of business in society are not new topics, though ethics emerged as a formal field study by management scholars and others beginning in the 1970s. Interest in business ethics accelerated dramatically during the 1980s and 1990s, both within major corporations and academia. **Business ethics** is a form of applied ethics or professional ethics that examines ethical principles and moral or ethical problems that arise in a business environment. Simply stated, ethics is the study of right and wrong. The focus of business ethics is on individuals and their ability and willingness to distinguish right from wrong and know when they are practicing one or the other in business settings. As such, business ethics is the application of ethical behavior, principles, and standards to guide the conduct of company managers and employees.

9.1 WHY IS IT SO DIFFICULT TO DISTINGUISH RIGHT FROM WRONG?

Determining right from wrong is not always obvious. When it comes to business ethics, a lot of "gray areas" exist that lack clear answers as to whether the practice in question is ethical. Why? Questions of ethics and one's understanding of ethical conduct can and do change over time and reflect the contextual environment in which business takes place. Researchers Hoyk and Hersey identified 45 traps "that every one of us falls prey to. Some of these traps distort our perceptions of right and wrong—so we actually believe our unethical behaviors are right." Among the 45 traps encountered by individuals in the workplace are: obedience to authority, faceless victims, getting lost in groups, money, time pressure, enacting a role, power, anger, alcohol, and low self-esteem.[40]

Ethical challenges also arise in business organizations because multiple stakeholders make conflicting demands on the firm, and these demands change over time. As we discussed previously, the range and quantity of business ethical issues can reflect the interaction of profit-maximizing behavior (operating under the classical single-sovereign model of the firm) with noneconomic concerns of the multiple-sovereign model. The single-sovereign model is **normative** in Friedman's prescription for business to always act in ways that maximize profits for stockholders, just as long as they play by the rules of the game. The stakeholder model is descriptive in that, at any point in time, some stakeholders are active and their actions can negatively (or positively) impact the firm. From this perspective, the multiple-sovereign model is descriptive, capturing "what is" or describing the current situation, versus Friedman's prescription of "what should be." Understanding the ethical implications of questionable management practices requires students to have an understanding of ethical standards and principles of ethical conduct. Several ethical standards or perspectives will be discussed in the next section.

9.2 ETHICAL UNIVERSALISM

This principle holds the belief that ethical standards should be universal and apply to all people throughout all of history regardless of cultural, political, social, or economic context. From this perspective, there are meta-ethics, or universal standards for behavior, that apply everywhere, no matter the location or country in which the business operates. For example, the command "Thou shall not kill" is universal, no matter the context or situation. The nonaggression principle, which prohibits aggression or the initiation of force or violence against another person, is a universal ethical principle. Examples of aggression include murder, rape, kidnapping, assault, robbery, theft, and vandalism. On the other hand, the commission of any such acts in response to aggression does not necessarily violate universal ethics. Universal ethics remains beneficial to society for many obvious reasons. For instance, if people were allowed to kill or steal, this would lead to widespread chaos and violence and prove detrimental to the well-being of society.[41]

9.3 ETHICAL RELATIVISM

This principle holds the belief that ethical standards are different across various peoples and cultures and is best captured by the saying, "When in Rome, do as the Romans do." Ethical relativism has existed throughout all of history and reflects cultural, political, social, or economic contextual differences among the moral judgments for different people and cultures. Descriptive moral relativism holds that some people do in fact disagree about what is moral. Metaethical moral relativism maintains that, in such disagreements, nobody is objectively right or wrong, whereas **normative moral relativism** holds that because nobody is right or wrong, we ought to tolerate the behavior of others even when we disagree about the morality of it. Ethical or moral relativism has been exposed, criticized, and debated for thousands of years, from ancient times to the present day, and is espoused in diverse fields, including philosophy, science, business and religion.[42]

9.4 UNITED NATIONS SOCIAL CONTRACT

Although not an ethical principle per se, the United Nations' Global Compact initiative attempted to implement guidelines that set universal morally right or wrong standards. The compact establishes a social contract, or contract with society, which is binding on all signees of the contract (individuals, organizations, groups, and businesses) in terms of establishing right and wrong and in drawing guidelines between ethical and unethical behavior. The UN Global Compact was initially launched in 1999, with a tenth principle against corruption (in accordance with the United Nations Convention Against Corruption) adopted in 2003. The UN Global

Compact is the world's largest corporate-citizenship initiative with 10,000 corporate participants and other stakeholders in more than 130 countries (see www.unglobalcompact.org/what-is-gc/mission/principles for the UN Ten Principles).[43]

9.5 ETHICAL PRINCIPLES

The principles of ethical conduct (an incomplete list subject to wide levels of interpretation and discussion) put forth by business scholars Steiner and Steiner[44] include:

- *The categorical imperative*: In the ethical system of moral philosopher Immanuel Kant, the categorical imperative holds an unconditional moral law that applies to all people, independent of any personal motive or desire. It is imperative that a person should always act only according to the principle that it should become a universal law.[45]
- *The conventional ethic*: Business is seen as a game with its own rules, and individuals should play by these rules as long as no laws are broken.
- *The disclosure rule*: How would it feel to explain this decision to a wider audience, such as a newspaper?
- *The golden rule*: Avoid committing intentional harm to others; do unto others as you would have them do unto you.
- *The might-equals-right ethic*: Seize the advantage if you are strong enough to take it.
- *The organization ethic*: The needs of the organization are more important than the needs of the individual.
- *The rights ethics*: Basic rights belong to individuals; business actions or decisions should not violate or interfere with those rights; in short, does the business action respect the rights of the individuals involved?
- *The theory of justice*: Maintaining the rights of the community is important because the community is where we live and work; thus, we must act "fairly" in maintaining relationships and mediate disputes between individual rights and those of the community—is the action consistent with the canons of justice?
- *The utilitarian ethic*: The greatest good for the greatest number; does it optimize the satisfaction of all constituents?

Thinking Critically Exercise 32

WHAT'S YOUR MORAL COMPASS?

A classmate has a copy of an upcoming accounting exam and offers to share it with you in return for some help with statistics. You are a whiz when it comes to statistics, but you have difficulty with accounting. In fact, you failed your first accounting exam, and your substantial scholarship from the university will be taken away if you fail accounting. Your classmate aced the first accounting exam and is majoring in accounting. You're pretty confident that the accounting instructor is oblivious to any cheating in the course, even though you know that your classmate had an advance copy of the first exam and had shared it with several other students. They all got A's on the exam.

    a. What would you do? How might you justify your actions if you actually take him up on his offer?

10. REFLECTION

This chapter presented the strategic management model concept and the style (or design) school of strategic thought as approaches to the study of strategy. The style school of thought focuses on the CEO as the chief designer or maker of strategy. Although the strategic management model represents a normative (or prescriptive) approach to strategy making and execution, it is driven by the manager's ability to act strategically and think critically. In other words, the model should be viewed as dynamic and action-oriented, not static. Taken from the style-school perspective, the strategic management model is driven by the CEO as primary designer of strategy. The CEO designs strategy and hands the strategy off to subordinates for implementation. This school is not overly formal or analytical but is based more on the CEO's position at the top of the organization.

The chapter also focused on PESTEL analysis, stakeholder analysis, business ethics, and sustainable business practices. Two competing models of the firm were presented: single-sovereign and multiple-sovereign. Models of the firm are important because they can help guide the strategist's resource-allocation decisions, ethical practices, and stakeholders' power, influence, and interest in the strategic actions of the firm. Strategists need to understand the impact of their strategic decisions and actions regarding the welfare of not only the firm but also the communities in which they operate. Values, ethics, sustainable business practices, and corporate social responsibility can and do have an important place in making and executing winning strategies.

| **Thinking Critically Exercise 33** | **SC JOHNSON'S SARAN WRAP DILEMMA (SEE SECTION 8, SC JOHNSON EXAMPLE)** |

If SC Johnson was a publically held company, do you think stockholders would have agreed with Fisk Johnson's actions regarding Saran Wrap, especially with the significant drop in market share? How would Milton Friedman view Johnson's decision? Using Carroll's responsibility framework as a guide, how might Fisk justify to stockholders his Saran Wrap strategy?

| **Thinking Critically Exercise 34** | **TYCO'S CORPORATE MALFEASANCE—MR. PIGGY** |

During Dennis Kozlowski's reign at Tyco, he became a CEO superstar, amassing large personal fortunes for himself, Tyco board members, and Tyco managers. He also became known as the archetype of avarice. In a March 2015 interview with *The New York Times* columnist David Kaplan, Kozlowski stated, "I was piggy. But I'm not that person anymore." Kozlowski acknowledged making mistakes. He told Kaplan, "I was too invested in the game." *The Times* article notes that, in just his last four years at Tyco, Kozlowski earned more than $300 million. "I'd go to Harvard Business School and get a standing ovation when I was introduced as the highest-paid CEO in the country." The courts found Kozlowski guilty of misusing his authority in distributing bonuses, extending loans, and misreporting material items.[46]

a. Although Kozlowski went to jail, Tyco's board was never accused of any wrongdoing. As agents of Tyco's stockholders, the board had legal obligations to fulfill. Using agency and stewardship theory, what is the role of the board? How do you account for Tyco's board's failure to carry out its fiduciary duties? Why did all of the board members simply disregard corporate and federal reporting rules?
b. How do you account for Kozlowski's behavior? What does it say about Harvard School students when they gave Kozlowski a standing ovation when he was introduced as the highest-paid CEO in the country?

CHAPTER ENDNOTES

1. Drucker, Peter F. *Managing in a Time of Great Change.* New York: Penguin Putnam, 1995.; Drucker, Peter F. *The Practice of Management.* New York: Harper Collins, 1986.
2. Thompson, James D. *Organizations in Action.* New York: McGraw-Hill, 1967.
3. Ibid.; Dill, William R. "Environment as an Influence on Managerial Autonomy." *Administrative Science Quarterly* 2, (1958): 409–43.
4. Macmillan, Douglas, Sam Schechner, and Lisa Fleisheruber. "Snags $41 Million Valuation." *Wall Street Journal,* December 5, 2014. http://www.wsj.com/articles/ubers-new-funding-values-it-at-over-41-billion-1417715938.
5. McGregor, Jena. "Uber's CEO Apologizes. Kind of." *Washington Post,* November 19, 2014. http://www.washingtonpost.com/blogs/on-leadership/wp/2014/11/19/uber-ceo-apologizes-kind-of/.
6. "Amazon's Vision and Mission Statements." Strategic Management Insight. http://www.strategicmanagementinsight.com/mission-statements/amazon-mission-statement.html.
7. Gamble, John E., Margaret A. Peteraf, and Arthur A. Thompson. *Essentials of Strategic Management.* 4th ed. New York: McGraw-Hill, 2015.; Thompson, Arthur A. *Strategy: Core Concepts and Analytical Approaches.* 3rd ed. e-text. Burr Ridge, IL: McGraw-Hill Education, 2014–2015.
8. Barney, Jay, and William S. Hesterly. *Strategic Management and Competitive Advantage.* 5th ed. Boston: Pearson, 2015.
9. Hamilton, Diana. "Top 10 Company Mission Statements." Wordpress. https://drdianehamilton.wordpress.com/2011/01/13/top-10-company-mission-statements-in-2011/.
10. Kotelnikov, Vadim. "Hierarchical Levels of Strategy." 1000 Ventures. http://www.1000ventures.com/business_guide/strategy_hierachical_levels.
11. Gitttell, Ross, Matt Magnusson, and Michael Merenda. "Brewing a Better World: Sustainable Supply Chain Management at Green Mountain Coffee Roasters, Inc." In *The Sustainable Business Case Book,* 211–213. Irvington, NY: Flatworld Knowledge, 2013. http://www.keurig-greenmountain.com/en/OurCompany/OurValues.aspx.
12. "Naveen Jain." BrainyQuote. http://www.brainyquote.com/search_results.html?q=jain.
13. Ansoff, H. Igor. "Competitive Strengths and Weaknesses." In *Business Strategy: Selected Readings.* New York: Penguin Modern Management Readings, 1978.; Ansoff, H. Igor. "Critique of Henry Mintzberg's The Design School: Reconsidering the Basic Premises of Strategic Management." *Strategic Management Journal* 12, (1991): 449–61.
14. Mintzberg, Henry. "The Design School: Reconsidering the Basic Premises of Strategic Management." *Strategic Management Journal* 11, no. 3 (1990): 171–95.
15. Ibid.; "Ten Major Strategic Management Schools: A Comparative Analysis." 1000 Ventures. http://www.1000ventures.com/business_guide/mgmt_inex_stategy_10schools.html.
16. Christenson, Clayton M. *The Manager's Dilemma.* Boston: Harvard Business School Press, 2000.
17. Chapman, Alan. "SWOT Analysis Methods." BusinessBalls. www.businessballs.com/swotanalysisfreetemplate.htm.
18. Petty, Art. "Tools for Developing as a Global Manager." The Balance. September 23, 2016. Accessed November 8, 2018. https://www.thebalance.com/tools-for-developing-as-a-global-manager-4046180.
19. "Infographics." Wikipedia. Accessed June 11, 2015. http://en.wikipedia.org/wiki/Infographic.
20. Friedman, Milton. *Capitalism and Freedom.* Chicago: University of Chicago Press, 1962.; Milton Friedman. "The Social Responsibility of Business is to Increase Its Profits," *New York Times Magazine,* September 13, 1970: 32.
21. Milton Friedman. "The Social Responsibility of Business is to Increase Its Profits," *New York Times Magazine,* September 13, 1970: 32.
22. Thompson, J.D. *Organizations in Action.* New York: McGraw Hill, 1967.
23. Donaldson, T.J., and L.E. Preston. "The Stakeholder Theory and the Corporation: Concepts, Evidence, and Implications." *Academy of Management Review* 20 (1995).
24. Donaldson, T. and T.W. Dunfee. "Toward a Unified Conception of Business Ethics: Integrative Social Contracts Theory," *Academy of Management Review* 19 (1994): 252.; Donaldson, T. and T.W. Dunfee. *Ties that Bind: A Social Contracts Approach to Business Ethics.* Boston: Harvard Business School Press, 1998.
25. Bebchuk, L.A., and J.M. Fried. "Executive Compensation as an Agency Problem." *Journal of Economic Perspectives* 17:71–92.; Bebchuk, L.A., J.M. Fried, and David Walker. "Managerial Power and Rent Extraction in the Design of Executive Compensation." *University of Chicago Law Review* 69 (2004): 751–846.; Carter, C.B., and J.W. Lorsch. *Back to the Drawing Board: Designing Corporate Boards for a Complex World.* Boston: Harvard Business School Press, 2003.; Eisenhardt, K. "Agency Theory: An Assessment and Review." *Academy of Management Review* 14, no. 1 (1989): 57–74. Also see: "The Shareholders' Revolt." *The Economist,* June 17, 2006: 71.; "A Bad Week to Be Bad." *The Economist,* June 23, 2005.; Bianco, A., W. Symonds, and N. Byrnes. "The Rise and Fall of Dennis Kozlowski." *Business Week Online,* December 23, 2002.
26. Freeman, R. Edward. *Strategic Management: A Stakeholder Approach.* Boston: Cambridge University Press, 2010.
27. Carroll, A.B. "A Three Dimensional Model of Corporate Performance." *Academy of Management Review* (1979).
28. Gitttell, Ross, Matt Magnusson, and Michael Merenda. "Government, Public Policy, and Sustainable Business." In *The Sustainable Business Case Book.* Irvington, NY: Flatworld Knowledge, 2013.
29. Burke, Michael. "CEO Explains Why SC Johnson Hobbled Saran Wrap." *Journal Times,* April 25, 2015. http://journaltimes.com/business/local/ceo-explains-why-sc-johnson-hobbled-saran-wrap/article_55000b9a-88cb-5786-a36e-3835f1d820ce.html.
30. Johnson, Fisk. "How I Did It … SC Johnson's CEO on Doing the Right Thing, Even When It Hurts Business." *Harvard Business Review,* 36 (2015).
31. Ibid., 34.
32. Ibid., 34.
33. Ibid., 36.
34. Burke, Michael. "CEO Explains Why SC Johnson Hobbled Saran Wrap." *Journal Times,* April 25, 2015. http://journaltimes.com/business/local/ceo-explains-why-sc-johnson-hobbled-saran-wrap/article_55000b9a-88cb-5786-a36e-3835f1d820ce.html.
35. Merenda, Michael, Allen Kaufman, and Alison Volk. "Tyco International: A Case of Corporate Malfeasance." In *Strategic Management: Competitiveness and Globalization, Text and Cases.* Edited by Michael Hitt, R. Duane Ireland, Robert Hoskisson. Cincinnati, OH: South-Western College Publishers, 2008.
36. "Leadership: Measuring the Return on Character." *Harvard Business Review* 20 (2015).

37. Ibid., 20.
38. Ibid., 20–1.
39. Ibid., 21.
40. Hoyk, R., and P. Hersey. *The Ethical Executive*. Stanford, CA: Stanford University Press, 2008.
41. Steiner, J., and G. Steiner. *Business, Government, and Society: A Managerial Perspective, Text and Cases*. 13th ed. New York: McGraw-Hill/Irwin, 2011.; "Ethical Universalism." Wikipedia. https://en.wikipedia.org/wiki/moral_universalism.
42. Steiner, J., and G. Steiner. *Business, Government, and Society: A Managerial Perspective, Text and Cases*. 13th ed. New York: McGraw-Hill/Irwin, 2011.; "Ethical Universalism." *Wikipedia*. https://en.wikipedia.org/wiki/moral_universalism.
43. "UN Global Compact." UN Global Impact. https://www.unglobalcompact.org/abouttheGC/thetenprinciples/index.html.; "UN Guide to Corporate Sustainability: Shaping A Sustainable Future." UN Global Impact. https://www.unglobalcompact.org/docs/publications/UN_Global_Compact_Guide_to_Corporate_Sustainability.pdf.
44. Partial list of ethical guidelines adapted from Steiner, J., and G. Steiner. *Business, Government, and Society: A Managerial Perspective, Text and Cases*. 13th ed. New York: McGraw-Hill/Irwin, 2011.
45. Kant, Immanuel. *Grounding for the Metaphysics of Morals*. 3rd ed. Translated by James W. Ellington. http://en.wikipedia.org/wiki/Categorical_imperative#cite_note-Ellington-1.
46. Kaplan, David A. "Tyco's 'Piggy,' Out of Prison and Living Small." *New York Times*, March 1, 2015. http://www.nytimes.com/2015/03/02/business/dealbook/dennis-kozlowskis-path-from-infamy-to-obscurity.html?_r=0.

CHAPTER 4

CRAFTING STRATEGY—EXTERNAL SITUATIONAL ANALYSIS AND COMPETITIVE FORCES STRATEGY SCHOOL

VIDEO 4.1 How Amazon, Apple, Facebook and Google Manipulate Our Emotions | Scott Galloway

SIZING UP THE PLAYERS IN MOBILE ADVERTISING

In 2014, Facebook, Apple, Google, Yahoo!, and others became locked in a fierce battle over online advertising revenues and market dominance. In 2013, internet advertising revenues reached an all-time high of $42.8 billion, surpassing broadcast television for the first time. Additionally, profits increased 17 percent over 2012's record-setting ad revenues. The Interactive Advertising Bureau (IAB) reported that, for the third year in a row, mobile ads achieved triple-digit growth year over year, rising to $7.1 billion in 2013—a 110 percent boost from the prior year's total of $3.4 billion.[a] Mobile ads accounted for 17 percent of 2013 revenues compared to 9 percent of revenues in 2012. Digital video, a component of display-related advertising, brought in $2.8 billion in 2013, up 19 percent over revenues of $2.3 billion in 2012. As a result, digital display advertising also increased its share to become the fourth-largest format, directly behind mobile ads. Search revenues totaled $18.4 billion in 2013, up 9 percent from 2012, when search revenues totaled $16.9 billion. Display-related advertising revenues in 2013 totaled $12.8 billion, or 30 percent of the year's revenues, a rise of 7 percent over $12 billion in 2012. Retail advertisers continue to represent the largest category of internet ad spending, responsible for 21 percent in 2013, followed by financial services and closely trailed by automotive, which account for 13 percent and 12 percent of the year's revenues,

---

a   IAB 2013 Global Mobile Advertising Revenue Report, August 21, 2014, http://www.iab.com/insights/iab-2013-global-mobile-advertising-revenue-report/.

respectively.[b] The financial stakes were high for Google, Facebook, Yahoo!, Apple, and Amazon. Google and Facebook captured the largest share of mobile advertising revenues, with 41 percent and 15 percent, respectively. Facebook grew into an internet advertising powerhouse, with revenues of $12.5 billion in 2014.[c]

FACEBOOK

When individuals signed up for Facebook's social network, Facebook's fine-print terms for users included permission to track personal information. This maintained its longtime practice of documenting websites its users visited when they were not on the social network, as well as keeping track of users' names. Facebook employed this data to build more detailed user profiles, allowing advertisers to target people with more personalized marketing pitches.[d] Facebook's strategy focused on expanding its advertising revenues by giving its ad customers wider access to Facebook's users' browsing history and personal information. Publishers on Facebook's multiple websites (Facebook, YouTube, Integra) found this very attractive because they would now have their content shared among Facebook's 1.3 billion users, and they hoped to win new readers. In addition, online retailers found this striking, as they wished to combine their data with Facebook's social network, helping them to better track existing and prospective customers online.[e]

While Google, Yahoo!, and Apple kept record of individuals who shopped on their sites (noting them by their computers), Facebook tracked real names. This allowed Facebook to do more with the information it accumulated about a person's browsing and shopping habits. Facebook could also follow users on their phones. Some mobile app publishers aimed to optimize their advertising on the social network by giving Facebook the unique hardware identifiers for their app users. This allowed Facebook to match the IDs to its own mobile users' IDs.[f] With this matching process, Facebook could more effectively monetize its websites by permitting its advertising customers (news media, manufacturers, online games, app writers, etc.) to tailor their ads to individuals browsing their sites. Among Facebook customers were *The New York Times*, Airbnb, Williams-Sonoma, Abercrombie & Fitch, and ESPN.[g] Although some advertisers initially resisted sharing user information with the social media giant, they eventually gave in as releasing data on Facebook's websites proved more cost-effective and enabled advertisers to target specific demographic groups in narrow geographic locations. *eMarketer* reported that advertisers would spend more on digital ads than either

---

b   Ibid.
c   Ibid.
d   Albergotti, Reed, "Websites Wary of Facebook Tracking," *Wall Street Journal*, September 24, 2014: B1.
e   Ibid.
f   Ibid., B1, B4.
g   Ibid.

newspapers or magazines in 2015, in part because advertisers could target digital ads to smaller subsections of potential customers.[h]

GOOGLE

Google, like Facebook, also tracked internet user browsing histories to sell targeted advertising. Although Facebook knew users' real identities, Google had to infer users' interests from their web browsing histories, which was misleading to its advertisers. As a result, Google moved aggressively to protect its leading position in online internet advertising, leading advertisers to pay more than $50 billion to the search giant for clicks that deliver potential customers to advertisers' web pages. When Google bought Android in 2005, it worried about proprietary mobile platforms dominating the mobile space and locking out future opportunities for Google to distribute services—and more importantly, sell ads on devices like smartphones. By 2010, Android became the top smartphone platform in the world. This was in sharp contrast to Apple's closed, curated iOS (operating system) smartphone platform. Google's strategy made its Android operating system open and essentially free to any smartphone manufacturer; but why would Google give it away at no cost? Because Google wanted a platform to sell online ads, not hardware or operating systems. Google's big gamble paid off handsomely. By 2014, most Android smartphone vendors, with the notable exception of Samsung, were not making a lot of money selling smartphones, but Google was making a substantial amount of money selling advertising space through its search engine and website portals.

APPLE

Apple neither pitched nor sold user privacy information on its iPhone, mobile devices, or services. Tim Cook, Apple's CEO, noted that Apple kept user information confidential and did not use it to sell targeted advertising. As such, Apple did not monetize user information stored on its devices or iCloud. Apple accounted for less than 3 percent of U.S. mobile advertising revenue in 2013.[i] Because of this, advertisers on Apple devices reached only Apple devices, not the 85 percent of smartphones running Google's Android operating system. Unlike Facebook and Google, Apple made a strategic decision not to tap its users' personal information. Instead, Apple's strategy under Jobs permitted its app developers to make money by allowing advertisers to create campaigns starting at $50. In general, Apple's advertising platform, iAd, proved more popular among large advertisers, such as Toyota, who were seeking to build a brand presence by crafting advertising campaigns that analyzed internet users' media consumption patterns, types of devices, and favored activities. Historically, major brands did not place ads on mobile devices.

YAHOO!

Meanwhile, Yahoo!'s CEO Marissa Mayer was finding it very difficult to grow its ad revenues. In fact, Yahoo! was rapidly losing its traditional advertisers to Facebook and Google. In July 2014, Yahoo! reported that second-quarter revenues fell 3 percent, its fourth decline in the past five periods and well below the company's estimates. Of particular concern was Yahoo's display ad revenue, which dropped 6.9 percent to $394 million. This was in contrast to earlier in the year when Yahoo! reported its first quarterly revenue growth in more than 12 months. In an effort to improve ad revenues and profits, Mayer personally approached advertisers, attempting to persuade them to shift their budgets from Google and Facebook to Yahoo! Although Yahoo!'s ad revenues initially declined because its advertisers were not willing to pay Yahoo!'s higher prices, the average

h   "Android vs. iOS: What Wins Where?" *eMarketer*, February 19, 2015, http://www.emarketer.com/articles/results.aspx?q=Apple percent-20Mobile percent 20Advertising percent202014.; Wakabayashi, Daisuke, "Apple's Latest Marketing Pitch: More Privacy," *Wall Street Journal*, September 24, 2014: B1–B4.
i   Wakabayashi, Daisuke, "Apple's Latest Marketing Pitch: More Privacy," *Wall Street Journal*, September 24, 2014: B1–B4.

price for Yahoo! ads dropped 24 percent in the second quarter of 2014. In addition, Yahoo!'s advertisers were moving away from higher-priced, graphic banner ads, which had been Yahoo's specialty. Advertisers were instead spending more on cheaper ads targeted to individual visitors, an area where Facebook and Google excelled. Consequentially, according to *eMarketer*, Yahoo's share of U.S. ad-display revenue was 6.4 percent in 2013, and that was expected to fall to 2.7 percent by 2014.[j]

Google, by comparison, was expected to remain steady in 2014 at 21.8 percent, whereas Facebook's share of ad-display revenue was estimated to fall to 46.4 percent from 50.5 percent. Another reason for Yahoo's decline stemmed from its search engines being primarily found on PCs and not mobile devices. As smartphones proliferated, clicks on Google ads rose, but ad prices continued to fall nearly 20 percent from the start of 2012. This was in part because clicks from a phone were not as valuable as clicks from a PC, as buyers searching for products on a phone completed purchases roughly one-third as often as those on PCs. The continued drop in ad revenue was a sign that Yahoo's new ad offerings, such as "in-stream" ads that appeared in the center of sites such as Yahoo! News and Yahoo! Finance, were not attracting much demand from advertisers. Yahoo! announced new ad offerings—such as native ads, digital magazines, and web video shows—but marketers believed Yahoo! lacked the popular appeal with consumers for these initiatives to payoff.[k]

THE BATTLE OVER MOBILE ADVERTISING

Amazon announced that it would challenge Google's dominance in the online advertising market by selling its own smartphones and tablets. Additionally, it would develop its own software for placing ads online that would leverage its knowledge of millions of web shoppers. Amazon planned on developing its own in-house ad-placement platform instead of using Google's platform for placing ads.[l]

In a counter move against Amazon, Google began offering expanded services to its search users instead of just connecting these users to other websites. If Google's new offerings were

Key Financials ($ Billions)	Apple	Google	Facebook	Yahoo!	
Market Cap	603.3	195.2	159.23	40.5	Table 4.1 Selected Financials: Apple, Google, Facebook, and Yahoo!
Revenue	178.0	63.1	12.5	4.68	
Net Income	38.6	13.2	2.4	1.4	
Total Assets	222.5	121.6	20.8	16.5	
Total Liabilities	101.6	25.9	2.4	3.8	
Shareholders' Equity	120.9	95.7	18.4	12.7	

Source: http://www.mergentonline.com.libproxy.unh.edu/companyfinancials.php?pagetype=asreported&compnumber=87948&period=Annuals&dataarea=PL&range=5&currency=AsRep&scale=AsRep&Submit=Refresh 12/31/15

j   "Yahoo Poised to Pass Twitter in US Mobile Ad Share by 2015," *eMarketer*, December 4, 2014, http://www.emarketer.com/Article/Yahoo-Poised-Pass-Twitter-US-Mobile-Ad-Share-by-2015/1011663.
k   Ibid., B4.
l   Winkler, Rolfe, and Bensinger, Greg, "Amazon Prepares Online Advertising Program," *Wall Street Journal*, August 22, 2014, http://www.wsj.com/articles/amazon-preps-a-challenge-to-googles-ad-business-1408747979.

perceived as favoring its own content over impartial search results, it risked the loss of some advertisers. Since adding the expanded services, Google's revenues rose 18 percent for the first six months of 2014 (compared with the first six month's revenues of the previous year). Its stock was up about 4 percent for the same period and up over 38 percent for the year. The rise in stock price makes Google the third-most valuable company in the United States behind Apple and Exxon Mobil. Google's ad-supported business proved highly profitable. It generated more operating profit in the first six months of 2014 than Amazon had since it was founded 20 years ago. See Table 4.1 for the partial financial data for Apple, Google, Facebook and Yahoo! as of December 31, 2014.

1. INTRODUCTION: QUESTIONS TO THINK ABOUT

- Why undertake an external environmental analysis?
- What is the competitive forces strategy school?
- What is an industry?
- What is a strategic group map?
- What is an analytical tool and how are they used to craft strategy?
- How do you conduct a competitive forces analysis?
- What might an infographic of an industry's competitive forces and factors model look like?
- What are entry and exit barriers?
- What is blue ocean strategy?
- What is a generic strategy?
- What are some commonly considered strategic alternatives?

Strategic thinking is about understanding and making sense of the external and internal environments of the organization and taking actions that capitalize on this sense making. To craft a competitive strategy, managers need to understand the competitive forces at work in the external environment. To do this, they must conduct external and internal situational environmental analyses. This chapter focuses on the external situational analysis. Critical inquiry analyzes the relevant information found in the organization's internal and external environments, and it aids managers in making the business case for strategy selection and action. Managers must create and extract customer value by strategically aligning or matching internal resources and capabilities to external opportunities while staving off or successfully countering external threats and internal weaknesses. They must continuously ask the right strategic questions, critically address these questions, and act on these questions. To successfully compete, strategists seek and exploit market opportunities by crafting strategies to improve organizational performance.

a. Describe Apple's, Google's, Facebook's, and Yahoo!'s internet advertising business models and customer value propositions. What's different or unique about each company's mobile advertising business model? How do you make money in internet advertising? What are the keys to success? Which company is in the best position to take advantage of the growth in internet mobile advertising? Why?
b. What technological and social forces are impacting the growth in mobile advertising? Why are ad agencies, media companies, and business enterprises devoting more of their advertising budgets to mobile devices?

1.1. WHY UNDERTAKE AN EXTERNAL ENVIRONMENTAL ANALYSIS?

To increase the organization's chances for success, managers must craft strategies that properly align the firm's resource strengths with customer-value creation opportunities. This takes place in the firm's external environment. The basic unit for understanding the firm's external environment is the industry(s) or customer market space in which it competes. When conducting an external situational analysis, the manager must answer the following strategic questions:

- Where should the firm "play" or compete externally?
- In what industries? Competitive markets?
- Is this an emerging or established industry?
- How attractive are the industries and markets?
- What customer segments best align with the firm's customer value proposition?
- How many customers will buy the firm's products and at what price?
- What strategic actions generate the greatest customer and firm value?

2. COMPETITIVE FORCES STRATEGY SCHOOL

The main focus of this chapter is on the competitive forces school as the dominant school in undertaking an external situational analysis. The school is considered to be one of the most dominant conceptual strategy schools of thought. The school provides several industry models and analytical tools for strategy making. The school is also known as the "five forces" school, the "industrial organization (IO)" school, and the "positioning" school. The school focuses on the attractiveness of a firm's products and services in the industry(s) it competes. It does this by critically addressing the question: *What is the market or industry potential for this product or service?* Porter prescribes competitive forces analysis as a way to answer this question by analyzing industries and competitors.[1] He asserts, "The essence of formulating competitive strategy is relating a company to its external environment."[2] As such, strategy making starts with an analysis of the competitive forces in the external environment. Competitive forces analysis has its roots in classical military strategy and industrial economics. Similar to the classical military general's need to assess the enemy's strengths and weaknesses and the environment or battlefield in which wars will be fought, the strategic manager must assess competitors and industries to determine a firm's market potential. Advocates of this school assume that all resources necessary for strategy execution are available to the firm or can easily be acquired. As with the style (design) school, structural analysis considers people as less important or secondary to competitive analysis. Porter argues that the collective strengths of the competitive industry forces determine the ultimate profit potential in the industry, where profit potential is measured in terms of return on invested capital.[3] Competition among rivals was best described as "monopolistic competition," where more than one rival could exert its power or influence over industry forces. This is in contrast to the classical economists' assumptions of perfect competition, where firms were powerless to act in the market. Managers must make strategies that give the firm a competitive advantage by exploiting competitive forces. This is done primarily by:

- Positioning the firm relative to the overall attractiveness of industry forces at any given time
- Assessing the firm's ability to influence these forces and competitive dynamics in its favor
- Exploiting its position and influence by shifting the balance of power in its favor and earning above-average return on investments (ROI)[4]

The competitive forces analysis is a simple yet powerful analytical tool used in assessing industry competitiveness and attractiveness. Strategic managers can use the tool to determine market entry, exit, and penetration strategies. Essential to a firm's competitive position is the firm's ability to differentiate itself through constant product and process innovation. Strategic managers can create competitive advantage by "perceiving or discovering new ways to compete in an industry and bringing these new ways to market—which is ultimately an act of innovation."[5] Innovation is defined as improvements in technology or better ways of doing things. Porter maintains that information plays a large role in the process of innovation—information that is not sought or available to competitors, or information available to others that is interpreted in new ways. He asserts that, with few exceptions, innovation is the result of unused effort.[6] A competitive forces analysis starts with identifying and assessing the competitive dynamics of the industry or industries in which the firm competes. But what is an industry, and how can rivals in an industry be grouped for competitive analysis?

2.1 WHAT IS AN INDUSTRY?

The basic unit for understanding the firm's external environment and conducting a competitive forces analysis is identifying the industry(s) in which the firm competes. A firm can compete in very narrow niches of an industry, broadly within an industry, or across several industries. An **industry** is a group of competitors that offers similar goods and services and compete directly with each other. An industry can also be identified through its customers, suppliers, rivals, and the extent to which it is regulated or governed by third parties (governmental or regulatory agencies). Customers determine which products or services offered by an industry's firms have value by their purchasing decisions. The aggregate number of customer purchases determines the level of demand, or the **demand curve**, for an industry's products and services. The firms in an industry determine the level of products or services available for sale to customers. The aggregate number of firms supplying products or services to customers determines the industry's **supply curve**. If demand outpaces the supply of goods and services offered for sale, then the industry is usually in its growth stage. During this stage, industry prices typically rise. If supply outstrips demand, the industry is usually faced with slowing growth. In this stage, industry prices generally drop.

In **perfectly competitive markets**, the firm is a **price take** because customers can shop around for the best price in rivals' similar products. The strategist goal is to create superior customer value for its products through product and service differentiation. If successful, then the firm engages in **monopolistic competition** where the firm is a **price setter**. Strategists strive to separate their firm's products and services from those of rivals and create unique customer value. If successful, they can differentiate themselves from rivals by generating entirely new industry segments or, in some cases, entirely new industries. In addition to rivals, customers, suppliers, and other institutions, organizations can play a significant role in the competitive dynamics of an industry. These include local, regional, and national governments; industry associations; educational institutions; consultants; supporting and relating industries; and basic and advanced factor conditions. For example, governments can play a key role in determining the availability and supply of all or some of an industry's products and services. In the United States, the government stands as the protector of society's well-being, keeper of competition, regulator of price and entry, as well as a valuable customer.

VIDEO 4.2 S-Curves in Innovation

2.2 THE S-CURVE

In business, the S-curve is a type of curve that illustrates the growth of one variable (e.g., sales in dollars) in terms of another variable (e.g., time), creating a pattern that usually takes the shape of the letter S.[7] S-curve graphs are extremely useful tools in conducting a situational analysis as a precursor to strategy making. The useful life of a physical entity (industry, company, and product) is similar to the human life cycle: birth, growth, maturity, decline, and, eventually, death. In addition to a product's life cycle, companies make extensive use of graphically trackable

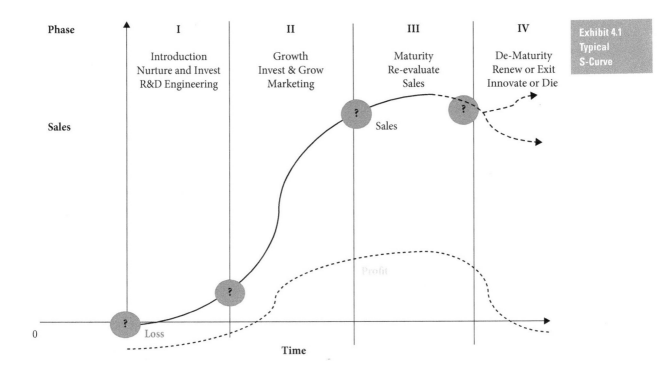

Phase

I	II	III	IV
Introduction Nurture and Invest R&D Engineering	Growth Invest & Grow Marketing	Maturity Re-evaluate Sales	De-Maturity Renew or Exit Innovate or Die

Exhibit 4.1
Typical
S-Curve

Sales

Sales

Profit

Loss

0

Time

performance by using S-curves. Other examples are industry life cycles and organizational life cycles (see Exhibit 4.1: Typical S-Curve). The S-curve portrays growth of company sales for a new product exhibiting a rapid, exponential increase in sales for a period, followed by a tapering or leveling off. The tapering occurs when the population of new customers declines. At this point, growth is slow or negligible and is sustained by existing customers who continue to buy the product. The strategic manager faces a critical decision at this point: either experience a decline or develop next-generation products to the existing product platform to regain growth. This phase is defined as *de-maturity*, or restoring growth to a mature, declining product. Fluctuations (high variability) in product or service demand over time signal a need for strategic action or critical decisions regarding the product's sustainable competitive advantage and performance at each stage of a product's S-curve. The length of time it takes a product to complete the S-curve could be less than a year for some high-technology products but decades for others. For example, Kodak was able to earn high gross margins for its film business for more than 80 years.

2.3. EXPERIENCE OR LEARNING CURVES

The experience- or learning-curve concept builds on the S-curve. The experience-curve concept can be simply expressed in the age-old adage: You improve with practice. The logic is based on the notion that unit labor cost decreases in a regular manner as experience making the product increases. For example, the direct labor cost associated with the 100th unit will be lower than with the first unit. The experience-curve concept is based on an extension of the learning curve to activities other than labor. According to Henderson and his colleagues at the **Boston Consulting Group** (BCG), the costs associated with an item's value will decline approximately

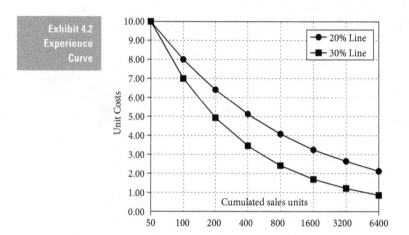

Exhibit 4.2
Experience
Curve

20 to 30 percent each time accumulated experience doubles.[8] Experience can be influenced by returns on human capital, labor efficiency, continuous improvement, total quality management, benchmarking, lean manufacturing, standardization, economies of scale, and continuous learning. Increased customer knowledge and experience with a product or service, combined with the firm's increased knowledge and experience with the product or service, will decrease the total cost of the product or service to the customer and the firm. As products or services move through the value chain, over time, costs to produce the product and customers' cost to acquire the product will decrease as experience with the product increases. That is, experience and knowledge determine the firm's value proposition and business model. In short, the strategy-making process needs to take into consideration the S-curve and experience-curve relationships (see Exhibit 4.2: Experience Curve).

2.4 S-CURVE AND CUSTOMER KNOWLEDGE

S-curves can also be used to track the amount of customer knowledge about a firm's products or services. Early phased high-technology products or complex products are usually high in firm knowledge (research and development, design, complexity, human capital) but low on customer knowledge. As a product moves through its life cycle, the amount of knowledge a customer needs to determine a product's value (and the related costs of acquiring the product) goes down as customer experience with the product increases. The reverse is also true for a company when making a decision to introduce a new high-technology or complex product to the market. These introductory staged products require significantly more technical, market, and other knowledge/expertise to determine the risk involved with selling the product, its value or selling price, and related costs associated with getting it to market. As such, high-technology and complex products usually require higher prices and gross margins in their early stages to recover the higher costs and investments in them. Therefore, early-stage product introductions that attract buyer attention and interests can usually command higher selling prices and margins. Products in the mature stage usually cannot attract higher purchasing prices from the customer because the customer has sufficient knowledge to make an informed purchasing decision and can shop around for the best price offered by a rival's similar products (see Exhibit 4.3: S-Curve and Customer Knowledge).

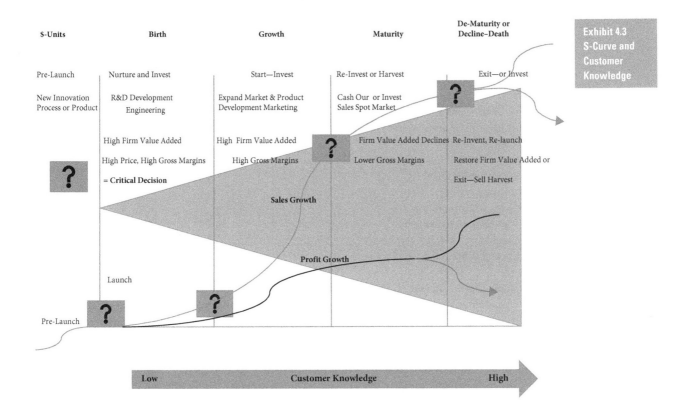

$-Units	Birth	Growth	Maturity	De-Maturity or Decline–Death

Exhibit 4.3
S-Curve and
Customer
Knowledge

Pre-Launch

New Innovation
Process or Product

Nurture and Invest

R&D Development
Engineering

High Firm Value Added

High Price, High Gross Margins

= Critical Decision

Start—Invest

Expand Market & Product
Development Marketing

High Firm Value Added

High Gross Margins

Re-Invest or Harvest

Cash Our or Invest
Sales Spot Market

Firm Value Added Declines

Lower Gross Margins

Exit—or Invest

Re-Invent, Re-launch

Restore Firm Value Added or

Exit—Sell Harvest

Sales Growth

Profit Growth

Launch

Pre-Launch

Low   **Customer Knowledge**   **High**

3. WHAT IS A STRATEGIC GROUP?

An industry's customers determine whether the products or services offered by firms have value. Customer value preferences aid firms in validating the fit between a firm's value proposition and customer value creation. Value creation and a firm's ability to create and sustain a competitive advantage are won in the external environment. Oftentimes, it is difficult to determine an industry's boundaries and its direct and indirect rivals. The strategic group map offers a convenient middle ground between industry-level analysis and firm-level analysis. It also assists in determining the firm's main rivals by focusing analysis on the extent to which rivals' strategic dimensions, market approaches, positioning, and customer value propositions are similar. Firms that offer comparable strategies and approaches form a **strategic group**.[9] **Homogeneity** of strategies is greater in the strategic group than outside the groups. Consequentially, competition in a strategic group is usually more intense than competition outside the group. A strategic group's competitive strategies and actions can coalesce along several dimensions including similarities in: technology, product quality, pricing, geographic footprint (number of locations), product depth, product breadth, services, and distribution channels. Membership within the strategic group defines the essential strategic dimensions that make up that group.

Strategic group maps help strategic managers focus an industry analysis on rivals with comparable strategies as well as the **competitive intensity** of rivals' strategies. Competitive intensity includes similarities in rivals' strategic actions and conduct that drive customer value creation. Among the competitive intensity factors are:

- Price
- Place or distribution channels (internet, whole, retail, private label, other)
- Product breadth (models offered)
- Product quality
- Continuous product and process innovation
- Technology development
- Design and style
- Advertising and promotion
- Use of celebrity endorsements
- Free shipping, rebates, delivery time
- Logistics and supply chain management

For example, Ford, Chrysler, General Motors, Volkswagen, Honda, Toyota, Tesla, BMW, and hosts of other firms all compete within numerous sectors of the global transportation industry. Although the internal combustion engine is still the dominant industry standard used in the vast majority of passenger vehicles sold annually, hybrid and all-electric cars are beginning to make headway as viable alternatives. Given the complexity and difficulty of analyzing all rivals that make passenger vehicles, a strategic group map can help focus the analysis. For instance, Tesla, General Motors, and VW are starting to market all-electric vehicles in the United States. A strategic group map of the all-electric vehicle segment of the transportation industry offers a convenient middle ground between analyzing internal combustion engine manufacturers and all electric manufacturers. Furthermore, all electric manufacturers can be subdivided based on the all-electric vehicle industry and firm-level analyses of their rivals' competitive intensity. All electric rivals can also be analyzed based on the homogeneity of rivals' strategies and their competitive intensity. Competitive intensity factors for all-electric vehicles include: vehicle size (full, intermediate, compact), quality (high-end luxury, lower-end affordability), amenities (infotainment system, sensor and telematics, safety features), and range (miles per charge). A strategic group map based on price/quality and range for the all-electric vehicle market is illustrated in Exhibit 4.4: Strategic Group Map—Competing All-electric Vehicle Market. Benefits of mapping strategic groups include:

- Helping to identify direct and indirect competitors (or possible partners) in a given sector, industry, or market
- Illustrating how easy or difficult it might be to move from one strategic group to another
- Helping to identify future opportunities or strategic problems in a given sector, industry, or market
- Ensuring that your firm takes your customers' or beneficiaries' views into account when developing or assessing existing strategies or crafting new strategies
- Assisting in strategy execution—what resources and competencies are needed to realize the crafted strategy[10]

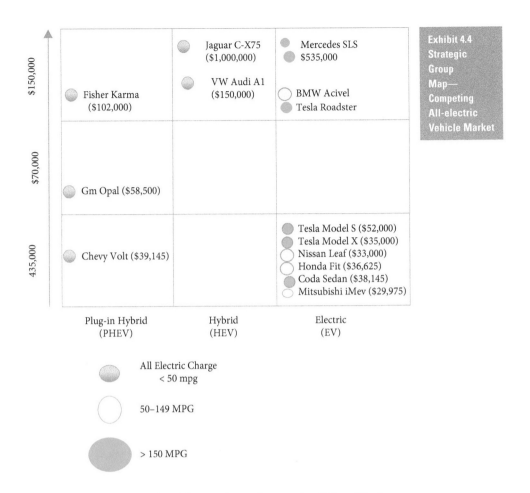

Exhibit 4.4
Strategic
Group
Map—
Competing
All-electric
Vehicle Market

Jaguar C-X75
($1,000,000)

Mercedes SLS
$535,000

VW Audi A1
($150,000)

BMW Acivel
Tesla Roadster

Fisher Karma
($102,000)

Gm Opal ($58,500)

Chevy Volt ($39,145)

Tesla Model S ($52,000)
Tesla Model X ($35,000)
Nissan Leaf ($33,000)
Honda Fit ($36,625)
Coda Sedan ($38,145)
Mitsubishi iMev ($29,975)

Plug-in Hybrid
(PHEV)

Hybrid
(HEV)

Electric
(EV)

All Electric Charge
< 50 mpg

50–149 MPG

> 150 MPG

Source: Michael J. Merenda–Adapted from: Paul Asquith, Parag A. Pathak, and Jay R. Ritter. Tesla Motors-Evaluating A Growth Company, Stanford Graduate School of Business, Case 209, 05/17/13: p. 17.

STRATEGIC GROUP MAP—U.S. RESTAURANT CHAINS

Thinking
Critically
Exercise 35

Industry rivals can be grouped by any number of strategic dimensions, such as similar business models, similar generic strategies, price/quality relationships, or degree of innovation. The number of groups within an industry and their composition depends on the dimensions used to define the groups. For example, a strategic group map for the restaurant industry might include fast food and fine dining based on variables like menu section and price. The graph below illustrates one procedure for plotting selected U.S. restaurant chains using menu selection and price (see Exhibit 4.5: Strategic Group Map—U.S. Restaurant Industry).

STRATEGIC GROUP MAP—U.S. RESTAURANT CHAINS

Using Exhibit 4.4, what other dimensions besides menu breadth or price could have been used in plotting rivals? Draw a new strategic group map using the new dimension(s). What are the strategic benefits of constructing your strategic group map compared to the original map?

Exhibit 4.5 Strategic Group Map—U.S. Restaurant Industry

Menu			
Full	Denny's iHop		Olive Garden Red Lobster Outback
Menu		Ponderosa Panera Bread Golden Corral	
Limited	Dunkin Donuts McDonald's Burger King Wendy's Sonic Taco Bell	Papa Gino's Pizza Hut KFC	Starbucks

Price →

Source: Michael J. Merenda 2018

3.1 CUSTOMERS DETERMINE COMPETITIVE ADVANTAGE

The strategist constantly searches for ways to create and sustain a competitive advantage over the firm's rivals. This is accomplished by delivering superior customer value. Only a firm's customers can determine whether a firm has achieved it because a firm's competitive advantage is based on customer purchasing decisions or, rather, the amount of money customers are willing to spend on one company's products over another's. Competitive advantage is when a firm can provide the same value as its competitors but at a lower price—or when it can charge higher prices by providing greater value through differentiation. Given this definition, there are several ways a firm can gain a competitive advantage. These include offering product and service benefits to customers (a firm's value proposition) that are:

- Superior to benefits of competitors' products or services
- Identical to benefits of competitors' products but offered at a lower price
- Superior to benefits of competitors' products and offered at a higher price [11]

3.2 INDUSTRY-DRIVING FORCES

A key to achieving competitive advantage is identifying and assessing the impact of an industry's driving forces on a firm's strategies and actions. Driving forces are forces outside the firm (external factors) that can trigger a change in the firm's strategies. Identifying, analyzing, and assessing driving forces and their impact on the firm is critical to the firm's success. Identifying industry-driving forces and ways to exploit these forces are prerequisites in determining a firm's potential ability to deliver superior customer value while simultaneously improving firm performance. Some examples of industry-driving forces are:

- Impact and spread of the internet, e-commerce, and the information technology (IT) revolution
- Globalization
- Changing demographics
- Rise of lean, agile, and sustainable business practices
- Breakthrough technologies, such as biotechnology, nanotechnology, and artificial intelligence
- Rise of borderless markets and rapidly falling temporal and spatial barriers
- Innovative business models, exploiting changes in cost and efficiency
- Rapid infusion and diffusion of technology within and across national borders
- Accelerated industry and product life cycles
- Rise of the knowledge worker
- Changes in the long-run industry growth rate
- Changes in who buys a product
- Changes in ways a product is used
- Entry or exit of a major firm, especially firms from unrelated industries or foreign countries
- Regulatory influences and government policy changes

3.3 KEY SUCCESS FACTORS

Strategists need to understand what it takes to be competitively successful, given industry dynamics and driving forces. That is, what is required to successfully compete in the industry or market space? Those elements or factors required for success are known as key success factors (KSF). KSFs are internal to the firm and make up the firm's core capabilities, distinctive competencies, actions, and activities employed to exploit industry-driving forces. They impact industry rivals' ability to effectively compete in the external environment. Identifying industry-driving forces and the keys to successfully exploiting them ultimately determines the competitive health of an industry and the competitive success or failure of industry rivals. As such, KSFs, by their very nature, are vital to the strategic management process and customer-value creation. Although all firms in the industry must pay close attention to them, only those firms with superior capabilities and competencies will be in a position to successfully align key success factors with industry-driving forces. The strategist needs to identify and understand industry-driving forces and key success factors as prerequisites for formulating and crafting strategy. Some examples of key success factors are:

- Information superiority
- Speed to market
- Customer response time
- Timely product or process innovations
- Superior knowledge management
- Innovative strategies and business models
- Superior technologies
- Superior management and employee know-how

SEARS AND TOYS 'R' US IT BATTLE

In June 2017, Sears Holdings Corp. announced it would close 72 Sears and Kmart stores. Sears followed that cull with another 20 closings the same month, 43 the following month, 28 that August, 63 that November, and 103 on January 4, 2018. *The Wall Street Journal* reported on October 24, 2017, that Sears would no longer sell the Whirlpool appliances it's carried since 1916. (An internal company memo cited pricing disputes.) Similarly, in March 2018, *The Washington Post* reported that Toys 'R' Us will sell or close all 800 of its U.S. stores, affecting as many as 33,000 jobs as the company winds down its operations after six decades. The news came six months after the retailer filed for bankruptcy. The company has struggled to pay down nearly $8 billion in debt—much of it dating to a 2005 leveraged buyout—and has (unsurprisingly) had difficulty finding a buyer.

a. Although Sears and Toys 'R' US have hit hard times, Amazon and Walmart have been able to use the internet and telecommunication technologies as sustaining technologies. What industry strategic drivers might have caused the demise of Sears and Toys 'R' Us?

b. What are some of the key success factors for competing in today's retail industry? How much of Sears's and Toys 'R' Us's troubles were driven by management's innovation dilemma—that is, did both stores hang on to their brick-and-mortar business models for too long?

Source: "Who Killed Sears? 50 Years on the Road to Ruin." *Investopedia.* https://www.investopedia.com/news/downfall-of-sears/#ixzz5FZAhGfGW.; Abha, Bhattarai. "Toys 'R' Us Will Close All 800 of Its U.S. Stores." *Washington Post.* March 2018. https://www.washingtonpost.com/news/business/wp/2018/03/14/toys-r-us-to-close-all-800-of-its-u-s-stores/?noredirect=on&utm_term=.dda06eed0103.

VIDEO 4.3 The Five Competitive Forces that Shape Strategy

4. FORCES DRIVING POSITIONING, INFLUENCING, AND EXPLOITING (PIE)

Advocates of the competitive forces school assume that the state of industry attractiveness for any firm is dependent on five forces and the interaction of these forces, as illustrated in Exhibit 4.6: Porter's Five Competitive Industry Forces. The five forces are: bargaining power of customers, bargaining power of suppliers, threat of new entrants, threat of substitute products, and intensity of competitive rivalry.[12] Several other macro factors can also drive the competitive forces and competitive dynamics in an industry. Examples of these macro factors are listed in Table 4.2: Macro Factors Driving Industry Forces. These factors can drive the strength of each force from more to less powerful, in the case of buyers and sellers; from low to high threat, in the case of new entrants and substitute products; and highly competitive (intense competition) to less competitive (low competitive intensity), in the case of each rival. For instance, Apple has been able to successfully position, influence, and exploit its new iPhone 8 and iPhone X in the global smartphone market. Its financial success and dominant position in large smartphones is highly unusual and rare in this fiercely competitive, cutthroat market. Apple was able to gain market share while also commanding higher prices in an industry where the average selling price for smartphones has been steadily reduced. Apple's strategic approach is about differentiating itself from rivals. Apple has pursued a closed, curated operating system

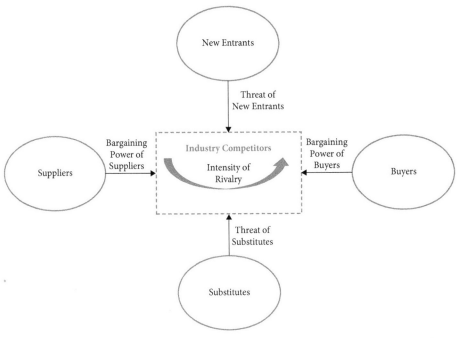

Exhibit 4.6
Porter's Five
Competitive
Industry Forces

Adapted from Michael E. Porter, "Note on the Structural Analysis of Industries," Boston, MA. Harvard Business School, 1975. p 2.

throughout most of its existence as a company. This strategy is drastically different from rivals' like Android, which sports an open operating system. Although the Android OS is used in more than 80 percent of all smartphones sold worldwide, Apple's strategy appears to be succeeding as its sales of the iPhone 8 and iPhone X have made Apple the number one company for market capitalization and profits[13].

Table 4.2
Macro Factors
Driving Porter's
Industry Forces

Bargaining Power Buyers
- Buyer concentration to firm concentration ratio
- Degree of dependency upon existing channels of distribution
- Bargaining leverage, particularly in industries with high fixed costs
- Buyer switching costs relative to firm switching costs
- Buyer information availability forcing down prices
- Availability of existing substitute products
- Buyer price sensitivity
- Differential advantage (uniqueness) of industry products
- Customer value proposition
- Buyer seller relationships

Bargaining Power of Suppliers
- Supplier switching costs relative to firm switching costs
- Degree of differentiation of inputs

- Impact of inputs on cost or differentiation
- Presence of substitute inputs
- Strength of distribution channel
- Supplier concentration to firm concentration ratio
- Employee solidarity (e.g. labor unions)
- Supplier competition: the ability to forward vertically integrate and cut ou
- Intensity of competitive rivalry

Threat of New Entrants
- The most attractive segment is one in which entry barriers are high and exit barriers are .
- Few new firms can enter and non-performing firms can exit easily.
- Patents, Copyrights, Trademarks, other intellectual property
- Government policy
- Capital requirements
- Absolute cost
- Cost disadvantages independent of size
- Economies of scale
- Economies of product differences
- Product differentiation
- Brand equity
- Switching costs or sunk costs
- Expected retaliation
- Access to distribution
- Customer loyalty to established brands
- Industry profitability (the more profitable the industry, the more attractive it will be to new competitors)

Threat of Substitutes
- Buyer propensity to substitute
- Relative price performance of substitute
- Buyer switching costs
- Perceived level of product differentiation
- Number of substitute products available in the market
- Ease of substitution
- Substandard product
- Quality depreciation

Intensity of Industry Rivals
- Sustainable competitive advantage through innovation
- Competition between online and offline companies
- Level of advertising expense
- Powerful competitive strategy
- Firm concentration ratio
- Degree of transparency

Source: Adapted from https://en.wikipedia.org/wiki/Porter_five_forces_analysis.

4.1 BARGAINING POWER OF BUYERS (AN INDUSTRY'S CHANNELS OF DISTRIBUTION AND CUSTOMERS)

Buyers comprise the market for a firm's output of products and services. Buyer bargaining power is based on the ability of a buyer to put the selling firm under pressure. Buyer pressure is usually measured in terms of either the buyer's ability to influence the price of outputs or the buyer's price sensitivity. The buyer power is high if the buyer has many buying alternatives that are equal to or better than the seller's output. The buyer power is low if the buyer highly values the seller's output and does not have any alternatives to buying the product from the seller. For example, if you own a bakery that sells 100 percent organically certified biscuits, there are no other bakeries that sell similar biscuits, and there are buyers (customers) who like and want only your biscuits, then buyer power would be low. This is especially true if you cannot or refuse to lower your selling price for the biscuit.

4.2 BARGAINING POWER OF SUPPLIERS (AN INDUSTRY'S FACTOR INPUTS)

Suppliers make up the market of inputs to a focal firm's products or services. Suppliers provide the inputs, such as raw material, parts and components, systems, networks, labor, services, and other factors that go into a firm's products or services. Firms can transform or transition factor inputs to products or services (market outputs) by adding their own value to inputs (a firm's value proposition). Similar to buyer power, supplier power is determined by its ability to influence or control input prices. When the firm needs or highly values the supplier's input and has no equal or better alternatives to the input, then the seller's power is high. If the firm has several equal or better alternatives, then the supplier's power is low. For example, if you are making 100 percent organically certified biscuits and your business depends on a certain flour, and there is only one supplier of this kind of flour, then the supplier power is high. This is especially true if the supplier refuses to work with the firm and charges excessively high prices for its unique input.

4.3 THREAT OF NEW ENTRANTS (POTENTIALLY NEW PLAYERS TO AN EXISTING INDUSTRY)

The threat of the entry of new rivals is determined by the market's output profitability. Markets that yield high returns will attract new firms. This results in many new entrants, which eventually will decrease profitability for all firms in the industry. Unless rivals block the entry of new firms, the abnormal profit rate of return will trend toward zero, thus moving the industry to what classical economists would define as perfect competition. New entrants bring many challenges to existing firms by delivering new capacity, the desire to gain market share, and, often, substantial resources. Again using the biscuit example, a new entrant may decide to go to the same supplier that your bakery is using and open a bakery next to yours. The new entrant determines that she can sell her rival biscuits for $1.00 less per biscuit and still make a good profit. She opens Tasty Biscuit right across the street from your bakery. If your customers find that the new entrant's products are of equal or better quality to yours, and they can buy them at a lower price without absorbing any additional costs (i.e., switching costs is zero or considerably less than $1.00), then buyer (customer) power is high.

4.4 THREAT OF SUBSTITUTE PRODUCTS OR SERVICES (PRODUCTS OR SERVICES WITH A POTENTIALLY BETTER CUSTOMER-VALUE PROPOSITION)

The existence of products or services that offer buyers (customers) a better value proposition outside the competitive markets or common market boundaries for products or services increases the propensity of buyers (customers) to switch to substitutes. For example, several of your loyal customers just learned that your 100 percent organically certified biscuit is made from wheat and other grains high in gluten. These customers also read the book *Wheat Belly* in which the author, a noted cardiologist, reported in great detail the health problems associated with consuming grains, especially on a daily basis.[14] They discover that 100 percent certified yogurt is not only better for them but also equally satisfying, so instead of stopping daily for their morning coffee and biscuit, they decide to buy yogurt at the nearby grocery store and stay at home. Not only is the yogurt better for them, but it also can save them significant money.

4.5 INTENSITY OF RIVALRY AMONG EXISTING COMPETITORS

For most industries, the intensity of competitive rivalry proves to be the major determinant of competitiveness. Porter notes, "Rivalry amongst competitors takes the similar form of jockeying for position—using tactics like price competition, advertising battles, product introductions, and increased customer services and warranties. Rivalry occurs because one or more competitors either feels the pressure or sees the opportunity to improve position."[15] For example, Tasty Biscuit decides to add yogurt to her menu and develop a 100 percent organic biscuit that is not only gluten-free but also tastes great. Her Tasty Biscuit and yogurt products take off and threaten not only your biscuit profits but also your entire bakery. Either you respond with an improved value proposition that better positions your bakery, or you risk going out of business. You attempt to regain your competitive advantage in the bakery business by better positioning and influencing competitive forces through building superior capabilities.

4.6 PESTEL FACTORS DRIVING INDUSTRY DYNAMICS

In addition to Porter's five forces, several other macro and mezzo factors can influence the competitive dynamics and intensity of industry rivals.. PESTEL factors include: political, environmental, social, technological, economic, and legal (see chapter 3).[16] Conducting a PESTEL analysis is useful in identifying, evaluating, and assessing the interplay among the five industry-level forces.. Forces and factors can be emergent (new developments), active (directly impactful), or latent (passive or no impact on forces). In Exhibit 4.7, Porter's forces are represented by the five rectangles. The PESTEL factors are further divided into three ovals: (1) technology (technological innovations), (2) political, environmental, social, legal, and (3) economic (including complements). Macro factors and mezzo forces can facilitate or hinder the demand for an industry's products and services either directly or indirectly, thus impacting industry and rivals' performance.

4.6.1 IMPACT OF TECHNOLOGICAL INNOVATIONS (TECHNOLOGY)

Markets and technologies can and do change over time. Change is driven by technological innovations. Every organizational leader must be a master at managing innovation. Industries and organizations go through constant evolutionary and revolutionary life cycles. **Evolutionary cycles** incrementally change industries and the way things are done. **Revolutionary cycles** shift the very nature of competition. Revolutionary change destroys the old order of things and brings in a new order. The source of technological innovation can come from inside

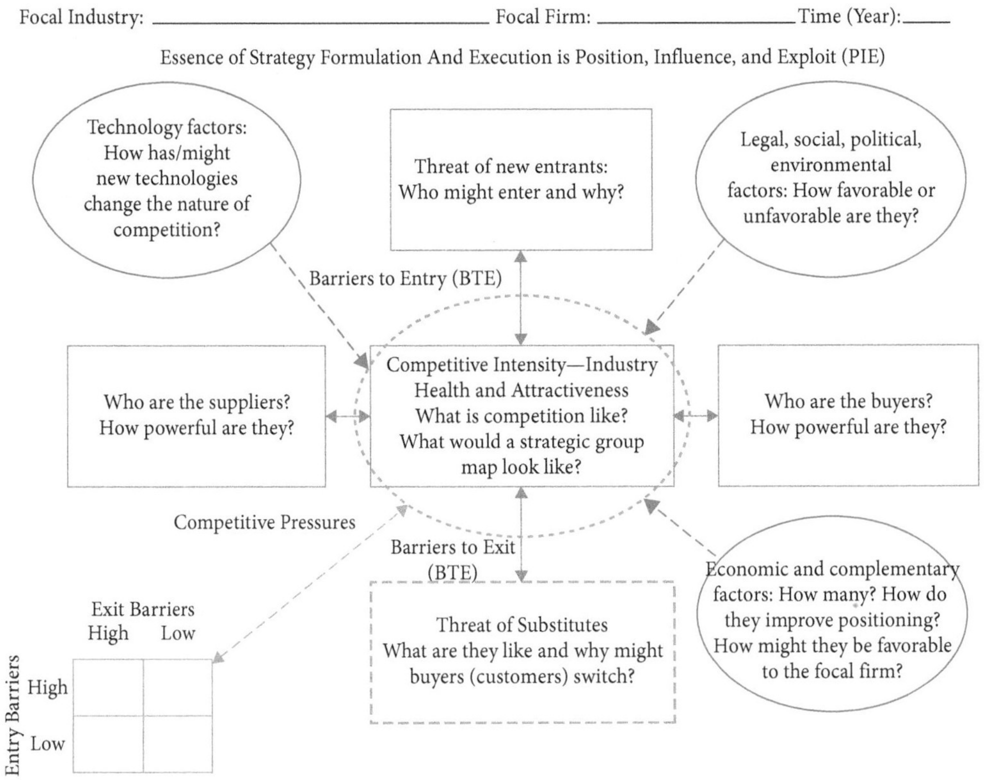

Focal Industry: _____ Focal Firm: _____ Time (Year):_____

Exhibit 4.7
Forces and
PESTEL Factors
Driving
Competition

Essence of Strategy Formulation And Execution is Position, Influence, and Exploit (PIE)

Technology factors: How has/might new technologies change the nature of competition?

Threat of new entrants: Who might enter and why?

Legal, social, political, environmental factors: How favorable or unfavorable are they?

Barriers to Entry (BTE)

Who are the suppliers? How powerful are they?

Competitive Intensity—Industry Health and Attractiveness What is competition like? What would a strategic group map look like?

Who are the buyers? How powerful are they?

Competitive Pressures

Barriers to Exit (BTE)

Threat of Substitutes What are they like and why might buyers (customers) switch?

Economic and complementary factors: How many? How do they improve positioning? How might they be favorable to the focal firm?

Exit Barriers
High   Low

Entry Barriers
High
Low

Critical Inquiry and Overall Assessment: Draw conclusions. Describe the overall attractiveness of the industry under analysis from highly attractive to highly unattractive?

Explain factor impact from favorable to unfavorable for the "focal firm".

Source: Adapted from: Source: Michael E. Porter, Competitive Advantage, New York: Free Press: 1985

---

the firm (research and development), within the firm's value chain, and from governmental, educational, and private research organizations.

4.6.2 IMPACT OF POLITICAL, ENVIRONMENTAL, SOCIAL, AND LEGAL FACTORS

Laws and regulations encourage businesses to conform to society's basic standards, values, and attitudes. Some growing concerns about legal and ethical issues in business that can impact the competitive forces in an industry are: antitrust violations, accounting fraud, cybercrimes, unfair competitive practices, and tax fraud. In some instances, competitive forces are influenced by social and political concerns and standards. Some of these concerns include noneconomic values (social and political beliefs that support or hinder a firm's ability to compete); socially desirable goods and services; protecting individual rights and privacy; resolution of national and global problems; regulation to benefit special groups; conservation of resources; and social value versus economic cost.

A **complement** is a product or service that can increase demand for an industry's products or services. Complements share similar demand curves or competitive dynamics; that is, the demand of one good is linked to the demand of another good. If a higher quantity is demanded of one good, a higher quantity will also be demanded of the other, and vice versa. When the prices of complementary goods are related, the rise in one complementary will also cause the related good's price to rise. With substitute goods, however, the price and quantity demanded of one good is related inversely to the price and quantity demanded of a substitute good, meaning that if the price or quantity demanded of one good rises, the price or quantity demanded of its substitute will fall. For example, the demand for smartphones is tied to the demand for content (movies), apps (fantasy football), services (bill pay), or network connectivity (social networks). An increase in any one or all of these complements could support greater demand for iPhones.

5. STEPS IN CONDUCTING A COMPETITIVE FORCES ANALYSIS

Competitive forces analysis begins with mapping out the playing field and boundaries that make up the industry (and the firms in the industry) being analyzed. The map needs to include the factors or variables that can positively or negatively influence the competitive dynamics of the industry. The map lays out the terrain and environmental forces that shape, influence, and ultimately determine the overall health and competitiveness of the industry and its rivals or competitors. See Exhibit 4.8 for the schematic drawing (or map) used to conduct a competitive forces analysis. The analysis provides an **information graphic** (infographic) or visual representation of the overall attractiveness of the industry, along with rivals' competitive positioning and influence within industry market segments.[17] The goal of the competitive forces analysis is to help improve the strategist's conceptual and cognitive abilities by utilizing graphics to enhance patterns and trends. The steps in conducting the competitive forces analysis, with the smartphone industry as an example, are discussed in steps 1–8.

STEP 1 IDENTIFY THE "FOCAL" FIRM AND "FOCAL" STRATEGIC GROUP (SUBINDUSTRY) FOR ANALYSIS

Porter cautions that it is not always clear where one industry's boundaries end and those for another industry begin. For example, where do you draw the line between an established industry and emerging industry; among competitors offering similar or dissimilar strategies or market approaches; among substitute products; between existing firms and potential entrants; between existing firms and suppliers; and between existing products and services, substitute products and services, and complementary products and services?[18] Let's consider the smartphone industry as the focal industry and Apple as the focal firm. Among a host of competitors in this industry are Google, Samsung, RIM, Palm, and Microsoft. The focal industry is smartphones. Apple sells many products and services, including Mac computers, iPad tablets, iPhone and iWatch devices, operating systems and apps, and services (iTunes, iCloud). Apple designs, assembles, and sells smartphones for buyers. Many vendor components and services (e.g., contract assemblers) go into making smartphones. Apple, and not the suppliers, is the focal firm. Also, Apple might sell its smartphones through **intermediaries** (Best Buy, Walmart, college tech stores) to final buyers (you and me). Other industry players may provide content (apps, movies, advertising) to be used on the smartphones by the focal firm (Apple) and sold to buyers (again, you and me). Some focal firms may be fully or partially **vertically integrated backward** (that is, they make all or some of the components that go into the manufacturing of smartphones), or they may be **vertically integrated forward** by selling directly to buyers (Apple stores) instead of through an intermediary.

The first step in conducting competitive forces analysis is to construct a strategic group map for the rivals competing in the smartphone industry.

STEP 2 IDENTIFY POTENTIAL NEW ENTRANTS

Two recent entrants to the smartphone industry are Xiaomi[19] and Amazon.[20] Although they are now full rivals in the smartphone industry, their entry was a potential threat to existing smartphone sellers. If benefits are greater than costs and reasonable profits can be made, then the **entry-deterring price** for potential competitors is low. If costs are greater than benefits, then potential new entrants will be deterred from entering.[21]

STEP 3 IDENTIFY BUYERS

Who are they and what are they buying? What would make them want to buy Apple's smartphones over another maker's smartphones? Consider the market segments and market characteristics in which the focal firm sells its products and services. For example, Apple sells to or through telecommunication companies (Verizon, AT&T), big-box retailers (Best Buy, Walmart), large enterprises (IBM), SMEs (small- and medium-size enterprises), governments, educational institutions, consumers, and directly through Apple brick-and-mortar stores (physical vs. online stores and online iStore). What will cause any one of these buyers to switch from buying Apple smartphones to buying Samsung smartphones?

STEP 4 IDENTIFY SUBSTITUTE PRODUCTS

What are they, and why might current buyers of Apple smartphones consider switching to substitute products? For example, Skype and other teleconferencing apps accessed through a computer would be a substitute for talking on smartphones. Other potential substitutes are PCs, tablets, and other internet-connecting devices (e.g., iWatch, wearables such as Google Glass, Apple's iTV, and Xbox).

STEP 5 IDENTIFY SUPPLIERS

Who are they, and what power do they have, if any, over the maker of smartphones? For example, Google provides its Android operating system practically free of charge to smartphone manufacturers. (The Android operating system is the killer app that makes smartphones run.) Google is the sole supplier of the Android operating system, which is used in more than 80 percent of all non-Apple smartphones sold worldwide. Other suppliers to Apple (as the focal firm) include component manufacturers (circuit boards, batteries, memory, other components), contract electronic manufacturers, telecommunication companies, software vendors, knowledge workers, etc.

STEP 6 IDENTIFY IMPACT OF NEW TECHNOLOGIES AND INNOVATION

How might innovation and technological advances impact the focal firm and competition among rivals? Is the technology a **sustaining technology** (advances the focal firm's existing product or services) or a **disruptive technology** (replaces the focal firm's products and services)? Is the focal firm in a good position to influence and exploit technological advances? Disruptive technologies come from radical innovations. Radical innovation can drastically reshape and change the nature of industry competition and competitive forces. Disruptive technologies are the catalysts for new and emerging industries. For example, digital photography emerged as a radical technology, replacing traditional film-based photography as a profitable industry.

STEP 7 IDENTIFY POLITICAL, ENVIRONMENTAL, SOCIAL, AND LEGAL FACTORS

Social, economic, political, and other macro factors need to be considered when conducting a competitive forces analysis. These forces can act as potential opportunities or threats to an industry's competitors. For example, in February 2015, the Federal Communications Commission passed a new "net neutrality or open Internet" regulation. The regulation is "designed to protect the free flow of content on the Internet." It is based on the principle that internet service providers (ISP) such as Verizon and AT&T "should give consumers access to all legal content and applications on an equal basis, without favoring some sources or blocking others."[22] The regulation prevents ISP from charging content providers, such as Netflix or Hulu, for speedier delivery of their content on "fast lanes" and deliberately slowing the content from providers that may compete with ISP. The net neutrality regulation has the full force of law and is being rigorously fought by the telecom providers.

STEP 8 IDENTIFY ECONOMIC FACTORS AND COMPLEMENTS

Are there available complements that could potentially positively or negatively impact the demand for smartphones? For example, the increased demand for peer-to-peer social networking could positively increase the demand for network devices such as Apple smartphones. Growth in the "sharing" economy services, such as the Uber app that provides individuals with an opportunity to earn money by ride sharing, could positively increase the demand for smartphones. Conversely, legislation or regulation that protects licensed city cab companies could slow demand for the Uber app or, in some instances, prevent it from competing in certain cities or towns.[23]

6. INDUSTRY ENTRY AND EXIT BARRIERS

Strategic managers engaged in crafting strategy must be constantly on guard for new rivals to their industry. New rivals or entrants to the industry can take sales and profits away from existing firms and challenge their ability to effectively compete. The general manager must determine who might enter the industry and why. New entrants will be attracted to an industry if the industry's profitability and its overall health remain appealing. They might also enter an industry in order to protect or advance their own strategies and profits regardless of the overall focal industry's attractiveness. The new entrant needs to assess the benefits of entering the industry against the costs to enter. If the benefits outweigh the costs, then there is a good chance for new firms to enter. Conversely, existing industry rivals need to constantly determine how to best respond to any new entrant. If the industry subgroup or focal firm's profitability is threatened, then it needs to determine how to best counter the new firm's entry. The ideal situation possesses high entry barriers for potential new entrants and low exit barriers for existing rivals.

For example, why would Google and Amazon enter the smartphone industry? Google realized that it needed to secure its search engine service on mobile devices to help protect its revenues from online advertisers, its main source of revenues and profits. Likewise, Amazon entered the industry with its Fire smartphone to secure its e-commerce sales as more and more people were using smartphones versus PCs for online purchases.[24] Interesting, Yahoo! failed to secure its search engine and advertising revenue when it did not transition services to the smartphone platform. Yahoo!'s failure to attract mobile advertising revenues on mobile devices resulted in a drastic deterioration of its sales and operating profits. The situation became so severe that Yahoo!'s Marissa Mayer and its board of directors were forced to sell the company to Verizon at a severely discounted valuation.

6.1 ASSESSING INDUSTRY ENTRY AND EXIT BARRIERS

Consider the approaches offered by Porter: Are economic and other barriers preventing new competitors from entering the industry? Conversely, does the focal firm possess dynamic capabilities allowing it to transition into new products and services when the timing is right (that is, industry exit barriers are low or manageable for the focal firm)? Each cell in the exit and entry matrix is discussed below:

Cell A: High entry barriers and high exit barriers—Protects focal firm or subgroup rivals already existing and future profits without the threat of new entrants. High entry barriers are extremely important when the subgroups or focal firms are enjoying supernormal return on capital reflective of a high-quality business well positioned in its industry subgroup. Supernormal profits provide a signal for other firms to enter the industry. High entry barriers block entry of new firms, preventing any new entrant from increasing the supply of goods offered for sale. A low entry barrier intensifies competition within the subgroup by increasing supply and lowering subgroup prices. This shifts the power away from rivals to buyers. New entrants will not challenge industry incumbents as long as entry barriers remain high. High exit barriers can pose new challenges for incumbents when the focal industry's attractiveness deteriorates from such factors as slowing growth, maturing of rivals' product lines, destabilizing industry boundaries, new entrants and availability of large number of substitutes.

Cell B: High entry barriers and low exit barriers—Signals an ideal situation for incumbent firms. High returns are protected during good times while allowing for exit from the industry when returns on invested capital do not meet the focal firm's investors' expectations. Although the financial risk remains low for the focal firm, the focal firm must decide how best to harvest or exit from the existing business and craft new strategies or adapt existing strategies for customers or new markets. Firms that possess dynamic strategies and capabilities that are flexible and valuable to buyers in other industries or markets are in a better position to move into these new markets or industries subject to favorable entry barriers.

Cell C: Low entry barriers and high exit barriers—This situation prevents high business and financial risks, especially in those situations where the focal firm and incumbent subgroup rivals' competitive advantage is seriously challenged.

Cell D: Low entry barriers and low exit barriers—This situation presents high business and financial risks to all firms in the subgroup and any firm entering the industry. Subgroups with these industry characteristics compete by offering similar products, face intense competition from rivals, and constantly threaten each firm's competitive actions and profits. Industries with low entry barriers and low exit barriers offer little chance in successfully growing profits and sales (see Exhibit 4.8: Entry and Exit Matrix).

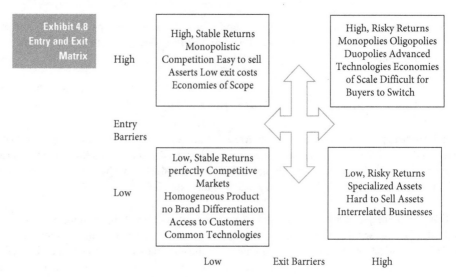

Exhibit 4.8
Entry and Exit
Matrix

Entry Barriers

High

High, Stable Returns Monopolistic Competition Easy to sell Asserts Low exit costs Economies of Scope	High, Risky Returns Monopolies Oligopolies Duopolies Advanced Technologies Economies of Scale Difficult for Buyers to Switch

Low

Low, Stable Returns perfectly Competitive Markets Homogeneous Product no Brand Differentiation Access to Customers Common Technologies	Low, Risky Returns Specialized Assets Hard to Sell Assets Interrelated Businesses

Low   Exit Barriers   High

Source: Michael J. Merenda 2018

6.2 DRAW CONCLUSIONS

The competitive forces and exit and entry barriers need be evaluated and assessed to determine:

a. The competitive health and strengths (opportunities) of the focal industry. Is this a competitively attractive industry for the focal firm? For rivals?
b. The power of buyers (customers) and rivals (incumbents). Is there a low, medium, or high threat of buyers (customers) shifting their purchasing decision away from the focal firm to either substitutes or other sellers (incumbents)? Buyers will change their purchasing decision if the cost to switch is low or nonexistent and the actual or perceived value received is greater.
c. The threat of new entrants. Is the threat of potential new entrants low, medium, or high?
d. The threat of substitutes. Is the threat of substitute products low, medium, or high? Buyers will shift to substitutes if they provide greater value at the same price of the focal firm's product or equal value to the focal firm, but at a lower price.
e. Macro factors. Are there other macro factors that could positively or negatively influence the competitiveness of the focal firm and industry? Is the impact on demand for the focal firm's product positive or negative?

Overall, is the industry segment or subgroup highly attractive, somewhat attractive, or not very attractive for the focal firm? Can the focal firm defend or advance its position against the competitive forces? The conclusions derived from the competitive forces analysis on industry attractiveness, dynamic capabilities, and entry and exit barriers are best used for:

a. Positioning the firm so that its capabilities provide the best defense against the existing array of competitive forces
b. Influencing the balance of forces through strategic moves, thereby improving the firm's relative position
c. Anticipating shifts in the factors underlying the forces and responding to them, hopefully exploiting change by choosing a strategy appropriate to the new competitive balance before rivals recognize it[25]

ENTRY AND EXIT BARRIERS FOR AIRLINES

Thinking Critically Exercise 37

The airline industry is highly competitive and capital-intensive. Because of this nature, fixed costs and barriers to exit are high. Competition in the airline industry is intense as barriers to entry remain low due to liberalization of market access, which is a result of globalization. According to the IATA (International Air Transport Association) about 1,300 new airlines were established in the past 40 years. The following summarizes the nature of competition in the airline industry:

- Competition increases when new airlines enter the market or when existing airlines expand services to new markets. Existing airlines benefit, however, from economies of scale and rights on airport slots. Hence, expansion into new markets has fewer entry barriers compared to new airlines.
- The capital requirement for aircraft acquisition is high and can deter new airlines from entering. However, the impact of this is reduced due to the availability of leasing options and external financing from banks, investors, and aircraft manufacturers.
- Switching cost is low for customers. Although loyalty programs are useful to retain customers across alliances, they are not very useful in retaining customers between airlines within an alliance.

   a. What strategic subgroups might be used to illustrate the different rivals competing in the airline industry?
   b. What would an entry and exit matrix look like for a low-cost airline such as Alaska Airlines?
   c. Can you think of another industry where competition is so fierce due to high exit barriers and low entry barriers?
   d. What is this industry, and what is competition like for rivals in this industry?
   e. What strategic subgroups might be used to illustrate the different rivals competing in this industry?
   f. What would an entry and exist barrier matrix look like for this industry?

Source: Cederholm, Teresa. "The Airline Industry's Growth and Impact on Economic Prosperity." *Market Realist.* December 29, 2014. Accessed March 27, 2017. http://marketrealist.com/2014/12/low-entry-barriers-intensify-competition-airline-industry/.

THE BATTLE BETWEEN WALMART AND AMAZON WILL BE EPIC

Thinking Critically Exercise 38

eMarketer estimated that in 2017 there were more than 2.4 billion smartphone users worldwide and by year end 2018, more than a third of the global population will be using a smartphone. In 2018, Amazon and Walmart are locked in a fierce battle over dominance of the online, ecommerce marketplace. Although many rivals exist in this space—Alibaba, eBay, Etsy, Sears—the biggest in the United States are Amazon and Walmart. *Forbes* reports, "There is an epic battle brewing between Amazon and Walmart" and the online marketplaces will be the main competitive space where this showdown will take place. According to *Forbes*, consumers already turn to Amazon first to look for products and reviews. Some 30 percent of shoppers begin their searches on Google while 49 percent start on Amazon. Unlike Amazon, Walmart does not have any of its own mobile devices (smartphones, tablets) as gateways to online markets.

7. GENERIC STRATEGIES

The two generic strategies for a firm to gain a competitive advantage are lower cost and differentiation. These two strategies can be further divided by their competitive scope: narrow and broad target markets. Exhibit 4.9: Porter's Generic Strategies is a 2×2 typology, or matrix, showing five types of generic strategies based on the source of competitive advantage (lower cost and differentiation) and competitive scope (narrow or broad): overall cost leadership, cost focus, overall differentiation, focused differentiation, and finally, best value or cost.

Exhibit 4.9 Porter's Generic Strategies

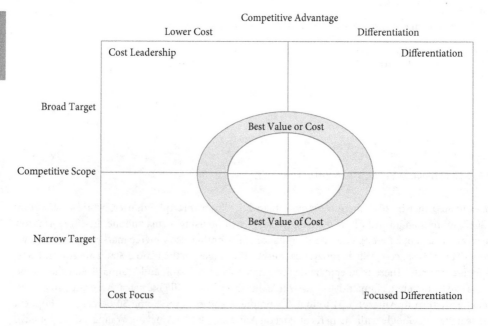

7.1 OVERALL COST LEADERSHIP

To assume a position of overall cost leadership for any specific product, service, or business, the firm must compete on price. To do so, the firm must possess core capabilities and competencies that focus on productivity improvements and cost efficiencies. Tight cost controls, efficient operations, economies of scale, and elimination of all marginal accounts and operations drive this strategy. The only way to gain a significant competitive advantage with an overall cost-leadership strategy is by outperforming your rivals based on cost. Low-cost strategies usually require high sales volume, standardized plants, set operating procedures, and extremely tight fiscal accountability in all functional areas (e.g., sales, marketing, manufacturing, R&D, administration). Overall, cost leadership is usually selected for a business or strategy center when the business unit's products are homogeneous and difficult to distinguish from competitive rivals'. Prime candidates for overall cost leadership strategies are natural resource companies (copper, steel, petroleum); fast-food companies (McDonald's, Wendy's, Burger King); low-cost airlines (Southwest, JetBlue); and some consumer product companies such as generics (private labels) or high-volume, low-cost items (bread, milk, paper, commodities).

7.2 OVERALL DIFFERENTIATION

The objective in a differentiation strategy is to create enough uniqueness (either perceived or actual) in a product so that customers will be willing to pay a premium price for the product, compared to rivals' products. This strategy is usually associated with high-margin, low-volume products. Differentiation can result from unique product features, customer service, quality, location, availability, product and process R&D, and brand image (i.e., upscale advertising and promotion). Rolex was able to achieve a differentiation strategy for its watches. Similarly, Jaguar's C-X75 hybrid electric vehicle (HEV) priced at $1.1 million sought differentiation over Mercedes' M Class HEVs priced at $47,000. Purdue Chicken, Stonyfield natural organic yogurts, and Apple smartphones are all examples of successful differentiation strategies. Other examples of differentiation strategies include Tesla Motors' all-electric Roadster and the Lincoln Continental for American-made automobiles; Mercedes and BMW for foreign imports; five star-restaurants; Cross Pens; the Four Seasons and The Ritz-Carlton in the hotel industry; and Disney World for family amusement parks.

7.3 COST-FOCUSED

A cost-focused strategy is based on a narrow target market. Firms that compete on cost focus limit the number of markets in which they sell their products. Cost-focused strategies are usually associated with high-volume, low-margin products. In executing this strategy, the firm must concentrate or focus its efforts and resources on a particular product, industry, or customer segment. Many contract electronic-component manufacturers or component-part manufacturers concentrate on manufacturing products produced in high volumes (economies of scale) and engineered, designed, and assembled according to customer specifications and strict standards. For example, many OEMs (original equipment manufacturers), such as Nike, Apple, and HP, use contract manufacturers (lower-cost manufacturers in China) to produce high volumes of electronic components at a lower cost for their end products (athletic footwear, smartphones, and PCs).

7.4 FOCUSED DIFFERENTIATION

Examples of vertical markets are very specialized niche markets found in large industries such as insurance, real estate, banking, heavy manufacturing, retail, aerospace, hospitals, and government. For example, a software developer may decide to sell its flight simulation software in the aerospace market and not in any other markets. As such, this company is selling its software aimed at a particular vertical market (commercial pilot training) and can be contrasted with horizontal market software (such as word processors and spreadsheet programs) that can be used in all industries. For instance, many smaller software companies could not compete with Microsoft and its Windows operating system or Apple and its iOS operating system. Because of this, smaller companies might elect to concentrate on developing specific spreadsheets or data-analytics software targeted for very specialized markets in terms of revenue and growth. These smaller companies might be in a better position to develop highly innovative software for smaller markets or emerging markets—markets that larger companies are not interested in due to small volume, minimal market attractiveness, etc.

Many smaller companies have successfully adopted a focused lower-cost or differentiation strategy when their industries' sales are concentrated and dominated by larger companies. Because the smaller company cannot possibly compete head-on with the industry majors, they must find a "niche" segment. Smaller companies may be able to operate at a lower cost because of their smaller size, or they may compete on differentiation by being more innovative than their larger rivals. Boutique wineries, craft beers, and specialty stores are all examples of companies pursuing a focused strategy in the industry in which they compete. Vertical marketing is another term for a focused strategy. A vertical market is a particular industry or group of enterprises in which similar products or services are developed and marketed using similar methods (and to whom goods and services can be sold).

For example, in the early 2000s, several major food companies began paying a premium for smaller organic companies. The higher price was based on the consistently faster sales growth and considerably higher profit margins for many of the so-called "green" start-ups. These acquisitions provided the majors with insights into how to inspire die-hard customer loyalty and new growth opportunities—two arenas in which the little guys regularly trounced the big guys.[26] It was reported that L'Oréal paid $1.4 billion (about 1.5 times annual sales) for The Body Shop in 2006; and in 2008, Clorox paid $913 million for Burt's Bees, more than 5.5 times Burt's annual sales at the time. Other notable acquisitions were (acquiring company in parentheses): Honest Tea (Coke), Ben & Jerry's (Unilever), Cascadian Farms (General Mills), Kashi (Kellogg), Stonyfield Yogurt (Groupe Danone), Tom's of Maine (Colgate-Palmolive), Naked Juice (PepsiCo), Dagoba Organic Chocolate (Hershey), Green & Black's chocolate (Kraft Foods), Earth's Best (Heinz), and The Organic Cow of Vermont (Dean).[27]

| Thinking Critically Exercise 39 | HAVING A GENERIC STRATEGY |

HAVING A GENERIC STRATEGY

Can the concept of a generic strategy be applied to individuals? For example, do you aspire to be a generalist or a specialist in your career? If you were a medical provider or caregiver, would you be a general practitioner, a primary care physician, a neurosurgeon, or a radiologist? Think of your career options; what management positions would emphasize the generalist's mindset? What about a specialist's mindset? What other dimensions beside costs might be used to define an individual's generic strategy? Would an individual have to be frugal and thrifty in order to work in a strategy position for a company that has a cost-focused strategy?

A best-cost strategy is based on offering customers value by combining reasonable value for a competitive price. This strategy emphasizes both lower cost and higher-quality products and services. The firm's value proposition is based on keeping costs and prices lower than those of other providers of comparable quality and features. For example, both Honda and Toyota car companies consistently rank higher on customer satisfaction surveys than rivals with much more expensive cars.

8. REFLECTION

This chapter focused on how to analyze a firm's external environments. It covered the competitive forces strategy school and several analytical tools and concepts used to conduct external situational analysis. An external situational analysis is usually the first step in crafting strategy. The second step in crafting strategy is to conduct an internal situational analysis. Both steps 1 and 2 are essential in effectively crafting and managing the strategic management process. Schools offer normative recommendations or prescriptions for managers' strategic actions, activities, and behaviors (what should be) but are based on positive, descriptive critical inquiry of the real world (what is). The competitive forces school is based on positive, descriptive real-world critical inquiry of the macro factors and industry forces that influence, shape, facilitate, or constrain a firm's ability to create and sustain competitive advantage. Although the descriptive forces school prescribes how the firm should behave, the strategist attempts to maximize stockholders' return on invested capital or wealth creation though positioning, influencing, and exploiting the five competitive forces. Thus, a precursor to all strategy making is external analysis and critical inquiry of the firm's competitive environment. An external situation analysis starts with understanding the firm's PESTEL macro factors, industry competitive forces, customers' value creation proposition, and the interdependence and interpenetrating nature of these factors and forces. A major tenet of the competitive forces school is that competitive advance is won in the external environment by customers' purchasing decisions.

Although the competitive forces school of thought is a useful tool for crafting strategy, it has its opponents. Critics argue that the external environment is unstable, dynamic, and constantly changing. They assert that customers, technologies, and markets can and do change. Although useful, the competitive forces school at best is only applicable in stable environments where little or no change occurs. Critics also argue that a competitive forces analysis is not realistic given the turbulence of rapidly changing markets and that the five forces school is too structured and deterministic to be of any value in fast-paced, uncertain environments. Another criticism is that industry boundaries are fluid and can quickly erode or destabilize. In these instances, firms find themselves being blindsided or competing in borderless markets where new rivals with radically different customer experiences and value propositions disrupt formerly distinct and clear industry practices. In response to some of these criticisms, several next-generation strategy schools have gained increasing prominence. One of these schools is the resourced-based view of the firm that will be discussed in the next chapter.

KODAK—THE FALL OF AN AMERICAN ICON

George Eastman founded his first photo plate company at the age of 23. In 1879, he invented a coating method that let him mass-produce photographic dry plates. In 1888, his company was incorporated in Rochester, New York, as Eastman Kodak Company (Kodak). By the 1930s, Kodak employed more than 135,000 people worldwide, with the majority of its employees located in Rochester. Throughout the twentieth century, the well-recognized brand was synonymous with film photography and enjoyed a dominant global position. It consistently earned record sales and above-average profits. By the 1950s, Kodak had become one of the most admired and respected global companies, known for its numerous innovations in the traditional photography industry. The tagline "Kodak Moment" not only captured a personal event that demanded to be recorded for posterity, but it also made Kodak an international household name. By the mid-1970s, Kodak possessed 90 percent of film sales and 85 percent of camera sales in the United States.

Throughout the twentieth century, Kodak held almost 50 percent of the global photography market. In the 1990s, Kodak planned a decade-long journey to move to digital technology. In 1995, Kodak's average stock price was $58.41, and the company recorded revenues and profits of $15 billion and $1.3 billion, respectively. As the twentieth century concluded, however, Kodak's fortunes turned for the worse, resulting in significant financial struggles. Even though Kodak invested more than $3 billion in the early 2000s into digital photography, its efforts to transition from traditional film-based photography to internet-focused digital photography failed miserably. Its "info-imaging strategy," as it was termed, proved disastrous despite the fact that Kodak had invented the digital camera and had more than 1,000 technology patents used in digital technologies. In 2004, Kodak announced it would cut between 12,000 to 15,000 jobs and divest one-third of its real estate worldwide.

In 2005, Antonio M. Perez, the former head of HP's inkjet-printer business, was named Kodak's CEO. At the time, Kodak's average stock price was down to $27.46, and net losses were $1.3 billion on revenues of $14.3 billion. In 2007, Kodak launched its low-cost, low-margin Easyshare camera and its All-in-One desktop inkjet-printer line. In addition, Perez sold its once highly profitable health-imaging business. In 2008, Kodak terminated its decades-old sponsorship of the Olympic Games after the Summer Olympics in Beijing, China. In 2009, Kodak ceased manufacturing and marketing its Kodachrome film and suspended its 25-cent semiannual dividend. Perez also stopped paying an annual wage dividend bonus to workers.

Despite these efforts, the CEO failed to turn the company around. In 2010, Kodak's average stock price dropped to $5.10, and it lost $687 million on revenues of $7.2 billion. In early 2011, Perez announced a new digital strategy that he projected would make the company profitable again by the end of 2012. This strategy called for growing commercial and consumer inkjet printing, as well as packaging printing and workflow software. His strategy also called for cutting back on its digital camera sales by concentrating only on profitable markets instead of worldwide distribution. Late in 2011, Perez warned analysts that Kodak could reach a point in 2012 when it would be unable to pay its bills unless it could raise cash through the sale of 1,100 digital-imaging patents. Perez also pinned hopes for a turnaround on winning lucrative settlements from lawsuits filed against Apple, Inc. and Research In Motion, Ltd. over alleged patent infringements.

At year-end 2011, Kodak reported revenues of $4.1 billion and a net loss of $1.4 billion. Perez's failure to garner enough cash and stem the financial losses forced Kodak to file for Chapter 11 bankruptcy protection in January 2012. In February 2012, Kodak announced that it would cease making digital cameras, pocket video cameras, and digital picture frames and instead focus on the corporate digital-imaging market. In August 2012, Kodak publicized the intention to sell its photographic film (excluding motion-picture film), commercial scanners, and kiosk operations as a measure to emerge from bankruptcy.

The Economist reported that at the time of Kodak's bankruptcy, though the former giant failed to make the transition to digital photography, its longtime rival, Fujifilm, did well. Fujifilm and Kodak had very similar business models, with Fujifilm enjoying a near-monopoly position in its home market in Japan. Both firms' traditional business models became obsolete with the rise of the internet. Whereas the rise of digital photography was a disruptive technology for Kodak, Fujifilm was able to reinvent itself. Fujifilm transformed into a solidly profitable business with a $12.6 billion market capitalization, dwarfing Kodak's comparative $220 million market capitalization.

Sources: "Kodak." Wikipedia. Last modified November 15, 2017. https://en.wikipedia.org/wiki/Eastman_Kodak.; "Kodak Timeline: 1878–Present." Democrat & Chronicle. Last modified January 19, 2012. http://www.democratandchronicle. com/story/money/2012/01/19/kodak-timeline-1878-present/77384948/.; "The Last Kodak Moment? Kodak Is at Death's Door; Fujifilm, Its Old Rival, Is Thriving. Why?" *Economist*. Last modified January 14, 2012. http://www.economist.com/ node/21542796.

a. What might an S-curve for Kodak's traditional photographic film business look like? That is, in 2012, where in its product life was Kodak's traditional film business? What might a product portfolio matrix look like for Kodak in 2012?

b. Why was Kodak unable to transition its considerable experience in traditional film and innovative digital technologies to digital photography? What were Kodak's traditional film customers like? What are customers of digital photography products and services like? Compare and contrast the value propositions for traditional and digital photography customers.

CHAPTER ENDNOTES

1. Porter, Michael E. *The Five Competitive Forces That Shape Strategy*. Boston, MA: Harvard Business School Press, Harvard Business Review, 1979. Reprint 2008.
2. Porter, Michael E. "The Competitive Advantage of Firms in Global Industries." In *Competitive Advantage of Nations*, 33. New York, NY: The Free Press, 1990.
3. Ibid., 35.
4. Porter, op. cit., 13–15.
5. Porter, Michael E. "The Competitive Advantage of Firms in Global Industries." In *Competitive Advantage of Nations*, 45–7. New York, NY: The Free Press, 1990.
6. Ibid., 45.
7. "S-Curve." Wikipedia. Last modified November 15, 2017. https://en.wikipedia.org/wiki/S_Curve.
8. Henderson, Bruce. "The Experience Curve—Reviewed (Part IV): The Growth Share Matrix or the Product Portfolio." The Boston Consulting Group, Inc., 1973. Accessed via *BCG Perspectives*. Last modified 2017. https://www.bcgperspectives.com/content/Classics/ corporate_finance_corporate_strategy_portfolio_management_experience_curve_reviewed_growth_share_matrix_product_portfolio/.; Henderson, B.D. *The Logic of Business Strategy*. Cambridge: Ballinger Publishing, 1984.; Stern, C.W., and G. Stalk Jr. *Perspectives on Strategy: From the Boston Consulting Group*. New York NY: John Wiley & Sons, 1998.; Ghemawat, P. *Building Strategy on the Experience Curve*. Boston, MA: Harvard Business School Press, Harvard Business Review, March–April 1985.
9. Gordon, Mary Ellen, and George R. Milne. "Selecting the Dimensions That Define Strategic Groups: A Novel Market Driven Approach." *Journal of Managerial Issues* 11, no. 2 (1999).
10. Lucco, Joseph. "Strategy Maps: 6 Benefits For Your Company." ClearPoint Strategy. August 18, 2015. Accessed November 8, 2017. https:// www.clearpointstrategy.com/software-banks-insurance-balanced-scorecard-strategy-maps/.
11. Porter, op. cit., 4–11.
12. Porter, op. cit., 4–11.
13. Tripp, Mickle. "iPhone Demand Charges Apple's Results." *Wall Street Journal*, November 2, 2017. Accessed November 8, 2017. https://www. wsj.com/articles/iphone-demand-charges-apples-results-1509654759.
14. Davis, William. "Not Your Grandma's Muffins: The Creation of Modern Wheat." In *Wheat Belly*, 12–30. New York: Rodale, 2011.
15. Porter, op. cit., 10–11.
16. Petty, Art. "Tools for Developing as a Global Manager." The Balance. September 23, 2016. Accessed November 8, 2018. https://www. thebalance.com/tools-for-developing-as-a-global-manager-4046180.
17. Porter, Michael E. *The Five Competitive Forces That Shape Strategy*. Boston, MA: Harvard Business School Press, Harvard Business Review, 1979. Reprint 2008.
18. Bensinger, Greg. "Amazon Fires up a Smartphone for Shopping," *Wall Street Journal*, June 19, 2014.; Winkler, Rolfe, and Greg Bensinger. "Amazon Prepares Online Advertising Program." *Wall Street Journal*, August 22, 2014.
19. Dau, Eva. "China's Xiaomi Aims to Export Its Success." *Wall Street Journal*, January 17–18, 2015: B4.
20. Porter, Michael E. *The Five Competitive Forces That Shape Strategy*. Boston, MA: Harvard Business School Press, Harvard Business Review, 1979. Reprint 2008.
21. Snider, Mike, Roger Yu, and Emily Brown. "What Is Net Neutrality and What Does It Mean for Me?" *USA TODAY*. February 27, 2015. Accessed May 20, 2015. https://www.usatoday.com/story/tech/2015/02/24/net-neutrality-what-is-it-guide/23237737/.

22. Yap, Chuin-wie, and Kersten Zang. "In Uber, Chengdu Cabs Meet an Enemy—and Maybe a Savior." *Wall Street Journal—China Online*. May 26, 2015. Accessed June 12, 2015. http://blogs.wsj.com/chinarealtime/2015/05/26/in-uber-chengdu-cabs-meet-an-enemy-and-maybe-a-savior/.
23. Porter, Michael E. *The Five Competitive Forces That Shape Strategy*. Boston, MA: Harvard Business School Press, Harvard Business Review, 1979. Reprint, 2008.
24. Eisen, Ben. "Shoppers Flock to Phones." *Wall Street Journal*, November 24, 2017.
25. Porter, Michael E. *The Five Competitive Forces That Shape Strategy*. Boston, MA: Harvard Business School Press, Harvard Business Review, 1979. Reprint 2008.
26. MacDonald, Christine. "Big/Green: Eco conscious Brands Are Increasingly Being Bought out by Giant Corporations. Can We Trust Them?" Newsreview.com. July 21, 2011. http://www.newsreview.com/sacramento/big-green/content?oid=2838435.
27. Howard, Philip H. "Consolidation in the North American Organic Food Processing Sector, 1997 to 2007." *International Journal of Sociology of Agriculture and Food* 16, no. 1 (2009): 13–30.

CHAPTER 5

CRAFTING STRATEGY—INTERNAL SITUATIONAL ANALYSIS AND RESOURCE-BASED VIEW STRATEGY SCHOOL

VIDEO 5.1
Kozlowski: The CEO
Who Went to Jail,
by Andrew Hill

TYCO INTERNATIONAL: AN ANATOMY OF A CONGLOMERATE

ARTHUR ROSENBERG, TYCO'S FOUNDER

Tyco, Inc. began in 1960 as an investment and holding firm in Waltham, Massachusetts. At that time, Tyco had two principle holdings: (1) Tyco Semiconductor and (2) the Materials Research Laboratory, which conducted industrial research and development in solid-state sciences and energy conversion. When Tyco merged these two divisions in 1962, its major customer remained the U. S. government. However, Arthur Rosenberg, Tyco's founder, saw further commercial opportunities. Over the next two years, Tyco became an industrial products manufacturer, going public in 1964. Tyco grew steadily over the next few years, adding an additional 16 companies by 1968. Five years later, Tyco generated $40 million in sales.[1]

JOSEPH GAZIANO, GROWTH THROUGH ACQUISITIONS

In 1973, Joseph Gaziano, an engineer trained at MIT, succeeded Rosenberg as president and CEO. Under his leadership, Tyco pursued a path of aggressive and often hostile acquisitions. Gaziano wanted to transform Tyco into a $1 billion company by 1985, using any means necessary. While Gaziano died of cancer in 1982, the company he left behind was large and diverse, possessing a net worth of $140 million and more than $500 million in sales. The conglomerate housed manufacturers of products as varied as undersea fiber optic cables, fire sprinkler systems, polyethylene film, and packaging materials.

JOHN FORT: PERFORMANCE OVER GROWTH

John Fort, an aeronautical engineer holding degrees from Princeton and MIT, became Tyco's third CEO in 1982. As Tyco's new president, Fort decided to set a different tone than his predecessor. He veered away from the acquisition-centered growth strategy of his forerunner by immediately trimming the tremendous debt that Gaziano had accumulated, instead focusing on cutting costs wherever possible. Fort informed investors, "The reason we were put on earth was to increase earnings per share."[2] He was thrifty and unglamorous, preferring to gain Wall Street's respect through his own economic restraint. Under Fort's leadership, Tyco became a company without frills. When it came time to find a location for the company's headquarters, Fort had builders clear land in Exeter, New Hampshire. The facility they later constructed consisted of three unpretentious, low-rise office buildings. There wasn't even a cafeteria on site. Fort drastically cut costs and discarded a number of businesses that were not directly related to Tyco's operations. He also separated the company's various businesses into three parts: fire protection, electronics, and packaging. This consolidation, however, did not signal an end to Tyco's acquisition strategy. Rather, Tyco simply became more selective about the companies it pursued. Fort's main focus remained on profits instead of growth. Consequentially, the company's stock price rose from $1.55 in January 1982 to $29.56 in July 1990, with sales increasing to $3 billion in 1991. Fort retired in 1992 after serving 10 years as CEO.[3] Dennis Kozlowski, Tyco's then chief operating officer, replaced him and further refined Tyco's art of acquisition.

DENNIS KOZLOWSKI: THE GREAT CONGLOMERATOR

Before he was carted off to prison for embezzling more than $600 million in Tyco funds, Kozlowski was referred to in the business press as "The Great Conglomerator." He reported, "I never started out with a game plan to be a $76 billion company. But I always envisioned one that had to grow every year in order to be successful."[4] During Kozlowski's 10-year reign at Tyco, the same word cropped up to describe him—*aggressive*. One Tyco board member explained, "Dennis has only one gear—forward at 300 miles an hour. There is no reverse." Kozlowski pursued acquisitions with a vigor that Tyco had not seen since the days of Gaziano. His style, however, was markedly different. Kozlowski told *The Boston Globe* that he always followed two rules for acquisitions: never do a hostile deal, and immediately cut costs at the new facility.[5] Tyco's newest CEO had learned from watching Gaziano that unfriendly takeovers often lead to failed business ventures. Kozlowski preferred deals to be made quickly and on good terms. When Kozlowski superseded Fort as CEO, Tyco was a $1.3 billion (net revenue) company divided into four divisions: fire protection; valves, pipes, and "flow control products"; electrical and electronic components; and packaging materials. Even though Tyco operated in many industries, the majority of its divisions sold products in the construction industry.

CHANGING THE PRODUCT MIX

Kozlowski wanted to decrease Tyco's reliance on the construction business (which is infamously unpredictable) and instead transition to manufacturing products in order to secure more reliable consumers. This desire led Kozlowski to buy Kendall International (a producer of medical supplies) for $1 billion in 1994. Tyco's board balked as Kendall had filed Chapter 11 bankruptcy just two years earlier. The company's dismal revenues were only increasing by 3 to 4 percent per year. Despite this, Kozlowski was determined to repair the failing company, and the board eventually agreed to the acquisition.

In the long run, Kozlowski's gamble paid off. After one year, the acquisition of Kendall International helped Tyco's earnings grow to $214 million. Kendall became the center of Tyco Healthcare, which in turn became a major producer of medical supplies, second in the country only to Johnson & Johnson. By 1998, Tyco had six divisions: fire protection, flow control, disposable medical products, Simplex Technologies, packaging materials, and specialty products. Between 1992 and 1998, Kozlowski perfected Tyco's acquisition strategy. (In many respects, it resembled the conglomerate strategy developed during the 1960s and abandoned by the 1980s.) Originally, conglomerates assembled businesses in unrelated fields to counter business cycle movements. When one business became strained during the downside of a business cycle, another division would be performing well. This portfolio approach was to ensure the corporate holding company a steady stream of cash. The central office functioned as a bank, using the operating firm's cash to weather economic storms, acquire new cash-generating companies, and divest those firms that no longer fit the conglomerate portfolio. As long as cash streams grew steadily, the conglomerate's stock price rose, allowing the company's stock to function as takeover currency.

EDWARD BREEN: REVIVING TYCO FROM THE SCANDAL

Edward Breen replaced Kozlowski as chief executive officer and chairman in 2002. Breen successfully led Tyco's turnaround strategy in the wake of the accounting scandal in the early 2000s. Breen's efforts extracted tens of billions of dollars in value for Tyco investors and led to the sale or spinoff of numerous Tyco businesses. By 2006, Breen was able to generate strong cash flow and revenue growth while decreasing debt. In 2006, Tyco's board of directors approved a plan to separate Tyco into three independent companies. Tyco believed this would allow for increased performance within each segment in its particular market, creating more value for its shareholders. In July 2007, Tyco formally separated into three publicly independent companies: Covidien Ltd. (formerly Tyco Healthcare), Tyco Electronics Ltd. (now TE Connectivity), and Tyco International Ltd. (formerly Tyco Fire & Security and Tyco Engineered Products & Services (TFS/TEPS)). Following the separation, Breen remained at the head of Tyco International, which was then composed of five major business segments: ADT worldwide, fire protection services, safety products, flow control, and electrical and metal products. The company generated revenue of $18.8 billion in 2007.

In September 2012, directors again announced plans to split the company once more, separating the company's flow control business, North America's residential security business, and its international fire and security business.[6] In November 2015, Breen stepped down as CEO of Tyco, appointing DuPont's chairman and chief executive officer in his place.

TYCO AND JOHNSON CONTROLS MERGER

In January 2016, *The Wall Street Journal* reported that Johnson Controls Inc. and Tyco International PLC agreed to a $14 billion merger. The merger would, according to the *Journal*, reflect a "growing push by some executives and shareholders toward companies that are bigger but more focused."[7] The merged companies would combine Johnson Controls' businesses in heating and air-conditioning equipment for skyscrapers, schools, hospitals, and other structures with Tyco's lines of security and fire-suppression gear, creating a company with more than $32 billion a year in sales. Under the agreement, Johnson Controls shareholders would own about 56 percent of the combined company shares and receive approximately $3.9 billion in cash consideration, whereas Tyco shareholders would own about 44 percent of the combined company shares. Tyco would also institute a reverse stock split so that Tyco shareholders would receive a fixed exchange ratio of 0.9550 shares of the combined company for each of their existing Tyco shares. Accordingly, Johnson Controls shareholders would receive one share of the combined company for each Johnson Controls share. They could also elect to receive cash equal to $34.88 per share for some or all of their Johnson Controls shares. (Johnson Controls shares would remain listed on NYSE under JCI.) The new companies' combined board of directors would consist of six directors from Johnson Controls and five directors from Tyco. Johnson Controls Chairman and CEO Alex Molinaroli would serve as chairman and CEO of the combined company for 18 months and then become executive chairman for 12 months. Meanwhile, Tyco's CEO George Oliver would serve as president and chief operating officer for 18 months, become CEO for 12 months, and then succeed to chairman and CEO of the new company. The combined companies would be renamed *Johnson Controls PLC* but maintain Tyco's Irish legal domicile.[8]

Tyco and Johnson Controls had both been pursuing an eradication of their numerous businesses as the companies had grown difficult to manage. At the time of the merger, Tyco posted revenues of $31 billion—$10 billion down from the $41 billion generated under Kozlowski's ambitious conglomeration strategy.[9] Sill, in 2016, Tyco possessed more than 3 million customers around the globe with more than 57,000 employees in 900 locations across 50 countries. Correspondingly, Johnson Controls served customers in more than 150 countries with just over 150,000 employees.

    a.   What type of company did Edward Breen inherit in 2002? How did he change Tyco's strategy? How did Breen and Tyco's board change Tyco's business model and company structure?

    b.   Why did Tyco's board agree to the $14 billion merger with Johnson Controls Inc.? What are the terms of the merger? What's in it for Tyco? For Johnson Controls?

1. INTRODUCTION: QUESTIONS TO THINK ABOUT

- What is the resource-based view (RBV)?
- What is portfolio analysis?
- What is value?
- What is a value chain?
- How do you extract value from the value chain?
- What is the difference between customer-value creation and firm-value appropriation?
- What is VIRO analysis?
- What is SPACE analysis?
- What is benchmarking?
- How do you know if a company's competitive advantage is sustainable?

This chapter examines strategic thinking and critical inquiry at the business level of the firm. Business-level strategy addresses **how** the firm will compete in each of its industries and markets. Whether strategy setting and appraisal is for a single or a multibusiness firm, the strategist must determine the overall success for the firm and for each of its businesses. For a firm to be successful, strategic managers must also know if the strategies and business models for each industry or market in which it competes are working. For firms with multiple businesses, how and in what ways is each business contributing to the overall success of the firm? Is the business creating value or destroying overall value for the firm? The resource-based view (RBV) or strategy school takes a decidedly **internal** view of what drives firm performance by asking: *Does the firm or business have a competitive advantage? If so, is the competitive advantage sustainable?* The source of sustainability of a firm's or its businesses' (for a multibusiness firm) competitive advantage lies in the competitive strengths and sustainability of its resources. Customer value creation superiority for a firm over its rivals is primarily based on the firm's superiority in resources.

2. WHY UNDERTAKE AN INTERNAL ENVIRONMENTAL ANALYSIS?

To increase the organization's chances for success, managers must identify internal customer value creation opportunities that also create above-average value for the firm (*firm value appropriation*). Firm value appropriation is a function of the firm's resource strengths as they relate to the cost, quality, and price of its products and services—that is, its business model. When conducting an internal situational analysis, the manager must answer the following strategic questions:

- What firm resource strengths best align with customer value creation opportunities?
- How does customer value creation equate to a firm's value appropriation (overall financial health and vision and mission alignment)?
- How dynamic are the firm's core capabilities and distinctive competencies in sustaining competitive advantage?
- What are the sources of competitive advantage, and can these sources be protected from imitators?
- How sustainable is the firm's competitive advantage long-term?

3. RESOURCE-BASED VIEW (RBV) STRATEGY SCHOOL

Contrary to the five forces school, resource school advocates argue that the external environment could be characterized as chaotic, uncertain, and unpredictable. The rules, or at least the ability to determine positioning based on relatively stable, predictable competitive dynamics do not hold much validity for proponents of the resource-based view (RBV). Competitive landscapes are fierce; thus, to sustain competitive advantage, longer-term capabilities must be both dynamic and flexible (lasting). The external environment is so uncertain and unstable that the main focus remains on the customer; that is, what does the customer value? **Dynamic capabilities** are defined as the firm's capacity to renew competencies for maintaining a competitive advantage through constant innovation.[10] The resource-based view focuses on an in-depth understanding of the firm's internal **tangible and intangible** resources, especially a firm's strengths, capabilities, core capabilities, and distinctive competencies. Penrose conceptualized the firm as a collection of resources, producing services at the request of the CEO or general manager. Penrose also refers to customer value creation as the creation of "productive opportunity of the firm." She saw this as a process of taking tangible and intangible resources as **inputs** or matter and changing these inputs to what she referred to as "energy" (products/services) or market outputs. Penrose maintains that this process is risky because it ultimately relies on **humans and psychological factors** like uncertainty and perceptions of risk.[11] Advocates of this view assume that firms can deliver and sustain competitive advantage when resources are managed in a way that competitors cannot **imitate. Unique or superior value** creating resources that are not imitable, rare (non-substitutable), and dynamic (adaptable) are ultimately the source of a firm's competitive advantage because they erect a competitive barrier for rivals. As such, the RBV takes a decidedly internal view of the firm, one in which **people** play a critical (if not superior) role to other factor inputs and the external environment. The school is based on three fundamental principles:

- Levels of tangible and intangible resource strengths—physical, intellectual, human, organizational
- Resources, core capabilities, and distinctive competencies—identification and assessment of each resource strength
- An in-depth understanding of a firm's culture, human capital, intellectual capacity, and participatory and collaborative relationships

Two critical assumptions of RBV are that resources must also be heterogeneous and immobile. **Heterogeneity** assumes the firm's resource strengths, both tangible and intangible, differ from its rivals' and other companies'. What separates a firm's strategy from those of its rivals is based on differences in **resource mix**. How a strategist differentiates and executes its core capabilities and distinctive competencies compared to rivals is the basis for continuous performance improvements and competitive advantage. If all firms had **homogeneous** resources and could not erect entry where no barriers to entering the firm's competitive space existed, then there would be perfect competition, resulting in all firms eventually reaching market equilibrium. Firms competing in perfectly competitive markets are powerless in regard to setting prices—that is, the firm is a price taker. In the real world, markets are far from perfectly competitive. Some companies are able to separate themselves from rivals on several strategic dimensions and resource strengths even though these firms are exposed to the same external competitive forces, factors, and industry drivers (e.g., same external conditions). Successful firms are able to implement different strategies to outperform rivals. Therefore, RBV assumes that a firm can achieve superior competitive advantage by using its different **bundles of resources**.[12]

Immobile assumes the firm's resource strengths are not mobile and thus do not move easily from the firm to its rivals. It takes a long time, if at all, for a rival to copy or imitate the firm's resource strengths, core capabilities, and distinctive competencies. At least in the short run, the firm has the power and ability to leverage its strategic resources for competitive advantage. (Due to this immobility, companies cannot replicate rivals' resources and implement the same strategies.) Intangible resources are usually immobile (e.g., brand equity, processes, knowledge and intellectual property).

3.1 WHAT ARE A COMPANY'S RESOURCE STRENGTHS?

What are the building blocks that make most organizations work? What drives a firm's strategy and competitive advantage? **Tangible** resources are physical and can be quantified either by total number of units or by assigning a market or financial value. Accountants can place a book value, market value, or replacement value on a firm's tangible resources (inventory, capital equipment, buildings). Because physical resources are easily introduced into the market, they usually provide no long-term superior competitive advantage. **Intangible** resources are not easily quantifiable, but they can be extremely valuable. Unlike tangible resources, it takes a long time for a company to earn and invest in brand reputation. The value of the firm's intellectual property, brand, and other intangible resources can also assess a market (premium paid over stock price) or financial value (assessed value of the firm's tangible and intangible assets). For example, the premium a company is willing to pay over the market value of another company's stock when acquiring the company is a surrogate measure of the acquired company's value based on intangible assets (brand, intellectual property, estimates of forward earning potential). Still, how does one place a value or quantify human intelligence? Although the value of a person's contribution to a firm is oftentimes measured by level of total compensation and other amenities, a person's actual versus perceived value is far more difficult to determine. Four types of resources are critical drivers of a firm's ability to create and sustain success: physical, intellectual, human, and organizational.

Physical capital: Tangible assets such as plant and equipment, materials, inventory, financials, location, technology, distribution, warehouses, transportation, and physical and cyber networks.

Intellectual capital: Tangible assets such as intellectual property, brands, patents, copyrights, trademarks, trade secrets, software, algorithms, customer databases, partnerships, and joint ventures.

Human capital: Intangible assets including intellect and knowledge. All organizations need human resources, especially people who are creative thinkers.

Organizational capital: Intangible assets such as culture, structure, processes, systems, dynamic learning, problem-solving capabilities, formal and informal working relationships, dynamic work design, and highly effective, high-performing teams.

Although all organizations may possess these resources, they are not always exploited or capable of providing the resource strengths needed for a firm to be successful. Critical to firm success (to create and sustain competitive advantage) is the strategist's ability to capitalize on its tangible and intangible resources. Resource strength is based on the overall capacity of the resource to create and provide intrinsic value to the customer. It cannot be easily copied or imitated by rivals. Resource strength, though extremely difficult to find, can be adapted or modified to external changes in technology, markets, and customers.

3.2 RESOURCE CAPABILITY HIERARCHY

The strategist's job is to continuously improve the firm's performance by maintaining or obtaining resources that are effective at exploiting external customer value, thereby creating opportunities while circumventing or staving off resource weaknesses and external threats to achieve organization purpose (vision, mission, goals, and objectives). Exhibit 5.1 depicts a typical resource capability hierarchy for a firm. The strategist is responsible for turning the firm's many strengths into strategic capital and capabilities. These strategic assets are valuable, inimitable (cannot be easily copied), rare, and dynamic. As discussed in Chapter 3, strengths are those resources that have the potential to add value to the firm. Conversely, weaknesses can become value killers. Capability is know-how, or the ability to actually carry out a given task, activity, or action. Capabilities represent what a company can actually do. Core capability is know-how that remains critical to a firm's success; it is not only what a company can do but also how it is done to move the company forward, increasing the firm's performance and chances for success. A distinctive competence is a core capability unique to the firm and difficult for rivals to emulate. Four criteria or questions are used to measure the firm's resource strengths at the highest level of the resource hierarchy:

- *The question of value*: Is the firm able to exploit an opportunity or neutralize an external threat with the resource/capability?
- *The question of rarity*: Is control of the resource/capability in the hands of a relative few?

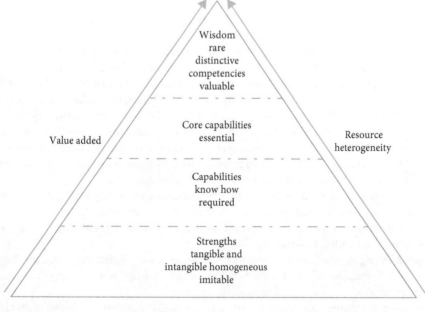

Exhibit 5.1 Resource Capability Hierarchy

Source: Michael J. Merenda 2018

- *The question of imitability*: Is the resource/capability difficult to imitate, disadvantaging the firm trying to obtain, develop, or duplicate it?
- *The question of organization*: Is the firm organized, ready, and able to exploit the resource/capability? Is the firm organized to capture value?[13]

3.3 PARTICIPATORY STRATEGIC MANAGEMENT

For the RBV of the firm, people and their human capital take a leading role in the success of the company. Unlike the competitive forces school where tangible, physical assets are viewed as the primary focus of the firm's competitive positioning and success, the RBV holds that strategic management is an inclusive **top-down** and **bottom-up** process involving all managers with inputs from their people as well as other stakeholders. RBV is based upon the belief that those responsible for a strategy and its execution, at any level of the firm (corporate, business, functional), understand that area of responsibility and have the capacity and ability to carry out their respective duties. The different perspectives of the firm's managers and employees can foster outside-the-box thinking, a thought process proven to be better suited for external environments that are unpredictable and constantly changing. The RBV holds that resource strengths and a strategic management participatory process can better capture creative thinking and build consensus and buy-in from managers and their employees.

Strategic managers must be critical of ideas, concepts, and long-held beliefs, but never their people. Building resource strengths must involve critical inquiry and strategic thinking at all levels of the firm. Because innovative ideas can also enter the organization from any level, RBV must support new ideas first and foremost, no matter their source, and allow these ideas to become fully developed. The strategic manager must ask *why not?* before asking *why?* For the resource-based view of the firm, participatory management, radically inclusive strategic thinking, and problem solving must challenge the firm's status quo. When appropriate, a new status quo can be introduced and enthusiastically supported until proven inadequate by the passing of time, accumulation of new data, or creation of better ideas. Friedman states that radically inclusive thinking "... involves bringing into your analysis as many relevant people, processes, disciplines, organizations and technologies as possible—factors that are often kept separate or excluded altogether."[14]

4. VIRO TEST FOR ASSESSING A FIRM'S SUSTAINABLE COMPETITIVE ADVANTAGE

Jay Barney and others advanced Penrose's notion of the firm as a bundle of resources offering the potential for superior performance over rivals. Barney identified three main bases of resources: physical, human, and organizational.[15] These different facets combine to create the source of the firm's competitive advantage. This advantage is also determined by the firm's ability to utilize its heterogeneous resources in unique ways that generate revenue and profits as well as protect against replication of the firm's resource strengths. That competitive advantage is based on the assumption that resource strengths are immobile, do not move easily from the firm to its rivals and are extremely difficult, for a rival to copy. As such, strategy is about being different by offering heterogenous resources that provide buyers unique value and, in turn, customer value creation opportunities for the firm. To this end, strategy making is about managing resources in ways that make them uniquely valuable to buyers, difficult to be imitated by rivals, special or rare (in that they are not easily obtained), and managed internally in ways that are specific to a firm's organizational competences. Organizational competencies are contained in a firm's culture, systems, processes, and nuances, as well as in the ways strategic leaders and managers craft and execute strategies within the firm. Organizational nuances and ways of doing business should be difficult, if not impossible, for rivals to understand or copy.

4.1 VIRO TEST

How do we know if a firm's competitive advantage is sustainable? One way is to perform a VIRO (valuable, imitable, rare, organizational) analysis. Strategic managers must develop and nurture only those resources, core capabilities, and distinctive competencies that pass this test. The test entails answering the following questions (see Table 5.1):

- Are there special historical conditions or factors that lead to acquisition of tangible and intangible resources that provide unique value to a firm's customers (valuable)?
- Is there organizational causal ambiguity that hinders rivals' understanding of how the resources are linked to competitive advantage? Are they difficult and costly for rivals to imitate (imitable)?
- Is there organizational social complexity that could be related to cultural attributes that facilitate competitive advantage not easily substituted by rivals (rare)?
- Are the resources dynamic and flexible with market changes (organizational)?[16]

Although, having heterogeneous and immobile resources is critical in achieving competitive advantage; alone, these are not enough to sustain it. A firm should periodically undertake a VIRO analysis to determine if its competitive advantage is superior and sustainable. In short, a

**Table 5.1
VIRO
(Valuable,
Imitable, Rare,
Organizational)
Test**

I. Strategy Overview

1. Company's name: _____

2. Company strategy (describe):

_____

_____

3. Does the company currently have a below average, average, or superior competitive advantage (provide financial support)?

_____

_____

_____

4. What is (are) the source (s) of its competitive advantage?

_____

_____

_____

II. Perform A VIRO Test (answer the following questions)

a. **Valuable:** Does the company have unique resources that provide customer value? → No → Can unique value be created in a reasonable time? → No

↓ Yes ← ← Yes → ↓ Competitive Disadvantage

↓

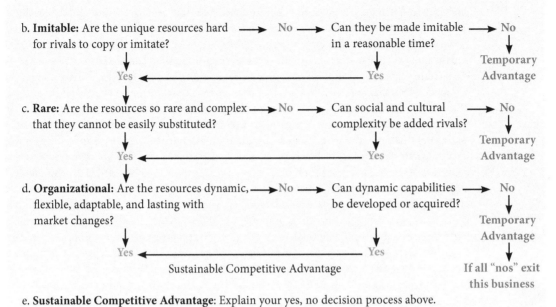

b. **Imitable:** Are the unique resources hard ⟶ No ⟶ Can they be made imitable ⟶ No
for rivals to copy or imitate?   in a reasonable time?

Yes ⟵ ——————————————————— Yes   Temporary
Advantage

c. **Rare:** Are the resources so rare and complex ⟶ No ⟶ Can social and cultural ⟶ No
that they cannot be easily substituted?   complexity be added rivals?

Yes ⟵ ——————————————————— Yes   Temporary
Advantage

d. **Organizational:** Are the resources dynamic, ⟶ No ⟶ Can dynamic capabilities ⟶ No
flexible, adaptable, and lasting with   be developed or acquired?
market changes?

                      Temporary
Advantage

Yes ⟵ ——————————————————— Yes
Sustainable Competitive Advantage   If all "nos" exit
this business

e. **Sustainable Competitive Advantage**: Explain your yes, no decision process above.

f. **Recommendation(s)**: What changes, if any, should be made to the current strategy?

Source: Michael J. Merenda, 2014; adapted from: Barney, Jay B and Hesterly, William S. Strategic *Management and Competitive Advantage: Concepts*. 2005 Pearson Education, Inc., Upper Saddle River, New Jersey, 07458; and Rothaermel's (2013) *Strategic Management*, McGraw-Hill Irwin p.91

PERSONAL STRATEGY—WHAT ARE YOUR UNIQUE TALENTS AND RESOURCES?

Thinking Critically Exercise 41

a. Do you have a competitive advantage in work? What mix of resource strengths separates you from others who may be vying for your job? Quickly list your strengths. What are your capabilities? What core capabilities are essential for you to effectively perform in your job? Are any of your core capabilities distinctive? Which ones?

b. Using the two critical assumptions that form the foundation of the RBV, are your resource strengths heterogeneous and immobile? What evidence do you have to support your conclusion?

VIRO analysis provides the means to constantly raise and test the two critical assumptions of RBV—resource heterogeneity and immobility for competitive advantage.

5. PRODUCT PORTFOLIO ANALYSIS

Another tool for assessing strategy at the business level is **product portfolio analysis**. Henderson and his colleagues at the Boston Consulting Group (BCG) not only developed this analytical tool,[17] but they also introduced the concept of experience curves (see Chapter 4) as a method for allocating scarce resources in companies with multiple products or businesses. Managers in multiproduct companies are faced with a dilemma: What products have the highest probability of success measured in return on invested capital? Product portfolio analysis is a strategy-making analytical tool that aids in mapping the firm's customer value proposition through the product's life cycle. Henderson and his colleagues use simple measures to track a product's competitive performance through its life cycle—the cost of value added for each additional unit produced and the unit's relative market share.[18] The BCG tracks product performance for several companies Ocompeting in different industries. Its economic and financial analysis for a large number of products reveals that the cost of added value declines each time accumulated experience is added. That is, a product's gross margin (selling price minus cost of goods sold) will improve each time experience is added. Experience is measured in terms of market share. The model is based on the assumption that the greater the market share and experience, the greater the gross margin will be for a particular product or business. As used in the product portfolio concept, experience is defined in terms of accumulated physical output for a product. A surrogate measure of physical output is relative market share. Relative market share is determined by dividing a firm's product market share by the market share of its largest competitors. A product or business's relative market share is plotted on the horizontal axis of a four-cell matrix. The vertical axis of the product portfolio matrix plots market growth rate for each of the company's products within the portfolio (high, average, low). The matrix is used to map and plot performance for each product or business measured in terms of free cash flow generated by each entity (see Exhibit 5.2: Product Portfolio Matrix). Depending on its place in the 2 × 2 matrix, a product or business can be classified as:

a. **Question Mark** (Quadrant I): Potentially high-growth product or business—selective investment is recommended
b. **Star** (Quadrant II): High-growth, high-profit-potential business—invest in these businesses
c. **Cash Cow** (Quadrant III): Low-growth, high-cash flow businesses—take cash from these businesses to invest in Star and Question Mark entities
d. **Dog** (Quadrant IV): Low-growth, low-cash flow businesses—divest or cut out these businesses

**Exhibit 5.2
Product
Portfolio Matrix:
Cash and
Product Flow**

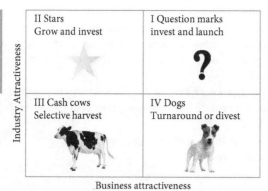

Industry Attractiveness

| II Stars Grow and invest | I Question marks invest and launch |
| III Cash cows Selective harvest | IV Dogs Turnaround or divest |

Business attractiveness
(relative marketshare)

Sources: Exhibit 5.3a: Copyright © 2014 / kritchanut.
Exhibit 5.3b: Copyright © 2014 / Best3d.
Exhibit 5.3c: Copyright © 2012 / lifeonwhite.
Exhibit 5.3d: Copyright © 2012 / lifeonwhite.

5.1 IMPORTANCE OF MAINTAINING A BALANCED BUSINESS PORTFOLIO

A **balanced portfolio** for a firm contains a proper mix of products in quadrants I, II, and III. The life of a product or business can be traced through each quadrant in the matrix. Quadrant I (conception to birth) represents early stage businesses and new products or markets that a firm might enter. These businesses have not yet developed superior or highly attractive resource strengths or capabilities. They are labeled Question Marks because the firm has to decide whether resource strengths can be applied or obtained to make these prospective entities attractive. Quadrant II (accelerated or high growth) represents growth-stage businesses. These firms either need further cash or investments to grow, or they are already high-cash-generating businesses. Offensive strategies are associated with high-growth firms because these businesses have superior resource strengths and capabilities and they compete in highly attractive industry environments. Quadrant III businesses compete in environmental settings that already are or are becoming less attractive. Although resource strengths and capabilities are still attractive, fewer customer value creating opportunities exist for these firms. Because of this, maintenance and offensive strategies often work best at this level. The firm must either rigorously defend or maintain its existing customer value by creating propositions (maintenance strategy) while developing new, more creative customer value propositions (offensive strategy). Quadrant IV businesses no longer create any customer value and actually detract value from the firm. These businesses are in the late stage of their life cycles and operate in highly unattractive, mature, or declining industry environments. These businesses' resources are no longer heterogeneous and their resource mix and capabilities can be copied or easily transferred to other firms. Defensive strategies are recommended for this stage. If it is highly likely that the business cannot be righted it should be closed, harvested, sold, or liquidated.

5.2 CASH FLOW

Businesses are either value-creating (net cash generators) or value-depleting (net cash deficits). **Quadrant I** (Question Marks) businesses are early in their life cycles and usually require significant financial investment to enter into the market and remain competitive. They also typically demand market research, staffing, and other tangible and intangible assets to separate them from rivals and exploit their potential. Quadrant I businesses that possess a strong potential for growth and sustained value should be invested in.

Quadrant II (Stars) firms are net value creators because they exist in the high-growth stage of their product life cycles. These businesses should be fully supported with the proper mix of resources and talent to successfully grow and maintain their value creation strategies. Funds invested in these firms can generate superior returns, providing the businesses with a major source of competitive advantage.[19]

Quadrant III (Cash Cows) businesses are considered steady sources of profit because they no longer generate sufficient value to warrant additional investments. Any investments in these businesses should be highly selective, and any value generated by these businesses should flow into quadrant I or II firms. Businesses in this area are regarded as "staid and boring" or "in a 'mature' market," yet corporations value owning them due to their cash-generating qualities. They are to be "milked" continuously with as little investment as possible as it would be wasted in an industry with such a low growth rate.

Quadrant IV (Dogs) firms at best break even, but they are more likely value-depleting. The **opportunity cost** to continue to invest in and support these businesses is greater than the benefits received from their continued operation. These firms do not generate enough value or cash to maintain the market share and, as such, depress the firm's overall profitability return on investment. These businesses are considered "dogs" because they perform poorly and operate in declining mature businesses or nonperforming businesses. The strategist is faced with shutting the company down immediately or letting the business slowly die (harvested) on its own, a situation that could seriously affect the well-being of its employees and people in the greater community (see Exhibit 5.3: Product Portfolio Matrix: Cash and Product Flow).

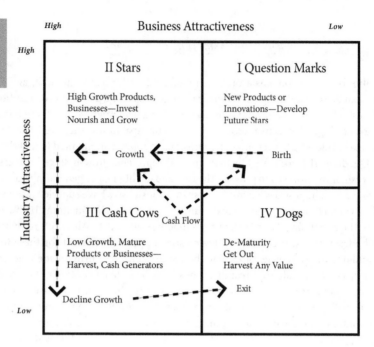

Exhibit 5.3
Product
Portfolio
Matrix

Exhibit 5.3 Product Portfolio Matrix

High   Business Attractiveness   Low

Industry Attractiveness — High / Low

II Stars

High Growth Products,
Businesses—Invest
Nourish and Grow

I Question Marks

New Products or
Innovations—Develop
Future Stars

Growth   Birth

III Cash Cows   Cash Flow

Low Growth, Mature
Products or Businesses—
Harvest, Cash Generators

IV Dogs

De-Maturity
Get Out
Harvest Any Value

Decline Growth   Exit

KODAK VS. FUJIFILM

VIDEO 5.3 Kodak - The Rise and Fall: Blue Chip to Bankruptcy

Fujifilm has remained an active dealmaker for years. In August 2017, it announced that the company plans to spend more than $4 billion over the next three years for acquisitions. One company under consideration is Xerox. Although Fuji has prospered in recent years, Kodak and Xerox have fallen on hard times. Once known mainly for photographic film and its global battle against Eastman Kodak Co. for consumer sales, Fujifilm today generates most of its more than $20 billion in annual revenue from products other than the one incorporated in its name. Fujifilm has branched out into medical equipment, such as mammography machines, as well as cosmetics and electronic materials. Even in photography, it focuses not on film but on hardware such as high-end, mirrorless digital cameras and its analog Instax instant camera, popular at weddings and birthday parties. Its printer and copier business continues to deliver significant profit despite facing long-term decline.

a. Go to the Fujifilm website at https://www.fujifilmholdings.com/en/investors/performance_and_finance/financial_highlights/index.html. Click on and review Fuji's Performance, Financial Condition and Efficiency annual data. What is Fujifilm's overall financial health in 2018? Go to: https://www.fujifilmholdings.com/en/business/field/index.html and click on "Business Field." What businesses is Fujifilm engaged in? What roles did Fujifilm's experience and dynamic competencies in digital photography and imaging play in the company's 2018 financial performance?

b. What competitive forces caused Kodak's position in digital and traditional photography to erode so quickly? What competitive forces might have led to Fuji's success and Kodak's lack of success?

Source: Merenda, Michael J., Mayumi Negishi, and David Benoit. "Fujifilm Sets Focus on Deal-Making after Surviving Fall of Film." *Wall Street Journal*, January 12, 2018.

6. WHAT IS A VALUE CHAIN?

VIDEO **5.4** Porter's Generic Value Chain Model

A firm's value chain analysis is used to map the activities, processes, and associated costs for doing business. A firm's value chain also examines the cost of acquiring, using, and maintaining the firm's mix of resources in relationship to creating value for the customer. The value created for the customer has to be equal to or greater than the firm's cost to create customer value. Simply stated, total revenues for the firm have to be greater than the cost or expense of producing this revenue. When a firm has superior profits and return on investments compared to its rivals, this signals that the firm's strategies have a superior competitive advantage. The appropriate level for constructing a value chain analysis is at the business level—that is, for each of the firm's products and services.[20] For a single business or product firm, the value chain analysis is at the firm level. A **value chain analysis** involves an analysis of a firm's costs of doing business. A firm's **business model** defines and identifies how it will make money.[21] The business model provides the economic justification that drives a firm's **value** creation proposition. A firm's **value proposition** is the mix of goods and services, price and payment terms, and other amenities offered by the firm to its customers. But what exactly is value? **Value** is the amount a buyer is willing to pay for products provided by a firm. Customers derive value from product differentiation, product cost, and the ability of the firm to meet their needs (service, response time, etc.) **Customer value** equals the benefits derived from the product or service minus the cost to acquire the product or service (purchase price plus any customer-added costs, such as storage, transportation, and employee training). Value for the selling firm (**firm value**) is measured in terms of profitability (revenues minus expenses) for the business overall or for each of its products and services. Value is created and extracted throughout a firm's supply chain.

6.1 VALUE CHANGE ANALYSIS

A **supply chain** is a system of organizations, people, technology, activities, information, and resources involved in moving a product or service from supplier to customer. Supply chain activities transform natural resources, raw materials, components, and the firm's mix of other tangible and intangible resources into finished products or services that deliver value to the end customer. According to Michael Porter, a firm's products "pass through a chain of activities in order, and at each activity the product gains some value. The chain of activities gives the products more added value than the sum of added values of all activities."[22]

A **value chain** is a model of a business process—it depicts the value creation process as a series of activities beginning with raw materials and ending with sales and services to end users—in other words, customers. Porter defines a firm's value chain as "an interdependent system or network of activities, connected by linkages."[23] The value chain describes a firm's activities and processes, along with trade-offs in costs or effectiveness among the various linkages. Porter also identifies two sets of activities: primary and secondary (or supporting) activities.[24] Primary and secondary activities are essentially the business itself—that is, all the informal and formal activities and functions used in the management of the business to earn a profit. Businesses convert market inputs into outputs, which in turn produce profits (or losses). A firm's value chain represents its **transaction costs** or the cost of doing business. The firm's value chain is embedded in a larger stream of activities that Porter calls "the **value system**." The value system includes suppliers (firm inputs), the firm's value chain (value-added activities), distributors and retailers (firm outputs), and the ultimate or final buyer (customers).[25] For a list of typical primary value chain activities, see Exhibit 5.4: Porter's Value Chain.

6.2 PRIMARY ACTIVITIES

Primary activities include:

- *Inbound logistics*: Arranging the inbound movement of materials, parts, and/or finished inventory from suppliers to manufacturing or assembly plants, warehouses, or retail stores
- *Operations*: Concerned with managing the process that converts inputs (in the form of raw materials, labor, and energy) into outputs (in the form of goods and/or services)
- *Outbound logistics*: The process related to the storage and movement of the final product and the related information flows from the end of the production line to the end user

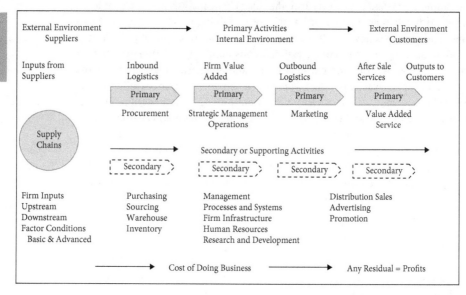

Exhibit 5.4 Porter's Value Chain

- *Marketing and sales*: Selling a product or service and processes for creating, communicating, delivering, and exchanging offerings that have value for customers, clients, partners, and society
- *Service*: All activities required to keep the product/service working effectively for the buyer after it is sold and delivered

6.3 SECONDARY (SUPPORTING) ACTIVITIES

Secondary activities include:

- *Infrastructure*: Consists of activities such as accounting, legal, finance, control, public relations, quality assurance, and general (strategic) management
- *Technological development*: The equipment, hardware, software, procedures, and technical knowledge used in the firm's transformation of inputs into outputs
- *Human resources management*: All activities involved in recruiting, hiring, training, developing, compensating, and (if necessary) dismissing or laying off personnel
- *Procurement*: The acquisition of goods, services, or works from an outside external supplier[26]

6.4 INDUSTRY SUPPLY (VALUE) CHAIN

An industry or traditional value chain is usually represented as a physical depiction of the players and various processes involved in producing goods and services. The chain illustrates clear distinctions among all the parties involved from sourcing raw materials to operations to the marketing and sale of the product/service to its customers. The physical chain is based on the assumption that clear distinctions and boundaries separate all activities found in the chain. Each player competes only within his or her place in the supply chain. Each player also competes for value added at each link or stage of production in the chain. The sum total of link activities yields total value of the industry value chain for a firm. A typical industry supply chain (also known as an industry value chain) is represented in Exhibit 5.5 (also see Chapter 1, Exhibit 1.1: Value Chain Activities and Internal and External Costs of Doing Business).

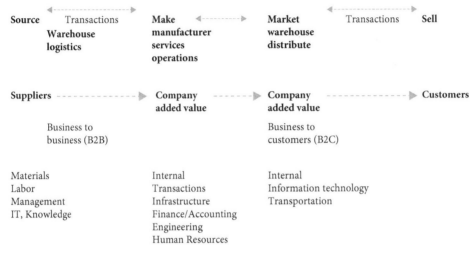

Exhibit 5.5 Typical Industry Supply Chain

Adapted from: "Porter, Michael E. Competitive Advantage of Nations." Copyright © 1990 by Model Free Press. Reprinted with permission.

Source: Michael J. Merenda 2018

6.5 VIRTUAL AND NETWORKED VALUE CHAINS

What happens when there is no clear line of demarcation between each player and link in an industry's value chain? Advances in telecommunications and information technology, artificial intelligence, automation, robotics, sensors, nanotechnology, material science, software, and integrated networks have blended in a new digital world. Developments in digital and related technologies have also accelerated the rate of change and ways of doing business. Digital technologies spawned the accelerated growth of the **internet of things**, innovative strategies, global strategy, mass customization of products and services, lean production processes, lean and other sustainable business practices. Telecommunications and digital technologies also set the stage for greater intra and inter-firm collaboration and flatter, virtual, decentralize structures replacing "top-down," command and control organizational structures. Digital technologies and the internet make it easier to collaborate and coordinate across organizational boundaries, including such practices as: **insourcing** (performing a business function internally in-house by bringing a third party outsourcer—another firm- into the business to perform the work); **offsourcing** (when a company relocates a business process to another country);.and **outsourcing** (transferring a portion of work or even an entire operation to outside providers or suppliers rather than completing it internally).

As we know, the firm's mix of resources and resource strengths ultimately determines the firm's competitive advantages and its sustainability. We also know that resource strength is a function of the heterogeneity and immobility of the firm's resources relative to those of its rivals. Resource strengths found in the firm's resource hierarchy create the foundation for generic strategies: cost, differentiation, or best value. A physical value chain is primarily based on tangible resources and clear and stable industry boundaries. Certainly, intangible resources (people, intellectual property, brand, patents, copyrights, etc.) are highly important and impactful in the physical value chain. A firm's relationships with rivals, suppliers, and customers are relatively stable, clear, and predictable. In this environment, intangible resources and human capital are less mobile and transparent. (The networked or virtual value chain is becoming more prominent in today's environment with current market turbulence and destabilization.) Firms, rivals, and suppliers find it extremely difficult to erect or maintain barriers to prevent entry or defend current position. Thus, they find themselves in hypercompetition with each other and or even distant industries.

In today's hypercompetitive digital world, intangible resources and understanding the power of networks (including human capital, artificial intelligence, deep data analytics, and other advanced technologies and concepts) are becoming ever more important and impactful. The virtual value chain expands globalization. It elevates awareness and accelerates growth in a global value chain, which increases the interconnectedness and interdependencies of firms, resources, and other entities across borders. It also links value chain activities more fluidly across physical borders, space, and time. Hence, in today's cyberworld, the firm will need to employ elements of both the virtual and physical value chains.

7. THE MULTIPLE BUSINESS FIRM

Companies can engage in singular or numerous industries, businesses, products, or services. The vast majority of firms today conduct business as a legal organizational entity, operating as a single business or multiple businesses. For example, Apple has many businesses or subsidiaries under its management. These separate business entities all perform unique operations that add value to Apple through diversification, revenue, earnings, research and development (R&D), and human resources. A multibusiness firm with several related businesses under one "roof" or operating structure is referred to as an **operating** company. A large company with a diversified portfolio of multiple businesses under one roof (legal structure) is known as a **diversified major**. Companies may become diversified by entering into new businesses on its own, by merging with another company, or by acquiring a company operating in another field or service sector. European diversified companies include Siemens and Bayer; Asian diversified companies include Hitachi, Toshiba, and Sanyo Electric. Some of the most well-known American diversified companies are GE, 3M, Sara Lee, and Motorola.

Similarly, Kraft Foods Group (KRFT), one of the largest diversified food and beverage companies, owns the following brands: Capri Sun, Country Time, Crystal Light, Gevalia, Kool-Aid, Maxwell House, MiO, and Tassimo. It also owns the brands A.1., Athenos, Breakstone's, Cheez Whiz, Claussen, Cracker Barrel, Jell-O, Lunchables, Miracle Whip, Oscar Mayer, Philadelphia, Planters, Polly-O, and Velveeta. Correspondingly, Proctor & Gamble (PG) remains one of the largest and most established consumer products companies in the world. Its best-known brands include: Bounce, Bounty, Cascade, Charmin, Downy, Febreze, Mr. Clean, and Tide. It also sells well-known beauty and health care products such as CoverGirl, Crest, Gillette, Olay, Old Spice, Oral-B, and Pantene Haircare. Some of the best-known single product companies include Chlorox, Nutrisystem, Scotts Miracle-Gro, Tootsie Roll, and WD-40.[27]

A **conglomerate** is made up of several different, unrelated businesses that each operate as an individual legal entity under a **parent or holding** company. The holding company manages the unrelated or subsidiary businesses independently. It can have full ownership (owning 100 percent of the business), majority ownership (controlling interest 50 percent or greater), or minority ownership (controlling interest less than 50 percent) in each of the subsidiary firms. The subsidiary businesses' managers report directly to the parent company's senior management team when the parent company owns the business outright (100 percent ownership) or has controlling interest. Well-known examples of conglomerate businesses include Berkshire Hathaway, General Electric, Textron, and Tyco and Siemens. Interestingly, Berkshire Hathaway as a conglomerate owns **majority** stake in more than 50 companies. It also possesses **minority** holdings in numerous other companies ranging from General Electric to Walmart. As a holding company, Berkshire possesses only 24 employees at its corporate headquarters.

Multibusiness firms aid in diversifying risk, growing sales and profits, innovating new concepts (R&D), and maximizing stockholder value. Additionally, firms with multiple businesses diversify risk by participating in a number of different markets, though some multibusiness firms compete in a single industry. For example, Walmart competes primarily in the discount retail industry, though it operates the vast majority of its super-stores as major malls with products and services ranging from groceries to hard goods (TVs, electronics), soft goods (clothing, shoes), banking, real estate, travel, pharmacy, and restaurants.

One of the challenges facing multibusiness companies is the need to continuously improve firm perfor-mance. Because firms compete in dynamic and contested markets, it is difficult for a single-product or single-industry firm to continue to improve its performance, let alone a multi-industry or multiproduct firm. The challenge for all firms is maintaining a strong strategic focus to produce solid financial returns for shareholders instead of diluting corporate value through ill-conceived business or product strategies, investments, expan-sions, or acquisitions.

8. WHAT IS A SPACE ANALYSIS (STRATEGIC POSITION AND COMPETITIVE ACTION EVALUATION)?

The SPACE matrix is a management tool used to analyze overall resource strengths and industry attractive-ness for a firm with multiple businesses. It combines both an internal and external situational analysis in the strategy-setting process. SPACE builds on the BCG's portfolio matrix by assigning economic values or measures to a firm's resource strengths, external industry conditions, and overall attractiveness. Similar to BCG analysis, SPACE determines what types of strategies or investments a company should undertake for each of its businesses, strategic business units, products, or companies. SPACE also employs specific environmen-tal, economic, financial, market, customer, and other stakeholder metrics to determine the relative business strength and performance, as well as market and industry attractiveness. The SPACE analytical tool is depicted as a four-cell matrix (see Exhibit 5.6) divided into two external factors representing overall industry attractive-ness—industry attractiveness (IA) and environmental stability (ES)—and two internal factors representing overall business attractiveness—financial strength (FS) and competitive advantage (CA).[28]

8.1 HOW TO CONDUCT A SPACE ANALYSIS

Step 1: Identify businesses for strategic positioning and competitive action evaluation.
Step 2: Identify relevant SPACE factors to measure environmental stability (ES). Examples of ES factors include:

- Political uncertainty; changes in national, state, and regional government policies or regulation
- Taxes
- Interest rates and federal reserve actions
- Inflation rates
- Industry cyclicality
- Social and legal uncertainty (climate change policies, EPA actions, etc.)
- Industry entry barriers (FTC, justice, or other administrative agencies' antitrust actions)
- Demand elasticity, fluctuations
- Industry average price trends
- Advances in technologies—accelerated or exponential growth in game-changing technologies (Moore's Law, Metcalfe's Law, advances in microchips, sensors, smart technologies, deep data analytics, artificial intelligence, etc.)

Step 3: Assign an ES score for selected factors from minus 1 (–1) for great to minus 6 (–6) poor in the SPACE analysis matrix.

Exhibit 5.6
SPACE Matrix

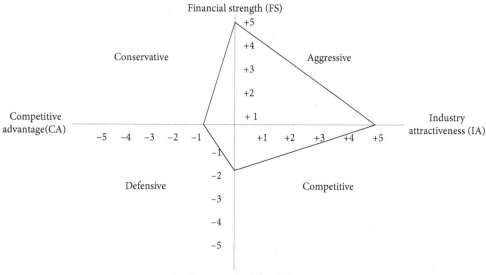

Environmental stability (ES)

Based on this position the firm has a favorable position. The recommended competitive strategy is aggressive growth support by a highly attractive industry, stable industry environment and strong financial strength. The firm has a superior competitive advantage that can be sustained

Source: Michael J. Merenda; Adapted from: Paul Simister, "SPACE Analysis—Strategic Position and Action Evaluation Matrix," September 1, 2011: at http://www.differentiateyourbusiness.co.uk/space-analysis-strategic-position-and-action-evaluation-matrix

Step 4: Calculate the overall ES average score.

Example:
Demand elasticity, fluctuations   –5 poor (highly elastic)

Industry average price trends	–4 poor (accelerated downward pressure on average price)
Taxes—business	–1 very favorable tax climate for businesses
Taxes—individual	–2 changes in tax policy, minimal impact on middle-income individuals
Interest rates	–2 limited federal action in low interest rate economy
Inflation rates	–3 neutral consumer price index, low inflation
Industry cyclicality	–4 poor, highly cyclical, erratic

Total score	**–21**
N = Factors	**7**
Average Score	**–3**

Step 5: Identify SPACE factors to measure industry attractiveness (IA). Examples of IA factors include:

- Industry growth rate
- Industry life cycle stage
- Threat of new entrants
- Power of buyers
- Power of suppliers
- Rival intensity
- Threat of substitute products
- Existence of complements
- Entry barriers
- Exit barriers

Step 6: Assign an IA score for selected factors from 6 (great) to 1 (poor) in the SPACE matrix.

Step 7: Calculate the overall IA average score.

Example:

Industry growth rate	6 explosive growth industry
Industry life cycle stage	6 early growth stage
Threat of new entrants	5 low, high entry barriers
Power of buyers	4 high switching cost
Power of suppliers	3 moderate risk of integrating forward
Rival intensity	4 low—room for more than one industry standard
Threat of substitute products	5 low
Existence of complements	4 strong ecology of supporting products and technologies

Total score	**37**
N = Factors	**8**
Average score	**4.625**

Step 8: Identify SPACE factors to measure financial strengths (FS).

Step 9: Assign a FS score for selected financial factors from 6 (strong) to 1 (weak) in the SPACE matrix. Examples include:

- Liquidity ratios
- Activity or turnover ratios
- Leverage ratios
- Profitability ratios
- Stock market ratios
- Horizontal analysis (three- to five-year trend analysis)
- Vertical analysis (three- to five-year trend analysis)
- Cash flow
- Market capitalization
- Access to strategic funds
- Stock price and performance
- Low fixed cost, low breakeven point

Step 10: Calculate the overall FS average score:

Example:

Liquidity ratios	5 strong
Activity or turnover ratios	6 very strong
Leverage ratios	3 average
Profitability ratios	5 strong
Horizontal analysis (three- to five-year trend analysis)	5 strong
Vertical analysis (three- to five-year trend analysis)	6 very strong
Total score	**30**
N = Factors	**6**
Average score	**5**

Step 11: Identify SPACE factors to measure competitive advantage (CA):
- Value chain strengths
- Transaction cost analysis
- Information superiority
- Speed to market
- Customer response time
- Timely product and process innovations
- Superior knowledge management
- Innovative business model
- Superior technologies
- Superior management and employee know-how
- Economies of scale
- Economies of scope
- Highly benchmarked products and processes

Step 12 : Calculate the overall CA average score from –1 (strong) to –6 (poor) in the SPACE matrix:

Example:

Value chain strengths	–1 very strong
Transaction cost analysis	–2 strong
Information superiority	–2 strong
Speed to market	–3 average

Customer response time	−2 strong
Timely product and process innovations	−3 average
Innovative business model	−1 very strong
Total score	**−14**
N = Factors	**7**
Average score	**−2**

Step 13: Find appropriate axis and scale in the SPACE matrix. Assign IA, ES, FS, and CA scores.

Step 14: Plot and connect IA, ES, FS, and CA scores in the matrix.

Step 15: Determine appropriate strategy position in the matrix: aggressive, conservative, defensive, or competitive.

Step 16: Draw conclusions.

8.2 AGGRESSIVE POSITION

An **aggressive** strategy is best when the business or product has superior financial resources and strengths and the external competitive market is highly attractive. In this situation, the business should also score high on its VIRO test to be considered for long-term investments and resource support. In these instances, the business's internal resource strengths are superior and the external assessment of the industry or market is highly attractive. For aggressive strategies, the business must employ its resource strengths to develop aggressive, offensive growth strategies such as market penetration and market development strategies, product development, horizontal integration (acquisition of a rival), or vertical integration (acquisition of a supplier).

8.3 CONSERVATIVE POSITION

A **conservative** or maintenance strategy is best pursued when a firm's current strategies are working but the industry or market is not attractive or exciting. The business barely passes the VIRO test and is trapped in a weak market position. Other situations that call for a conservative strategy are: (1) The business's or product's competitive markets are relatively predictable or stable, but unexciting; (2) the business has an acceptable or desired position in markets short term, but longer-term industry attractiveness is unfavorable; or (3) the competitive environment is so uncertain or unpredictable that altering current strategies or making resource commitments would be extremely risky and costly.

8.4 DEFENSIVE POSITION

Defensive strategies are associated with poor industry and business attractiveness. A VIRO test shows that the business' strategies are vulnerable and not sustainable. A defensive strategy does not necessarily mean business performance is poor. The business's relative market share and favorable profit margins might dictate short-term defensive moves to protect its position while considering long-term actions to harvest or exit from the market or industry.

A **competitive strategy** is called for when the business scores favorably on its industry attractiveness and competitive advantage scores but unfavorably on its financial strengths and environmental stability scores. The key to business success is to strengthen financial resources (balance sheet, income statement, cash flow) to offset the environmental uncertainty and instability. If the business can acquire the financial investments or improve its financial health, then it will be better positioned to move aggressively in its market or industry.

Thinking Critically Exercise 43	SPACE—HOW TO CONDUCT A SPACE ANALYSIS

Go to section 8.1 above.

    a. Using the scores for each of the four SPACE dimensions (FS, CA, ES, IA) draw a SPACE assessment using the SPACE matrix. What is the recommended strategy for this firm? What risks and opportunities are identified with this strategy?

    b. What are some of the advantages for using a SPACE analysis as a predictive tool? What are some of its limitations?

9. BENCHMARKING

Benchmarking is the continuous process used by a firm to learn about or take advantage of the best industry or organizational practices. Best practices can be found in the multibusiness firm within the firm's subsidiaries, strategic business units, divisions, departments, or functions. Benchmarking can also take place outside the firm or its multiple businesses to discover what exceptional industry or organizational practices, products, processes, or ways of doing business (business models) are driving another organization's strong performance. A firm can take advantage of benchmarking by observing and learning about another firm or industry's performance drivers. Benchmarking can be applied against any product, process, function, or approach in business. Common focal points for benchmarking initiatives include measures of time, quality, cost, effectiveness, and customer satisfaction. The intent of benchmarking is to compare a firm's operations against competitors' to generate ideas for improving processes, refining approaches and technologies to reduce costs, increasing profits, and strengthening customer satisfaction and loyalty.[29]

9.1 TYPES OF BENCHMARKING

Almost any product, process, activity, or way of conducting business can be benchmarked. Before starting, the firm must first determine what is to be benchmarked. What are the goals or expected outcomes for benchmarking? What measures or metrics are to be benchmarked? What is to be compared? What is the best way to access and collect data? How will the benchmarked data be used? Three broad types of benchmarking include product benchmarking, process benchmarking, and strategic benchmarking.

    Product benchmarking is undertaken when one company's product or service continuously outperforms its rivals' in terms of total sales, profit margins, performance, quality, customer satisfaction, or special features. For example, firms in high-technology industries are notorious for copying or stealing product ideas, technologies, or other features. For instance, Apple's introduction of the smartphone in 2007 disrupted sales of mobile phones and upset product sales in other industries including cameras and film, record sales and record stores, newspapers, computers, and media publishers. Although Apple has legally challenged rivals' actions in court, competing smartphone manufacturers have discovered ways to bypass legal restrictions. In 2012, Apple won a lawsuit against Samsung. The jury awarded Apple $1 billion after concluding that Samsung "ripped off" the innovative technology employed in the iPhone and iPad. Similarly, Green Mountain Coffee Roasters settled a lawsuit against Kraft Foods Global for patent infringement that violated its intellectual property rights. Green Mountain asserted that Kraft infringed on Keurig's brewing and K-Cup technologies. Kraft paid Green Mountain $17 million to settle the suit. As part of the settlement, Green Mountain licensed its brewer and cartridge technologies to Kraft.[30]

There are several ways a firm's products can be benchmarked, such as reverse engineering, licensing and royalty agreements, patent purchases, buying the company, and acquiring the rights to the benchmarked products. **Reverse engineering** is the reproduction of another firm's product following detailed examination of its construction or composition. The product is literally taken apart and studied by the firm's engineers. In some instances, firms will partner with other firms to acquire products, product technologies, people, processes, or practices. For example, in recent years, many traditional automobile companies have set up research and development offices in Silicon Valley to be close to software companies working on next-generation smart technologies for vehicles.

Process benchmarking is undertaken to learn about another firm's method of operations. It can include how firms employ best practices in one or more points on its value chain, such as best practices associated with inbound logistics, operations, outbound logistics, customer relationship management, human resources, and other supporting activities. Walmart's supply chain is one the most heavily benchmarked, not only in the discount retail industry but also by firms in other industries like manufacturing, chemicals, pharmaceuticals, and defense. Walmart has consistently lowered costs while continuously accelerating the flow of a greater number of items (millions) through its value chain. The retail giant's automated distribution centers; geographic configuration of distribution centers and stores; use of artificial intelligence, deep-dive analytics, and tracking technologies; store-within-a-store design; in-house teleconferencing with store managers; use of lean business practices; and collaborative relationship with suppliers have all led to its becoming one of the most benchmarked firms in the retail discount industry.

Strategic benchmarking examines the actions other organizations are taking to improve performance and maintain long-term organizational vitality. This style of benchmarking focuses on the best practices found in the strategic management process. It includes study of strategic management practices, human resource management and development, and advanced management frameworks and analytical tools. Strategic benchmarking aims at answering the question *why do some firms consistently remain top performers while other firms fail?* Strategic benchmarking surveys the best practices in terms of strategy setting and execution (why are some firms more flexible and better able to adapt to environmental change?), investments in technologies and innovation (a company's investment in the future), organization culture and structure, and investments in development of human resources. *Fortune's* 2017 top 10 most admired and benchmarked U.S. companies (in order of ranking) are: Apple (computers), Amazon.com (internet services and retailing), Starbucks (food services), Berkshire Hathaway (property and casualty insurance), Disney (entertainment), Alphabet (internet services and retailing), General Electric (industrial machinery), Southwest Airlines (airline), Facebook (internet services and retailing), and Microsoft (computer software).[31]

10. IS YOUR COMPANY'S COMPETITIVE ADVANTAGE SUSTAINABLE?

In assessing the sustainability of a company's competitive advantage, strategic managers must constantly develop, nurture, and monitor only those resources, core capabilities, and distinctive competencies that invariably support winning strategies. A winning strategy is one that creates value for the customer while simultaneously creating value for the firm. Winning strategies demand constant evaluation to ensure maximum effectiveness and sustainability. Managers must continually ask several strategic questions to assess the sustainability of a firm's competitive advantage including:

1. Do the firm's resources, core capabilities, and distinctive competencies offer unique value to the firm's customers?
2. Is this unique value difficult and costly for rivals to imitate?
3. Are the firm's tangible and intangible resources, core capabilities, and distinctive competencies so rare that rivals or others cannot easily substitute them?
4. Are the tangible and intangible resources, core capabilities, and distinctive competencies dynamic and flexible so they can be successfully adapted to change in customers' value creation expectations?
5. Are there new value creation opportunities outside existing industry and market boundaries that open up entirely new customers and markets?
6. Do the firm's customer value creation strategies and activities align with its vision, mission, goals, and objectives?

If any of the answers to these questions is no, then the sustainability of the firm's competitive advantage is at risk. The level of said risk is determined by the firm's ability to counter rivals' competitive moves or rivals' failure to capitalize on their favorable competitive position. Either case calls for continuous critical inquiry, strategic thinking, and action on the part of the firm's strategic managers.

11. REFLECTION

Chapter 5 covers internal environmental analysis and strategy crafting with a focus on the resource-based school of strategic thought and business-level strategy. This school advances the notion that competitive advantage is earned internally by assessing the firm's ability to develop and nurture heterogeneous tangible and intangible resources. The firm's resource strengths, core capabilities, and distinctive competencies can be nurtured and developed in offering customers a superior (over rivals') value proposition. The chapter shows how to conduct a VIRO (valuable, imitable, rare, and organizational) test, a SPACE (strategic position and competitive action evaluation) analysis, and the Boston Consulting Group's (BCG) product portfolio analysis, as well as how o identify and assess the potential sources of a firm's competitive advantage in the primary and supporting activities in its supply and value chains. Other topics covered in the chapter are the multiple business firm, the conglomerate firm, and benchmarking as tool for evaluating a firm's products, processes, or strategies. The overall purpose of a situational analysis is to facilitate strategy crafting. The situational analysis is a precursor to all strategy making, implementation, execution, and control included in the strategic management conceptual model. The situational analysis is based on continuous critical inquiry, strategic thinking, and action.

a. What do you want to achieve in your lifetime? Do you have a strategy for accomplishing your lifelong goals? If so, what is it? On a piece of paper, write the phrases "cool" and "crappy" on the upper right hand corner of the paper. Put a current date on the paper. Giving yourself three minutes maximum, list all your lifetime goals. Now take another three minutes and rewrite your lifetime goals, this time trying to separate what you consider "cool" and what you consider "crappy". Fold the paper and put it in a safe place. Take a week or two and think about your lifetime goals. Redo the assignment a second time. This time, take an additional three minutes and list the strategies and actions that will move you toward your lifetime goals, along with those obstacles or constraints that might prevent you from attaining those objectives.

b. Are there individuals, corporate leaders, or coaches that you admire? What is it that you admire most about these individuals? If you were to use these individuals to benchmark your lifetime goals and individual performance, what benchmarking attributes would you find most useful?

CHAPTER ENDNOTES

1. "History." Tyco.com. http://tycoint.com/tyco/history.asp.
2. Ibid.
3. Ibid.
4. Bianco, Anthony, William Symonds, and Nanette Byrnes with David Polek. "The Rise and Fall of Dennis Kozlowski." *Business Week Online,* 2002.
5. Syre, Steven, and Charles Stein. "The Quiet Giant: Tyco International Takes Unglamorous Road to Riches." *Boston Globe,* 1999.
6. "Tyco International." Wikipedia. https://en.wikipedia.org/wiki/Tyco_International.
7. Tita, Bob, and Dana Mattioli. "Johnson Controls, Tyco to Merge in Inversion Deal." *Wall Street Journal,* January 25, 2016. https://www.wsj.com/articles/johnson-controls-tyco-to-merge-in-inversion-deal-1453724828.
8. Johnson Controls PLC. "Johnson Controls and Tyco." Management PowerPoint Presentation to Investors. January 26, 2016. http://investors.johnsoncontrols.com/.
9. History." Tyco.com. http://tycoint.com/tyco/history.asp.
10. Porter, Michael, E. "Toward a Dynamic Theory of Strategy." *Strategic Management Journal* (2007): 95–117.
11. Penrose, Edith. *The Theory of the Growth of the Firm.* New York: Oxford University Press, 1959.
12. Barney, Jay. "Firm Resources and Sustained Competitive Advantage." *Journal of Management* 17, no. 17 (1991): 99–120.
13. Jurevicius, Ovidijus. "VRIO Framework." *Strategic Management Insight.* October 21, 2013. https://www.strategicmanagementinsight.com/tools/vrio.html.
14. Friedman, Thomas. *Thank You for Being Late.* New York: Picador, 2016.
15. Barney, Jay. "Firm Resources and Sustainable Competitive Advantage." *Journal of Management* (1991): 99–120.; Peteraf, J. "The Cornerstones of Competitive Advantage." *Strategic Management Journal* (1993).; Penrose, Edith. *The Theory of the Growth of the Firm.* New York: Oxford University Press, 1959.
16. Barney, Jay. "Firm Resources and Sustainable Competitive Advantage." *Journal of Management* (1991): 99–120.; Peteraf, J. "The Cornerstones of Competitive Advantage." *Strategic Management Journal* (1993).; Penrose, Edith. *The Theory of the Growth of the Firm.* New York: Oxford University Press, 1959.
17. Henderson, Bruce. "The Experience Curve—Reviewed IV. The Growth Share Matrix or the Product Portfolio." The Boston Consulting Group, Inc. (1973): 1–3.
18. Ibid., 1–3.
19. Porter, Michael E. "The Competitive Advantage of Firms in Global Industries." In *Competitive Advantage of Nations.* New York: The Free Press, 1990.
20. Porter, Michael E. *The Competitive Advantage: Creating and Sustaining Superior Performance.* New York: The Free Press, 1985.
21. Porter, Michael E. "The Competitive Advantage of Firms in Global Industries." In *Competitive Advantage of Nations.* New York: The Free Press, 1990.
22. Porter, Michael E. *The Competitive Advantage: Creating and Sustaining Superior Performance.* New York: The Free Press, 1985.
23. Ibid.
24. Ibid.
25. Ibid.
26. Porter, Michael E. "The Competitive Advantage of Firms in Global Industries." In *Competitive Advantage of Nations.* New York: The Free Press, 1990.
27. Pylypczak-Wasylyszyn, Daniela. "Companies That Own the World's Most Popular Brands." dividend.com. October 28, 2014. http://www.dividend.com/how-to-invest/9-companies-that-own-the-worlds-most-popular-brands/.
28. "Application of Space Matrix." SCRIBD. https://www.scribd.com/document/109265501/Application-of-SPACE-Matrix.
29. Reh, F. John. "Benchmarking Overview, Practices, and Approaches in Business." the balance. March 31, 2017. https://www.thebalance.com/overview-and-examples-of-benchmarking-in-business-2275114.
30. Green Mountain Coffee Roasters, Inc. 2009 Annual Report on Form 10-K, For Fiscal Year Ended September 26, 2009.
31. "World's Most Admired Companies." *Fortune,* 2017. http://fortune.com/worlds-most-admired-companies.

BROADBAND 2030: THE NETWORKED FUTURE

BY ROUZBEH YASSINI

THE FUTURE, BROUGHT TO YOU BY BROADBAND

Rouzbeh Yassini,
"Broadband 2030: A
Networked Future," pp.
3-9. Copyright © 2013
by University of New
Hampshire Broadband
Center of Excellence.
Reprinted with
permission.

Thirty years ago the Internet was an R&D project that connected a few thousand Ph.D.-level researchers at an average of about 500 bits per second per person, each in a fixed location limited to universities in the U.S. and Europe. That's a total network capacity of about 1 million bits per second.

Today, that capacity has grown to 2 million megabits per second for close to 1 billion people, a majority of them now connected to mobile broadband networks. The total network capacity has grown to petabits (that is 10^{15} bits per second). To put that in common terms, that's about the same information rate equivalent to transferring 15,000 full length high definition movies per second. Not bad. It reflects a factor of 1 billion in 30 years, an exponential growth rate doubling each year.

Now for the fun part. Let's assume that growth rate will continue. The number of people won't double each year (we hope), but the number of connected devices will increase by a factor of 1 million to 10^{15} (peta) devices—producing a forthcoming "big bang" of connectedness that will inspire huge improvements in broadband network performance. Each device will be connected at a speed of 1 gigabit per second. The devices will be connected wirelessly, and at some point it won't matter where they are: anywhere on the surface of the earth or in the sky or under the sea or in space within the orbit of the moon. The total network capacity will be 10^{24} bits per second—a yottabit per second, or the equivalent to transferring 15 thousand-billion full length high definition movies per second. Yowza!

In this emerging world, the possibilities start to expand dramatically as we move toward a world a reality where a full range of business services, government services and personalized services are made possible by applying intelligent, automated software over broadband networks.

For one thing, forget tablets and smartphones. The broadband device of the future could just as well be part of your outfit for the day: a hat, let's say. Place it on your head and you're connected to an immersive virtual reality world, thanks to brain research that will have shown engineers how to wirelessly connect directly into our visual, spatial and olfactory sensory nerve centers at 1 billion bits per second. Think of where you want to go and you'll be transported there, virtually. Entrepreneurs can attend a business meeting on the moon with their professional colleagues to discuss the challenges of colonizing Mars with the raw materials available on the moon. A surgeon in Boston can perform a delicate procedure on a patient's heart in Los Angeles. Engineers will collaborate on world-changing projects such as fusion-based clean energy. Students from hundreds of countries can come together on the same day to learn from one another thanks to simultaneous language translation driven automatically by broadband's toolkit. Infants will effectively grow up in a world without boundaries. And we will all enjoy entertainment and art no matter where we are. You'll simply need your ultra-broadband connected-hat. ultra broadband-connected hat. Pretty cool, yes?

This is where thinking about the future of broadband starts to get fun. Rather than look to existing applications and practices and marveling about how next-generation networks will affect them, why not theorize about an entirely new range of possibilities?

Adopting this wider lens lets us escape the relatively narrow trappings of the voice-video-data heritage. Much of what today's multi-megabit broadband networks do is to make familiar Internet applications work better than they did in the dial-up era. That's an improvement, but it's not a revolution.

BETTER WAYS

A more telling way to express the possibilities of broadband is to look at ahead-of-their time companies like Amazon, which exemplifies a transformational embrace of connectivity, automation and intelligent software that is achievable through broadband. Amazon has transformed an industrial-age business—the selling of physical, printed books—into an integrated goods delivery platform. It has done so by integrating a suite of fully automated, broadband-connected services that together create a nearly friction-free, highly efficient commerce environment. Broadband touches nearly everything Amazon does, from ingesting and distributing enormous amounts of data at server farms to integrating knowledge about customer habits with price and merchandise information. Amazon has coupled software tools with broadband to collapse and flatten its internal organization in a way that hints at how networked collaboration can improve economic performance in a hybrid industrial-information age.

Imagine how a similar transformation might impact thousands of global companies and millions of individual entrepreneurs who will be able to conduct commerce at a fraction of current costs thanks to the adoption of smart tools and automation. When the independent plumbing contractor shows up at your doorstep knowing in advance what pipe is leaking, what parts he needs to fix it and which of your preferred accounts to bill electronically, we'll know broadband has truly arrived.

NEXT INGREDIENT: SOFTWARE

But that's not going to happen without a concerted effort by software developers who hold the keys to making broadband integration accessible, secure and foolproof for organizations of all types and sizes.

Cable and telco providers have invested mightily in creating user-friendly, powerful and robust delivery platforms that scale to serve massive amounts of customers. Wireless network operators have revolutionized our world by introducing the concept of connected mobility to the lives of billions of people.

Now, a similarly vigorous effort should be directed toward devising intelligent and rigorously tested software solutions associated with broadband-enabled nanotechnology, biotech and information technology. Software is the glue that tightly couples these technologies with broadband to produce breathtaking advancements in health care, education, business and governance that will touch every connected citizen in the world.

It's a grand ambition, but recent developments points to our ability to achieve it. The type of seamless, automated, integrated experiences Amazon has demonstrated in post-industrial retailing can be associated with almost any element of life. This is how we will advance and grow a global economy in the post-industrial era: with a combination of intelligent networks and software that allows anyone, from the solo entrepreneur to the large corporation, from the municipal mayor to a national government, to leverage the power of sophisticated software applications enabled by broadband.

There are examples already emerging everywhere. In agriculture, farmers can now apply software and broadband-connected devices to maintain watch of growing conditions, market prices, inventory yields and other critical information with newfound efficiency. This sort of nanotechnology application is emblematic of the emerging Internet of Things revolution that will infuse the world with new knowledge thanks to findings reported by billions of miniature devices connected to broadband.

In biotechnology, the broadband-plus-software pairing will provoke enormous advancements by enabling simple, easy and inexpensive monitoring of indicators like blood pressure, heart rate and neural activity that used to require time-consuming and expensive in-person visits with physicians and caretakers.

Broadband also has enormous influence in academic research. Believe it or not, academic and industry researchers who specialize in research subjects such as gene sequencing still commonly overnight computer disks to one another because they're unable to move massive amounts of information over available access networks. The combination of advanced software and multi-gigabit networks will change that, enabling real-time Big Data analysis and collaboration that inspires scientific breakthroughs.

Business and commerce are poised for revolution as well. Consider just one category: e-commerce. Many providers have taken advantage of broadband capabilities to present merchandise in more attractive ways using multimedia tools. That's terrific. But what if instead of changing the color of the shirt displayed on a shopping site's web page, you could render a holographic 3D model of how you would look wearing it? And even touch it to feel the fabric? Samsung's Advanced Institute of Technology is among those working to deliver vibrational feedback in response to touch so that users can feel and interact with 3D objects—an endeavor that has almost limitless implications across the spectrum of business, government and personalized broadband services.

A final indicator has to do with the most important application of all: human interaction. Today we marvel that we can see the image of a friend or family member on a screen while we talk live over the Internet. But we're only skirting the surface of more immersive "presence" applications that have the potential to redefine the way people participate in relationships, communicate with one another, and create or maintain friendships in communities large and small, anywhere in the world.

The academic and writer Susan Crawford is among those who believe advanced broadband networks hold the key to technology breakthroughs that can help restore notions of belonging and even self-esteem that early-stage social media applications have struggled to produce. "We're getting closer to full-bandwidth communications. That's presence. That's the killer app," Crawford said in a June 2013 speech at a conference organized by US Ignite, a gigabit network advocacy group. "We may be able to figure out how to make authentic friendship possible over high-capacity networks. That's what's next. Presence; visual literacy; a new form of relating."

CONNECTING EVERYTHING—INCLUDING CARS

We often think of broadband connectivity as a conduit to two types of devices—homebound machines like computers or appliances and mobile marvels like tablets and smartphones. But in the emerging networked ecosystem, everything will be connected. And that includes another place where we spend much of our time—in vehicles.

Within 10 to 15 years, your car will be part of your connected personalized broadband world. Connected vehicles will enable safer operating, better fuel efficiency and more pleasant traveling environment for passengers with potential for these technologies to improve several aspects of existing transportation systems.

The broadband-meets-vehicle ecosystem comprises three distinct types of connectivity: intra-vehicle, vehicle-to-vehicle and vehicle to infrastructure vehicle-to-infrastructure. Among its possibilities:

1. Providing standardized interfaces for intra-vehicle applications promises to reduce the weight of the cabling harness and provide a high-performance high-reliability communications infrastructure that will connect life-critical systems such as braking and steering along with information distribution and presentation systems such as dashboard indicators, heads up displays and infotainment systems.
2. Providing standardized interfaces for vehicle-to-vehicle communications will help realize the vision of Dedicated Short Range Communications (DSRC) applications that will help reduce collisions, improve road safety, and enable fuel savings by more efficient operation of single vehicles as well as vehicle "platoons."
3. Using DSRC to enable vehicle-to-roadway communications that will allow roadway conditions to be communicated to vehicles enabling them to operate more safely as well as detect and avoid other potentially dangerous situations. Of course, all of these capabilities will have to be built on top of hardened communication systems that will be highly reliable and impervious to malicious attacks.

The connected vehicle is another missing piece of ubiquitous connectivity and personalized services we all will experience as networks increasingly reshape the experience of personalized communication.

SOBERING SIDE

As I said, it's fun to theorize about the future. But there's a sobering side, too. Although broadband's rise has been impressive, a communications system that many believe is essential to future social and economic welfare is still present in the lives of only a minority of the world's population. According to a September 2013 report from the International Telecommunications Union, roughly 4.4 billion people, or 60 percent of the global population, lack access to the Internet at all. Fewer still have (or can afford) broadband access.

If broadband is to achieve the high goals many people believe it can, wider adoption is essential. But that's only one obstacle the world needs to overcome to realize the full potential of this powerful communications tool. At the University of New Hampshire's new Broadband Center of Excellence (UNH BCoE), where I serve as acting Executive Director, we've identified seven impediments to a full realization of broadband as a tool

Obstacles: Creating a truly connected global population requires overcoming seven impediments to broadband ubiquity.

for a global, connected civilization. They are availability, adoption, affordability, performance, utilization, ease of use and service development.

Overcoming these obstacles requires a collaborative interplay among governments and policymakers, investors and corporations, entrepreneurs and community activists.

Among other things, it requires a willingness to experiment with new delivery technologies such as TV White Space, a promising approach that uses fallow broadcasting spectrum to supply wireless broadband connectivity. The UNH BCoE is now engaged in a trial deployment of TVWS to connect underserved New Hampshire communities wirelessly at broadband speeds.

Additionally, we've identified a number of policy and market approaches that can help inspire ideas to overcome broadband's most pressing obstacles, and do so in a time frame that delivers on the promise of the broadband-meets-software revolution.

An early glimpse of this promise is evident today within the university community, where many of the forward-looking services and capabilities of broadband are visible. The University of New Hampshire system has deployed hundreds of advanced services powered by intelligent software applications running over multi-gigabit networks. UNH is a living, working, visitor-friendly showcase representing these new possibilities. Within this advanced environment, UNH BCoE is working to enable a broad cross-section of students, government, researchers, faculty and business organizations to learn how to use broadband and associated software to advance strategic goals and provoke economic growth. We conduct research on broadband technologies and broadband's role in fostering community development while advising practitioners on resources available to leverage broadband capabilities in any location.

The truth is that in the end, we don't know exactly what a fully integrated, broadband-connected, software-infused world will look like. But there is a broad consensus around the world that broadband is an essential ingredient in the transformation from an industrial economy to something new and different and promising. More than 130 nations, advanced and developing alike, have adopted national broadband plans that seek to gain the fullest advantage of broadband connectivity for their citizens. They believe in broadband's ability to enable positive change across critical social, political, economic and cultural dimensions of life. So do I. If we do it right, broadband can be a key to unlocking new possibilities for reducing poverty, elevating opportunity, improving global understanding and building prosperity across the world. Those are ambitious goals, yes. But in broadband, we're known for making big things happen.

a. What are the main characteristics of broadband technologies and devices? A broadband ecosystem?

b. Yassini believes that lives are improved by having access to affordable, ubiquitous broadband connections. He notes that, similar to electricity a century ago, broadband is the driver for this generation's modern revolution. The broadband ecosystem already touches every aspect of our personal lives and work environment. What is the modern broadband revolution? How are our lives touched and improved through broadband ecosystems?

c. What are some of the implications of a world powered by the internet and broadband? What are some of the limitations or concerns that go with today's fast-paced, interconnected, virtual, ubiquitous internet; internet devices; and internet products and services?

d. What advice would you give to a dad who succumbs to the pleas of his 8-year-old daughter to buy her an iPhone X?

1. INTRODUCTION: QUESTIONS TO THINK ABOUT

- What is corporate-level strategy?
- What is firm vitality?
- What is radically inclusive strategic thinking?
- What is exponential growth?
- What is accelerated change?
- What is Metcalfe's Law?
- What is Moore's Law?
- What are maintenance strategies?
- What are offensive strategies?
- What are defensive strategies?
- What are the implications of digital economy on corporate level strategy?

1.1 WHAT IS CORPORATE-LEVEL STRATEGY?

As explained previously, strategic actions are necessary at three levels of the organization: corporate, business, and functional. **Corporate**-level strategy focuses on the firm's overall vision, mission, core purpose, goals, and objectives. Simply stated, corporate-level strategy primarily focuses on **what** industries and businesses the firm will compete with and how it will be judged. (Contrastingly, business-level strategy primarily focuses on **how** business-level managers compete in these industries.) The authority and responsibility to make corporate-level decisions rests with a company's board of directors, CEO, and other senior-level managers. Decisions at this level usually, but not always, must be approved by a company's stockholders if the company is publically traded. Typical characteristics of corporate-level strategy are:

- Primarily concerned with complex strategic decisions that affect the total or overall performance of the firm
- Also concerned with long-term profits, vitality, and viability of the firm
- Effectively create and manage large-scale strategic and organizational change in light of simultaneous acceleration in technology, globalization, and climate change
- Overall success is based on the firm's ability to adapt to and cope with dynamic and turbulent environments

- Concerned with the proper identification and allocation of limited resources across all organizational entities and units
- For multibusiness firms, corporate-level strategy coordinates and delegates strategy crafting and execution to business and functional-level managers

Corporate-level strategy is based on what matters to the firm. In other words, what are the firm's interests regarding:

- Profit, survivability, and growth
- Social impact and business ethics
- Return on investments for shareholders
- Satisfaction of stakeholders, near and far
- Resolving stakeholder conflicts of interests
- Legal and regulatory compliance

VIDEO 6.1 Philip Evans: How Data Will Transform Business

2. MAINTAINING VITALITY

How does a firm maintain its vitality? Vitality is defined as a firm's ability to explore new options, renew its strategies, and grow sustainability.[1] Few firms are able to maintain their vitality long-term as they grow in complexity, size, and scope. A Boston Consulting Group (BCG) study found that just 7 percent of companies that were market leaders in their industries were also profit leaders. That decline in vitality renders large companies increasingly vulnerable to change.[2] This is normal as firms advance through several stages of organizational growth and complexity and through their competitive advantage life. Constant renewal, adapting to or driving the way customer and firm value is created, requires constant higher-order thinking, critical inquiry, reflection, and creativity at the highest level of the firm. Correspondingly, strategic problem solving at the utmost level of the firm requires "inside the box," "outside the box," and "where there is no box at all" kinds of thinking.[3] The latter type of thinking—where there is no box at all—is driven by the "simultaneous acceleration in technology, globalization and climate change, all interacting with another."[4] Friedman calls this approach to problem solving and thinking being **radically inclusive**. He also states that radically inclusive thinking "... involves bringing into your analysis as many relevant people, processes, disciplines, organizations, and technologies as possible—factors that are often kept separate or excluded altogether."[5]

Thinking Critically Exercise 45

FORTUNE'S 50 COMPANIES WITH BEST PROSPECTS FOR GROWTH

BCG, a well-known strategy consulting company, defines **vitality** as the capacity of a company to explore new options, renew its strategy, and grow sustainably. In a 2015 study on what drives vitality in companies, BCG notes that "preserving past advantages and position is not sufficient to thrive in today's complex and dynamic business environment. In a fast-changing world, only the vital will survive." The high growth rates typical of younger companies are hard to sustain. But in the long run, the majority of returns for shareholders are driven by revenue growth. For companies to prosper and deliver for investors well past the startup stage, they must learn the secrets of staying vital. Using the BCG study, *Fortune* developed an index for the 50 U.S. companies with the best prospects for growth. The index has two pillars: (1) a market view of growth potential and (2) an assessment of the firm's actual capacity to deliver that growth based on four dimensions: strategy, technology and investments, people, and structure. The result is a composite score that represents both a new metric and a new perspective for business analysis.

Go to your library's online listing of periodicals or fortune.com/2017/10/19/future-50-companies-intro/. Select the *Fortune* article from October 19, 2017, by Martin Reeves entitled "In Search of 'Vital' Companies." Read Reeves's article and review *Fortune*'s top 50 U.S. company vitality rankings.

  a. Critique the rankings. Any surprises? What conclusions can be drawn about the role of strategy in helping firms foster vitality?
  b. Reeves notes that the Future 50 is not a crystal ball. Effective strategy does not always follow precedents or aggregate patterns. Circumstances change, and good strategies can be undermined by better ones or by poor decisions. What advice would you give the CEO of a company that is a market share leader but whose overall profits and financial performance are poor?

Source: Reeves, Martin. "In Search of 'Vital' Companies." *Fortune*, October 19, 201: 44–45

---

a   Reeves, Martin. "In Search of 'Vital' Companies." *Fortune*, October 19, 2017: 44

3. ASSESSING CORPORATE-LEVEL STRATEGY: GE/MCKINSEY SPOTLIGHT MATRIX

Corporate-level strategy is primarily concerned with identifying the industry or industries in which the firm will complete. One of the earliest, and still one of the most popular, analytical tools for assessing industry attractiveness at the corporate level is the GE/McKinsey's **spotlight framework** or nine-cell matrix. As of 2016, GE operates in the following business segments: aviation, digital, energy connections, global research, health care, lighting, oil and gas, power, renewable energy, transportation, financial services, medical devices, life sciences, pharmaceutical, automotive, software development, and engineering.[6] How do a company's managers, specifically its corporate-level managers, determine what industries in which it will compete? The GE/McKinsey nine-box matrix is a strategy tool that offers a systematic approach for the multibusiness corporation to prioritize its investments among its business units.[7] McKinsey recommends that GE create **strategic business units** (SBUs) that report directly to GE's corporate-level managers. McKinsey also recommends the development of **investment priority screens** that will be used to review the performance of each business and determine an appropriate investment strategy for SBUs (see Exhibit 6.1: GE/McKinsey Spotlight Matrix).

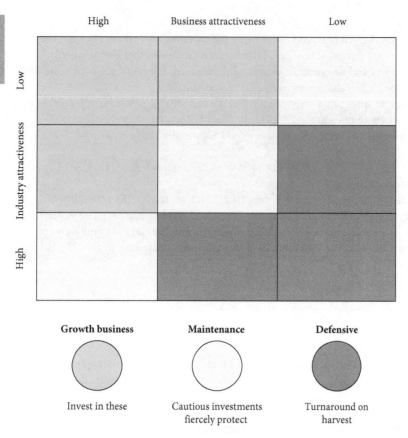

Exhibit 6.1 GE/McKinsey Spotlight Matrix

High   Business attractiveness   Low

Industry attractiveness — Low / High

Growth business

Invest in these

Maintenance

Cautious investments
fiercely protect

Defensive

Turnaround on
harvest

Source: Michael J. Merenda; Adapted from: *McKinsey Quarterly* September 2008

"Enduring Ideas: The GE–McKinsey nine-box matrix:" at: https://www.mckinsey.com/business-functions/
strategy-and-corporate-finance/our-insights/enduring-ideas-the-ge-and-mckinsey-nine-box-matrix

3.1 STEPS IN CONDUCTING A SPOTLIGHT ANALYSIS

Step 1:   Identify businesses for strategic review by corporate-level managers (see Table 6.1 Opal's Pearl Brewery: Product Categories).

Step 2:   Conduct an external situational analysis of the industries and markets in which the business competes.

Step 3:   Assign a weight (.01, not important, to 1.0, very important) and value (1, not attractive, to 5, highly attractive) to each of the most important driving forces and factors. Calculate an overall industry attractiveness score (see Table 6.1a below).

Step 4:   Conduct an internal situational analysis of competitive intensity factors for each business. For each business, compare its competitive intensity factors to those of its rivals. These include:

- Price
- Market share
- Place or distribution channels (internet, whole, retail, private label, etc.)
- Product breadth (models offered)

- Product quality
- Continuous product and process innovation
- Technology development
- Design and style
- Advertising and promotion
- Use of celebrity endorsements
- Free shipping, rebates, and delivery time
- Logistics and supply chain management

Step 5:   Assign a weight (.01, not important, to 1.0, very important) and value (1, not attractive, to 5, highly attractive) to each of the most important competitive intensity factors. Calculate an overall business attractiveness score (again, see Table 6.1b).

Step 6:   Position each business in the nine-cell matrix according to its overall score on its business attractiveness and industry attractiveness scores.

Step 7:   Draw conclusions. Based on the overall scores and position in the matrix, determine the appropriate investment strategy according to its color: green, yellow, or red light.

A. *Green light or aggressive position*: Businesses designated high on both business and industry attractiveness. Invest in these businesses; offensive strategic actions are recommended.

B. *Yellow light or conservative and maintenance positions*: High on business attractiveness but low on industry attractiveness. These businesses can usually represent the complete spectrum of investment strategies, such as market penetration and development (offensive strategy). Rigorously defend current position, and selectively harvest (defensive strategy). A yellow light indicates proceed with caution because the investment strategy or industry attractiveness and business attractiveness are uncertain (see Exhibit 6.2: GE Spotlight Example—Opal's Pearl Brewery).

C. *Red light or defensive position*: Businesses that are in undesirable strategic positions on the matrix (low industry and low business attractiveness) and require a divestment or turnaround investment decision.

Step 8:   Execution. Business managers are charged by corporate-level managers to implement the recommended course of action. At GE, managers' compensation is partially based on performance; that is, how they execute the given set of investment strategies. At GE, performance screens are also used in developing individualized appraisal systems. The appraisal system reflects the differences in strategic actions required for each set of recommendations (individualized evaluations and performance screens that underlie each type of strategic action: green, yellow, and red light positions). Each position requires a different set of strategies and corresponding managerial skills and expertise.

Step 9:   Strategic follow-up and continuous assessment. The spotlight approach to strategic management is a continuous process requiring constant corporate-level strategic appraisal and assessment of the industry attractiveness, business attractiveness, and business-level managers' effectiveness in carrying out the recommended strategy.

Table 6.1 Opal's Pearl Brewing— Craft Brewers Industry	Five Product Categories*	Business Score	Industry Score
	A – Unicorn Blond	2.76	3.62
	B – Marshmallow IPA	4.2	4.0
	C – Strawberry Larger	1.5	2.0
	D – Red Apple Hard Cider	3.0	3.0
	E – Cotton Candy Nitro	5.0	2.0

*B,C, D, & E Scores Given—Not Shown

Example: Business Attractiveness Score For Unicorn Blown

Table 6.1a Industry Attractiveness	Unicorn Blown		
	Weight	Value	Score
Industry Growth Rate	0.3	5	1.5
Industry Life Cycle	0.2	4	0.8
Threat of New Entrants	0.2	2	0.4
Power of Buyers	0.8	5	4
Power of Suppliers	3	5	15
Rivalry Intensity	0.6	2	12
Threat of Substitute Products	0.3	2	0.6
Complements	0.7	5	3.5
PESTEL	0.8	7	5.6
I			**3.622**

Table 6.1b Business Attractiveness	Unicorn Blown		
Industry Attractiveness			
Beara Irish Beer	**Weight**	**Value**	**Score**
Price	0.5	5	2.5
Market Share	0.7	2	1.4
Product Quality	0.4	5	2
Product Depth	0.4	2	0.8
Innovation	1	5	5
Logistics Input	0.6	4	2.4
Logistics Output	0.7	5	3.5
Marketing/Promotion	0.9	5	4.5
Overall Average Score			**2.7625**

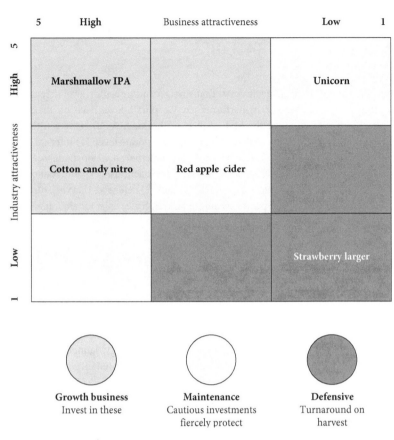

Source: Michael J. Merenda: Adapted from *McKinsey Quarterly* September 2008

"Enduring Ideas: The GE–McKinsey nine-box matrix:" at: https://www.
mckinsey.com/business-functions/strategy-and-corporate-finance/our-insights/
enduring-ideas-the-ge-and-mckinsey-nine-box-matrix

3.2 ADVANTAGES OF DOING A SPOTLIGHT ANALYSIS[8]

- Aids in prioritizing the limited resources in order to achieve the best returns
- Managers become more aware of how their products or business units perform
- More sophisticated business portfolio framework than the BCG matrix
- Identifies the strategic steps the company must take to improve the performance of its business portfolio

3.3 DISADVANTAGES OF SPOTLIGHT ANALYSIS

- Requires a consultant or a highly experienced person to determine the industry's attractiveness and business unit strength as accurately as possible
- Costly to conduct
- Does not take into account the synergies that could exist between two or more business units

4. TYPES OF CORPORATE-LEVEL STRATEGIES: ALTERNATIVE INVESTMENT STRATEGIES

Numerous investment strategies exist that a board and/or senior-level managers can make at the corporate level to improve a firm's long-term performance. Corporate-level decision making requires strategic thinking and in-depth critical inquiry at the highest level of thinking. As discussed in the spotlight matrix analysis, two essential elements of strategy making occur at the corporate level: (1) internal situational analyses of strengths and attractiveness of the firm's businesses and (2) an external situational analysis of industry or attractiveness. Gupta and others identify three broad categories of strategic actions: (1) maintenance (hold or continue as strategies); (2) offensive (build or aggressive grow strategies); and (3) defensive (harvest, turnaround, or sell strategies)[9] For each of these overall investment positions, numerous strategies exist for a company to consider.

4.1 MAINTENANCE OR CONTINUE AS IS STRATEGIES

A maintenance strategy is best pursued when a firm's current strategies are working and pass the VIRO test. A maintenance strategy is usually recommended when: (1) a firm's competitive markets are relatively predictable or stable; (2) the firm has an acceptable or desired position in markets; or (3) the competitive environment is so uncertain or unpredictable that altering current strategies would prove extremely risky and costly. Southwest Airlines's highly successful and consistent low-cost strategy, launched in the early 1970s in the fiercely competitive airline industry, is an example of a successful maintenance strategy. Alternative maintenance strategies include *profit focus*, *stabilize*, and *proceed with caution*.

Continue As Is. This position requires little or no change to the firm's current set of strategies for green light businesses. The existing strategies are working extremely well and a VIRO test for the business or product shows a superior competitive advantage that is sustainable over the foreseeable future. Companies that are well-positioned in highly attractive industries to influence and exploit its favorable condition should continue with existing strategies.

Profit Focus. A short-term, profit-oriented strategy is usually associated with businesses or products that are in the mature, slow, or no-growth stage of its life cycle. The strategist's objective is to maximize profits in the short term so it can pursue more profitable strategies long-term. A short-term, profit-focused strategy is recommended for yellow-positioned businesses. For example, cigarette companies face stiff government regulation and are at the mature stage in their industry life cycle. Because of this, these companies should pursue profit-focused strategies by drastically curtailing advertising and promotion, reducing sales and operating staff, and depleting inventories.

Stabilize. These businesses are in the enviable position of achieving rapid growth with their present or current strategies at the expense of profits or profitless growth. Examples include the prompt success of many person-to-person (trust-based) social network companies like Uber and Airbnb. Although these entities have experienced rapid growth, they also have generated little to no profit. Under such situations, these businesses begin guaranteeing product deliveries and services but are unable to deliver on time as promised because they try to meet demand as quickly as possible without managing costs and expenses. For example, though Tesla Motors has assisted in fostering a significant growth in demand for electric vehicles, it consistently posts net losses and constantly revises production forecasts. (Tesla's lower-priced Model X SUV is more than two years behind its scheduled launch.)

Proceed with Caution. Although current strategies are considered appropriate, the uncertainty in predicting future industry trends or impact of competitive intensity factors in the external environment puts the business in a maintenance or conservative investment position. The recommended strategy is proceed "as is" with caution until new and sufficient information can be gained or the uncertainty facing the industry has been clarified.

4.2 OFFENSIVE OR "GROWTH" STRATEGIES

Offensive strategies are most appropriate when the business is positioned to take advantage of very favorable industry forces and markets. The VIRO test for these businesses supports a superior and sustainable competitive advantage. The industry's competitive forces and overall attractiveness, and the businesses' position in the industry, are also highly attractive. Favorable industry attractiveness and a VIRO test for the business support an aggressive offensive growth strategy. For example, when Microsoft acquired Nokia, in 2013 it was adopting an offensive strategy. Microsoft expected that the combined companies would be better able to compete, first by pooling resources and second by immediately increasing market share. However, in July 2015, Microsoft admitted failure of the Nokia acquisition and wrote-off $7.6 billion.[10] When Groupe Danone, a major French food company, purchased Stonyfield Farm's yogurt, it was not only adding a new line of organic yogurts to its existing line of dairy products, but it was also increasing market share across several international markets.

Horizontal Integration. Horizontal integration is undertaken when a firm acquires or merges with a company (former rival) that sells similar products or services. Horizontal integration is an inorganic growth strategy because it adds products or markets from former rivals through acquisition.

Vertical Integration. Vertical integration is aimed at increased control over either a former supplier or customer.

Forward Integration. Forward integration occurs when a company acquires or buys a present customer (e.g., Google's acquisition of YouTube). Shortly after the Justice Department unsuccessful attempt to block AT&T merger with Time Warner in federal anti-trust proceedings, AT&T announced in June 2018, it had completed its $85.4 billion merger Time Warner. The merger gave AT&T, Time Warner's vast media and entertainment portfolio including HBO and CNN, rights to major sports leagues and valuable film franchises such as "Harry Potter."[11]

Backward Integration. Backward integration occurs when a firm buys or acquires a former supplier (e.g., Yahoo!'s acquisition of Maven Networks, a supplier of internet video players and video advertising tools for approximately $160 million).

Market Penetration. This strategy is aimed at increased market share by means of selling more of the same products to existing customers or taking market share from competitors. Apple's joint venture with IBM is an example of Apple's attempt to grow the sale of smartphones and other devices to large corporate customers.

Market Development. This strategy calls for marketing existing products to new geographic markets or new segments or niches within existing markets. For example, Google's announcement that it is investigating the development of an all-electric, driverless vehicle (if it comes to fruition) would be both a market development and new product development strategy.

Product Development. This strategy aims at increasing sales by modifying or improving existing products and services. Apple's introduction of the iWatch, Google's launch of Google Glass and Google Mini, and Green Mountain's introduction of Keurig Gold Drink Maker are examples of product development strategies.

Concentric Diversification. Concentric diversification occurs when a company adds new but related products to its existing product offerings. Google's expansion into Google Glass, electric vehicles, and satellite communications are examples of concentric diversification because these entities propagate Google's Android operating system and other software apps across an array of product platforms and customer markets.

Conglomerate Integration. Growth can also be achieved through conglomerate integration, which is the acquisition of completely unrelated products or services. Berkshire Hathaway, GE, Siemens, Tyco International, and United Technologies are examples of companies known for

VIDEO 6.2 Google Buys YouTube for $1.6B: CBS News

VIDEO 6.3 AT&T-Time Warner Leading to Future Media Deals?

their conglomerate strategies. Conglomerate strategies provide growth opportunities while lowering or spreading business and systems risk across several industries and markets. Corporate-level conglomerate strategies are analogous to investment strategies that focus on index mutual funds.

Joint Ventures. Joint ventures occur when a business elects to work with another business on special projects or investment opportunities. For example, Tesla Motors and Mercedes-Benz teamed up in a joint venture to develop the next generation of electric vehicles. Tesla also formed a joint venture with Panasonic to develop large-scale manufacturing of lithium-ion batteries.

Concentration Strategies. Concentration strategies are adopted when a company concentrates all its resources on a particular product, market, or technology. For example, Southwest and Jet Blue are examples of airline companies pursuing this type of strategy by focusing entirely on becoming lower-cost airlines.

4.3 DEFENSIVE STRATEGIES

Defensive strategies are associated with poor industry attractiveness and poor business attractiveness. A VIRO test shows that the business' strategies are vulnerable and not sustainable. Because the business faces such an unfavorable situation, it must take decisive and critical action to reverse it. If the business cannot alter the unfavorable situation, then it must be harvested, liquidated, or divested. No new investments will be made in these businesses. Any funds earned from harvesting, selling, or liquidating the business now become available for investments in green- or yellow-positioned businesses. For example, GE's decision to spin off its GE Capital business, though profitable, was based on the company's need for other investment opportunities. Examples of defensive strategies include *turnaround*, *harvest or exit*, and *divest or sell*.

Turnaround. A turnaround strategy is adopted when a business holds value but is experiencing poor performance. It must be "turned around" from the unprofitable or less-than-desirable situation to a profitable or more desired position. Furthermore, the present or near-term financial prospects for the business require an immediate strategic action. In a turnaround situation, the business manager is faced with: (1) a current downturn or slump in its market or industry condition, though a more favorable market is forecasted or (2) is currently poorly positioned to capitalize on existing industry attractiveness, though it has a good chance of reversing its placement. For instance, in 2012, Yahoo!'s CEO Melissa Mayer was appointed in an effort to alter the company's troubled online-ad business. Failure to do so resulted in Yahoo!'s acquisition by Verizon.

Harvest or Exit. Harvest strategies are advised when the business is underperforming and competing in mature or declining industries or markets. Both industry and business attractiveness are so unfavorable that corporate management has no choice but to disengage from the troubled business.

Spin-off or Divest. Spin-off or divestment strategies take place when a company's directors decide to sell (or spin off) an existing business or product. This strategy is required when:

- A change occurs in the overall corporate mission of the firm (e.g., the business no longer "fits" with the mission of the firm)
- Funds and additional resources are needed to devote to growth businesses
- Limited financial resources exist at the corporate or firm level (e.g., the business must be sacrificed because the immediate cash it can generate through its sale is needed for the survival of the firm)
- The market value of the business is greater than its book value

Liquidation. A liquidation strategy is adopted when a business faces such poor financial health that it has no tangible or intangible valuable assets to attract potential suitors. Furthermore, the overall expectations for the business are so dire that its chances for survival are extremely low. As such, the business's assets or market value is so minimal that it must be sold at a loss or "liquidated" (e.g., closed immediately with the assets retired or sold at auction to the highest bidder, usually at a fraction of their book value).

In 2006, Google bought YouTube for $1.65 billion. That figure at the time was an outrageous sum to pay for a startup only 18 months-old. Some analysts and competitors said Google overpaid. Mark Cuban noted the search giant was "crazy" to take on YouTube's many legal liabilities. Google itself later acknowledged that YouTube wasn't worth anywhere near the price tag at the time of the acquisition.

A decade later, however, the YouTube buy is widely considered to be one of the best consumer tech acquisitions ever. Other acquisitions, such as Yahoo! scooping up Flickr and Google's $50 million acquisition of Android in 2005, also are considered among the best attainments. The difference for Google's acquisition of Android was that, at that time, no one outside Silicon Valley knew what Android was. YouTube was already world-famous when Google snapped it up, and its price tag according to some analysts was ridiculous by conventional standards. It was one of the first wild bets a tech giant made following the dot-com crash.

Using commonly considered alternatives as a reference, what type(s) of strategic action was Google pursuing with its acquisition of YouTube? What type of strategic action was its acquisition of Android? Why would a search engine company—whose revenue model is based on advertising revenue—want to get into other businesses and markets?

Source: Luckerson, Hugo. "A Decade Ago, Google Bought YouTube—and It Was the Best Tech Deal Ever." *The Ringer*. October 10, 2016. Accessed March 28, 2017: https://www.theringer.com/2016/10/10/16042354/google-youtube-acquisition-10-years-tech-deals-69fdbe1c8a06

5. RADICALLY INCLUSIVE STRATEGIC THINKING IN A DIGITAL WORLD

Advances in technology have altered the dynamics of well-established companies and industries by completely changing how the rules of the game are played and by creating entirely new industries. Whether it was the advent of the telescope, steam power, electricity, the light bulb, the telephone, the microprocessor, the automobile, the computer, the internet, or the smartphone, technology has a way of sneaking up on and displacing conventional thinking, industry attractiveness, and business competitiveness.

What makes today's technology revolution different from previous technological revolutions (see: Exhibit 3.2 Radically Inclusive Thinking)? First, rapid advances in **telecommunications** and **information technology** (referred to in this chapter as the **digital world**) drive it. Accelerated technological growth stems from advances in telecommunication networks, microprocessors (chips), sensors, and software development (operating systems and applications). Second, the digital revolution's growth has demonstrated **pervasiveness** across all industries, sectors of the economy, and country borders. In other words, it is a global phenomenon. Third, it has spread quickly as a result of a drastic drop in the cost of telecommunication networks, network devices (any device that connects to networks), and network products and services. Fourth, rapid infusion and diffusion of digital technologies has disrupted and **destabilized industries' boundaries** as well as relationships between the firm and its rivals, suppliers, and customers (an industry's supply chain or value-generating network). Lastly, this digital revolution has enabled firms to problem solve, continuously innovate, and upgrade capabilities (deep data analytics, artificial intelligence, automation, enhanced learning communities, etc.).

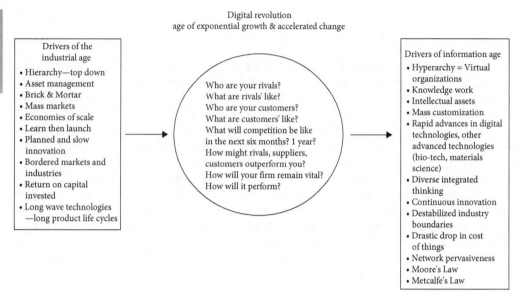

**Exhibit 6.3
Radically
Inclusive
Thinking**

Digital revolution
age of exponential growth & accelerated change

Drivers of the
industrial age

• Hierarchy—top down
• Asset management
• Brick & Mortar
• Mass markets
• Economies of scale
• Learn then launch
• Planned and slow
  innovation
• Bordered markets and
  industries
• Return on capital
  invested
• Long wave technologies
  —long product life cycles

Who are your rivals?
What are rivals' like?
Who are your customers?
What are customers' like?
What will competition be like
in the next six months? 1 year?
How might rivals, suppliers,
customers outperform you?
How will your firm remain vital?
How will it perform?

Drivers of information age

• Hyperarchy = Virtual
  organizations
• Knowledge work
• Intellectual assets
• Mass customization
• Rapid advances in digital
  technologies, other
  advanced technologies
  (bio-tech, materials
  science)
• Diverse integrated
  thinking
• Continuous innovation
• Destabilized industry
  boundaries
• Drastic drop in cost
  of things
• Network pervasiveness
• Moore's Law
• Metcalfe's Law

*The Internet is a petri dish for innovation. Advances in mobile technology, super chips, nano technology, broadband, the "invisible"
Internet, and information technologies will create whole new industries and the rapid rise and demise of organizations. Only those
strategic managers who can think clearly, master creative destruction, and lead their organizations through continuous change and
transformations will succeed in the new. It inside the box, out side the box and where is no box at all strategic thinking.*

Source: Michael J. Merenda

5.1 RAPID ADVANCES IN DIGITAL TECHNOLOGIES

Advances in telecommunications and information technology, artificial intelligence, automation, robotics, sensors, nanotechnology, material science, software, and integrated networks have ushered in a new digital world. Development in digital and related technologies has accelerated the **rate of change** and reinvented **ways of doing business**. Over the past 10 years, firms have witnessed an exponential growth in digital technologies, especially information technologies, telecommunications, and the rise of the integrated internet. The internet has since become more valuable as the number of nodes (N) connecting to it has increased. **Metcalfe's Law** states that where N is the number of nodes, the power of the network is N squared (N^n).[12] If you double the number of nodes, you quadruple the overall value of the network. The network gets more valuable to each user as new users join. The explosive growth in business-to-business networks (B2B), business-to-consumer networks (B2C), person-to-person social networks (P2P), and the internet of things have all dramatically increased a network's power and value. The **internet of things** is commonly defined as the network of physical devices, vehicles, home appliances, and other items embedded with electronics, software, sensors, actuators, artificial intelligence (AI), virtual network connectivity-enabled devices, and individuals connected to exchange data and information.

Further expanding the scalability and value of the internet and digital technologies has been the durability of the principles that underlie **Moore's Law**. Gordon Moore, Intel's co-founder, first published what later became known as "Moore's Law" in a 1965 *Electronics Magazine* article entitled "Cramming More Components onto Integrated Circuits."[13] He predicted that the performance capacity of the microprocessor (computer) would double and the cost of manufacturing the microprocessor with be cut in half every two years. Moore's prediction has held true since it was first proposed, paralleling the rapid growth of the mini computer and workstations in the late 1960s and 1970s, followed by the explosive growth of the mini and personal computer in the 1980s and 1990s, as well as the integrated internet, cloud technologies, and other digital devices and advances in the 2000s and 2010s. Today, Moore's Law has become known as the "law of **exponential growth**" or the "law of **accelerating change**."[14] The emergence and exponential growth of high technology, telecommunications, media and publishers, e-commerce, social networks, and other supporting and relating industries (as a result of the dramatic growth of digital technologies) have infinitely increased the power and value of today's integrated network.

5.2 NETWORK PERVASIVENESS

In 1969, the internet attained 50 million users, and its usage has doubled every year since. By 2014, the number of internet hosts (websites) passed 1 billion. By 2016, the networking giant Cisco estimated that global internet traffic surpassed 1 zettabyte (1 trillion gigabytes).[15] In 2017, the number of Facebook users surpassed 2 billion, doubling the 1 billion it had in 2012.[16] In today's world, any individual who possesses access to the internet can start a global business, teleshop, telebank, teledesign, telemanufacturer, teleteach, or telecommute. The accelerated growth experienced in the network and digital technologies traverses all industries, economic sectors, national borders, and company functions. In short, it is astronomically persuasive.

Unlike other technology revolutions, the digital revolution is both a factor of production (input) and a specific product or service (output). As an **input**, digital technologies are capable of revolutionizing production, manufacturing systems, and processes. Advances in computer technologies (speed, storage, killer apps), sensors, storage/memory, automation, artificial intelligence, and robotics have changed the very way work is organized and performed. It has also transformed manufacturing, design, engineering, and other scientific and professional services, jobs, and activities. Revolutions in technology have also altered how products and services are distributed and channeled through the supply chain, oftentimes displacing intermediaries and traditional brick-and-mortar entities. Significant decreases in the cost of digital technologies have also greatly reduced procurement, transaction, transmission, and processing costs (across all firm functions), while decreases in factor cost (inputs) have increased the added value and productivity of firms.

Digital technologies have spawned the accelerated growth in globalization, global strategy, the flattening of organizational structures, rise in big data and data analytics, mass customization of products and services, and host of lean, agile, and sustainable business practices. Digital technologies have not only forged intra- and interfirm collaboration but also accelerated the growth in insourcing, outsourcing and offshoring (see chapter 5). These technological advances have changed how people work, communicate, learn, think, find jobs, and socialize.

As an **output**, digital technologies have generated entirely new industries and services. In many cases, it has enabled companies to introduce next-generation products or services, enhancing their ability to sustain competitive advantages and continuously improve performance. For example, Walmart has been able to gain a competitive advantage and become the largest global company in terms of total sales as a result of its information superiority and use of digital technologies. Walmart was one of the first companies to use point-of-sale digital systems, its own private satellite network, and digital technologies to work with suppliers, forecast sales trends, manage supplier relationships, monitor store operations, schedule pickup and deliveries of goods to and from stores, and promote online retail.

In other instances, digital technologies as an output have created countless innovative products and services that **disrupt** or displace companies unwilling or unable to change. A firm's inability to demonstrate agility and adaptation in changing environments brought about by accelerated growth in digital technologies will greatly hinder its survival. Amazon, Google, Facebook, Apple, and other high-technology companies have disrupted and changed the nature of competition across numerous industries. In many cases, altering the nature of competition has forced many traditional brick-and-mortar and traditional service and manufacturing businesses to either adapt how they do business or close (see Exhibit 6.4: Rate of Change, Agility, and Adaptation). Increasingly, human adaptability lags behind the pace of Societal change in an age of exponential growth and accelerated change. Closing the human adaptability and rate of change gap requires faster and continuous learning, resilience and agility.

Exhibit 6.4
Rate of Change, Agility, and Adaptation

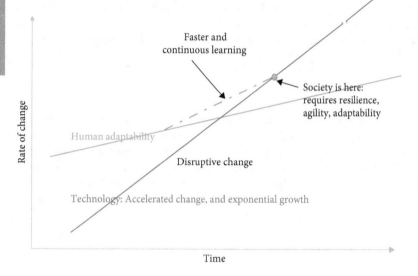

Source: Michael Merenda 2018; Adapted from: Friedman, Thomas, *Thank You For Being Late, Picador*, 2016:p 29–37; Friedman describes the presentation and graphical illustration of Eric "Astro" Teller, CEO of Google's X research and development lab. Teller's graph showed the impact of accelerated growth and society's constant challenge to adapt to this change. Teller graphical presentation highlights the gap between accelerated change and human adaptability.

Thinking Critically Exercise 47

FCC VOTES TO DISMANTLE NET-NEUTRALITY RULES

In December 2017, the Federal Communications Commission (FCC) voted to significantly curtail the Obama administration's far-reaching rules governing net neutrality. The administration required broadband providers to treat all internet traffic equally, without blocking or slowing content, or providing fast lanes for favored sites and services. FCC's net-neutrality rollback is expected to benefit cable and wireless providers and transform consumers' online experiences. Advocates of the rollback argue that the shift will unwind what they consider to be a regulatory overreach, restoring vitality to the broadband economy and benefiting consumers with more choices and lower prices. Under the new ruling, internet service providers such as Comcast, Verizon Communications, T-Mobile, and others would be free to implement big changes like offering new packages with pricing schemes that deliver some kinds of content but not others. One type of service that could proliferate in the new regime is zero-rating deals, where specific websites or services are exempted from a mobile carrier's data caps.

Opponents of the rollback view a tightly regulated, open internet as a powerful force for democracy and opportunity. They argue that the change threatens to hit consumers with higher prices and to Balkanize the internet.

a. What is net neutrality?
b. What is the potential impact of the rollback on the Obama administration's net-neutrality regulation on ISP telecommunication companies such as Verizon, AT&T, Sprint, T-Mobile, etc.?

c. How will the new net neutrality rules affect content providers such as Time Warner, Disney, and Comcast?

d. How will the FCC's ruling on net neutrality affect sellers of smartphones? How will net-neutrality rules affect you?

e. How might the internet of things change after net neutrality is repealed? Could websites be slower? Blocked?

Source: McKinnon, John D. "FCC Votes to Dismantle Net-Neutrality Rules." *Wall Street Journal,* Dec. 14, 2017. https://www.wsj.com/articles/fcc-readies-unwinding-of-net-neutrality-regime-1513247401.

5.3 DRASTIC DROP IN THE COST OF THINGS

The true measure of the acceptance and impact of any new technology is the drastic cost in either developing the technology or acquiring it. A rapid drop in cost of a technology is also a measure of the speed in which the technology is used within and across industries. Compared to previous technology introductions, the pace at which digital technology cost, acceptance, and use as a factor in input and output has proved staggering. No other technology revolution has experienced the exponential growth, accelerated change, and increased value added as seen today. For example, the cost of steam power generation was not all that much cheaper than waterpower. In real terms, steam power cost barely changed between the 1790s and 1830s. It was not until 1850 that its cost decreased by half. Additionally, it took another 40 years (from 1890 to 1930) for the cost of electricity to decrease by half. In comparison, the cost of computer processing power has declined 30 percent per year in real terms over the past two decades. As a comparison, if cars had developed at the same pace of the microprocessor, they would cost $5 and get 250,000 miles per gallon. Today's iPhone has more computer power than the first lunar landing craft did in 1969. As such, a $300 smartphone is many times more powerful than a 1970s $10 million mainframe.

The accelerated and drastic drop in the cost in digital technologies has propagated its rapid infusion and diffusion across industries and firms, as well as organizational and national borders. For instance, in the 1860s, it cost £1 per word to send a transatlantic message from London to the United States. In 1960, a transatlantic telephone cable could carry only 138 conversations simultaneously. By the mid-1980s, with the introduction of the fiber optic cable, 1.5 million conversations could be carried at once. Today's fiber optic cable is the diameter of a human hair and can carry 153 years of telephone conversations simultaneously.

Digital technology's rapid decline in cost has accelerated the growth of globalization and the rise of high-technology companies and rivals in developed, emerging, and newly emerging or developing countries worldwide. In 2016, the top five nations with the most internet users (in millions of users and as a percent of the total worldwide users) were: China, 657.7 (19.9 percent of worldwide users), India, 326.4 (9.86 percent), United States, 289.5 (8.75 percent), Brazil, 123.0 (3.72 percent), and Japan, 111.9 (3.38 percent).[17] Interestingly, in 2014, the tiny country of Estonia became the first nation in the world to offer noncitizens e-residency in the form of a government-issued transnational digital identity.[18] In 2016, the top five nations with the highest percentage of their population using the internet were: Iceland (98.40 percent), Liechtenstein (98.90 percent), Bahrain (98.00 percent), Andorra (97.93 percent), and Luxembourg (97.49 percent).[19] Surprisingly, the United States was not listed in even the top 20 nations for internet use.[20]

In short, the drastic drop in digital technology's costs have, in turn, decreased the cost of business operations and exponentially increased the functionality and carrying capacity of networks creating customer value creation opportunities for firms. These opportunities include rapid growth in globally integrated internet; internet devices; and internet services such as computers, smartphones, internet devices (Xbox, digital TVs), search engines, digital content, mobile advertising, video cases, and a host of other technology-related products and services.

5.4 DESTABILIZED INDUSTRY BOUNDARIES[21]

One of the biggest challenges faced by corporate strategists today is the degree to which a firm can exploit the accelerated growth in digital technologies and gain a competitive advantage. The business press is littered with the obituaries of companies that have failed to effectively compete in today's rapidly changing environment. Digital and other advanced technologies are destabilizing the relationship of the firm between its rivals, customers, and suppliers. This disruption has also accelerated the erosion of formerly distinct boundaries, thus radically altering the manner in which firms conduct business. Exhibit 6.5: Technology Impact on Market Erosion and Relationships examines the different types of change on industry relationships.

Quadrant A: Quiescent. Quadrant A represents a quiescent or quiet (steady) state where the boundaries between the firm and its rivals, customers, and suppliers are fixed. Thus, the competitive environment is relatively stable. Industry change is incremental or evolutionary within its boundaries. As such, each player (firm, rival, customer, supplier) has the capability to adjust or adapt to change in a timely manner. Any technology advances have capacity to sustain (not disrupt) the firm's rivals' and suppliers' business models. Any variations to the customers' value propositions remain relatively slow and predicable.

Quadrant B: Prospecting. This stage depicts a situation where an industry's competitive dynamics are "heating up" and being steered in accordance with technological advances. Technology in this stage acts as a catalyst for softening an industry's boundaries, though its boundaries remain relatively fixed and clear. The firm's relationship to its customers, rivals, and suppliers remains relatively predictable, though new relationships are emerging. Although industry change is still incremental, the pace and frequency of change is starting to accelerate. Any technological change is sustainable in the short term for the firm and its rivals and suppliers. Change to customer value creation proposition is in its incipient or early stage. Firms, rivals, and suppliers should start prospecting for innovation and upgrade in capabilities. Customer switching cost remains relatively high, but advances in digital product and technologies are starting to decrease the cost to change over.

Quadrant C: Agitation. This stage reflects an increased agitation or the "stirring up" of industry dynamics and relationships. Advances in technology are also starting to "heat up" at a more accelerated pace. Change is no longer incremental but rather borders on revolutionary. Industry boundaries are fading fast. Firms', rivals', and customers' once stable relationships are no longer clear (that is, becoming blurred), forcing each player to seek new opportunities to move into another's space. Suppliers may move laterally forward as they are no longer a subcontract but a rival. Customers may move laterally backward, no longer a customer but a new rival. The firm itself may also move laterally into adjacent industries, becoming a rival to its former suppliers and customers. Finally, other rivals may make similar lateral strategic moves in not only their own industry but the industries of their suppliers and customers as well. Change is beginning to disrupt industry dynamics and firm, rival, supplier, and customer relationships. Revolutionary alteration is drastically reshaping the industry's competitive dynamics. Firms, rivals, and suppliers pursue both inorganic and organic growth opportunities inside and outside their traditional industries. Customer value creation models are also rapidly evolving, permitting customers to have more choice and greater value creation opportunities.

Quadrant D: Turbulence. This stage reflects a highly chaotic and turbulent environment. Exponential technological growth and accelerated change has stirred up the agitation stage to such a degree that radical inclusive thinking is becoming the predominant environmental paradigm and mental model. The pace of change has also "heated up" to the point where change is no longer discrete and evolutionary but rather quantum

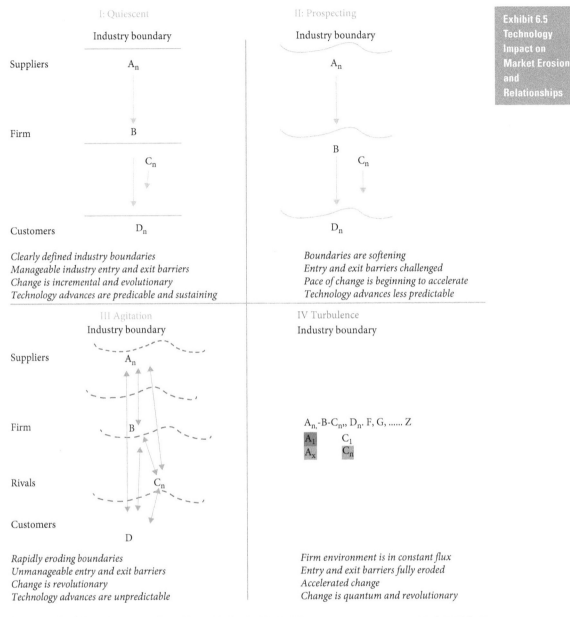

Source: Michael Merenda; Adapted from: Manley Rutherford Irwin. *Telecommunications America: Markets Without Boundaries* Westport, Conn. : Quorum Books, 1984; and. Manley R. Irwin and Michael J. Merenda, "Corporate Networks, Privatization and State Sovereignty: pending issues for the1990s?' *Telecommunications Policy*, Vol 13, No 4, December 1989, p 332.

and revolutionary. Consequentially, the firm's competitive environment remains in constant flux. Industry boundaries are no longer clear. Firms, rivals, and suppliers find it extremely difficult to maintain or erect barriers to prevent entry or defend current positions. Firms, rivals, and suppliers also find themselves in hypercompetition with each other, from others outside, as well as those from adjacent or even distant industries. In this final stage, emergence players and industries have now replaced what were once separate and distinct industries and relationships. Power has shifted to customers, who have access to digital and other advanced technologies, products, and services that enhance purchasing power and increase value creation opportunities (see Exhibit 6.6 Change, Ideals, and Radically Inclusive Thinking).

Exhibit 6.6
Change, Ideas,
and Radically
Inclusive
Thinking

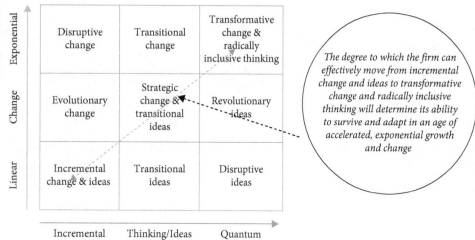

Source: Michael Merenda, 2018; adapted from Noel M. Tichy and Stratford Sherman, *Control Your Destiny or Someone Else Will: How Jack Welch is Making General Electric the World's Most Competitive Company*, New York, Doubleday 1993: 326: Also see Ibid, Noel M. Tichy, "Handbook for Revolutionaries," pp303–373.

In sum, technological advances in digital technologies have increasingly softened clear-cut distinctions between firms, rivals, suppliers, and customers across several industries, including financial technologies (fintech); banking (bitcoins); brokerage (online and high-speed trading); retailing (e-commerce); manufacturing (industrial internet, online collaborative networks); advertising (mobile advertising); media and content (digital content); education (online courses and content); publishing (digital content); music (web service); photography (digital devices); and a host of others. For example, in the computer industry, 70 percent of the industry's sales now come from products introduced to the market in the past two years. Amazon completely revolutionized the way business is conducted in the retail industry. The online giant not only changed the rules of the game but also all but eliminated third-party intermediaries, threatening the very existence of brick-and-mortar shopping malls. Additionally, the acquisition of Whole Foods by Amazon and the merger of Aetna and CVS are just two examples of unlikely partners coming together and simultaneously changing long-standing relationships between firms, rivals, suppliers, and customers.

In 2015, PWC Auto Industry Trend reported that several movements were reshaping the automobile industry, including shifts in consumer demand, expanded regulatory requirements, and increasing availability of data and information. Regarding the first major trend, PWC states that consumers appeared to be rethinking their long love affair with individual automobile brands, instead opting to view cars more as transportation machines.[22] This swing in consumer behavior began to affect how much buyers were willing to pay for their automobiles given that brand differentiation and quality were rapidly converging. This trend impacted consumers' purchasing decisions by devaluing brand differentiation. Consequentially, consumers began to demand the more sophisticated infotainment systems and features (standard on high-priced models) at a lower cost.

The PWC also notes that consumers are inundated with easily accessible information about automobile specifications, prices, discounts, quality, and performance, giving buyers greater bargaining power. These trends caused rivals to pour money into software, services, electric vehicles, and other game-changing technologies. Driving the industry's transformation were several radical technological, political, and social factors including internet manufacturing, all-electric vehicles, driverless cars, and the internet of things.[23] Business models more representative of high-technology software companies have started to upstage and challenge traditional auto companies and their once stable business models. Examples of outside industry rivals developing their own versions of next-generation all-electric vehicles include Tesla, Google, Apple, Amazon, Uber, as well as several other high-tech software and technology companies. All these new rivals engaged in the radical redesign of the transportation industry seek to install driverless cars and trucks as the transportation mode of the future. And these companies continue to challenge traditional carmakers by racing to cement the all-electric vehicle as the industry standard by 2030.[24] As a result, traditional competitive forces and the relationships between the auto firms and their rivals, suppliers, and customers are unraveling at an accelerated rate. Traditional car companies are now locked in a fast-paced race to form joint ventures, acquire high-technology start-ups, transform their business models, and change how they engage workers and organize operations.

In short, the traditional auto companies are currently experiencing a full-on assault. Apple, Google, Amazon, Uber, and a host of others outside the auto industry threaten to extract most of the profits generated by car sales, turning traditional automakers into low-margin equipment suppliers.[25] This radical deconstruction of the industry's supply and value chain is very similar to what occurred in the computer industry during the 2000s when mainframes and PCs were replaced by smartphones and cloud technologies. The automobile, according to industry followers, is rapidly becoming a bundle of software apps, information, and data networks, busting with valued-added after-sales services.

a. What is competition like in the global automobile industry? What are the major trends and characteristics of this industry?
b. What key challenges need to be addressed by CEOs of traditional automakers given the potential threat or opportunity of the passenger car or pickup truck becoming a smartphone on wheels?

5.5 ENABLING FIRMS TO PROBLEM SOLVE AND CONTINUOUSLY INNOVATE

As previously discussed, the digital revolution has significantly reduced factor inputs while simultaneously growing primarily **intangible** products and services. The digital revolution provides firms with increased access to information, artificial intelligence, deep data analytics, and next-generation knowledge workers. Information technologies and telecommunications bridge **temporal** (time), **physical** (organizational), and **spatial** (distance) boundaries while extending the **richness** (quality) and **reach** (spread) of information. Although prior technology revolutions were predominantly consumers of physical finite resources, the digital revolution is foremost a generator of intangible and infinite resources. Intangible resources come in the form of intellectual property, knowledge, the creative use of information, problem solving and learning, and artificial intelligence. Access to firm and market information, knowledge, creativity and innovation, big data, and artificial intelligence can improve industries' and markets' efficiency and competitive edge. Porter argues that the health of a nation or region is dependent on the competitiveness and health of its industries. The competitiveness and health of an industry is driven by constant productivity improvements. Productivity improvements in an industry are dependent on the capacity of its firms to continuously **innovate** and upgrade.[26] Advances in digital technologies, the internet, and telecommunication have all acted as catalysts for constant change and innovation and continuous cost reduction. The degree to which the firm can effectively move from incremental change and ideas to transformative change and radically inclusive thinking will determine its ability to survive and adapt in an age of accelerated exponential growth and change (see Exhibit 6.6: Change, Ideas, and Radically Inclusive Thinking above).

The digital revolution, by providing virtual access to information and new knowledge, can drive economic growth and innovation. In turn, it has the capacity to render knowledge work and the knowledge worker as more productive.[27] Intangible resources such as intellectual property, software, cloud technology, artificial intelligence, learning communities, and deep data analytics are more traceable, mobile, expandable, and valuable than ever before. It is now just as easy for a software engineer in India to design software for Ford Motors as it is for a software engineer living in Detroit. The rapid growth of Amazon's e-commerce businesses, web and portal services (business hubs, content, mobile advertising, services), and cloud technologies has largely contributed in making Jeff Bezos (its founder and CEO) one of the wealthiest individuals in the world. A 2016 article by the *World Economic Forum* reports:

> Digitalization is converging all technologies, from cloud-based IT and the Internet of Things (IoT) to big data. Digitalization is driving the next digital revolution and leading to a new wave of productivity. Old business models are being shattered, with disruption driving new innovation, new ways of thinking through problems, and new solutions.
>
> In previous years, there has been a clear distinction between what tech companies and non-tech companies do. But with access to supercomputing and aligned technologies … non-tech companies can now leverage data to make more informed business decisions. With access to historic and real-time data, companies can upsell and cross-sell to customers and deliver better customer service. Without the digital revolution, leveraging data to extend business capabilities would have been impossible.[28]

VIDEO 6.4 The Explainer: Blue Ocean Strategy

6. BLUE OCEAN STRATEGY

In 2005, Kim and Mauborgne introduced the concept of blue ocean strategy. Through company histories and archival data, these researchers studied 150 strategic moves of companies in 30 industries over more than 100 years.[29] They found that companies could succeed by not competing directly with industry rivals, but rather by creating open space, or **blue ocean.** Blue oceans represent "open water" or uncontested market space. The research team reported that by finding uncontested markets, a firm could create greater value opportunities for buyers as well as for the company. Blue oceans provide the company with new demand while making former rivals irrelevant. Contested markets are called **red oceans**, which represent all the industries in existence today in the known competitive space. Companies pursuing a blue ocean strategy define their own industry boundaries. These firms have a **first-mover advantage**, where the competitive "rules of the game" are not established. Red ocean industries have inherent **legacy effects**, where industry players conform to the existing industry's known competitive rules. In existing industries, competitors try to outperform one another by fighting for greater market share. As the market space gets crowded, commodities force prices down and create cutthroat competition, turning the blue ocean "bloody" (competitive space) and, thus, into the red ocean.[30] Although traditional competition-based strategies (red ocean strategies) are necessary, they are not sufficient to sustain a firm's high performance. Fighting over market share in mature or declining industries eventually turns into a zero-sum game in which one company's gain is achieved at another company's loss. Because the total profit level of the industry is also determined by structural factors, firms principally seek to capture and redistribute wealth instead of creating wealth; that is, they focus on dividing up the red ocean, where growth is increasingly limited.

Blue ocean strategy, on the other hand, is based on the view that market boundaries and industry structures are not given or predetermined and can be reconstructed by the actions and beliefs of the strategists who are finding or creating blue oceans for their companies. Kim and Mauborgne assume that structure and market boundaries exist only in managers' minds and that blue ocean practitioners do not let existing market structures limit strategic thinking. These strategists believe that demand is out there, largely untapped. The crux of the problem is how to create it. This, in turn, requires a shift of attention from supply to demand; from a focus on competing to a focus on **value innovation**—that is, the creation of innovative value to unlock new demand. Competition in the old game is therefore rendered irrelevant. By expanding the demand side of the economy, new wealth is created. Such a strategy, therefore, allows firms to largely play a non–zero-sum game with high payoff possibilities. Kim and Mauborgne identify several company examples of blue ocean strategies (see Table 6.2).[31]

Table 6.2 Company Examples of Blue Ocean Strategies

Apple: First Company to successfully design, develop, manufacturer and market high technology proprietary products (personal computers, tablets, smartphones) and services to everyday consumers through a unique technology eco-system.

Amazon: Transformational approach to retailing through the use of net-centric based strategies and the Internet

Curves: redefining market boundaries between health clubs and home exercise programs for women.

New Chapter: Unique development of the herbal supplements, organic whole foods, and dietary remedies markets long before these markets became stables in the Lifestyle of Health and Sustainability (LOHAS) industry.

Netjets: Development of the fractional jet ownership market.

Purdue Chicken: The first company to successfully brand a commodity and staple in American diets—chicken.

Southwest Airlines: Unique approach in offering point-to-point, quick turnaround, lower cost business and commercial air travel comparable to Indy pit crews turnaround of formula one race cars during races.

Uber: Revolutionary approach to ride sharing based on exploiting a "sharing" economy.

Walmart: Revolutionary approach to discount retailing becoming the world's largest company in terms of sales.

Xiaomi: Founded in 2010 by entrepreneur Lei Jun, the Chinese Company has become the leading manufacturer and marketer of low price, low cost, high-quality smart phones and other high technology products in China by incorporating customer "fan" feedback into its products.

Sources: Kim, W. Chan and Mauborgne, Renee, "Blue Ocean Strategy, (Boston Ma. Harvard Business Review, October 2004); Reconstruct the Automobile Industry," (Boston, Ma. Harvard Business School Press. Retrieved March 12, 2015) Downloaded at: https://en.wikipedia.org/wiki/Blue_Ocean_Strategy; accessed June 12, 2015; A conversation with W.Chan Kim and Renee Mauborgne". INSEAD. 2005. Downloaded at: http://en.wikipedia.org/wiki/Blue_Ocean_Strategyy; accessed June 12, 2015

<table>
<tr><td>Thinking
Critically
Exercise 49</td><td></td></tr>
</table>

BLUE OCEAN STRATEGY AND INNOVATION

Since 2000, we have witnessed several game-changing innovations including GPS, hybrid cars, Wikipedia, text messaging, nanotechnology, genome mapping, music streaming, social networks, medical imaging, life-changing drugs, and a host of other products and services. These innovations have made several entrepreneurs and investors extremely rich. Identify a game-changing technology introduced since 2000. Next, identify the entrepreneur, entrepreneurial team, or company that has benefited the most from this technology by employing a blue ocean strategy.

What factors drive the blue ocean strategy? Compare it with the mindset of the entrepreneur. Is blue ocean strategy just another name for entrepreneurship or entrepreneurial strategy?

7. MAINTAINING VITALITY AND AGILITY IN A DIGITAL WORLD

What does it take for an organization or individual to survive in today's environment of rapid and radical change? Change management requires both the firm and people who lead it to pivot and adapt quickly to new ways of doing things.[32] It also demands the organization be agile and efficient at the same time. Change management mandates a variation in the way strategic leaders and workers think about their organizations, their jobs, and their competitive markets. It necessitates, as Friedman maintains, **radically inclusive thinking**. This thinking process provides critical inquiry with strategic decisions that include as many relevant people, processes, disciplines, organizations, and technologies as possible—factors, Friedman indicates, that are often kept separate or excluded altogether.[33] (See Exhibit 6.7: Traditional vs. Agile Organizations.)

7.1 DYNAMIC WORK DESIGN

Organizations are designed and structured to solve customer problems. When the external environment is relatively stable and predictable, then hierarchical and mechanistic structures work best. Frederick W. Taylor, an early advocate and pioneer of the mechanistic approach to organizational design, maintained that if work is regularly repeated, it can be studied and improved via motion studies and observation—a theory and process that eventually became known as **scientific management**.[34] But what happens when efficiency in organizations is trumped by uncertainty? Repenning, Kieffer, and Repenning investigated agile principles that underlie software development by studying Toyota's well-known flexible production system. These researchers sought to understand how organizations could balance Taylor's stable and efficient work principles to environments that require organizations to be agile and flexible. They recommended a **dynamic work design** framework that "enables managers to create work processes in their own organizations that are both more flexible and more efficient."[35] Dynamic work design maintains the traditional mechanistic work design while empowering workers to override the mechanistic approach when things go awry. For example, at Toyota, when a problem in the assembly line develops, a worker can push a button to stop the line. The worker can then go into collaborating problem-solving mode with other workers. Once the problem is solved, the assembly line is returned to its serial design. Workers at Toyota are given several mechanisms and the best practices to collaboratively cycle back and forth between well-defined factory-style tasks and more agile dynamic work designs. The authors maintain that "agile development methods work by channeling the creativity of software engineers through frequent team meetings and customer interactions."[36]

7.2 ONE EXAMPLE OF THE AGILE ORGANIZATION

In today's rapidly changing environments, the same agile and problem-solving capabilities are needed not only in assembly line operations but also throughout the organization. In order to examine an agile organizational structure, Birkinshaw conducted an empirical case study of ING's agile organizational work structure.[37] He interviewed 15 executives and several front-line workers at ING's headquarters in the Netherlands. At the conclusion of the case study, the researcher offered five lessons for overcoming the challenges of building dynamic agile work teams at ING:

1. Decide how much power you (CEO and top-level managers) are willing to give up. Agile shifts power away from the top into the hands of those closest to the action.
2. Prepare stakeholders for the leap. ING executives had to sell agile to nervous stakeholders, including board members, employees, and bank regulators.
3. Build the structure around customers and keep it fluid. Agile is focused on what is best for the customer, so organizations must conform to this standard.
4. Give employees the right balance of oversight and autonomy. Agile has been a learning process at ING that sets ambitious quarterly goals for ING work groups.
5. Provide employees with development and growth opportunities. Change can be scary for employees, so ING's HR department mapped out personal development for its personnel. It also provided career progression paths for employees and mainstream career trajectories of industries.[38]

One of the hardest parts of ING's transformation to a dynamic, agile structure was finding the proper coaching and support for agile and the new long-term responsibilities the employees had to face.[39]

8. SKILLS TO REMAIN VITAL AND AGILE

What personal traits are required for individuals to not only survive but also thrive in environments that are characterized by rapid and dynamic change? Individuals, similar to organizations, must be agile and capable of adapting quickly to new ways of learning and working. Michelman sees the challenges for the individual "along three dimensions, each of which can be captured as a personal trait: skill, will, and velocity."[40] He describes each dimension as follows:

Skill. In a changing world, skill is no longer just about the capabilities required to succeed in your present role. (Presumably, you possess those already.) You also need the ability to excel in what your role will become. Are you able to adapt your skill sets and adopt new tools to succeed as the environment transforms?

Will. Will is about desire and tenacity. Do you have the appetite to evolve and the nerve to try new things? Are you legitimately interested in helping chart a new future for your organization?

Velocity. Change usually requires a new speed or a higher gear than you are accustomed to. And this pace won't let up: Digital life moves fast. Can you shift up to keep up? Some might argue that a focus on velocity can be counterproductive and that decision making is more important than ever. I believe that is a false argument. You must be able to move quickly and make smart bets at the same time.[41]

VIDEO 6.5 Your Elusive Creative Genius | Elizabeth Gilbert

8.1 RADICALLY INCLUSIVE THINKING AND ACTING

Many highly successful people (whom some would call "genius" in their thinking and action) were self-taught, willing their way to success.[42] We are not all blessed with the high intelligence that fashions the complex into something simple to understand. And not all highly intelligent people are successful; they too might find it difficult to succeed in everyday life, let alone in environments that remain in constant flux. Several studies give us clues as to how we can learn what makes a person a genius and what drives his or her success. Drucker argues that today's worker must act and think like a CEO. Knowledge, work, and the knowledge worker dominate today's work environment.[43] This is increasingly true in today's digital world. To be successful, one must act and think like a CEO and learn like a seasoned scholar—in some ways, even like a genius. In her article "Who is Genius?" Claudia Kalb notes that no single source of understanding exists to define what genius is: "Instead we try to understand it by unraveling the complex and tangled qualities—intelligence, creativity, perseverance, and simple good fortune to name a few—that entwine to create a person capable of changing the world."[44] Steve Jobs, to some researchers and scholars, epitomizes these personal traits and characteristics of a genius. Still, Jobs would not have been successful with intelligence alone; his success was driven by good fortune, creativity, perseverance, a nurturing environment, passion, and supporting social networks.

Assume that you are going in for a job interview at Technology Business Research, Inc. (TBR) headquartered in Hampton, New Hampshire. TBR is recognized as one of the leading high-tech market research and consulting firms, specializing in the analyses of computer, application, networking, wireless, and professional services companies. TBR serves international clientele of high-tech manufacturers, IT (information technology) professionals, end users, and financial executives. The company has continually distinguished itself in the marketplace by providing high-quality information and market research in a format that is uniquely responsive to its clients. TBR clients include a who's who of high-technology companies as well as small- to medium-size enterprises (SMEs). TBR is looking for a high-energy junior salesperson with the drive to be successful in selling IT research services to the high-tech industry. This is an entry-level position, providing a ground-floor opportunity to learn and advance at TBR. This position also provides on-the-job training and exposure to the highest levels of the F100 (Fortune 100) accounts in the IT industry. Your interviewer, Greg Richardson, has reviewed your resume and is an alumnus of the same college that you attend. In addition to your resume, Richardson asks you to bring in a list of your strengths and weaknesses, including a personal values statement. He also asks you to identify the top driving forces operating in the high-technology mobile advertising industry. Your interview is scheduled in three days.

    a. Go to TBR's webpage at tbri.com. What does TBR do? What is its value proposition? What key success factors has TBR capitalized on?

    b. What are your strengths and weaknesses regarding this job position?

    c. Describe your personal values statement.

    d. What are some of the top driving forces operating in the high-tech mobile advertising industry?

9. REFLECTION: HOW TO THINK AND ACT LIKE A GENIUS

Corporate-level strategy focuses on the firm's overall vision, mission, core purpose, goals, and objectives. Simply stated, corporate-level strategy primarily emphasizes what industries and businesses the firm will compete in and how it will be judged. There are numerous investment strategies that a board and/or senior-level managers can make at the corporate level to improve a firm's long-term performance. Corporate-level decision making requires strategic thinking and in-depth critical inquiry at the highest level of thinking. How well the firm can exploit the accelerated growth in digital technologies and gain a competitive advantage is one of the biggest challenges faced by corporate strategists today.

Isaacson, in his masterful book *Leonardo Da Vinci*, notes that though Da Vinci was not superhuman—studying and understanding his methods of thinking and acting can bring intellectual rewards to anyone.[42] When Da Vinci was around 30 years old, he wrote a letter to the ruler of Milan applying for a job. In 10 carefully numbered paragraphs, he listed his skills in engineering, including his ability to design bridges, waterways, cannons, and armored vehicles. At the end of his letter, as an afterthought, he added an eleventh paragraph stating that he was also an artist. He writes, "Likewise in painting, I can do everything possible."[45] Da Vinci looked at his many diverse talents in art, theater, music, engineering, and his treatises "as part of a dynamic process always receptive to refinement by the application of new insight." In other words, Da Vinci exemplified today's **radically inclusive** thinker and problem solver. His thinking was not only out of the box but also completely free of boxes. He viewed his work with the perspective that there was always something more to learn. In fact, right up to the end of his life, he viewed his masterpiece *The Mona Lisa* as unfinished, still requiring additional paint strokes to bring it closer to perfection.

What lessons can we learn from Da Vinci's way of thinking and the way he approached life? One basic lesson is that as knowledge workers and students of business, your work and learning as an individual is never finished. This is especially true in a fluctuating digital world. As such, how can you remain vital and agile in today's fast-paced and rapidly changing work environment?

Da Vinci's creativity set him apart from the common person. Few others were as accomplished in so many different fields. His curiosity compelled him to try to know all there was to know about everything that could be known. His outlook on life epitomized his desire and passion to understand all of creation, including how we fit into it.[46] Isaacson concludes his book with some lessons that we can learn from the Italian master:[a]

- *Be curious, relentlessly curious*—Something we all can do every day of our lives.
- *Seek knowledge for its own sake*—Not all knowledge needs to be useful; seek it for pure pleasure.
- *Retain a childlike sense of wonder*—Never outgrow these formative years of discovery.
- *Observe*—One of Da Vinci's greatest skills was his acute ability to observe things and wonder how they work.
- *Start with the details*—Da Vinci took copious notes, 7,200 pages of them in fact, containing everything from scribbles to detailed lists and observations.
- *See things unseen*—Da Vinci made connections throughout his life, tying together his seemingly disparate and diverse interests.
- *Go down rabbit holes*—Do not be afraid try new things or to start the journey without necessarily knowing where it might take you.
- *Get distracted*—His curiosity of almost everything fostered a richness in his mind and filled it with deeper connections.
- *Respect facts*—Combine observational experimentation with critical thinking; do not be afraid to change your mind based on new information (facts).
- *Procrastinate*—Take the time to pause, think, and reflect.
- *Let the perfect be the enemy of the good*—Like Da Vinci's own quest for perfection, do not let go until it is perfect.
- *Think visually*—Too often, when we learn by rule or formula, we fail to visually comprehend how things work; that is, how elements fit into nature and the world beyond mathematical formulas.
- *Avoid silos*—Da Vinci possessed "a free range mind that merrily wandered across all the disciplines: art, sciences, engineering, and the humanities" (this coincides with Steve Jobs's belief that Apple's creative success stemmed from the intersection of "liberal arts and technology streets").
- *Let your reach exceed your grasp*—Do not be afraid to dream about new things and wonder how they might work.
- *Indulge fantasy*—Da Vinci not only "blurred the lines between science and the arts, he also did so between reality and fantasy."
- *Create for yourself, not just for patrons*—Do things because you want to do them, not because others want you to.
- *Collaborate*—"Genius starts with individual brilliance" requiring singular vision, but "executing it often entails working for others." "Innovation is a team sport. Creativity is a collaborative endeavor."
- *Make lists*—"Make lists and be sure to put odd things on them."
- *Take notes on paper*—Even after 500 years, Da Vinci's notes are "still around to astonish and inspire us."
- *Be open to mystery*—"Not everything needs sharp lines."[47]

---

a   Please note that the brief summary of comments not in quotations is this author's interpretation of Issacson's lessons. The author apologizes for any misinterpretations of Issacson's insights and descriptions on the lessons we can take from Da Vinci's genius and life's work.

Clearly, many of the above lessons are an "idealized" description of what individuals might take away from Da Vinci's way of thinking and acting. As unique individuals, we exemplify these characteristics in different ways and to different degrees. Still, the closer a person gets to satisfying all these conditions, the more that person fits the model of a genius—the model of thinking and acting like successful CEOs. Many of these lessons can help firms and individuals succeed by maintaining vitality and staying agile. We can all learn by being radically inclusive thinkers, no matter the degree of uncertainty or change in one's environment. Setting strategy at the corporate level requires the strategist to be good at several things, not just business acumen. Among other things, it requires corporate-level strategy crafted and executed by senior-level managers and leaders (and leaders at all levels of the firm) to be a radically inclusive thinkers and problem solvers, be able to respect the facts, see the unseen, seek knowledge for its own sake, take detailed notes, collaborate, and be open to mystery that requires skill, will, and velocity.

 VIDEO 6.6 Apple: Five Years with Tim Cook

Thinking Critically Exercise 51

TIM COOK'S APPLE—INCREMENTAL, EVOLUTIONARY, OR REVOLUTIONARY CHANGE

In July 2014, Apple's CEO Tim Cook announced that the company would offer the iPhone with 4.7- and 5.5-inch screen sizes (iPhone 6 and iPhone 6 Plus), which were significantly larger than the company's current models. The larger-screen iPhones were developed in response to Samsung's and other manufacturers' models with large screens that utilize the Android OS (operating system). Large-screen Android smartphones featuring a display larger than 5 inches sold at a premium price—an area that had been previously dominated by Apple. More than 98 percent of Android smartphones sold globally were priced at the equivalent of $400 or more.

Under co-founder Steve Jobs, Apple was one of the world's most innovative and successful companies by 2011. Jobs's passion was to build a lasting and enduring organization. Under his leadership, Apple introduced game-changing products and services across an array of industries. Chief among these was the iPhone. Never before did one firm change the competitive dynamics so drastically in so many industries from computers, mobile phones, and tablets to music, movies, photography, electronic components, newspapers, and print media, among many others.

Jobs desired to build a company that would survive changes in its leadership and the dynamism of competitive markets. The co-founder's untimely death in October 2011 raised questions about Apple's future. Would Apple's new CEO Tim Cook be able to sustain the company's strong financial performance and its competitive advantage over rivals? Apple's financial performance and parade of spectacular new products under Jobs made it the most valuable global company in terms of market capitalization at the time of his death. No one expected Apple to continue to perform to such a degree, but the decline in its stock price and market capitalization raised questions about Cook's leadership and ability to sustain such a high level of success. Under Cook, Apple's string of successive big-hit, innovative product introductions had slowed, and Apple was again at a crossroads. Even after three years with Cook at the helm, industry analysts and others wondered whether Apple would prosper or suffer under his leadership. *The Wall Street Journal* reported on May 14, 2018, that Taiwan-based Foxconn technology posted a worse than expected 15 percent drop in first-quarter net profit after Apple (its biggest customer) reported modest growth in iPhone shipments. In 2018, Foxconn relied on Apple for about 54 percent of its revenue. The *Journal* reports that though Apple does not offer a breakdown of shipments by iPhone models, the growth pace of the number of iPhones shipped has decreased. At the end of the first quarter of 2017, Apple posted a modest 3 percent increase in the number of iPhones shipped. Still, Apple's revenues from its iPhone rose 14 percent to $38 billion during the quarter, driven largely by the launch of the $1,000 iPhone X.

Go to Apple's webpage and click on its "Investors" link (investor.apple.com/investors). Select Apple's quarterly 1Q report.

a. How has Apple performed under Tim Cook's leadership?

b. Has Cook presided over something truly revolutionary at Apple during his leadership?

c. What will competition be like for Apple in the next six months? One year?

d. How might rivals, suppliers, and customers outperform Apple?

e. Using the BCS Vitality Index as a guide, how confident are you that Apple will remain vital in an age of exponential growth and accelerated change? Has Cook done enough to maintain Apple's market cap leadership and strong performance?

Sources: Fisher, Dan, "Apple and the Fear of Flopping." news.cnet.com. July 18, 2013.; Gallagher, Dan. "Apple's Cook Can't Afford to Miss a Beat." *Wall Street Journal*, May 29, 2014.; Gallagher, Dan. "Apple Takes Its Business Seriously." *Wall Street Journal*, July 16, 2014: C1.; Isaacson, Walter. *Steve Jobs.* Simon & Schuster: New York, 2011.; Wakabayashi, Daisuke, "Tim Cook's Vision for 'His' Apple Begins to Emerge." *Wall Street Journal*, July 7, 2014.; Wakabayashi, Daisuke, Greg Bensinger, and Alistar Barr. "Apple Boss Makes His Boldest Bets Yet." *Wall Street Journal*, September 10, 2014: A1–A2.; Kubota, Yuba. "Foxconn's Profit Drops as iPhone Shipment Growth Slows." *Wall Street Journal*, May 14, 2018. www.wsj.com/articles/foxconns-profit-drops-as-iphone-shipment-growth-slows-1526306939?mod=searchresults&page=1&pos=2.

CHAPTER ENDNOTES

1. Reeves, Martin. "In Search of 'Vital' Companies." *Fortune*, November 1, 2017: 44–5.
2. Ibid.,44–5.
3. Friedman, Thomas. *Thank You for Being Late*. New York: Picador, 2016.
4. Ibid.
5. Ibid.
6. "General Electric." Wikipedia. https://en.wikipedia.org/wiki/General_Electric.
7. "Enduring Ideas: The GE/McKinsey Nine-box Matrix." McKinsey & Company. Last modified 2008. http://www.mckinsey.com/insights/strategy/enduring_ideas_the_ge_and_mckinsey_nine_box_matrix.; "BCG Matrix & GE/McKinsey Matrix." McKinsey & Company. Last modified 2008. http://wiki.telfer.uottawa.ca/ci-wiki/index.php/BCG_Matrix_%26_GE/McKinsey_Matrix.
8. Ovidijus, Jurevicius. "GE/McKinsey Matrix." *Strategic Management Insight*. Last modified August 19, 2014. https://www.strategicmanagementinsight.com/tools/ge-mckinsey-matrix.html.
9. Gupta, A.K. and Govindarajan, V. "Build, hold, harvest: Converting strategic intentions into reality." *The Journal of Business Strategy*, 4 (3), (1984): 34–47
10. Keizer, Gregg. " Microsoft writes off $7.6B, admits failure of Nokia acquisition." *Computerworld*. July 8, 2015: https://www.computerworld.com/article/2945371/smartphones/microsoft-writes-off-76b-admits-failure-of-nokia-acquisition.html
11. Lee, Edmund Lee and Kang, Cecilia. "AT&T Closes Acquisition of Time Warner." *The New York Times*. June 14, 2018. https://www.nytimes.com/2018/06/14/business/media/att-time-warner-injunction.html
12. "Metcalfe's Law." Business Dictionary. http://www.businessdictionary.com/definition/Metcalfe-s-Law.html.
13. Friedman, Thomas. *Thank You for Being Late*. New York: Picador, 2016.
14. Moore, Gordon. "Cramming More Components onto Integrated Circuits," *Electronics Magazine* 38, no. 8 (April 19, 1965).
15. Janssen, Sarah. *The World Almanac and Book of Facts: 2018.* New York, NY: World Almanac Books, 2017.
16. Ibid. *The World Almanac and Book of Facts: 2018:*
17. Ibid. *The World Almanac and Book of Facts: 2018:*
18. Ibid. *The World Almanac and Book of Facts: 2018:*
19. Ibid. *The World Almanac and Book of Facts: 2018:*
20. Ibid. *The World Almanac and Book of Facts: 2018:*
21. Irwin, Manley R. "Markets Without Boundaries." *Telecommunications Policy* 8, no. 1 (1984): 12–4. https://doi.org/10.1016/0308-5961(84)90055-7.
22. Hirsh, Evan, Arjun Kakkar, Akshay Singh, and Reid Wilk. "2015 Auto Industry Trends, Strategy: Turbulence and Technology." *PWC*, April 5, 2017. http://www.strategyand.pwc.com/trends/2015-auto-trends.

23. Sharman, Andy. "Tyred and Wired." *Financial Times*, April 5, 2015: 4.

24. Drvies, Alex. "Power Play: The Inside Story of How GM (Yes GM!) Beat Elon Musk in the Race to Build a True Electric Car for the Masses," *Wired*, February 2016: 59–71.

25. Ewing, Jack. "As Apple and Google Rethink Cars, Automakers Plan Their Defense," *New York Times*, September 18, 2015: B4.; Clark, Pilita, and Andy Sharman. "Fallout Threatens to Choke Diesel Cars." *Financial Times*, September 23, 2015: 17.

26. Porter, Michael E. "Competitive Advantage of Nations." *Harvard Business Review* (1990). https://hbr.org/1990/03/the-competitive-advantage-of-nations.

27. Edersheim, Elizabeth Hass. *The Definitive Drucker*. New York: McGraw-Hill, 2007.

28. Raina, Savita. "The Digital Revolution Is Creating New Opportunities for Leadership." *World Economic Forum*. Last modified October 5, 2016. https://www.weforum.org/agenda/2016/10/the-digital-revolution-is-creating-new-opportunities-for-leadership.

29. Kim, W. Chan, and Renée Mauborgne. *Blue Ocean Strategy: How to Create Uncontested Market Space and Make the Competition Irrelevant*. Boston, MA: Harvard Business School Press, 2005.; Siegemund, Carsten. *Blue Ocean Strategy for Small and Mid-sized Companies in Germany: Development of a Consulting Approach*. Hamburg, DEU: Diplomica Verlag, 2008. ProQuest, November 2015.

30. "A Conversation with W. Chan Kim and Renée Mauborgne." INSEAD. 2005. Accessed June 12, 2015. http://en.wikipedia.org/wiki/blue_ocean_strategyy.

31. Blue Ocean.

32. Michelman, Paul. "Survival Skills for a Digital World." *MIT Sloan Management Review* (2018): 1.

33. Friedman, Thomas. *Thank You for Being Late*. New York: Picador, 2016.

34. Dininni, Jeanne. "Management Theory of Frederick Taylor." business.com/managing. May 16, 2017. https://www.business.com/articles/management-theory-of-frederick-taylor/.

35. Repenning, Nelson P., Don Kieffer, and James Repenning. "A New Approach to Designing Work." *MIT Sloan Management Review* (2018): 30–1.

36. Ibid., 38.

37. Ibid., 91.

38. Birkinshaw, Julian. "What to Expect from Agile." *MIT Sloan Management Review* (2018): 34–8.

39. Ibid., 42.

40. Michelman, Paul. "Survival Skills for a Digital World." *MIT Sloan Management Review* (2018): 1.

41. Ibid., 1.

42. Isaacson, Walter. *Leonardo Da Vinci*. New York, NY: Simon & Schuster, 2017.

43. Edersheim, Elizabeth Hass. *The Definitive Drucker*. New York: McGraw-Hill, 2007.

44. Kalb, Claudia. "What Makes a Genius?" *National Geographic* (2017): 36–55.

45. Isaacson, Walter. "The Lessons of Leonardo: How to Be a Creative Genius." *Wall Street Journal*. Last modified September 29, 2017. https://www.wsj.com/articles/the-lessons-of-leonardo-how-to-be-a-creative-genius-1506690180?mg=prod/accounts-wsj.

46. Isaacson, Walter. *Leonardo Da Vinci*. New York, NY: Simon & Schuster, 2017.

47. Ibid.

CHAPTER 7

STRATEGY EXECUTION, LEARNING, AND CHANGE

GE'S STRATEGY CRAFTING AND EXECUTION CHALLENGES

In November 2016 at GE's two-day tech show in San Francisco, GE CEO Jeff Immelt took the stage and asked the audience, "Why not us? Why can't we make ourselves into a digital company?" The company is "all in" Immelt said, on crafting itself in the image of a tech and computing disruptor, which included becoming a "top 10" software company by 2020. To achieve this goal, GE invested heavily in building software and wireless capability to connect machines like wind turbines, trains, and jet engines. It was also buying the latest algorithms to better monitor and control its machines and industrial products. Similar to his former boss, Jack Welch, Immelt was looking to get more value added products and services by developing a technology ecosystem for its global network of employees, suppliers, customers, and in some cases, rivals. As part of its transformation strategy, GE acquired about $2 billion worth of technology startups over the past several years. For example, in 2016 alone GE acquired ServiceMax, a cloud-based field service management (FSM) solutions company for $915 million, and Meridium an data analytics company for $495 million. (Meridium was a developer of asset performance management (APM) software for machine-heavy industries such as oil, gas, electricity and chemicals.) In another high profile strategic acquisition, Immelt, in early 2017, completed a merger with Baker Hughes (BH) combining oil and gas units with GE's oil and gas equipment and services operations. The merger created the world's second-largest oilfield service provider by revenue. GE paid $7.5 billion in cash and transferred 37.39% of GE Oil & Gas business assets and liabilities in exchange for 62.61% of BH assets and liabilities.[a] Ahmed Hashmi, Head of Upstream Technology at BP, a GE customer, noted at the time of the BH merger that BP was also going through its own disruption. Shortly after Immelt's presentation at the San Francisco tech show, Hashmi noted, "Our industry needs a transformation, and digital is our biggest lever." GE calls its transformation the "digital internet." A major investment to connect these machines was GE's Predix software, which extracts, crunches, and employs data from machines to increase efficiency, saving GE's customers money, time, and energy. For GE, it's a huge investment. But it is also somewhat of a risk: this is a "transformation, not a task" and an "all-encompassing change," said Immelt.

In October 2017, Immelt abruptly announced that he was immediately retiring and was stepping down as a GE director and board chairman. Immelt had been promoted to CEO in 2001 shortly after the 9/11 terrorism attacks on the U.S., replacing Jack Welch, who many consider one of the greatest CEOs of all time. John Flannery, 55, a long time GE executive replaced Immelt in June 2017 as GE's CEO. Flannery formerly led GE's healthcare division. GE reported that Immelt opted to step aside from his board leadership post early because of his "determination that the CEO transition has proceeded smoothly" and that Flannery "was ready to succeed" him as chairman. Brian Langenberg, an industrial analyst who covered GE, said he expected Flannery would keep GE's focus on cutting costs and spending while it reconfigured itself as an institution. Under Immelt, GE was transformed from a sprawling conglomerate to an industrial company focused on the faster-growing industrial and power sectors.

Immelt sold or spun off major businesses, including appliances, insurance and plastics, as well as NBC Universal, among others. During Immelts' tenure as CEO, GE's stock price fell 27 percent. In October 2015, Trian Fund Management, led by Nelson Peltz, made a $2.5 billion investment in GE making it one of its top 10 shareholders. At the time of its investment, Peltz demonstrated that GE could be worth approximately $40 to $45 billion by the end of 2017. Peltz, an activist investor, put considerable pressure on GE's board to boost profit by drastically reducing costs and overhauling executive compensation. Under fire from Peltz, Immelt began shedding billions in annual industrial costs. Peltz hailed the cost cutting as a positive step. By the end of 2017, GE shares closed at $17.45, 41% lower than Train's mid-point estimate.

Prior to Immelt stepping down as GE's CEO, Scott Davis, an analyst at Barclays, noted to his clients that Immelt was "likely in the final inning of what we see as a rather unspectacular 15-year run. It will likely be Mr. Immelt's successor who reaps the rewards of an improved GE." Davis also stated that GE's next leader "will inherit a transformed, simplified portfolio with optionality to do more. ... GE Capital has been shrunk down

---

a   Honeywill, Robert. "GE: Understanding The Baker Hughes Transaction." *seekingalpha.* November 13, 2017: https://seekingalpha.com/article/4124379-ge-understanding-baker-hughes-transaction

to its core financing subsidiaries, the power business has been beefed up with the Alstom acquisition, and non-core assets are quickly being sold off."[b]

SOURCES:

Miller, Ron. "GE Digital snags ServiceMax for $915 million." *techcrunch.com*. November 14, 2016: https://techcrunch.com/2016/11/14/ge-digital-snags-servicemax-for-915-million/; Fehrenbacher, Katie. "GE's CEO Reveals How to Transform into a Digital Company." *Wall Street Journal*, November 15, 2016. Accessed April 2, 2017. http://fortune.com/2016/11/15/ges-ceo-digital-remake; Kellner, Tomas. "GE Buys $500 Million Machine Analytics Firm." *GE Reports*. September 14, 2016: https://www.ge.com/reports/ge-buys-500-million-machine-analytics-firm/; Sources: Cheng, Evelyn and Daniels, Jeff.. "GE Chairman Jeffrey Immelt steps down earlier than expected." *CNBC*. October 2, 2017: https://www.cnbc.com/2017/10/02/ge-chairman-jeffrey-immelt-steps-down-earlier-than-expected.html; Shell, Adam. "Jeff Immelt exits as GE chairman months earlier than planned." *USA Today*. Oct. 2, 2017: https://www.usatoday.com/story/money/2017/10/02/jeff-immelt-exits-ge-chairman-months-earlier-than-planned/724926001/; "GE: What Did Nelson Peltz And Trian Get Wrong?" *Cornerstone investments.* January 31, 2018 https://seekingalpha.com/article/4141869-ge-nelson-peltz-trian-get-wrong

a. What challenges faced Immelt as he transformed GE into a digital company? GE calls its transformation the "digital internet." How is GE remaking itself as a digital internet company? (See GE's Digital Strategy at www.gereports.com/ges-2017-annual-outlook-changing-game-digital-industrial-strategy/.)

b. Immelt stated, "Why not us? Why can't we make ourselves into a digital company?" How might you respond to his question: "Why not us?"

c. Why do you think Immelt abruptly relinquish his position as board chairman? What impact did the company's faltering stock price have on Immelt's stepping down as CEO and his abrupt retirement?

d. What role did Peltz and Train Investment play in GE's decisions to cut costs and divest several of its core businesses?

e. Go to GE annual report at: https://www.ge.com/investor-relations/ar2017/ceo-letter. What is your overall assessment of GE's financial and strategic health as reported in its 2017 annual report?

f. How difficult is it for a CEO to effectively craft and executive strategy when he or she faces constant pressure from an activist investor and a falling stock price?

1. INTRODUCTION: QUESTIONS TO THINK ABOUT

- Who are the strategic leaders and what do they do?
- What is the learning school of thought?
- What is meant by strategy implementation, execution, and control?
- How do you know if your strategies are working as crafted?
- What are the challenges of executing strategy?
- What are the different types of organizational change?
- What are the different types of organizational structure?
- What is change management?
- What are the characteristics of high-performing teams?
- What are the common stages of managing change?

---

b   Langford, James. "Nelson Peltz's Trian Links GE Performance Target to Immelt's Bonus."March 23, 2017: https://www.thestreet.com/story/14057514/1/nelson-peltz-s-trian-links-ge-performance-target-to-immelt-s-bonus.html

Less than one-third of all newly crafted strategies succeed in their execution.[1] A survey by the Conference Board on strategy execution reported, "Chief executives are so concerned about strategy execution that they rated it as both their number one and number two most challenging issues."[2] The American Management Association (AMA) estimates that more than 60 percent of strategies are not successfully implemented.[3] This chapter focuses on the strategic management concept model.

Although treated as separate steps, strategy implementation, execution, and strategic control are closely intertwined in the strategic management conceptual model. To achieve the intended results, the crafted strategy must prove functional. Strategic leaders provide the vision and direction for sustaining organizational success and skillfully manage all the steps in the strategic management model. The model can also be viewed as a process for managing organizational change. In its broadest sense, the model is about managing for the future. Managing change for the future is a complex, ambiguous process requiring strategic leaders who not only provide a sense of direction but also build ownership and alignment within the organization. Strategy implementation requires making tough resource-allocation decisions. To be effective, strategic leaders must balance customer value creation opportunities with the firm's value appropriation opportunities and exploit these opportunities through execution. Execution is as much a human activity or function as it is a resource allocation process. Similar to a football coach crafting a game plan prior to the actual game, the strategy itself is only as good as the assumptions on which it was based. The game plan also heavily depends upon the ability of the coaches and players to carry it out—in other words, the execution of the game. Seldom is a game plan executed as intended. The ability of coaches and players to adapt and change to actual game conditions ultimately determines their success or failure. Newly crafted strategies in the workplace are only as good as the assumptions on which they are based. They are also heavily contingent on the capabilities of those charged with its implementation.

2. STRATEGY IMPLEMENTATION, EXECUTION, AND STRATEGIC CONTROL

Strategy implementation and execution (step 6) and strategic control (step 7) focus on making newly crafted or designed strategy operational. We will refer to step 6 as "execution" and step 7 as "strategic control." Steps 6 and 7 can be viewed as a continuous process for strategy implementation (see Exhibit 7.1: Strategy Implementation, Execution, and Control Process). Unlike an ordinary plan, continuous learning, innovative actions, critical inquiry, strategic thinking, analysis, assessment, and action drive the strategic management model. Some of the basic elements of strategy implementation, execution, and strategic control are listed in Table 7.1. Strategy execution and control are continuous processes of managing the organization for improved performance via:

- Visionary, committed strategic leaders at the top of the organization
- Leaders at all levels of the organization
- Constant strategy alignment with the organization's vision and mission
- Constant adapting and monitoring of strategy against organizational goals and objectives
- Making tough resource allocation decisions
- Collaborating and coordinating across organizational functions, units, and activities
- Sharing knowledge and information internally and with key value chain partners and stakeholders
- Building trust throughout the organization and across organizational borders
- Ethical decision making
- An openness to strategic change

Exhibit 7.1
Strategy
Implementation,
Execution and
Control Process

Strategy implementation, execution and control process: IEC

Strategy implementation: Who, What, Why and When

Strategic control: Re-invest, Re-new, Re-Launch

Strategy Execution: How Learning, Leading Innovating

Source: Michael J. Merenda 2018

Table 7.1
Basic Elements
of Strategy
Implementation,
Execution, and
Control

Strategic Leadership	Strategic Leadership	Strategic Leadership
A: Strategy Implementation (Who, What, Why, and When)	B: Strategy Execution (How) (Learning, Leading, Innovating)	C: Strategic Control (Re-invest, Renew, Re-lauch)
Clearly state the new strategy. What does it entail?	Ongoing CEO strategic leadership and management of organizational change.	Is the strategy aligned with the vision and mission?
Communicate why a change in strategy is necessary.	Engage the organization in technical learning—identify major elements of the strategy and how it will work and be operationalized.	Does the strategy meeting specify goals and objectives?
Identify what individual or work teams should lead the implementation.	Engage in behavioral learning and training—identify what professional, managerial, inter-personal, and group development are needed.	Is the strategy working as intended, or does it need to be changed, altered, or adjusted?
Determine what cross function units, departments, and other organizational activities are required.	Foster leaders and leadership teams throughout the firm that will facilitate, coach, mentor, and champion the strategies, ongoing development, and implementation.	If the strategy has changed, how has it changed and why was it changed?
Determine what organizational resources and investments are required and where these resources will come from.	Look for leaders and innovation at every level of the organization that support and complement strategy execution.	If the strategy changed, what changes are now needed for its implementation and execution?
Determine if the firm's organizational structure needs to be changed in implementing the strategy.	Foster learning communities that rewards and compensates performance and fit with organizational values and philosophies.	Continue to monitor, evaluate, and determine if the strategy and its execution is under control—the strategy is meeting its intended purpose.
Determine what policies, systems, manuals, capital budgets processes, and other standard operating procedures need to be changed, modified, or added.	Provide timely feedback and support to all individuals and work groups involved with implementing and executing strategy.	Continue in the ongoing management of the of the strategic management process.
Set challenging metrics to measure whether or not the strategy is achieving intended results.	Engage in managerial succession planning, hiring, and human resource restructuring as needed.	Engage the organization in continuous learning.
Establish a clear timeframe for implementing the strategy with key milestones, actions, and activities and major events identified.		Engage the organization in continuous innovation.
		Engage in the continuous management of the competitive advantage life cycle.

2.1 STRATEGY IMPLEMENTATION

Strategy implementation requires consideration of how the formulated strategies will be carried out (executed) by the firm. What resources are needed? Who will be responsible for implementing the strategies, and over what time period? Strategy implementation addresses how the organization is to use its people and resources to achieve a competitive advantage and improve the firm's performance.

2.2 STRATEGY EXECUTION

Strategy execution is the actual carrying out of the steps and actions involved in implementation. Sull, Homkes, and Sull define strategy execution as "seizing opportunities that support the strategy while coordinating with other parts of the organization on an ongoing basis."[4] Strategy execution is dynamic, not static. Strategy crafting sets the stage for strategic action. Execution is the active, constant, and daily management of strategies, resources, systems, people, and other required activities and tasks to improve organizational performance. Although execution requires constant action and monitoring, it's still strategic, not tactical. As such (according to Bossidy and Charan), strategic leaders need to keep three essential points in mind to understand strategy execution:[5]

- Execution is a discipline and integral to strategy.
- Execution is the major job of the business leader.
- Execution must be a core element of an organization's culture.

2.3 STRATEGIC CONTROL

Strategic control describes the process by which organizations control the formation, implementation, and execution of strategies. This step assesses whether the formulated strategies (step 5) and executed strategies (step 6) are producing the intended or desired outcomes. Strategic control asks the questions: *Are these the right strategies for the intended results? Were they properly executed and carried out?* If the answer to either question is no, then a return to steps 1 through 6 is required. Control, in the broadest sense, requires identifying what activities, programs, and processes need to be managed. Usually, control takes place in closed-system logic with set parameters, guidelines, measures (or metrics), and boundaries. Unlike controlling an operation or activity, strategic control must handle complexity, uncertainty, and ambiguities associated with the total strategic management of the firm that competes in dynamic, constantly changing, competitive environments. Unlike operational controls, strategic control focuses on the achievement of future goals rather than the evaluation of past performance.

Through constant monitoring and evaluation of a strategy's implementation and execution, strategic control acts as a timely barometer of whether the strategy, its implementation, and its execution are working. If they are successful, then the processes are under control. If not, then changes to the strategy, its implementation, or its execution are required. As emphasized and explained in Chapter 1, there is no endpoint to strategy.[3]

3. CHALLENGES ASSOCIATED WITH STRATEGY IMPLEMENTATION AND EXECUTION

Strategic leadership drives strategy execution. To be successful, leaders have to be ruthless in the execution of strategies. The key purpose of strategy implementation and execution is to make crafted strategies work. The strategic leader's challenge is to know when a strategy is working, when a strategy is not working, and when a change in strategy is required. In implementing and executing strategy, the general manager confronts a number of challenges, including organizational size, operational scope and diversity, external pressure to perform and complexity of products, services, and business models.

3.1 ORGANIZATIONAL SIZE

Smaller organizations are usually more agile and adaptable to change, especially given the close working relationships with strategic leaders and the organization's employees. But smaller organizations might not possess the needed resources or expertise to carry out the change, requiring additional help from outside the company.

3.2 OPERATIONAL SCOPE AND DIVERSITY

Companies operating in several locations, especially across national borders, face more coordination (locus of decisions and authority), configuration (location of operations), and cultural challenges. Cultural diversity could make communicating and building trust, especially virtually through the internet and other information technologies, more difficult.

3.3 COMPLEXITY OF PRODUCTS, SERVICES, AND BUSINESS MODELS

Companies competing in hypercompetitive, high-technology industries with advanced, sophisticated products, services, and business models require constant adjustments to strategies and their execution. In some cases, completely new transformative strategies are necessary over a short period of time. Strategy implementation, execution complexity, and challenges are directly proportional to the organization's increase in size and the degree of organizational, product, service, people, and cultural differences or diversity within the firm. This, in turn, can present challenges to the implementation and execution of the company's business model.

3.4 RESISTANCE TO CHANGE

In order for strategies to be properly implemented and executed, individuals must understand the level of change needed (incremental, strategic, transformative) and why change is important. Managing change effectively is a journey and a learning process. People resist change if it is not properly communicated because change can threaten people and remove them from their comfort zones. Resistance to change, especially significant or transformative change, is unfortunately not that uncommon. Employees can resist change overtly and covertly. Overtly by openly challenging change through actions such as banding together, work stoppage, etc. Covertly, a group or individual can fight change through false rumors, deception, and defiance. In either case, the organization is challenged with conflict and confrontation, and these, along with resistance to change, can block or delay strategy implementation. If properly done, however, change can be an opportunity for growth and actualization.[6]

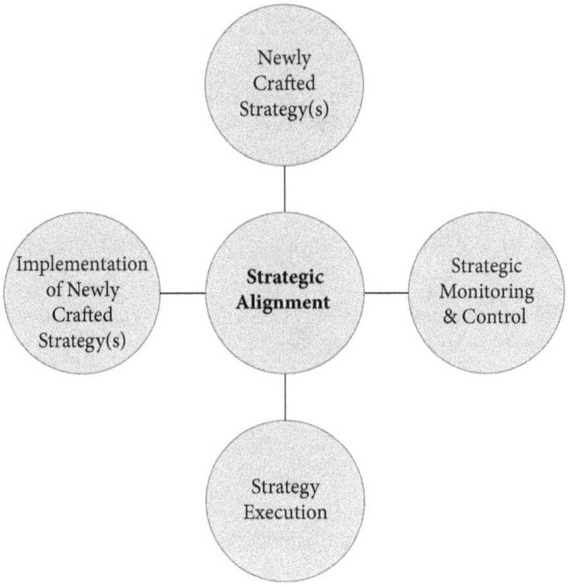

4. ALIGNING NEWLY CRAFTED STRATEGIES: STRATEGY IMPLEMENTATION, EXECUTION, AND CONTROL

Strategy crafting, implementation, execution, and control are continuous processes. These processes must be properly aligned, however, to improve organizational performance and gain a competitive advantage. Crafted strategies also require effective implementation, execution, monitoring, and reevaluation if they begin to fail. We can conceptualize this as a constant alignment process (see Exhibit 7.2: Strategy Alignment Process). Execution encompasses how decisions are made and what critical resources are allocated. Firms exist in constantly changing markets and environments. As such, implemented strategies need continual surveillance to determine if they are working as planned and achieving the desired end goal. If not, the strategies must then be recrafted or adapted as circumstances dictate. Strategic leadership is required in the strategy implementation, execution, and control processes.

Exhibit 7.2 Strategy Alignment Process

5. IMPLEMENTATION—WHO, WHAT, WHY, AND WHEN?

Simply stated, implementation mandates that planned actions occur at a certain point in time. This signals the start of putting crafted strategies into action. Similar to strategy development, there is no endpoint to implementation; rather, it's a journey where planned actions and steps will change over time. The implementation process focuses on the following questions:

- Who will be charged with implementing crafted strategies?
- What are the new strategies?
- Why are new strategies required?
- When and over what time period will the implementation process take place?

5.1 WHO ARE THE LEADERS OF THE STRATEGIC CHANGE?

Who is the person(s) that has the authority and responsibility to implement the strategy? What about for making decisions? Who in the organization will be involved with the implementation? Who and what units need to work together, exchange/share information, and provide the talent, resources, and other inputs to carry out the strategic change?

5.2 WHAT ARE THE CHANGES TO EXISTING STRATEGIES?

What changes to existing strategies are needed, and what new strategies are being implemented—that is, what programs, strategies, and past actions are being abandoned? Which ones are being modified? What new strategies are being pursued? What structural and system changes are required?

5.3 WHY ARE CHANGES NEEDED TO EXISTING STRATEGIES?

Why are changes to existing strategies and actions needed, and why at this time? What is the rationale and case for making strategic changes?

5.4 WHEN WILL CHANGES BE MADE?

When will major decisions need to be made? When will communications to key stakeholders take place, and what needs to be communicated? When will funds and other resources need to be committed? How will resources be managed? When will key milestones and events be reached?

6. EXECUTION: LEARNING AND LEADING

Execution encompasses how the implementation process will take place on a daily basis. Typically, this process of change is led from the top of the organization. Senior leaders need to champion the strategy implementation process over time and adjust and change the implementation plan as circumstances warrant. Strategic leadership, organizational learning, and constant innovation are essential elements of strategic change. Change can be incremental, strategic, or transformative. Strategic leaders must be skilled in managing each type of change.

6.1 CHANGE CAN BE INCREMENTAL, STRATEGIC, OR TRANSFORMATIVE

Strategy implementation and execution is change (see Exhibit 7.3: Incremental, Strategic, Transformative Change Model. Organizations can experience:

- **Incremental Change**: A small adjustment made toward an end result. In a business environment, making an incremental change to the way things are done typically does not significantly threaten existing power structures or alter current methods. Practices associated with incremental change are TQM (total quality management), benchmarking, Six Sigma, and continuous product and process improvements.[7]
- **Strategic Change**: A restructuring of an organization's business or strategies that is typically performed in order to achieve an important objective. For example, a strategic change might include shifts in a corporation's policies, target market, mission, or organizational structure.
- **Transformational or Radical Change**: Transformational change is driven by radical technological innovations or shifts in the external environment. For example, the shift from gas-powered vehicles to electric vehicles is driving radical or transformative changes in the automobile industry. Uber's car-sharing app is driving transformative change in the taxi industry. Radical or technical change is not a new phenomenon; it happens to all industries and all companies. Radical technical change is transformative to traditional business products and processes and usually necessitates a shift in the firm's culture and strategic management. A transformational change is designed to be organization-wide and is enacted over a period of time.

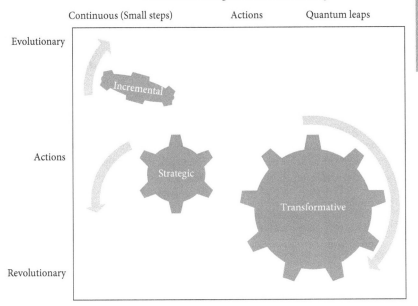

Incremental, strategic, transformative change

Exhibit 7.3
Incremental,
Strategic,
Transformative
Change Model

Once an organization embarks on transformational change, it cannot go back to the old way of doing business. Transformative change radically alters the culture, strategies, business model, and mental models of the firm.[8]

6.2 TECHNICAL AND ORGANIZATIONAL LEARNING

Strategy execution requires learning at two levels—technical learning and organizational learning:

- **Technical Learning**: Defines and specifies the main elements, characteristics, and components of a newly crafted strategy (e.g., what it is, what its components are, and what differences and similarities exist among current strategy(s) and the newly crafted strategy(s)). Technical learning specifies the type of generic strategy the organization is pursuing and what key success factors, critical resources, core capabilities, and distinctive competencies are needed to make it work from a technical and operational perspective. Technical learning has a focus on the firm's business (the economics of the strategy) and the programs, systems, actions, staffing, and resources needed to pursue this particular strategy or set of strategic actions. For example, if the generic strategy is based on low cost, then technical learning is required to understand the firm's cost structure and how cost efficiencies can be achieved. Technical learning provides the specifications, elements, and characteristics of newly crafted strategies.
- **Organizational Learning**: Enhances the firm's collective ability to accept, make sense of, and respond to internal and external change on an organization-wide level. Organizational learning is more than the sum of the information held by employees. It requires systematic integration and collective interpretation of new knowledge that leads to collective action. It also involves risk taking in experimentation. In sum, organizational learning details the organizational-wide learning required to implement the newly crafted strategy.[9]

7. STRATEGIC CONTROL: REINVEST, RENEW, RELAUNCH

Strategic control monitors and evaluates the effectiveness of the newly crafted strategy and its implementation. This step assesses whether the crafted strategy(s) (step 5) and the implemented and executed strategy(s) (step 6) are producing the intended or desired outcomes. One analytical tool or conceptual model employed in strategic control is gap analysis. **Gap analysis** determines whether the intended results are being achieved, or are likely to be achieved, through the newly crafted and executed strategies.[10] It is a check on the previous steps in the strategic management conceptual model. Gap analysis consists of (1) listing the characteristic factors (such as attributes, competencies, and performance levels) of the present situation (i.e., what is), (2) listing the factors needed to achieve future objectives (i.e., what should be), and (3) highlighting the gaps that exist and need to be filled. Gap analysis forces a company to reflect on whether the crafted strategies are working as intended and, if not, what needs to change. Gap analysis can also be depicted as the ongoing management of the firm's competitive advantage through its life cycle (see Exhibit 7.4: Gap Analysis). Competitive advantage for any organization is difficult to sustain over long periods of time. A firm's competitive advantage life cycle mirrors the firm's organizational and product life cycles. A firm's realized competitive advantage is challenged by rivals and environmental change and erodes over time. To sustain a competitive advantage, the firm requires renewal or investment in strategic change via innovative strategies and activities.

(See Exhibit 7.5: Competitive Advantage Life Cycle.)

**Exhibit 7.4
Gap Analysis**

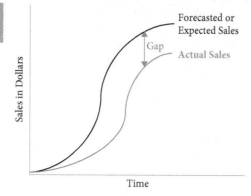

**Exhibit 7.5
Competitive
Advantage Life
Cycle**

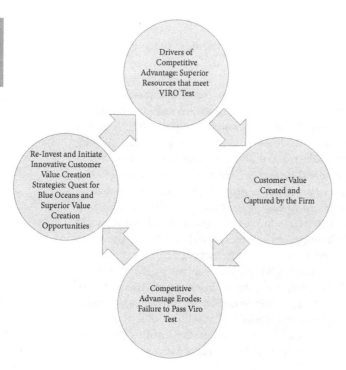

In June 2018, GE was dropped from the S&P Dow Jones industrial index. The removal from the Dow ended GE's more than 100-year run in the 30-company blue chip index. The company was an original member of the Dow Jone index dating back to 1896. If the removal was not bad enough for this iconic global conglomerate, GE was also under investigation by the Securities and Exchange Commission for a $15 billion write-off used to cover miscalculations in its insurance unit. Warren Buffet noted just prior to GE's removal from the DOW: "The best thing to happen to us is when a great company gets into temporary trouble. … We want to buy them when they're on the operating table."[a] This was the third time that GE was removed from the index. Other notable companies removed from the Dow when they faced financial difficulties and their stock underperformed are AT&T, Honeywell, and General Motors.

Sources: Veiga, Alex. "General Electric to End Its More Than 100-Year Run on the Dow Jones." *Time*. June 19, 2018: http://time.com/5316708/general-electric-delisted-dow-jones/; "If General Electric Gets Kicked Out Of The Dow, So What?" *Seeking Alpha*. February. 27, 2018: https://seekingalpha.com/article/4151339-general-electric-gets-kicked-dow

1. What is the DOW Jones Industrial Average? How important is being listed in this index for a company?
2. Why would someone like Warren Buffet want to buy GE stock when it is "on the operating table" and its future is unknown?
3. Should GE management be concerned that it was removed for the DOW index? Why or why not?

---

a   "If General Electric Gets Kicked Out Of The Dow, So What?" *Seeking Alpha*. February. 27, 2018

8. WHAT NEEDS TO BE ALIGNED IN STRATEGY IMPLEMENTATION AND EXECUTION?

Strategy execution is closely associated with the concept of strategic fit or alignment. One cannot hope to effectively implement and execute a newly crafted strategy(s) without a clear alignment to the firm's strategic intent, vision, mission, goals and objectives, values, culture, and structure.

8.1 STRATEGIC INTENT

It is not enough to focus on the drivers of competition alone to gain a position of market leadership. Strong leadership and a determination to realize a clear vision for the future is also required.[11] Hamel and Prahalad, in *Competing for the Future*, describe **strategic intent** as a dream that energizes a company. In their terms, strategic intent is an animated dream, driven and shaped by capstone strategic architecture that not only "points the way to the future" but also provides the emotional and intellectual energy needed for the journey. **Strategic architecture** is the brain (intellectual energy), and strategic intent is the heart (emotional energy). Strategic intent implies a significant **stretch** for the organization.[12] With this as the organizational mindset (a strategic leader's focus on strategic intent and stretch), the disparities and gaps between existing organizational resources and future goals become challenges (opportunities) rather than constraints (obstacles). With strategic intent and stretch, the strategic leaders' focus on winning becomes a core obsession, capable of sustaining a sense of urgency in the organization and in strategy execution. Strategic intent does more than just paint a vision; it signals the desire to win. Most organizations will not have the resources or capabilities to reach their most ambitious goals. As such, strategic intent forces the firm to think critically and strategically in obtaining resources and developing key capabilities. Stretch reflects the recognition that successful strategies are built as much around "what can be" as around "what is,"

VIDEO 7.2 The Mission, Vision, and Values Statements

8.2 VISION

A key to implementing and executing a strategy is the leader's ability to create a vision for the organization. Leaders must craft a clear, concise strategy and a set of actions for realizing the vision. Vision entails a set of ideals and priorities for the business; it paints a picture of the future as well as a sense of what makes the business unique. The vision typically outlines a broad set of compelling criteria that set the boundaries in executing newly crafted strategies.

8.3 MISSION

The mission of the business identifies the "where" and "how" of the actual "territory" in which the organization will compete. It defines the scope of the organization's products and services, markets, customers, and geographic coverage. A mission statement often contains a code of conduct and principles to guide management in implementing and executing strategy. A mission statement implies that, throughout the business, there is a common thread or unifying theme that provides a guide for carrying out the business's vision and strategic intent.

8.4 GOALS AND OBJECTIVES

Goals are open-ended statements pertaining to desired outcomes; that is, what the business would like to achieve in being a profitable market leader. Objectives act as benchmarks to identify the results the business must achieve if it is to be successful in executing its strategy. In executing strategy, objectives should be quantifiable, challenging, and attainable.

8.5 VALUES

Values are the beliefs one holds. These beliefs usually act to legitimize one's behavior. In determining a business's vision, mission, goals, objectives, and understanding of values, both individual and group inputs are necessary. Values formulate the basis for ideas and encompass the emotional energy for acting on one's beliefs. Values signal what is important to the individuals responsible for implementing and executing strategies.

8.6 CULTURE

Culture is the shared values held by the strategic leaders of an organization that are passed down from one generation of the organization's people to the next. Culture encompasses the values, core principles, norms of behaviors, and beliefs that drive the business in both good and bad times.

An organization's culture can be the major force in moving the organization forward, or it can be its greatest obstacle. In a four-year study of nine to 10 firms in 20 industries, Kotter and Heskett found that firms with a strong corporate culture (based on shared values) outperformed the others by a significant margin.[13] The authors also note the cultures of winning firms emphasized three constituents: customers, employees, and shareholders. Strong corporate culture alone is not enough; it must be combined with an appropriate business strategy for the competitive environment. This requires strong leadership at all levels of the organization, not just the top.

8.7 ORGANIZATIONAL STRUCTURE—STRUCTURE "ALWAYS" FOLLOWS STRATEGY

One of the earliest and most widely accepted models on management is Alfred Chandler's theory that a firm's organizational structure follows strategy; that is, a corporate structure is created in order to implement a given corporate strategy.[14] Chandler substantiated his thesis in the 1960s with case studies of four U.S. conglomerates that dominated their industries from the 1920s onward. Chandler describes how the chemical company DuPont, the automobile manufacturer General Motors, the energy company Standard Oil of New Jersey, and the retailer Sears Roebuck managed a growth and diversification strategy by adopting the revolutionary multidivision form (M-form). The **M-form** is a corporate federation of semi-independent **product or geographic groups** plus a headquarters that oversees the corporate strategy and coordinates interdependencies. Although the organizational M-form was implemented differently by each of the organizations, Chandler demonstrates that the need to restructure arose from a strategic shift driven by new technologies and market changes. Chandler also describes corporate strategy as (1) the determination of long-term goals and objectives and (2) the adoption of courses of action and associated allocation of resources required to achieve goals. Accordingly, **structure** is the design of the organization through which strategy is implemented and executed. Chandler's thesis argues that new organizational forms are no more than a derivative of strategy.

9. DESIGNING ORGANIZATIONS TO SOLVE PROBLEMS

All firms need to have structure in order to effectively craft and carry out strategy. A clearly designed structure helps to organize a firm's functions, business units, work teams, and people. Structure is critically important for managing people and information flows; coordinating decisions; and configuring organizational units and activities. Boards of directors and senior managers design structures to aid the firm in addressing several strategic, functional, and human processes. Structure enables the firm to meet various demands placed on environmental change and stakeholders. In designing an optimum structure for the firm, the strategic manager must address several questions including:

- What structure is best for each stage of a firm's growth and development?
- What organizational, managerial, people, and decision-making problems need to be solved?
- What structure best addresses customer value creation?
- What structure promotes efficient operations?
- What structure best solves problems and facilitates organizational effectiveness?

Strategists have numerous options in designing not only the structure but also the ways in which the firm's decisions, processes, tasks, and activities are carried out. No one best organizational structure exists because all businesses are different in the ways they manage resources and interact with customers, employees, and other stakeholders. Still, there are several common or generic models of structure that can be used to guide strategists in designing a structure that fits the needs and challenges of their organization. We will briefly examine the advantages and disadvantages of the following organizational structure models: simple, functional, multidivision, and matrix.[15]

9.1 SIMPLE STRUCTURE (OWNER–MANAGER-CENTERED)

Simple structure is the most common and centers on the founder(s) or owner-manager's personal approach to managing resource dependency (access to limited resources). This structure is usually associated with small- to medium-sized firms in their early stage of growth. The firm typically has a limited number of products and minimal staff. The key to firm success lies within the abilities and expertise of the owner-manager. Decision making is centralized in the hands of the owner or a small number of partners or staff (see Exhibit 7.6: Simple Structure (Owner–Manager-Centered)). Unlike other organizational structures, the simple, or flat, structure does not have formal departments or other layers of management.[16] The advantages of the simple structure are decision-making authority is clear and rests with the owner-manager; the small size fosters speed and flexibility in responding to customers and changes in the external environment; communication is simplified, given the small size and limited number of employees; and expertise is focused on one product and/or customer group. Small entrepreneurial start-ups are more creative in finding effective ways of using limited resources, a concept know as *bricolage*. **Bricolage** is defined as the creative rearrangement of resources to generate true novelty. In entrepreneurial settings, bricolage is the "creative organization." The use of social networks and extremely limited resources for better outcomes create unique products and services that challenge silos or bureaucracy found in larger organizations.[17] Some disadvantages of this structure include the organization's heavy dependence on the expertise of the owner-manager, availability or access to resources to grow the business may be limited, and a lack of professional and functional expertise may also hinder the success of the company.

Exhibit 7.6 Simple Structure (Owner–Manager-Centered)

SOLE PROPRIETOR—ALL DECISIONS MAKE BY THE OWNER-MANAGER

Most small businesses

Owner's personal approach to managing resource dependency

Simple structure is the most common and centers on the founder(s) or owner-manager personal approach to managing resource dependency (access to limited resources). This structure is usually associated with small-to medium-sized firms in their early stage of growth.

9.2 FUNCTIONAL STRUCTURE

Functional structures are designed around the firm's activities and tasks performed. The primary and secondary activities in the firm's value chain mirror the professional expertise and skills found in the functional structure. Primary activities are those activities, functions, or work groups that are directly engaged in the operational and technical core profit-generating activities of the firm. Profit-generating activities are also referred to as **line** activities. In the manufacturing firm, line activities include all functions that are directly engaged in the procurement, value added operations (manufacture), and distribution of the final product to customers. In the service firms (e.g., legal, professional, financial services), line function and activities generate fees and profits through the services provided to clients. Secondary activities support the primary or line activities but are not directly engaged in generating profits. Secondary activities are also referred to as **staff** functions. These functions provide support for line functions (e.g., engineering, advisory (legal), service (human resources), or control (accounting) groups). Staff groups support those engaged in the core or primary activities of the enterprise. Thus, staff groups create the infrastructure of the organization. Human resources, information technologies, and finance are infrastructural functions. Staff groups provide analysis, research, counsel, monitoring, evaluation, and other activities that would otherwise reduce organizational efficiency if carried out by the primary activities. As such, functional structures group a company's activities and tasks by common primary and secondary functions. Although the various functions must collaborate and coordinate specialized tasks and activities, they are managed and grouped independently of one another (see Exhibit 7.7: Functional Structure). Functional structures are best when the external environment is relatively stable and predictable and the firm has a small number of products or services that can be mass-produced for mass (large) markets. The advantages of this type of structure include centralized and streamlined decision making that allows for more efficient and effective management of diverse activities. Conversely, some disadvantages are that decision making can become bureaucratic within functions and functional areas can turn into silos that stifle change, creativity, interdisciplinary learning, and bricolage opportunities.

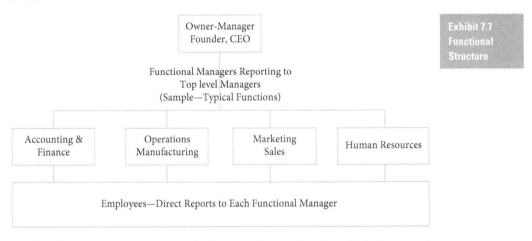

Functional structures are designed around the firm's activities or tasks performed. The primary and secondary activities in the firm's value chain mirror the professional expertise and skills found in the functional structure. Above functions are by example only - can you think of other functions that would be included in this type of organization structure?

9.3. MULTIDIVISIONAL (M-FORM)

As tasks, activities, products, and markets grow in complexity and diversity, the crafting and execution of strategies becomes more challenging and difficult, especially for firms with functional structures. Growth brings on new organizational challenges and problems requiring a change in the way things are done. This usually necessitates an alteration in organizational structure. The division structure clusters the firm's functions, tasks, and activities by product groups, customer groups, or geographic regions or countries. The firm is now composed of several divisions with each division overseen by a CEO, president, or general manger. This leader typically has profit and loss responsibility for the division. The division groups or units engage in its primary (line) and secondary (staff) functions. Some secondary functions like treasury (equity and financing), human resource management, and research and development are either centralized at corporate (headquarters) or shared equally or partially with the divisions. Primary functions remain the domain of the division. Division mangers are responsible for determining **how** the division will compete and position its products in customer or geographic markets (see Exhibit 7.8: Multi-Divisional Structure). One advantage of a divisional structure is greater strategic fit between the division's products, customers, and geographic markets with its expertise and talents. Strategic managers act as chief strategists and have profit and loss responsibilities. These skilled individuals tactically position their division or business unit to better anticipate and adapt to customer and industry changes. Another advantage of the divisional structure is that decision making is decentralized to units' strategic managers who can lobby for limited resources and build strong cultures for divisions. Conversely, the main disadvantage of the divisional structure is that it can generate infighting and acrimony among divisions. For example, divisional silos can develop within the division and between the firm's other divisions. Thus, one division will sometimes act to undermine another division or resist change introduced by corporate. As such, division compartmentalization could inhibit the firm's ability to make timely and critical strategic decisions.

**Exhibit 7.8
Multidivisional
Structure**

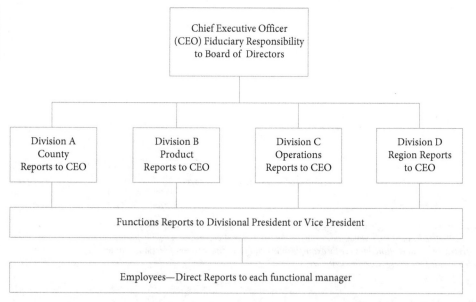

*The division structure clusters the firm's functions, tasks, and activities by product groups, customer groups, or geographic regions or countries. Each division is overseen by a president, or general manager and reports to corporate management (CEO, Corporate). Divisional managers typically have profit and lost responsibility for the division.. Primary functions remain the domain of the division. Division mangers are responsible for determining **how** the division will compete. Division managers usually have responsibility for some, but not all secondary functions.*

9.4 MATRIX STRUCTURE

This structure combines the best of functional and divisional structures. A matrix organization utilizes teams of employees to accomplish activities by: (1) taking advantage of the firm's many resource strengths and (2) limiting or designing around the weaknesses or disadvantages found in the functional and division structures. The matrix structure is based on two principles: the authority of functional knowledge or expertise and the authority of knowledge of managing people and work teams. As such, in a matrix structure, employees within the work team (also referred to as a "project group") answer to more than one manager. The functional managers are charged with overseeing the functional expertise while the project manager is responsible for planning, managing, and delivering the project from inception to completion. Matrix structures are not new. For example, many defense contractors and aerospace firms use the matrix structure to manage large-scale government projects and contracts. For each new program or contract, a team of managers, both functional and project, are given the authority and responsibility to manage the program throughout its entire life cycle (see Exhibit 7.9: Matrix Structure). The advantages of the matrix structure include the combination of expertise over several functions; decisions are made on the authority of knowledge and not necessarily on one's position or politics in an organization; project teams share a common vision and purpose; and multiple goals and values can guide and motivate the project team. The disadvantages of the matrix structure are increased complexity, resulting in coordination and communication challenges; reporting to more than one manager could lead to conflict of power, unclear direction, favoritism, and ineffective decision making; and close-knit project teams could spiral into group think or decisions that support their own interests but not necessarily the interests or needs of project customers. Complicated and confusing reporting structures can also incur unnecessary costs to the project and delay time of completion.

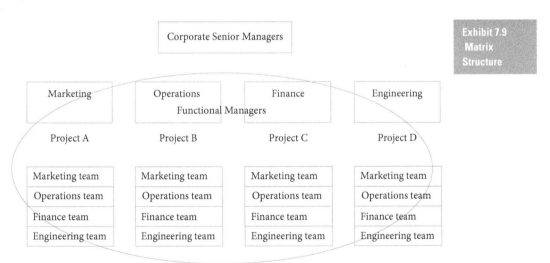

Exhibit 7.9 Matrix Structure

Matrix structure combines the best of functional and divisional structures. A matrix organization utilizes teams of employees to accomplish activities by: (1) taking advantage of the firm's many resource strengths, and (2) limiting or designing around the weaknesses or disadvantages found in the functional and division structures. The matrix structure is based on two principles – the authority of functional knowledge or expertise, and the authority of knowledge of managing people and work teams..

10. THE LEARNING STRATEGY SCHOOL

Strategic managers must create and extract customer value by tactically aligning internal resources and capabilities with external opportunities. This must be done while successfully countering external threats and internal weaknesses. Schools offer mental models and normative recommendations or prescriptions for managers' strategic actions, activities, and behaviors (what should be) but are based on positive, descriptive, critical inquiry of the real world (what is). The learning strategy school of thought took shape in the late 1980s and early 1990s, though its conceptual roots are based in behavioral theory of the 1950s and 1960s.[18] Researcher Herbert Simon argued that, unlike the classical economic assumptions of perfect information and profit maximization, firms consist of coalitions that operate under the notion of bounded rationally, logical incrementalism, and "satisficing" (good enough) behavior. The underlying logic is that competitive advantage is built more on learning and less on controlling resources or commanding people.

10.1 LEARNING BY DOING

Advocates of this school share the belief that "we act in order to think as much as we think in order to act."[19] Wang Yang Ming's 1498 proverb, "Knowledge is the beginning of practice; doing is the completion of knowing,"[20] captures the essence of the learning school of thought. The best-designed strategy is useless unless the organization has the knowledge, people, and resources needed to actually execute the strategy.

10.2 BUILDING LEARNING COMMUNITIES BASED ON INFORMATION SUPERIORITY

Learning school advocates argue that a firm's competitive landscape is not static with well-defined rules or principles for maximizing behavior but rather dynamic, constantly changing, hypercompetitive, and unpredictable. These competitive dynamics make it difficult for any firm to sustain its competitive advantage for an extended period of time. This school operates under the premise that strategists must create learning organizations that regularly adapt strategies through continuous learning that is retrospective, reflective, and active.[21] As such, firms constantly identify, obtain, manage, and develop information and knowledge management systems that provide opportunities to sustain and improve organizational performance—or competitive advantage—by means of information superiority over rivals. Information superiority supplies strategists with the means to help solve customer product, service, and organizational problems. Information superiority and problem-solving capabilities are achieved through continuous organizational and individual learning and knowledge management. From this perspective, strategy is crafted and executed through a series of "nibbles" (**incremental** and **evolutionary** actions or steps) as opposed to one large bite (**discrete** or **revolutionary** actions or steps).[22] Because competitive environments are constantly changing and unpredictable, organizations need to continually learn by building and fostering learning communities. "**Learning community**" is a term coined by Peter Senge and his colleagues. A learning community (and organization) is an institution that facilitates the learning of its members and continuously transforms itself.[23] Senge describes a learning organization as a group of people working together collectively to enhance their capacities to create results they really care about.

10.3 FIVE DISCIPLINES OF A LEARNING ORGANIZATION

Senge advanced five disciplines of a learning organization:

Systems Thinking: Organizations are a system of interrelationships. To become more successful, we need to analyze these relationships and find the problems within. This will allow an organization to eliminate the obstacles to learning.

Personal Mastery: An individual holds great importance in a learning organization. Continuous self-improvement holds as much significance as commitment to the organization. Employees must grow and work on their own goals. Learning school advocates argue that there is a competitive advantage for an organization whose workforce can learn more quickly than the workforces of other organizations.

Mental Models: The assumptions held by individuals and organizations are called "mental models." Mental models drive company culture and the diverse theories and mindsets that serve as a framework for the functioning of the organization. Learning organizations look for how these affect organizational development.

Shared Vision: A learning organization's employees all share a common vision. Personal goals must be in sync with the goals and vision of the organization. The development of a shared vision is important in motivating the staff to learn, as it creates a common identity that provides focus and energy for learning through the organization.

Team Learning: The accumulation of individual learning constitutes team learning. For a team to learn, its members must be in sync and reach agreement. The benefits of team or shared learning are that staff grow more quickly and the problem-solving capacity of the organization is improved through better access to knowledge and expertise.[24]

10.4 THE LEADER'S ROLE IN THE LEARNING ORGANIZATION

The learning school encourages organizations to shift to a more interconnected way of thinking. Organizations need to become more like communities to which employees can feel a commitment. Senge argues that learning is the only way to address two deep-seated problems embedded in hierarchical organizations:

- Leaders in hierarchical organizations are ill-prepared to manage rapidly changing complex environments.
- Leaders are also unprepared to harness the intelligence and spirit of people at all levels to continually build and share knowledge.[25]

This view requires profound rethinking of the basic tenets underlying strategic leadership. Leadership is not top-down. Learning organizations are knowledge-creating organizations that require leadership in order for knowledge to be distributed among a diverse array of individuals and teams. Strategy is both emergent and deliberate. Emergent strategies can be found throughout the organization and grow out of individuals instead of being immaculately conceived or analytically derived at the top of the organization. Advocates of this school note that for learning to endure in organizations, the organization needs to concentrate on three interrelated activities:

- Research and the disciplined pursuit of discovery and understanding that leads to generalizable theory and methods
- Capability-building by the enhancement of people's abilities and knowledge to achieve results in line with their deepest personal and professional aspirations
- Practice, or the "stuff" that happens in organizations every day; that is, people working together to achieve practical outcomes and building practical know-how in the process[26]

Many reasons exist as to why an organization may have trouble transforming itself into a learning organization. The first is that an organization does not have enough time. Employees and management may have other issues that take priority over attempting to effect change in the culture of their organization. Second, the firm may not have the resources, appropriate staff, or training and development programs required to be a learning organization. Finally, for an organization to be able to change, it needs to know the steps necessary to solve the problems it faces. Changing to a learning organization may not be relevant to the organization's needs or problems. To combat this challenge, a strategy must be built. The organization should determine what its problems are before transforming itself into a learning organization.

VIDEO 7.3 5 Ways to Lead in an Era of Constant Change | Jim Hemerling

11. STRATEGIC LEADERSHIP

What is strategic leadership? What does it take to assume the role of strategic leader in the twenty-first century's age of information? Critical inquiry and strategic thinking are the responsibility of all leaders. To increase the organization's chances for success, strategic leaders must be skilled at making and executing strategy. The strategic management conceptual model can act as an information "hub" and knowledge management system that turns data into information and information into the pertinent knowledge that drives critical inquiry, strategic thinking, and action (execution). Knowledge is the basis for action. It manifests itself in the core capabilities and distinctive competencies that set the organization apart from rivals. It is the responsibility of the strategic leader to develop and effectively execute core capabilities and distinctive competencies with the sole purpose of value creation. In the industrial age organization, a relatively small number of strategic managers were responsible for making and executing strategy. In the information age organization, it takes leaders throughout the organization to effectively make and executive strategy. All strategic leaders in the twenty-first century must develop the creative vision of a seasoned entrepreneur and the mindset of a skilled CEO.[27] Today's leaders must be active learners and teachers who think and act like CEOs. Although the CEO is the chief architect of strategy as well as the organizational builder and doer, it takes leadership at all levels of the organization to effectively execute strategy.[28] In a study of leadership in great family businesses, the authors reported, "The competencies most frequently required for success at the top of any size business include strategic orientation, market insight, results orientation, customer impact, collaboration and influence, organizational development, team leadership, and change leadership."[29]

11.1 TRADITIONAL LEADERSHIP DEFINED

Dahl and Lindblom noted the difficulty sociologists and political scientists have had in finding a useful operational definition of leaders. This is no less so for the management scholar and student of strategy. Dahl and Lindblom provide us with a starting point for our understanding of leadership. They note that, in defining leadership, "A good first approximation is to say that if individuals in groups were ranked according to the extent of their control over another, the leader or leaders would be those with significantly greater control." Conversely, if no one had significantly greater control in the group, then the group would be without a leader. Thus, one could locate control relationships along a virtual continuum of equal control to disparate control. Leaders, in their view, are those with disparate control or influence. What is disparate control? **Disparate control** can be defined in terms of a person's authority or position in the organization and the ability of this person to influence and control the action of others. One's position in the organization does not always define one's ability to lead. As Barnard noted in his seminal theory of the CEO's or senior executive's function, authority is delegated upward; that is, as director (or leader) of an organization, you have no power that is not granted to you by your subordinates. Within the content of disparate control, three distinct types of leaders have emerged: transactional, charismatic, and transformational.[30]

11.2 TRANSACTIONAL LEADERS

Transactional leadership occurs when one person takes the initiative in making contact with others for the purpose of exchanging something valued; that is, leaders approach followers with an eye toward exchanging. In this arrangement, both the superior and subordinate influence one another reciprocally so that each receives something of value. Transactional leadership is contingent upon the leader's ability to satisfactorily meet and respond to the reactions and changing expectations of the followers. Transactional leadership, to a large extent, is based on the leader's ability to satisfy the needs and desires of the followers in the exchange process. If what is received is of greater value than what has to be given in return (for both parties), then a mutually agreeable exchange will take place. In Barnard's terms, there is a "zone of indifference" to the order as long as the exchange taking place is of value to the person.[31]

The transactional-leadership approach is characteristic of the style that was in vogue during most of the twentieth-century industrial age. The manager is described as transactional because he or she keeps practicing the same kind of exchanges with employees, customers, shareholders, and society at large. The information age ushered in a radical change in this type of classical thinking. Information and knowledge have grown exponentially in the information age, and these two factors are rapidly infused and diffused throughout industries and organizations. The explosion in information and knowledge across all disciplines and society, primarily through the rapid growth in the internet and information technology, has changed the nature of competition and the nature of the organization. This has, in turn, revolutionized our understanding of what leadership is and what it means to be a leader in the twenty-first-century information age. The **information revolution** has resulted in hypercompetition and a delayering of the organization—a flattening of the organization's hierarchy. Being fast to market with the "next new thing" or improved products and services requires a different type of leader and organization. It requires the leader to be simultaneously charismatic *and* transformational. It also requires the leader to be an active learner, teacher, and entrepreneur whose conduct and reasoning parallels that of a seasoned CEO.

11.3 CHARISMATIC LEADERS

Charisma is a Greek word meaning "a gift." In biblical times, charisma was associated with leaders and certain religious members. From these early beginnings, much study on personal attributes and characteristics of charismatic leadership has been undertaken. The concept includes any authority that derives its legitimacy from a "devotion to the specific and exceptional sanctity, heroism, or exemplary character of an individual person, and of the normative patterns or orders revealed or ordained by him,"[32] rather than from rules, position, or tradition. In more recent studies (especially from the organizational theorists' point of view), the personal attributes of charismatic leaders are vision, appealing ideological goals, behavior that instills confidence, an ability to inspire and/or create inspirational activities, dominance, rhetorical or articulating ability, and unconventional and/or counternormative behavior.[33]

Followers of charismatic leaders exhibit attributes such as an unquestioning acceptance of the leader; trust in the leader's beliefs; affection for the leader; willing obedience to the leader; emulation or an identification with the leader; similarity of the follower's beliefs with those beliefs of the leader; emotional involvement of followers in the mission; heightened goals of the followers; and feelings on the part of followers that they are able to accomplish or contribute to the leader's and organization's vision and mission.

11.4 TRANSFORMATIONAL LEADERS

Transformational leaders act from deeply held value systems that include standards like justice and integrity. These values are end values—that is, values that cannot be negotiated. As a result of these values, the transformational leader is able to raise the level of performance in the followers and change followers' goals and beliefs.[34] The personal characteristics of the transformational leader include self-confidence, dominance, and a strong conviction in the moral righteousness of one's beliefs. The key behaviors of successful transformational leaders include articulating goals, building an image, demonstrating confidence, and arousing motivation. Transformational leaders attempt and succeed in raising colleagues, subordinates, followers, clients, or constituents to a greater awareness of self and performance. These leaders have a passion for what they do and maintain a drive to succeed and gain results. They have a passion for the journey it will take to create and sustain value for the business and the people they lead. In contrast to the charismatic leader (though attributes of the charismatic leader are found in all transformational leaders), nonleaders follow, not necessarily from blind faith or inspiration but from a strong understanding and belief in the ideas and values of the leader, their own values and beliefs, and strategic thinking. It makes strategic sense based on their knowledge, expertise, and their own leadership ability.[35]

12. CHANGE MANAGEMENT

Strategic management is about change and the process of organizational learning and adaptation. Research has shown that individuals do not necessarily resist change; they just need to understand why change is needed for the firm and for themselves. Change can be exhilarating for individuals and work groups if it is approached with the understanding of why it is needed and individuals are provided with the resources and support necessary to carry it out. Change can be debilitating if not understood and approached by strategic leaders who do not bring the vision, integrity, and commitment required to effectively manage the adjustment. As such, change needs to be viewed as a process and activity that can be strategically and organizationally managed. (See Table 7.1: Strategy Implementation, Execution and Control Process.)

12.1 THE NATURE OF STRATEGIC CHANGE

Change in organizations is both constant and necessary. Without change, organizations will stagnate and eventually decay. This especially holds true in today's fast-paced and radically changing environment. Although change is necessary, it is not always embraced, especially when it comes to strategic and transformative change. The management of change must be viewed as a continuous learning process. To be successful, strategic leaders at all levels of the organization need to be open to and embrace change. But what does this entail? The type of change (incremental, strategic, or transformative) will determine the time, organizational energy, and resources committed to bringing about the desired change. There are several formal and informal activities and processes that can be used to help people navigate and manage change. In addition to technical learning associated with change, behavioral (organizational) learning is also extremely important; both types of learning are required to bring about desired change. Kanter, in her seminal book entitled *The Change Masters*, wrote, "The individuals who will succeed and flourish in the times ahead will be masters of change: adept at reorienting their own and others' activities in untried directions to bring about higher levels of achievement."[36] Change usually progresses through several cycles or stages. Bringing individuals and work teams through these cycles is critically important to implementing and executing strategy.

When change occurs, leaders and the people they lead must manage both the **things** that are changing and the **feelings** they are having about the change. Strategic decisions encompass altering some or all things, such as products, services, processes, activities, locations, resources, people, and the ways things "used to be done." Transformative change modifies most, if not all, of the former ways of doing business. Once transformative change has commenced, a return to the way things used to be done proves impossible. Transformative change embodies a complete revolution. Similarly, strategic change is associated with altering most of the organization's structure and prior methods of doing business. Strategic and transformative change, if not managed correctly, can evoke strong feelings and emotions. These emotions include positive feelings, such as joy, excitement, engagement, empowerment, openness, satisfaction, and sense of self-worth, as well as negative feelings, such as anger, frustration, helplessness, denial, dissatisfaction, uncertainty, powerlessness, and self-deception. As such, feeling and emotions can either substantively facilitate or block the change process. Even incremental change, such as adding a new total quality management program, can evoke strong positive or negative feelings and emotions. Feelings and emotions transcend formal policies, procedures, and structures. They evoke strong, formal and informal personal interactions with one another. As such, all change, no matter its frequency and magnitude, must be clearly thought through, critically analyzed, and consciously executed. Change must be seen as a continual learning process.

HOW DO YOU MANAGE CHANGE IN YOUR LIFE?

Think of a recent significant change in your life. What changed? What surroundings drove the change? How did you respond to the change? Did you resist the change, seeing it as a threat to the way you normally do things? Did you begrudgingly cope with it but still feel it was not needed? Or did you openly embrace the change and see it as a potential opportunity? And finally, did you knowingly drive the change to improve your life and future success?

12.2 THE CHANGE CYCLE

Change is a normal aspect of daily life (personal, political, technological, and organizational (work), etc.). And without it, there would be few opportunities for individuals to grow and prosper and improve their quality of life, both on a personal and a career level. Change and our reaction to it go through a recognizable cycle. Understanding this cycle and its characteristics helps us to harness the emotional side, seeing fewer threats and more opportunities. Each step is important. Although some steps can be moved through at a faster pace, no step can be skipped altogether. In order to effectively implement and execute strategy, key managers must understand and properly manage the change process. The **change process** includes the following steps or phases: unawareness, awakening, reordering and chaos, transforming, commitment, implementation, and integration.[37]

- *Stage 1:* **Unawareness**. In stage 1, there is a feeling of comfort with the way things are normally done. No feeling of urgency, need, or desire to change exists. Many people (and organizations) fail because they become too comfortable with their surroundings and the way of doing business. Being too blind or unaware of the world around them can lead to complacency, inaction, and a false sense of comfort. Individuals and organizations need to be open to the world around them, to be observant and perceptive of what is different and changing in their world. They also need to be open to and develop a capacity to acknowledge that change is always present, even if it might be problematic.

- *Stage 2:* **Awakening**. In this stage, the individual becomes aware that things are changing and that better ways of doing things might exist. They become aware that the status quo might present a threat. While becoming aware and gaining an understanding for a possible need for change, the individual still does not understand how change will come about. They need to understand what is driving change and why individual change might be needed. A lack of understanding can lead to instability and uncertainty, disrupting the harmony of stage 1.

- *Stage 3:* **Reordering and Chaos**. Analyzing the existing situation and challenging the status quo becomes commonplace. With an increased awareness of surrounding change, a frenetic type of energy starts to catch hold for the individual fueling more questions and more challenges. Turmoil increases as possible issues and implications become more fully realized. Roles become unclear, workloads increase, and direction seems unfocused. In this stage, individuals begin to understand that a change in their mindset, mental models, and the way they do things might be required.

- *Stage 4:* **Transforming**. Transforming requires creating a compelling vision from analyzing and assessing the information and feelings identified in stages 1 through 3—a clear image of what is to be achieved that will inform every step taken toward the desire vision and goals. Organizations can have the most impact on the success of a change effort during the transformation stage. At this point, energy must be harnessed and focused on a common vision. The successful concentration on achieving a better state equates to opportunity. Allowing emotions to run rampant equates to threat. Fear of losing the security of the old can be offset by the enthusiasm for the potential of the new.

- *Stage 5:* **Commitment**. Taking responsibility for the implementation of the vision. Leaders must find a means to channel the once frenetic energy of the individual into a focused drive toward vision. Conflict and discomfort arise between the individual wanting to go back for security and comfort in the previous methods for doing things and the excitement in potential opportunities of new vision and transformative ways of doing things. The best way for the individual to adapt to change is for them to see change as an opportunity and not a threat.

- *Stage 6:* **Implementation**. Implementation requires bringing the transformation vision into the daily activities of the individual. Strategic leaders need to balance the tempo of implementing change with the human needs of the organization. Leaders need to "walk the walk," not just "talk the talk." Without commitment and leadership at all levels of the organization, strategic and transformative change is doomed from the start. Implementation is a continuous process led by committed leaders at all levels.

- *Stage 7:* **Integration**. Understanding and believing that the changes are real and here to stay. Leaders need to build a solid foundation of trust, cooperation, and honesty to accelerate peak performance.

VIDEO 7.4 Kotter's 8 Step Change Management Model

John Kotter, a professor at the Harvard Business School, conceptualized eight essential steps in managing the change process for successful organizational transformation in his book *Leading Change*. (Kotter's model is depicted in Exhibit 7.10: Eight Steps for Effective Change.) There are numerous change models with similarities, such as creating a clear vision, conducting good communication regarding the new vision, empowering employees, leading by example, and celebrating successes. There is no one change model, but some models may be a better fit for an organization based on the type and nature of change the organization is experiencing.[38]

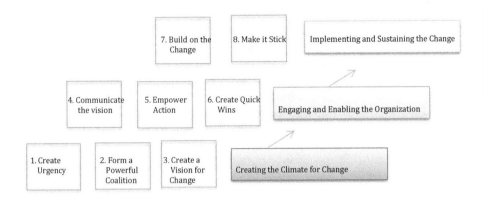

Exhibit 7.10
Kotter's Eight
Steps for
Effective
Change

7. Build on the Change

8. Make it Stick

Implementing and Sustaining the Change

4. Communicate the vision

5. Empower Action

6. Create Quick Wins

Engaging and Enabling the Organization

1. Create Urgency

2. Form a Powerful Coalition

3. Create a Vision for Change

Creating the Climate for Change

Source: Adapted from: Kotter, J.P. (1996). Leading Change. Harvard Business School Press. ISBN 9780875847474; at https://www.kotterinc.com/8-steps-process-for-leading-change/

CHANGING THE CULTURE AT GE

In October 2017 Jeffrey Immelt, GE's longtime CEO, announced his retirement stepping down in June 2017. The announcement was not all that surprising given the company's weak financial performance. In May 2016 at a company event, Immelt stated that "GE was a strong, very strong company." At the event he defended his long-held 2018 profit goal, an optimistic benchmark Wall Street had long abandoned. "It's not crap. It's pretty good really," (refering to GE's financial performance). "Today (May 2016), when I think about where the stock is compared to what the company is, it's a mismatch." On that day of the event, GE shares traded near $28. GE's stock would go on to collapse over the next six months while the stock market set new records. GE shares traded below $15 when Immelt announced he was stepping down as CEO. GE's precipitous fall followed years of treading water while the overall economy grew. According to the WSJ, the downfall was exacerbated by what GE insiders called GE's " success theater." "The history of GE was to selectively only provide positive information," said an industry analyst. Insiders noted that "there is a credibility gap between what GE is reporting and the reality of what is to come." Within weeks of the 2016 meeting, Immelt announced his retirement. By the end of 2017, GE's new CEO John Flannery cut GE's dividend in half and started restructuring the company—moves that were expected to eliminate thousands of jobs and cast off more than $20 billion worth of assets. In November 2017, just four months after GE combined its oil and natural gas unit with Baker Hughes technical services business, GE's CFO Jamie Miller announced that it might divest its interest in Baker Hughes in an effort to find exit optionality and increase much needed cash. In addition, CEO Flannery announced plans to drastically shrink the company founded by Thomas Edison by selling multiple business lines, downsizing the board of directors and slashing the dividend. The dividend cut was only the second time since the Great Depression.[a]

a   Carroll, Joe. "The GE-Baker Hughes Romance May Be Ending After a 4-Month Run." *Bloomberg*. November 14, 2017: https://www.bloomberg.com/news/articles/2017-11-13/the-ge-baker-hughes-romance-may-be-ending-after-a-4-month-run

a. Go to your library online periodicals or other sources and conduct a strategic and financial audit pre- and post-Immelt's retirement. How has GE fared under Flannery's leadership? What is GE's overall financial health?

b. What type of leadership is needed in an old-line industrial company like GE when faced with doing business in the digital age?

c. Go to GE Investor Update, November 13, 2017 at: https://www.ge.com/investor relations/sites/default/files/GE%20Investor%20Update_Presentation_11132017.pdf. What is your assessment of CEO Flannery's strategy presentation to investors, and plans for the future?

d. What does the GE saga say about the difficulty in transforming a company by changing its culture, business model, and ways of doing business?

e. What goes into a company's transformation, especially for a company like GE? How important is participatory management in transforming a company like GE?

Sources: Gryta, Thomas, Joann S. Lublin, and David Benoit. "How Jeffrey Immelt's 'Success Theater' Masked the Rot at GE." *The Wall Street Journal*, February 21, 2018. https://www.wsj.com/articles/how-jeffrey-immelts-success-theater-masked-the-rot-at-ge-1519231067?mod=searchresults&page=1&pos=9; Henning, Peter J. "Accounting Investigation Adds to Challenges Facing G.E." *The New York Times*. February 2, 2018: https://www.nytimes.com/2018/02/02/business/dealbook/general-electric-accounting-investigation.html

13. MANAGING HIGH-PERFORMING TEAMS

Why do some teams consistently perform at a high level? Whether it is firms that are unfailingly ranked high on *Fortune*'s Most Admired Companies list, Dale Earnhardt's high-performing pit crew, or the captain of the space shuttle navigating a successful mission, high-performing teams are rare but powerful contributors to success.

Research has shown that high-performing teams have several characteristics or elements in common. Building successful teams requires strong leadership and commitment at all levels of the organization. High-performing teams also require constant nurturing, managing, developing, and honing in on a common goal. High-performing teams exponentially add to a firm's resource strengths, core capabilities, and distinctive competencies. Teams, their structure, composition, behaviors, and performance can make a significant difference in effectively implementing and executing strategic and transformative organizational change. Firms do not maintain their vitality or sustainable competitive advantage from tangible resources alone, however. People, teams, and the relations they form with each other (both inside and outside the organization) drive and sustain firm success. High-performing teams are hard to find and even tougher to build, but it can be done. Crone identifies 10 elements of high-performing teams:[39]

1. *Vision:* An understanding of the team's vision and how this vision relates to and supports the firm's vision is vital. A vision provides a broad set of compelling criteria for the team to act on and evaluate performance against. The vision also provides the big-picture perspective and long-term view of what the firm will be like.

2. *Common Purpose:* Why is the team in place, and what is expected of the team? Without a clear team mission, charge, and purpose, performance is compromised

and, thus, doomed from the start. A common purpose or mission provides a mutual thread or unifying approach to guide the team's charge, member responsibilities, and roles. Winning sports teams have a clear overall vision and defined expectations.

3. *Culture and Team Dynamics*. What individual and team mental models, philosophies, core values, and principles will guide and support team decisions, actions, and behaviors? High-performing teams cannot afford "lone wolves" who do not support the culture and expected behaviors.

4. *Clear Roles and Responsibilities*. "Just do your job." The famous mantra of Coach Bill Belichick of the New England Patriots embodies this element of high-performing teams. But what does it mean to do one's job? Team members must know why they are part of the team and what roles and responsibilities they are expected to carry out. This does not mean to do your job independent of other team members. Rather, it requires understanding the connectedness, interrelationship, and interdependence of all roles and responsibilities of the team members in order for the team to perform at its highest level. Knowing one's role and responsibility demonstrates trust, confidence, and respect for all other members of the team.

5. *Efficient and Effective Processes*. Success does not solely stem from knowing what to do; it comes from hard work and performance. Whether it's the high-performing elite military teams (such as of the Navy Seals), the talented and skilled team of doctors and nurses performing critical surgery, or highly effective and efficient teams of first responders to national emergencies, there is no substitute for a team's continuous learning, practice, and preparedness to efficiently and effectively do their job.

6. *Shared and Collective Leadership*. Leadership is not just vertical—it is also horizontal and interactive. Leadership goes vertically up and down and horizontally back and forth. In today's world, we sometimes get overly focused on algorithms, frameworks, formulas, and artificial intelligence to make informed decisions, but there is no substitute for strong leadership at all levels of the organization. Reflection and collective learning and action ensures team and organizational success.

7. *Solid Relationships*. High-performing teams do not work in isolation of other teams and parties. Coordination and collaboration between and among teams is critical to team and organizational success. High-performing teams are part of a large and fluid network of relationships. Knowing how to work and succeed in an interconnected work environment is critical to team success. It takes integrated, diversified thinking and actions in teams, as well as the relationships they form with others inside and outside the organization.

8. *Communication, Information, and Knowledge*. Communication is a two-way street. High-performing teams are clear on their purpose, tasks, and responsibilities. They know how to receive, process, and act on information as well as communicate within and across groups. As continuous learners, high-performing teams work from facts and are open to change when the facts and circumstances change. Acting on false or untrustworthy information can bring down not only the team but the firm as well.

9. *Skill Diversity or Team Mix*. Strategic decisions and actions requires "inside the box," "outside the box," and "where there is no box at all" thinking. The simultaneous acceleration of all three of these external forces necessitates thinking where there are no clear industry boundaries or "rules of the game" and thinking where there are no industry boundaries (or boxes) at all. It requires radically inclusive thinking and action. This type of thinking and action requires teams to be skilled in a number of diverse areas and talents. It also requires individuals and teams to be open to and embrace change both inside and outside the firm.

10. *Embrace Change*. High performing teams are change agents that continually look for ways to improve. Change is viewed as an opportunity and not a threat. They have the passion and enthusiasm to embrace change and continuously improve performance, even if things are not broken.

14. WHAT DOES IT TAKE TO BE A SUCCESSFUL CEO AND LEADER?

Bennis and Nanus,[40] two well-known leadership scholars, note that a business corporation is not only an economic entity but also a community, possibly the central community of our times. The leader, according to Bennis and Nanus, hopes to unite the people in the organization into a responsible community. The two scholars studied successful chief executive officers across 90 businesses and organizations of all types and sizes. They found that there seemed to be no obvious pattern for CEO success. The CEOs they studied "were right-brained and left-brained, tall and short, fat and thin, articulate and inarticulate, assertive and retiring, dressed for success and dressed for failure, participative and autocratic."[41] Still, after reviewing the interviews in further detail and revisiting the CEOs over another two-year time period, they were able to conceptualize four major themes and areas of competencies that all 90 leaders embodied:

- *Attention through vision*: Management of attention through vision is the creating focus for a business. All 90 people interviewed had an agenda and an unparalleled concern with outcome. Leaders are the most results-oriented people in the world, and results get attention.
- *Meaning through commitment*: Leaders have a capacity to illustrate a compelling image of a desired state of affairs—the kind of image that induces enthusiasm and commitment in others.
- *Trust through position*: Trust is the lubrication that ensures function on an organizational level. Trust implies accountability, predictability, and reliability. It is what sells products and keeps organizations humming. Trust—the glue that maintains organizational integrity—requires knowing where the organization is going and what steps are necessary to get there.
- *The deployment of self through positive self-regard*: Positive self-regard consists of three major components: knowledge of one's strengths, the capacity to nurture and develop those strengths, and the ability to discern the fit between one's strengths and weaknesses and the organization's needs.[42]

Thinking Critically Exercise 55

LEADERS YOU ADMIRE

What kind of leader inspires you? Think about people/leaders who have been influential in your life. What makes you want to follow them? What do you imagine your leadership style will be/should be to be successful? Do different kinds of organizations need different types of leaders at different times? Why or why not?

15. REFLECTION

Strategy making is useless unless the newly crafted strategies can be effectively executed. Strategic leaders spend as much time on executing strategy as they do on crafting strategy. Similar to the distinction between a strategy and a plan, as there is no endpoint to strategy, there is no end point to execution. Execution is a continuous process. Because environments are dynamic and unstable, strategies start out as deliberate actions, but these actions need to be altered or adapted to changing circumstances. As such, strategy implementation, execution, and monitoring require an open-system logic and mindset. Strategy, by definition, is about change, change directed at how best to effectively manage the organization for continuous performance improvement, with the end goal of achieving organizational purpose. Both strategy making and execution are steps in the strategic management model that focus on change management. Change can be incremental, significant, and transformative. Change requires both technical and organizational learning. It also necessitates visionary and creative leaders.

Change, always future-oriented, moves toward a future that is unpredictable, consequential, uncertain, and dynamic. Directing, motivating, stewarding, envisioning, organization building, communicating, and managing the strategic management model require leaders at every level of the organization. Successful strategy execution and strategic control require effective, ethical, and committed leaders. At every step along the way, the leader has to act strategically and think critically. Leaders, though they cannot predict the future with certainty, can help increase the odds for a successful outcome in the firm's favor.

Strategy execution requires constant and effective decision making by those responsible for implementing strategy across all organizational units. It involves making difficult decisions aimed at solving organizational problems or removing obstacles that can hinder or block the execution of a newly crafted strategy(s). This encompasses acquiring, managing, and allocating company resources, as well as motivating and engaging people to work together across units with its implementation and execution. This process also mandates strategic control or the process of monitoring the crafted strategies for their effectiveness. Effectively executed strategies improve the firm's performance by aligning with the organization's vision, mission, goals, and objectives. The proper execution of strategy depends heavily upon the magnitude of organizational change—incremental, strategic, or transformative. The latter type of change is the most difficult and involves high degrees of organizational technical and behavioral learning. Strategy execution requires leaders to be both managers and entrepreneurs. In summary, managing change for the future is a complex, ambiguous process requiring strategic leaders who not only provide a sense of direction but who can also build ownership and alignment within the organization. As Robert Buckman, CEO Buckman Labs, so eloquently stated in recounting his 15 year journey to implement a knowledge management and transfer system at his company:

> You need to change the way you relate to one another. If you can't do that, you won't succeed … but it boils down to: Do you trust the people who give you the information? … What you need is persistence. This whole thing is a journey—a journey without end, and it has to invade the fabric of our corporation. This is not a project, with clearly defined, finite goals, with a beginning and an end … it was a continual cut-and-try process, an evolutionary process.[43]

For Belichick, coach of the New England Patriots, to properly execute a game plan and to constantly win both on and off the playing field requires every player, coach, and staff member to "just do their job, and do it well."[44] It is no different whether the firm is a new venture or an established multinational company—they both require leadership, communication, vision, commitment, trust, learning, feedback, and, most importantly, for everyone across the organization to do their job—and do it well.

PERSONAL STRATEGY ACTION PLAN (PSAP)

Do you have a life plan and vision? Throughout this textbook we have empathized the importance of always acting strategically and thinking critically. Strategy frameworks and concepts can be equally effective for an organization and for an individual. It is time to take stock on your life, and a personal strategy action plan (PSAP) can help you do so. At a minimum, your PSAP should include answers to the following questions (see chapter 1, section 11.1 Managing Oneself):

- *What is my vision?* Consider including a personal vision statement and some specific objectives and lifetime goals. Vision statements should inspire and guide you on a daily basis.
- *What are my strengths?* Most people, according to Drucker, know what they are "not" good at, but they do not know what they *are* good at.
- *What values do I hold dear?* Personal values are those beliefs that legitimatize your behavior. They are the catalyst and the motivation behind how you use your time. What do you enjoy doing?
- *What are my core capabilities and distinctive competencies?*
- *Where do I belong?* Knowing your strengths, capabilities, and values will help you figure out where you belong. What should you contribute to your company, family, and society? Where you can make the greatest contributions to what needs to be done?
- *What results have to be achieved in the next three to five years to make a difference in my career and in my life? Over the next 10 years? For your career?*
- *How do I define a successful career? Successful life? What will be your legacy?*

Finally: have fun with this assignment. Be creative. Make it something that will help you make strategic decisions and take action throughout your life.

  a. Take the time to write a PSAP. What additional questions would you include?
  b. Use the PSAP to take stock of where you have been and where you are heading in your career and personal life. Use it for feedback analysis. What items are you on a clear path to achieve? What strengths and competencies are facilitating your achievement?
  c. At no specific time interval, refer to your PSAP. Revise it as needed. Use it as a guide—as you know, there is no endpoint in strategy.

CHAPTER ENDNOTES

1. Huy, Quy. "Five Reasons Most Companies Fail at Strategy Execution." Forbes Asia January 8, 2016.: https://www.forbes.com/sites/insead/2016/01/08/five-reasons-most-companies-fail-at-strategy-execution/#207759e03348

2. R. Adl, The Heat is On: CEOs Under Pressure to Perform Strategy Execution Proves Key to Success, Downloaded at: http://www.bts.com/docs/newsletter/BTS-Insight-Strategy-Execution-Heat-Is-On.pdf?sfvrsn=0, Retrieved 3/26/15

3. "The Keys to Strategy Execution: A Global Study of Current Trends and Future Possibilities: 2006–2016." American Management Association. http://www.amanet.org/training/articles/what-is-strategy-execution.aspx.

4. D. Sull, R. Homkes, C. Sull, Why Strategy Execution Unravels – and What to Do About it," Harvard Business review March 2015, pp. 59-66

5. Bossidy, Larry, Ram Charan, and Charles Burck. Execution: The Discipline of Getting Things Done. London: Random House Books, 2002.

6. Heathfield, Susan M. "What Is Resistance to Change?" the balance. January 16, 2017. https://www.thebalance.com/what-is-resistance-to-change-1918240.

7. Utterback, J.M. Mastering the Dynamics of Innovation: How Companies Can Seize Opportunities in the Face of Technological Change. Boston: Harvard Business School Press, 1994.

8. Christensen, C.M. The Innovator's Dilemma. Boston: Harvard Business School Press, 2000.; J.M. Utterback. Mastering the Dynamics of Innovation: How Companies Can Seize Opportunities in the Face of Technological Change. Boston: Harvard Business School Press, 1994.; J.Tichy. The Leadership Engine. New York: Harper Business, 1997.; and Hodges, Julie and Gill, Roger. Sustaining Change in Organizations. London: SAGE Publications, 2015.

9. Argote, L. "Organizational Learning Research: Past, Present and Future." Management Learning 42, no. 4 (2011): 439–46.; "Organizational Learning." Wikipedia. Last modified January 18, 2018. http://en.wikipedia.org/wiki/organizational_learning.

10. Fox, Carol. "Recognizing the Gaps in Gap Analysis." Risk Management. October 3, 2016: http://www.rmmagazine.com/2016/10/03/recognizing-the-gaps-in-gap-analysis/

11. Hamel, G., and C.K. Prahalad. Competing for the Future. Cambridge: Harvard Business School Press, 1996.; Welch, J. Jack: Straight from the Gut. New York: Warner Business Books, 2001.

12. Hamel, G., and C.K. Prahalad. Competing for the Future. Cambridge: Harvard Business School Press, 1996.

13. Kotter, J.P., and J.L. Heskett. Corporate Culture and Performance. New York: The Free Press, 1992.

14. Chandler, A.D. Jr. Strategy and Structure: Chapters in the History of Industrial Enterprise. Cambridge: MIT Press, 1962.; Freeland, R.F. "The Myth of the M-Form? Governance, Consent, and Organizational Change." American Journal of Sociology (1996): 102.

15. Sullivan, Janie. "Four Basic Elements of Organizational Structure," Chron, January 18, 2018. http://smallbusiness.chron.com/four-basic-elements-organizational-structure-288.html.

16. Ashe-Edmunds, Sam. "Simple Organizational Structure." Chron, January 18, 2018. http://smallbusiness.chron.com/simple-organizational-structure-63451.html.

17. Earle, Andrew, Michael Merenda, Marc Sedam, Kevin Short, and Mei-Win Thein. "Lean Collaboration on Campus? A Social Network and Bricolage Approach." 3E Conference—ECSB Entrepreneurship Education Conference in Cork, Ireland, May 10–12, 2017.

18. Simon, H.A. "A Behavioral Model of Rational Choice." Quarterly Journal of Economics (1955): 99–118.

19. Ten Major Strategic Management Schools: A Comparative Analysis." 1000ventures. http://www.1000ventures.com/business_guide/mgmt_inex_stategy_10schools.html.

20. Yangming, Wang. "Internet Encyclopedia of Philosophy (IEP)." http://www.iep.utm.edu/wangyang/.

21. Freedman, L. Strategy: A History. New York: Oxford University Press, 2013.; Handy, C. "Managing the Dream." In Learning Organizations, edited by S. Chawla and J. Renesch. Portland: Productivity Press, 1955. Cited in M. Driver. "The Learning Organization: Foucauldian Gloom or Utopian Sunshine?" Human Relations 55 (2002): 33–53.; Senge, P. The Fifth Dimension: The Art and Practice of the Learning Organization. New York: Doubleday, 1990; Mintzberg, H. "Rebuilding Companies as Communities." Harvard Business Review (2009): 140–3.

22. Irwin, Richard D. "J.B. Quinn Strategies for Change: Logical Incrementalism." Boston: The Irwin Series in Management and the Behavioral Sciences, 1980.

23. Senge, P. The Fifth Dimension: The Art and Practice of the Learning Organization. New York: Doubleday, 1990.

24. Ibid.

25. Ibid.

26. Drucker, P.F., E. Dyson, C. Handy, P. Saffo, and P.M. Senge. "Looking Ahead: Implications of the Present." Harvard Business Review (1997).

27. Edersheim, E. Hass. The Definitive Drucker. New York: McGraw-Hill, 2007.

28. Bower, J.L., C. A. Barlett, C.R. Christensen, A.E. Pearson, and K.R. Andrews. "The Chief Executive's Job: Roles and Responsibilities." Business Policy: Text and Cases. Boston: Irwin, 1991.

29. Fernandez-Araoz, C., S. Iqbal, and J. Ritter. "Leadership Lessons from Great Family Businesses." Harvard Business Review (2015): 86.

30. Dahl, R.A., and C. Lindblom. Politics, Economics, and Welfare. New Brunswick, NJ: Transaction Publishers, 2000.

31. Barnard, C.I. The Functions of the Executive. Cambridge, MA: Harvard University Press, 1968.; The Functions of the Executive: 30th Anniversary Edition. Cambridge, MA: Harvard University Press, 1971.

32. Riggio, Ronald E. "What Is Charisma and Charismatic Leadership? Is Charisma Born or Made? What Makes Leaders Charismatic?" Cutting-Edge Leadership. October 7, 2012. https://www.psychologytoday.com/blog/cutting-edge-leadership/201210/what-is-charisma-and-charismatic-leadership.

33. Ibid.

34. Barnard, C.I. The Functions of the Executive. Cambridge, MA: Harvard University Press, 1968.; The Functions of the Executive: 30th Anniversary Edition. Cambridge, MA: Harvard University Press, 1971.

35. Tichy, N.J. The Leadership Engine. New York: Harper Business, 1997.;Hodges, Julie and Gill, Roger. .Sustaining Change in Organizations. London: SAGE Publications, 2015.

36. Moss-Kanter, Rosabeth. The Change Masters. New York: Simon & Schuster, 1983.

37. Adapted from Ela, John. "Change Management: It's A Process." Ela Management Group, PowerPoint Presentation April 20, 2017.; Purnell-Webb, Patricia, Ian Glendon, and Peter Creed. "Understanding Spirituality in the Workplace: A Qualitative Study." Journal of Spirituality, Leadership and Management 1 (2002): 1–3.

38. eba. "Kotter's 8 Step Process: Identifying Important Elements to Successful Organisational Change." http://www.educational-business-articles.com/8-step-process/.

39. Crone, Mike. "High Performing Teams Have These Ten Elements." Linkedin.com. July 30, 2015. https://www.linkedin.com/pulse/high-performing-teams-have-10-key-elements-mike-crone-ccp/.

40. Bennis, Warren, and Burt Nanus. *Leaders: The Strategies for Taking Charge*. New York: Harper & Row, 1985.

41. Ibid.,175–6.

42. Barnard, C.I. *The Functions of the Executive*. Cambridge, MA: Harvard University Press, 1968.; *The Functions of the Executive: 30th Anniversary Edition*. Cambridge, MA: Harvard University Press, 1971.

43. Fulmer, W.E. *Buckman Laboratories (A)*. Boston: Harvard Business School Publishing, 1999.

11. Kerr, James M. "How Bill Belichick's 'Just Do Your Job Mantra' Applies to Leadership." Inc.com. January 26, 2015. http://www.inc.com/james-kerr/how-do-your-job-can-be-a-difference-maker-for-your-company.html.; Halberstam, David. *The Education of a Coach*. New York: Hyperion, 2005.

CHAPTER 8

COMPETITIVE ADVANTAGE IN THE INTERNATIONAL, ENTREPRENEURIAL, AND SOCIAL ORGANIZATION

ADVERTISING'S 'MAD MEN' BRISTLE AT THE DIGITAL REVOLUTION

PUBLICIS GROUPE IS TRYING TO FORCE OLD-SCHOOL 'CREATIVES' TO WORK MORE CLOSELY WITH NEW TECHNOLOGY HIRES TO HANG ON TO BIG CLIENTS

By Nick Kostov and David Gauthier-Villars

One of the world's biggest ad agencies, Publicis Groupe SA, PUBGY -0.86% fully felt the disruptive power of advertising's digital revolution when McDonald's Corp. , a huge client, put its account into play.

The fast-food chain wanted a marketing plan covering everything from social-network posts to food-tray liners, according to people involved with the account. McDonald's thought Publicis's Leo Burnett unit, its main advertising agency at the time, wasn't adept enough at using data to quickly produce online ads and target minute slices of its customer base, these people say.

Publicis had an army of copywriters, art directors and computer engineers, but when senior executives gathered in 2016 to come up with a pitch for McDonald's, debates erupted over the meaning of such basic terms as "data" and "content," recalls Britt Nolan, chief creative officer of Leo Burnett USA.

Publicis lost the McDonald's contract to Omnicom Group Inc., which had worked with Facebook Inc. and Alphabet Inc.'s Google to assemble a team of creative talent and data experts.

That blow convinced current Publicis Chief Executive Arthur Sadoun of the need to more quickly shatter the boundaries between the sprawling company's many fiefs, which includes such agencies as Saatchi & Saatchi and Razorfish.

"There is a big debate: Where is our industry going?" he said in a recent interview. "You have very different people that need to work together."

The ad industry is in upheaval as it grapples with the rise of big data and analytics. Ad giants such as WPP PLC, Omnicom and Publicis have gone on acquisition sprees, bringing legions of information-technology experts into their ranks.

The influx has opened a cultural divide on Madison Avenue between the new arrivals and an old guard of "creatives"—the pitchmen, copywriters and artists that have shaped advertising since the end of World War II. The digital talent has questioned the attachment of traditional agencies to TV ad campaigns, while creatives have complained about engineers interfering with carefully honed client pitches.

Since he was picked last January to become chief executive, Mr. Sadoun has been trying to force the tribes to work together. He worked with a tech entrepreneur to overhaul Leo Burnett's U.S. business, and has assembled a team of programmers to design an algorithm to identify talent from different in-house agencies to work together on single projects.

"We have to find the right alchemy between creativity and technology, and that's both difficult and tiresome," Mr. Sadoun says.

Clients are pressuring ad firms to embrace technological change. Big advertisers such as Bridgestone Corp. and Procter & Gamble Co. are seeking more transparency on whether ad campaigns are effective. They also expect guidance on how to survive the digital disruption.

That is blurring the lines between traditional ad firms and consulting firms. Publicis, for example, spent $3.7 billion to buy information-technology consultancy Sapient in 2015. In late 2016, Accenture PLC acquired Karmarama, a U.K. advertising agency known for its creative edge. Last April, WPP acquired Deeplocal Inc., a small Pittsburgh-based lab with skills ranging from robotics to software development to industrial design.

When Mr. Sadoun began his career at Omnicom in the late 1990s, creative directors called the shots, building story lines that defined brands. He was a fixture at glitzy events such as the industry's annual award ceremony held in Cannes, where, as head of Omnicom's French agency, he collected several Agency of The Year awards.

At that time, Maurice Lévy was running Publicis, which he had joined decades earlier as head of its budding IT department. He worked to shed his tech background and blend in with creative staffers who wore jeans and sneakers to work. "The creatives called us the suits," Mr. Lévy recalls.

Mr. Sadoun said he was drawn to Publicis by the opportunity to work with Mr. Lévy. When he arrived in 2006, Publicis's creative directors still wielded considerable power at their respective agencies. Leo Burnett was known for its storytelling, having created such iconic campaigns as the Marlboro Man. Saatchi & Saatchi was known for its edge. Mr. Sadoun was tapped to run Publicis Conseil, the company's French agency.

The internet and smartphones presented a challenge to ad agencies. Brands wanted to know all about consumers' online spending habits and target them as they searched for directions, chatted with friends and planned vacations. No single agency had the resources to track such activity on its own, Publicis executives say.

Publicis tried to bridge the technology gap by acquiring digital-marketing specialists, including Digitas Inc. in 2007 and Razorfish from Microsoft Corp. in 2009. Yet creative staffers at the traditional agencies were reluctant to work on digital projects, Publicis executives say. Many creatives, they say, considered online banner ads inferior assignments.

The digital talent, meanwhile, chafed over TV campaigns they considered retrograde and a waste of time. "What am I doing filming cars driving through the desert when brands are being built on Instagram?" says Jeffrey Dachis, a Razorfish co-founder who left the company and started other tech firms.

Management responded by moving entire accounts to Digitas, telling creative staffers that anyone who refused to work on digital projects would miss out on bigger annual bonuses, according to the Publicis executives.

Still, Mr. Lévy recalls worrying that forcing digital operations and traditional agencies to work together would create "a kind of Quasimodo-Frankenstein animal that wouldn't function."

In 2013, Procter & Gamble Co. was concerned about its online ads, including some that Leo Burnett made for Always feminine-care products. The company wanted to make sure people wouldn't scroll right past them, according to Krister Karjalainen, a former P&G executive who tested some of the ads.

Through a partnership with tech company Sticky, now a unit of Sweden's Tobii AB, P&G had tracked the eye movements of millions of consumers using their webcams. That allowed P&G to measure how the people, who were paid to participate in the research, were responding to the placement of its logos.

P&G requested changes to the size and location of the logos, Mr. Karjalainen says, but Leo Burnett's creative team balked, saying it would make the ads look bad.

He says he shut down the conversation by citing the eye-tracking data. "You know what? The logo should be here," he recalls telling the creatives. "They didn't appreciate the conversation because it was like we were stepping into their world."

Former Leo Burnett executive Tony Wallace, who has made videos for the P&G account, said eye-tracking technology and other forms of market research made "creatives a lot of times just roll their eyes. You have people sitting behind the glass window eating their baloney sandwiches telling you to make the logo bigger."

In late 2015, Mr. Sadoun and hundreds of other Publicis executives gathered at a retreat in Silicon Valley to discuss how to get its disparate units to work together more closely. The company had recently purchased Sapient, bringing thousands of engineers and India-based computer coders into the company, and needed to find a way to dissolve internal barriers, the Publicis executives say.

The group decided to appoint a chief talent officer, meeting participants say. They also rallied around a novel concept: Using algorithms to assign employees to projects, regardless of their agency affiliation.

After the meeting, Mr. Lévy said he wanted to unify the company before stepping down as CEO, slated for June 2017. He appointed Mr. Sadoun to oversee all of the creative agenciesand Alan Herrick, the chief executive of Sapient, to run all digital and technology operations.

In spring 2016, Messrs. Sadoun and Herrick corralled senior executives from Digitas, Razorfish, Sapient and others at Leo Burnett's Chicago headquarters for a series of meetings to try to save the McDonald's account. Leo Burnett had a big chunk of McDonald's nearly $1 billion of annual ad spending in the U.S., all of which was up for grabs.

To retain the account, Publicis needed its different agencies to work together seamlessly. Instead, the executives gathered in Chicago stepped on each other's toes, according to people at the meeting. Mr. Nolan, Leo Burnett's chief creative officer, recalls cutting into one discussion and asking in frustration: "Now what exactly are we looking for here?"

McDonald's spokeswoman Terri Hickey says Omnicom won the account with an approach that was "fast, fluid and flexible."

With Mr. Lévy preparing to step down as CEO, Mr. Sadoun started to champion digital change. Months before taking over, Mr. Sadoun assembled a secret team of computer engineers, including Sapient staffers, to develop the algorithm dreamed up at the Silicon Valley meeting.

The idea was to develop a computer system to comb a database containing résumés and other data on nearly 80,000 Publicis employees—including account managers, coders, graphic designers and copywriters—then pick a team from around the world for a project or client pitch. The algorithm would use a set of criteria to score employees and determine how well they match with a given campaign.

"We keep saying our clients need to transform digitally," Mr. Sadoun explains. "It was time we did it ourselves."

Mr. Sadoun went on a hunt for tech talent and began to integrate more technology into the traditional agencies he oversaw.

He flew to New York to woo Andrew Swinand, a former Publicis executive and the founder of a startup incubator. Over $50 steaks, Mr. Sadoun told him Publicis would buy some of the incubator's businesses if Mr. Swinland joined Publicis as head of Leo Burnett's North American business.

In January 2017, Publicis hired Mr. Swinand to shake up Leo Burnett and announced Mr. Sadoun would succeed Mr. Lévy as CEO.

Mr. Swinand's recruits from the tech world began colonizing Leo Burnett's offices. He poured resources into Greenhouse, the agency's video unit for social media, building a 630-person outfit to crank out videos at a fraction of the time and cost it takes to produce a traditional TV ad.

Leo Burnett shot more than two dozen different ads for a new online campaign for Bridgestone Corp's Firestone tire brand. Through a partnership with Facebook, Google and other data platforms, the agency combed the feeds of social-network users and determined what kind of cars they drove. The result: SUV owners saw ads showcasing Firestone tires on SUVs blazing through dirt while sports-car owners saw ads of high-performance cars ripping around a track.

The agency then used Google's geo-localization tool to determine whether people who had seen their videos visited a Firestone dealer in the next 30 days.

"We're now all about targeting and retargeting," said one creative director at Leo Burnett who is skeptical of the digital overhaul. "Who's thinking about what people are going to be dreaming about?"

In June, Mr. Sadoun arrived at the Cannes award ceremony to make his debut as chief executive. He made a surprise announcement: In 2018, the company's creative teams wouldn't come to Cannes and other award ceremonies. The budget, he said, was being redirected to help fund the algorithm project, which was code-named Marcel and expected to cost tens of millions of dollars.

Thousands of miles away, in the Chicago skyscraper that houses Leo Burnett's headquarters, employees were shocked, according to several of them. If the algorithm assembled teams from across the entire Publicis workforce, they feared, Leo Burnett's ranks would shrink and its brand would fade.

At the foot of the building, someone covered the agency's granite sign with a flimsy sheet of paper bearing the letters "MARCEL." The stunt was a thinly veiled reference to a retirement speech by the agency's founder. In 1967, Leo Burnett had told his successors to rename the company if they ever strayed from his philosophy of placing creativity at the heart of their business.

A few weeks later, Mr. Sadoun flew to Chicago. "Who put up that sign?" he asked a room of about 200 executives gathered on the 21st floor. As unease spread across the room, the CEO explained he was proud to see creative spirit was alive at the agency.

"I don't want to fire them," he said. "I want to congratulate them."

Appeared in the Wall Street Journal *January 20, 2018, print edition as 'Digital Revolution Upends Ad Industry.'*

1. How has the digital revolution disrupted the advertising powerhouse Publicis Groupe S.A's culture and business model?
2. What factors led McDonald's to drop Publicis's Leo Burnett as its premiere advertising agency? Why did the Omnicom agency win the MacDonald's account from Burnett?
3. In what ways did the digital revolution cause a cultural divide at Publicis agencies between the arrival of new high technology, digital creatives, and its old guard of "creatives"—the pitchmen, copywriters, and artists who shaped advertising since the end of World War II?
4. Why did the traditional TV ad agency creatives at Publicis agencies resisted change and complain about the new generation of data analysts, software, and engineers whom they claimed were interfering with carefully honed client pitches and were blurring the lines between?
5. Are digital technologies, sustaining technology or disruptive technologies for a company like the Publicis Groupe S.A's?
6. How difficult is it for a global company, like Publicis, to compete internationally and be entrepreneurial, creative and innovative in the digital age?

1. INTRODUCTION: QUESTIONS TO THINK ABOUT

- What is Porter's diamond model of a nation's competitive advantage?
- What is globalization?
- What are the implications of globalization?
- What is global strategy?
- What is multi-domestic strategy?
- What is transnational strategy?
- What are the advantages and disadvantages of doing business across national borders?
- What is pest?
- What are some strategies for entering international markets?
- What is the entrepreneurship school of strategic thought?
- What is the innovator's dilemma?
- What is first mover advantage?
- What is social entrepreneurship?
- What is a not-for-profit business?
- How do you foster creativity and innovation?
- What are some legal forms of business ownership?
- What are some useful ways to distinguish small business entrepreneurial ventures?

1.1 INFLUENCES ON FIRMS' STRATEGIC BEHAVIOR

Strategy is about having a theory of what actions and activities will improve future performance.[1] Strategic managers are constantly testing their theories of strategy and ascertaining their effectiveness across varying business models, products, services, processes, and markets—that is, does a company's strategy work across different formats? A firm's **theory of strategy** is succeeding if it can create and sustain a competitive advantage over its rivals.[2] For instance, Walmart's success at improving company performance in the United States with its everyday low prices, convenience, and variety of products has not proved so successful in foreign markets, especially in China and Germany. Why? What is different about its theory of strategy in the United States versus competing in international markets? The principles of strategy making and execution are the same whether the firm is facing domestic or global competition. The **context**, however, is different in that global competition adds extra layers of complexity due to the variety of ways customers, markets, and institutions can differ when competing in new and untested markets.

2. COMPETITIVE ADVANTAGE OF NATIONS

The challenge for strategic managers when trying to compete globally is to determine the root differences found in a country's culture, subcultures, institutions, technologies, industries, markets, customers, and peoples.[3] According to Porter, it is primarily the firm's **proximate** environment that improves technological innovation. A firm's ability to achieve competitive advantage stems from value creation in the firm's approximate environment, which is ultimately an act of innovation. Whether the firm competes domestically or internationally, its location and its relations with suppliers, rivals, customers, and other stakeholders—**its proximate environment**—will influence its ability to gain a competitive advantage. Porter and his colleagues conducted empirical research on the competitive advantage of nations. Why are some countries' industries and products considered world-class? And why have some countries and its industries been able to continually lower product costs while continuously improving product quality? Research on the competitive advantage of nations found that the dynamic interdependent of four sets of internal and external variables influence a firm's ability to gain competitive advantage (see Figure 8.1: Porter's Diamond Model). These four variables include: (1) factor conditions (natural resources, geographic location); (2) demand conditions (demand requirements of the firm's most sophisticated customers); (3) relating and supporting industries (geographic grouping of industries into clusters); and (4) firm strategy, structure, and rivalry (the systematic differences in how firms compete within and across industries). The strengths of the interaction between these determinants of national competitive advantage depends on geographic concentration in the industry and the tendency to be located within particular cities or regions. Porter argues that such proximity accelerates diffusion of innovation, facilitates investment in skills, and encourages the development of supporting industries.[4]

The four sets of dynamic variables or factors form a diamond model and are known as the *Porter Diamond Theory of National Advantage*. All four sets of factors are important in global business competition. Porter assumes that the competitiveness of businesses is related to the performance of other firms and factors that link the firm's value chain to a global value chain either in a long-distance relation (from the home country) or a local or regional context (doing business directly in the host country). Firms use the Diamond Model to establish how they can translate its competitive advantages

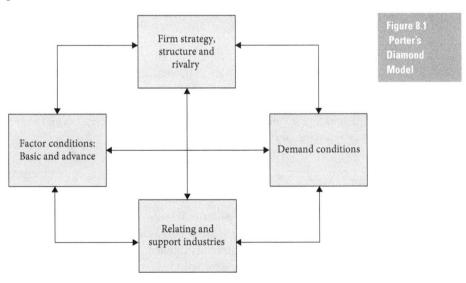

Source: Michael E. Porter. "The Competitive Advantage of Nations," *Harvard Business Review*, April 1990; at: https://hbr.org/1990/03/the-competitive-advantage-of-nations

Figure 8.1 Porter's Diamond Model

(or disadvantages) into international advantage. Researchers have added two other conditions or variables to the interrelated dynamic factors: (1) the role and support of the host country's governments (national, regional, and local) and (2) chance events. Both government support and chance events can facilitate or hinder a firm's ability to gain a competitive advantage in the host country's industries and markets (see Figure 8.2: Diamond Model—Common Factors).

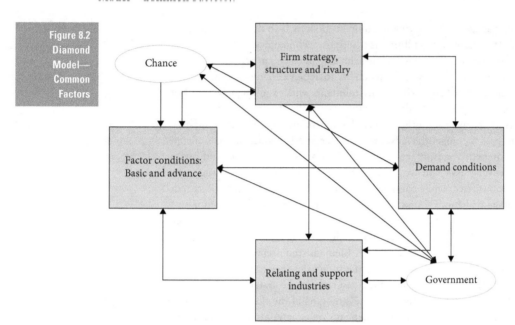

Figure 8.2 Diamond Model— Common Factors

Source: Michael E. Porter. "The Competitive Advantage of Nations," *Harvard Business Review*, https://hbr.org/1990/03/the-competitive-advantage-of-nations.

2.1 FACTOR CONDITIONS

Factor conditions can be subdivided into two groups: basic and advanced. Basic factors include availability and access (location) to natural resources (forests, ores, climate); physical infrastructure (roads, airports, deepwater harbors); and labor force and skills (availability and access to low-cost labor). Advanced factors include: advanced telecommunication networks, world-class universities and colleges, cutting-edge research centers and think tanks, proprietary technology, highly qualified scientists and engineers, capital markets, and access to equity financing, health care, and quality of life.

2.2 RELATED AND SUPPORTING INDUSTRIES

Porter found that a firm's competitive advantage is not necessarily tied to a single firm but rather to the interpenetrating and interdependence of the firm to its **industry cluster**, suppliers, and other organizations. A business cluster is a geographic concentration of interconnected businesses, suppliers, and associated institutions within a particular field. Clusters are considered to increase the productivity with which companies can compete both nationally and globally (see Exhibit 8.1: Innovative Firm Cluster). A firm can possess several sources for innovation including how it links to firms in its industry cluster and value chain. For example, original equipment manufacturers (OEMs: General Motors, General Electric, General Foods, DuPont/Dow Chemical) can perform two important roles in the value chain: act as sophisticated customers or learn from more advanced suppliers and related industries. In both cases, innovation is found not only internal to the firm (patents, research centers, creative and entrepreneurial talent) but also external to the firm in how it collaborates with other companies in supporting and relating industries (supplier density, networks, resource strengths). Local industries with international success (world-class products, technologies, best-in-class management practices) can provide efficient and cost-effective access to factor inputs (land, labor, resources).[5]

A firm's innovation is not tied to the size of the firm but to the quality of the business relationship that links the firms and supporting organizations to one another.[6] The key unit of analysis is no longer the single company but a decentralized network of companies. Research conducted by Rothwell and Dodgson demonstrated that firms extensively network in order to improve innovation potential.[7] In summary, the work on competitive advantage and technological innovation suggests that a firm's performance is positively affected by both the degree to which it engages in continuous innovation/knowledge creation and the quality of its collaborative relations with customers and suppliers. Porter proposes that the existence of regional concentrations of customers, suppliers, and competitors may favorably affect innovation and organizational upgrading and improvement.

2.3 DEMAND CONDITIONS AND SOPHISTICATED CUSTOMERS

Several factors exist that aid in determining a host country's demand conditions. This includes the industry's life cycle (birth, early growth, high growth, maturity), standard of living, economic indicators, demographics, government policies, culture, and other macro (PESTEL), mezzo (industry competitive forces), and micro (firm-level heterogeneity) factors. Other demand conditions include the degree of access the entering firm has to a host country's **sophisticated** customers. Porter argues that cultural and physical proximity to sophisticated customers can influence the entering firm's perception of new market needs and opportunities. Demanding sophisticated customers (buyers) can exert substantial pressure on entering firms' brands, products, processes, business models, or technology standards. Porter also argues that national (or state/regional) passions and pride in having world-class industries, industry clusters, companies, and products will usually translate into internationally competitive industries (i.e., the United States's high technology, software, and biotechnology; Italy's high-end fashion and passion for sports cars; France's fine wines; Cuba's cigars; South Korea's consumer electronics; Germany's advanced manufacturing and precision engineering; etc.) These demand factors—as well as others—influence industry dynamics and the host country's attractiveness to the prospective entering firm. The entering firm must determine not only the strategic dimensions that will drive demand but also how to capitalize on demand opportunities. The entering firm must examine all host country value chain transaction costs and its ability to create customer and firm value.

2.4 STRATEGIES, STRUCTURE, AND RIVALRY

A country and its regions or geographic areas, rivals, and proximate environments may differ greatly from one another. Regional differences like intra- and inter-region firm rivalry, industry clusters, strategic industry groups, customers, and demand conditions can differ significantly from one country (and within a country) to another. Differences in firms' strategies, business models, and other strategic dimensions can affect the attractiveness of a country's industries. Furthermore, differences in strategies, industry structure, and intensity of rivals can also pose both advantages and disadvantages for firms entering international markets. The domestic rivalry and the continuous search for industry (and firm) competitive advantage through constant productivity improvements and technological innovation advances can help firms achieve advantages on an international scale. In this regard, a firm's or industry's competitive advantages are not constrained by a nation's physical boundaries or borders. As such, an entity can extend its operational structure and strategies (where it competes) beyond a nation's borders.

For example, the world's five largest companies in 2016 were: Walmart, USA ($485.8 billion in total revenue); State Grid, China ($315.0 billion); Sinopec, China ($267.5 billion); China National Petroleum, China ($262.6 billion); and Toyota Motor, Japan ($254.7 billion).[8] A strong measure of a country's strength in technology and innovation is the number patents (all types) received by foreign companies from the U.S. Patent and Trademark Office. The top five countries (outside the United States) ranked by number of U.S. patents in 2015 were: Japan (52,409 patents), South Korea (17,925 patents), Germany (16,549 patents), Taiwan (11,690 patents), and China (8,116 patents). By comparison, the number of U.S. patents granted to U.S. firms in 2015 was 140,969.[9]

2.5. GOVERNMENT: NATIONAL, REGIONAL, AND LOCAL

Porter maintains that differences in government policies and roles in shaping industry competitiveness can vary widely across nations. Governments play a significant role in influencing a nation's competitive advantages by acting as a major customer, protector of society's well-being, regulator of price and entry, and guardian of its fiscal and monetary policies. (These include the financing and construction of infrastructure (roads, airports) as well as investment in education and health care.) Moreover, governments may encourage companies to comply with climate change regulation (e.g., the required use of alternative energy or alternative environmental systems), which can affect production and climate change. Governments can also provide entering firms with substantial tax incentives, work force training, or facilitating permitting and licensing for plant construction and other capital projects.

2.6 CHANCE EVENTS

Porter maintains that disruptive developments outside the control of firms and governments in the host country may allow new firms to enter these countries. New firms may be better able to exploit opportunities arising from a reshaped industry structure caused by chance events. For example, rapid introductions of radical innovations, unexpected rise in commodities or oil price, insurgents or revolutions, civil or border wars, climate change, or national disasters may be the catalyst for new firms to enter international markets. New firms might also be in a better position than host governments, industries, or firms to provide innovative and entrepreneurial approaches to addressing critical problems and challenges brought on by disruptive events. For example, the exact degree of impact on international trade, currencies, immigration, and terrorism following Great Britain's monumental decision to exit the European Union (EU), commonly referred to as "Brexit," are still unknown. In May 2017 at the G20 trade union event held in Berlin, German Chancellor Angela Merkel told reporters, "Everything from just-in-time auto supply chains to the free movement of workers and even their pet cats and dogs will be thrown into question by Britain's exit from the European Union. ... The fact that so many areas of policy have for decades operated under EU rules meant that the disruption following Brexit could extend into wholly unexpected parts."[10]

3. COMPETING ACROSS BORDERS: INTERNATIONAL, GLOBAL, AND TRANSNATIONAL STRATEGY

We live in a global world. More and more strategic managers are discovering that their firm's products are competing with not only domestic rivals but global rivals as well. U.S. society and its economic well-being are integrally linked to actions from other nations, organizations, companies, and ideologies. Whether it's environmental pollution spreading across the Pacific from Asia or immigration and emigration of people and companies across national borders, our way of life and even the way we act and think is affected by globalization. **Globalization** is the increasing interaction of people, states, or countries through the growth of the international flow of money, ideas, and cultures. It is primarily an integration process that encompasses political, social, economic, technical, environmental, and legal dimensions. Globalization is not a new phenomenon. However, now more than ever, industries are driven by person-to-person personal and social networks, rather than nations, trading companies (mercantilism), and multinationals as seen in the past.[11] **Globalization** is the cross-integration and interdependence of countries, companies, organizations, and people driven by:

VIDEO 8.1 What is Gloablization?

- **Global economics**. Global economics is the interdependence of national economies through foreign direct investment (FDI), trade agreements, global institutions (trading of stock on foreign stock exchanges), migration of firms (knowledge transfer), people (immigration), and other resources (offshoring and outsourcing resources across international borders).
- **Global industries**. Firms whose products compete globally dominate several industries. These industries include: air transport; shipping; natural resources (e.g., oil exploration, production, distribution); computers/smartphones; financial services and brokerage houses; hospitality, travel, and tourism; manufacturing (availability of a low-cost workforce, cheap energy, etc.); and mining (extractive industries such as precious metals).
- **Global institutions**. The rise of nonstate players such as: World Trade Association (WTA); NGOs (nongovernmental organizations, such as the Red Cross or Greenpeace, and terrorist groups, such as ISIS and Al Qaeda); global brands (accelerated growth in the number of firms competing globally); and Trans-Pacific Partnership (TPP), World Trade Organization (WTO), North American Free Trade Agreement (NAFTA), and other regional trade organizations that have lowered international trade and investment barriers.
- **Advanced technologies**. The accelerated increase and widespread use of advanced technologies, especially information technologies, social networks, virtual networks, data analytics, nanotechnologies, and AI (artificial intelligence). Digital technologies have spawned the exponential growth of the internet of things (including mass customization of products and services); production processes; lean and sustainable business practices—insourcing, offsourcing, and outsourcing of services—manufacturing, engineering, and technical services; and the flattening and decentralization of a firm's structures and business activities. These technological advances have revolutionized how people work and communicate with one another, learn, think, take care of themselves, find jobs, and socialize, among other learned human behaviors.
- **Demographics**. Changes in national demographics, such as birth rates, aging populations, growth in college graduates, advanced degrees (Master's, PhD), and STEM declines, have altered the relationship among emerging, newly developed, and developed nations. For example, of the world's 2.725 billion people in 2015, China and India share approximately 37 percent (China, 1.4 billion, and India, 1.3 billion). In comparison, the total U.S. population is 325 million people (4.4 percent). In contrast to the 150 percent expansion of the population aged 65 and older in the next 35 years, the youth population (younger than age 20) is projected to remain almost flat, 2.5 billion in 2015 and 2.6 billion in 2050. Over the same period, the working-age population (aged 20 to 64) will increase only a moderate 25.6 percent. The working-age population's share of total population will shrink slightly in the decades to come, largely due to the impact of low fertility.[12]

Some major implications of globalization are:

- Expanded foreign competition
- Rise in borderless markets and destabilized value chains (see Chapter 6)

- Continued push by rivals for productivity improvements and efficiency
- Rapid product life cycles and obsolesces
- Rise in knowledge, information, and service industries
- Rapid change in nature of organizations—the emergence of new management paradigm (e.g., the way things are done)
- A change in the way we think and see the world

Thinking Critically Exercise 57

HEURISTICS AND PERCEPTIONS OF DIFFERENT COUNTRIES

In psychology, heuristics are simple, efficient rules that people often use to form judgments and make decisions. They are mental shortcuts that usually involve focusing on one aspect of a complex problem and ignoring others.[a] These rules work well under most circumstances, but they can lead to systematic deviations from logic, probability, or rational choice theory. The resulting errors are called "cognitive biases," and many different types have been documented. These have been shown to affect people's choices in situations, such as making a gaffe when traveling internationally, valuing a house, deciding the outcome of a legal case, or making an investment decision. Heuristics usually govern automatic, intuitive judgments but can also be used as deliberate mental strategies when working from limited information. Cognitive scientist Herbert A. Simon originally proposed that human judgments are limited by available information, time constraints, and cognitive limitations, terming this phenomenon "bounded rationality."

    a. What five things quickly come to mind when you hear the term *globalization*? What about when you think of traveling to China for business? To Italy for pleasure? To Russia?

    b. What advice would you give to a friend who is thinking about international travel and a career in international management? How might a heuristic help you in your decision making regarding international travel?

    c. How might your personal heuristic or mental models cause you to make cognitive errors in judgment?

---

a   Lewis, Michael. The Undoing Project: A Friendship That Changed Our Minds. W. W. Norton & Company, 2016.; "Heuristics in Judgment and Decision-Making." Wikipedia. https://en.wikipedia.org/wiki/heuristics_in_judgment_and_decision-making.

Sources: Lewis, Alan. *The Cambridge Handbook of Psychology and Economic Behaviour.* Cambridge University Press, 2008.; Harris, Lori A. *CliffsAP Psychology.* John Wiley & Sons, 2007.; Nevid, Jeffrey S. *Psychology: Concepts and Applications.* Cengage Learning, 2008.; Bazerman, M. H. (2017). "Judgment and Decision Making." In Noba Textbook Series: Psychology, ed. R. Biswas-Diener and E. Diener. Champaign, IL: DEF publishers, 2017.

3.1 INTERNATIONAL STRATEGY

International strategy involves offering a firm's products and services in more than one nation but not globally. For example, Lululemon Athletica, Inc., a Canadian company, sells its athletic sportswear in its home country as well as in the United States and Australia. In determining its strategy, goals, objectives, and opportunities for growth, it is considering expanding to other countries. Lululemon's growth path has taken it from selling domestically to globally by expanding its presence in other nations.

3.2 MULTIDOMESTIC STRATEGY

Porter identifies two forms of international industries: multidomestic industries and global industries.[13] **Multidomestic** industries are represented by competition in which one country's industry and institutional environment is independent of another country's industries or cultural institutions. For example, in 1998, Microsoft acquired a very successful South Korean software company that specialized in office software and later adapted it for its Microsoft Office platform in South Korea.[14] Microsoft's entry into this market was a disaster. Not only did the company fail in meeting its ambitious goal of capturing 100 percent of market share through the combined companies, but it also nearly caused a national revolution when thousands of South Koreans flooded the streets in protest of Microsoft's acquisition of the South Korean company.

Microsoft's changes to the specialized South Korean software also incited older South Koreans, who recalled the Japanese colonial occupation of South Korea in the early 1900s. During the occupation, Japan forbade the use of Hangul, South Korea's official language, declaring Japanese to be the only official language in 1938. By 1940, South Koreans were forced to change their family names and use only Japanese surnames. When South Korean independence was restored at the end of World War II, the preservation of Hangul became a priority. Microsoft, a multibillion-dollar global company, became viewed as a return to colonial rule. Microsoft's dream of dominating the South Korean software market was destroyed, and its multimillion-dollar investment in the South Korean company was a failure. Microsoft learned a hard lesson: Not all software industries and institutional cultures are the same across nations. Microsoft's entry in South Korea called for a **multidomestic** market strategy, not a global market strategy.

3.3 GLOBAL STRATEGY

Global strategy entails determining what you want to achieve globally and setting the course of action to achieve it. It is about having a theory on how to globally improve a firm's performance.[15] Global strategy is when a firm sells in many, if not all, of the countries that have, or potentially have, representative markets for a firm's products and services. Determining global strategy starts with answering the question, *Is your theory of strategy at home (home country markets and industries) transferable to another country's markets and ways of doing business?*[16] Crafting global strategy requires the "same thought process whether it's local, national, international or global strategy."[17] The essential question is *When and how is the sum of international whole [for a firm] greater than the sum of the domestic [firm's] whole?* A **global market** is one where a firm's products and services are sold across several markets, with little or no change to the product or service. For example, Ford's concept of a global car, the sale of Boeing aircrafts in all nations with domestic carriers, and the dominance of the Apple iPhone in numerous countries are just some examples of global markets. Another example of a global market is Uber's innovative ride-sharing app, which faced stiffer obstacles and barriers in Europe than it did in the United States due to different government regulations and stronger cabbie unions.

3.4 TRANSNATIONAL STRATEGY

A **transnational business strategy** combines global configuration and coordination of business activities with local responsiveness and continued organizational learning.[18] **Configuration** determines the firm's physical footprint of its value chain activities, facilities, and operations in its domestic and international markets. **Coordination** determines where and how decisions are made for a firm's facilities and operations.[19] Coordination determines the extent and method that activities and decisions are coordinated across a global value chain. Decision structures can be viewed as a pendulum from highly centralized to decentralized.

Centralized decisions are made at the highest level of the firm, in the firm's home (headquarters), or in the divisional offices (divisional vice presidents), usually by a small number of senior strategic managers.

Decentralized decisions are localized and made lower down in the firm by strategic managers in the firm's several domestic and international facilities (sales offices, business offices, research and development centers, field engineering) and operations (manufacturing, warehousing, distribution centers). Decentralized decisions are made in closer proximity to the suppliers and customers (local control) found in the firm's domestic and international markets. Senior managers remain in the constant process of balancing efficiency and effectiveness in decision making. Centralized decisions promote greater efficiency and economies of scale where "one size" fits all national and international markets. Decentralized decisions are considered more effective because decisions are made closer "to the ground" and can be tailored to the differences in markets, customers, cultures, and technologies found in a firm's geographically spread-out operations and facilities. A transnational strategy offers the centralization benefits provided by a global strategy along with the local responsiveness of domestic strategies (see Figure 8.3: Global, Transnational, International, Multidomestic Strategy). A firm using a transnational strategy seeks a middle ground between a multidomestic strategy and a global strategy. Such a firm attempts to balance the desire for efficiency with the need to adjust to local preferences within various countries.[20]

Figure 8.3 Global, Transnational, International, Multidomestic Strategy

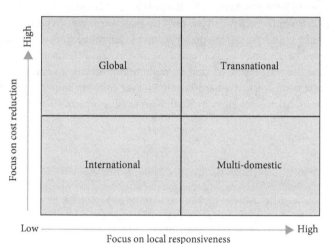

Source: Adapted From: Hill, Charles W.I. Global Business Today, Sixth Edition, Boston, McGraw-Hill/Irwin: P 396

4. ADVANTAGES OF DOING BUSINESS ACROSS BORDERS

What determines the success or failure of firms on an international level? Firms expand internationally for a number of reasons with the foremost being to improve firm performance. As we discussed earlier, a firm's competitive advantage undergoes several cycles of growth and decline. Each cycle brings new opportunities and new challenges. As we know, firms compete in contested and dynamic markets. Strategy links a firm's international resources, actions, activities, and processes to its external environment to determine how it will compete in contested and dynamic markets. Rivalry among firms and the dynamism of industries and markets constantly challenge a firm's strategies and ability to create customer and firm value. Expanding internationally, if done correctly, can be a critical source and driver of firm success. If done poorly, it can be a costly and—in extreme cases—debilitating factor in firm success. As such, strategists must apply the same strategic thinking and critical inquiry to analyzing international entry strategies as they do in analyzing domestic strategies and actions. Critical inquiry and thinking at the highest level will provide the means for weighing the advantages and disadvantages of going international and arriving at an informed decision.

4.1 GROWTH OPPORTUNITIES AND ACCESS TO NEW CUSTOMERS

Firms look toward international markets to find new growth markets for its products and services. This is especially the case when home markets are saturated or in a mature or declining stage of growth. The challenge for strategists is to craft international strategies that can renew and reshape existing strategies and resource strengths for sustained competitive advantages. Growth opportunities can be found in developed, emerging, and newly developing countries. In developed countries, the strategist is looking for large markets where the firm's products and services change the dynamics and status quo of existing industry players (rivals, suppliers, and customers). Entry strategies for already developed markets can include bringing new and innovative technologies, business models, strategies, processes, products, services, and management concepts to these markets.

In emerging or developing countries and markets, the strategist's job is to find markets where the firm can gain a foothold in markets and industries that are expected to experience rapid growth in demand. In emerging markets, government control over or regulation of entry into these markets requires the entering firm to collaborate with local governments and other parties in the host country's industries and markets. Collaborative strategies could include: sharing or committing advanced technologies or other resource strengths (core capabilities, management practices, and concepts); investment strategies (partnerships and joint ventures with host countries' firms); local content (buying from host country suppliers), and labor contracts.

4.2 LOWER INPUT OR FACTOR COSTS

A country can offer both a **competitive** and **comparative** advantage for entering firms. A competitive advantage occurs when the country has a monopoly. For example, it is the only source of an item, the only producer of an item, or the most efficient producer of an item. Entering firms can benefit from a country's competitive advantage through partnerships, joint ventures, and other arrangements with firms in the host country. **Comparative advantage** exists when a country specializes in products that it can supply more efficiently or at a lower cost than it can produce other items. Entering firms can greatly benefit by taking advantage of a host country's comparative advantages. International expansion can provide the firm access to lower factor costs like labor, natural resources, transportation, taxes, and investment capital. Access to low-cost factor inputs can provide entering firms greater competitive advantage opportunities. Lower factor costs can also produce higher gross and net margins for firms' generic strategies (cost, differentiation, and best cost). For instance, access to cheaper raw materials and labor can lead to considerable **outsourcing** (moving some noncritical value activities to other countries) and **offshoring** (moving physical plants and facilities to other countries). The cost benefits of outsourcing and offshoring need to be weighed against the risk of losing a firm's distinctive competencies to foreign rivals, as well as the added cost of effectively outsourcing and offsourcing activities (added governance agreements and management, etc.). China, for example, had a comparative advantage in an abundant supply of cheap labor. The availability of cheap labor made China one of the most manufacturing-friendly and efficient operations in the world. As such, many U.S. companies forced its suppliers to move their manufacturing operations to China (like Walmart did to maintain its "everyday low price" strategy). Sharing manufacturing expertise and technologies in China or India while providing significant reductions in labor and material costs needs to be weighed against foreign partners copying and using the manufacturing expertise for their own benefit (see Exhibit 8.1: China's Global Competitive Edge).

4.3 BUSINESS RISK MANAGEMENT

Business risk refers to the normal risks of doing business, such as poorly crafted strategies, ineffective execution, inability to capitalize on industry opportunities, or failure to adapt to changing market forces and conditions. Competing in multiple markets allows the strategist to better manage risk by spreading it across many economies and customers. The firm manages risk by taking advantage of the differences in demand conditions across international markets. Several multiproduct companies have business operations in numerous countries to offset the risk of business failure in one country against business success in another. For example, American cigarette companies like Philip Morris and R. J. Reynolds, when challenged by laws restricting the advertisement of tobacco products and prohibiting smoking in public areas, responded to the adversity in U.S. markets by expanding their operations within countries where smoking is popular and firm profits attractive.

4.4 POLITICAL RISK MANAGEMENT

Political risk deals with the stability and challenges that face host governments and institutions. Political risk can harm a firm's business success. Many western countries' home markets are governed by democratic principles and (for the most part) free and open markets compared to other parts of the world. For example, the term "Arab Spring" has been used to refer to a series of uprisings within countries such as Tunisia, Egypt, Libya, Bahrain, Syria, and Yemen in 2011. Unstable governments associated with such demonstrations and unrest make it difficult for firms to plan for the future. Over time, a government could become increasingly hostile to foreign businesses by imposing new taxes and new regulations. In extreme cases, a firm's assets in a country can be seized by the hostile national government or apprehended as political retaliation against other countries' actions. The nationalization of U.S. firms in foreign countries is, unfortunately, not that uncommon in countries that are hostile to the United States or that face strong civil unrest. For example, In 2008, Venezuela's President Hugo Chávez's nationalization took control over foreign companies in the oil, cement, steel, and glass industries by nationalizing these industries.[21]

4.5 CULTURE RISK

Culture risk deals with a firm making poor strategic decisions because of a lack of understanding of the values, norms, social customs, and belief systems of the people and social institutions of the host country. Many businesses fail to achieve their international goals not because of business or political risks but because they neither understand nor adapt to a country's cultural norms. For instance, western business practices can differ considerably from the way business is conducted in India or other Asian countries. Newspapers and personal accounts contain scores of stories detailing failed international expansions due to major cultural gaffes or clumsy social error or misstep. When KFC opened in Beijing, China, in the late 1980s, the restaurant had accidentally translated its famous "Finger-lickin' good" slogan to a not-so-appetizing phrase: "Eat your fingers off." While many western nations use rule-centered approaches to build business agreements and settle disputes, in eastern countries, business managers rely on establishing individual relationships with their business partners rather than depending on lengthy contracts and teams of attorneys. In conservative Muslim countries like Saudi Arabia, people pray five times per day. During this time, all establishments are required to close. Additionally, there are neither public movie theaters and public concerts nor bars or pubs because the sale of alcohol is prohibited. Customary dress is required in the workplace, and no premarriage contact between men and women is permitted. Married men and women cannot mingle with each other or single members of the opposite gender. A comprehensive understanding of the cultural values and customs of the prospective foreign market is critical to a firm's success in that region.

Thinking Critically Exercise 58

PERCEPTIONS ON GLOBALIZATION

a. What are the drivers of globalization? What are some of the implications of globalization on one's career choices?
b. What advice would you give to a friend who is thinking about international travel and a career in international management? What are some of the benefits of living and working in a foreign country?

5. PEST: A CRITICAL FIRST STEP IN GOING INTERNATIONAL

 VIDEO 8.2 PEST Analysis

Before entering new and untested international markets, firms must first conduct an in-depth situational analysis to determine the attractiveness of entry. One useful tool for this analysis is PEST (political, economic, social/cultural, and technological environments). The strategist needs to analyze each PEST factor to determine the difference between a firm's home market competitive dynamics and those of another country. This process proves invaluable in identifying the opportunities and threats of doing business internationally. For example, though there are numerous PEST variances across countries, competition against rivals in markets with similar institutions, values, and belief systems remains more accessible to entering firms than competing against rivals with dissimilar institutions, values, and beliefs systems (see Table 8.1: Understanding Business Culture—West and East).

5.1 POLITICAL FACTORS

A handful of factors that aid in assessing the impact of a country's political environment are: the stability of the national, regional, and local governments; regulatory policies and tax structures; and differences in political systems and philosophies. For example, many countries operating under socialism believe that economic inequality is detrimental to society. Rather, the government is responsible for reducing inequality via programs that benefit the poor (free public education, free or subsidized health care, social security for the elderly, higher taxes on the rich, etc.) Conversely, capitalists believe that the government does not use economic resources as efficiently as do private enterprises. Therefore, society is better off with the free market determining economic winners and losers.[22] The differences in socialism and capitalism can impact a country's trade and tariff policies, licensing, regulation, antitrust, control over industries, and government control of factor inputs such as labor (human rights), environment (climate control), and justice systems (due process, intellectual property, personal property rights).

Table 8.1 Understanding Business Culture—West and East	Cultural Values Expressed	West (America & most European countries)	East (The Chinese and Most Asian cultures)
	Type of Logic	Linear (More causal relationships and direct associations between A and B)	Spiral (more roundabout and subtle)
	Expression of Agreement and Disagreement	More argumentative, willing to express disagreement verbally	More difficult to say no even if one means no, disagreement expressed nonverbally
	Communication of Information	More meaning is in the explicit, verbal message. Use of direct language	Meaning is often implied or must be inferred Use of indirect language patterns
	Expression of Honesty	More overt, one is more likely to ask the person to "speak their mind" or "get it out on the table"	Subtle, nonverbal
	Expression of Self	"I"-oriented Sender-oriented	"We"-oriented Receiver-sensitive
	Thinking Orientation	More rule based or based on application of abstract principles such as regulations or laws	Tends to take context and the specific situation into account in rule interpretation
	The Individual	Has to have rights and greater need for autonomy and individual achievement	Group duty preservation of harmony
	Nature of the Business Relationship	Less important, tend to substitute relationship for written agreement, superficial, easy to form, not long lasting	Most important business cannot occur until relationship if sound, written agreement secondary to quan xi, hard to form, long lasting
	Conflict Resolution	Trial or confrontation, use of lawyers and courts	More mediation though trusted third parties
	Time Sense During Meetings	Be on time and end on time.	Appointments less driven by exact start and end times
	Conflict results	Perception of two states: win or lose	Win-Win To lose is to win Lose in order to win

Source: https://www.legacee.com/the-global-leader/chinese-business-culture/

5.2 ECONOMIC FACTORS

Economic factors must be identified and assessed to determine host entry strategy, home firm resource commitments (investment strategy), and timing. Among the economic factors that need to be analyzed are: GDP (gross domestic product) growth rates, tax policies, rate of inflation, interest rates, exchange rates, unemployment and the labor supply, income distribution, and long-term prospects for economic growth.

5.3 SOCIAL FACTORS

Social factors include: cultural norms, values, and belief systems; work ethic (attitudes toward work and family life balance); social, religious, and ethical beliefs (fairness, open-system thinking, human rights); demographics (age, education, income, growth rates); class structure; psychographic factors; and lifestyle considerations (see *Demographics* above).

5.4 TECHNOLOGICAL FACTORS

Technology encompasses both tangible and intangible factors. Tangible factors include intellectual capital, productivity and innovation, advanced factor conditions (infrastructure—roads, airports, ports, public transportation networks), telecommunication networks (broadband), education, research centers, advances in digital technologies), and Moore's and Metcalfe's laws (see Chapter 6). Conversely, intangible factors include intellectual property (patents, trademarks, copyrights), software, sensors, storage, cloud technologies, deep data analytics, availability of skilled talent, knowledge workers (professional, technical, and administrative talent), and overall innovation and creativity intellectual quotient. A creativity intellectual quotient refers to one's **ability** to come up with new and creative ideas through mental processes. These processes can include models for connecting existing concepts, continuous learning, entrepreneurial mindset, capacity to see market asymmetries, problem solving, market opportunism, and ASTC (acting strategically, thinking critically).

6. STRATEGIES FOR ENTERING FOREIGN MARKETS[23]

A firm can elect to enter international markets in a variety of ways. Each entry strategy is influenced by a number of factors including the firm's tolerance for risk, cost to enter, timing of entry, learning curve effects, and sustainability of competitive advantage in home markets. Although these factors and others will influence firm-specific entry strategy, several generic options are open for consideration as well. Some examples are direct exporting, licensing, franchising, strategic partnering, joint ventures, and foreign direct investments.

6.1 DIRECT EXPORTING

Some methods of directly marketing and selling a firm's products and services to customers in international markets are: company webpage, e-commerce (Amazon.com), mobile adverting and publishing, and social media (Facebook). Ecommerce opportunities include: B2C (business to customers), B2B (business to business), and P2P (person to person—e.g., Craigslist). A firm can also elect to outsource marketing and distribution of products through host country sales agents and distributors (third-party intermediaries located in the host country), foreign sales agents or sales representatives, state and regional import/export agencies, industry associations, and international trade shows or by forming collaborative partnerships with foreign companies and governmental agencies.

6.2 LICENSING

Licensing consists of formal contractual arrangements where the home county firm transfers the rights to use its products and services to a firm in the host country. Licensing is used when the firm purchasing the license is a major player in a highly attractive industry or strategic group in the host country. Licensing agreements are used as an entry strategy for manufacturing, marketing, and distributing a firm's product or services or by granting technology rights (patents, trademarks, copyrights, proprietary technologies and processes) for use by authorized users in the purchaser host country.

6.3 FRANCHISING

Franchising can be used for rapid international expansion into one or more international markets. Franchising can also be used as a way to quickly finance international expansion. Franchisees pay a share of the cost to set up host country operations including location and construction costs of operations, staffing, and selling the franchisor's products and services in the host country. Franchising is used by start-up firms to finance international expansion and establish companies that have scalable business models and brands. Some well-known brands with scale business models employing a franchisee cost to acquire a franchise are:

- Subway: $15,000, a minimum net worth of $80,000, and minimum liquid assets of $30,000
- Pizza Hut: $25,000, a required net worth of $700,000, and liquid assets of $350,000
- Ben & Jerry's: $37,000, a minimum net worth of $350,000, and minimum liquid assets of $100,000
- Dunkin' Donuts: $40,000 to $90,000, a minimum net worth of $250,000, and minimum liquid assets of $125,000
- McDonald's: $45,000 and minimum liquid assets of $750,000

6.4 STRATEGIC PARTNERING

A **strategic partnership** (sometimes referred as **strategic alliance**) is a relationship between two commercial enterprises, usually formalized by one or more business contracts. Strategic partnerships can take on various forms from informal arrangements to detailed alliance and partnership agreements. Strategic partnerships can also include formation of a joint venture (equity agreements) or cross-holdings and ownership in each partner's products, services, processes, or technologies. Typically, two companies form a strategic partnership when each possesses one or more business assets or has expertise that will help the other by enhancing their firm. Partnering is required in some foreign markets, especially in China. Partnerships with developing countries in Eastern Europe and Asia ("Asian Tiger" countries) are common. The four Asian tigers—Hong Kong, Singapore, South Korea, and Taiwan—have consistently maintained high levels of economic growth since the 1960s, fueled by strategic partnerships, exports, and rapid industrialization, which enabled these economies to join the ranks of the world's richest nations. Currently in China, it is accepted wisdom that a non-Chinese company cannot possibly be successful without a Chinese intermediary or partner well-versed in the Chinese language, customs, and laws. The partnership becomes mutually beneficial when the non-Chinese company provides the Chinese company with technology or management expertise in return for access to its vast markets.

6.5 JOINT VENTURES

A **joint venture** (JV) is a business entity created by two or more parties, generally characterized by shared ownership, shared returns and risks, and shared governance. Typically, the JV takes the form of two partnerships coming together to create a third, interdependently owned and managed company. Two examples of JVs are Tesla Motors and Panasonic to create lithium-ion batteries and Sony and Ericsson to produce cellphones.

Companies typically pursue JVs for several reasons, including:

- Access a new market, particularly emerging markets
- Gain scale efficiencies by combining assets, operations, and lower factor inputs
- Gain economies of scope (complementary and supporting products and/or technologies)
- Share risk for major investments or projects
- Access skills and capabilities

6.6 FOREIGN DIRECT INVESTMENTS (FDI) (MERGERS AND ACQUISITIONS)

On a broad scope, foreign direct investment entry strategies can include: mergers and acquisitions, building new facilities (greenfield investments), reinvesting profits earned in the host country back into the host country, and intracompany loans (to host country licensees, franchisees, strategic partners, and joint ventures). Generally, FDI refers to investing in new facility and direct investments in tangible resources while maintaining a lasting management interest (owning 10 percent or more of voting stock in a foreign enterprise). FDI also includes foreign acquisitions. Acquisition targets can include rivals, suppliers, contract manufacturers, and channel distributors. This may be because the foreign entity has substantial market share, is a direct competitor, or is required by host country governments.

6.7 OTHER—EXPATS AND SERENDIPITY EVENTS

Individuals, especially individuals seeking new adventure and entrepreneurial opportunity, move to foreign countries to learn professional practices and start their own businesses. For example, Elon Musk is founder or co-founder of several entrepreneurial start-ups, including Tesla Motors, SpaceX, SolarCity, PayPal, Neuralink, and The Boring Company. Musk was born in 1971 in Pretoria, South Africa. He moved to Canada at the age of 17 for his undergraduate studies. Musk transferred two years later to the University of Pennsylvania, where in 1997 he received a Bachelor of Science degree in physics from its College of Arts and Sciences and a Bachelor of Science degree in economics from its Wharton School of Business. Musk holds triple citizenship in South Africa, Canada, and the United States.[24]

BECOMING AN EXPAT

Prepare a PowerPoint presentation for a publically traded company (New York Stock Exchange, NASDAQ (an Electronic Exchange) in the industry of your choice. Assume that you are presenting to the company's board of directors. Your company's senior management team is looking for recommendations about conducting business in a host country of your choice. Assume that you will be given a one-year (minimum) appointment to set up the business in the host country. This is a promotion that comes with a significant pay raise. Prepare a senior management briefing (PowerPoint presentation) on your company, industry, and country. Assume this is your employer's first direct investment in this host country. Incorporate the following:

a. What is your company? Conduct a strategic audit of this company. What is its overall financial health?

b. What industry or product segment will you be analyzing? (If the company has several products or industries it serves, pick one for your analysis.) What are the key industry characteristics for your company in this country? Who are the main competitors in your industry, and what are they like?

c. What is your country? What is your country's population density, average educational level, per capita income, climate, form of government, dominant racial-ethnic group, dominant religion, living standard and economic growth (GDP and PPP), quality of life (Human Development Index and Economic Freedom Index), and exchange rate compared to the United States. How stable is your country politically and economically?

d. Go to your company's website. Which stakeholders are most important to your company and why? Build a table showing the key financials for the previous five years. Conduct a financial audit with a summary assessment of the company's financial health. Is the company's business model working? How successful are its international operations? What does it mean to be a "global citizen" (corporate social responsibility and ethical policies) at your company?

e. What is the appropriate protocol when conducting business in your country (greeting people, negotiating a contract, gift-giving, appropriate topics for conversation, etc.)?

f. What type of living conditions can an expat expect for themselves and their family in this country?

g. What are some of the PEST issues facing your company's entry into your host country? What is the climate for doing business in your host country? What challenges do you expect the company to encounter while doing business in this country? What personal challenges and opportunities do you expect to encounter while living and working in this country?

h. What career opportunities are there in working and living as an expat in a foreign country?

7. ENTREPRENEURSHIP STRATEGY SCHOOL

The entrepreneurship strategy school offered a new theory of entrepreneurship. Typically, entrepreneurship was applied to particular individuals and contextual situations, start-ups, niche players, privately owned companies, and turnaround situations. Unlike the other strategy schools, the entrepreneurial school is rooted in the "mysteries" of intuition, improvisation, and imagination. It shifts strategic thinking away from precise design, plans, positioning, specialized capabilities, and learning to the creative and visionary mind of the entrepreneur. This school recognizes the importance of visioning or perspectives as typically seen through metaphors. Visioning and concept generation stimulates entrepreneurs to move quickly in order to gain first-mover advantage. These factors also drive the underlying logic behind new strategies, business models, and the entrepreneur's innovative and creative thinking.

An entrepreneur always searches for change, responds to it, and exploits it as an opportunity.[25] An **entrepreneur** can be defined as an innovative visionary who creates value by mobilizing resources to exploit market opportunities. They see market asymmetries that others do not and take bold action to exploit these irregularities. The entrepreneurial school argues that strategic managers must be skilled at not only innovation but also management. This focus on entrepreneurship shifts from a particular individual or context to the CEO as entrepreneur and strategic leader. As such, strategic management and entrepreneurship are inseparable concepts. All organizations, no matter their size or context, need to be innovative to sustain performance and thrive. The purpose of a business is to "… provide value to the customer—to provide something that an independent and knowledgeable outsider who can choose whether or not to buy is willing to get in exchange for his or her purchasing power."[26] From this strategic marketing perspective, an organization's customer value creation and capture is driven by human creativity, imagination, intellectual expertise, and action. The CEO as entrepreneur is on a constant search for opportunities. Strategic managers as entrepreneurs are opportunity-driven and need to utilize their creative and innovation talents to capitalize on opportunities. In order to grow and sustain a firm's competitive advantage, strategists must have strong leaders with complementary strengths and abilities in business acumen and entrepreneurship. Entrepreneurs do not necessarily cause change; they just need to recognize and exploit opportunities that swings in markets, technology, and customers create.[27]

7.1 ENTREPRENEURIAL MANAGEMENT OF INNOVATION AND TECHNOLOGY

Entrepreneurial school advocates hold the view that innovation and technology can be managed. This school maintains that technological upgrading and innovation is not an exogenous phenomenon but can be internally and creatively managed and used in the creation of competitive advantage.[28] This is accomplished through the development of processes or frameworks that facilitate technological innovation and knowledge creation. **Technology** is defined as a process by which a stock of knowledge is made available to reduce uncertainty in achieving some desired end. The basic assumption is that technological information or knowledge facilitates the organization's ability to make strategic decisions that ultimately lead to organizational upgrading and improved performance; that is, technology is viewed as a process for creating solutions to problems.[29] Innovation requires the ability to gain access to information and process that information effectively.

7.2 THE INNOVATOR'S DILEMMA

According to Peter Drucker, management can be viewed as a two-sided coin with one side representing the CEO's or strategist's business acumen and leadership skills and the other side the entrepreneur's innovative and creative talents.[30] As such, a firm's wealth or value creation and realization comes from human creativity and imagination, intellectual expertise, and fast action. It requires letting go of the past—the very things, capabilities, and thinking that drove a firm's success—and moving on to new things, new capabilities, and new thinking. Deciding when to let go and when to move on is a critical strategic choice, resulting in what Christensen calls the *innovator's dilemma*.[31] For example, Kodak's inability to transition from its traditional film business to digital photography caused the firm to spiral downward and eventually enter bankruptcy.

VIDEO 8.3 "The Innovator's Dilemma" by Clayton Christensen—Video Book Summary

In your opinion, what are the top five all time most innovative products or services introduced in your lifetime? What was innovative about each product or service? How disruptive were each of these innovative products or services to the existing products, services, or companies already on the market?

7.3 STRATEGY AS CREATIVE DESTRUCTION

The entrepreneurial school line of reasoning can be traced to the work of Austrian economist Joseph Schumpeter in the 1930s.[32] Schumpeter offers his theory of creative destruction, which focuses on strategy as change. According to Schumpeter, **creative destruction** describes the "process of industrial mutation that incessantly revolutionizes the economic structure from within, incessantly destroying the old one, incessantly creating a new one."[33] Schumpeter argues that industries, customers, and technologies are constantly changing—some more quickly than others. All organizations must undergo a constant renewal and readjustment to the needs of their customers and the market. Failure to monitor, accommodate, and respond to these needs threatens the viability of the firm. In responding to these needs, every organizational leader must master managing change because all industries and organizations go through constant evolutionary and revolutionary life cycles. Evolutionary cycles incrementally change industries and the means by which business is conducted. **Revolutionary** cycles alter the very nature of competition, thereby completely transforming the way things are done. In short, it's about "the gales of creative destruction," a term coined by Schumpeter.[34]

7.4 FIRST-MOVER ADVANTAGE

The concept of **first-mover advantage** is similar to the old adage, "The early bird gets the worm." Being the first company to sell a new product may (but not always) provide long-lasting benefits and competitive advantages.[35] Most researchers use the term "first mover" to refer to the first company to enter a market, not the first company to develop a product (the inventor). For example, Amazon.com was the first major online bookstore, getting a head start on later entrants. Established book retailers Barnes & Noble and Borders were quick to develop their own websites. However, Amazon maintained its first-mover advantage by branching out beyond books, developing sophisticated web-based technology and advanced inventory and supply chain management infrastructure and systems.

VIDEO 8.4 Michael Porter: Why Business Can Be Good at Solving Social Problems

8. SOCIAL ENTREPRENEURSHIP

The study of social entrepreneurship is a subset of the entrepreneurship field. The social enterprise seeks to gain a better understanding of the business context and develop action steps for achieving long-term, mission-related social impact.[36] Martin and Osbery note that "the social entrepreneur aims for value in the form of large-scale, transformational benefit that accrues either to a significant segment of society or to society at large."[37]

Phills, Deiglmeier, and Miller make a distinction between economic and social innovation. Social innovation aims at providing "a novel solution to a **social problem** that is more effective, efficient, sustainable, or just than existing [market] solutions and for which the value created accrues primarily to society as a whole rather than private individuals."[38] Profit and market forces drive **economic innovation**. **Social innovation** can be defined as "new ideas that work in meeting social goals" and draw distinctions between innovation and improvement, creativity and invention.[39] Mullen and Shepherd noted, "Not all innovation comes from new organizations. Many come from existing organizations learning to renew themselves." They also observed that "any successful organization needs to be simultaneously focused on existing activities, emerging ones and more radical possibilities that could be the mainstream activities of the future."[40]

The social enterprise's ability to attract supplementary revenues is based on the extent of its social impact on its customers and communities.[41] The **social entrepreneur** makes the social mission explicit and central to the purpose of the social enterprise. The mission-related impact becomes the central criterion, not wealth creation. Wealth is just a means to an end for social entrepreneurs. Dees notes that to offset the value capture problem, social entrepreneurs rely on subsidies, donations, and volunteers. Their ability to attract philanthropic resources may provide some indication of value creation in the eyes of the resource providers.

Dees also emphasizes the important role social entrepreneurs play as change agents in the social sector by:

- Adopting a mission to create and sustain social value (not just private value)
- Recognizing and relentlessly pursuing new opportunities to serve that mission
- Engaging in a process of continuous innovation, adaptation, and learning
- Acting boldly without being limited by resources currently in hand
- Exhibiting heightened accountability to the constituencies served and for the outcomes created[42]

Dees cautions that this is clearly an "idealized" definition. Social sector leaders will exemplify these characteristics in different ways and to different degrees. The closer an individual gets to satisfying all these conditions, the more that person fits the model of a social entrepreneur.

8.1 NOT-FOR-PROFITS

The entrepreneur's creativity and innovative talents also apply to the not-for-profit (NFP) organization. A **not-for-profit** organization is formed to serve some public purpose or good rather than for financial gain. As long as the NFP's activities are for charitable, religious, educational, scientific, or literary causes, it is exempt from paying income taxes. The term *not-for-profit organization* is broad-based, encompassing all organizations that are known variously as charities, nonprofits, nongovernmental organizations (NGOs), private voluntary organizations (PVOs), and civil society. Nonprofits are generally associated with social clubs or associations designed to serve the association or club's membership or support a community need. For example, a group of people might come together as a nonprofit to raise money for families who lost their homes in a national disaster or to raise money for a person with a serious illness (See Exhibit 8.2: Types of Not-for-Profits).

NFPs have no equity owner. Its assets are considered public assets under the management of the NFP's board of directors. Not-for-profits provide for many of society's essential needs that cannot or should not be provided by for-profit businesses. They help to address both positive externalities (external to the natural interplay of market forces), such as quality of life, education, and health care initiatives, as well as negative externalities, such as pollution, global warming and climate change, fair trade, environmental degradation, human rights violations, and animal rights.

Exhibit 8.2
Types of
Not-for-Profits

Types of not-for-profit organizations (Adapted from Coulter, Mary *strategic management in action,* pearson/prentice-hall, chapter 8: Special topics, figure 8-3, p257)

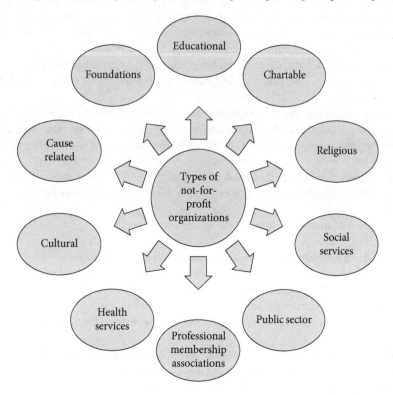

Not-for-profit & special type of organizations

Not-for-profits do not have the same market discipline as for-profit businesses. Success for the latter is based on creating customer value and market-driven competitive advantage. Success for the former is centered around creating social, community, and market-driven competitive advantage. The NFP's ability to creatively solve customer problems that are not or cannot be solved in the market alone addresses a social need deemed important by society. The NFP then fills a revenue and profit gap in the marketplace. Sources of revenues and funds for not-for-profits, include:

- Fees for Services
- Charitable Contributions
- Corporate Philanthropy
- Federal, State, and Local Governments
- Federated Funds—Community-based efforts such as United Way, Red Cross
- Grant-Making Public Charities, Community

The concept of customer value creation can be applied to the NFP firm and the social enterprise. A useful tool for defining and assessing a firm's value proposition is the customer value proposition canvas.[43] Similar to a for-profit business, the customer value proposition needs to be both determined and evaluated for the NFP, but its customer value proposition addresses a social need. Charitable donations, government support, or community aid going to the NFP fill the gap between the NFP's earned fees and mission. This is one measure of the effectiveness of NFP strategies and customer value proposition. The NFP's managers as social entrepreneurs in crafting strategy need to ask: *What is to be gained by the customer and community by purchasing or supporting the NFP's programs or services? What basic service or need (illness, poverty, education, team-building) is the NFP providing and to whom? What benefits will the client receive that are not accessible or available through for-profit businesses? What economic or financial barriers are removed or lessened by the social enterprise? What emotional, psychological, or social barriers are addressed that cannot be or are not addressed by a for-profit?* Unlike the for-profit enterprise, the social enterprise needs to determine the fit or gap between the costs to provide its programs and services with the fees received for these programs and services. Any gap must be made up through supplementary revenue from donors, grants, and contributions. As such, the social enterprise needs to determine what the minimum viable program or services are required to address customer needs.[44]

9. FOSTERING CREATIVITY AND ENTREPRENEURSHIP

Entrepreneurs are creative visionaries who create customer and firm value by mobilizing resources to exploit market opportunities. Entrepreneurs are CEOs and strategic leaders who see market asymmetries and take bold action to exploit them. Some strategic actions and concepts associated with entrepreneurship within organizations (known as **intrepreneurship**) and outside the organization are:

- Creatively managing company spin-offs, harvesting or downsizing a business, and/or letting go of   existing company business models or processes
- Innovatively relaunching or repositioning established businesses with new business models or new product and service platforms
- Establishing skunkworks (stand-alone units) designed to foster innovation and creativity without the entrapments of organizational bureaucracies
- Forming collaborative, strategic R&D alliances and partnerships
- Exploiting value chain relations by working with sophisticated customers, suppliers, and other value chain entities (assumption is that the source of innovation is embedded in value chain relationships)
- Rewarding and recognizing creative ideas and innovation no matter their sources or level within the firm
- Engaging and hosting entrepreneurial events and competitions with significant prizes for the most creative and innovative ideas and business proposals

Cash awards and other incentives have long been used by public and private entities to spur creativity, innovation, and entrepreneurial initiatives. It has also been well-documented that creativity and innovation spur entrepreneurship, job creation, productivity, and firm competitive advantage.[45] Research funded by the Kauffman Foundation consistently demonstrates that all new jobs created in the United States come from start-up companies that are fewer than five years old.[46] Corporate- and university-sponsored business plan competitions can act as catalysts for venture creation and wealth generation.

a. Have you ever entered a business plan competition? Do you know someone who has? What might attract you to enter one? What is the connection between entrepreneurial strategy, strategic management, and strategy execution?

10. CHOOSING THE LEGAL FORM OF OWNERSHIP FOR YOUR BUSINESS

Start-up companies come in all forms and sizes, ranging from small businesses owned by a sole proprietor to high-growth, high-technology entrepreneurial ventures. Three common forms of business start-ups are: small- to medium-sized businesses (the most common in number of established and legal form of organizational structure); start-ups revolving around technology; and high-growth, high-potential, nontech ventures. A useful way to distinguish high-technology growth companies from small- to medium-sized companies is by growth rate (sales) and rate of innovation. Very small companies and medium-sized companies are sometimes referred to as **mice** or **ants**—though small in number, their cumulative and aggregative effect on a community and society is large. Slow-moving, larger companies are referred to as **elephants** or **dinosaurs** because they have failed to adapt to disruptive changes in the market. High-growth technology businesses are sometimes referred to as **gazelles** because of their speed and accelerated market growth rather than their absolute size. As such, they can range in scope from small companies to very large enterprises. David Birch of Cognetics is a well-known entrepreneurial school advocate and researcher who conferred the name "gazelle" on fast-growing companies. He also distinguished these speedy firms from the "mice" on Main Street and the "elephants" on the Fortune 500.[47]

High-growth, nontechnology businesses are sometimes referred to as **unicorns** because they are so rare in number. Aileen Lee first used the term in 2013. She defined *unicorn* as a start-up company valued at more than $1 billion, choosing the mythical animal to represent the statistical rarity of such successful ventures. Similarly, the term *decacorn* is used for those start-up companies with more than $10 billion, and *hectocorn* is the appropriate term for a company valued at more than $100 billion. According to TechCrunch, there were 223 unicorns as of March 2017.[48] *Business Insider* in January, 2017, ranked the top 8 decacorn start-ups:[49]

Rank	Company	Valuation
8	Dropbox	(2014* Valuation: $10 billion)
7	Pinterest	(2015 Valuation: $10.47 billion)
6	SpaceX	(2015 Valuation:$12 billion
5	WeWork	(2016 Valuation: $16.9 billion)

4	Snap	(2016 Valuation: $18.19 billion)
3	Palantir	(2015 Valuation: $20.53 billion)
2	Airbnb	(2016 Valuation: $30 billion)
1	Uber	(2016 Valuation: $68 billion)

*Year Achieved

10.1 LEGAL FORMS OF BUSINESS OWNERSHIP

The most common form of legal structure and ownership for entrepreneurial ventures are sole proprietorships for small businesses (mice and ants) and general and professional partnership for small- to medium-sized enterprises (SMEs) and medical, legal, and services enterprises (e.g., law, accounting). Partnerships and general partnerships can grow to significant size and reputation. A partnership occurs when business ownership and control is shared by more than one owner or associate (partners). The partners may be individuals, businesses, interest-based organizations, schools, governments, or a combination of these entities. A partnership may result in issuing and holding equity, or it may be governed only by a contract. For tax purposes, income generated by the partners is shared (based on the partnership agreement) and treated as personal income. In other words, income is **passed through** the partnership to the partners and taxed as personal taxes rather than a business tax. The partnership has the added benefit of avoiding double taxation by corporations when the business pays federal and state taxes. Gross income earned by the corporation and after tax net income is distributed to stockholders in dividends. Other advantages of forming a partnership are: the joining of partners may increase the likelihood of amplifying their reach and achieving their mission; added skills and competencies; added resources (equity and other financial contributions); and decreased risk from sharing among the partners. Disadvantages of partnerships include: limited access to equity capital, business risks caused by the actions of one partner over another, liability risks of partners' actions, and business continuity upon the departure or death of a partner. Partnerships need to register with the state. The best practices call for a carefully crafted partners' charter and articles of agreement to help address some of the disadvantages that come with a partnership structure.

10.2 LIMITED LIABILITY COMPANY

A **limited liability company** (LLC) is a business structure that combines the pass-through taxation of a partnership or sole proprietorship with the limited liability of a corporation. An LLC is not a corporation in and of itself; it is a legal form of a company that provides limited liability to its owners in many jurisdictions (not all U.S. states recognize LLC as a legal form of ownership). The LLC provides an added degree of flexibility to a start-up's founders, but how much depends on the state where the LLC was formed. The LLC founders may elect to use corporate tax rules instead of being treated as a partnership. Under certain circumstances, an LLC may be organized as not-for-profit. The LLC has the added benefit of treating business income as personal income and is taxed accordingly. Some states do not allow the LLC form of ownership for professional service businesses that require state professional licensing or certification (e.g., legal or medical services). In these instances, the state may allow the professional service enterprise to organize as a special form of LLC, known as a **professional limited liability company** (PLLC). The disadvantage of LLC is that it may be not recognized or it may be treated differently for enterprises conducting multistate or international business. Also, the LLC restricts not only the number of domestic shareholders but also the number of shares they can hold. LLCs do not allow foreign equity ownership. These constraints restrict access to and the amount of equity funds that the LLC can raise.

C Corporation (C-Corp) under U.S. law is taxed separately from its owners. As such, the C-Corp is a legal entity and is taxed separately from its stockholders (owners). Most major companies (and many smaller companies) elect to form as a C-Corp for expanded flexibility and access to equity funds (issuance of stock) and limited liability exposure. The business may qualify as a C Corporation without regard to any limit on the number of shareholders, foreign or domestic. Regarding liability exposure, the C-Corp is considered a separate legal entity that owns the assets and risks associated with the business. The personal assets of founders and stockholders are separate from the assets and risks of the business and are protected from lawsuits and other legal actions. This protection extends only to owners who do not attempt to violate U.S. protection through malfeasance. In cases of malfeasance, the C-Corp liability shield and limited liability protection is broken. A disadvantage of the C-Corp is the added cost to incorporate, additional state and federal regulation, strict state governance oversight and regulation (board members and meetings per year), added incorporation costs and filings (Incorporation Charter) , and double taxation. The C-Corp stockholders can avoid double taxation if they elect to be treated as a flow-through entity known as an **S (Sub) Corporation**. An S Corporation is not itself subject to income tax. Rather, shareholders of the S Corporation are subject to tax on a prorated share of income based on percent of ownership. To qualify to make the S Corporation election, shares must be held by residents, individuals, or certain qualifying trusts.

10.4 B (BENEFITS) CORP

Certified B Corporations are firms certified by the nonprofit B Lab to have met rigorous standards of social and environmental performance, accountability, and transparency. B Corp certification is similar to **LEED** certification for green buildings, Fair Trade certification for produce or products produced in low-wage countries (certified that a "living" wage is being paid), and for certification of organic and all-natural products such as 100 percent organic coffee. B Lab is a nonprofit organization "that serves a global movement of people using business as a force for good. Its vision is that one day all companies compete not only to be the best in the world, but the Best for the World' and as a result society will enjoy a more shared and durable prosperity."[50]

11. WRITING A BUSINESS PLAN FOR A START-UP: ESSENTIAL QUESTIONS

Have you ever thought about starting your own business but have no idea where to begin? A good place to start is to write a business proposal or business plan. Writing out your business plan forces you to review everything that goes into a new product or business proposal including the feasibility and appropriateness of the idea or new venture. A business plan also contains an assessment of the customer value proposition, goals, required management competencies, potential strengths and areas of weaknesses, opportunity recognition, potential threats, and assumptions about how your business will function (management, marketing, operations, accounting, finance plan, and staffing plans). Robbins reports that in going through the business plan writing process, "You'll end up spotting connections you otherwise would have missed." For example, if your marketing plan projects 10,000 customers by year two and your staffing plan provides for two salespeople, that forces you to ask, *How can two salespeople generate 10,000 customers?* The answer might lead you to conclude that forming partnerships, targeting distributors, and concentrating on bulk sales to large companies would be your best tactic initially.[51] A business plan facilitates strategic thinking and critical inquiry. Whether it's for a start-up or moving a firm into new markets or products, a business or strategic plan is essential. The basic questions that all entrepreneurs must answer in writing a business or strategic plan are in Table 8.2.

Table 8.2
Business Plan
Essential
Questions

- What is the envisioned product or service and what does it do? What is the appropriate revenue streams or business model? What are the customer benefits your business model provides?
- What are the top 2 or 3 competitive products or services currently on the market? Why will prospective customers buy your product or service over rivals'? Compared to competitor products and services, how is your product, service, or business unique and/or innovative?
- What is the underlying technology (if any) for your product, service, or your innovative business approach compared to competitors'?
- What is your initial target market for your product/service and what is this market like? Is there a clear window of opportunity for the product, service, or innovative business approach?
- What is the estimated size of your initial target market (in units and sales dollars)? What is the estimated growth potential of your product or service in actual units sold and/or annual percentage growth in sales?
- How much are your potential customers willing to pay (your initial selling price) for your product/service? How did you arrive at this amount?
- How might your product or service contribute to a more sustainable economy, a more sustainable environment, or otherwise contribute to society?
- What is the current stage of your product/service, and what is your plan for making your product/service ready for sale?
- What is your estimate of monthly sales and expenses for years one and two? What are your estimated quarterly sales and expenses for year three? Clearly state your assumptions behind your estimates for sales and expenses.
- What are your estimated costs to launch your business? What are your financing needs? How do you plan to finance the start-up? Please provide a day one (the launch date of your venture) sources and uses of funds statement.
- How much will it cost to produce a unit of product/service for sale? What is your break-even point in units and sales for your product or service? In calculating break-even, please use the following equation: Break-even point equals fixed costs divided by unit contribution. Unit contribution equals selling price per unit minus variable cost per unit.
- For small businesses, cash is king. Cash flow is the movement of money in and out of your business. Provide a monthly estimate of cash inflows and outflows for years one and two of your venture and a quarterly cash flow statement for year three. Include a pro forma statement.
- What is the estimated financial return or financial pay-off to investors and management teams from the sale of your products or services?
- What are the barriers or challenges associated with entering and competing in your initial market? What could go wrong? How might these concerns or barriers be addressed?
- What is your exit strategy? How will you as an entrepreneur extract value from the start-up and early investors? Will it be through an IPO (initial public offering), selling the company and cashing out, or management buy-out? The form of business ownership will help to drive this decision and get maximum value for your start-up or venture.

12. REFLECTION: MANAGING ONESELF

It is only proper that we conclude this book and our study of acting strategically and thinking critically (ASTC) with the entrepreneurial school of strategic thought, going international, and social enterprise. We live in exciting and dynamic times, requiring everyone to think and act like a CEO and entrepreneur. The modern world is ample with disruptive change and accelerated growth. Opportunities are abundant for those individuals who can engage in diversified and integrated thinking and demonstrate an ability to employ open systems, as well as innovative thinking and actions. Today's rapidly changing industries and markets require our current and next-generation business leaders to think inside the box, outside the box, and where there is no box at all. It requires our leaders in all walks of life to be able to think globally and act locally. It requires leaders to be ethical and fair in their critical thinking and actions. The U.S. National Intelligence Council conducted a survey of their readers' 2030 global trends predictions. The council's *The Global Trends 2030: Alternative Worlds* (GT 2030), reported six key "looming" challenges for global trends in 2030 (see Table 8.3: Global Trends 2030—An Overview):

1. A greater focus on the role of the United States in the international system. The key looming issues for GT 2030 was "how other powers would respond to a decline of a decisive re-assertion of U.S. power."

2. A clearer understanding of the central units in the international system. Previous works detailed the gradual ascendance of nonstate actors but did not clarify their role versus the role of states. GT 2030 reviewers suggest that the Council delve more deeply into the dynamics of governance and explore the complicated relationships among a diverse set of actors.

3. A better grasp of time and speed. Past Global Trends works "correctly foresaw the direction of the vectors: China up, Russia down. But China's power has consistently increased faster than expected … . A comprehensive reading of the four reports leaves a strong impression that [we] end toward underestimation of the rates of change …"

4. Greater discussion of crises and discontinuities. The reviewers note that the use of the word "trends" in the title suggests more continuity than change. GT 2025, however, "with its strongly worded attention to the likelihood of significant shocks and discontinuities, flirts with a radical revision of this viewpoint." GT 2030 reports that the authors recommend developing a framework for understanding the relationships among trends, discontinuities, and crises.

5. Greater attention to ideology. The authors of the study admit that "ideology is a frustratingly fuzzy concept … difficult to define … and equally difficult to measure." They agree that grand "isms" like fascism and communism might not be on the horizon. However, "smaller politico-pychosocial shifts that often don't go under the umbrella of ideology but drive behavior" should be a focus.

6. More understanding of second- and third-order consequences. Trying to identify looming disequilibria may be one approach. More war gaming or simulation exercises to understand possible dynamics among international actors at crucial tipping points was another suggestion.[52]

Table 8.3
Global Trends
2030—An
Overview

Megatrends		
Individual Empowerment	Individual empowerment will accelerate owing to poverty reduction, growth of the global middle class, greater educational attainment, widespread use of new communications and manufacturing technologies, and health-care advances.	
Diffusion of Power	There will not be any hegemonic power. Power will shift to networks and coalitions in a multipolar world.	
Demographic Patterns	The demographic arc of instability will narrow. Economic growth might decline in "aging" countries. Sixty percent of the world's population will live in urbanized areas; migration will increase.	
Food, Water, Energy Nexus	Demand for these resources will grow substantially owing to an increase in the global population. Tackling problems pertaining to one commodity will be linked to supply and demand for the others.	
Game-Changers		
Crisis-Prone Global Economy	Will global volatility and imbalances among players with different economic interests result in collapse? Or will greater multipolarity lead to increased resiliency in the global economic order?	
Governance Gap	Will governments and institutions be able to adapt fast enough to harness change instead of being overwhelmed by it?	
Potential for Increased Conflict	Will rapid changes and shifts in power lead to more intrastate and interstate conflicts?	
Wider Scope of Regional Instability	Will regional instability, especially in the Middle East and South Asia, spill over and create global insecurity?	
Impact of New Technologies	Will technological breakthroughs be developed in time to boost economic productivity and solve the problems caused by a growing world population, rapid urbanization, and climate change?	
Role of the United States	Will the US be able to work with new partners to reinvent the international system?	
Potential Worlds		
Stalled Engines	In the most plausible worst-case scenario, the risks of interstate conflict increase. The US draws inward and globalization stalls.	
Fusion	In the most plausible best-case outcome, China and the US collaborate on a range of issues, leading to broader global cooperation.	
Gini-Out-of-the-Bottle	Inequalities explode as some countries become big winners and others fail. Inequalities within countries increase social tensions. Without completely disengaging, the US is no longer the "global policeman."	
Nonstate World	Driven by new technologies, nonstate actors take the lead in confronting global challenges.	

Global Trends 2030: National Intelligence Council, "Global Trends 2030: An Overview," https://www.dni.gov/files/documents/GlobalTrends_2030.pdf.

GLOBAL TRENDS AND MANAGING ONESELF

Using the information in Table 8.3: Global Trends 2030—An Overview, how might these trends change the way work is currently performed in your present job? Way of life? What the implications of these trends on your choice of a career? What trends take high priority for you? How might you influence these trends in your current or future work? In your everyday life?

ANALYTICAL TOOLS AND STRATEGY EXECUTION

Former British Telecom (BT) CEO Lord Livingston claimed that he used the same set of strategy slides when he arrived at the telecom company in 2008 as on the day he left in 2013. He stated in an interview with *The Financial Times:* "People often think business is about strategy but it's actually one part strategy and nine parts execution." In the same article Andy Mattes, CEO of Diebold, a U.S. supplier of ATM machines, said, "A mediocre strategy well executed will yield far better results than a perfect idea poorly done." *The Financial Times* notes that "demand for (analytical) tools and frameworks to help business plot a path through uncertainty is as great as ever."[53]

Has the usefulness of strategic tools and frameworks diminished over time? Some business schools have questioned whether strategy concepts such as Porter's strategic competitive advantages are still useful in a world where everything is in flux. *The Financial Times* reports that "flexibility in using strategic tools and frameworks is more important than ever as new corporate forms, such as networked organizations, and mature insights into human behavior improve and technology advances."[54]

Freedman, in his book *Strategy* argues, "Everyone needs a strategy." He cautions that when using tools and frameworks, there is a lot to be said about using them "as long as you don't make such copious notes that it (the framework) becomes an alternative to thought rather than a stimulus to thought."[55]

a. What inferences can be drawn from the statements in the *Times* article regarding the usefulness of analytical tools and frameworks when crafting and executing strategy?
b. How is it possible for Livingston to claim that he used the same set of strategy slides when he arrived at the telecom company in 2008 as on the day that he left in 2013? Isn't strategy dynamic based on an open-system logic that requires constant changes and adjustments to strategies and their execution?
c. How might analytical tools and frameworks help one to act strategically and think critically?

MANAGING ONESELF AND SELF-REFLECTION

a. Are you achieving your lifetime goals? How do you know? List them. Identify core competencies and strengths that will move you toward your lifetime goals. Identify potential threats or personal deficiencies that might block you from achieving your goals. What are your tangible and intangible resources?
b. How do you allocate your resources and spend your time? Start tracking your performance toward achieving your lifetime goals. What gaps exist? What actions do you need to take to keep you moving in a direction that is favorable to achieving your lifetime goals?

CHAPTER ENDNOTES

1. *Peng, Mike W. Global Strategy. United States: Thompson/Southwestern, 2006.*
2. Ibid.
3. Porter, Michael E. *The Competitive Advantage of Nations.* New York: The Free Press, 1990.
4. Porter, Michael E. *The Competitive Advantage of Nations.* New York: The Free Press, 1990.; Grant, Robert M. "Porter's Competitive Advantage of Nations: An Assessment." Strategic Management Journal 12 (1991): 535–48.
5. "Porter's Chapter Summaries—Chapter 3: Determinants of National Competitive Advantage." MBA Boost. https://www.mbaboost.com/porters-chapter-summaries-chapter-3-determinants-of-national-competitive-advantage/#factor_conditions_demand.
6. Howard, Robert. "Can Small Business Help Countries Compete?" Harvard Business Review (November–December 1990): 88–103.
7. Rothwell, Roy, and Mark Dodgson. "External Linkages and Innovation in Small- and Medium-Sized Enterprises." R&D Management: 21 (1991): 125–37.
8. Janseen, Sarah. "World's Largest Companies, 2016." In The World Almanac and Book of Facts 2016. Simon & Schuster, 2016.
9. Ibid.
10. Escritt, Thomas. "From Carmakers to Cats, All Face Brexit Disruption." Reuter, *World News.* May 17, 2017. https://www.reuters.com/article/us-britain-eu-merkel/from-carmakers-to-cats-all-face-brexit-disruption-merkel-says-idUSKCN18D1U5.
11. Friedman, Thomas. The World Is Flat. New York: Farrar, Straus, Giroux, 2005.
12. He, Wan, Daniel Goodkind, and Paul Kowal. "An Aging World: 2015 International Population Reports." U.S. Census Bureau (2016): 3.
13. Porter, Michael E. *Enhancing Competitive Advantage Through a Global Strategy.* Boston: Harvard Business School Press, 1998.
14. Zonis, Marvin, Dan Lefkovitz, and Sam Wilkin. *Kimchi Matters: Global Business and Local Politics in a Crisis-Driven World.* Evanston, IL: Agate Publishing, 2003.
15. Porter, Michael E. *The Competitive Advantage of Nations.* New York: The Free Press, 1990.
16. Porter, Michael E. *Enhancing Competitive Advantage Through a Global Strategy.* Boston: Harvard Business School Press, 1998.
17. Ibid.
18. Atwell, Paula. "What Is a Transnational Business Strategy?" *azcentral.* Downloaded January 25, 2018. https://yourbusiness.azcentral.com/transnational-business-strategy-27176.html.
19. Porter, Michael E. "Changing Patterns of International Competition." *California Management Review* 28, no. 2 (1986): 9–40.
20. Atwell, Paula. "What Is a Transnational Business Strategy?" azcentral. https://yourbusiness.azcentral.com/transnational-business-strategy-27176.html.
21. "Mastering Strategic Management." University of Minnesota Libraries Publishing. http://open.lib.umn.edu/strategicmanagement/.
22. "Capitalism vs. Socialism." Diffen. https://www.diffen.com/difference/capitalism_vs_socialism.
23. "Market Entry Strategies." Tradestart.ca. http://www.tradestart.ca/market-entry-strategies.
24. Vance, Ashlee. "Elon Musk: Tesla, SpaceX, and the Quest for a Fantastic Future." New York: Harper Collins, 2015.
25. Dees, Gregory J. "The Meaning of 'Social Entrepreneurship.'" Kauffman Foundation and Stanford University, Kansas City, MO. May 2001. https://entrepreneurship.duke.edu/news-item/the-meaning-of-social-entrepreneurship/.
26. Edersheim, E. Hass. *The Definitive Drucker.* New York: McGraw-Hill, 2007.
27. Dees, Gregory J. "The Meaning of 'Social Entrepreneurship.'" Kauffman Foundation and Stanford University, Kansas City, MO. May 2001. https://entrepreneurship.duke.edu/news-item/the-meaning-of-social-entrepreneurship/.
28. Drucker, Peter. F. Innovation and Entrepreneurship. New York: Harper & Row, 1985.; Quinn, James B. "Managing Innovation: ontrolled Chaos." Harvard Business Review 62, no. 3 (1985): 73–84.
29. Methe, D. Technological Competition in Global Industries. Westport, CT: Quorum Books, 1991.
30. Edersheim, E. Hass. *The Definitive Drucker.* New York: McGraw-Hill, 2007.
31. Christensen, C. M. *The Innovator's Dilemma.* Boston: Harvard Business School Press, 2000.
32. Colander, L. *History of Economic Thought.* Boston: Houghton Mifflin Company, 2002.; Bygrave, W.D. "The Entrepreneurship Paradigm (I) Revisited." In *Handbook of Qualitative Research Methods in Entrepreneurship, edited by* H. Neergaard and J.P. Uhoi. Cheltenham, UK: Edward Elgar, 2007.; Oster, S. *Modern Competitive Analysis.* New York: Oxford University Press, 1990.
33. Schumpeter, J.A. *Capitalism, Socialism and Democracy.* London: Routledge, 1942.
34. Śledzik, Karol. "Schumpeter's View on Innovation and Entrepreneurship." Electronic Journal (April 2013): 89–95.
35. Barney, J., and W.S. Hesterly. *Strategic Management and Competitive Advantage.* Boston: Pearson, 2015.; Oster, S. *Modern Competitive Analysis.* New York: Oxford University Press, 1990.
36. Ibid.
37. Martin, Roger L., and Sally Osberg. "Social Entrepreneurship: The Case for Definition." Stanford Social Innovation Review. Accessed August 14, 2017: https://ssir.org/articles/entry/social_entrepreneurship_the_case_for_definitionarticles/entry/social_entrepreneurship_the_case_for_definition.
38. Phills, J.A., Jr., K. Deiglmeier, and D.T. Miller. "Rediscovering Social Innovation." Stanford Social Innovation Review. 2008: Retrieved June 23, 2009. http://www.ssireview.org/images/articles/2008FA_feature_phills_deiglmeier_miller.pdf.
39. Mullen, Jeffrey S., and Dean A. Shepherd. "Entrepreneurial Action and the Role of Uncertainty in the Theory of Entrepreneurship." The Academy of Management Review 31, no. 1 (January 2006): 132–52.
40. Ibid,
41. Phills, J.A., Jr., K. Deiglmeier, and D.T. Miller. "Rediscovering Social Innovation." Stanford Social Innovation Review. 2008. Retrieved June 23, 2009. http://www.ssireview.org/images/articles/2008FA_feature_phills_deiglmeier_miller.pdf.
42. Dees, Gregory J. "The Meaning of 'Social Entrepreneurship.'" Kauffman Foundation and Stanford University, Kansas City, MO. May 2001. https://entrepreneurship.duke.edu/news-item/the-meaning-of-social-entrepreneurship/.
43. Osterwalder, A., Y. Pigneur, P. Papadakos, G. Bernarda, and A. Smith. Value Proposition Design: How to Create Products and Services Customers Want. Wiley, 2015.
44. Ibid.
45. Porter, Michael. *Competitive Advantage of Nations.* New York: The Free Press, 1990.
46. Luthje, C., and N. Franke. "Fostering Entrepreneurship Through University Education and Training: Lessons from Massachusetts Institute of Technology." 2nd Annual Conference on Innovative Research in Management. European Academy of Management, 2002.

47. Case, John. "The Gazelle Theory: Are Some Small Companies More Equal Than Others?" Inc.com. May 15, 2001. https://www.inc.com/magazine/20010515/22613.html.

48. Lee, Aileen. "Welcome to the Unicorn Club: Learning from Billion-Dollar Start-ups." TechCrunch. November 2, 2013. https://techcrunch.com/2013/11/02/welcome-to-the-unicorn-club/.

49. Hartmans, Avery. "THE $10 BILLION CLUB: Meet the 8 most valuable startups in the US." January. 2, 2017: http://www.businessinsider.com/most-valuable-us-startups 2016-12.

50. "About B Lab." B Lab.TM https://www.bcorporation.net/what-are-b-corps/about-b-lab.

51. Robbins, Steve. "Why You Must Have a Business Plan: It's More Than a Tool for Getting Funding. Think of It as the Road Map to Your Business's Future." Entrepreneur.com. http://www.entrepreneur.com/article/74194.

52. "The Global Trends 2030: Alternative Worlds." U.S. National Intelligence Council. https://www.dni.gov/files/documents/globaltrends_2030.pdf.

53. Hill, Andrew. "Wanted: Flexible Corporate Strategies for Fast Times." *Financial Times*, March 25, 2015. http://www.ft.com/cms/s/0/81f5bd8e-cd65-11e4-9144-00144feab7de.html#axzz3sJcUaurG.

54. Ibid.

55. Ibid.

PART 2

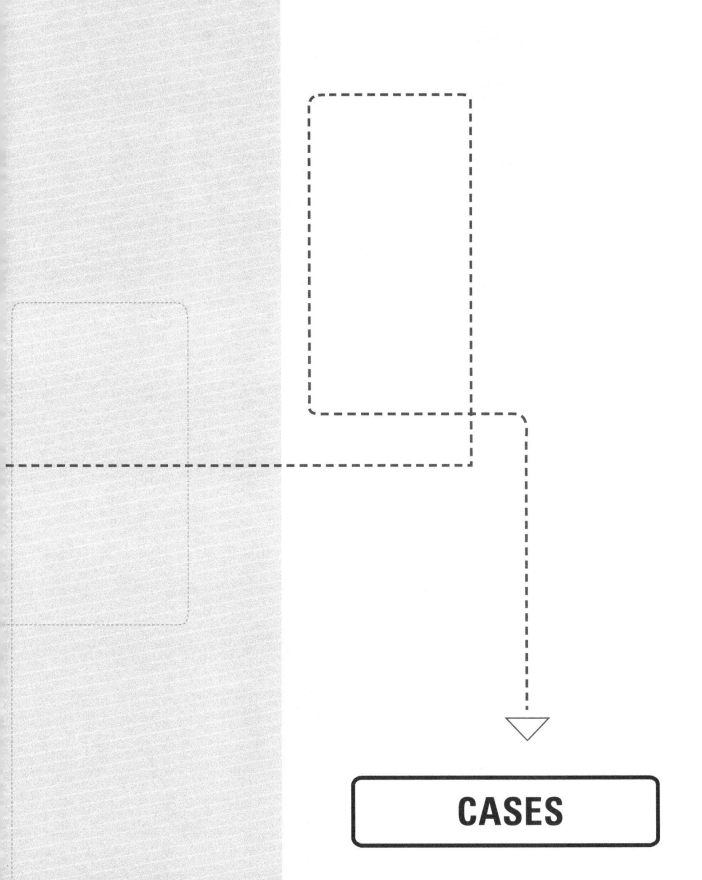

CASES

BY MICHAEL J. MERENDA

LEARNING OBJECTIVES

- The evolution of industry structure over time and its implications for strategic positioning
- The nature of sustainable competitive advantage
- The timing of strategic moves
- Multisided business platforms
- The challenge of reinvigorating competitive advantage through innovation
- The role of technology standards in competitiveness
- Role of the CEO as chief strategist, organization builder and doer

INTRODUCTION

Despite beating market projections for fiscal first quarter (Q1) results 2014, Apple, Inc. headquartered in Cupertino, California, disappointed industry analysts and Apple watchers when it reported iPhone sales grew at a 7% rate, falling short of Wall Street expectations of a 15% increase.[1] Apple's supremacy as the top dog in the fiercely contested high technology consumer electronics industry, especially in the U.S. was under attack. Since 2011, Apple was constantly losing ground to the Android operating system in the battle for smartphone supremacy at home and abroad.[2] Analysts were looking for Tim Cook, Apple's CEO to quickly act to prevent further market erosion and stem the advances of competitors.[3]

Apple was one of the most innovative companies of all times under Steve Jobs' leadership introducing game changing products and services across an array of industries. Chief among the game changing products was the iPhone. Never before did one firm change the competitive dynamics so drastically in so many industries from computers, mobile phones, music, tablets, movies, photography, electronic components, newspapers and print media, as well as other industries.

Eric Schmidt, Google's CEO, who once served on Apple's board of directors challenged Apple's lead in smartphones and tablets by offering the Android operating system (OS) free or at minimal charge to smartphone manufactures. Google's open system approach of giving its Android OS away free of charge was a sharp contrast with Apple's closed system, curated approach for its iOS (Operating System) used only in Apple devices.

Walter Isaacson commissioned to write Job's autobiography, interviewed Jobs. Isaacson wanting to know if Jobs made a strategic and costly mistake by keeping the Mac operating system a closed system, unlike Microsoft's Windows operating system that was available to computer manufactures at a minimal cost. Eventually the open system's Windows became the dominant OS capturing 98% of global personal computer (PC) market. Open versus closed system approaches were a matter of great debate in the digital age. Schmidt interviewed for the Jobs' book, commented: "Steve has a particular way that he wants to run Apple, it's the same as it was twenty years ago, which is that Apple is a brilliant innovator of closed system.[4] Schmidt later commented that, "The benefit of closed systems is control. But Google has a specific belief that open is the better approach, because it leads to more options and competition and consumer choice." Bill Gates weighing in on the discussion agreed with Schmidt, arguing that, "Competition among a variety of devices and manufacturers leads to greater consumer choice and more innovation."[5]

In response to Schmidt's comment Jobs stated:

> Google says we exert more control than they do, that we are closed and they are open. Well look at the results—Android's a mess. It has different screen sizes and versions, over a hundred permutations. … I like being responsible for the whole user experience … We do not do it for the money. We do it because we want to make great products, not crap like Android.[6]

Apple was the most profitable company in the high technology industry. Its profit for the fiscal year ended September 2013 were triple Google's 2013 earnings and $9 billion more than its nearest competitor, Samsung Electronics. The profit and revenue results for Apple remained strong for the first quarter of 2014. (See Exhibit 1)

In addition to competitor challenges to its smartphones and other mobile devices, Tim Cook, Jobs' hand-picked successor faced criticism for Apple's contract labor practices and its management of the environment. The nonprofit, *China Labor Watch* reported in July 2013 that Pegatron and Jabill Circuit two Apple suppliers were violating workplace standards. The nonprofit levied a formal complaint against Taiwan-based Pegatron for reportedly violating several major safety and environmental standards, and was now similarly accusing U.S. based Jabil Circuit, which was responsible for producing Apple's low-cost iPhone.[7, 8]

Even with this criticism *Fortune* magazine named Apple the most admired company in the world from 2008 to 2012. On September 30, 2013, Apple surpassed Coca-Cola to become the world's most valuable brand in the *Omnicom Group's* "Best Global Brands" report. Omnicom Group reported that value of the Apple brand at $98.3 billion, up 28 percent from the 2012 report. Coca-Cola was valued at $79.2 Billion.[9] Apple was the world's second-largest information technology company by revenue after Samsung Electronics and the world's second largest smartphone manufacturer after Samsung. Apple was the largest publically traded corporation in the world by market capitalization with an estimated capitalization of $462.3 billion as of October 2013.[10] (See Exhibit 2)

Under Cook Apple's string of successive big hit, innovative and unique products had stalled and Apple was again at a crossroads in its terms of its future direction. Apple's ability to introduce game changing innovative products and its ability to charge premium prices for smartphones were being called into question. Would the company flourish or flop under Cook's leadership?

APPLE'S PRODUCT INFORMATION

Apple was unique in that it was one of just a few companies that designed, manufactured and marketed both hardware and software products first with its line of Macs and then with its array of high technology consumer

EXHIBIT 1: APPLE'S SELECTED FINANCIAL INFORMATION

Apple Selected Financial Information

(In millions, except number of shares which are reflected in thousands and per share amounts)

	Sep-13	Sep-12	Sep-11	Sep-10	Sep-09
Net sales	170,910	156,508	108,249	65,225	42,905
Cost of sales	106,606	87,846	64,431	39,541	25,683
Gross Margin	**64,304**	**68,662**	**43,818**	**25,684**	**17,222**
Gross Margin Percentage	**37.6%**	**43.9%**	**40.5%**	**39.4%**	**40.1%**
Research and development	4,475	3,381	2,429	1,782	1,333
R&D as a % of net sales	3%	2%	2%	3%	3%
Selling, general, and administrative	10,830	10,040	7,599	5,517	4,149
SG&A as a % I net sales	6%	6%	7%	8%	10%
Total operating expenses	**15,305**	**13,421**	**10,028**	**7,299**	**5,482**
Owners' Equity as a % net sales	9%	9%	9%	11%	13%
Operating income (loss)	48,999	55,241	33,790	18,385	11,740
Other income and expenses	1,156	522	415	155	326
Income before provision for income taxes	50,155	55,763	34,205	18,540	12,066
Provision for income taxes	13,118	14,030	8,283	4,527	3,831
Net income (loss)	**37,037**	**41,733**	**25,922**	**14,013**	**8,235**
Return on sales	22%	27%	24%	21%	19%
Total Assets					
Cash, cash equivalents and marketable securities	146,761	121,251	81,570	51,011	33,992
Net Property, Plant and Equipment	16,597	15,452	7,777	4,768	2,954
Total assets	207,000	176,064	116,371	75,183	47,501
Return on Assets	18%	24%	22%	19%	17%
Total liabilities	83,451	57,854	39,756	27,392	15,861
Total shareholders' equity	123,549	118,210	76,615	47,791	31,640
Return on Equity	30%	35%	34%	29%	26%
Earnings per share					
Basic	$40.03	$44.64	$28.05	$15.41	$9.22
Diluted	$39.75	$44.15	$27.68	$15.15	$9.08
Share used in computing earnings per share					
Basic	925,331	934,818	924,258	909,461	893,016
Diluted	931,662	945,355	936,645	924,712	907,005
Cash Dividends per common share	$11.40	$2.65	$0.00	$0.00	$0.00

Source: Apple, Inc., *10K Report* September 28, 2013: Complied from data found in Apple's 10K; See: http://investor.apple.com/financials.cfm;

Comparison of 6 Year Cumulative Total Return

Among Apple Inc., the S&P 500 Index, the S&P Computer Hardware Index, and the Dow Jones US Technology Supersector Index

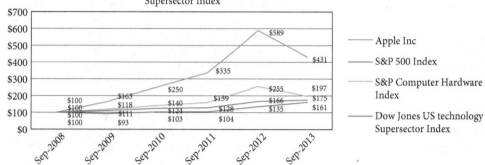

devices. The Company was renamed Apple Inc. on January 9, 2007, to reflect its shift from selling mainly computers toward a focus on consumer electronics.

Apple products included mobile communication and media devices, personal computers, and portable digital music players, and sold a variety of related software, services, peripherals, networking solutions, and third-party digital content and applications. It's products and services included: iPhone®, iPad®, Mac®, iPod®, Apple TV®, a portfolio of consumer and professional software applications, the iOS and OS X® operating systems, iCloud®, and a variety of accessory support offerings. Apple sold and delivered digital content and applications through the iTunes Store®, App StoreTM, iBooksStoreTM, and Mac App Store. The Company sold its products worldwide through its retail stores, online stores, and direct sales force, as well as through third-party cellular network carriers, wholesalers, retailers, and value-added resellers (See Appendix A for a brief overview of Apple's Products).[11]As of June 2014, Apple maintained 25 retail stores in fourteen countries, as well as the online Apple Store and iTunes Store, the latter of which was the world's largest music retailer. The company had 73,000 permanent full-time employees and 3,300 temporary full-time employees worldwide. Its annual revenue in 2013 totaled $170 billion. As of Q1 2014, Apple's five-year growth average was 39% for top line growth and 45% for bottom line growth. In May 2013, Apple entered the top ten of the Fortune 500 list of companies for the first time, raising 11 places above its 2012 ranking to take the sixth position[12] (See Exhibit 3).

STEVE JOBS – "THE FATHER OF THE DIGITAL REVOLUTION"

On April fool's day 1976, out of his parents' garage in Los Altos, California Steve Jobs with his high school friend Steve Wozniak founded Apple computer to develop and sell personal computers. Mike Markkula, an angel investor joined the two Steves in their fledging partnership turning it into Apple Computer Co. in January 1977, valued at $5,309.[13] Four years later the partners took the company public becoming the most oversubscribed IPO (initial public offering) since Ford Motors in 1956. By December 1980, Apple was valued at $1.79 billion and in the process it would make three hundred people millionaires.[14]

EXHIBIT 3

Apple, Inc.'s Net Sales by Operating Segment, Net Sales by Product, and Unit Sales by Product, 2011–2013

The following table shows net sales by operating segment and net sales and unit sales by product during 2013,–2012,–2011 (dollars in millions and units in thousands)

	2013	Change	2012	Change	2011
Net Sales by Operating Segment:					
Americas	62,739	9%	57,512	50%	38,315
Europe	37,883	4%	36,323	31%	27,778
Greater China (a)	25,417	13%	22,533	78%	12,690
Japan	13,462	27%	10,571	94%	5,437
Rest of Asia Pacific	11,181	4%	10,741	8%	9,902
Retail	20,228	7%	18,828	33%	14,127
Total net sales	$170,910	9%	$156,508	45%	$108,249
Net Sales by Product:					
iPhone(b)	91,279	16%	78,692	71%	45,998
iPad(b)	31,980	3%	30,945	61%	19,168
Mac(b)	21,483	-7%	23,221	7%	21,783
iPod(b)	4,411	-21%	5,615	-25%	7,453
iTunes, software and services(c)	16,051	25%	12,890	38%	9,373
Accessories(d)	5,706	11%	5,145	15%	4,474
Total net sales	170,910	9%	156,508	45%	108,249
Unit Sales by Product:					
iPhone	150,257	20%	125,046	73%	72,293
iPad	71,033	22%	58,310	80%	32,394
Mac	16,341	-10%	18,158	9%	16,735
iPod	26,379	-25%	35,165	-17%	42,620

(a) Greater China includes China, Hong Kong and Taiwan.

(b) Includes deferrals and amortization of related non-software services and software upgrade rights.

(c) Includes revenue from sales on the iTunes Store, the App Store, the Mac App Store, and the iBooks Store and revenue from sales of AppleCare, licensing and other services.

(d) Includes sales of hardware peripherals and Apple-branded and third-party accessories for iPhone, iPad, Mac and iPod.

Source: Apple, Inc., 2013 10-K reports. P27
See: http://investor.apple.com/financials.cfm

Apple, under Steve Jobs became one of the most successful companies of all times. Jobs' passion was to build an enduring organization. Steve Jobs born in 1955 died of pancreatic cancer on October 5, 2011. At the time of his death Jobs was hailed as one of America's most successful and celebrated entrepreneurs. Through Apple, he was widely recognized as a charismatic pioneer of the personal computer revolution. His influential career in computers and consumer electronics transformed several industries from computers and smartphones to music and movies.

Jobs was the first to see the commercial potential of Xerox PARC's mouse-driven graphical user interface, which led to the creation of the Apple Lisa and shortly after the successful line of Macintosh computers. Jobs played a key role in introducing the LaserWriter, one of the first widely available laser printers.

After a power struggle with Apple's Board and Apple's CEO John Scully in 1985, Jobs was forced out of Apple and founded NeXT, a rival computer platform development company to Apple specializing in the higher education and business markets.[15] When Jobs left Apple he owned 6.5 million shares of the company's stock, 11% of the company, worth more than $100 million. He quickly sold his shares and within five months dumped all but one share so he could attend shareholders meetings if he wanted.[16] In turn, Apple's Board elected to sue NeXT and Jobs on claims that Jobs was using Apple's proprietary technology in the NeXT platform. Eventually, Scully and Jobs reached an out-of-court agreement involving no financial damages.[17]

For a few years after Jobs departure, Apple was able to coast comfortably with high profit margins based on its temporary dominance in desktop publishing. Scully, buoyed by Apple's Board backing and the continued high profit margins boastfully proclaimed that "Jobs wanted Apple 'to become a wonderful consumer products company', ... 'this was a lunatic plan. ... Apple would never be a consumer products company. ... We couldn't bend reality to all our dreams of changing the world [some called the counter-intuitive, ambitious, demands of Steve Jobs on his company and its employees as Jobs'reality distortion field]. ... High tech could not be designed and sold as a consumer product."[18]

In 1986, Jobs acquired the computer graphics division of Lucas film, which was subsequently spun off as Pixar. He was credited in Toy Story (1995) as an executive producer. Walt Disney eventually purchased Pixar Animation Studios. In 1996, after Apple had failed to deliver its operating system, called Copland, then Apple's CEO Gil Amelio turned to NeXT Computer and its NeXTSTEP platform. The NeXTSTEP platform became Apple's primary operating system and the foundation for the Mac OS X operating system. At Amelio's request, Jobs returned to Apple as an advisor, and reluctantly took control of the company as interim CEO. By that time Apple was on its fourth CEO in just a few years.

Michael Dell at the time of Jobs appointment as Apple's interim CEO stated, "It (Apple) was on the rocks," When he was asked what would he do with Apple, he stated, "I'd shut it down and give the money back to the shareholders," Jobs noted, that "Apple was about 90 days from going bankrupt ... and it was much worse than I thought when I went back initially."[19] As the new CEO of the company, Jobs oversaw the development of the iMac, iTunes, iPod, iPhone, and iPad, and on the services side, the company's Apple Retail Stores, iTunes Store and the App Store. The success of these products and services provided Apple with strong financial returns. Making many industry analysts and Apple watcher described the reinvigoration of Apple by Jobs as one of the greatest turnarounds in business history

After Jobs' death accolades and honors poured in. Jobs was recognized for his influence in the technology and music industries and was called: legendary, a futurists and a visionary, the Father of the Digital Revolution, master of innovation, the master evangelist of the digital age and a design perfectionist.[20]

APPLE'S HISTORIC COMPETITIVE ADVANTAGE

Under Jobs leadership, Apple built its strategy and business model on several key factors. The Company's business strategy leveraged its unique ability to design and develop its own operating systems, hardware, application software, and services to provide its customers new products and solutions with superior ease-of-use, seamless integration, and innovative design.

First was the way it designed its PCs and subsequently its electronic consumer products to be easy to use, most often letting customers use or play with the product right out of the box. Key to the strategy was the Macintosh's user-friendly graphical user interface, (GUI) which was acquired at a minimal cost from Xerox Corporation in 1979. Jobs and his engineers were able to significantly improve the GUI making it a prime feature and differentiator of Apple's computers in the rapidly emerging PC industry.[21]

Second, whether it was an obsession for total control of Apple, its products, and technology Jobs maintained a closed system, proprietary environments with its computers, IPhone, IPad, and iTunes operating systems. This was contrary to the open system approached used by Bill Gates and Microsoft Corporation that made its Windows operating system designed to operate on Intel's microprocessors available at a minimal cost to PC manufacturers in the early days of the computer industry. Eventually, Microsoft's open systems approach closed the gap between Apple's lead in proprietary technology and its rivals spurring the rapid growth of the PC industry. With the introduction of Windows 3.0 in 1991 Apple computer business was on a path toward history.

Apple was well recognized for being a leader in designing and introducing, branded "Insanely great products with high innovation content that attracted strong buyer loyalty. Its digital hub strategy was the basis for its eco-system approach to high technology." For Jobs, Apple operated at the nexus of Science, Technology and the Arts.[22]

Rapid growth of its products and services afforded Apple the economies of scale (e.g., one of the largest purchasers of flash memory in the world) that significantly lower its supply chain costs and provided the company bargaining power with its vendors. The success of its product line and its eco-system, digital hub strategy provided Apple with economies of scope (e.g., the ability to cross-sell iPhones, iPads, Macs, iTouch, Apps and services online and through Apple's retail stores and its major big box vendors, retailers and other distributors.

Apple's unique and innovative business model allowed it to charge higher than average industry selling prices and earning it higher than industry average gross margins. For example Apple's average selling price for its iPad was $600 while the industry average price was closer to $300. Buyers could purchase Amazon's Kindle Fire HD 7" 8GB Tablet for $139. Apple also had a significant price premium on its iPhones compared to similar competitors' models. In 2013, IDC expected smartphone ASPs (average selling prices) to hit $337, down 12.8% from the $387 recorded in 2012.[23] Premium pricing and differentiation fueled Apple's growth and provided the funds for next generation products.

GLOBAL SMARTPHONE INDUSTRY

The smartphone industry was a hyper-competitive, global market characterized by aggressive price cutting that resulted in downward pressure on industry profits and gross margins. Competitors frequently introduced new products that resulted in short product life cycles, evolving industry standards, continual improvement in product price/performance characteristics, rapid adoption of technological and product advancements by competitors, and price sensitivity on the part of consumers.[24] One of the factors contributing to smartphone growth was the convergence of several Internet technologies including PCs and tablets as more and more consumers and businesses were switching away from computers to tablets and smartphones.

TECHNOLOGY CONVERGENCE: PCs, TABLETS AND SMARTPHONES

PC shipments were declining in every region of the world. International Data Corp. (IDC) reported worldwide PC shipments would decline about 6% in 2014. PC shipments declined 9.8% in 2013. Declines stemmed from a lack of innovation by PC manufacturers coupled with an increased in popularity for smartphones and tablets. For example, the success of Apple's iPad mini had cannibalized sales of MacBook.[25] Worldwide tablet shipments were forecasted to grow from 221 million units in 2013 to 386 million units by 2017 for a 15% compounded annual growth rate (CAGR). By value, tablet shipments would grow at an 11.5% CAGR from $79.4 billion in 2013 to $123 billion in 2017.[26]

Smartphones were gradually replacing traditional mobile phones (non-smartphones) and this trend was expected to continue. Worldwide smartphone shipments by dollar value were expected to grow at an 11.5% CAGR between 2014 and 2018. Smartphone unit shipments were expected to grow at an 11.5% CAGR from 1.2 billion in 2014 to 1.7 billion in 2018. While mobile phone unit shipments were forecasted to grow at a 4% CAGR from 1.8 billion in 2013 to 2.2 billion in 2018.[27]

WORLDWIDE SMARTPHONE SHIPMENTS

In 2013, North America accounted for 15% of global smartphone shipments; Latin America, 9%; Europe, the Middle East, and Africa (EMEA), 24%; and Asia Pacific, (APAC) 52%. This would change by 2017 with a shift to 11% for North America, 9% Latin America, 21% EMEA, and 59% APAC. It was expected that smartphone shipments would grow at a CAGR of 5.7% in North America, 14.1% in Latin America, 10.4% in EMEA, and 16.8% in APAC. (S&P) between 2013 and 2017.[28] The ratio of non-smartphones to smartphones is expected to change from 45%/55% in 2013 to 25%/75% by 2017.[29]

Demand for smartphones was largely driven by replacements by current mobile phone users as well as first-time users. Competition amongst smartphone manufacturers, especially in Asia was forcing down prices making smartphones affordable to the middle class and accelerating penetration. The increased competition within Android-based smartphones was forcing vendors to innovate, introduce differentiated smartphones and reduce prices all contributing to an increase in demand for smartphones. Samsung accounted for 31.3% of worldwide smartphone shipments in 2013; Apple, 15.2%; LG, 4.5%; Huawei, 4.8%; Lenovo, 4.7%; and others, 39.5%. (See Exhibits 4 and 5).[30] Android dominate the market on a global scale with devices running Google's Android O.S., capturing 79% of the entire smartphone unit shipments. Apple's iOS platform captured 15.2% of global share in 2013 down from 19% in 2012. While Apple›s global share had declined, Apple captured sizable profits on its iPhone compared to rival smartphone manufacturers and Apple's iPhone sales were expected to significantly grow in China and the rest of Asia.[31]

REACHING MARKET SATURATION IN THE U.S.

In 2013, Smartphone penetration in the U.S was at 68%, with 80 million users still without a smartphone. The iPhones remained enormously popular in U.S. with a market share of 57.6% at the end of March 2014. This was an increase from the 50.3% market share at the end of November 2013. The Android operating system was not far behind with a 35.9% market share, a decline of 7.8% from the same period a year earlier. For Q1 2014, Apples iPhone lost ground in the U.S. to Android.[32]

Apple commanded over 50% share of AT&T and Verizon smartphone sales in the U.S. The gap between Apple and Samsung's share of Sprint's smartphone sales was a bit closer with Apple sitting at 36% versus Samsung's 30%. Samsung captured the majority of T-Mobile's sales (See Exhibit 6).[33]

Apple was the top original equipment manufacturer (OEM) vendor in U.S. with 41.3% of the smartphone OEM market. Windows Phones was the least selling, with just 5.3% of the market share, an overall decline of 0.3% from the same period last year.

Companies selling the Android O.S. could not match Apple's iOS platform as a major source of income. InfoTech reported that for the 2013 holiday season iOS users were 5 times more likely to purchase online and that these purchases average $93.94 compared to $48.10 for Android transactions. The report noted that the iOS dominated revenue for app developers with $21,276 average revenue per developer on iOS compared

EXHIBIT 4

Global Apple iPhone sales from 3rd quarter 2007 to 2nd quarter 2014 (in million units)

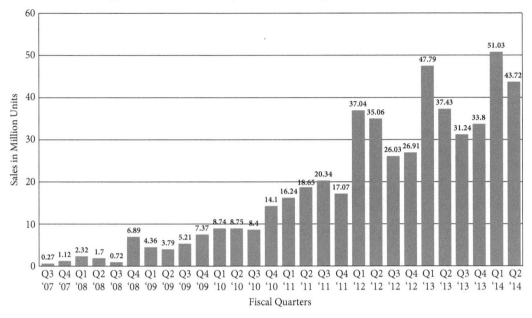

EXHIBIT 5

Global market share held by the leading smartphone operating systems in sales to end users from 1st quarter 2009 to 3rd quarter 2013

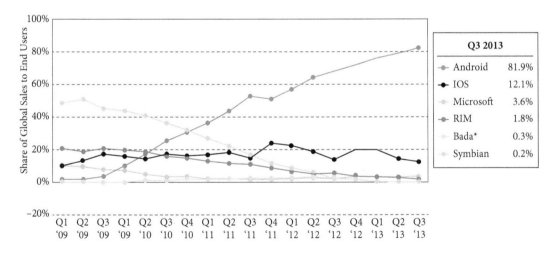

Source: Sourabh, "3 Android Data Showing 'Why Android is the New King of Technology?'" *SourceDigit*, January 15, 2014

EXHIBIT 6

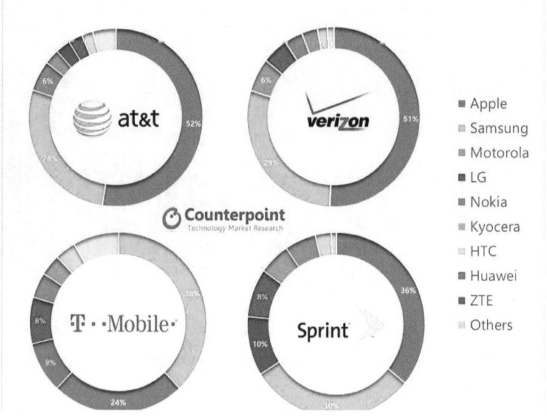

Source: Lee, Taylor, "Apple is the Leading Smartphone Vendor in U.S." *Ubergizmo*, May 21, 2014

to $6,000 revenue per developer for Android. The report concluded that Apple had control over that part of the online market that was very comfortable with buying apps online and that it "wasn't a far stretch to assume that they also experience high purchases for other Apple products, iTunes store downloads and App store downloads" (See Exhibit 7).[34]

Microsoft had emerged as the latest smartphone OEM vendor, after its acquisition of Nokia Corporation devices and services. Nokia Lumia devices accounted for 93.5% of all Windows Phone 8 powered devices, Nokia remained a popular brand global. However, *Kantar World Panel ComTech* reported the Windows Phone faced an uphill battle in most countries, even as sales of cheaper Android phones were growing in China, U.K and U.S.[35]

CHINA

Android captured 80% share of the market for smartphones in China. Android growth in sales were partly a result of a price war for low priced smartphones being waged by local vendors such as ZTE Corporation and Xiamoi. These vendors wanted to bring out the cheapest Android

EXHIBIT 7

iOS   VS. Android

THE INEQUALITY OF MARKET SHARE AND MONEY

Over the past four years Android devices have exceeded **iOS**, continuously winning increasing market share.

- iOS
- ANDROID
- BLACKBERRY OS
- WINDOWS MOBILE
- SYMBIAN (NOKIA)
- OTHER MOBILE OS%

WORLDWIDE MARKET SHARE

2009
2010
2011
2012
2013

The 2013–2014 holiday season revealed something unusual about purchases on mobile devices:

iOS users were 5 times more likely to buy online
(than Android users)

23% of all online sales were made on iOS

—VS—

4.6% of all online sales were made on Android

$93.94 average iOS transaction

—VS—

$48.10 average Android transaction

Source: Train, Phi, "Inequality Between iOS and Android Market Shares," *Infographic: Social Times*, March 26, 2014

products possible in a country with 700 million smartphone users, most of whom could not afford a premium models, like the iPhone. Apple iPhones sales (Q1, 20140) accounted for 17.9% of market share in China, a decline from 23.3% market share achieved during the same three-month period a year earlier.[36]

EUROPE, JAPAN, AND AUSTRALIA

Apple posted strong sales of the iPhone 5s in Europe, Japan and Australia during a three-month period ending March 31, 2014. Apple iPhone was the leader in Japan, with 57.6% of the smartphone market. iPhone sales were helped by the decline of Blackberry OS, lack of momentum in Android sales, and having a stronger relationship with NTT Docomo its Japanese partner. The market share of Windows phones was under 1%, despite the low 40% Smartphone penetration in Japan (See Exhibit 8: Is Android Becoming the New Windows?).[37]

In all the top five European countries, Great Britain, France, Spain, Germany and Italy, Android and Apple shares were helped by a rapid decline of Blackberry, Nokia and other operating systems For Q1 2014, Android phones accounted for 70.7% of the smartphone market, while

EXHIBIT 8

Is Android Becoming the New Windows?

Global connected device shipments broken down by operating system* (in million units)

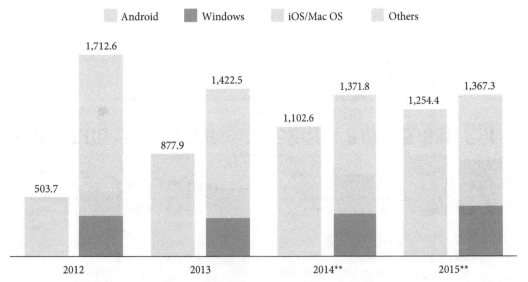

*Incl. PCs, mobile phones, tablets and other ultramobiles
**Forecast

Source: Sourabh, "3 Android Data Showing "Why Android is the New King of Technology?" *SourceDigit*, January 15, 2014

Apple iPhone stood at 19.2%. The market share of iPhone grew steadily in France, Great Britain and Spain during the first quarter of 2014. The share of Windows phones jumped to 10.0%, towards the end of November 2013, but slumped ever since to 8.1%, a decline of 20% in just four months.[38]

THE OPERATING SYSTEMS BATTLE: GOOGLE VS. APPLE

Apple under Jobs revived its personal computer business increasing its U.S market share to 8% by the time of was death. This growth was driven by Apple's innovative digital hub strategy that linked Apple's eco-system of mobile devices, services, iTunes, iStore, and apps to Apple's line of Mac computers. Powerful rivals such as Google, Samsung, Amazon, Microsoft and others were now replicating Apple's digital hub strategy and offering their own smartphones and tablet computers.

By 2010, Android share of the smartphone market exceeded Apple for the first time. By 2011, Android operating systems were on over 170 devices while Apple's iOS system was on 5 devices, all Apple products (2 iPhone models, 2 iPad models and iTouch). Google also changed the relationship between the major operating system companies and the telecom carriers. In its deal with Verizon, Google agreed to give Verizon and other telecom carriers 30% of app revenue. Google also gave app developers 30% of app revenues. Finally Google gave Verizon a small percent of Google's mobile advertising revenues. Sharing revenue with telecom carriers gave carriers incentives to sell smartphones with the Android O.S. and provide additional bandwidth and network capacity to handle the increasing volume of data and services flowing through the network (voice, video, data, software, etc.). While Apple shared 30% of app revenue with app developers, it did not share app or advertising revenue with its major carrier AT&T.[39] Both Apple and Google launched their app stores in 2008. Since then Apple users download significantly more apps than Android users, although Android app buyers were growing at a faster rate.[40]

A Yankee Group survey from April 2013, found that the buying intent for new customers to iOS and Android was about the same, but loyalty to one ecosystem or the other was not. Only 9 percent of the Apple device owners surveyed said they would switch to another platform with their next phone purchase, while 24 percent of Android owners plan to abandon the Android platform. And Apple buyers were more likely to adopt other parts of the product lineup, such as the $99 Apple TV, which was the top selling Internet streaming device.[1]

AMAZON'S FIRE

Jeff Bezos, Amazon's founder and CEO announced in June that Amazon would start selling a smartphone called Fire using the Android OS exclusively through AT&T starting at the end of July, 2014. The Fire when purchased through AT&T's two-year contract would cost $199 to $299. Amazon's price cut the equivalent iPhone 5s 32-gigabyte and 64-gigabyte handsets by $100 each. Without a contract the Fire would sell for $649 to $749. One feature of the Fire was Firefly that used the devices' camera and sensors to recognize merchandise, signs, music or television shows. Bezos strategy was to use Fire as a mobile cash register to boost ecommerce sales to Amazon.[42, 43]

TIM COOK LEADERSHIP AT APPLE

Tim Cook joined Apple in 1998 after 10 years at IBM. At Apple, Cook was responsible for most of Apple's day-to-day operations and was credited with revamping Apple's global supply chain, making it one of the most efficient and effective in the industry. Cook was named CEO of Apple Inc. on August 24, 2011.[44]

Cook, steadily introduced and announced several product upgrades and updates. While some Apple watchers believed Cook's was slow to respond to competitors moves and their string of several innovative product introductions, Cook was crafting a new strategy and approach for Apple.[45]

From October 2011 to March 2012, Apple under Cook's leadership added upgrades to its iOS 5, iPhone 4S, Siri, iCloud, iPad and Apple TV. At its June 2012 World Wide Developers Conference (WWDC) Cook introduced the iOS 6 and the Mac OS X Mountain Lion. Upgrades were announced for the MacBook Air and Pro lines, Airport Express N Routers and Time Capsules. In October Cook announced a new iPhone 5, updated iPad Mini, iPad, iMac, MacBook Pro, a new iPod Touch and iTunes 11.[46]

Cook changed several members of Apple's executive team. In October 2012, Scott Forstall resigned as senior vice president of iOS, becoming an advisor to Cook until his departure in 2013. John Browett, who was SVP of retail, was dismissed after six months on the job having received 100,000 shares worth $60 million when he joined. Jonathan Ives, design SVP was made head of Apple's Human Interface team. Craig Federighi became the head of iOS software engineering and services chief Eddy Cue took over responsibilities for Maps and Siri. These moves came when revenues and profits for Apple's 3 quarter 2012 results were less than predicted. One analyst commented that Forstall was forced to step down as Cook "has decided to lance the boil as internal politics and dissent reached a key pitch." Cook›s direction since becoming CEO was to build a culture of harmony, which meant "weeding out people with disagreeable personalities—people Jobs tolerated and even held close, like Forstall." Other analysts questioned the moves noting that, "Apple›s ability to innovate came from tension and disagreement."[47]

In April 2012, *Time* included Cook on its annual 100 Most Influential People in the World list. By year-end, Apple had experienced its most productive year with over 15 products released.

During 2013, Apple introduced a cheaper iPod Touch model, announced an updated MacBook Pro and released iOS 7 and Mac OS X Mavericks. It also introduced a new MacBook Air carrying Intel's latest Haswell CPUs and the latest WiFi technologies.[48]

COOK'S NEW APPLE

After three years of what some analysts saw as small moves. Cook'vision and bolder strategy for Apple was taking shape. In February 2014, Cook made headlines when he challenged shareholders to "get out of the stock" if they didn't share the company's views on sustainability and climate change. Cook wanted Apple to be more collaborative as it faced new challenges, particularly from Google and its Android mobile operating system. Cook broadened the company's legendary laser focus by looking outside Apple for innovative technologies, joint ventures and partnerships.[49]

In April 2014, after several rounds of negotiations with investor Carl Ichan, Cook with the Board's approval bought back $100 billion of its shares—more than any company in U.S. history—after years of hoarding cash. Also in April, Apple settled a feud with Google, a rivalry that Steve Jobs once called a "holy war."[50]

In late May, while analyst were still looking for the next new thing regarding Apple's mobile devices and perhaps a SmartWatch, Cook took a risky and bold move for Apple by acquiring Beats Electronics headphone business for $3 billion. The deal was striking in that it diverged from Apple's past strategy of acquiring smaller firms and immediately submerging them into the Apple culture and brand. With Beats, Apple acquired a well-known brand with more than 500 employees. Beat was started and led by two strong willed entrepreneurs Jimmy Iovine and hip-hop artist Dr. Dre. Iovine and Dre were two high-powered music executives not known for marching to someone else's beat. Beats' streaming service was the key attraction for Apple in making the acquisition. Customer reaction to Apple's owns iTunes Radio service had been lukewarm compared to rivals such as Spotify and Pandora Media at the time of the deal. In late July 2014, Bose filed suit against Beats and Apple claiming that Beats and Dr. Dre had infringed on several Bose's noise cancelation patents. Apple's Board was expected to approve the purchase of Beats at their September meeting.[51]

In June 2014, Cook and IBM's CEO Ginni Rometty announced a partnership between their companies. The partnership would enhance IBM›s business apps to its customers while providing Apple access to IBM›s large corporate customers, a historically weak market segment for Apple. Apple and IBM would work together to create easy-to-use business apps and sell iPhones and iPads to IBM›s corporate customers. IBM and Apple were archrivals under Steve Jobs when the two companies fought bitterly for over 30 years in the PC industry. In 1981, IBM offered a PC in direct competition to Apple›s line of computers. In a major strategic error, IBM's gave Bill Gates and Microsoft rights to own and license the DOS operating system to IBM and PC manufacturers. IBM argued that the money was in the hardware, not the software. DOS was the forerunner of Windows and became the dominate industry standard operating on billions of computers capturing over 98 percent of the global market. Questions arose as to whether or not the two former enemies could work together given their past history and their divergent organization cultures and customer focus. The possibility of a larger Apple presence in the enterprise segment might lead to some tension between end-users and information technology professionals, who were traditionally Windows supporters.[52]

On July 22nd, Cook announced that Apple would offer iPhones with *4.7-Inch and 5.5-Inch Screen Sizes*, significantly larger than the iPhone's 4 inch screen. The larger screen iPhones were in response to Samsung and other manufacturers models with large screens utilizing the Android O.S. Large screen Android smartphones were sold a premium price an area that was dominated by Apple. Over 98% of Android smartphones sold globally priced at the equivalent of $400 or above featured a display greater than 5 inches according to Counterpoint Research. Samsung was feeling the pinch in emerging markets where its low-to-mid-end smartphones faced intense price competition from rival Asian handset makers Lenovo Group Ltd. and XiaomiInc.[53]

Earlier in 2014, Apple announced that it had formed a partnership with China Mobile, Ltd. to sell Apple's iPhones. China Mobile was that country's largest telecommunications carrier. Apple expected demand for its iPhones to surge from the partnership with China Mobile. Bigger-screen smartphones were popular in China and other emerging markets where the smartphone was replacing the personal computer as a main computing device. To fulfill demand Apple told its two main iPhone contract assemblers Pegatron Corp. and Foxconn to ramp up capacity in its plants for up to 120 million iPhones by year-end. Apple was expecting a much higher than normal failure rate for its iPhone because of the newer larger screen's more complicated technology.[54]

CONCLUSION: WILL APPLE FLOURISH OR FLOP?

Was Cook doing enough to maintain Apple's lead in breakthrough technology in smartphone and Apple's other mobile device? Cook noted,

> We have to focus on products, making the best products … If we do that right and make great products that enrich peoples' lives, then the other things will happen.[55]

Was Cook just replicating Steve Jobs "build it and they will come" approach or was he truly overseeing a new and revolutionary Apple under his leadership? While Apple had more than one million customers visit its Apple Stores daily, and had nearly 600 million online App Store accounts was this enough to keep Apple's momentum going in the right direction? Was there was more to Apple's success formula than setting out to build great products and cathedrals to attract loyal customers?[56]

Although Apple's profits and revenues were growing at double digits, the overall rate was slowing down (See Exhibit 9). Apple's stellar financials belied the fact that Apple was losing market share both at home and abroad for its smartphones to rival manufactures utilizing Google's Android operating system. Apple's iPhone was now competing against a host other companies, including Samsung, HTC, Microsoft, Amazon and several others. As one Apple observer commented, "the halo starts to wear off unless the seeming miracles that transform markets or industries keep happening."[57]

EXHIBIT 9

Net Sales, Gross Margin, and Net Income (Loss)
2009–2013

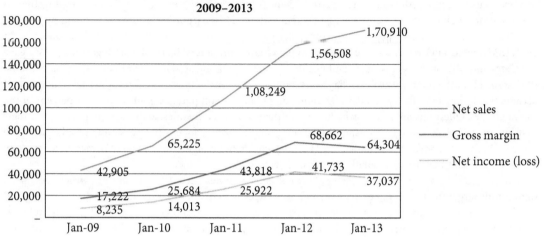

Source: Apple, Inc., *10K Report* September 28, 2013: Complied from data found in Apple's 10K;

APPENDIX A: BRIEF OVERVIEW OF APPLE PRODUCTS AND SERVICES

iPhone: Apple's line of *iPhone* (smartphones) combined a phone, music player, and internet device in one product, and was based on Apple's iOS Multi-Touch™ operating system. IPhone had an integrated photo and video camera and photo library app, and on qualifying devices, also included Siri®, a voice activated intelligent assistant. IPhone works with the iTunes Store, the App Store and iBooks Store for purchasing, organizing and playing music, movies, TV shows, podcasts, books, and apps.

IPad: iPad and iPad mini™ were the Company's line of multi-purpose tablets based on Apple's iOS Multi-Touch operating system

Mac: Mac was the Company's line of desktop and portable personal computers. Macs feature Intel microprocessors, the OS X operating system and included Mail, Safari web browser, Messages, Calendars, Apple's desktop computers included iMac®, Mac Pro® and Mac mini. The Company's portable computers included MacBook Pro® and MacBook Air®.

IPod: The Company's iPod line of portable digital music and media players included iPod touch, iPod nano®, iPod shuffle® and iPod classic®. All iPods work with iTunes to purchase and synchronize content.

ITunes and the iTunes Store: Apple's iTunes app, available for both Mac and Windows personal computers, keeps users' music, movies, and TV shows organized in one place. ITunes was integrated with the iTunes Store, the App Store and the iBooks Store. The iTunes Store allowed users to purchase and download music and TV shows and to rent or purchase movies. The App Store allowed customers to discover and download apps and purchase in-app content. The iBooks Store features e-books from major and independent publishers

Mac App Store: The Mac App Store allowed customers to discover, download and install Mac apps. The Mac App Store offers applications in education, games, graphics and design, lifestyle, productivity, utilities and other categories. The Company's OS X operating system software and its iLife, iWork and other application software titles were also available on the Mac App Store.

iCloud: iCloud was the Company's cloud service, which stores music, photos, applications, contacts, calendars, documents and more, keeping them up-to-date and available to multiple iOS devices and Mac and Windows personal computers.

Operating System Software
iOS: iOS was the Company's Multi-Touch operating system that serves as the foundation for iOS devices. iOS 7 was the current version and was released in September 2013. Apps delivered with iOS for qualifying devices included Safari web browser, FaceTime video calling, Maps with turn-by-turn directions, Mail, Contacts, Calendar, Clock, Weather, Calculator, Notes, Reminders, Stocks, Compass, and Messages. Devices running iOS were compatible with both Mac and Windows personal computers and Apple's iCloud services.

BOS X: OS X, the Company's Mac operating system, was built on an open-source UNIX-based foundation and provides an intuitive and integrated computer experience. OS X Mavericks, released in October 2013, was the tenth major release of OS X. Support for iCloud was built into OS X so users can access content and information from their other Macs, their iOS devices and other supported devices and access downloaded content and apps from the iTunes Store. In addition to Mail, Safari web browser, Messages, Calendars, Reminders, Contacts and theiLife® suite of software apps, Mavericks also included a new Maps app and a new iBooks app that both work with their iOS counterparts.

Application Software included: iLife, iWork and Other Application Software

ENDNOTES

1 Yerram, Siddarth, "Google Inc. (GOOG)Is Capturing U.S. Smartphone Market Faster Than Apple," *Info: Report:* September 11, 2013

2 "The Latest Market Research Shows that Android Smartphones rule the World," February 16, 2014

3 Gallagher, Dan, "*Apple's Cook Can't Afford to Miss a Beat*," *Wall Street Journal* May 29, 2014

4 Isaacson, Walter *Steve Jobs*, Simon & Schuster: New York 2011, p.513

5 Ibid., Issaacson, *Steve Jobs, p:514*

6 Ibid., Issaacson, *Steve Jobs, p:514*

7 Smith, Dave, "Apple Labor Issues Continue: iPhone Supplier Jabil Circuit Accused Of Major Violations," *International Business Times*, September 5, 2013; Downloaded at: http://www.ibtimes.com/apple-labor-issues-continue-iphone-supplier-jabil-circuit- accused-major-violations-1402951; Accessed: July 23, 2014

8 Smith, Dave, "Foxconn Riot: Largest Apple Supplier Suffers Another Violent Outbreak," September 24, 2013 *International Business Times*, Downloaded at: http://www.ibtimes.com/foxconn-riot-largest-apple-supplier-suffers-another-violent-outbreak-1410316; Accessed August 7, 2014

9 Elliott, Stuart "Apple Passes Coca-Cola as Most Valuable Brand," New York Times September 29, 2013

10 Elmer-DeWitt, Philip, "*Google's jumps to No. 3, after Apple and Exxon, in market cap*," *Fortune*, October 19, 2013: Downloaded at: http://fortune.com/2013/10/19/googles-jumps-to-no-3-after-apple-and-exxon-in-market-cap/; Accessed August 7, 2014

11 Apple, Inc., *10K Report* September 28, 2013: Downloaded at: http://investor.apple.com/financials.cfm; Accessed: July 30, 2014

12 Elmer-DeWitt, Philip, "*Apple cracks the Fortune 10*," Fortune: May 6, 201; Downloaded at: http://fortune.com/2013/05/06/apple-cracks-the-fortune-10/; Accessed August 7, 2014.

13 Isaacson, Walter *Steve Jobs*, Simon & Schuster: New York 2011, p.102

14 Ibid., Issaacson, *Steve Jobs, p. 103*

15 Isaacson, Walter *Steve Jobs*, Simon & Schuster: New York 2011, p.217

16 Ibid., Issaacson, *Steve Jobs, p. 217*

17 Ibid., Issaacson, *Steve Jobs, pp. 221-222*

18 Ibid., Issaacson, *Steve Jobs, p. 295*

19 Millian, Mark, "14 years later, Dell founder backtracks on Apple attack*" CNN Tech:* October 18, 2011, Downloaded at: http://www.cnn.com/2011/10/18/tech/web/michael-dell-apple/; Accessed July 24, 2014

20 Wikipedia, *Steve Jobs* Downloaded at: http://en.wikipedia.org/wiki/Steve_Jobs Accessed: June 20, 2014

21 Wikipedia, *Steve Jobs* D

22 Ibid., Issaacson, *Steve Jobs, p.*

23 Nair, Smita, "Apple's premium pricing strategy and product differentiation *Yahoo Finance, Market Realist* , January 28, 2014; Downloaded at: http://finance.yahoo.com/news/apple-premium-pricing-strategy-product-191247308.html; Accessed August 7, 2014

24 Apple, Inc., *10K Report* September 28, 2013: Downloaded at: http://investor.apple.com/financials.cfm; Accessed: July 30, 2014

25 Zino Angelo, CFA Report: "Current Environment: *Mobility to drive hardware, as personal computer spending contracts.*" *Standard & Poor Advantage: Industry Surveys; Computer Equipment:* April, 2014: Downloaded at:*http://www.netadvantage.standardandpoors.com.libproxy.unh.edu/NASApp/NetAdvantage/showIndustrySurvey.do?code=coh*; Accessed July 24, 2014

26 Ibid., Zino Angelo, *Standard & Poor Advantage: Industry Surveys; Computer Equipment*

27 Ibid., Zino Angelo, *Standard & Poor Advantage: Industry Surveys; Computer Equipment*

28 Ibid., Zino Angelo, *Standard & Poor Advantage: Industry Surveys; Computer Equipment*

29 Ibid., Zino Angelo, *Standard & Poor Advantage: Industry Surveys; Computer Equipment*

30 Ibid., Zino Angelo, *Standard & Poor Advantage: Industry Surveys; Computer Equipment*

31 Train, Phi, "Inequality Between iOS and Android Market Shares," *Infographic: Social Times*, March 26, 2014

34 Train, Phi, "Inequality Between iOS and Android Market Shares," *Infographic: Social Times*, March 26, 2014

32 Yerram, Siddarth, "Google Inc. (GOOG) Is Capturing U.S. Smartphone Market Faster Than Apple," *Info: Report:* September 11, 2013

33 Lee, Tyler, "Apple is the Leading Smartphone Vendor in U.S." *Ubergizmo:* May 21, 2014

34 Train, Phi, "Inequality Between iOS and Android Market Shares," *Infographic: Social Times*, March 26, 2014

35 Yerram, Siddarth, "Google Inc. (GOOG) Is Capturing U.S. Smartphone Market Faster Than Apple," *Info: Report:* September 11, 2013

36 Luk, Lorraine, "Apple Readies a Big Bet on Big Screen Phones," *Wall Street Journal* July 22, 2014: Downloaded at: *http://online.wsj.com/articles/apple-suppliers-gear-up-for-large-screen-iphones- 1405985788?KEYWORDS=Apple+Luk*; Accessed July 22, 2014

37 "The Latest Market Research Shows that Android Smartphones rule the World," February 16, 2014

38 "The Latest Market Research Shows that Android Smartphones rule the World," February 16, 2014

39 Vogelstein, Fred "The Android Explosion," *Wired, p.*

40 Ibid, Vogelstein, Fred "The Android Explosion," *p.*

41 Gallagher, Dan, "Apple Takes Its Business Seriously," *Wall Street Journal,* July 16, 2014, p.C10

42 Bensinger, Gregg, "Amazon Fires Up a Smartphone for Shopping," *Wall Street Journal*, June 19, 2014, p.B5

43 Gottfried, Miriam and Gallagher, Dan, "Amazon's Smartphone: Where There's Fire There's Smoke," *Wall Street Journal* June 19, 2014, p. C10

44 Apple, Inc. http://investor.apple.com; Accessed: June 19, 2014

45 Fisher, Dan, "Apple and the Fear of Flopping," *News.cnet.com*: July 18, 2013

46 Ibid., Fisher,"Apple and the Fear of Flopping"

47 Wakabayashi, Daisuke, "Tim Cook's Vision for 'His' Apple Begins to Emerge" *Wall Street Journal:* July 7, 2014 Downloaded at: http://online.wsj.com/articles/ tim-cooks-apple-takes-shape- 1404757939?KEYWORDS=Apple%27s+Cook Accessed July 7, 2014

48 Ibid.,Wakabayashi, "Tim Cook's Vision for 'His' Apple Begins to Emerge"

49 Ibid.,Wakabayashi, "Tim Cook's Vision for 'His' Apple Begins to Emerge"

50 Ibid.,Wakabayashi, "Tim Cook's Vision for 'His' Apple Begins to Emerge"

51 Gallagher, Dan, "*Apple's Cook Can't Afford to Miss a Beat,*" *Wall Street Journal* May 29, 2014

52 Wakabayashi, Daisuke, "Apple, IBM in Deal to Create Apps, Sell Phones Tech Firms Plan to Create Business Apps and Sell iPhones, iPads to IBM›s Corporate Customers," *Wall Street Journal,* July 15, 2014

53 Luk, Lorraine, "Apple Readies a Big Bet on Big Screen Phones," *Wall Street Journal* July 22, 2014: C10; Downloaded at: *http://online.wsj.com/articles/apple-suppliers-gear-up-for-large-screen-iphones- 1405985788?KEYWORDS=Apple+Luk;* Accessed July 22, 2014

54 Ibid., Luk, "Apple Readies a Big Bet on Big Screen Phones," *Wall Street Journal* July 22, 2014

55 Wakabayashi, Daisuke, "Tim Cook's Vision for 'His' Apple Begins to Emerge" *Wall Street Journal:* July 7, 2014

56 Fisher, Dan, "Apple and the Fear of Flopping," *News.cnet.com*: July 18, 2013

57 Ibid., Fisher, "Apple and the Fear of Flopping,"

⛊IVEY | Publishing

INTRODUCTION

James Neuhausen was a U.S. stock analyst tasked with preparing a recommendation on what his firm, a large U.S. investment house, should do with its stake in Walmart Stores, Inc. It was an unseasonably warm day in early February 2012, and Neuhausen was reviewing his notes on the firm. Walmart, the world's largest retailer, was trying to recover from a series of missteps that had seen competitors such as Dollar Stores and Amazon.com close the performance gap. Competitors had copied many aspects of Walmart's distribution system, including cross-docking product to eliminate storage time in warehouses, positioning stores around distribution centres and widespread adoption of electronic data interchange (EDI), to manage ordering and shipping from suppliers. Neuhausen stated:

> Walmart is believed to have one of the most efficient supply chains in the retail world. What impact will the increasing variety of product, store formats and the growing importance of international stores have on the way it distributes product? What improvements to its supply chain does the company need to make in order to continue to stay ahead of competitors?

Last year, Walmart suffered nine consecutive quarters of declining same store sales. Procter & Gamble's Chief Executive, Robert McDonald, pointed out that part of the problem was that there were execution issues at Walmart's U.S. stores.[b] More nimble competitors such as Dollar General are rolling out small format stores that are eating into Walmart's share. In the online space, Amazon.com has become a major threat. Walmart has also changed over the years and it now operates a variety of store formats under 60 different banners

---

a   This case has been written on the basis of published sources only. Consequently, the interpretation and perspectives presented in this case are not necessarily those of Walmart or any of it employees.

b   http://operationsroom.wordpress.com/2011/03/07/is-Walmart-losing-focus/, accessed January 4, 2012.

around the world. International sales hit US$109 billion in fiscal year 2011, more than a quarter of its business. Can its supply chain keep up and still deliver efficiency gains?

THE RETAIL INDUSTRY

U.S. retail sales, excluding motor vehicles and parts dealers, reached US$3.9 trillion in 2011. Major categories in the U.S. retail industry included general merchandise, food and beverage, health and personal care and other categories as can be seen in Exhibit 1. In the United States, retailers competed at local, regional and national levels, with some of the major chains such as Walmart and Costco counting operations in foreign countries as well. In addition to the traditional one-store owner-operated retailer, the industry included formats such as discount stores, department stores (selling a large percentage of soft goods, or clothing), variety and convenience stores, specialty stores, supermarkets, supercentres (combination discount and supermarket stores), Internet retailers and catalog retailers. Online retail sales were rising in importance, accounting for US$197 billion in 2011.[c]

The top 200 retailers accounted for approximately 30 per cent of worldwide retail sales.[d] Major retailers competed for employees and store locations as well as customers. There were two broad strategies in global retailing: variable pricing, or "hi-lo pricing," and everyday low price (EDLP). Hi-lo pricing, practiced by retailers for decades, involved adjusting the retail price of items to optimize gross margins. For example, at traditional grocery stores, while prices of key items—such as milk, sugar, eggs and butter—were kept consistently low, items such as toothpaste, detergent and tissue had high prices. The goal in a hi-lo environment was to generate increased sales by having the manufacturer fund the trade promotions on some items—lowering prices by 25 to 30 per cent—every month or quarter.

On the other hand, an EDLP strategy meant that prices on items were generally consistent from week to week but were kept as low as possible so as to generate the highest consumer foot traffic. Running an EDLP strategy generally required the retailer to focus on keeping operational costs as low as possible and investing any savings into lowering retail prices. The goal, in an EDLP environment, was to generate higher aggregate gross profit by increasing the volume of items sold.

As many of the top global retailers faced intense competition in their home markets, a growing trend for these global retailers was international expansion, especially into developing markets such as Asia, South America and Africa. The objective of international expansion was to find a way to continue to grow earnings at a faster pace than was possible domestically. Retailers going abroad sought to capitalize on global purchasing economies of scale and to leverage international expertise from one market to another. But international expansion was fraught with risk, and it was not uncommon for retailers to pull out of a market if they were unable to build profitable operations.

WALMART STORES, INC.

Based in Bentonville, Arkansas and founded by the legendary Sam Walton, Walmart was the number one retailer in the world with fiscal year 2011 net income, from continuing operations, of US$16 billion on sales of US$419 billion. It had over 2 million employees and 8,500 stores in 15 countries, the result of a series of acquisitions over the past 20 years. Beginning with its "big box" discount store format in the 1960s, Walmart's store formats around the world had grown to include supercentres, which were a larger version of a discount store that included groceries, supermarkets, wholesale outlets, restaurants and apparel stores. Globally, it served about 200 million customers per week.[e]

c   http://mashable.com/2011/02/28/forrester-e-commerce/, accessed January 15, 2012.
d   http://www.uneptie.org/pc/sustain/reports/Retail/Nov4Mtg2002/Retail_Stats.pdf, accessed May 10, 2006.
e   "WMT — 17th Annual Meeting for the Investment Community," Thomson StreetEvents, October 13, 2010, accessed January 5, 2012.

Walmart's strategy was to provide a broad assortment of quality merchandise and services at "everyday low prices" (EDLP) and was best known for its discount stores, which offered merchandise such as apparel, small appliances, housewares, electronics and hardware. In the U.S. general merchandise arena, Walmart's competitors included Sears and Target, with specialty retailers including Gap and Limited. Department store competitors included Dillard, Federated and J.C. Penney. Grocery store competitors included Kroger, Albertsons and Safeway. The major membership-only warehouse competitor was Costco Wholesale. Walmart was facing growing competition for large ticket general merchandise products and from online retailers such as Amazon.com.

THE DEVELOPMENT OF WALMART'S SUPPLY CHAIN

Before he started Walmart Stores in 1962, Sam Walton owned a successful chain of stores under the Ben Franklin Stores banner, a franchisor of variety stores in the United States. Although he was under contract to purchase most of his merchandise requirements from Ben Franklin Stores, Walton was able to selectively purchase merchandise in bulk from new suppliers and transport these goods to his stores directly. When Walton realized that a new trend, discount retailing—based on driving high volumes of product through low-cost retail outlets—was sweeping the nation, he decided to open up large warehouse-style stores in order to compete. To stock these new stores, initially named "Walmart Discount City," Walton needed to step up his merchandise procurement efforts. As none of the suppliers were willing to send their trucks to his stores, which were located in rural Arkansas, self-distribution was necessary.

Walmart undertook an initial public offering in 1969 to raise funds to build its first distribution centre in Bentonville, Arkansas. As the company grew in the 1960s to 1980s, it benefited from improved road infrastructure and the inability of its competitors to react to changes in legislation, such as the removal of "resale price maintenance," which had prevented retailers from discounting merchandise. To keep an eye on his growing network, Walton piloted a small single-engine airplane, which he would land at air strips close to his new stores.

Walmart's supply chain, a key enabler of its growth from its beginnings in rural Arkansas, was long considered by many to be a major source of competitive advantage for the company. It was one of the first firms to rely on data to make operational decisions, using bar codes, sharing sales data with suppliers, controlling its own trucking fleet and installing computerized point-of-sale systems that collected item-level data in real time. When Walmart was voted "Retailer of the Decade" in 1989, its distribution costs were estimated at 1.7 per cent of its cost of sales, comparing favourably with competitors such as Kmart (3.5 per cent of total sales) and Sears (5 per cent of total sales).[f]

Its successes were widely publicized, and competitors had adopted many of Walmart's management techniques. Yet Walmart continued to lead the industry in efficiency, achieving inventory turns of 11.5 times in fiscal year 2011. For perspective, for the same period, key U.S. competitors Target Corp., Amazon.com and Sears had inventory turns of 8.7 times, 6.2 times, and 4.7 times, respectively. But Kroger Co., the second largest grocery retailer in the United States, had inventory turns of 14.2 times, primarily due to its focus on high-turning perishable food items.[g]

PROCUREMENT

As his purchasing efforts increased in scale, Walton and his senior management team would make trips to buying offices in New York City, cutting out the middleman (wholesalers and distributors). Walmart's U.S. buyers, located in Bentonville, worked with suppliers to ensure that the correct mix of staples and new items were

---

f   *"Low Distribution Costs Buttress Chain's Profits," Discount Store News, December 18, 1989.*
g   *Inventory turns calculated from respective firms' 10-K filings.*

ordered. Over time, many of Walmart's largest suppliers maintained offices in Bentonville, staffed by analysts and managers supporting Walmart's business.

In addition, Walmart started sourcing products globally, opening the first of these offices in China in the mid-1980s. Walmart's international purchasing offices worked directly with local factories to source Walmart's private label merchandise. Private label products were appealing to customers as they were often priced at a significant discount to brand name merchandise; for Walmart, the private label items generated higher margins than suppliers' branded products. Private label sales at Walmart, first developed in the 1980s, were believed to account for just 16 per cent of Walmart's sales, compared to 25 per cent at U.S. rivals Safeway and Kroger.[h] This was because Walmart's stated strategy was to be a "house of brands," procuring top brands in volume and selling them at low prices.[i]

Every quarter, buyers met in Bentonville to review new merchandise, exchange buying notes and tips and review a fully merchandised prototype store, which was located in a warehouse. In order to gather field intelligence, buyers toured stores two or three days a week and worked on sales floors helping associates stock and sell merchandise.

Walmart wielded enormous power over its suppliers. For example, observers noted that increase bargaining clout was a contributing factor in Procter & Gamble's (P&G) acquisition of chief rival Gillette.[j] Prior to the acquisition, sales to Walmart accounted for 17 per cent of P&G's and 13 per cent of Gillette's revenues.[k] On the other hand, these two suppliers combined accounted for about 8 per cent of Walmart's sales.[l] Some viewed Walmart's close cooperation with suppliers in a negative light:

> Walmart dictates that its suppliers . . . accept payment entirely on Walmart's terms … share information all the way back to the purchasing of raw materials. Walmart controls with whom its suppliers speak, how and where they can sell their goods and even encourages them to support Walmart in its political fights. Walmart all but dictates to suppliers where to manufacture their products, as well as how to design those products and what materials and ingredients to use in those products.[m]

When negotiating with its suppliers, Walmart insisted on a single invoice price and did not pay for cooperative advertising, discounting or distribution. Globally, Walmart was thought to have around 40,000 suppliers, of whom 200—such as Nestle, P&G, Unilever, and Kraft—were key global suppliers. With Walmart's expectations on sales data analysis, category management responsibilities and external research specific to their Walmart business, it was not uncommon for a supplier to have several employees working full-time to support the Walmart business.

DISTRIBUTION

Walmart's store openings were driven directly by its distribution strategy. Because its first distribution centre was a significant investment for the firm, Walton insisted on saturating the area within a day's driving distance in order to gain economies of scale. Over the years, competitors had copied this "hub-and-spoke" design of high volume distribution centres serving a cluster of stores. This distribution-led store expansion strategy persisted for the next two decades as Walmart added thousands of U.S. stores, expanding across the nation from its headquarters in Arkansas.

---

h   http://www.ft.com/intl/cms/s/0/762b1f80-1259-11de-b816-0000779fd2ac.html#axzz1lv8XtooH, accessed January 15, 2012.
i   http://www.bloomberg.com/apps/news?pid=newsarchive&sid=a8ErNwolNpAw, accessed January 15, 2012.
j   http://www.newyorker.com/talk/content/?050214ta_talk_surowiecki, February 7 2005, accessed January 15, 2012.
k   Larry Dignan, "Procter & Gamble, Gillette Merger Could Challenge Walmart RFID Adoption," Extremetech.com, January 31, 2005. http://www.extremetech.com/article2/0,1558,1758152,00.asp, accessed January 15, 2012.
l   Mark Roberti, "P&G-Gillette Merger Could Benefit RFID", RFID Journal, February 4, 2005.
m   Barry C. Lynn, "Breaking the Chain," Harper's Magazine, July 2006, p. 34.

Stores were located in low-rent, suburban areas close to major highways. In contrast, key competitor Kmart's stores were thinly spread throughout the U.S. and located in prime urban areas. By the time the rest of the retail industry started to take notice of Walmart in the 1980s, it had built up the most efficient logistics network of any retailer. Walmart's 75,000-person logistics and its information systems division included the largest private truck fleet employee base of any firm—6,600 trucks and 55,000 trailers, which delivered the majority of merchandise sold at stores. [n] Its 150 distribution centres, located throughout the United States, were a mix of general merchandise, food and soft goods (clothing) distribution centres, processing over five billion cases a year through its entire network.

In the United States, Walmart's distribution centres received about 315,000 inbound truckloads, of which 115,000 were shipped "collect," which meant they were picked up directly from suppliers' warehouses by Walmart's trucking fleet, The remaining 200,000 loads were shipped by suppliers' trucks or by logistics providers. The goal at Walmart's distribution centres was for high turning items—such as fresh food or other perishable merchandise—to be cross-docked, or directly transferred from inbound to outbound trailers without extra storage.

The average distance from distribution centre to stores was approximately 130 miles. Each of these distribution centres were profiled in a store friendly way, with similar products stacked together. Merchandise purchased directly from factories in offshore locations such as China or India were processed at coastal distribution centres before shipment to U.S. stores.

On the way back from delivering product to stores, Walmart's trucks generated "backhaul" revenue by transporting unsold merchandise on trucks that would be otherwise empty. Walmart's backhaul revenues—its private fleet operated as a for-hire carrier when it was not busy transporting merchandise from distribution centres to stores—were more than US$1 billion per year. [o] In mid-2010, Walmart was looking to expand its backhaul program, to pick up more product directly from suppliers' factories. It was seeking, in some cases, a 6 per cent reduction in the manufacturer's selling price. For perspective, suppliers estimated the actual transportation expense was just 3 per cent of the selling price. [p]

Because their trucking employees were non-unionized and in-house, Walmart was able to implement and improve upon standard delivery procedures, coordinating and deploying the entire fleet as necessary. Uniform operating standards ensured that miscommunication between traffic coordinators, truckers and store level employees were minimized. During an analyst meeting in October 2011, Johnnie Dobbs, Walmart Stores' (Walmart's) EVP Logistics, had stated:

> Everyday low cost is the foundation for everyday low prices. So our focus across the organization is delivering products that our customers need in the most efficient method and process available. So, here's an example of a sustained cost reduction in our transportation area. We have improved visibility and routing tools. We've reengineered processes that have decreased the number of empty miles and out-of-route miles that our drivers drive. Our merchants and our suppliers have improved packaging, and we've adjusted methods that we use to load our trailers, resulting in increased cases in cube in every trailer that we ship. . . . (This year) we'll ship 335 million more cases while we'll drive 300 million fewer miles. [q]

STORE NETWORK

In the early years, Walmart grew rapidly as customers were attracted by its assortment of low-priced product. Over time, the company copied the merchandise assortment strategies of other retailers, mostly through observation as a result of store visits. It bought in bulk, bypassing distributors, and passed savings on to consumers.

---

n   http://walmartprivatefleet.com/AboutUs/LeadershipProfiles.aspx, accessed January 2, 2012.
o   http://www.dcvelocity.com/articles/july2004/inbound.cfm, accessed August 19, 2006.
p   http://www.businessweek.com/magazine/content/10_23/b4181017589330.htm, accessed March 3, 2012.
q   "WMT — 18th Annual Meeting for the Investment Community," Thomson StreetEvents, October 12, 2011, Investext, accessed January 12, 2012.

Each Walmart store aimed to be the "store of the community," tailoring its product mix to appeal to the distinct tastes of that community. Thus, two Walmart Stores a short distance apart could potentially stock different merchandise. In contrast, most other retailers made purchasing decisions at the district or regional level.

The display of merchandise was suggested by a store-wide template, with a unique template for each store, indicating the layout of Walmart's various departments. This template was created by Walmart's merchandising department after analyzing historical store sales and community traits. Associates were free to alter the merchandising template to fit their local store requirements. Shelf space in Walmart's different departments—from shoes to household appliances to automotive supplies—was divided up, each spot allocated to specific SKUs.

Unlike its competitors in the 1970s and 1980s, Walmart implemented an EDLP policy, which meant that products were displayed at a steady price and not discounted on a regular basis. In a "hi-lo" discounting environment, discounts would be rotated from product to product, necessitating huge inventory stockpiles in anticipation of a discount. In an EDLP environment, demand was smoothed out to reduce the "bullwhip effect." Because of its EDLP policy, Walmart did not need to advertise as frequently as their competitors and channeled the savings back into price reductions. To generate additional volume, Walmart buyers worked with suppliers on price rollback campaigns. Price rollbacks, each lasting about 90 days and funded by suppliers, had the goal of increasing product sales between 200 and 500 per cent. A researcher remarked: "Consumers certainly love Walmart's low prices, which are an average of 8 per cent to 27 per cent lower than the competition." [r]

The company also ensured that its store level operations were at least as efficient as its logistics operations. The stores were simply furnished and constructed using standard materials. Efforts were made to continually reduce operating costs. For example, light and temperature settings for all U.S. stores were controlled centrally from Bentonville.

As Walmart distribution centres had close to real-time information on stores' in-stock levels, the merchandise could be pushed to stores automatically. In addition, store level information systems allowed manufacturers to be notified as soon as an item was purchased. In anticipation of changes in demand for some items, associates had the authority to manually input orders or override impending deliveries. In contrast, most of Walmart's retail competitors did not confer merchandising responsibility to entry level employees as merchandising templates were sent to stores via head office and were expected to be followed precisely. To ensure that employees were kept up-to-date, management shared detailed information about day/week/month store sales with all employees during daily 10-minute long "standing" meetings.

INFORMATION SYSTEMS

Walton had always been interested in gathering and analyzing information about his company operations. As early as 1966, when Walton had 20 stores, he attended an IBM school in upstate New York with the intent on hiring the smartest person in the class to come to Bentonville to computerize his operations. [s] Even with a growing network of stores in the 1960s and 1970s, Walton was able to personally visit and keep track of operations in each one, due to his use of a personal airplane, which he used to observe new construction development (to determine where to place stores) and to monitor customer traffic (by observing how full the parking lot was).

In the mid-1980s, Walmart invested in a central database, store level point-of-sale systems and a satellite network. Combined with one of the retail industry's first chain-wide implementation of UPC bar codes, store level information could now be collected instantaneously and analyzed. By combining sales data with external information such as weather forecasts, Walmart was able to provide additional support to buyers, improving the accuracy of its purchasing forecasts.

---

r   William Beaver, "Battling Walmart: How Communities Can Respond," Business and Society Review 110.2, Summer 2005, p. 159.
s   http://www.time.com/time/time100/builder/profile/walton2.html, accessed August 23, 2006.

In the early 1990s, Walmart developed Retail Link. At an estimated 570 terabytes—which, Walmart claimed, was larger than all the fixed pages on the Internet—Retail Link was the largest civilian database in the world. By 2008, Retail Link had 2.5 petabytes (2,500 terabytes) in data storage capacity, second only to eBay's 4-petabyte installation.[t] For a description of how Retail Link fits in with Walmart's supply chain, see Exhibit 2. Retail Link contained data on every sale ever made at the company during a two-decade period. Walmart gave its suppliers access to real-time sales data on the products they supplied, down to individual stock-keeping items at the store level. In order to harness the knowledge of its suppliers, key category suppliers, called "category captains," first introduced in the late 1980s, provided input on shelf space allocation. As an observer noted:

> One obvious result [of using category captains] is that a producer like Colgate-Palmolive will end up working intensively with firms it formerly competed with, such as Crest manufacturer P&G, to find the mix of products that will allow Walmart to earn the most it can from its shelf space. If Walmart discovers that a supplier promotes its own products at the expense of Walmart's revenue, the retailer may name a new captain in its stead.[u]

In 1990, Walmart became one of the early adopters of collaborative planning, forecasting and replenishment (CPRF), an integrated approach to planning and forecasting through sharing critical supply chain information, such as data on promotions, inventory levels and daily sales.[v] Walmart's vendor managed inventory (VMI) program (also known as continuous replenishment) required suppliers to manage inventory levels at the company's distribution centres, based on agreed service levels. The VMI program started with P&G diapers in the late 1980s and by 2006 had expanded to include all major suppliers.[w] In some situations, particularly grocery products, suppliers owned the inventory in Walmart stores up to the point that the sale was scanned at checkout.

Retail Link had an estimated 100,000 registered users, working for suppliers, who accessed the system. They ran approximately 350,000 weekly queries of the data warehouse that contained two years of weekly point-of-sale information.[x] Walmart buyers held regular meetings with category captains, who would come to the meeting prepared with category analyses and recommendations for how shelf space for the various competitors should be allocated. In exchange for providing suppliers access to these data, Walmart expected them to proactively monitor and replenish product on a continual basis.

To support this inventory management effort, supplier analysts worked closely with Walmart's supply chain personnel to coordinate the flow of products from suppliers' factories and resolved any supply chain issues, from routine issues such as ensuring that products were ready for pick up by Walmart's trucks and arranging for the return of defective products, to last minute issues such as managing sudden spikes in demand for popular items. When Walmart buyers met, on a frequent basis, with a supplier's sales teams, two important topics of review were supplier's out-of-stock rate and inventory levels at Walmart, indications of how well replenishment was being handled. Suppliers were provided targets for out-of-stock rates and inventory levels.

In addition to managing short-term inventory and discussing product trends, Walmart worked with suppliers on medium- to long-term supply chain strategies including factory location, cooperation with downstream raw materials suppliers and production volume forecasting. Walmart's satellite network, in addition to receiving and transmitting point-of-sale data, also provided senior management with the ability to broadcast video messages to the stores. Although the bulk of senior management lived and worked in Bentonville, Arkansas, frequent video broadcasts to each store in their network kept store employees informed of the latest developments in the firm. In an effort to emulate Walmart's ability to share information with suppliers,

---

t   http://www.informationweek.com/news/software/info_management/228800661, accessed March 3, 2012.
u   Barry C. Lynn, "Breaking the Chain," 33.
v   A.H. Johnson, "35 Years of IT Leadership: A New Supply Chain Forged," Computerworld, September 30, 2002, pp. 38-39.
w   T. Andel, "Partnerships With Pull," Transportation and Distribution, July 1995, pp. 65-74; http://www.industrialsupplymagazine.com/pages/Print-edition--MayJune10IsVMIForYou.php, accessed April 10, 2012.
x   http://findarticles.com/p/articles/mi_m0FNP/is_17_44/ai_n15624797, accessed January 15, 2012.

Walmart's competitors began developing systems similar to Retail Link. Available through Agentrics LLC, a software service provider, the software platform, built with the input of dozens of global retailers, was made available through a subscription and collected and made available store level data by retailer. Agentrics' customer base included many of the world's top retailers including Carrefour, Tesco, Metro, Costco, Kroger and Walgreen's. Many of these retailers were also investors in Agentrics.

RFID

To ensure that cases moved efficiently through the distribution centres, Walmart worked with suppliers to standardize case sizes and labeling. Since 2003, Walmart had required its top 100 suppliers to affix RFID (radio-frequency identification) tags to shipping cases to facilitate the tracking and sorting of inbound product.

RFID tags allowed Walmart to increase stock visibility as stock moved in trucks through the distribution centres and on to the stores. Walmart would be able to track promotion effectiveness within the stores while cutting out-of-stock sales losses and overstock expenses. The company placed RFID tag readers in several parts of the store: at the dock where merchandise came in, throughout the backroom, at the door from the stockroom to the sales floor and in the box-crushing area where empty cases eventually wound up. With those readers in place, store managers would know what stock was in the backroom and what was on the sales floor.

According to researchers, about 25 per cent of out-of-stock inventory in the United States was not really out of stock: the items could be misplaced on the floor or mis-shelved in the backroom. U.S.-wide, about 8 per cent of merchandise was out of stock at any given time, leading to lost sales for retailers. [y] In a study performed by the University of Arkansas, Walmart stores with RFID showed a net improvement of 16 per cent fewer out-of-stocks on the RFID-tagged products that were tested. However, RFID tags cost approximately 17 cents each. [z] It was estimated that Walmart saved US$500 million a year by using RFID in its operations. [aa]

HUMAN RESOURCES

By visiting each store and by encouraging associates to contribute ideas, Walton was able to uncover and disperse best practices across the company in the 1960s and 1970s. To ensure that best practices were implemented as soon as possible, he held regular "Saturday morning meetings" that convened his top management team in Bentonville. At 7:00 a.m. each Saturday, the week's business results were discussed and merchandising and purchasing changes implemented. Store layout resets were managed on the weekend, and the rejigged stores were ready by Monday morning. Walton and his management team often toured competitors' stores, looking for new ideas to "borrow."

Walmart believed that centralization had numerous benefits including lower costs and improved communications between different divisions. All of Walmart's divisions, from U.S. stores, International and Sam's Club, to its logistics and information systems division, were located in Bentonville, a town of 28,000 people in Northwest Arkansas. Regional managers and in-country presidents were the few executives who were stationed elsewhere. Another key to Walmart's ability to enjoy low operating costs was the fact that it was non-union. Without cumbersome labour agreements, management could take advantage of technology to drive labour costs down and make operational changes quickly and efficiently. Being non-union, however, had its drawbacks. As its store network encroached on unionized grocers' territory, unions, such as the United Food

---

y   http://knowwpcarey.com/article.cfm?aid=803, accessed April 10, 2012.
z   http://knowledge.wpcarey.asu.edu/index.cfm?fa=viewfeature&id=1205, accessed March 3, 2012.
aa   http://www.rfidprivacy.org/walmarts-supply-chain-management-and-rfid.htm, accessed March 3, 2012.

and Commercial Workers' Union, started to become more aggressive in their anti-Walmart publicity campaigns, funding so-called grassroots groups whose goals were to undermine Walmart's expansion. Walmart's size also made it a target for politicians: every stumble was magnified and played up in the press.

FOCUSING ON THE SUPPLY CHAIN

Walmart remained focused on improving its supply chain. A recent initiative was Remix, which was started in the fall of 2005 and aimed at reducing the percentage of out-of-stock merchandise at stores by redesigning its network of distribution centres. As Walmart stores increased its line-up of grocery items (Walmart was the U.S's largest grocer in 2005), the company noticed that as employees sorted through truckloads of arriving merchandise to find fast-selling items, delays in restocking shelves occurred. [ab]

Moving from its original model of having distribution centres serve a cluster of stores, Walmart envisioned that fast-moving merchandise, such as paper towels, toilet paper, toothpaste and seasonal items, would be shipped from dedicated "high velocity" food distribution centres. Food distribution centres—of which there were 40—were designed to handle high-turn food items.

High velocity distribution centres differed from general merchandise distribution centres in the following ways: as primarily food distribution centres, they were smaller and had temperature controls and less automation. [ac] In contrast, general merchandise distribution centres required automation and conveyor belts to move full pallets of goods. Walmart did not elaborate on how much savings this move was expected to generate, but it was believed to be an incremental improvement to the current system. Walmart's CIO, Rollin Ford, stated:

> We could have done nothing and been fine from a logistics standpoint . . . but as you continue to increase your sales per square foot, you've got to do things differently to make those stores more productive. [ad]

In 2006, Walmart continued to seek improvements to its supply chain. Although the company publicly declined to outline its targets for inventory reduction, its suppliers stated that Walmart's top executives spoke in January 2006 about eliminating as much as $6 billion in excess inventory. [ae] In addition, the firm was undertaking a significant program to remodel most of its U.S. stores to improve "checkout speed, customer service and store appearance."

The company reported that remodeled stores could drive 125 to 200 basis points of improvement in both sales and gross margin and 8 to 9 per cent in lower inventories. [af] From fiscal year 2008 to fiscal year 2011, Walmart had remodeled just under 70 per cent of its store base. The company was opening fewer large format supercenters, down to 113 a year in fiscal year 2011 from 277 in fiscal year 2006, and was facing competition from online competitors such as Amazon.com, which enjoyed annual sales increases of 40 per cent from 2009 to 2011. And smaller format stores, or Dollar Stores, which were 10,000 square feet in size or smaller, were becoming popular. Walmart had a small store format as well, Walmart Express, aiming to be a fill-in store for space-constrained urban areas. But even as competitors such as Dollar General were opening over 500 new stores in 2011, Walmart seemed hesitant with its small store format, opening only 35 small stores that year (see Figure 1). [ag]

ab   Kris Hudson, "Walmart's Need for Speed," The Wall Street Journal, September 26, 2005.

ac   http://knowwpcarey.com/article.cfm?aid=803, accessed April 10, 2012.

ad   http://cincom.typepad.com/simplicity/2005/09/index.html, accessed August 23, 2006.

ae   Kris Hudson, "Walmart Aims To Sharply Cut Its Inventory Costs," The Wall Street Journal, April 20, 2005.

af   Patrick McKeever, "Walmart Stores," MKM Partners, May 28, 2010.

ag   Charles Grom, Paul Trussell, Shane Higgins, and Matt Siler, "Broadline Retail Initiation," Deutsche Bank, September 14, 2011, page 106.

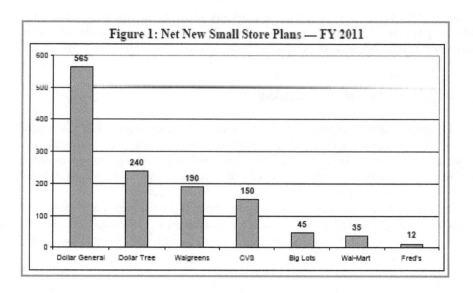

Figure 1: Net New Small Store Plans — FY 2011

But execution issues at the store level and disruption from the remodeling had a negative impact on Walmart's sales. There was also the financial crisis that started in 2008, along with a cutback on staffing levels. The result was nine consecutive quarters of same store sales decline starting in the second quarter of 2009. [ah]

Figure 2: Wal-Mart Same Store Sales Increases (Decreases)

By October 2011, due to its lacklustre topline and earnings growth prospects, Walmart's stock price had languished in the $45 to $55 dollar range for the entire decade. The stock price seemed to be a topic of conversation

---

ah   Charles Grom, Paul Trussell, Shane Higgins, Matt Siler, "Broadline Retail Initiation," page 106; Walmart press releases.

at every analyst meeting that Neuhausen had attended for the past few years. This year, however, he wondered whether Walmart's management's efforts to drive additional gains from its already efficient operations could help its lagging stock price.

NEW INITIATIVES AND A REORGANIZATION

There were three significant initiatives at Walmart whose goals were to improve its supply chain as the firm operated an increasingly varied number of store types and grew its global operations. There were changes to the way it procured product (Global Sourcing), optimizing product delivery to stores to increase on-shelf availability (Project One Touch) and finding ways to leverage its strength in physical store locations to boost its online business (Multi-Channel). To facilitate the improvements, Walmart reorganized, combining its real estate division with store operations and logistics. Walmart was split into three geographic business units (GBUs) in the United States: West, South, and North. [ai]

GLOBAL SOURCING

In February 2010, the Walmart buying group was reorganized into Global Merchandising Centers: general merchandise; food; consumables, health and wellness and Walmart.com; and softlines. [aj] For its private label business, instead of purchasing directly from factories, it entered into a partnership with Li & Fung. The latter would assist with product sourcing in a range of categories and markets where Walmart did not "have the scale or the competencies and skills to leverage." [ak] In 2010, the first year of the agreement called for approximately $2 billion in goods to be purchased through Li & Fung. [al] Walmart was targeting 5 to 15 per cent savings on the $100 billion in product it was purchasing through non-direct channels. [am]

PROJECT ONE TOUCH

"Across the organization, we're focused on the supply chain all the way down to the customer," said Dobbs. "Improvements in our DCs [distribution centres] and our transportation operations generate savings, but if you improve processes at the store level, you have a significant multiplier, when you think about the 3,800 plus stores out there (in the United States)." He continued:

> So we've been working with our store operations team and our innovations teams to develop what we call Project One Touch. We aligned the merchandise flow, our delivery schedules, and the store labor schedules together. Then, we reorganized our high velocity distribution centers to deliver category group pallets that allow our associates to easily transfer product from our trailers to the sales floor. Then, we added aisle and modular locations to the general merchandise case labels to make it easy for our store associates to get these types of products onto the shelf. And finally, this past year, we installed a systems-driven process that dramatically improves the less than case back processing in our back rooms. [an]

---

ai http://www.chainstoreage.com/article/walmart-reorganization-designed-increase-efficiency, accessed January 15, 2012.
aj http://www.massmarketretailers.com/inside-this-issue/news/09-20-2010/changes-at-walmart, accessed January 15, 2012.
ak http://www.storebrandsdecisions.com/news/2010/02/02/walmart-creates-global-merchandising-centers-to-streamline-sourcing,   accessed March 15, 2012.
al http://www.chainstoreage.com/article/walmart-reorganization-designed-increase-efficiency accessed January 215, 012.
am Charles Grom, Paul Trussell, Shane Higgins, Matt Siler, "Broadline Retail Initiation," p. 118.
an "WMT — 18th Annual Meeting for the Investment Community."

In the 10 months from January to October 2011, Walmart's on-shelf availability increased by 5.7 per cent to over 90 per cent. On key items, it had 93 per cent availability. In addition, as a result of reorganizing its logistics, Walmart was able to reinvest the US$2 billion in cost reductions into reducing prices at store level. [ao]

THE MULTI-CHANNEL STRATEGY

Walmart aimed to build a "continuous channel approach" to leverage both its physical store and distribution centre infrastructure and its growing presence online. Walmart.com aimed to carry a broader selection of items not available in stores. In addition, the firm looked to find ways to use the stores to drive online business. Joel Anderson, EVP and president of Walmart.com, stated:

> Our store teams next year (in 2012) will get sales credit for both store sales and .com sales. This is like unleashing a sales force of over 1 million people. That is a differentiation that will be hard to replicate. Secondly, I want to focus on access. Several pilots are currently in place to leverage our ship food storage capabilities. We will offer next day delivery at a very economical price. We will use these capabilities to reach customers in urban areas that we have not yet penetrated. And finally, our online marketing efforts will over index in these areas we haven't penetrated so that we can continue to provide access to the Walmart brand. The third area is fulfillment. We already have unlimited assets in place. Nearly 4,000 stores, over 150 DCs, this will give us the flexibility to offer our customers best in class delivery options.

> For example, last week, we transitioned several disparaged shipping offers into one comprehensive fulfillment program. We are now offering three compelling free shipping programs. This is an excellent example of multi channel strategy beginning to come to life. Let's look at this one a little bit closer. We call it fast, faster, fastest. You have our site to store offer. And this offers our broadest merchandise assortment beyond the stores. Site to store allows a customer to pick it up in our store or hundreds of urban FedEx locations for free. Home free in the middle is our new faster program.

> This launched just last week. Home free allows our customers to bundle their items into one order and have it delivered to home for free. And there are no membership fees like some other online retailers currently charge. Pickup today . . . is our third program. It is our fastest option, and it provides the convenience of same day pickup in our stores for free. Pickup today is available in every one of our stores on the hottest assortment we have to offer. [ap]

DECISION—HOLD, BUY, OR SELL?

Neuhausen put his notes down and walked into the conference room where his analyst team was assembled. He switched on the projector and clicked through the Walmart stock presentation to the comparative information slides that included financial information (see Exhibit 3) and a description of each competitor (see Exhibit 4). Neuhausen hit "enter" and brought up Walmart's stock performance over the past 10 years (see Exhibit 5). He concluded:

---

ao   Ibid.
ap   Ibid.

We've owned Walmart stock for the past decade, and it's been basically flat over that period. During the same time, we'd have made more money had we been invested in the S&P 500 index of the largest 500 U.S. stocks. Should we continue to hold Walmart stock?

I'd like to find out your views on Walmart's key competitive advantages, especially its supply chain strategy, and whether these advantages are sustainable. The data suggest that new competitors, especially the Dollar Stores, Amazon.com and Tesco,[aq] are gaining in popularity in the United States. Is Walmart's high volume "buy it low, stack it high, sell it cheap" model still valid today?

---

aq   Tesco opened four "Fresh & Easy" food markets in California, Arizona and Nevada. http://www.freshandeasy.com/whereweare.aspx, accessed January 15, 2012.

EXHIBIT 1
U.S. RETAIL CATEGORIES (PARTIAL LIST)

Category	2011 (US$ billions)
General merchandise stores	630.9
Food and beverage	615.4
Food services and drinking places	494.2
Gasoline	533.6
Building materials and gardening equipment and supplies	300.2
Furniture, home furnishings, electronics and appliances	190.9
Health and personal care	274.9
Clothing and clothing accessories	226.5
Sporting goods, hobby, books, music	88.9

Source: http://www.census.gov/retail/index.html#arts, accessed January 20, 2012.

EXHIBIT 2
WALMART'S RETAIL LINK DATABASE

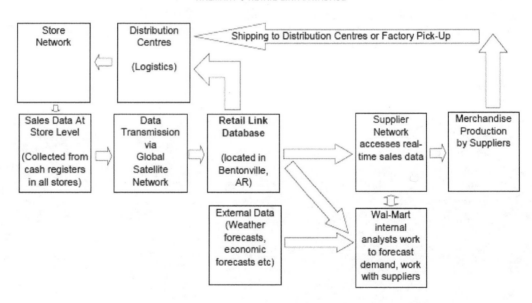

Source: Case writers.

EXHIBIT 3

WALMART AND COMPETITORS—FINANCIAL RESULTS, 2002–2011

FISCAL YEAR	2011	2010	2009	2008	2007	2006	2005	2004	2003	2002
Walmart										
Sales	418,952	405,046	401,244	374,526	344,992	312,427	285,222	256,329	244,524	217,799
COGS	315,287	304,657	306,158	286,515	264,152	240,391	219,793	198,747	191,838	171,562
Operating expenses	81,020	79,607	76,651	70,288	64,001	56,733	51,105	44,909	41,043	36,173
Net income	16,993	14,848	13,400	12,731	11,284	11,231	10,267	9,054	8,039	6,671
Inventories	36,318	33,160	34,511	35,180	33,685	32,191	29,447	26,612	24,891	22,614
Total assets	180,663	170,706	163,429	163,514	151,193	138,187	120,223	104,912	94,685	83,451
Target Corp										
Sales	68,466	65,786	63,435	62,884	61,471	57,878	51,271	45,682	46,781	42,722
COGS	47,860	45,725	44,062	44,157	41,895	39,399	34,927	31,445	31,790	29,260
Operating expenses	14,106	13,469	13,078	12,954	13,704	12,819	11,185	9,797	10,696	9,416
Net income	2,929	2,920	2,488	2,214	2,849	2,787	2,408	3,198	1,841	1,654
Inventories	7,918	7,596	7,179	6,705	6,780	6,254	5,838	5,384	5,343	4,760
Total assets	46,630	43,705	44,533	44,106	44,560	37,349	34,995	32,293	31,392	28,603
Kroger Co										
Sales	90,374	82,189	76,733	76,000	70,235	66,111	60,553	56,434	53,791	51,760
COGS	71,494	63,927	58,958	58,564	53,779	50,115	45,565	42,140	39,637	37,810
expenses	15,345	13,811	13,398	12,884	12,155	11,839	11,027	10,611	10,354	9,618
Net income	596	1,133	57	1,249	1,181	1,115	958	-100	315	1,205
Inventories	6,157	5,793	5,705	5,659	5,459	5,059	4,886	4,729	4,493	4,175
Total assets	23,476	23,505	23,093	23,211	22,299	21,215	20,482	20,491	20,184	20,102
Costco										
Sales	87,048	76,255	69,889	70,977	63,088	58,963	51,862	47,146	41,693	37,993
COGS	77,739	67,995	62,335	63,503	56,450	52,745	46,347	42,092	37,235	33,983
Operating expenses	8,682	7,840	7,252	6,954	6,273	5,732	5,044	4,598	4,097	3,576
Net income	1,542	1,323	1,086	1,283	1,083	1,103	1,063	882	721	700
Inventories	6,638	5,638	5,405	5,039	4,879	4,569	4,015	3,644	3,339	3,127
Total assets	26,761	23,815	21,979	20,682	19,607	17,495	16,514	15,093	13,192	11,620
Safeway										
Sales	43,630	41,050	40,851	44,104	42,286	40,185	38,416	35,823	35,553	32,399
COGS	31,837	29,443	29,157	31,589	30,133	28,604	27,303	25,228	25,019	22,303
Operating expenses	10,659	10,448	10,348	10,662	10,381	9,981	9,898	9,423	9,231	7,719
Net income	518	591	-1,098	965	888	871	561	560	-170	-828
Inventories	2,470	2,623	2,509	2,591	2,798	2,643	2,766	2,741	2,642	2,493
Total assets	15,074	15,148	14,964	17,485	17,651	16,274	15,757	15,377	15,097	16,047

EXHIBIT 3 *(continued)*

WALMART AND COMPETITORS—FINANCIAL RESULTS, 2002–2011

FISCAL YEAR	2011	2010	2009	2008	2007	2006	2005	2004	2003	2002
Amazon.com										
Sales	48,077	34,204	24,509	19,166	14,835	10,711	8,490	6,921	5,264	3,933
COGS	37,288	26,561	18,978	14,896	11,482	8,255	6,451	5,319	4,007	2,940
Operating expenses	9,773	6,131	4,300	3,452	2,689	2,057	1,560	1,112	896	813
Net income	862	1,406	1,129	842	655	389	432	440	271	64
Inventories	4,992	3,202	2,171	1,399	1,200	877	566	480	294	202
Total assets	25,278	18,797	13,813	8,314	6,485	4,363	3,696	3,249	2,162	1,990
Dollar General										
Sales	14,807	13,035	11,796	10,458	5,571	9,170	8,582	7,661	6,872	6,100
COGS	10,109	8,858	8,107	7,397	4,000	6,802	6,117	5,398	4,854	4,376
Operating expenses	3,207	2,902	2,737	2,449	1,325	2,120	1,903	1,706	1,497	1,297
Net income	767	628	339	108	-5	138	350	344	301	265
Inventories	2,009	1,765	1,520	1,415	1,289	1,432	1,474	1,377	1,157	1,123
Total assets	9,689	9,546	8,864	8,889	8,656	3,041	2,992	2,841	2,653	2,333
Dollar Tree										
Sales	6,631	5,882	5,231	4,645	4,243	3,969	3,394	3,126	2,800	161
COGS	4,252	3,769	3,374	3,053	2,782	2,612	2,222	2,013	1,787	114
Operating expenses	1,596	1,458	1,344	1,226	1,131	1,046	889	819	719	55
Net income	488	397	321	230	201	192	174	180	178	-11
Inventories	867	803	680	676	641	605	577	615	526	438
Total assets	2,329	2,381	2,290	2,036	1,788	1,873	1,798	1,793	1,480	1,304
Big Lots										
Sales	5,202	4,952	4,727	4,645	4,656	4,743	4,430	4,375	4,174	3,869
COGS	3,132	2,940	2,807	2,788	2,816	2,852	2,698	2,598	2,428	2,237
Operating expenses	1,635	1,577	1,532	1,524	1,515	1,622	1,596	1,606	1,616	1,485
Net income	207	223	201	155	151	113	16	30	91	77
Inventories	825	762	731	737	748	758	836	895	830	776
Total assets	1,641	1,620	1,669	1,432	1,444	1,721	1,625	1,734	1,785	1,642
Fred's Inc.										
Sales	1,842	1,788	1,799	1,781	1,767	1,589	1,442	1,303	1,103	911
COGS	1,315	1,289	1,296	1,291	1,272	1,141	1,036	935	798	661
Operating expenses	451	434	450	445	425	380	338	317	262	218
Net income	30	24	17	11	27	26	28	34	28	20
Inventories	313	294	302	320	305	304	275	240	194	164
Total assets	596	571	545	551	516	498	465	414	346	284

FISCAL YEAR	2011	2010	2009	2008	2007	2006	2005	2004	2003	2002
Sears										
Sales	41,567	43,326	44,043	46,770	50,703	53,012	48,911	19,701	17,072	6,181
COGS	30,966	31,448	31,824	34,118	36,638	37,820	35,505	14,670	13,084	4,762
Operating expenses	10,664	10,571	10,654	11,060	11,468	11,581	10,759	4,156	3,577	1,421
Net income	(3,147)	150	297	53	826	1,490	858	1,106	248	(862)
Inventories	8,407	9,123	8,705	8,795	9,963	9,907	9,068	3,281	3,238	4,431
Total assets	21,381	24,268	24,808	25,342	27,397	30,066	30,573	8,651	6,084	6,660
Walgreen										
Sales	72,184	67,420	63,335	59,034	53,762	47,409	42,202	37,508	32,505	28,681
COGS	51,692	48,444	45,722	42,391	38,518	34,240	30,414	27,310	23,706	21,076
Operating expenses	16,561	15,518	14,366	13,202	12,093	10,467	9,364	8,055	6,951	5,981
Net income	2,714	2,091	2,006	2,157	2,041	1,751	1,560	1,360	1,176	1,019
Inventories	8,044	7,378	6,789	7,249	6,791	6,050	5,593	4,739	4,203	3,645
Total assets	27,454	26,275	25,142	22,410	19,314	17,131	14,609	13,342	11,406	9,879
CVS										
Sales	107,100	96,413	98,729	87,472	76,330	43,814	37,006	30,594	26,588	24,182
COGS	86,539	76,156	78,349	69,182	60,222	31,875	27,105	22,563	19,725	18,113
Operating expenses	14,231	14,092	13,942	12,244	11,314	9,497	7,882	6,577	5,439	4,863
Net income	3,457	3,424	3,696	3,212	2,637	1,369	1,225	919	847	717
Inventories	10,046	10,695	10,343	9,153	8,008	7,109	5,720	5,454	4,017	4,014
Total assets	64,543	62,169	61,641	60,960	54,722	20,570	15,283	14,547	10,543	9,645
Carrefour										
Sales	106,205	105,212	112,336	113,648	107,352	101,801	97,352	94,963	92,111	89,815
COGS	84,827	83,595	88,990	89,789	84,432	79,981	76,613	74,557	71,391	69,498
Operating expenses	18,255	17,634	19,112	18,759	17,867	16,851	15,986	15,535	15,000	14,923
Net income	-2,878	444	646	1,990	2,677	2,640	2,556	2,542	2,537	2,303
Inventories	8,949	9,140	8,716	9,005	8,974	7,907	7,985	7,346	7,437	7,479
Total assets	62,636	70,110	67,369	68,061	67,865	62,116	60,440	55,257	51,048	50,866
Tesco plc										
Sales	96,608	90,233	86,137	74,992	67,609	62,556	53,696	53,206	45,367	40,675
COGS	88,585	82,928	79,449	69,237	62,471	57,755	49,518	45,861	39,285	35,315
SG&A	2,657	2,421	1,979	1,628	1,438	1,308	1,161	1,343	1,145	1,027
Net income	4,235	3,704	3,434	3,377	3,011	2,499	2,136	1,744	1,500	1,316
Inventories	5,013	4,327	4,232	3,853	3,062	2,321	2,075	1,896	1,779	1,440
Total assets	74,847	72,971	73,018	47,826	39,332	35,774	31,956	29,431	26,163	21,493

Sources: Mergent, various company annual reports. Note that Tesco plc's calculation of COGS (which includes some operating expenses) may not be directly comparable to other firms' COGS figures. Tesco's SG&A for 2002–04 have been estimated using figures from 2005–11. Kmart Holdings Corporation purchased Sears, Roebuck and Co. on November 17, 2004, and the new firm was renamed "Sears Holding Corp."

EXHIBIT 4
COMPETITORS—DESCRIPTION

Target Corporation
Target operates as two reportable segments. Its Retail Segment includes its merchandising operations, including its online business. Its Credit Card Segment provides the Target Visa and the Target Card credit cards, as well as the Target Debit Card. Target's Canadian segment consists of its leasehold interests in Canada. It operates Target general merchandise stores and SuperTarget® stores, providing a range of general merchandise and food. The company's merchandise includes household products, hardlines, apparel and accessories, food and pet supplies and home furnishings and decor. As of January 28, 2012, Target had 1,763 stores in 49 states and the District of Columbia.

Kroger Co.
Kroger operates retail food and drug stores, multi-department stores, jewelry stores and convenience stores. It also manufactures and processes some of the food for sale in its supermarkets. As of January 29, 2011, Kroger operated, either directly or through its subsidiaries, 2,460 supermarkets and multi-department stores, 1,014 of which had fuel centres. In addition, as of January 29, 2011, it operated through subsidiaries 784 convenience stores and 361 fine jewelry stores. Additionally, 87 convenience stores were operated through franchise agreements. These convenience stores offer an assortment of staple food items and general merchandise and, in most cases, sell gasoline.

Costco Wholesale Corp.
Costco Wholesale operates membership warehouses. Its products include sundries, such as candy, snack foods, tobacco, alcoholic and nonalcoholic beverages and cleaning and institutional supplies; hardlines, such as appliances, electronics, health and beauty aids, hardware, office supplies, cameras, garden and patio, sporting goods, toys, seasonal items and automotive supplies; food, such as dry and packaged foods; softlines, such as apparel, domestics, jewelry, housewares, media, home furnishings and small appliances; fresh food, such as meat, bakery, deli and produce; and ancillary and other, such as gas stations, pharmacy, food court, optical, one-hour photo, hearing aid and travel.

Safeway Inc.
Safeway is a food and drug retailer in North America, with 1,678 stores at December 31, 2011. Its U.S. retail operations are located principally in California, Hawaii, Oregon, Washington, Alaska, Colorado, Arizona, Texas, the Chicago metropolitan area and the Mid-Atlantic region. Its Canadian retail operations are located principally in British Columbia, Alberta and Manitoba/Saskatchewan. Its stores provide an array of grocery items tailored to local preferences. Most stores provide food and general merchandise and include specialty departments such as bakery, delicatessen, floral, seafood and pharmacy. The majority of stores provide Starbucks coffee shops and adjacent fuel centres.

Amazon.com
Amazon.com serves consumers through its retail websites. It provides merchandise and content purchased for resale from vendors and those provided by third-party sellers; it also manufactures and sells the Kindle e-reader. It provides services such as Amazon Web Services; fulfillment; miscellaneous marketing and promotional agreements, such as online advertising; and co-branded credit cards. It has two principal segments: North America, which consists of retail sales of consumer products and subscriptions through North America-focused websites; and International, which consists of retail sales of consumer products and subscriptions through internationally focused locations.

Dollar General

Dollar General is a discount retailer. As of February 25, 2011, it operated 9,414 retail stores located in 35 states in the southern, southwestern, midwestern and eastern United States. It provides a selection of merchandise, including consumables, seasonal, home products and apparel. Its products portfolio includes home cleaning supplies, food, beverages and snacks, personal care products, pet supplies, decorations, toys, batteries, small electronics, greeting cards, stationery, prepaid cell phones and accessories, gardening supplies, hardware, and automotive and home office supplies, as well as a selection of home products and apparel products.

Dollar Tree, Inc.

Dollar Tree is an operator of discount variety stores providing merchandise at the fixed price of $1.00. Its merchandise mix consists of consumable merchandise, which includes candy and food and health and beauty care, and household consumables such as paper, plastics, house chemicals and frozen food; variety merchandise, which includes toys, housewares, gifts, party goods, greeting cards, softlines and other items; and seasonal goods, which include Easter, Halloween and Christmas merchandise. At January 28, 2012, it operated 4,252 stores in 48 states and the District of Columbia, as well as 99 stores in Canada under the Dollar Tree, Deal$, Dollar Tree Deal$, Dollar Giant and Dollar Bills names.

Big Lots, Inc.

Big Lots is a broadline close-out retailer. Its merchandising categories consist of Consumables, which include food, health and beauty, plastics, paper, chemical and pet departments; Furniture, which includes the upholstery, mattresses, ready-to-assemble and case goods departments; Home, which includes domestics, stationery and home decorative departments; Hardlines, which include electronics, appliances, tools and home maintenance departments; Seasonal, which includes lawn and garden, Christmas, summer and other holiday departments; and Other, which includes toy, jewelry, infant accessories and apparel departments. At January 29, 2011, it operated a total of 1,398 stores in 48 states.

Fred's Inc.

Fred's operates discount general merchandise stores and pharmacies. Its stores generally serve low, middle and fixed income families located in small- to medium-sized towns. It also markets goods and services to its 24 franchised stores. Its stores stock over 12,000 purchased items that address the needs of its customers, including brand name products, its label products and off-brand products. Its FRED'S brand products include household cleaning supplies, health and beauty aids, disposable diapers, pet foods, paper products and a variety of food and beverage products. As of January 29, 2011, it had 653 retail stores and 313 pharmacies in 15 states primarily in the southeastern United States.

Sears Holding Corp.

Sears Holdings is the parent company of Kmart Holding Corporation (Kmart) and Sears, Roebuck and Co. (Sears). It is a broadline retailer with 2,172 full-line and 1,338 specialty retail stores in the United States operating through Kmart and Sears and 500 full-line and specialty retail stores in Canada operating through Sears Canada Inc., a 95%-owned subsidiary. As of January 28, 2012, it operated three reportable segments: Kmart, Sears Domestic and Sears Canada.

Walgreen Co.

Walgreen, together with its subsidiaries, operates a retail drugstore chain. It sells prescription and non-prescription drugs as well as general merchandise, including household products, convenience and fresh foods, personal care, beauty care, photofinishing and candy. Its pharmacy, health and wellness services include retail, specialty, infusion and respiratory services, mail service, convenient care clinics and worksite clinics. In addition, its Take Care Health Systems, Inc. subsidiary is a manager of worksite health centres and in-store convenient care clinics. As of August 31, 2011, it operated 8,210 locations in 50 states, the District of Columbia, Puerto Rico and Guam.

CVS Caremark Corporation

CVS Caremark, together with its subsidiaries, is a pharmacy health care provider in the United States. Its segments include Pharmacy Services, which provides a range of pharmacy benefit management services including mail order pharmacy services, specialty pharmacy services, plan design and administration, formulary management and claims processing; and Retail Pharmacy, which sells prescription drugs and a range of general merchandise, including over-the-counter drugs, beauty products and cosmetics, photo finishing, seasonal merchandise, greeting cards and convenience foods. As of December 31, 2011, it had 7,300 CVS/pharmacy® retail stores.

Carrefour S.A.

Carrefour is a distribution group based in France. It engages in retailing business primarily in Europe, Asia, and Latin America. It operates under four main grocery store formats: hypermarkets (offers food and non-food product lines); supermarkets; hard discount (offers a reduced range at discount prices); and convenience stores, which included Cash & Carry stores (which are conveniences stores for professionals) and E-commerce. Some of its trade names are Carrefour, Carrefour Market, GB, GS, Dia, Ed, Shopi, Marche Plus, 8 a Huit, Proxi, Promocash and Docks Markets. As of December 31, 2010, it operated 15,937 stores worldwide.

Tesco plc.

Tesco is engaged in retailing and associated activities. Its core U.K. segment consists of four different store formats: Express, Metro, Superstore and Extra, as well as one trial format called Homeplus. Its Non-Food segment includes merchandise such as electricals, home entertainment, clothing, health and beauty, stationery, cookshop and soft furnishings, and seasonal goods such as barbecues and garden furniture in the summer. Its Retailing Services segment consists of several operations, including Tesco Personal Finance, Tesco.com and Tesco Telecoms. Its International segment operates in 13 markets outside the United Kingdom in Europe, Asia (including India) and North America.

Source: Mergent.

EXHIBIT 5
WALMART STOCK PRICE
FEBRUARY 2002 TO FEBRUARY 2012

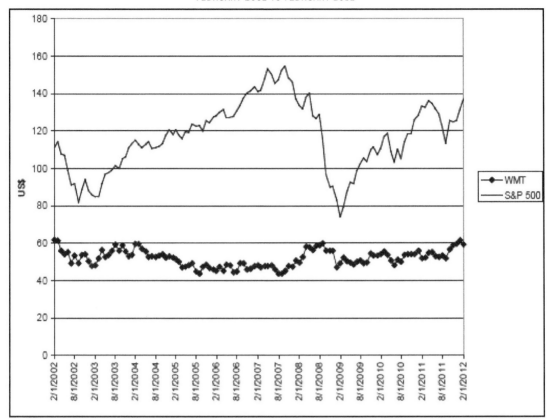

Source: Yahoo! Finance.

3 TESLA MOTORS: EVALUATING A GROWTH COMPANY

BY MAUREEN MCNICHOLS, ANNE CASSCELLS, AND JACLYN FOROUGHI

TSLA down ~$500M Friday, but back up ~$500M today. Sorry for the roller coaster.

—Elon Musk, co-founder and CEO, Tesla Motors

In January 2010, Tesla Motors filed Form S-1 with the U.S. Securities and Exchange Commission, indicating its intention to register for a proposed initial public offering (IPO). Over the next five months, world stock markets wavered as a result of the European sovereign debt crisis, and volatility soared following the "Flash Crash" that left U.S. exchanges with their largest intraday losses ever. Despite worldwide market and economic uncertainty, Tesla debuted its stock in June 2010 on the NASDAQ Stock Market (Ticker Symbol: TSLA). The stock price jumped over 40 percent in its first day of trading to close at $23.89 in an upsized deal that valued the company at $2 billion and raised over $226 million (see **Exhibit 1** for Tesla's annotated stock chart from IPO through first quarter 2013). It was the first initial public offering by an American automaker since Ford's debut in 1956.

While the primary market showed strong enthusiasm for the stock, the secondary market was much less convinced. Concerns were raised about the long-term viability of the company stemming from a limited operating history, a long history of losses, liquidity issues, unreliable consumer demand, expensive battery technology, and competition from traditional automakers. As a result, the stock was frequently the subject of high short interest, a predictor of lower investment performance (see **Exhibit 2** for Tesla's short interest ratio from IPO through first quarter 2013).[a] The question plaguing investors was: were the short-sellers correct in their bearish sentiment or was a short squeeze imminent?

Maureen F. McNichols, Anne Casscells, and Jaclyn Foroughi, "Tesla Motors: Evaluating a Growth Company," Stanford Graduate School of Business. Copyright © 2013 by Stanford Graduate School of Business. Reprinted with permission.

---

[a] Paul Asquith, Parag A. Pathak, and Jay R. Ritter, "Short Interest and Stock Returns," National Bureau of Economic Research Working Paper No. 10434, April 2004.

Jaclyn Foroughi, CFA, Anne Casscells, Principal of Aetos Capital and Lecturer, and Professor Maureen McNichols prepared this case as the basis for class discussion rather than to illustrate either effective or ineffective handling of an administrative situation.

TESLA HISTORY

ROAD TO IPO

Founding

Engineers Martin Eberhard and Marc Tarpenning originally incorporated Tesla Motors Inc. in July 2003, and were later joined by Elon Musk as chairman of the Board, JB Straubel as CTO and Ian Wright as VP of Vehicle Development (see **Exhibit 3** for Tesla's timeline from 2003 through 2012).[b] Eberhard assumed the role of CEO while Tarpenning became CFO. The original business model focused on building the first high-performance fully electric vehicle with a high price point to defray start-up costs.[c]

Concurrent with his role as chairman of the Board, Musk took an active part in the design of the company's first production vehicle, the Roadster. He was also the controlling investor in Tesla from the first financing round, leading or co-leading nearly every round until February 2008, just prior to the initial public offering (see **Exhibit 4** for a list of Tesla's private funding sources).

Tesla management targeted an original delivery date of June 2007 for the Roadster and by late 2007, the company had already taken pre-sales of 570 2008 Roadsters; however the first Roadster was not delivered until February 2008.[d] In fact, the company stopped taking reservations and instead initiated a waiting list, charging customers $5,000 for the opportunity to purchase the sports car priced at over $100,000. With the delay in Roadster delivery and significant cost overruns, Eberhard was asked to transition out of his role as CEO, a position that was assumed by Elon Musk in October 2008.

Elon Musk Takes Over

After having sold his prior ventures, Zip2 to Compaq's AltaVista division in 1999 and PayPal to eBay in 2002, and founding SpaceX in 2002, Musk had already built up a reputation as "an entrepreneurial legend."[e] However, by the time Musk assumed the helm as CEO, Tesla had already gone through three CEOs and was named in a number of lawsuits.

Despite the contentious management turnover, Musk forged ahead with Tesla's "master plan" as posted on Tesla's blog:

1. Build sports car
2. Use that money to build an affordable car
3. Use *that* money to build an even more affordable car
4. While doing above, also provide zero emission electric power generation options[f]

In order to reach his goal, Musk continued to develop Tesla's proprietary electric powertrain technology, which incorporated commoditized lithium-ion battery packs at lower cost and higher energy relative to competing battery makers. In doing so, the company amassed a portfolio of significant intellectual property that formed the foundation for future vehicles.[g]

---

b   All five men were later cited as founders of the company following an out-of-court settlement to a lawsuit filed in 2009. See "Judge Strikes Claim on Who Can Be Declared a Founder of Tesla Motors," Tesla Motors press release July 29, 2009, http://www.teslamotors.com/de_CH/about/press/releases/judge-strikes-claim-who-can-be-declaredfounder-tesla-motors (April 19, 2013).

c   Martin Eberhard, "The Future of Cars is Electric," Tesla Motors, August 7, 2007, http://webarchive.teslamotors.com/display_data/pressguild.swf (April 19, 2013).

d   Tesla Form S-1, p. 22.

e   Owen Thomas, "Tesla's Elon Musk: 'I ran out of cash'," VentureBeat, May 27, 2010, http://venturebeat.com/2010/05/27/elon-musk-personal-finances/ (April 19, 2013).

f   Tesla Blog, http://www.teslamotors.com/blog/secret-tesla-motors-master-plan-just-between-you-and-me, August 2, 2006 (April 19, 2013).

g   Tesla Motors 2012 Annual Report, p. 5.

An early prototype of the Model S sedan was introduced in March 2009 with a base price of $49,900. Unlike the Roadster, which was developed using a Lotus Elise glider, the Model S was designed "with an adaptable platform architecture and common electric powertrain to provide ... the flexibility to use the Model S platform to cost efficiently launch new electric vehicle models subsequent to the start of production of the Model S."[h]

The adaptability of Tesla's technology led to a relationship with Daimler AG in March 2008. Under the agreement, Tesla would provide up to 1,000 battery packs and chargers for the Daimler Smart fortwo electric vehicles (and later, the A-Class and B-Class electric vehicles). Subsequently, in May 2010, Tesla entered into a relationship with Toyota Motor Corporation to develop a full electric powertrain system for the Toyota RAV4 EV. In return, Toyota was to support Tesla "with sourcing parts and production and engineering expertise for Model S."[i] This included a $50 million investment by Toyota to finance a portion of the purchase of a defunct auto manufacturing plant in Fremont, California, less than twenty miles away from the Tesla headquarters in Palo Alto.[j] The intended use of the facility was for the production of the Model S as well as future electric vehicles.

The End of the Roadster

By the end of 2009, Tesla had sold over 900 Roadsters to customers in 18 countries and marked its first month of profitability in July 2009 when the company shipped a record 109 vehicles.[k] Still, from its inception in 2003 to September 30, 2009, the company had generated net losses of $236.4 million on revenues of $108.2 million. Thus, while Musk had accomplished his initial goal of building a sports car, he had not been successful in generating significant cash to build a more affordable car—the Model S.

Consequently, Tesla continued to secure additional sources of funding including two rounds of financing led by Daimler, which resulted in a 10 percent stake in the company in mid-2009. Around the same time, Tesla also obtained a $465 million loan from the U.S. Department of Energy (DOE), which had indicated that strategic partnerships with creditworthy companies would be a major advantage in its award of loan guarantees.[l] As part of the loan agreement, Tesla would use the DOE funds to support two specific projects: the production, engineering, and assembly of the all-electric Model S sedan, and a powertrain manufacturing facility to build advanced electric vehicle powertrain components for other automakers.

With an improving financial market and a renewed focus on a more affordable sedan, Tesla turned to the equity market to raise an additional $100 million. Instead, the company raised over double that amount as a result of enthusiasm surrounding the company's vision and the potential of the electric vehicle market.

ELECTRIC VEHICLE MARKET

GLOBAL ELECTRIC VEHICLE GROWTH

From 2007 to 2011, the global electric vehicle market grew at a compound annual growth rate (CAGR) of 135 percent, which was substantially higher than the global internal combustion engine growth rate of 2 percent over the same period.[m] Driven by a desire to improve fuel efficiency and minimize carbon dioxide (CO_2) emissions, both consumer demand and production efforts to meet those demands increased greatly. In 2011,

---

h   Tesla Motors Form S-1, p. 6.
i   Ibid, p. 15.
j   "Tesla Notifies SEC of Agreement with Toyota to Develop Electric Version of RAV4," Tesla Motors press release, October 13, 2010, http://ir.teslamotors.com/releasedetail.cfm?releaseid=518184 (April 19, 2013).
k   "Tesla Motors Attains Profitability Milestone," Business Wire, August 7, 2009, http://money.cnn.com/2009/08/07/technology/tesla_profitability/ (April 19, 2013).
l   "Advanced Technology Vehicles Manufacturing Incentive Program," Section 136 *Code of Federal Regulations*, Pt. 611. 2008 ed.
m   Ryan Brinkman, Amy L. Carroll and Samik Chatterjee, "Tesla Motors: Initiate TSLA at Neutral, on Combination of Clear Investment Positives with Execution Risk and Full Valuation," J.P. Morgan, December 18, 2012.

the total units of light vehicle production were 77 million, with electrical vehicles comprising 0.1 percent of total global production (see **Exhibit 5** for electric vehicle global market penetration forecasts).

Though a small market compared to global production, electric vehicle production was projected to continue to grow at an annual rate of 26 percent during 2012 to 2020, while internal combustion engine production was expected to grow at an annual rate of 3 percent over the same period. At this rate, electric vehicles were expected to comprise 0.8 percent of total global production in 2020. Musk, meanwhile, had suggested that electric vehicles would be the only cars sold in America by 2030 and the only vehicles on the road by mid-century.[n]

MODEL S RESERVATION GROWTH

Less than 24 hours after the Model S was revealed to the public, over 500 reservations were received with a minimum refundable deposit of $5,000 (see **Exhibit 6** for Model S reservations, production, and deliveries from the first quarter of 2009 through 2012).[o] Nearly nine months later, reservations swelled to approximately four times that amount. While orders stabilized over the three years ending December 31, 2012, the positive momentum continued with reservation payments for the Model S growing at a 64 percent compound annual growth rate.

Because of its reputation as "the first company to commercially produce a federally-compliant, fully electric vehicle that achieves market-leading range on a single charge,"[p] Tesla was able to generate significant reservation growth without the use of conventional means of advertising:

> To date, media coverage and word of mouth have been the primary drivers of our sales leads and have helped us achieve sales without traditional advertising and at relatively low marketing costs. We also use traditional means of advertising including product placement in a variety of media outlets and pay-per-click advertisements on websites and applications relevant to our target demographics.[q]

Contributing to demand was the desire by customers to limit or fully extinguish any reliability on petroleum-based transportation due to rising fuel costs and a desire to mitigate the environmental impact from carbon emissions. Unlike hybrid vehicles, which combine a conventional internal combustion engine with an electric powertrain, fully electric vehicles rely solely on an electric powertrain and batteries that are charged by plugging the vehicle into an electric power source. Although most U.S. electricity production contributes to air pollution because of its use of fossil fuels, the U.S. Environmental Protection Agency categorizes all-electric vehicles as zero-emission vehicles because they produce no direct exhaust or emissions.[r] Finally, Tesla estimates that the Model S could save consumers approximately $1,800 per year in fuel costs relative to a comparable premium internal combustion engine sedan.[s]

Another factor increasing demand for Tesla's electric vehicle was the sleek design and leading performance. These unmatched characteristics helped the Model S claim both the 2013 *Automobile Magazine* Automobile of the Year and 2013 Motor Trend Car of the Year:

n   Elon Musk, "Past, Present and Future," Clean Tech Investor Summit 2011, The Renaissance Esmerelda Resort and Spa, Indian Wells, CA, January 19, 2011.
o   Tesla Motors Spring 2012 Investor Presentation, p. 14.
p   Tesla Motors 2012 Annual Report, p. 11.
q   Tesla Motors 2012 Annual Report, loc. cit.
r   "All-Electric Vehicles," U.S. Department of Energy: Alternative Fuels Data Center, April 19, 2013, http://www.afdc.energy.gov/vehicles/electric_basics_ev.html (April 19, 2013).
s   Assumes an average of 12,000 miles driven per year, an average electricity cost of 11.2 cents per kilowatt-hour and an average gasoline price of $3.32 per gallon over the full ownership of the vehicle. (Tesla Motors 2012 Annual Report, p. 10).

The 2013 Motor Trend Car of the Year is one of the quickest American four-doors ever built. It drives like a sports car, eager and agile and instantly responsive. But it's also as smoothly effortless as a Rolls-Royce, can carry almost as much stuff as a Chevy Equinox, and is more efficient than a Toyota Prius. Oh, and it'll sashay up to the valet at a luxury hotel like a supermodel working a Paris catwalk. By any measure, the Tesla Model S is a truly remarkable automobile, perhaps the most accomplished all-new luxury car since the original Lexus LS 400.

That's why it's our 2013 Car of the Year. Wait. No mention of the astonishing inflection point the Model S represents—that this is the first [Car of the Year] winner in the 64-year history of the award not powered by an internal combustion engine? Sure, the Tesla's electric powertrain delivers the driving characteristics and packaging solutions that make the Model S stand out against many of its internal combustion engine peers. But it's only a part of the story. At its core, the Tesla Model S is simply a damned good car you happen to plug in to refuel.[t]

REGULATORY INCENTIVES

Another driver of producer supply and consumer demand in the electric vehicle market was regulatory incentives. Under the U.S. Internal Revenue Service's New Qualified Plug-in Electric Drive Motor Vehicle Credit, consumers were entitled to a federal tax credit up to $7,500 for new qualified plug-in electric vehicles. The credit is comprised of a $2,500 fixed amount in addition to $417 for each kilowatt-hour of battery capacity over 4 kilowatt-hours not exceeding $5,000. As a result, electric vehicles such as the Model S qualified for the full $7,500 credit while the Toyota Prius Plug-in Hybrid was only eligible for a $2,500 credit due to its smaller battery capacity. Buyers of electric vehicles were also allowed various additional state and local incentives including reduced home electricity bills, free parking, and use of High-Occupancy Vehicle (HOV) or carpool lanes.

Electric car manufacturers were also entitled to a number of regulatory incentives including zero emissions vehicle (ZEV) and greenhouse gas (GHG) credits as well as low-interest loans. Under California's Low-Emission Vehicle Regulation, vehicle manufacturers were required to ensure that a portion of vehicles delivered for sale were zero emission vehicles. Because Tesla was a manufacturer of zero emission vehicles only, they earned credits on each vehicle sold and could then sell those excess credits to manufacturers with deficits. Similarly, under the Environmental Protection Agency's national greenhouse gas emission standards, manufacturers were required to meet average fleet-wide carbon dioxide emissions standards; those manufacturers whose fleet-wide average performed better earned credits, which they were permitted to sell to manufacturers whose fleet failed to meet the required standards. As a result, Tesla had earned revenue from the sale of such credits in the amounts of $40.5 million, $2.7 million, and $2.8 million for the years ended December 31, 2012, 2011, and 2010, respectively.

Under the Department of Energy's Advanced Technology Vehicles Manufacturing (ATVM) Loan Program, Tesla received a loan in June 2009 that provided "for projects that reequip, expand, and establish manufacturing facilities in the United States to produce light-duty vehicles and components for such vehicles, which provide meaningful improvements in fuel economy performance beyond certain specified levels."[u] The loan had a weighted-average interest rate of approximately 1.5 percent,[v] which was "equal to the cost of funds to the Department of the Treasury for obligations of comparable maturity" set at the time

t   Angus MacKenzie, "2013 Motor Trend Car of the Year: Tesla Model S," *Motor Trend*, January 2013.
u   *Code of Federal Regulations*, op. cit., p. 66721.
v   Tesla Motors 2012 Annual Report, p. 85.

loans were disbursed, and significantly lower than the prevailing U.S. private sector lending interest rate of 3.3 percent at the time.[w]

INDUSTRY CHALLENGES

BATTERY TECHNOLOGY

One of the key challenges facing the electric vehicle market was "range anxiety," or a fear that an electric vehicle had limited drivable miles per charge and would strand its occupants. As a result, a demand for extensive public charging networks developed to help alleviate this concern. Tesla's strategy addressed these needs in two ways: first, management sought to develop a vehicle with exceptional range, performance, and styling; second, the company introduced a network of fast charging Superchargers along key routes in North America.

The Roadster had a range of 236 miles while the Model S had a range of up to 265 miles on a single charge.[x] Meanwhile, mass-market competitors such as Nissan launched the fully electric Nissan Leaf with a range of 100 miles. The notably wider range of Tesla vehicles was principally due to substantially larger battery-packs deployed in their vehicles. While Tesla's battery pack had over 7,000 cells and up to 85 kilowatt-hours, the Nissan Leaf had fewer than 200 cells and 24 kilowatt-hours.

Mass-market competitors relied on a public electric vehicle charging network known as ChargePoint® developed by an independent third party. Tesla, however, developed and constructed its own proprietary Supercharger network that was offered free to vehicles with the largest 85 kilowatt-hour batteries and as an upfront option for 60 kilowatt-hour owners. Whereas it took over seven hours to replenish 50 percent of the Model S at a ChargePoint location, the Supercharger was able to do the same in 30 minutes, saving customers hours in charging time.[y]

Despite addressing concerns over "range anxiety," consumer demand for electric vehicles remained muted relative to overall vehicle production in 2011, capturing just 0.1 percent of the market, as mentioned earlier.[z] This was due in part to high electric vehicle prices as a result of costly batteries. A report by technology research firm Gartner Inc., suggested that electric vehicles were in a "trough of disillusionment" and would not experience full production for more than ten years:

> Due to high battery costs, EVs should initially be offered as premium vehicles with sport and technology sophistication or as small city cars. A breakthrough in battery technology, subsequent cost reductions and capacity increases will be needed to achieve broad market adoption.[aa]

Unlike its competitors, Tesla used thousands of small cylindrical lithium-ion cells, which were commoditized and provided a cost advantage relative to competitors' prismatic cells. And while prismatic cells offered reduced complexity, Tesla developed a proprietary battery management system to optimize performance, safety and useful life.

---

w   "Lending Interest Rate (%)," The World Bank: World Development Indicators, April 19, 2013, http://data.worldbank.org/indicator/FR.INR.LEND (April 19, 2013).
x   http://www.fueleconomy.gov/feg/evsbs.shtml (April 19, 2013).
y   Assumes the use of a 30 amperage J-1772 adapter and an additional 26 miles of driving per hour of charging.
z   Brinkman, Carroll, and Chatterjee, op. cit., p. 11.
aa   Simon Mingay and Stephen Stokes, "Hype Cycle for Sustainability and Green IT, 2012," Gartner Inc., July 31, 2012, p. 92.

While traditional automakers launched versions of electric vehicles to meet consumer and regulatory demands for more stringent fuel economy standards, these vehicles mainly targeted the mass market (see **Exhibit 7** for competing electric vehicle launches). The Model S, on the other hand, while more affordable than the Roadster, was still priced at the mid- to high-end of the luxury market. This made comparable analysis difficult, particularly given Tesla's newly developed and highly differentiated business model.

Tesla focused purely on electric vehicles as opposed to most competitors who diversified their strategies with hybrids or internal combustion engine vehicles. In addition, Tesla developed and manufactured the majority of its parts internally, while most of its competitors outsourced similar parts.[ab] And while larger automakers operated on much greater scales and benefited from brand recognition, larger distribution networks and access to financial resources, they were also encumbered with hefty costs associated with pensions and other post-employment benefits (OPEB).

TESLA'S FINANCIAL PERFORMANCE

REVENUE ANALYSIS

While Tesla historically derived revenues primarily from the sales of the Roadster and from electric powertrain development services, the Model S became the primary contributor to revenue beginning in the fourth quarter of 2012. For the year ended 2012, total revenues for the company were $413 million, which was composed of $386 million in automotive sales (93 percent of total revenues) and $28 million in development services (7 percent of total revenues). Automotive sales were further segmented into vehicle, options, and related sales (86 percent of total revenues) and powertrain component and related sales (8 percent of total revenues). Vehicle, options, and related sales (86 percent of total revenues) incorporated sales of the Model S and Roadster, vehicle options, accessories and destination charges, and service provided by Tesla Rangers, along with regulatory credit sales and lease revenue. Meanwhile, powertrain component and related sales (8 percent of total revenues), included sales of battery packs and drive units to other manufacturers. Development services (7 percent of total revenues) included revenue earned from Daimler and Toyota agreements (see **Exhibit 8** for Tesla's revenue trend from 2008 through 2012).

COST ANALYSIS

Cost of Revenues
Automotive sales costs for the year ended 2012 were $372 million while development services were $12 million. Costs of automotive sales (97 percent of total cost of revenues) included "direct parts, material and labor costs, manufacturing overhead, including amortized tooling costs, royalty fees, shipping and logistic costs and reserves for estimated warranty expenses."

Adjustments to warranty expenses and charges for inventory were also included in automotive sales costs. Development services costs (3 percent of total cost of revenues) included development expenses, such as engineering support and testing, direct parts material and labor costs and manufacturing overhead incurred in the performance of services under development agreements (see **Exhibit 9** for Tesla's cost of revenue and operating costs trend from 2008 through 2012).

---

ab   Dan Galves, Rod Lache, and Patrick Nola, CFA, "Tesla Motors: Initiating coverage with a Hold recommendation," Deutsche Bank, August 9, 2010.

Operating Costs

Tesla's operating costs consisted primarily of research and development, sales, general and administrative costs, and share-based compensation. Research and development accounted for 65 percent of total operating costs for the year ended 2012, as the company focused its efforts on the development of its planned Model X crossover sports utility vehicle and electric powertrain components and increased production capacity to produce the Model S and electric powertrain components. Sales, general and administrative costs (35 percent of total operating costs) and stock-based compensation (12 percent of total operating costs) continued their upward trajectory in 2012 as the company focused on opening new Tesla sales and service centers, expanded its Supercharger network, and compensated staff with stock-based incentives.

Capital Expenditures

Following the purchase of its manufacturing facility in May 2010, Tesla had to continually invest in manufacturing equipment and supplier tooling in order to ready the plant for scale production (see **Exhibit 10** for Tesla's capital expenditures schedule from 2008 through 2012). As a result, capital expenditures in 2012 were $239 million, a 30 percent increase from the prior year, and 58 percent of total revenues in 2012. The company planned to spend significantly less on capital expenditures in 2013.

BOTTOM LINE

In its ramp to steady state production, the company experienced a widening net loss in 2012 relative to prior years of operation. For the year ended 2012, Tesla's net loss was $396 million, a 56 percent increase in losses from the prior year, and greater than the expected consensus estimate loss of $366 million (see **Exhibit 11** for Tesla's consolidated income statement, balance sheet and cash flow statements).

LIMITED OPERATING HISTORY

With just over five years of experience in the delivery of vehicles, Tesla had a very limited operating history available upon which to accurately evaluate the business. As the company admitted in its Form S-1 prior to its IPO, and in subsequent annual reports, "We have no experience to date in high volume manufacturing of our electric vehicles."[ac] As a result, analysts at the time of the IPO were quick to identify execution risk as a primary limitation in the company's ramp from niche to volume manufacturing:

> Though the successful launch of the Roadster provides proof-of-concept and valuable brand cachet, Tesla faces substantial execution risk as it burns roughly $650 million to get its luxury sedan to production. Multiple major auto firms plan to launch competing electric vehicles by 2011 and Tesla's integrated sales model is untested at scale.[ad]

Indeed, the company underwent a fundamental shift in design, manufacturing, and sales efforts from 2008 to 2012 as it transitioned away from the niche Lotus Elise glider-based Roadster to an entirely new luxury sedan concept with a much broader customer base. Not only was the Model S conceived from the ground up but management also faced the challenge of building it to scale, while conceptualizing an entirely new approach to distribution.

---

ac   Tesla Motors Form S-1, p. 22.
ad   Renaissance Capital IPO Research, "Tesla Motors (TSLA)," August 6, 2010.

Instead of leveraging an independent dealer network, Tesla sold its vehicles directly to the consumer over the phone and Internet, and later through sales and service storefronts throughout North America, Europe, and Asia. While this distribution approach had a number of advantages such as the ability to charge retail versus wholesale prices, generate profits from warranty repairs, and ensure the strategic position of each location, it was also the subject of legal action and strategic impediments as a result of various laws in jurisdictions that restricted its vehicle reservation practices.[ae]

Accentuating its limited operating experience in vehicle manufacturing were significant production delays and safety recalls with its first produced vehicle, the Roadster. The company initially announced plans to deliver the Tesla Roadster in June 2007, but due to various design and production delays, the company did not deliver its first Roadster until eight months later in February 2008. As a result, the company suffered further costs and adverse publicity, as well as a significant number of order cancellations. In addition, the company experienced two product recalls for the Roadster in May 2009 and October 2010, which adversely affected the company's brand.

VIABILITY ISSUES

As the company noted in its Form S-1, "We have a history of losses and we expect significant increases in our costs and expenses to result in continuing losses for at least the foreseeable future." While this risk was updated two years later in the 2012 Tesla Motors Annual Report to read, "We have a history of losses and have to deliver significant cost reductions to achieve profitability in 2013 and long-term commercial success," the message was the same: the company had a long history of losses.

With net losses in each quarter and over $1 billion in accumulated losses since inception, it was imperative for the company to achieve planned cost reductions and control operational costs in the ramp to volume production of the Model S. For the year ended 2012, the company generated a cash deficit of $396 million, or roughly $33 million per month, suggesting the need for an additional capital raise.[af] Meanwhile, for the year ended 2012, working capital turned negative for the first time since 2008, and negative free cash flow swelled to $505 million.

During the month of December 2012, however, the company generated positive free cash flow, through increasing sales and careful working capital management:

> Since we are now producing cars at steady state production, we have shifted our focus to cost reduction. As a result, the cost of producing Model S is beginning to decline. Our operations in 2013 are already more efficient compared to Q4, as we continue to stabilize and improve the production process. In addition, further cost reduction efforts undertaken by both us and our suppliers will continue to reduce costs in Q1 and in upcoming quarters. Consequently, we expect gross margin to continue to improve towards our 25 percent target by year-end.[ag]

MANAGEMENT ISSUES

Fair Disclosure

While Musk "lends visionary leadership, and is backed by a management team with solid functional strength,"[ah] he was just as readily referred to as a "prickly interlocutor."[ai] His use of social networking sites such as Twitter

ae   Tesla Blog, http://www.teslamotors.com/blog/tesla-approach-distributing-and-servicing-cars, October 22, 2012 (April 19, 2013).
af   Brinkman, Carroll, and Chatterjee, op. cit., p. 5.
ag   Tesla Motors 2012 Shareholder Letter, p. 3.
ah   Brinkman, Carroll, and Chatterjee, op. cit., p. 3.
ai   John Reed, "Elon Musk's Ground-Breaking Electric Car," *Financial Times*, July 24, 2009.

to post material facts about the company's financials or upcoming announcements stoked controversy as some questioned whether this medium was a fair manner, as outlined by the SEC's Regulation Fair Disclosure (Reg FD), in which to disclose information:

> Elon Musk, CEO of electric car and component maker Tesla Motors, arguably has garnered the most attention for his use of Twitter to release–or preview–company news.
> The latest example came last week, when Musk signaled that he would make another investment in the company by tweeting 'am going to put my money where my mouth is in a major way.'
> That followed an early December tweet in which Musk said he was 'happy to report that Tesla was narrowly cash flow positive last week' and that 'continued improvement was expected through year end.'[aj]

Unreliable Guidance

Tesla management faced particular criticism for repeated missed guidance with respect to production delays and financial guidance. Production delays began with the postponed delivery of the Roadster from June 2007 to February 2008 due to "various design and production delays." This was followed by the delivery of 2,650 Model S vehicles relative to guidance of 5,000 for all of 2012 due to "stringent quality standards."[ak] At the same time, deliveries for the company's planned future crossover, the Model X, was delayed from late 2013 to late 2014 as the company focused on production and deliveries of Model S.

In addition to production delays, the company's financial guidance has also missed on repeated occasions:

- In its first quarter 2012 earnings call, management indicated that Model S vehicles would be available for test drives in all Tesla stores by the end the month (May 2012). Test drives for the Model S were exclusively offered to current reservation holders in late June 2012.[al]
- In its second quarter 2012 Shareholder Letter, management reported expectations for positive automotive sales gross margin just before the end of the third quarter. The company later reported automotive sales gross margins of -17.5 percent for the third quarter.
- In its second quarter 2012 Shareholder Letter, management reported expectations for "close to flat" free cash flow at the end of the fourth quarter of 2012. The company later reported negative free cash flow of $102 million for the fourth quarter of 2012.
- In its third quarter 2012 Shareholder Letter, management reported expectations for positive free cash flow at the end of 2012. The company later reported negative free cash flow of $505 million for the year.
- In its third quarter 2012 Shareholder Letter, management reduced prior revenue guidance for 2012 provided in its second quarter 2012 Shareholder Letter from a range of $560 million to $600 million to a range of $400 million to $440 million. The company later reported 2012 revenues of $413 million.

Stock Options

In August 2010, Tesla began reporting quarterly results through press releases or Shareholder Letters on its website in addition to filing with the SEC. In its non-SEC communications, however, the company consistently reported earnings on a non-GAAP basis, which excludes the impact of stock options. Meanwhile, management earned much of their compensation in the form of equity or stock options. For example, in August 2012, Musk, who earned a salary of [one dollar],[am] was granted over 5 million stock options "to create incentives for

---

aj   John Shinal, "New Tech Economy: Musk's Tesla Tweets Still Upbeat," *USA Today*, March 31, 2013, http://www.usatoday.com/story/tech/columnist/shinal/2013/03/31/tesla-elon-musk-twitter/2034905/ (April 19, 2013).
ak   Tesla Motors 2012 Shareholders Letter, p. 1.
al   Tesla Blog, http://www.teslamotors.com/blog/inside-tesla-060512, June 5, 2012 (April 19, 2013).
am   Tesla Form S-1, p. 134.

continued long term success beyond the Model S program and to closely align executive pay with increases in stockholder value."[an] In addition, various members of senior management were awarded stock option grants in June and September 2010, while certain non-employees were awarded stock options in 2011 and 2010. Prior to the company's initial public offering, Musk was awarded nearly 7 million stock options in December 2009.

CONCLUSION

By the end of the 2012 fiscal year, Tesla's share price was at odds with itself. Its short interest ratio remained elevated, while over half of the analysts covering the company rated the stock a "buy." In fact, since its IPO, the stock had, on average, never been rated below a "hold." Meanwhile, analyst price targets consistently forged ahead of the stock price, indicating that some additional value had yet to be realized in the stock. Does a high short interest ratio predict lower investment performance or is Tesla a compelling business opportunity with potential future growth that will offset that bet?

EXHIBIT 1
Tesla Motors (TSLA) Annotated Stock Chart Since IPO

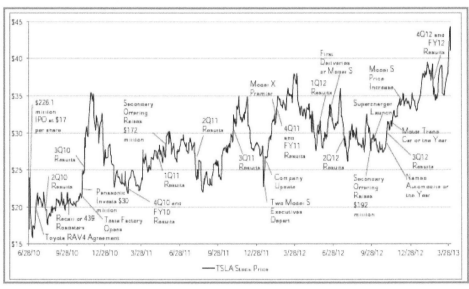

Source: Compiled from Bloomberg and company data.

---

an   Tesla 2012 Annual Report, p. 73.

EXHIBIT 2
Tesla Motors (TSLA) Short Interest Since IPO

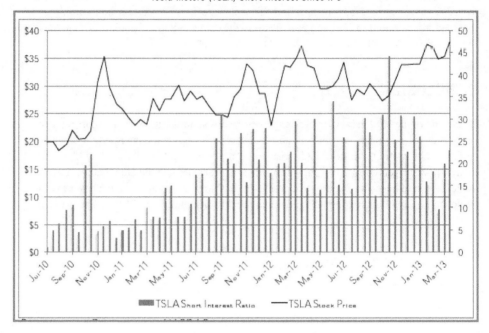

Source: Compiled from Bloomberg and NASDAQ data.

EXHIBIT 3
Tesla Motors Timeline (2003–2012)

7/03: Tesla Motors Founded

4/04: $7.5 million Series A Led by Elon Musk

2/05: $13 million Series B Led by Musk

2/07: Transmission Redesign

2/08: First Roadster Delivery

5/09: Daimler Acquires Equity Stake; First Store Opens in LA

6/10: IPO Raises $226 million

6/12: First Deliveries of Model S

Late 2012: 2013 Motor Trend Car of the Year and Automobile of the Year

8/04: Battery Development Begins

7/06: Roadster Engineering Prototype Unveiled

4/07: $45 million Series D Led by Technology Partners, Musk and Vantage Point

10/08: Musk Assumes CEO Role

1/10: Battery Partnership with Panasonic Begins

5/11: Secondary Offering Raises $172 million

2/04: Business Plan Complete

2003 2004 2005 2006 2007 2008 2009 2010 2011 2012

3/04: Private Fundraising Begins

10/04: Drivetrain Design Begins

5/06: $40 million Series C Led by Vantage Point

Late 2007: 570 Roadster Pre-Sales

3/09: Model S Prototype Unveiled

5/10: Toyota Relationship Begins; Manufacturing Plant Acquired in Fremont

2/12: Model X Unveiled

9/12: Supercharger Network Unveiled; Secondary Offering Raises $192 million

1/04: Roadster Development Begins

7/04: Lotus-based Development Begins

10/05: Motor Process Developed

Venture Partners and Musk

3/07: Validation Prototype Completed

3/08: Daimler Relationship Begins

6/09: $465 DOE Loan Approval

11/10: Panasonic Invests $30 million

Source: Compiled from company data.

EXHIBIT 4
Private Funding Sources

Date	Series	Source	Amount
April 2004	A	Elon Musk Compass Technology Partners	$7.5 million
February 2005	B	Elon Musk Compass Technology Partners Valor Equity Partners	$13 million
May 2006	C	VantagePoint Venture Partners Elon Musk Capricorn Management Compass Technology Partners Google Inc. JP Morgan Valor Equity Partners Sergey Brin Larry Page Nick Pritzker Jeff Skoll Draper Fisher Jurvetson (DFJ)	$40 million
May 2007	D	Technology Partners Venture Capital Elon Musk VantagePoint Venture Partners Capricorn Management Compass Technology Partners Draper Fisher Jurvetson (DFJ) JP Morgan Valor Equity Partners	$45 million
February 2008	E	Elon Musk	$40 million
May 2009	F	Daimler	$50 million
September 2009	Venture Round	Fjord Ventures Daimler Aabar Investments	$82.5 million
November 2010	Venture Round	Panasonic	$30 million
October 2012	Venture Round	California Energy Commission	$10 million
November 2008	Debt	Existing Investors U.S.	$40 million
June 2009	Debt	Department of Energy	$465 million

Source: Compiled from company data and CrunchBase.

EXHIBIT 5
Electric Vehicle Global Market Penetration Forecasts (2007–2020)

Units of production in thousands

000 units	2007	2008	2009	2010	2011	2012	2013	2014	2015	2016	2017	2018	2019	2020
EV	1	4	4	14	71	100	220	355	425	469	553	660	766	879
PHEV	—	—	5	7	32	89	116	176	475	639	771	920	1,017	1,125
HEV	552	594	837	1,060	1,051	1,811	1,952	2,119	2,205	2,449	2,718	2,973	3,335	3,743
ICE	70,031	66,948	58,675	73,305	75,684	79,138	80,474	84,960	89,657	93,675	96,829	99,264	100,818	102,396
Global LV Production	**70,585**	**67,546**	**59,521**	**74,386**	**76,839**	**81,146**	**82,771**	**87,611**	**92,763**	**97,233**	**100,871**	**103,825**	**105,937**	**108,143**
EV as % of global production	*0.0%*	*0.0%*	*0.0%*	*0.0%*	*0.1%*	*0.1%*	*0.3%*	*0.4%*	*0.5%*	*0.5%*	*0.5%*	*0.6%*	*0.7%*	*0.8%*
PHEV as % of global production	*0.0%*	*0.0%*	*0.0%*	*0.0%*	*0.0%*	*0.1%*	*0.1%*	*0.2%*	*0.5%*	*0.7%*	*0.8%*	*0.9%*	*1.0%*	*1.0%*
HEV as % of global production	*0.8%*	*0.9%*	*1.4%*	*1.4%*	*1.4%*	*2.2%*	*2.4%*	*2.4%*	*2.4%*	*2.5%*	*2.7%*	*2.9%*	*3.1%*	*3.5%*
ICE as % of global production	*99.2%*	*99.1%*	*98.6%*	*98.5%*	*98.5%*	*97.5%*	*97.2%*	*97.0%*	*96.7%*	*96.3%*	*96.0%*	*95.6%*	*95.2%*	*94.7%*

Source: IHS Automotive and J.P. Morgan estimates.

EXHIBIT 6

Tesla Motors Model S Reservations, Production and Deliveries (in Units)

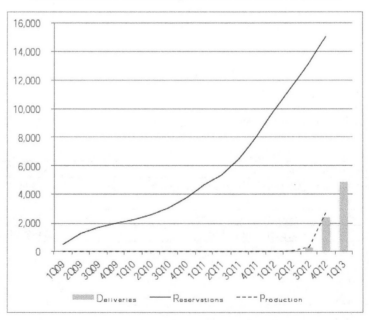

Source: Company data.

EXHIBIT 7
Competing Electric Vehicle Launches (Mainstream and High-End Vehicles)

Mass-Market Vehicles

Manufacturer	Model	Launch Date	Type	MPG (Highway)	Battery Type	Energy Density (kWh)	Power Density (kW)	All-Electric Charge miles/charge)	Performance (0–60mph)	Starting Price ($US)
Mitsubishi	iMiev	2010	EV	112	Lithium-ion	16	47	80	—	$29,975
Nissan	Leaf	2010	EV	99	Lithium-ion	24	90	100	—	$33,000
Ford	Lincoln MKZ Hybrid	2011	HEV	45	Nickel Metal Hybride	—	—	—	—	$35,925
Ford	Focus Electric	2011	EV	105	Lithium-ion	—	—	—	—	—
GM	Chevrolet Volt	2011	PHEV	40	Lithium-ion	16.5	111	38	—	$39,145
Ford	Fusion E Hybrid	2012	HEV	47	Lithium-ion	—	—	—	—	$27,995
Ford	C-Max Hybrid	2012	HEV	47	Lithium-ion	—	—	—	—	$25,995
Ford	C-Max Energi n	2012	PHEV	92	Lithium-ion	—	—	—	21	$32,950
Toyota	Lexus CT 200h	2012	HEV	40	Nickel Metal Hybride	—	—	—	9.8	$31,850
GM	Opel Ampera	2012	PHEV	235	Lithium-ion	—	111	35	—	$58,500
Toyota	Prius	2012	PHEV	95	Lithium-ion	—	—	—	—	$32,000
Coda	Sedan	2013	EV	—	Lithium iron phosphate	31	100	125	—	$38,145
Ford	Fusion Energi	2013	PHEV	47	Lithium-ion	—	—	—	—	$39,495
Mercedes	B Class E Cell	2013	EV	—	Lithium-ion	—	—	—	—	—
Honda	Fit EV	2013	EV	105	Lithium-ion	20	100	82	—	$36,625
Toyota	Lexus ES Hybrid	2013	HEV	39	—	—	—	—	8.1	$38,850
Ford	Lincoln MKZ Hybrid	2014	PHEV	—	—	—	—	—	—	—
Volvo	70 Series Hybrid	2015	PHEV	—	—	11	—	31	8.9	—

Notes: EV are Electric Vehicle, HEV are Hybrid Electric Vehicle and PHEV are Plug-in Hybrid Electric Vehicle

High-End Launches

Manufacturer	Model	Launch Date	Type	MPG (Highway)	Battery Type	Energy Density (kWh)	Power Density (kW)	All-Electric Charge miles/charge)	Performance (0–60mph)	Starting Price ($US)
Toyota	Lexus GS 450h	2010	HEV	34	Nickel Metal Hydride	—	—	—	5.7	$59,825
BMW	ActiveHybrid 7	2011	HEV	30	Lithium-ion	—	—	—	—	$84,000
Fisker	Karma	2011	pHEV	52	Lithium-ion	20.1		50	6.3	$102,000
Mercedes	M Class Hybrid	2011	HEV	28	Lithium-ion	—	—	—	—	$47,270
VW	VWTourareg Hybrid	2011	HEV	23	Nickel Metal Hydride	—	—	—	6.2	$62,055
BMW	ActiveHybrid 5	2012	HEV	30	Lithium-ion	—	—	—	5.7	$61,100
BMW	ActiveE	2012	EV	—	Lithium-ion	32		100	<9.0	
Nissan	Infiniti M35h	2012	HEV	32	Lithium-ion	1.3		—	—	$54,200
Porsche	Panamera Hybrid	2012	HEV	30	Nickel Metal Hydride	1.7	34	—	6	$96,150
Mercedes	E Class Hybrid	2013	HEV	30	Lithium-ion	—	—	—	—	$55,800
GM	Cadllac Escalade	2013	HEV	23	Nickel Metal Hydride	—	—	—	—	$73,850
Porsche	Cayenne Hybrid	2013	HEV	24	Nickel Metal Hydride	—	—	1.2	6.1	$69,850
Tesla	Model S	2013	EV	90	Lithium-ion	40–85		160–300	5.6	$52,400
Toyota	Lexus RX 450h	2013	HEV	28	Nickel Metal Hydride	—	—	—	7.5	$45910
BMW	i3	2014	BEV	—	Lithium-ion	—	125	—	<8.0	—
Mercedes	S Class Hybrid	2014	HEV	25	Lithium-ion	—	—	—	—	$92.350
Mercedes	SLS AMG E-Cell	2014	EV	19	Lithium-ion	48	392	155	4	$535.000
GM	Cadillac ELR	2014	PHEV	—	Lithium-ion	18–20		—	—	—
Honda	Acura MDX Hybrid	2014	HEV	20	—	—	—	—	7.8	—
Honda	Acura RLX Hybrid	2014	HEV	—	—	—	—	—	—	—
Nissan	Inifiniti LE	2014	EV	—	Lithium-ion	24		100	—	—
Porsche	918 Spyder Hybrid	2014	HEV	78	Lithium-ion	6		15.6	3.2	—
Tesla	Model X	2014	EV	—	Lithium-ion	—	—	—	—	—
Jaguar	C-X75	2015	HEV		Lithium-ion	19.6		37	3.4	$1,100,000
Toyota	Lexus SC 600h	2015	HEV	23	-	—	—	—	5.5	$122,750
VW	Audi R8 e-Tron	2015	HEV	—	-	—	—	—	-	—
VW	Audi A1 e-Tron	2018	HEV	148	Lithium-ion	45	230	31	5.9	$150,000

Notes: EV are Electric Vehicle, HEV are Hybrid Electric Vehicle and PHEV are Plug-in Hybrid Electric Vehicle

Source: J.P. Morgan, Ward's Auto, Motor Trend, company reports and company websites.

EXHIBIT 8
Tesla Motors Revenue Trend (2008–2012)

(in thousands)	2012	2011	2010	2009	2008
Automotive sales	385,699	148,568	97,078	111,943	14,742
- Vehicle, options and related sales	354,344	101,708	75,459	111,555	—
- Regulatory credit sales	40,500	2,700	2,800	—	—
- Powertrain component and related sale	31,355	46,860	21,619	388	—
Development services	27,557	55,674	19,666	—	—
Total revenues	**413,256**	**204,242**	**116,744**	**111,943**	**14,742**

(Percent of total revenues)	2012	2011	2010	2009	2008
Automotive sales	93%	73%	83%	100%	100%
- Vehicle, options and related sales	86%	50%	65%	100%	—
- Regulatory credit sales	10%	1%	2%	—	—
- Powertrain component and related sale	8%	23%	19%	0%	—
Development services	7%	27%	17%	—	—

Source: Company data.

EXHIBIT 9
Tesla Motors Cost of Revenue and Operating Costs Trend (2008–2012)

(in thousands)	2012	2011	2010	2009	2008
Automotive sales	371,658	115,482	79982	102408	15883
Development services	11,531	27,165	6031	—	—
Total cost of revenues (1)	**383,189**	**142,647**	**86,013**	**102,408**	**15,883**

(in thousands)	2012	2011	2010	2009	2008
Research and development (1)	273,978	208,981	92,996	19,282	53,714
Selling, general and administrative (1)	150,372	104,102	84,573	42,150	23,649
- Stock-based compensation	50,145	29,419	21,156	1,434	437
Total expenses	**807,539**	**455,730**	**263,582**	**163,840**	**93,246**

(1) Includes stock-based compensation expense

Source: Company data.

EXHIBIT 10
Tesla Motors Capital Expenditure Schedule (2008–2012)

(in thousands)	2012	2011	2010	2009	2008
Capital expenditures spending	239,228	184,226	40,203	11,884	10,630
Capital expenditures (percent of total revenue)	58%	90%	34%	11%	72%

Source: Company data.

EXHIBIT 11
Excerpts from Tesla's 2012 Annual Report

Consolidated Balance Sheets	Year Ended December 31,	
(in thousands, except share and per share data)	2012	2011
Assets		
Current assets		
Cash and cash equivalents	$ 201,890	$ 255,266
Short-term marketable securities	—	25,061
Restricted cash	19,094	23,476
Accounts receivable	26,842	9,539
Inventory	268,504	50,082
Prepaid expenses and other current assets	8,438	9,414
Total current assets	524,768	372,838
Operating lease vehicles, net	10,071	11,757
Property, plant and equipment, net	552,229	298,414
Restricted cash	5,159	8,068
Other assets	21,963	22,371
Total assets	$ 1,114,190	$ 713,448
Liabilities and Stockholders' Equity		
Current liabilities		
Accounts payable	$ 303,382	$ 56,141
Accrued liabilities	39,798	32,109
Deferred revenue	1,905	2,345
Capital lease obligations, current portion	4,365	1,067
Reservation payments	138,817	91,761
Long-term debt, current portion	50,841	7,916
Total current liabilities	539,108	191,339
Common stock warrant liability	10,692	8,838
Capital lease obligations, less current portion	9,965	2,830
Deferred revenue, less current portion	3,060	3,146
Long-term debt, less current portion	401,495	268,335
Other long-term liabilities	25,170	14,915
Total liabilities	989,490	489,403
Commitments and contingencies		
Stockholders' equity:		
Preferred stock; $0.001 par value; 100,000,000 shares authorized; no shares issued and outstanding	—	—
Common stock; $0.001 par value; 2,000,000,000 shares authorized as of December 31, 2012 and 2011, respectively; 114,214,274 and 104,530,305 shares issued and outstanding as of December 31, 2012 and 2011, respectively	115	104
Additional paid-in capital	1,190,191	893,336
Accumulated other comprehensive loss	—	(3)
Accumulated deficit	(1,065,606)	(669,392)
Total stockholders' equity	124,700	224,045
Total liabilities and stockholders' equity	$ 1,114,190	$ 713,448

Source: Tesla Motors 2012 Annual Report.

EXHIBIT 11 (continued)

Excerpts from Tesla's 2012 Annual Report

Consolidated Statement of Operations	Year Ended December 31,		
(in thousands, except share and per share data)	2012	2011	2010
Revenues			
Automotive sales	$ 385,699	$ 148,568	$ 97,078
Development services	27,557	55,674	19,666
Total revenues	413,256	204,242	116,744
Cost of revenues			
Automotive sales	371,658	115,482	79,982
Development services	11,531	27,165	6,031
Total cost of revenues	383,189	142,647	86,013
Gross profit	30,067	61,595	30,731
Operating expenses			
Research and development	273,978	208,981	92,996
Selling, general and administrative	150,372	104,102	84,573
Total operating expenses	424,350	313,083	177,569
Loss from operations	(394,283)	(251,488)	(146,838)
Interest income	288	255	258
Interest expense	(254)	(43)	(992)
Other expense, net	(1,828)	(2,646)	(6,583)
Loss before income taxes	(396,077)	(253,922)	(154,155)
Provision for income taxes	136	489 173	
Net loss	$ (396,213)	$ (254,411)	$ (154,328)
Net loss per share of common stock,			
basic and diluted	$ (3.69)	$ (2.53)	$ (3.04)
Weighted average shares used in computing net loss per share of common stock,			
basic and diluted	107,349,188	100,388,815	50,718,302

Source: Tesla Motors 2012 Annual Report.

EXHIBIT 11 (continued)
Excerpts from Tesla's 2012 Annual Report

Consolidated Statement of Cash Flows	For the Year Ended December 31,		
(in thousands, except share and per share data)	2012	2011	2010
Cash Flows From Operating Activities			
Net loss	$ (396,213)	$ (254,411)	$ (154,328)
Adjustments to reconcile net loss to net cash used in operating activities:			
Depreciation and amortization	28,825	16,919	10,623
Change in fair value of warrant liabilities	1,854	2,750	5,022
Discounts and premiums on short-term marketable securities	56	(112)	—
Stock-based compensation	50,145	29,419	21,156
Excess tax benefits from stock-based compensation	—	—	(74)
Loss on abandonment of fixed assets	1,504	345	8
Inventory write-downs	4,929	1,828	951
Changes in operating assets and liabilities:			
Accounts receivable	(17,303)	(2,829)	(3,222)
Inventories and operating lease vehicles	(194,726)	(13,638)	(28,513)
Prepaid expenses and other current assets	1,121	(248)	(4,977)
Other assets	(482)	(288)	(463)
Accounts payable	187,821	19,891	(212)
Accrued liabilities	9,603	10,620	13,345
Deferred development compensation	—	—	(156)
Deferred revenue	(526)	(1,927)	4,801
Reservation payments	47,056	61,006	4,707
Other long-term liabilities	10,255	2,641	3,515
Net cash used in operating activities	(266,081)	(128,034)	(127,817)
Cash Flows From Investing Activities			
Purchases of marketable securities	(14,992)	(64,952)	—
Maturities of short-term marketable securities	40,000	40,000	—
Payments related to acquisition of Fremont manufacturing facility and related assets	—	—	(65,210)
Purchases of property and equipment excluding capital leases	(239,228)	(184,226)	(40,203)
Withdrawals out of (transfers into) our dedicated Department of Energy account, net	8,620	50,121	(73,597)
Increase in other restricted cash	(1,330)	(3,201)	(1,287)
Net cash used in investing activities	(206,930)	(162,258)	(180,297)
Cash Flows From Financing Activities			
Proceeds from issuance of common stock in public offerings, net	221,496	172,410	188,842
Proceeds from issuance of common stock in private placements	—	59,058	80,000
Principal payments on capital leases and other debt	(2,832)	(416)	(315)
Proceeds from long-term debt and other long-term liabilities	188,796	204,423	71,828
Principal payments on long-term debt	(12,710)	—	—
Proceeds from exercise of stock options and other stock issuances	24,885	10,525	1,350
Excess tax benefits from stock-based compensation	—	—	74
Deferred common stock and loan facility issuance costs	—	—	(3,734)
Net cash provided by financing activities	419,635	446,000	338,045
Net increase (decrease) in cash and cash equivalents	(53,376)	155,708	29,931
Cash and cash equivalents at beginning of period	255,266	99,558	69,627
Cash and cash equivalents at end of period	$ 201,890	$ 255,266	$ 99,558
Supplemental Disclosures			
Interest paid	$ 6,938	$ 3,472	$ 1,138
Income taxes paid	117	282	9
Supplemental noncash investing and financing activities			
Conversion of preferred stock to common stock	—	—	319,225
Issuance of common stock upon net exercise of warrants	—	—	6,962
Issuance of convertible preferred stock warrant	—	—	6,294
Issuance of common stock warrant	—	—	1,701
Acquisition of property and equipment	44,890	15,592	4,482

Source: Tesla Motors 2012 Annual Report.

VW TAKES AN ETHICS HIT

INTRODUCTION

When Volkswagen AG the parent company of the Volkswagen brand disclosed that it top engineers installed software in its diesel-powered cars to by-pass emission control standards during routine EPA testing, the disclosure shocked the company and revealed a tangled web of deceit and mismanagement. The admission also raised social and governmental concerns about the entire global auto industry pattern of unethical behaviors and competitive practices.

The increased public and congressional scrutiny for VW was coming at time when automobile manufacturers were facing increased worldwide turbulence and uncertainty. Slowing growth in emerging markets, international currency instability and volatility, regulatory reform, and a rising pro-labor populist movement were confounding Müller's turnaround strategy.

As Matthias Müller, CEO of the Volkswagen Group A.G. prepared to pay the latest settlement of $10.03 billion to buy back or fix nearly a half million diesel cars equipped with defeat devices, he wondered if he had finally reached then end of the road in the costly scandal.[1] While there were positive signs that the new strategies he orchestrated were moving his company in the right direction, he was concerned if it would be enough to profitably transform his company. His vision was to turn VW into a technology company were the real money was to be made from software and services. The strategy also called for increased production of all-electric vehicles by 2025.[2] The technology and service transition would turn the company from primarily a metal, internal combustion engine, carmaker and marketer into a technology company. As industry analysts and next generation car markers had predicted, the automobile was rapidly being turned into a modern day version of a smartphone on wheels.[3] This transformation was turning the car into a connected Internet device reshaping the whole transportation infrastructure and car buyers' purchasing experience and decision. By early 2017, VW's U.S. bill for the emissions scandal was $15.3 billion and rising. In all, analysts and researchers estimated the entire U.S. and European settlement charges and penalties would be a record $50 billion.[4] The scandal resulted in Volkswagen reporting it largest ever, annual loss in 2015 and the prospects for 2016 were not much better. It also caused the VW's stock to lose 35% of its value in the week following the scandal and had continued to underperform. (See Exhibit 1: Volkswagen Group Financial Highlights and Exhibit 2: Volkswagen Stock Performance—Pre-Post Scandal Compared to DJI).

EXHIBIT 1
Volkswagen Group Financial Highlights

Source: Google Finance: https://www.google.com/finance? 4-10-17

EXHIBIT 2
Volkswagen Stock Performance—Pre-Post Scandal Compared to DJI

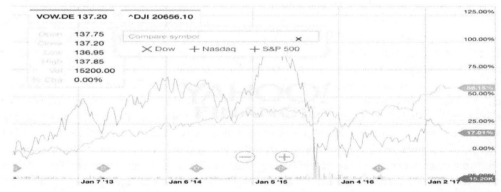

Source: Yahoo Finance: https://finance.yahoo.com/chart/VOW.DE? 4-10-17

Müller and Winterkorn have denied any culpability and knowledge of the wrongdoing prior to September 2015, when an independent research agency and the EPA made their investigation of VW public.[5] Winterkorn and Herbert Diess, head of VW's passenger car brand, were facing a probe by German prosecutors for not informing investors quickly enough about the potential losses in connection with the defeat device scandal. In March 2016, *Fortune* reported that Müller infuriated US regulators when he stated in a National Public Radio interview in January that the emission testing software installed in the US cars was an honest mistake. He blamed it on a technical problem. He stated, "We had not the right interpretation of the American law … we didn't lie. We didn't understand the question first."[6] *Fortune* reported, "VW's misbehavior did not come out of nowhere. The company had a history of scandals and episodes in which it skirted the law. Each time—till now—it has escaped without dire consequences."[7] The mal-behavior of VW executives revealed a complex VW system where the iconoclastic Company seemed immune from public scrutiny, especially in Germany.

VW COMPANY BACKGROUND

The VW Group, headquartered in Wolfsburg, Germany is a leading manufacturer of automobiles and commercial vehicles and the largest carmaker in Europe. Volkswagen operated more than 100 factories worldwide and had over 600,000 employees. The Group was spawned out of post WW II Germany, when the company founded by Hitler in 1936, was re-organized under a new governance structure. The company was rescued by the British army after the war and then privatized in 1960.[8] The German State of Lower Saxony and early on, the German Federal government, were given special ownership rights and board seats. The new system was designed around deep connections between management, workers (unions and work councils) and local politicians.

The Group developed, designed, manufactured and marketed 12 brands of cars and trucks worldwide. The Brands included: Volkswagen Passenger Cars (50% of all Group sales), Audi, SEAT, ŠKODA, Bentley, Bugatti, Lamborghini, Porsche, Ducati, Volkswagen Commercial (Truck) Vehicles, Scania and MAN. In 2016, the company was the largest automaker in the world with sales of 10.3 million units, overtaking Toyota. It had maintained the largest market share in Europe for over two decades. It ranked seventh in the 2016 Fortune Global 500 list of the world's largest companies.[9] By the end of 2015, VW sold over 10.8 million diesel powered vehicles worldwide with 2.8 ad 1.2 million sold in Germany and UK respectively.

FERDINAND PIËCH: ARCHITECT BEHIND VW'S SUCCESS

An industrial scion and engineer, Piëch transformed VW from a regional carmaker into a global powerhouse during his 32 year reign as CEO and Board Chairman. Piëch was the grandson of Ferdinand Porsche, who introduced the Porsche sports car and developed the classic VW Beetle. The elder Piëch, developed the VW Beetle under a 1934 contract with Hitler. The younger Piëch started his career at Porsche, before leaving for Audi after an agreement that no member of the Porsche or Piëch families should be involved in the day-to-day operations of the company. After leaving Porsche, Piëch became the head of VW's Audi brand. He was credited with evolving and growing Audi into a competitor that equaled Mercedes-Benz and BMW.[10]

In 1993, Ferdinand Piëch, became Chairman and CEO of Volkswagen Group. At that time, Volkswagen was only three months from bankruptcy. He was credited with orchestrating VW's dramatic turnaround.

Piëch led VW as chief executive from 1993 to 2002 and was widely known as one of the last towering figures in the auto industry. Under his leadership VW was transformed from a European regional car marker into one of the auto industries largest automobile manufactures. Piëch aggressively moved VW into new markets.

Among Piëch major acquisitions were the purchases of Lamborghini and Bentley, as well as the founding of Bugatti Automobiles. Piëch integrated the Volkswagen, Škoda, SEAT and Audi brands into a ladder-type structure similar to that used by Alfred Sloan at General Motors. In 1998, when VW's former CEO, Carl Hahn efforts to revitalize Volkswagen market share in North America failed, Piëch reversed VW's fortunes by manufacturing the Volkswagen New Beetle. The move boost Beetle sales and market share in North America.[11]

In 2002, per VW policy, Piëch at age 65 retired as VW's longtime CEO. He remained on as Chairman of the Company's Board of Directors. As Chair, he was actively involved in the company's strategic decisions. In 2011 *Automobile Magazine* named Piech its "Man of the Year." In April 2015, shortly before the news of VW's emissions scandal broke, Piech resigned as Board Chairman, but stayed on the Board.[12]

THE AUTO INDUSTRY: A CHANGING ROAD

Competition in the global automobile was fierce in early 2017. Rivals were pouring money into software, services, electric vehicles and other game changing technologies. In addition to the macro-economic, political and social uncertainty all automobile manufacturers were up against several major transitions in its traditional markets that were rapidly transforming its industry. Driving the industry's transformation were several radical technological, political and social drivers. Some game changing technological innovations coming into the industry were Internet manufacturing, all electric vehicles, driverless cars, and the "internet of things."[13] In addition, car companies faced stricter regulatory requirements for safety, fuel economy and the environment. All these factors, while presenting opportunities, came at an added cost of doing business, shrinking short-term operating margins and profits. Business models more representative of high technology software companies were challenging traditional auto company business models. For example, Google and Apple were developing their own versions of game changing next generation all electric vehicles. Uber, Amazon, and others were engaged in the radical redesign of the transportation industry with their efforts to make driverless cars and trucks the transportation mode of the future. Tesla, several traditional carmakers and venture backed technology start-ups were racing to make the all-electric vehicle the industry standard by 2030.[14] As a result, traditional competitive forces of the auto industry were undergoing an all out assault. The risk was that Apple, Google, Amazon, Uber, and a host of others outside the auto industry would extract most of the profits generated by car sales turning traditional automakers into low margin, equipment suppliers.[15] Similar to what was happening in the computer industry were mainframes and PCs were being replaced by smartphones and cloud technologies, the automobile, according to industry followers, was rapidly becoming a bundle of software apps, information and data networks, and valued added after sales services.[16]

In 2015, PWC *Auto Industry Trend* reported that several trends were reshaping the automobile industry: Shifts in consumer demand, expanded regulatory requirements, and increasing availability of data and information. Regarding the first major trend, PWC reported that consumers appeared to be rethinking their long love affair with individual automobile brands and were beginning to view cars more as transportation machines.[17] This shift in consumer behavior was affecting how much consumers were willing to pay for their automobiles given that brand differentiation and quality were converging across brands. This trend would impact consumers purchasing decisions by making once higher regarded brand differentiation less important as consumers demanded more sophisticated infotainment systems and features that were standard on high priced models at lower price. PWC reported that consumers were inundated with easily accessible information about automobile specifications, prices, discounts, quality, and performance, giving buyers greater bargaining power.

Secondly, expanded regulatory requirements for tighter corporate average fuel economy (CAFE) regulations in the United States and the rest of the world made it more expensive for automakers. Regulators were also adding to vehicle costs by mandating that more safety-related features, such as backup cameras, collision avoidance systems, and advanced monitoring devices be standard. In order to comply Automobile companies needed to achieve higher volume sales to amortize the increased costs.

Finally, increased availability of data and information regarding vehicle usage and driver behavior usage was proliferating as sensors and telematics systems became more common. According to PWC report, while all players across the automotive value chain were interested in collecting more customer and car data, there was widespread uncertainty in the industry as to how to use and monetize this data.[18]

THE DEFEAT DEVICE EMISSION SCANDAL

On September 18, 2015, The US EPA announced that Volkswagen had installed a defeat device software code in the diesel models sold in the US since 2008. The code was intended to detect when an emissions test was being conducted, and altered emissions controls for better compliance. Off the test stand, the controls were relaxed, and emissions jumped 35 to 40 times regulatory levels according to investigators at West Virginia University and the California Air Resources Board. The defeat device was installed on 482,000 vehicles in the US resulting in a potential $18 billion ($37,500 per violation) in fines, penalties, and criminal and civil ligation.[19]

The admission resulted in the resignation of CEO Winterkorn and prompting an apology from its U.S. President Michael Horn at a contentious U.S. congressional subcommittee investigation. Because of WV's indiscretions it announced in early October 2015 that it would stop selling diesel powered vehicles in the U.S. for the foreseeable future because it fail to receive U.S. certification for carbon emissions standards.[20] Volkswagen also halted production at its plant Chattanooga, Tennessee plant. The plant accounted for over one-third of its diesel car output. The Company was unclear as to how it was going to rectify the lack of EPA certification for its U.S. diesel powered cars. VW owners were not only driving vehicles that failed U.S. emission tests their vehicles were now practically worthless in the resale markets. Similarly, VW dealers and suppliers were stuck with an inventory of unsellable cars and components.[21]

ROBERT BOSCH GMBH: SUPPLIER INVOLVEMENT

The probe of the VW emission scandal went beyond the Company when investigators expanded it to include Robert Bosch GmbH, one of the world's biggest auto suppliers.[22] German investigators found that Bosch informed VW in a September 2007 letter to company management that the software provided by Bosch could be illegal. In a June 2008 email from a Bosch employee concerned about getting caught, the employee suggested that Bosch could rig engines to recognize when they were being tested. In another email exchange between the two companies, Borsch demanded that Volkswagen indemnity Bosch of any anticipated liability arising from the Bosch created defeat device. Prosecutors claimed that Winterkorn was not only aware of the exchanges, but took part in the negotiations. Volkswagen defended Winterkorn by suggesting that as CEO he was inundated with emails and never saw the email exchanges with Bosch.[23] By the end of 2016, industry analysts and investors were predicting that the emission scandal would cost VW upwards of $46 billion.[24] VW senior management blamed the scandal on the actions of a few senior engineers and has repeatedly denied any knowledge of the defeat devices scandal prior to the company's September 2015 admission of guilt.[25]

VW: A PATTERN OF SCANDALS

Scandals for VW Group unfortunately was nothing new. In 2003 and 2005 VW experienced industrial espionage, prostitution and bribery scandals, respectfully. Early on in 1993, Piëch started one of the biggest fights in the auto industry when he orchestrated a hostile pirating away of Jose Ignacio Lopez, from General Motors. This action resulted in an onslaught of insults, lawsuits and criminal investigations between the two companies alleging espionage, stolen documents and patent infringements. Lopez had a reputation on squeezing suppliers, negating long-term contracts and relentlessly cutting costs. Piech wanted Lopez to help turnaround VW's dire financial situation. The controversy ended when Lopez was forced to leave VW.[26]

In 2005, VW became embattled in a prostitution and bribery scandal. Klaus Volkert, head of VW's powerful works council and a supervisory board member was found guilty of breach of trust by illegally receiving a 2 million euros payment from a VW Board member. The illegal payment came at the same time when members of the works council went on trips allergically involving prostitution, shopping excursion for wives, and "Viagra paid by Piech. Chairman Piech told a court, "The scandals were 'irregularities' of which he had known nothing."[27]

In 2015, in addition to the emissions scandal, VW was embroiled in another scandal revolving around a safety flaw in the keyless ignition of Volkswagen and other vehicles, including the VW Brand. Volkswagen management spent the prior two years trying to keep reports of the flaws in the keyless ignition from the public domain.[28]

Just prior to the VW scandal, the EPA reached 14 settlements and won court orders against several auto manufacturers for not complying with the Clean Air Act rules. A number of these cases involved Chinese-made all-terrain vehicles and motorcycles, and Honda and Kia vehicles. The biggest case prior to the VW scandal was in 1995, when the EPA and Justice Department collected $11 millions in fines form GM for installing "defeat devices" that overrode emission control testing on 470,000 Cadillacs.[29]

ETHICS VIOLATIONS IN THE AUTOMOBILE INDUSTRY

Several analyst and industry insiders noted several factors behind VW's and other automakers ethics violations. The deadly consequences of several auto manufacturers' failure to disclose vehicle safety defects in a timely fashion added to a host of governmental, regulatory, social and legal pressures and demands on an already fiercely competitive industry. GM's defective push button ignition switches, Takata's malfunctioning vehicle airbags, and the sudden and uncontrollable acceleration of Toyotas, where just a few of the high profile governmental investigations, resulting in billions of dollars in penalties, fines, legal costs and damaged brand. These included industry-wide behaviors where auto industry executives engaged in questionable actions as a competitive game to keep up with rivals, playing it as long as they could, until or if, getting caught. They assumed the added risk based on the benefits of playing this game out weighed the cost of playing it. Still others believe that they had to engage in this behavior because of burdensome government regulation. Industry executives argued that government market interference took investment dollars away from needed research and development and other investments. Stricter regulations were coming at a time when the automobile industry was going through major change. Fast moving change, some industry experts foresaw, was transforming automobile companies from one of making cars to one turning the automobile into a smartphone on wheels.[30]

FACTORS DRIVING VW'S EMISSION SCANDAL

What factors might have accounted for WV' emission scandal? Several factors, according to numerous sources were behind its current emissions scandal. These included: Ambitious Sales Goal—to become the number one global brand in total units and revenues by 2018; abnormally high labor and manufacturing costs; and the "VW System -an unwieldy, complex governance structure and culture that fostered dysfunctional behaviors.

AMBITIOUS REVENUE AND VEHICLE GOALS

VW's leading position as the world's largest automobile company was seriously being threatened as a result of its rigged carbon testing. In 2014, Volkswagen generated $246 billion in revenue and $13.2 billion in net income with 592,586 employees. Toyota had $227 billion in revenues and $18.1 billion in net income with 344,109 employees. General Motors had revenues of $155.9 billion, net income of $3.95 billion with 216,000 employees.[31] Winterkorn had set a goal of annual production of 10,000,000 cars by 2018. Ironically, he reached that goal in 2014.[31] VW struggled to remain profitable under Winterkorn's and Müller's leadership. VW had been plagued with high labor and manufacturing costs, too many unprofitable or low margin cars, too many brands and models, and unbridled spending as it raced to overtake Toyota and GM in sales and profitability. While VW's global expansion into other markets went well as it doubled the number of plants worldwide, expanding in the North America, as well as China, Russia, Brazil and other emerging markets, only China provided any significant growth.[32] VW's troubles were made more difficult by taking fluctuating currency exchange rate hits and significantly higher operating costs, particularly in Germany, compared to arch rivals Toyota and GM.

HIGH LABOR AND MANUFACTURING COSTS

In testifying to the subcommittee Horn noted that the cheating scandal may have been prompted by cost pressure at home and in the U.S. and difficulty of VW engineers to develop a diesel powered engine that would deliver on its carbon emissions and MPG (miles per gallon) efficiency goals. While refusing to give full refunds to U.S. customers for their cars, when asked by U.S. lawmakers Horn noted that Volkswagen had set aside $7.5 billion to help address the problem. Horn reported he recently learned that the cheating was the work of senior engineers: Ulrich Hackenberg, Audi's chief engineer; Wolfgang Hatz, developer of racing engines; and Hienz-Jakob Neussr, head of development for the Volkswagen brand.[33] Several early attempts at rationalizing and restructuring VW labor and manufacturing costs did not produced the desired results. VW manufacturing plants made most of its parts, as separate components unit for each of its 12 brands. Previous plans to consolidate manufacturing plants and add more efficiency into its development and manufacturing of components were blocked by strong work councils and board members, particularly the State of Lower Saxony. Cost cutting efforts included job reductions, internal biddings across its internal component manufacturers and outsourcing more components to external suppliers. One long-time VW employee commented, restructuring would require "… a sea change in the way VW does business. He noted that the complete absence of competition for supplying parts led to internal inefficiencies. VW needed cost reductions to boost profitability because material cost at VW plants was large, rising from 80 billion euros in 2010 to 144 billon euros in 2015.[34]

THE VOLKSWAGEN GROUP'S SYSTEM

Several analysts blamed the company's inability to learn from its past transgressions and current scandal on what they refer to as the VW system. The emission scandal revealed a complete system failure, according to Richard Milne.[36] He blamed the emissions scandal on the VW system, a structure that fostered a dysfunctional culture where company politics blocked real change. VW Board of Directors, unlike US companies, operated under the principle of co-determination. This principle divided the Board into two groups, each with 10 seats. A supervisory Board made up the work council seats and a second group of Porsche and Piech family members (five seats), German State of Lower Saxony (2 seats), Country of Qatar Investment Group (one seat), IG Metall union (one seat), and one held by the CEO of Swedish bank SEB. The German State of Lower Saxony held 12.7% of the company's shares, granting it 20% of the voting rights. According to governance experts, the VW system closely aligned the Board Chair with the work council board members. This close relationship was evident when the head o the IG Metall union was appointed Interim Board Chair when Winterkorn's resigned.[35] Shortly afterwards, Hans Dieter Potsch was appointed Board Chair. Potsch was previously VW Group's finance director and was close to family members on the Board. The VW system was made even more complex by several layers of family and state ownership on its Board. After the 2005 scandal, VW changed it governance structure when the Porsche and Piech families and later the country of Qatar, joined Lower Saxony as VW Group's dominant shareholders. For local politicians, the union and Saxony, the VW system was crucial for protecting jobs.

For investors and non-workers, critics claimed that the Board had no independent, outside members. They argued that since SEB was an advisor to one of VW's 12 brands this Board member it should be disqualified as an independent director. They argued that the Board was dominated by family ownership intertwined with a complex company culture and structure making it difficult for members to exercise their fiduciary responsibilities. The system, they asserted, fostered a dysfunctional corporate culture that stressed profitability.[37]

MATTHIAS MÜLLER'S: STEERING A NEW STRATEGIC COURSE

In June 2016, Müller announced VW's 2025 strategy as the company struggled to keep pace with industry leaders as its profits lagged behind its main rivals Toyota Motor and General Motors. Müller aimed to streamline VW's company operations by cutting 5% of its workforce and rationalizing manufacturing, including cutting 30,000 jobs in Germany. Müller wanted to increase VW's operating margins to 6% by 2025 at a time when industry margins were being squeezed. His strategy entailed moving aggressively into electric vehicles, self-driving cars and digital mobility. He told company top executives, "We have to catch up with the best." Müller reported that he intended to use the scandal, "… as a catalyst to impose cost discipline, and make the 12 brand group a big player in electric cars, producing between two and three million vehicles by 2025."[38] To meet his electric car goal VW would need 150 gigawatt hours of battery capacity. Other elements of Mueller's 2025 strategy included:

- Selling 1 million all electric cars per year
- Build them in US beginning in 2021
- Invest in technology and limit R&D spending to 6% of sales
- Find investment funds by reduced costs and productivity improvements
- Achieve short-term cost savings without mandatory job reductions through attrition.[39,40]

A pillar of VW's strategy was to restructure VW's component business that was widely regarded by industry analysts as a black hole. Critics noted that real change and cost reductions would be difficult. Union Chief Bernh Osterloh claimed that Müller and Diess were using in the scandal as an excuse for cutting costs and job reductions. In a scathing letter addressed to both leaders, Osterloh demanded protection of 12,000 of the 120,000 VW jobs at German factories. The letter signaled a major break in the union's collaborative relationship with management. Osterloh wrote that the work council did not share the same close relations that it had with Winterkorn. Osterloh warned of a "grave lost of trust" between the unions and State of Saxony where most of the jobs were located.[41] He noted, with Winterkorn labor disputes were kept in the background.

Müller's strategy had other critics besides labor. These critics asserted that any VW "Pact for the Future" with unions would be futile. They noted that even after planned labor reductions, VW's labor cost would only be second to BMW. They also noted after previous rounds of reductions in 2006, VW's head count reductions quickly recovered. They wanted to know: Can electric cars be made more appealing to European drivers? Could VW's higher costs of developing and manufacturing electric cars be sufficiently reduced without cutting operating margins? One analyst, Arndt Ellinghorst, at Evercore ISI, noted, "… the bulk of VW's rising costs stem from unnessary complexity and out-of-control engineering projects." He added, "Cost savings are not about squeezing suppliers, but managing the business well."[42]

CONCLUSION: A FAMILY DIVIDED

In early April 2017, former Chairman Ferdinand Piech agreed to sell his 14.7% ownership stake in Porsche Automobile Holdings (PAH). PAH controlled 52.2 percent of the voting shares in Volkswagen A.G. and planned on exercising its right of first refusal on buying Piech shares. Since the emissions scandal, Piëch relationship with VW's Board and family members soured. Piëch resignation from the board and disputes with Winterkorn and family board members caused a major chasm in the company's governance structure. Piëch was ousted as VW's chairman in 2015, months before the emissions scandal broke. Piëch battled on the board with his billionaire cousin Wolfgang Porsche, the chairman of Porsche. Porsche and other top players on VW's Board, sided with Winterkorn in the dispute with Piëch. The media reported in February 2016, that Piëch had told investigators that his cousin and other board members knew about the emissions test cheating earlier than stated in public.[43] Müller the former Chair of Porsche took over as CEO of VW when Winterkorn resigned under pressure from the emissions scandal. Winterkorn was Müller mentor at Porsche. Since quitting as chairman, Piech has become reclusive and unwilling to defend the Company that he brought to Global prominence. Was Piëch decision to sell his ownership stake and disinfection with VW's Board the final straw that derails VW emission scandal defense and Müller's 2025 turnaround strategy? Or could Müller actually overcome the scandal and restore trust and profitability back to the Company? Many stockholders, analyst and industry experts questioned whether VW would ever change.[44] The company they argued needed a radical overall, but believed it would never happen given its legacy of a complex governance system that fostered interpersonal rivalries, competing interests and inefficiencies.

ENDNOTES

1 William Boston, "VW Readies New Strategy," *Wall Street Journal*, June 16, 2016
2 Patrick McGee, "US Settlement closes latest chapter in saga of VW's diesel emissions scandal." *Financial Times*, 29 June 2016; Patrick McGee, "VW's criminal settlement rounds off years of emission deceit and denial." *Financial Times*, 12 January 2017
3 Andy Sharman, "Tyred and wired," *Financial Times*, 4 April/5April 2015
4 Patrick McGee, "VW's criminal settlement rounds off years of emission deceit and denial." *Financial Times*, 12 January 2017
5 William Boston, "VW Brand's Chief Faces Tough Slog," *Wall Street journal*, June 19, 2015; William Boston, "Former VW Leader Faces Probe," *Wall Street journal*, June 21, 2015
6 Geoffrey Smith and Roger Parloff, "Hoaxwagen: Inside Volkswagen Diesel Fraud," *Fortune*, March 7, 2016: at http://fortune.com/inside-volkswagen-emissions-scandal/
7 Ibid. Smith, et. al.
8 Wikipedia, Ferdinand Piëch, Downloaded: April 7, 2017, https://en.wikipedia.org/wiki/Ferdinand_Pi%C3%ABch
9 Ibid. Ferdinand Piëch
10 Andreas Cremer, "Architect of modern VW cuts ties with share sale," April 3, 2017, *Rueter.com* http://www.reuters.com/article/us-volkswagen-piech-idUSKBN1751KY
11 Wikipedia, Ferdinand Piëch, Downloaded: April 7, 2017, https://en.wikipedia.org/wiki/Ferdinand_Pi%C3%ABch
12 Andreas Cremer, "Architect of modern VW cuts ties with share sale," April 3, 2017, *Rueter.com* http://www.reuters.com/article/us-volkswagen-piech-idUSKBN1751KY
13 Andy Sharman, "Tyred and wired," *Financial Times*, 4 April/5April 2015
14 Alex Drvies, "Power Play: The Inside Story of How GM (Yes GM!) Beat Elon Musk In the Race to Build A True Electric Car for the Masses," Wired, February 2016: 59–71.
15 Jack Ewing, "As Apple and Google Rethink Cars, Automakers Plan Their Defense," *The New York Times*, September 18, 2015: B4; Pilita Clark and Andy Sharman, Fallout threatens to choke diesel cars," *Financial Times*, September 23, 2015: p.17
16 Andy Sharman, "Tyred and wired," *Financial Times*, 4 April/5April 2015
17 Evan Hirsh, Arjun Kakkar Akshay Singh, Reid Wilk, "2015 Auto Industry Trends, Strategy: Turbulence and Technology," PWC, Downloaded April 5, 2017, http://www.strategyand.pwc.com/trends/2015-auto-trends
18 Ibid., Hirsh, et.al.
19 Mike Spector and Amy Harder, "VW's U.S. Chief Apologizes, Says Engineers at Fault," *The Wall Street Journal*, October 9, 2015:B1, B2
20 Mike Spector and William Boston, "VW to Halt New Diesel Sales in U.S.," The *Wall Street Journal*, October 8, 2015: p. B1 and B2;
21 Dan Neil, VW Lost Its Moral Compass in Quest for Growth," *The Wall Street Journal*, September 24, 2015
22 Peter Campbell and Michael Stothard, "Prosecutors widen probes into VW," *Financial Times*, 9 March 2016

23 Ibid. Campbell

24 Jeff Bennett, "VW Scandal Threatens Suppliers," The Wall Street Journal, September 28, 2015, B6

25 Patrick McGee, "VW's criminal settlement rounds off years of emission deceit and denial." *Financial Times*, 12 January 2017; Mike Spector and Amy Harder, "VW's U.S. Chief Apologizes, Says Engineers at Fault," *The Wall Street Journal*, October 9, 2015:B1, B2

26 Geoffrey Smith and Roger Parloff, "Hoaxwagen: Inside Volkswagen Diesel Fraud," *Fortune*, March 7, 2016 http://fortune.com/inside-volkswagen-emissions-scandal/

27 Richard Milne, "System Failure," *Financial Times*, 5 November 2015: Richard Milne, "Volkswagen choked by cost and complexity," *Financial Times*, 11 November 2015

28 Milne, 5 November 2015

29 David Shepardson "VW not alone in evading emissions rules," *The Detroit News*, 9/21/15 http://www.detroitnews.com/story/business/autos/foreign/2015/09/21/vw-alone-evading-emissions-rules/72599274/

30 Andy Sharman, "Tyred and wired," *Financial Times*, 4 April/5April 2015

31 Mergent Online: http://www.mergentonline.com.libproxy.unh.edu/competitors.php?compnumber=8830&isprintpage=1&orderby=[1,%22 desc%22

32 William Boston, "VW Readies New Strategy," *Wall Street Journal*, June 16, 2016

33 Mike Spector and Amy Harder, "VW's U.S. Chief Apologizes, Says Engineers at Fault," *The Wall Street Journal*, October 9, 2015:B1, B2

34 Geoffrey Smith and Roger Parloff, "Hoaxwagen: Inside Volkswagen Diesel Fraud," *Fortune*, March 7, 2016: at http://fortune.com/inside-volkswagen-emissions-scandal/

35 Richard Milne, "System Failure," *Financial Times*, 5 November 2015: Richard Milne, "Volkswagen   choked by cost and complexity," *Financial Times*, 11 November 2015

36 Ibid., Milne

37 Ibid., Milne

38 William Boston, "VW Readies New Strategy," *Wall Street Journal*, June 16, 2016

39 Ibid., Boston

40 "Together 2025," *Volkswagen Group Annual Report*, https://www.volkswagenag.com/en/InvestorRelations.html

41 Henry Foy and James Politi, "Volkswagen scandal fuels fears for jobs across Europe," *Financial Times*, October 13, 2015; Patrick McGee, "VW aims to ensure union backing for electric push," *Financial Times*, 17 June 2016

42 Patrick McGee, Volkswagen chief executive seeks to avoid past failures," Financial Times, 16 JUNE; Peter Campbell, VW scandal drags on sales of diesel cars in Europe," *Financial Times* 21 June, 2016 2016; William Boston, "VW Holders Scold Top Management," *Wall Street journal*, June 23, 2016

43 Patrick McGee Former Volkswagen chairman to sell majority of Porsche stake," Financial Times, April 3, 2017; Andreas Cremer, "Architect of modern VW cuts ties with share sale," April 3, 2017, *Rueter.com* http://www.reuters.com/article/us-volkswagen-piech-idUSKBN1751KY

44 Geoffrey Smith and Roger Parloff, "Hoaxwagen: Inside Volkswagen Diesel Fraud," *Fortune*, March 7, 2016: at http://fortune.com/inside-volkswagen-emissions-scandal/

5 ASHOKAN CENTER: FOSTERING DEEP CONNECTIONS

BY MICHAEL J. MERENDA

The mission of The Ashokan Center is to teach, inspire, and bring people together through shared experiences in nature, history, and the arts (See http://ashokancenter.org/).

Ashokan has done its work when visitors go home inspired by a strong desire to keep their positive feelings alive and spread the word to others, be they students whose live have been changed by their Ashokan experience, teachers who've found new ways to engage and inspire their students, retreat attendees who start experiential learning programs of their own, or people who've simply found new meaning in their lives and shared it with others.[1]

—Jay Ungar and Molly Mason

INTRODUCTION

As Jay Ungar, Board Chair and Interim Executive Director of the Ashokan Center, Inc. (ACI or Ashokan), prepared for the upcoming June 2017 board meeting, several questions raced through his mind as he contemplated the events that had transpired since the March meeting. Shortly before the March meeting, Gina Gould announced that she would be leaving her position as ACI's Executive Director. At the January meeting Gould reported on the progress the Center had made under her leadership and stressed the need for the Board to continue to work on discovering the right mix of revenue producing programs that best met the Center's mission. She also emphasized the importance of finding the proper balance between the Center's environmental education school programs and it music, arts, and events programs. Gould was able to get a small grant for the Harvard Business School Club of New York Community Partners (HBSCP) to study the Center's revenues and cost by program. The goal for HBSCP was to "identify the mix of program and service offerings that would best fulfill the Center's mission and ensure financial stability through increased revenue diversity."[2] Despite Gould's announcement, Jay noted continued high staff moral and approval of Ashokan at the March meeting.

Jay was excited about the Center's prospects. In March he announced that ACI would receive $2.76 million from the New York City Department of Environmental Protection (NYCDEP). The money was to be allotted toward the preservation and repair of the

Center's historic 1885 covered bridge. Repairing the bridge was estimated to cost $755,000. The remaining $2 million would be invested with income from the investment unrestricted for AFI use.

JANUARY 2017 BOARD MEETING

At the January meeting Gould, a former Associate Professor of Environmental Science, desired the Center to increase its school programs beyond environmental education to other STEM disciplines (Science, Technology, Engineering, Math). Gould was concerned about having adequate funds and staff to effectively deliver its school programs, however. At the September 2016 board meeting, Patrick, a board member with a financial background presented a detailed cash flow analysis. The analysis projected that ACI would need $4 million through 2023 to cover deferred maintenance on its buildings and campus. Patrick reported:

> If we value the Center's assets at $6 million, we would need between 5% and 10% per year for mainte-
> nance ($300,00 to $600,000). And this does not include forest/natural resource maintenance. I don't
> see the current business model generating that much net income nor will a large push in fundraising.
> I don't believe the current program/activity mix can financially support the Center.

Ungar noted that proper management of the Center's core assets was essential to achieving Ashokan's vision and mission and critically important to its viability (See Exhibit 1: Experience + Inspiration = Ashokan Center). The situation was additionally concerning because net cash assets generated since 2009 were insufficient to grow programs and cover deferred expense. Although, cumulative net cash assets were positive ($146,207) under ACI management compared to cumulative negative net assets (-$328,514) under SUNY: New Paltz Management). Ashokan Foundation holds the montage for the Center and helps with fund raising.[3]

EXHIBIT 1
Experience + Inspiration = Ashokan Center

As you pass through Ashokan Center's main gate, the natural world comes alive. You've entered a place where people open up to nature and each another—a place that sparks inquiry—where joy and community become a backdrop for the exploration of critical topics.

At Ashokan Center people of all ages learn and grow by doing, whether by forging iron with 18th century tools; walking a woodland trail; seeing beaver in the pond, or a heron flying overhead; hiking through 385 million year-old rock formations in Cathedral Gorge; writing a song; learning a musical instrument; meeting and speaking with writers, painters, or musicians; singing and dancing; or simply sharing ideas and forming new friendships.

Ashokan has accomplished its work when visitors go home inspired to keep their positive feelings alive and spread the word to others, be they students whose lives have been changed by their Ashokan experience, teachers who've found new ways to engage and inspire their students, retreat attendees who start experiential learning programs of their own, or people who've simply found new meaning in their lives and shared it with others.

Jay Ungar and Molly Mason

Source: Ashokan Documents

ASHOKAN BACKGROUND

Ashokan operates as a 501(c)(3) legal entity located in the foothills of the Catskill Mountains in upstate New York. ACI's land consists of 320 secluded acres adjacent to the Ashokan Reservoir and wilderness areas in the Catskill Forest Preserve. The Ashokan Center was formerly the Field Campus of SUNY (State University of New York) New Paltz since its opening in 1967. In May 2008, the Open Space Conservancy (OSC) in conjunction with the newly established Ashokan Foundation Inc. (AFI) acquired the Field Campus. OSC became the land acquisition affiliate of the Open Space Institute (OSI). As part of the purchase and sale agreement, OSI transferred 65 acres to the New York City Department of Environmental Protection (NYCDEP) to facilitate the water supply management of the Ashokan Reservoir—the main source of drinking water for the City of New York.

The remaining portion of the property (320 acres) including educational buildings, meeting facilities, and several 18th century historic buildings, were transferred to the Foundation. As part of the acquisition agreement, AFI received $5 million from NYCDEP. Joe Martens, OSI's President noted at the signing of the historic agreement, "Thanks to a concerted effort on the part of SUNY, NYCDEP, and the Ashokan Foundation, school children and adults will continue to benefit from a one-of-a-kind outdoor learning experience … this is truly a win-win situation."[4] The $5 million was used to replace five principal campus buildings situated along the Esopus River, a designated emergency flood zone. The $5 million was augmented with a $2 million loan to AFI to build state-of-the-art and energy-efficient educational buildings. By August 2012, replacement buildings (main lodge, bunk halls, dining hall, recreation halls, and kitchen) were rebuilt on higher ground to accommodate water releases from the reservoir. The building project was completed in August 2012. (See Exhibit 2: Ashokan Foundation (AFI) Profit and Loss Statement and Exhibit 3: Ashokan Foundation (AFI) Balance Sheet).

EXHIBIT 2
Ashokan Foundation (AFI): Profit and Loss Statement, January through May 2017

Ordinary Income/Expense	
Income	2,755,000
NYC DEP Covered Bridge Fund	27,721
Donations	6,680
Interest Income	0
Total Income	**2,789,401**
Expenses	
Covered Bridge Repair & Maintenance Contract	755,000
Solar Panel Expense	2,000
Winter Hoot 2015	69
Consultant/Account	500
Fundraising Expense	409
Interest Expense	14,929
Repair and Maintenance	6,250
Insurance	3,628
Bank Service Charges	54
Total Expenses	**782,839**
Net Ordinary Income	2,006,562
Net Income	**2,006,562**

EXHIBIT 3
AFI Balance Sheet as of May 31, 2017

ASSETS		
Current Assets		
Cash	$127,782	
Other Current Assets		
Due From ACI (Note 1)	–$1,779	
NYDEP Grant (Note 2)	$2,000,000	
Total Other Current Assets	$1,998,221	
Total Current Assets		**$2,126,003**
Long Term Fixed Assets		
Bath House	$115,750	
A/D Office Equipment (OE)	$9,189	
OE Depreciation	–$2,704	
Land	$745,000	
Land Improvements	$213,624	
Land Improvements Depreciation	–$32,044	
A/D Buildings Depreciation	–$365,288	
A/D Furniture, Fixtures & Equipment	$155,527	
A/D FF&E Depreciation	–$48,724	
A/D Equipment	$18,419	
A/D Equipment Depreciation	–$6,504	
Total long Term Fixed Assets		**$802,245**
Other Assets		
Promises to Give	$107,562	
Buildings	$6,858,540	
Construction in Progress	$976	
A/A Closing Costs	–$7,001	
Loan Closing Costs	$25,986	
Total Other Assets		$6,986,063
TOTAL ASSETS		**$9,914,311**
LIABILITIES		
Current Liabilities	$0	
Long Term Liabilities		
Mortgage (Note 3)	$1,484,163	
Total Long Term Liabilities		$1,484,163
TOTAL NET ASSETS		**$8,430,148**
EQUITY		
Opening Balance Equity (Note 4)	–$1,536,679	
Temporary Restricted Net Assets	$111,792	
Unrestricted Net Assets	$6,687,468	
Retained Earnings	–$418,139	
Net Income	$6,563	

| TOTAL EQUITY | $4,851,005 |
| TOTAL LIABILITIES AND EQUITY | $6,335,168 |

Note 1: Due from ACI- Interest on AFI Mortgage; Interest & Principal starting in 2018

Note 2: $2,755,000 NYDEP Grant for historic bridge; 755,000 transferred to ACI for repair bridge;
   Grant Principal Restricted for Bridge Maintenance; Interest Earned is unrestricted

Note 3: AFI $2 million Construction Mortgage

Note 4: Includes $5 million NYDEP Grant for Building Construction New ACI Campus

Source: Ashokan Center, Financial Reports

SOCIAL ENTREPRENEURS

Internationally acclaimed musicians Jay Ungar and Molly Mason led AFI's formation. Since 1980, the SUNY New Paltz campus had been home to Ungar and Mason's Ashokan Music & Dance Camps. Ungar and Mason assembled a Board of Directors and Advisory Board for AFI, composed mainly of attendees of the M&D camps. The AFI Board, inspired by Ungar and Mason, envisioned a living and working teaching campus with a focus on sustainability and protection of the physical environment and open space.

By 2010, a separate ACI Board of Directors was established with several AFI board members serving on both boards including Ungar. The Board's vision focused on reconnecting people to the natural environment, as well as educating, engaging, and empowering individuals to live more respectfully, simply, and sustainably. The Center also encouraged individuals to work together to find solutions to the environmental and economic challenges of the 21st century. Ungar and Mason planned to continue the field campus as a fee-based outdoor environmental education center with a focus in natural science. For over 40 years SUNY New Paltz has hosted environmental education programs annually to over 5,000 school children primarily in the fourth, fifth, and sixth grades. (The children came mostly from the City of New York, New Jersey, and surrounding school districts.) The AFI Board planned to expand current programs and create new programing for the music camps, living history, and cultural arts.

MISSION[5]

The mission of the Ashokan Center is to provide a learning environment where schools, organizations, families, and individuals can reconnect with nature and build community through shared experiences in environmental education, living history, art, music, and dance. The Ashokan Center seeks to practice stewardship and teach green sustainable living by example. The Center also strives to decrease its carbon footprint while increasing its use of local food and materials. The Board believes that innovations in green building technologies and the creative use of existing resources will provide a dynamic, experiential, lasting and meaningful learning experience for all children and adults. Ungar explains, "We get fifth and sixth graders primarily from New York, they come here and spend either a three-or five-day program learning about the outdoors in the outdoors. So we get between five and six thousand kids a year coming through Ashokan and are hands-on in helping collect eggs and see sheep being shorn-it makes it real. It is just no longer food from a supermarket."[6]

TRANSFORMING THE CENTER

Ungar and Mason share the belief that people today are growing increasingly isolated from one another and from nature. The name Ashokan means "place of many fishes" or "where waters converge." They envisioned

Ashokan as a physical and emotional place where nature, music, arts, and other disciplines can bring people together in a shared community experience. Their vision is also reflected in their politics and music. Through their M&D camps at SUNY New Paltz, the duo developed a strong connection to the land and acknowledged the transformative power that both out door environmental education and the arts have on individuals of all ages. (Ungar was so inspired by the place that he composed his Grammy winning waltz, *Ashokan Farewell*, while sitting on the banks of the Ashokan reservoir.)

Mason notes, "When the Dance Camps began in 1980, we realized how important it was for people to come to this beautiful, natural place, spend time out in the woods and out in the field, see nature and play music and get away from the world's busyness." For many children, the environmental camps provide their first experience of education in a natural setting free from the classroom's four walls. (See Exhibit 1: Molly's and Jay's Inspirational Vision Statement for ACI).[7] Unger explains, "There's a big difference from telling people that they should preserve the environment and keep it clean because it's the right thing to do and inspiring them."[8] Ungar in sharing his vision for ACI, highlights the Center's resource strength:

> Through its professionally trained staff, natural resources, and teaching campus, the Board envisioned a special place that helped shape the belief systems of children and all who visited Ashohan. The transformative experience on people would be fostered through a deeper understanding of diversity, greater sense of the complexity and interconnectedness of people and the natural world, critical thinking, problem-solving skills, ethical behavior, sustainable livingand stewardship of natural resources.[9]

Ungar continues:

> To keep Ashokan open and operating with energy and food costs rising would not really be viable unless we look at sustainable ways to heat, to provide electricity and to provide food. Sustainability is not only a practical imperative, but will enable the Ashokan Center to leverage its competencies as environmental educators offering programs in innovative green facilities to develop a niche growth strategy and sustain a competitive advantage.[10]

Welch, a social researcher, writes:

> Ungar and Mason might be counted among the growing number of "cultural creatives," whose attributes include "deeply caring about ecology and saving the planet, human relationships, peace, social justice, self-actualization, spirituality, and self-expression. They are inner-directed and socially concerned. They are activists, volunteers, and contributors to good causes.[11]

ACI'S MARKETS AND BUSINESSES

The Ashokan Center operates in several markets including outdoor environmental education, music and dance, arts, weddings, festivals, and conferences. SUNY's field campus (now called Ashokan) is one of the oldest outdoor environmental education programs in New York. For each niche business, the Center faces a wide range of direct and indirect rivals including: large corporations (hotel chains, corporate training and development programs, events, concert organizers); private and public universities; religious organizations and affiliates; SMEs (small to medium size enterprises); and consultants. Without support from governmental agencies, corporate and nonprofit foundations, and donors, many non-profit service establishments that offer similar school programs would not survive. The Bureau of Labor Statistics (BLS) reported that on average 35% of net revenues for educational, non-profits came from governmental agencies and donations.[12]

The nonprofit sector of the outdoor, experiential education industry (NAICS 611: Educational Services Support, NEC) traditionally had low operating margins and net cash assets. (The ACI's primary industry classification was NAICS 611430 Schools and Educational Services, NEC (Not Elsewhere Classified). The Educational Services Sector includes programs in scientific, engineering, and technical training, trade, arts, music, and language schools to consulting and professional development programs. The large industry offers a diverse array of educational services and programs. In 2012 (latest available data) BLS (Bureau of Labor Statistics) reported that well over 68,000 establishments for this industry classification.[13] These establishments generated over $57 billion in receipts and had 669,908 total paid employees. The industry was also widely viewed by analysts as extremely fragmented, highly volatile, cyclical, and mature with excess capacity and a small number of industry leaders within well-defined market segments. Analysts reported that industry volatility implied a high level of risk, negatively affecting long-term strategic decisions. If a firm made poor investment decisions, it not only faced the risk of underutilized capacity when demand fell, but also capacity constraints when demand increased.[14] For an illustration of volatility risk versus growth for the Summer Camps Industry see Chart 1. Also see Chart 2: Summer Campus Tools of the Trade: Growth Strategies for Success. In 2014, outdoor recreational summer camps generated $2.9 billion in total revenue and $253 million in profits. At least 53 percent of New York residents annually participated in outdoor recreation activities and camps annually.

COMPETITORS

ACI's rivals are an average of 64 miles from the Ashokan Center. On average, 11 programs were offered per competitor. Bed capacity per rival ranged from a low of 85 to a high of 1,000+ beds. The quality of facilities offered in the industry ranged from rustic, dorm facilities or campsites to high-end, superior rooms and accommodations. It was not uncommon to find extremely high quality, high end rivals such as Rhinebeck's Omega Center to low-end, low-priced rivals competing in the same markets. As such, program pricing was directly related to the quality of accommodations, amenities offered, program programs available, as well as customer service quality. ACI's main competitors include:

Rhinebeck's Omega Center: In 2014 this large nonprofit organization had 23,000 patrons of all, ages. Customers attended workshops and educational programs on leadership, sustainability, health and healing, the arts and music. Omega locations comprise a 250-acre Rhinebeck, New York campus; a yoga retreat in Costa Rica; and conferences in New York City. The Omega Center heavily promoted its programming and retreat facilities spending 8-10 percent of total program revenues on marketing annually. In 2014 Omega had $18.94 million in revenues, $3.35 million in donations, and $21.8 million in expenses. Rhinebeck also reported in 2014 that its net assets (revenues minus expenses) increased by $474,499 (see http://www.eomega.org/visit-us/rhinebeck-ny)

Frost Valley YMCA: Frost offers several environmental and specialty programs for individuals of all ages. It also offers day and residential programs throughout the year. Its school programs are held on 6,000 aces in Catskills Forrest Preserve, two hours north of metro New York and New Jersey. Frost Valley has provided natural experiences for school children for over 50 years and attracts outdoor environmental educators from all over the U.S. and other countries (see http://frostvalley.org/).

Timberlake Lake Camp (TLC) and Timber Lake West (TLW): Timberlake facilities are located on two separate campuses spanning across 500 acres in New York's Catskill Mountains. TLC campers range from 7 to 16 years-old. Timberlake offers traditional co-ed campsites on well-maintained properties and facilities that feature two private spring-fed lakes, as well as an array of facilities on manicured grounds. Its Timber Lake West

CHART 1
Summer Camps: Volatility vs Growth

A higher level of revenue volatility implies greater industry risk. Volatility can negatively affect long-term strategic decisions, such as the time frame for capital investment.

When a firm makes poor investment decisions it may face underutilized capacity if demand suddenly falls, or capacity constraints if it rises quickly.

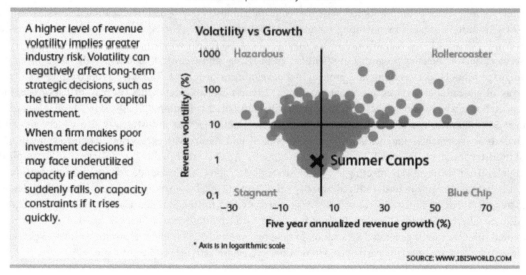

Source: Source: Yuanfei Tang, Graduate Assistant, Ashokan Center Business Plan Part 1: Industry Research, Feb.27,2015; IBIS, "Summer Camps": See: IBIS World Industry Report OD5349-Summer Camps in the US and https://www.ibisworld.com/industry/summer-camps.html; Accessed May 25, 2017

CHART 2
Summer Campus Tools of the Trade: Growth Strategies for Success

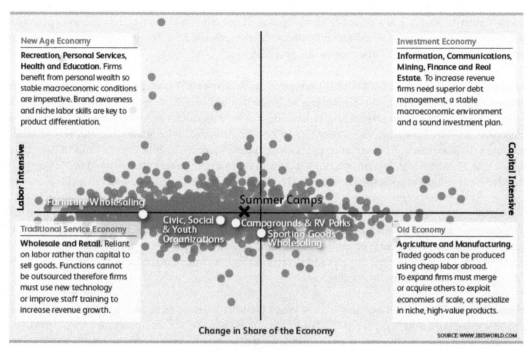

Source: Yuanfei Tang, Graduate Assistant, Ashokan Center Business Plan Part 1: Industry Research, Feb.27,2015; IBIS, "Summer Camps": See: IBIS World Industry Report OD5349-Summer Camps in the US and https://www.ibisworld.com/industry/summer-camps.html; Accessed May 25, 2017

(second campus) offers an assortment of amenities including rental facilities for up to 500 people. The TLW facilities comprise a variety of outdoor and indoor athletic facilities, a private spring-fed lake, two heated pools, high and low ropes challenge course with a 40-foot climbing tower, assembly hall/theater, and game room. Timberlake offers several other day camps and day schools in addition to TLC and TLW, including: Tyler Hill Camp, North Shore Day Camp & School, Hampton Country Day Camp, and Southampton Racquet Camp & Club. The Timberlake family of camps and rental facilities supports the Foundation for Children, a 501C-3 not-for-profit. The foundation is dedicated to promoting the health, education, welfare, and betterment of children throughout the world. Founded in the mid-1980s, this institution has donated $4.5 million to worthy causes (see http://www.camptlc.com/).

Nature's Classroom: Nature's Classroom offers similar environmental education programming in partnership with YMCAs, Universities (Boston Universities Sargent Environmental Center), and other entities at competitive prices. Nature's Classroom possesses 13 different locations in the Northeast (including New York at Silver Bay), as well as associated sites in other regions of country.

Hofstra University: Hofstra, located on New York's Long Island, offers environmental education programs for boys and girls entering grades 4-9 (see: http://www.hofstra.edu/Academics/CE/SC/index.html).

ACI PROGRAMS AND CAMPUS

ACI's 320-acre campus includes: hiking trails, streams and waterfalls, camping for groups and program participants, as well as other outdoor activities and amenities. The campus is located in Olivebrigde, New York, adjacent to the Ashokan Reservoir in the Catskills Mountains. Ashokan facilities encompass a 14,000 ft^2 main lodge; a 5,570 ft^2 barn dormitory; a 1,200 ft^2 teacher's cabin; and relocated and reconstructed historical buildings including an Indian village. Facilities include: 63 private/semi-private beds, 96 shared bunkhouse beds, 4 semi-private rooms, a 200-seat dining hall, an inside stage and dance hall, and two outside stages. (The two outside stages are named for Peter and Toshi Seeger. Peter, an iconoclastic folk hero, lived in nearby Beacon, New York and was a longtime friend and associate of Ungar and Mason.)

ACI'S PROGRAMS AND EVENTS

Ashokan's programs are divided into five broad areas that emphasize:

- Outdoor Education: learning respect for and stewardship of our natural environment while having fun in the great outdoors.
- Arts & Cultural Expression: having joyful, meaningful experiences in music, dance, literature, and the graphic arts.
- Sustainable Living: taking part in green, sustainable living, efficient energy use, onsite agricultural projects, and finding ways to do more with less.
- Living History: seeing, hearing, and feeling what life was like in a simpler time, with an eye toward finding old ways to solve the problems of today and tomorrow.
- Building Community: bringing people together to accomplish shared goals, experience new things, and enjoy a beautiful natural setting. Ashokan offers residential and day programs for students and teachers of all ages:
- Natural Science: including watershed studies and ecology, living history, culture, music, dance, and team-building.

SOURCES OF REVENUE

The board knows that financial stability is essential to achieving ACI's mission. As such, the Center has four sources of revenue:

- *Education Programs:* residential three- to five-day programs designed for school groups with all programming provided by the Ashokan Center staff. Single-day field trips with outdoors, environmental, and cultural arts programs for school groups, scout groups, staff training groups, senior citizens and other adult groups.
- *Retreat and Conference Groups:* non-Ashokan Center programming held during the summer months and on weekends throughout the entire year; these account for factors in age, purpose, facility, and program needs. Groups include camps for children and adults, yoga retreats, board meetings, scout groups, colonial craft groups, reunions, weddings, and religious gatherings.
- *Public Programs and Special Events:* programs with themes related to nature and the environment, arts in education, history, and personal development. Ashokan also has special events such as Civil War reenactments and Hoot Americana Music Festivals (since February 2013).
- *Loans, Grants and Donations:* AFI negotiated a $2 million bank loan in 2009 and received a $5 million grant from NYCDEP in 2008. The loan and grant were used to renovate older building and construct new structures for its envisioned teaching campus. In May 2017, AFI received a $2.76 million grant from NYCDEP to repair and maintain its 1885 covered bridge. The Foundation acted on behalf of the Center and functioned as its main fundraiser and source of donated funds and loans. The Ashokan Foundation managed the grants and donations on behalf of the Center. AFI grants and donations were used to fund and operationalize the ACI's vision, programs, and campus.

SCHOOL AND RETREAT REVENUES AND CAMPER DAYS UTILIZED

The Ashokan Center's education programs not only serve as a complement to New York State's primary and middle-school classroom curriculum, but also help schools achieve compliance with New York State learning standards. For example, in 2014, 28 schools sent students to the residential camps, and 23 schools and other organizations (e.g., Girl and Boy Scouts of America, Girls of Today/Tomorrow, Manhattan College) sent students to the day camps. Camper days utilized were 90, 59, and 23 days for retreats, residential schools, and day schools, respectively, for a total of 172 days utilized. Camper days (campers x camper days utilized) totaled 12,505. Music and dance camps generated total revenue of $236,154 and had an 83% gross margin.

For 2017, ACI budgeted $795,181 in School Group revenues based on 42 school groups with an average of 70 attendees per group at $270 per attendee. School groups were the largest revenue source for the Center at 45% of total revenues. Music and Dance camps were the second largest revenue source at $322,350 representing18% of total revenue. The Center budgeted 2017 revenues, expenses, and income at $1,780,109, $1,751,678 and $28,431, respectively. The 2017 budgeted numbers reflected 4% revenues and expenses increase and an 8% increase of net assets over 2016 actuals. ACI budgeted less than 2% of revenues for marketing (see Exhibit 4: Ashokan Center, Inc (ACI) Statement of Financial Position, and Exhibit 5: Ashokan Center, Inc (ACI) Income Statement 2016 and 2017).

MUSIC AND DANCE CAMPS

ACI's most popular non-school offering was Ungar and Mason's music & dance camps. The M&D camps took place 14 times per year with a focus on attracting people interested in learning or advancing their skills in

EXHIBIT 4

Ashokan Center, Inc (ACI): Statement of Financial Position, August 31, 2016

CURRENT ASSETS	
Cash	$99,153
Account Receivable	191,878
Inventory	4,825
Prepaid Expenses	69,404
Total Current Assets	365,260
NONCURRENT ASSETS	
Property & Equipment	
(Net of Acc. Dep. Of 93,096)	106,878
Total Assets	472,138
CURRENT LIABILITIES	
Account Payable	39,372
Accrued Expenses	30,564
Customer Deposits	73,488
Notes Payable-Current Portion	57,920
Total Current Liabilities	201,344
LONG TERM LIABILITIES	
Notes Payable–Long Term Portion	9,528
Total Liabilities	210,872
NET ASSETS	
Unrestricted	261,266
Total net Assets	261,266
TOTAL LIABILITIES AND NET ASSETS	$472,138

Source: Ashokan Center, Financial Reports

becoming fiddlers, guitarists, mandolin players, uke players, percussionists, singers, dancers, and teachers. Ashokan's art and music programs and events were incorporated into the majority of its school programs where the Center regularly partnered with musicians and other organizations to host cultural events. Long-time customers included Summersongs, Wayfinders, Northeast Herbal Association, and Northeast Blacksmith Association. The music and dance camps were scheduled around school programs and helped to fill rooms and utilize staff when school programs were not in session. Ungar and Mason started renting out the music halls in 1980 to host music retreats and community dances. These programs have become staples of the ACI over the years when schools are not in session. In 2006, when SUNY field campus was put up for sale, the musicians who had been attending the M&D camps banded together to save Ashokan's unique education initiatives and its beautiful environment for music making.

HOOT FESTIVALS

The Hoot Music Festivals were co-founded by Ruth Ungar (Jay's daughter) and her husband Mike in 2012. (Ruth was herself a second-generation music and dance camps attendee.) Hoot festivals were held on weekends in February and August. Attendance at the Hoots was growing with over 600 and 1,000 festival goers attending the winter and summer 2017 festivals respectively. The festivals generated positive net receipts after expenses in 2017. Ruth, like her father, was an accomplished musician and performer teaching at the music and dance camps. She also toured professionally with her husband Mike in the Mike and Ruthy Band. From an early age Ruthy regularly participated in her dad's music and dance camps. Having grown up with the Askohan music and dance camps, playing and performing along side her dad, step-mom, and mom, Lynn Hardy, Ruthie too shared Ungar and Mason's vision for Ashokan. In an interview with No Depression, Ruthy commented:

> There's a strong theme of preservation at Ashokan. A connection between the drive to understand ecology and the relationship humanity [has] to the environment and preserving the planet—and preserving the old ways of doing things that are gentler on the environment, that stem from a timeless tradition. That might be clawhammer banjo or making a broom by hand. But that's the through-line that makes everything about Ashokan part of one thing: Preserving what's timeless."[15]

EXHIBIT 5

Ashokan Center, Inc (ACI) Income Statements 2016 and 2017 (Budget)

REVENUES	2016 (Actual)	%Rev	2017 (Budget)	%Rev	Yr. over Yr. %
School Groups	782,381	46%	796,181	45%	2%
Day Programs	60,223	4%	55,000	3%	−9%
Retreat Groups	214,275	12%	241,800	14%	13%
Ashokan Events (Hoot Festivals)	113,683	7%	121,612	7%	7%
Ashokan Music and Dance Camps	307,000	18%	322,350	18%	5%
Summer Camps	1,175	0%	—		—
Weddings	154,224	9%	142,000	8%	−8%
Ashokan Store (Net)	13,216	1%	23,666	1%	79%
Fundraising	51,885	3%	70,000	4%	35%
Grants	19,185	1%	7,500	0%	−61%
TOTAL REVENUES	$1,717,247	100%	$1,780,109	100%	4%
EXPENSES					
Facilities	181,800	11%	294,200	17%	62%
Kitchen	213,816	12%	338,920	19%	59%
Program	139,697	8%	277,660	16%	99%
Administration (Note 1)	351,939	20%	695,713	39%	98%
Development	8,374	0%	13,824	1%	65%
Marketing	31,651	2%	37,200	2%	18%
Ashokan Events	71,453	4%	94,161	5%	32%
Salaries/Benefits (Note 1)	407,714	24%	—		—
Fixed Expenses (Note 1)	284,583	17%	—		—
TOTAL EXPENSES	1,691,027	98%	1,751,678	98%	4%
NET INCOME					
Net Income	$26,220	2%	$28,431	2%	8%

Note 1: Salary/Benefits, Fixed Expenses in 2017 Administration Expenses

Source: Ashokan Center, Financial Reports

Jay Ungar, building on Ruthy's comments, notes, "Part of our mission is to be an example of how those things fit together."[16] He further explains:

Most of the music that happens here happens on hand-held instruments and some on instruments made from wood that was from trees that were felled hundreds of years ago. There are definitely deep connections. Another part of it too is that when people learn environmental science and how the earth works, where their food comes from, if you connect that [education] with song, music, ad social dance experiences, it goes very deep. It becomes part of your heart and it stays with you.[17]

COMMUNITY PARTNERS: INITIAL FINDINGS

In May 2017, HBSCP made its preliminary findings stating that ACI was a high fixed-cost, low marginal-cost business, with variable cost of 20-40% of revenues. This cost structure was similar to those of hotels. It did not see much opportunity to increase school prices; rather, the best way to increase profits was increased group size and days booked. The Center was booked on average 275 days per year. If ACI could improve room days booked by 45 days at $4,000 average contribution per day, an additional $180,000 in revenue could be earned. In comparison, to raise $180,000 with 275 days booked the center would have to increase group size by 12 students at $60 per student, or ACI would have to raise contributions per day by $655, or 11 students at $60 per student. The partners reported that while the interviewed teachers and administrators were satisfied with ACI programs, they cautioned that the Center undertake further market research before making any major changes

The partners' cost analysis revealed that neither of the two major customers (schools and music camps) was more profitable materially than the other. Given that both programs were established over many years and were important contributors to current financial stability, ACI should focus their efforts on growing both in number of participants and program days, supplemented by retreats, weddings, and increased activities attractive to local communities. The partners also recommended that the Board strongly consider acquiring or forming a partnership with Ungar and Mason for the music and dance camps. Additionally, the partners noted that no succession plan was in place for the leadership of ACI or the music camps.

CONCLUSION: MOVING FORWARD

As the sun set over the Catskill mountains, Ungar was ready to travel back the thirty miles to his home after a long day at the Center. He could not help thinking about the long journey he and Mason had made from their early days at the field campus. He and Mason were proud of what they had been able to achieve, breathing new life into the field campus and saving it from demolition; but they realized that the Center still faced several challenges. While the Board was firmly committed to its mission, they were concerned about having the funds and community backing to support its campus and programs long-term. The Board knew that Ungar's song *Ashokan Farewell* had a lot to do with saving the Center.[20] The song was introduced to the general public when Ken Burns, the widely acclaimed documentary film maker, used it as the haunting background music for his mini series *The Civil War*.[21] The song evoked strong emotions and feelings from those who tuned into the mini-series. It also opened the door to New York Governor Pataki, who attended a function in 1999 where Ungar performed it. Subsequently the Governor connected Ungar to the Open Space Conservancy, paving the way for the eventual transfer of the SUNY's field campus to AFI. Ungar told the *New York Times*, "I've gotten hundreds of letters and e-mails from people saying the song figured in a transitional moment in their lives ... It's a healing a healing experience."[22]

Ungar knew there was a healing and inspirational power to his song that connected people to Ashokan. *But how could this powerful connection be used to create a sustainable competitive advantage for the center? As he prepared for the upcoming June board meeting, several questions raced through his mind: Are we spending enough on marketing and advertising? How should we invest the $2 million after the bridge was repaired? How might we grow program size and days booked? And how should we go about transferring or partnering with the Center for the M & D camps? How much longer can we maintain the pace the camps require?* We already donated all the M & D revenues to the Center. While we were glad to do it, I have been thinking about transferring ownership. How do you put a monetary value on our camps? As he finalized the agenda, he thought about the song he would open the board meeting with and what he had recently read about innovation:

Not all innovation comes from new organizations. Many come from existing organizations learning to renew themselves. Any successful organization needs to be simultaneously focused on existing activities, emerging ones, and more radical possibilities that could be the mainstream activities of the future.[23]

He wondered, *Have we been were radical enough? Will the fact that an overall strategy has not been formally developed inhibit efforts to effectively use our resources?*

ENDNOTES

1. Jay Ungar and Molly Mason, *Experience + Inspiration = Ashokan Center*. Statement prepared by Jay Ungar and Molly Mason: See: http://ashokancenter.org/about/missionhistory/
2. HBSCNY (Harvard Business School Club of New York: Community Partners), Draft Report, January 27, 17: PowerPoint presentation for ACI Board of Directors.
3. ACI changed its financial from a calendar year to a fiscal year in 2016. Fiscal Year not ends July 31tst. The change was made to better represent program revenues from Schools.
4. Martens, OSI quote
5. See: ACI Mission at: http://ashokancenter.org/about/missionhistory/
6. DeWan, D. (2009). Interview, Jay Ungar, Overview of 2009 ACI Strategic Plan and Description of Existing business, history of Ashokan Center; and DeWan, D. (2009). The Ashokan Foundation: Bridge to a Sustainable Future. *The Ashokan Center Foundation*.
7. Ibid., DeWan, D. (2009) and The Ashokan Foundation website video, 2008: http://www.ashokanfoundation.org/video.shtml
8. Ibid., DeWan, D. (2009)
9. Ibid., DeWan, D. (2009)
10. Ibid., DeWan, D. (2009)
11. Welch, W. (2008). Tactics of Hope: How Social Entrepreneurs are Changing Our World. San Rafael: Earth Aware.
12. See: "2012 NAICS: 611–Educational services," *US Census of Manufacturers* at: https://www.census.gov/econ/isp/sampler.php?naicscode=611; and "Industries at a Glance, Educational Services: NAICS 61," *Bureau of Labor Statistics*, at https://www.bls.gov/iag/tgs/iag61.htm, Accessed: May 25, 2017
13. Ibid., Educational Services: NAICS 61, Accessed: May 25, 2017
14. IBIS, "Summer Camps": See: IBIS World Industry Report OD5349-Summer Camps in the US and https://www.ibisworld.com/industry/summer-camps.html; Accessed May 25, 2017
15. Ruehl, Kim, "Part Of Your Heart," *No Depression*, in Summer Hoot 2017 Program
16. Ruehl, ibid., No Depression
17. Ruehl, ibid., No Depression
18. HBSCNY (Harvard Business School Club of New York: Community Partners), Draft Report, January 27, 17: PowerPoint presentation for ACI Board of Directors
19. Ibid., HBSCNY, January 27, 2017
20. Gaffney, Dennis, "Catskill Cultural Center Saved, and Renewed, Thanks to a Fiddler's Tune," *New York Times*, May 12, 2013
21. See: PBS Series, The Civil War: A Film by Ken Burns. Originally aired, September 1990, re-aired September 7-11, 2015, at http://www.pbs.org/kenburns/civil-war/, Accessed May 25, 2017
22. Ibid., Gaffney, *New York Times*, May 12, 2013
23. Mulgan, G. (2007). "Social Innovation: What it is, why it matters and how it can be accelerated," Skoll Centre for Social Entrepreneurship, Oxford Said Business School. Retrieved June 23, 2009, at: www.youngfoundation.org/files/images/SI-sp.pdf
24. Ashokan Document, Prepared Statement by Jay Ungar and Molly Mason

REFERENCES

Ashokan Center website http://ashokancenter.org/

Ashokan Center website, Featured Video: https://vimeo.com/32189450

Ashokan Center website, School Programs: http://ashokancenter.org/natural-history-education-research/

Ashokan Center, Music and Arts: http://ashokancenter.org/arts-music/

Ashokan Center, Facilities and Rentals: http://ashokancenter.org/facilities-rentals/

The Ashokan Foundation: Bridge to a Sustainable Future, Brochure, 2008 www.fuqua.duke.edu/centers/case/documents/dees_SE.pdf

DeWan, D. (2009). The Ashokan Foundation: Bridge to a Sustainable Future.

DeWan, D. (2009). Interview, Jay Ungar, Overview of 2009 ACI Strategic Plan and Description of Existing business, history of Ashokan Center

Mulgan, G. (2007). "Social Innovation: What it is, why it matters and how it can be accelerated," Skoll Centre for Social Entrepreneurship, Oxford Said Business School. Retrieved June 23, 2009: www.youngfoundation.org/files/images/SI-sp.pdf

Welch, W. (2008). Tactics of Hope: How Social Entrepreneurs are Changing Our World. San Rafael: Earth Aware.

Zald, M.N. (Summer 2004). Making Change: Why Does the Social Sector Need Social Movements? Stanford Social Innovation Review, Retrieved June 23,2009: http://www.ssireview.org/pdf/2004SU_feature_zald.pdf?PHPSESSID=d4f5b9f25c6dc9b5c7aeeb789114772a

6 YAHOO!: ARE THE PARTS GREATER THAN THE SUM?

BY ALOK KAVTHANKAR AND INDU PEREPU

On Feb 2, 2016, US-based technology company Yahoo Inc. (Yahoo!), released its 4th quarter and full year 2015 results. Yahoo!'s yearly revenue had grown by 7% but its cost of revenue had increased by 266% and the company had written off $ 4.461 billion owing to goodwill impairment of its recent acquisitions. Yahoo! had also announced to cut 15% of its workforce. *(Refer to Table 1 for Yahoo's Fourth Quarter and Full year results)*

TABLE 1
Yahoo's Fourth Quarter and Full Year 2015 Results

				(In $ millions)
	Q4 2014	Q4 2015	Full Year 2014	Full Year 2015
GAAP revenue	$1,253	$1,273	$4,618	$4,968
Cost of revenue—TAC	$74	$271	$218	$878
Goodwill impairment	$88	$4,461	$88	**$4,461**
Income (loss) from operations	$32	($4,530)	$143	($4,748)
Non-GAAP income from operations	$256	$63	$755	$342
Adjusted EBITDA	$409	$215	$1,362	$952
Net earnings	$166	($4,435)	$7,522	($4,359)
GAAP net earnings per share diluted	$0.17	($4.70)	$7.45	($4.64)
Non-GAAP net earnings per diluted share	$0.30	$0.13	$1.57	$0.59

Source: Yahoo!

The Chairman of Yahoo!, Maynard Webb, said, "The Board believes that exploring additional strategic alternatives, in parallel to the execution of the management plan, is in the best interest of our shareholders. In addition to continuing work on the reverse spin, which we've discussed previously, we will engage on qualified strategic proposals."[a]

Analysts decoded 'strategic alternatives' to mean "Yahoo! on sale". Apparently, the turnaround initiatives spearheaded by the CEO Marissa Mayer (Marissa), who joined the company in 2012, had yielded to the continual erosion of Yahoo!'s core business[b]—targeted advertising through its search engine and display advertising through Yahoo.com

---

a   Yahoo press release , "Yahoo To Improve Profitability and Accelerate Growth By Sharpening Focus," February 2, 2016
b   Yahoo Core comprised its search and display advertisement services. Search advertising was targeted advertising against the user search results while display advertising was essentially placing display banners against the type of content on Yahoo! as well as affiliate websites.

and auxiliary sites which produced original content. In 2015, Yahoo!'s five-year CAGR (compound annual growth rate) was—0.0651%, clearly indicating stagnancy *(Refer to Table 2 for Yahoo's Statement of Operations).*

TABLE 2
Yahoo!—Statement of Operations

(in US$ Billion)

Year	2010	2011	2012	2013	2014	2015
Revenue	6.325	4.984	4.987	4.68	4.618	4.968
Total operating expenses	5.552	4.184	4.42	4.09	4.475	9.716
Income (loss) from operations	0.773	0.8	0.566	0.59	0.143	(4.748)
Other income (expense)	0.298	0.027	4.648	0.043	10.369	0.075
Provision for income tax	(0.222)	(0.242)	(1.94)	(0.153)	(4.038)	0.089
Earnings in equity interest	0.396	0.477	0.676	0.897	1.058	0.383
Net income attributable to Yahoo!	1.232	1.049	3.945	1.366	7.522	(4.359)

Source: Annual Reports

Marissa maintained that it would take at least 3-5 years for the turnaround efforts to show results. But analysts labeled Yahoo! as a 20-year-old dinosaur in the technology business and described "3 years as a geographical epoch and 5 years as a near eternity" in the hi- tech business.

BACKDROP

In 2015, Yahoo! was one of the last bastions of the Dotcom era, with its humble beginnings in Stanford University. Yahoo! was founded in 1994 by two electrical engineers, Jerry Yang (Yang) and David Flo (Flo). The website then was called Jerry and David's guide to the World Wide Web. The guide was a directory to their favorite websites organized category-wise with an index. In the subsequent years, the list of websites grew and Yahoo! successfully monetized its search results by selling ads against the search queries generated by its users. Yahoo! went public in 1996 and, by 1998, its revenues had reached $203 million. Yahoo! also started adding communication services to its portfolio like Yahoo! Chat and Yahoo! Mail. Yahoo! Auction, an online marketplace, was launched in 1998. Yahoo! became content-oriented toward the late 1990s to increase traffic to its site. It introduced content like sports news, movies reviews, real estate, games, and weather. Yahoo.com thus became a single portal where the users could access most of the Yahoo! services.

Toward the early 2000s, the effort seemed to be to diversify revenue streams. The dotcom bubble had recently burst and recession had hit the ad revenues of Yahoo!. In 2001, revenue had slumped by 35%, taking the company into the red. Though ad revenue remained the principal contributor to the top line, in the 2001 annual report, Yahoo! said, "Our strategy is to: Build a diversified global business by focusing our efforts and leveraging our core strengths to provide deeper, more valuable solutions for our consumers and business partners." It added, "To achieve this, we are committed not only to growing our marketing services revenue, but also to broadening and growing diversified revenue streams such as listings and fees and transactions."

The new strategic shift to diversify led to the hiring of a new CEO, Terry Semel (Terry). Terry had previously served as Co-CEO and Co-Chairman of Warner Brothers, a well-known Hollywood production studio. Terry's appointment came as a surprise to Yahoo!'s top executives owing to his non-technical background but Yang was full of praise for Terry and reckoned that he would be a great asset to Yahoo! and his background would help the company to innovate for future growth. Over the next two years, Yahoo! recovered significantly, with revenue of $1.6 billion in 2003 and the marketing services contributing 74% to the top line. The contribution hadn't changed much from 2001.

Even as Yahoo! was focused on diversifying its portfolio, there were new focused start-ups like Google exploring the search engine arena. Google was founded by Larry Page and Sergey Brin at Stanford University. Google's search engine had a better algorithm patented as 'PageRank' (Larry Page as its namesake). Many analysts believed that Google's technology was superior to that of other search engines and hence Google was able to charge premium for displaying more relevant ads against its search results. Similarly, other start-ups which emerged focused on one single product. For example, Craigslist focused on classifieds and eBay on auctions.

In 2005, Yahoo! entered into a strategic tie up with Alibaba, a leading Chinese online marketplace, and purchased 46% of its outstanding common stock for $1 billion in cash. Yahoo! owned a 34% stake in Yahoo! Japan which was a publicly traded company whose majority stake was owned by SoftBank Corp. In 2005, Yahoo! acquired the remaining shares of its joint ventures in Europe and South Korea. Such moves would give Yahoo! a greater flexibility and control to take advantage of growth opportunities in these countries.

To strengthen its search advertising arm, Yahoo! devised two ways to increase its ad business. The first was to increase its reach inorganically through acquisitions of new products and services. Alternately it could demand higher ad prices through building rich content which drew more traffic. Yahoo! acquired search engine Overture Services for $1.63 billion followed by smaller acquisitions like image hosting website Flikr and media company LAUNCH Media. It continued to increase its revenue in the subsequent years and went on to become the most visited site. At its peak, Yahoo! had a market cap of $128 billion.

In 2006, Yahoo! framed its mission statement as "To connect people to their passions, their communities and the world's knowledge". Yahoo! focused on "Project Panama", its new search advertising platform which had taken longer than anticipated but was critical for Yahoo!'s intention to become a customer-focused organization. Panama, which was launched in 2006, did not perform as expected.

Toward the late 2000s, stagnation started to set in. Yahoo!'s revenue started growing in low single digits as opposed to the double digit growth of early days. The 2008 recession added to its woes. Moreover, with advertising becoming a cut-throat business, Yahoo! found itself losing traffic to its competitors.

Even as it struggled to improve, it saw four CEOs come and go between 2007 and 2012. Throughout the slack times, when its stock bottomed, Yahoo! became an easy target for hostile takeovers, which it kept at bay by adopting desperate measures like manipulating its stock price and offering expensive severance packages to employees in case they were fired after Yahoo! had been acquired by another company. Yahoo! evaded Microsoft's advances by using this technique, which would have resulted in Microsoft spending several million dollars on acquiring Yahoo! Such strategy was termed as poison pill defense. Microsoft's unsolicited $44.6 billion bid failed.

Yahoo! also became a target of investor activists like Carl Icahn who demanded a board seat to navigate Yahoo! toward maximizing shareholder value. In 2012, it was Daniel Loeb, another activist shareholder, who made Scott Thompson (Yahoo!'s then CEO) resign by publishing a letter accusing him of fabricating a Computer Science degree. Thompson's predecessor, Carol Bartz, was fired on the phone, which resulted in a media blitz, bringing Yahoo!'s management under public scrutiny for all the wrong reasons. Mounting mistrust in Yahoo!'s governance led to more investor activists who started training their guns on Yahoo!'s board. Investors not only demanded a turnaround and change in leadership but eyed Yahoo!'s Asian holdings (Alibaba and Yahoo! Japan stake) which were now ripe and amounted a large portion of Yahoo!'s value.

In 2012, analysts opined that Yahoo!'s overdependence on the PC platform was hurting its business. The world was going mobile. Social media sites like Facebook and Twitter were drawing online traffic. Google had evolved into the most preferred search engine and had developed Android, a mobile OS (operating system), bundled with its Chrome browser and other applications, which directed more traffic toward its search platform. Apple too had built its own hardware moat bundled with a slew of exclusive applications. There was a massive shift in the pattern in which people consumed content. Yahoo! had neither a browser nor an OS (operating system). Nor did it have a strong social media platform. Post 2001, Yahoo! defined itself as a media company and focused on building content rather than technology which could have channelized people to that content. Yahoo! needed a CEO with a strong technical and product oriented background. Since Terry's appointment, all the subsequent CEOs (except Yang) had lacked the experience to run a technology enterprise. Yahoo! didn't have to look far for its next CEO—one of Google's homegrown top executives was at its disposal.

MARISSA'S MANEUVERS

Marissa, a Google top executive, joined Yahoo! in July 2012. She was Google's 20th employee and had played an instrumental role in designing Google's web services. Marissa had been responsible for several of Google's successful products like Google Maps, Google Earth, Street View, Google News, and Gmail.

Marissa described Yahoo's position in online display and search advertising as 'strong' and hoped to "inject some innovation and some new ways of advertising" into its business model.

From late 2012, Yahoo! went on an acquisition spree (Refer to Exhibit I for Yahoo's Acquisitions under Marissa). The first acquisition in October 2012 was a mobile app named Stamped which allowed users to share things or places with their friends. "We're looking for smaller-scale acquisitions that align well overall with our businesses,"[c] Marissa had said at a shareholder conference call. By the end of 2013 there were 37 acquisitions and aqui-hires[d]. The biggest acquisition was Tumblr, an internet blogging service which Yahoo! bought for $1.1 billion in cash, outbidding Facebook by $200 million. After Tumblr, Yahoo! attempted to bid for Hulu, a movies and TV show streaming service. But when the bidding topped $1billion, the deal didn't work out. The acquisition spree continued in 2014 but at a relatively slower pace, mobile apps being the major targets. Clearly, Marissa's focus was turning to mobile followed by video streaming.

Yahoo!'s revival strategy was driven around "Mavens", an acronym for mobile, video, native, and social. Yahoo! launched its own video division named Yahoo! Screen in 2012 to produce rich original content and focus on video advertising. Marissa started Yahoo! online magazines which covered diverse areas like health, parenting, fashion and beauty, and spent millions of dollars on hiring talent. She placed her bets on the magazines as a key to reinvent Yahoo! as a one stop destination for rich content. Another acquisition was that of Polyvore, a clothing e-Commerce website owned by an ex-colleague of Marissa's at Google. The Polyvore deal was seen as a wrong move by Yahoo! investors. Eric Jackson (Eric), manager of hedge fund Spring Owl, said, "It is unacceptable to pay $230 million for zombie companies run by former Googlers."[e]

Apart from a series of acquisitions, Marissa also focused on shaping the Yahoo! culture. As soon as she joined, she launched a policy that food should be made free at Yahoo! offices. A year after joining, she banned Yahoo!'s popular telecommuting (work from home) policy. Then there was the extravagant 1920's Gatsby theme party in 2015, on which Yahoo! spent $7 million, much to the annoyance of investors. The party was in the news for the anger it created among shareholders rather than the exuberance it exhibited.

By 2015, in the three years in which Marissa was at the helm, the revenues from Mavens climbed from about 12% in 2013 to 25% of the total revenues in 2014. But mobile and video sites did not show much growth. The number of employees fell by 29% mainly as Yahoo! exited from several products. At the same time, several high profile executives from companies like Amazon, Google, and AoL who had joined Yahoo! in top positions, left the company. Yahoo! spent a lot of money on their compensation and severance.

Experts pointed out that some of the projects through which Marissa had planned to revive Yahoo! failed to take off. The mobile development app failed to increase its market share in the mobile search engine market. When it came to advertising, Marissa felt that the homepage ad increased the load time of Yahoo! Mail, and had

---

c   David Benoit, "Yahoo CEO Mayer Expects to Make Small Acquisitions," http://blogs.wsj.com, October 22, 2012.

d   Aqui-hiring is an act or instance of buying out a company primarily for the skills and expertise of its staff, rather than for the products or services it supplies.

e   Maya Kosoff, "Hedge Funder Slams Yahoo: 'It is Unacceptable to pay $230 million for Zombie Companies run by Former Googlers,'" www.businessinsider.in, December 14, 2015.

it removed in order to improve user experience. This led to a loss of more than $ 70 million in ad revenue for the company. Yahoo! Gemini, a search and native advertising solutions provider, also failed to take off.

As Marissa had predicted, photo sharing and sharing multimedia content took off in a big way, but Tumblr remained stagnant while others like Instagram and Pinterest grew popular. The digital magazines did not generate any enthusiasm among the audience, and the video content on which Yahoo! had spent more than US$ 100 million did not attract many new visitors.

During the three years, revenues, however, declined by 3% a year. Though $ 6 billion had been invested on product development and acquisitions, the returns were yet to be seen. Analysts also pointed out that under Marissa, the core business had declined by half. *(Refer to Table 3 for EBITDA of Yahoo's Core Business)*

TABLE 3
Yahoo!—EBITDA

US $ Million

Quarter	EBITDA
Q1 2012	303
Q2 2012	321
Q3 2012	309
Q4 2012	405
Q1 2013	281
Q2 2013	262
Q3 2013	234
Q4 2013	309
Q1 2014	203
Q2 2014	181
Q3 2014	186
Q4 2014	221
Q1 2015	76
Q2 2015	100
Q3 2015	99
Q4 2015	96

Compiled from various sources

Despite all the initiatives and action, investors claimed that Marissa had failed to turn the organization around. Meanwhile, the majority of analysts valued Yahoo! Inc as worthless, as Yahoo!'s market value less its holdings in Alibaba and Yahoo! Japan and marketable securities resulted in a negative figure (Refer to Exhibit II for Yahoo's valuation).

Activist investors were back, this time it was Eric Jackson (Eric) who managed Spring Owl Asset Management LLP, a New York-based hedge fund, and Jeffery Smith (Smith), managing member of Starboard Value, a New York-based financial advisory. Though both the activist investors had shown distrust in the management to create shareholder value, they had proposed two different approaches for the Yahoo! Board and Marissa to take.

MAXIMIZING SHAREHOLDER VALUE

In early 2015, the Yahoo! Board authorized a tax-efficient plan to pursue the spin-off of all remaining holdings in the Alibaba Group, then valued at $32 billion, which was a 15% stake. Yahoo! had previously sold $10 billion in Alibaba shares, taking a tax hit of $3 billion. Being a US company, Yahoo! faced a federal tax bill of about 35% when it sold stock in other enterprises for cash.

In the 2014 annual report, Yahoo! wrote to its shareholders "Yahoo's Board of Directors and executive team are committed to delivering shareholder value through sustained growth. In 2012, our leadership team began a multiyear transformation to return an iconic company to greatness, shifting from a declining desktop strategy to a mobile-first strategy that has already yielded significant results. Our strategy to reinvent our business has made Yahoo one of the top three players in mobile, and we're just getting started."

Yahoo! bought back $9.1 billion of shares from July 2012 through the end of 2014. So combined with the Alibaba spin-off, Yahoo! promised to create $40 billion of value to its shareholders. But in late 2015, Yahoo! was still indecisive about spinning off its Alibaba holdings. Further, the activist shareholders were relentlessly targeting the Yahoo! Board and Marissa for their indecisive stance, often writing letters which gave rise to a great amount of public scrutiny.

Yahoo! had planned to spin off the Alibaba shares into a new company called Aabaco, an independent company mostly comprising Alibaba shares which would be then distributed to Yahoo! shareholders on a pro-rata basis. When Yahoo! proposed this plan to the IRS (Internal revenue service), the IRS refused to allow the Aabaco spin-off.

When the tax-efficient plan came to a halt, Starboard Value wrote a letter to the Yahoo! Board suggesting the action Yahoo! should take.

STARBOARD'S PROPOSITION

The letter came in the wake of Yahoo!'s Board being indecisive about the Alibaba spin-off due to the tax risk. Instead, the company announced that it would explore the reverse spin-off[f] of Yahoo!'s assets and liabilities other than the Alibaba and Yahoo! Japan stake, which would then trade as separate companies.

"In addition to our efforts to increase value and diminish uncertainty for investors, the ultimate separation of our Alibaba stake will be important to our continued business transformation,"[g] Marissa said in a statement. "In 2016, we will tighten our focus and prioritize investments to drive profitability and long-term growth. A separation from our Alibaba stake, via the reverse spin, will provide more transparency into the value of Yahoo's business."[h]

The letter from Starboard highlighted Yahoo!'s declining EBITDA adjusted to its core business and further expressed mistrust in the management's ability to turn the Yahoo! business around. Smith further suggested that instead of eroding Yahoo!'s core value through failed attempts, it was the right time to seek a financial or strategic buyout (*Refer to Table 4 for Starboard's plan*). Alternatively, there had to be a dramatic change in the composition of the Yahoo! Board along with cost-cutting initiatives and selective investment in certain parts of the business.

---

f   Seperating Yahoo Assets and Liabilities and the Asian stakes. Thus forming two separate companies.
g   Julia Greenberg, "Yahoo will Lay off 15 Percent of its Workforce," www.wired.com, February 02, 2016.
h   "Yahoo Provides Update on Planned Spin Off of Remaining Stake in Alibaba Group," www.businesswire.com, December 09, 2015.

TABLE 4

Starboards Plan

Sell Yahoo! core to Strategic buyers to increase shareholder value , form a shell company which will mostly contain Yahoo!'s Asian stakes, i.e. Alibaba and Yahoo! Japan		
Yahoo! Core (C+ D)* will earn	$8.2 B	Z
Value created per share Z/ Total Shares (S)	$8.6 per share	N
Yahoo! CMP	$27	Y
Appreciated market price (N+Y)	$35.6	
Total Valuation of Yahoo! (S X35.6)	$33 Billion	
* Go through Exhibit II for more details		

Source: Starboard

The letter concluded with Smith's warning, "If the Board is unwilling to accept the need for significant change, then an election contest may very well be needed so that shareholders can replace a majority of the Board with directors who will represent their best interests and approach the situation with an open mind and a fresh perspective."[i]

The Yahoo! Board then decided to spin off its core business and its Yahoo Japan stake. The company would then be left with only the stock of Alibaba; the Yahoo core business and Yahoo Japan would trade under a different ticker.

SPRING OWL PROPOSITION

Spring Owl was against this proposal and came out with its own suggestions. The Spring Owl proposition was not a letter but a 99-page, exhaustive presentation titled as "A better plan for Yahoo! shareholders" which it shared in December 2015. Spring Owl agreed with Starboard on the radical degradation of Yahoo's! core business and need for changes at the top including a new CEO who must have Tech/Digital/Media industry experience. Eric strongly disagreed with Starboard's proposition to sell the Yahoo! core at a low, which would only create value of $3-$4 per share, Valuating Yahoo! only at $6 billion.

Instead, Eric laid out a plan for Yahoo!'s revival and for investing resources in Yahoo!'s Core, creating $60 dollar per share of additional value compared to Smith's plan. Eric suggested strong cost-cutting measures in the form of stopping the free food policy and laying-off staff in verticals having poor prospects. He further suggested chopping the Yahoo! head-count to 3000 employees, his rationale being that Facebook had $15 billion in revenues with a head count of just 11000 whereas Yahoo! generated approx. $5 billion of business and had under 12000 employees.

---

i   "Starboard Delivers Letter to Yahoo's Board of Directors," www.finance.yahoo.com, January 06, 2016.

TABLE 5
Spring Owl's Plan

Action	Result	
Wait for Alibaba returning to $120/share and Yahoo! Japan increasing in value by 12%	adds $31.78 to per share	I
Buy back 24% shares of Yahoo! below $45 per share using $1.8B proceeds from selling property, reducing cash reserves by $4 B and raising debt of $4B. Retire 226 million shares at $43.36 per share	adds $23.47 to per share	II
Attain 8x EV/EBITDA Multiple for Core business adding $3B ($750M Normal EBIDTA+ plus $2.25B gain through Headcount Reductions)	adds $22.46 to per share	III
Yahoo! CMP (Current market price)	$27	IV
Share price appreciation after optimization of Asian stakes and buyback and laying off (I+II+III+IV)	$100 +	
Total valuation of Yahoo! as a single entity after retiring 24% shares (944million—226 million) X 100	$71 billion	

Eric further said that buying back the shares for the sake of buyback would not create value; Yahoo! had spent $2.5 billion in share buy-backs in 2013. However, Eric suggested that at the existing stock prices, buyback made sense. Yahoo! had $5.5 billion in cash reserves and its Sunnyvale campus with 1 million sq. ft. of property could fetch $1.5 billion. Also, bringing the cash levels down to their historically normalized $1.5 billion level and taking a debt of $4 billion, Yahoo! could retire 24% of its outstanding share, thus boosting the stock value of its remaining shares substantially. The report further suggested that Yahoo! should wait until its Asian holdings tracked to higher values. *(Refer to Table 5 for Spring Owl's Plan).*

THE RECOURSE

A week after Yahoo! released its 4th quarter and full year 2015 results, things weren't the same at Yahoo!'s Sunnyvale headquarters. In accordance with the announcement that 15% of the Yahoo! workforce would be laid off, Marissa announced lay-off Wednesdays, wherein employees would be laid off in tranches with effect from April 2016. Yahoo! announced that several of its digital magazines would be shuttered and the salvage would be shifted to Yahoo! News. Marissa thus wanted to focus on most successful content areas, which were finance, news, sports, and lifestyle.

All the years since Marissa's appointment, Yahoo! had been the shadow stock of its Asian holdings, mainly Alibaba (Refer to Exhibit III to see how Yahoo!'s stock was tracking Alibaba's stock). The spinning-off of Yahoo! Core or even seeking strategic buyers seemed to be the logical way out. U.S. based telecom carrier Verizon was one such strategic buyer which had previously bought search engine major AOL for $4.4 billion. However, Verizon's was ready to offer only between $2-3 billion, much below Yahoo!'s marketable and cash security of $6.8 billion. The other buyers lined up were Comcast and AT&T. There were also non-strategic buyers, mainly private-equity players like Bain capital and Vista equity partners.

In April 2016, Yahoo! ceded to the proxy war raged against it by Starboard. It announced in a press release that it would welcome four new board members from Starboard, including Smith. Maynard Webb, chairman of Yahoo's board of directors, said, "We are pleased to welcome these four new highly respected, independent directors to our board. The additional board members will bring valuable experience and perspectives to Yahoo! during this important time for our company."[j]

Yahoo!'s levers were again in the hands of an activist investor. Yahoo! had four options:

1. Make a second attempt to spin off its Asian holdings after the denial of IRS. The shell company would then trade under a different ticker, bringing transparency into the valuation of Yahoo! Core.
2. Reverse spin-off. This proposition was pushed by Starboard Value, spinning off of the Yahoo! Core and Yahoo! Japan holding while holding on to the Alibaba shares which would then transform into a shell company. Reverse spin-off is complicated and would take at least a year.
3. Re-organizing: Yahoo! had a confused identity; it had to choose between being a Tech company or a Media company. Yahoo! had let each new wave of Technology pass-by, be it Search, Social or Mobile. Yahoo! had also hired McKinsey to identify which business to shut and which to focus on. Having written off 4.5 billion dollars, the acquisition spree led by Marissa was questionable.
4. Firing Marissa and pruning the workforce and following other measures in the Spring Owl proposition. Firing Marissa would also incur a hefty severance amount to the tune of $55 million.
5. Outright sale of Yahoo! to strategic buyers or private equity.

EXHIBIT 1
Yahoo Acquisitions Since 2012

Date	Company	Business	Value US$ Million
Oct-12	Stamped	Social Recommendation	3
Dec-12	OnTheAir	Video Chat	4
Jan-13	Snip.it	Social Network	10
Feb-13	Alike	Social Recommendation	1
Mar-13	Jybe	Social Recommendation	1
Mar-13	Summly	News Aggregation	30
May-13	Astrid	Productivit y	2
May-13	GoPollGo	Real time survey	1
May-13	MileWise	Flight Rewards	2.5
May-13	Loki Studios	Mobile Gaming	1
May-13	Tumblr	Blogging	1100
May-13	PlayerScale	Online gaming	1
Jun-13	GhostBird Software	Mobile Photography App	1
Jun-13	Rondee	Video Conferencing	1
Jun-13	Bnignoggins Productions	Fantasy Sports	1
Jun-13	Qwiki	Automated Video Production	50
Jun-13	Xobni	CRM	60
Jun-13	Ztelic	Social Analytics	1

---

j   "Yahoo Announces Board Changes and Agreement With Starboard," www.businesswire.com, April 27, 2016.

EXHIBIT 1 (continued)
Yahoo Acquisitions Since 2012

Date	Company	Business	Value US$ Million
Jun-13	Lexity	ecommerce Analytics	35
Aug-13	Rockmelt	News Aggregation	70
Aug-13	IQ Engines	Image Recognition	4
Sep-13	Hitpost	Sports	2
Oct-13	Bread	Advertising	3.5
Oct-13	LoofFlow	Image Recognition	1
Dec-13	SkyPhrase	Natural Language Processing	1
Dec-13	Ptch	Video Sharing	7
Dec-13	EvntLive	Live music playing	2.3
Dec-13	Quik.io	Cross poltform video streaming	1.3
Dec-13	PeerCDN	Content Delivery Network	1
Jan-14	Aviate	Intelligent homescreen	80
Jan-14	SPARQ	Mobile Marketing	1.7
Jan-14	Cloud Party	Virtual world gaming	1
Jan-14	Tomfoolery	Converstaion Platfrom	16
Jan-14	Incredible Labs	Time Management	1
Feb-14	Wander	Social Diary	1.2
Feb-14	Distill	Technical Recruiting	1.3
Mar-14	Vizify	Social Media Information	1.5
May-14	Blink	Mobile Messaging	2
Jun-14	PhotoDrive	Photo Management	1
Jul-14	RayV	Video Streaming platform	16
Jul-14	Flurry	Mobile Analytics	300
Aug-14	ClarityRay	Ad Security	1
Sep-14	Luminate	Advertising	30
Sep-14	Bookpad	Document Handling	25
Oct-14	LittleInc	Messaging App	1
Nov-14	BrightRoll	Online Video Advertising	715
Dec-14	Coollris	Photo Viewing	28
Dec-14	Media Grou pOne	Advertising and Online Video	1
Jul-15	Polyvore	Clothing E-commerce	230
		Total	**2852.3**

Source: Presentation by Spring Owl

EXHIBIT 2

Yahoo! Valuation Math (March 2016)

Yahoo! number of shares outstanding	944	S
Number of shares in Alibaba	*383 million (15% Holding)*	
Value of Yahoo! stake in Alibaba at $60 CMP	$22.98B	X
After Tax 35%	$14.93B	A
Number of Shares in Yahoo! Japan	*2021.54 million (35% holding)*	
Value of Yahoo! stake in Yahoo! Japan at CMP	$ 7.6 B	J
After Tax 35%	$4.94B	B
Yahoo! cash and marketable security	$6.8B	C
Convertible Debt	$(1.4)B	D
Yahoo!'s value if liquidated after selling stakes in Alibaba and Yahoo! Japan and then deducting tax (A+B+C-D)	$25.27B	E
Yahoo! current market cap	$25.8B	F
How market values Yahoo!'s core business (F-E)	$0.53 B	G
Yahoo! present value the way market values it F-X+J+C-D	Negative $12.98 B	H
The valuation of Yahoo! implies either a massive tax liability on Yahoo!'s minority equity interests in Alibaba and Yahoo! Japan Corporation ("Yahoo Japan") or that the remaining operating assets of Yahoo! are worthless, or a combination of the two.		

Compiled by the author

EXHIBIT 3
How Yahoo! is Tracking Alibaba

Source: Spring Owl

EXHIBIT 4
Stock Price Chart of Yahoo!

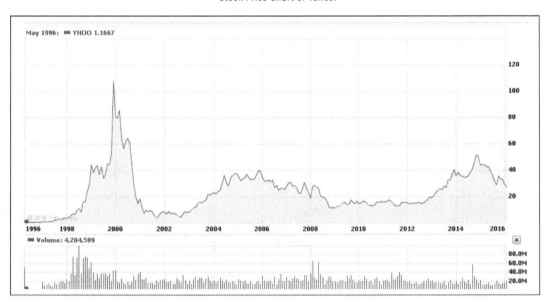

Source: Yahoo Finance

EXHIBIT 5

Net Search Ad Revenues—Worldwide

US$ Billion

	2014	2015	2016
Google	**38.41**	**43.98**	**47.57**
– % Change	17.70	14.50	8.20
– % of total	60.80	58.90	55.20
Baidu	**5.35**	**6.91**	**8.71**
– % Change	41.00	29.10	26.10
– % of total	8.50	9.20	10.10
Microsoft	**1.90**	**2.48**	**2.94**
– % Change	11.90	30.20	18.60
– % of total	3.00	3.30	3.40
Yahoo	**1.78**	**1.62**	**1.41**
– % Change	4.80	(9.20)	(12.70)
– % of total	2.80	2.20	1.60
Sohu.com	**0.32**	**0.47**	**0.61**
– % Change	78.10	47.00	29.50
– % of total	0.50	0.60	0.70
Other	**15.41**	**19.27**	**25.01**
– % Change	19.30	25.10	29.80
– % of total	24.40	25.80	29.00
Total Search Spending	**63.17**	**74.72**	**86.25**

Source:Marketeer.com

ADDITIONAL READINGS:

1. Julia Greenberg, **"Yahoo will Lay off 15 Percent of its Workforce,"** www.wired.com, February 02, 2016.
2. Maureen Farrell, **"What Yahoo's Main Business Might Be Worth,"** blogs.wsj.com, December 2, 2015
3. Leslie Picker, **"How To Value Yahoo's Core Business,"** www.nytimes.com, December 9, 2015

7 XIAOMI IN CHINA: STRUGGLING WITH "COOLING" GROWTH

BY GARIMA RATNA

"Disruptive Chinese phone maker Xiaomi is now five years old. In that time it has accomplished a lot more than pretty much any other half-decade-old company—it has diversified from smartphones to all manner of smart gadgets, expanded out of China, made headlines around the world, formed a legion of passionate fans, and risen to become one of the world's top phone brands. While all that was happening, Xiaomi has pushed HTC to the edge of the abyss, terrified the life out of Samsung, and perhaps even given Apple some food for thought."[a]

—Steven Millward[b]

It took a short span of five years for the China based tech start-up-Xiaomi to be hailed as 'The Apple of China'.[c] The title was well justified. Xiaomi offered features comparable to the best smartphone in the market at very competitive prices. This led to Xiaomi witnessing a meteoric rise in its fortunes and soon occupying the *numero uno* position in the smartphone market of China. The feat was remarkable as China's market was inundated by tech behemoths like Apple, Samsung, Huawei, etc. However, the extremely successful run of Xiaomi went for a toss in the year 2015. The curtailing of annual sales target by the company and not so overwhelming response to the company's smartphones were an indication that the company was losing its grip on the market. The fact that China's smartphone market was maturing only added to Xiaomi's woes in 2015. Analysts had also started doubting the company's much hyped $45 billion valuation (as of 2014). While all this was creating a buzz in the market, Xiaomi was setting its eyes on the overseas markets. Was Xiaomi making a right choice with overseas expansion instead of consolidating in the home turf?

---

a   Millward Steven, "Xiaomi at 5 years old (INFOGRAPHIC)", https://www.techinasia.com/history-of-xiaomi-infographic, August 14th 2015.
b   He is a tech blogger and Editor-in-Chief at Tech In Asia.
c   Ahmad Daniel, "A brief history of Xiaomi—China's tech success story!", http://www.gizchina.com/2014/04/18/brief-history-xiaomi-chinas-tech-success-story/, April 18th 2014 "© 2016, Amity Research Centers HQ, Bangalore. All rights reserved."

XIAOMI: THE MAKING OF A CHINESE BRAND

CHARACTERISTICS OF CHINA'S SMARTPHONE MARKET

According to IDC[d], China's smartphone market was headed towards saturation in 2015.[e] For the first time in six years, China's smartphone market shrunk by nearly 4% YoY in the first quarter of 2015. On the quarter to quarter, basis the market reportedly shrunk almost 8%. Kitty Fok, Managing Director at IDC China, stated thus on the maturing China's smartphone market, "Smartphones are becoming increasingly saturated in China. China is oftentimes thought of as an emerging market but the reality is that the vast majority of phones sold in China today are smartphones, similar to other mature markets like the US, UK, Australia, and Japan. Just like these markets, convincing existing users as well as feature phone users to upgrade to new smartphones will now be the key to further growth in the China market."[f]

Going by a Nielsen[g] report in 2015, smartphone penetration in urban China had already exceeded 90%.[h] Amongst the medium to high income group and below 30 age group consumers, the smartphone penetration level was above 80%. The same report further stated that the availability of more smartphones in the market was no longer a key trend and Chinese customers were increasingly inclined to look for quality and performance of smartphones while making purchasing decisions. Oliver Rust (Rust), Managing Director of Nielsen China, made a pertinent point when he stated, "Despite the fact that the penetration rate of smartphones is close to reaching maturity within urban areas and middle to high income groups, we still see big opportunities for consumption from these same segments. Their demand stems from the upgrading of equipment and consumers are continuing to pay more attention to the quality and performance of smartphones."[i] Rust further stated, "With the penetration rate of smartphones already above 80% for urban consumers, we expect an overall upgrading trend in China's smartphone market. It is expected that middle and high-end smartphones will be the primary source of growth in 2015. Manufacturers who are able to leverage the trend of premiumization to build higher performing products will have a greater chance at success."[j]

Occupying the top throne in the Chinese smartphone market had become a game of 'musical chairs' for the multitudes of smartphone companies playing in the China market. According to a press release of IDC, "Apple was the top smartphone vendor in China in the first quarter of 2015, with consumers still having a strong appetite for the larger screens on the iPhone 6 and iPhone 6 Plus. Xiaomi slipped to the second position as it faced strong competition from other vendors in the low to mid-range segment of the market, while Huawei maintained third position as it saw a good uptake in the mid-range segment. Samsung and Lenovo both led the market at least once last year, but rankings have since changed quickly, highlighting the volatility of consumers' brand preference in China."[k] As per strategists, other trends that ruled the year 2015 included employing multi-brand strategies and seeking overseas expansion[l] (Exhibit 1).

---

d   International Data Corporation (IDC), an American market research, analysis and advisory firm, specializes in information technology, telecommunications, consumer technology and Software Development.
e   "China's Smartphone Market Contracts Year Over Year for the First Time in Six Years, According to IDC", https://www.idc.com/getdoc.jsp?containerId=prSG25614115, May 10th 2015.
f   ibid.
g   Nielsen Holdings N.V. is an American global information and measurement company with headquarters in New York and Diemen, the Netherlands.
h   "Nielsen: Chinese Smartphone Market Now Driven By Upgrading", http://www.nielsen.com/cn/en/press-room/2015/Nielsen-Chinese-Smartphone-Market-Now-Driven-by-Upgrading-EN.html, June 17th 2015.
i   ibid.
j   ibid.
k   "China's Smartphone Market Contracts Year Over Year for the First Time in Six Years, According to IDC", op.cit.
l   ibid.

EXHIBIT 1
Popular Trends in China's Smartphone Market (2015)

- **Multi-brand strategies**. Huawei and ZTE were positioning younger sub-brands Honor and nubia, respectively, to chip away at Xiaomi's user base, and to attempt to gain a loyal fanbase. Lenovo was also getting into the mix with the Motorola acquisition, not to mention its upcoming online-focused Shenqi division.
- **Higher price tier competition**. More vendors like Huawei, Lenovo, and even Xiaomi were trying to push higher into the mid to high-end segment.
- **Non-traditional channel strategies**. Reduced operator subsidies meant that vendors would further expand channels into more vendor-branded retail shops, direct online sales, and eTailers instead. In particular, they were trying to save on the cost that they had to pay to the traditional dealers/distributors in the past.
- **Expansion into overseas markets**. With the market in China slowing down, Chinese vendors focused on increasing their presence in India as well as more Southeast Asia countries in 2015.

Source: Compiled by the Author from- "China's Smartphone Market Contracts Year Over Year for the First Time in Six Years, According to IDC", https://www.idc.com/getdoc.jsp?containerId=prSG25614115, May 10th 2015

Additionally, China was on the verge of a big 3G and 4G revolution.[m] As revealed by a GSMA[n] study, users of 3G and 4G smartphones would constitute nearly two-thirds of China's mobile connections by the end of 2015. Further, nearly 68% (913 million) of the estimated 1.3 billion mobile connections in China would be on smartphones by the end of 2015. Incidentally, smartphone adoption in China had touched 62% at the end of the Q1 of the year 2015 when the European average was 55%. As stated by Hyunmi Yang (Yang), the GSMA's Chief Strategy Officer, "Our study published today reveals a vibrant domestic device market that has established the smartphone as a lifestyle hub and digital platform for millions of Chinese citizens"[o] **(Exhibit 2)**.

Apart from the increase in smartphone adoption, there were major Chinese companies (China Mobile, China Unicom and China Telecom) which were investing heavily in 4G infrastructure in China. It was also predicted that the number of 4G smartphone connections would touch the figure of one billion by 2020 from 100 million as reported at the end of 2014.[p] Transaction volume of China's smartphone market was expected to become 470 million units in 2016 and according to expert analysis, would gear towards saturation.[q] Despite the fact the China's smartphone market was reaching maturity phase, the fact remained that, as of 2015, the country accounted for nearly 28.3% of the global smartphone users and by 2019, nearly half (49.8%; 687.7 million Chinese) of the population would possess a smartphone and use it at least once in 30 days.[r]

m   Perez Bien, "China has more smartphone users than US, Brazil, and Indonesia combined", http://www.businessinsider.com/china-has-more-smartphone-users-than-us-brazil-and-indonesia-combined-2015-7?IR=T, July 13th 2015

n   The GSM Association, formed in 1995, is an association of mobile operators and related companies devoted to supporting the standardising, deployment and promotion of the GSM mobile telephone system.

o   "China has more smartphone users than US, Brazil, and Indonesia combined", op.cit.

p   ibid.

q   Wang Amy, "Android OS Dominates China Smartphone Market", http://www.chinainternetwatch.com/16230/smartphone-market-overview-2015/, December 16th 2015

r   "Asia-Pacific Boasts More Than 1 Billion Smartphone Users", http://www.emarketer.com/Article/Asia-Pacific-Boasts-More-Than-1-Billion-Smartphone-Users/1012984, September 16th 2015

EXHIBIT 2

Percentage of Smartphone Users in China (2010–2015)

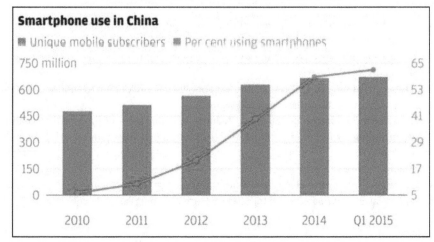

Source: Perez Bien, "China has more smartphone users than US, Brazil, and Indonesia combined", http://www.busines-sinsider.com/china-has-more-smartphone-users-than-us-brazil-and-indonesiacombined-2015-7?IR=T, July 13th 2015

Notably enough, Chinese smartphone brands were set to benefit from the rise of smartphone adoption in China as according to Yang, "They are benefiting from a rich local smartphone manufacturing and design ecosystem, which is allowing them to compete effectively with foreign smartphone brands."[s] Apart from this, Android OS seemed to have found preference amongst Chinese buyers. The reason behind iOS not being popular enough was that Chinese smartphone users were reluctant to pay for software[t] **(Annexure 1–4)**. Moreover, according to a press release of Strategy Analytics[u], "Led by Huawei and Xiaomi, domestic brands in China are gaining market share from global brands. More Chinese-branded Android-based smartphones are now providing greater usability for core daily features and are attracting consumers with innovations in industrial design and localized experiences."[v] The Chinese brands that ruled the roost were Huawei, Xiaomi, Lenovo, ZTE, Alcatel, Vivo and Oppo.[w] And amongst these brands, the most interesting success story was that of Xiaomi.[x]

---

s   "China has more smartphone users than US, Brazil, and Indonesia combined", op.cit.
t   Carmen, "Smartphones usage in China", http://zeendo.com/info/smartphones-usage-in-china/, December 12th 2013
u   It is a firm involved in market research and has worked with CEOs, product planners and managers, research managers, product development teams and financial and business managers.
v   Brown Paul and O'Neill Diane, "Chinese Smartphone User Evaluation: Domestic Brands Gaining Market Preference", https://www.strategyanalytics.com/strategy-analytics/news/strategy-analytics-press-releases/strategy-analytics-press-release/2015/10/07/chinese-smartphone-user-evaluation-domestic-brands-gaining-market-preference#.VnoRiLZ95kg, October 7th 2015
w   Gilbert David, "Chinese Brands Huawei, Lenovo, Xiaomi And More Dominate Global Smartphone Industry", http://www.ibtimes.com/chinese-brands-huawei-lenovo-xiaomi-more-dominate-global-smartphone-industry-2078834, September 2nd 2015
x   Osawa Juro, et al., "Xiaomi Becomes World's Most Valuable Tech Startup", http://www.wsj.com/articles/xiaomi-becomes-worlds-most-valuable-tech-startup-1419843430, December 29th 2014

Xiaomi was founded by eight co-founders in April 2010, the prominent being Lei Jun.[y] Other two prominent partners of this eight-member collaboration were Qualcomm (mobile chip developer) and Temasek Holdings (an investment firm owned by the Singaporean government).[z] One year later, Xiaomi released its first product-a smartphone named Xiaomi M1.[aa] The mobile was launched in the market in October 2011 and in December 2011 good news awaited the company as the smartphone was the most searched after device on Chinese search engines. If the year 2011 ushered in encouraging response for Xiaomi's tech products, the year 2012 was even better. A funding round of $216 million led to Xiaomi being considered at par with the iconic BlackBerry. The company registered a sale of 7.19 million phones. Once establishing itself in the top league, Xiaomi started experimenting with its product offerings. It launched Mi2, and Xiaomi Box for streaming media to televisions apart from selling phones on Sina Weibo—a Chinese twitter like platform.[ab]

In the year 2013, the company set its eyes on markets outside China. Xiaomi prepared to set its foot in Hong Kong and Taiwan. Xiaomi also launched its first budget phone-the Hongmi (or Redmi) priced at a modest $129. In the same year, Xiaomi introduced new products like Mi3 phones and MiTV. Xiaomi was certainly making its way in the China's smartphone of the time, but the best news came in the month of August 2013 when Canalys–a prominent research firm announced Xiaomi to be ahead of the iconic smartphone brand–Apple. Xiaomi was number sixth in the ranking and Apple was at seventh. Almost 18.7 million Xiaomi phones were sold in 2013.[ac]

In the year 2014, Xiaomi treaded further and set foot on Singapore soil. Apart from this, in the same year, the company launched MiPad. Xiaomi ventured into the smartphone markets of other Asian economies–India, Philippines, Malaysia and Indonesia. The company conscientiously stayed away from US market and sought to venture into third world markets as growth seemed to lie there. Apart from venturing into other Asian markets, Xiaomi continued its 'new product launch spree'. Consequently, Mi4 phone, Mi Band fitness tracker, smart home gadgets and smart air purifiers were released in the market.[ad] According to media reports, Xiaomi's valuation jumped somewhere between $40 billion and $50 billion. Further, as reported by Bloomberg, the company registered an impressive $12 billion in revenues the same year. Although the figure was small when compared to Apple's revenues ($182.8 billion) or Samsung's revenue ($200 billion), it was quite remarkable by its own standards.[ae]

The year 2014 probably brought in the best news in Xiaomi's short corporate life. The brand had toppled Samsung and became the *numero uno* smartphone brand in Chinese market, according to Canalys. In the same year, Xiaomi clocked in a whopping $163 million during one of China's 24 hours shopping sales. This sale included 1.2 million Xiaomi smartphones amongst other Xiaomi products. Overall, in the year 2014, Xiaomi managed an impressive 61.12 million phone sales. The following year, the company launched Xiaomi Note in the Chinese market. But then, the successful stint was interrupted by some bad news in the year 2015 when Apple toppled Xiaomi to occupy the top slot in the Chinese smartphone market.[af] In the same year, Xiaomi expanded beyond Asian markets and ventured into Brazil. Apart from this, the company started manufacturing the Redmi 2 Prime in India.[ag] Juro Osawa and Eva Dou of the Wall Street Journal remarked with regards to the meteoric rise of Xiaomi, "Over the past few years, Xiaomi has thrown the country's traditional electronics

y   "Xiaomi at 5 years old (INFOGRAPHIC)", op.cit.
z   Abbruzzese Jason, "What is Xiaomi? Getting to know the Chinese company that is taking on Apple", http://mashable.com/2015/01/18/what-is-xiaomi/#cpXZaUDLMSqp, January 19th 2015
aa   "Xiaomi at 5 years old (INFOGRAPHIC)", op.cit.
ab   ibid.
ac   ibid.
ad   ibid.
ae   "What is Xiaomi? Getting to know the Chinese company that is taking on Apple", op.cit.
af   "Xiaomi at 5 years old (INFOGRAPHIC)", op.cit.
ag   "Xiaomi at 5 years old (INFOGRAPHIC)", op.cit.

makers into disarray. The company's buzzy online sales and rock concert-like product launches netted the company a $46 billion valuation, making it China's most valuable startup."[ah]

Aaron Back (Back) of the Wall Street Journal attributed the success of Xiaomi to its business model, pricing policy and its ability to build 'a distinct software ecosystem on top of the Android platform that is not easily copied'.[ai] In the words of Back, "Xiaomi's business model, though, is no Apple clone. While the U.S. Company earns the bulk of its profits from sales of high-price hardware, Xiaomi pushes cheap devices and turns them into a platform to distribute software. Besides frequent over-the-air updates of the operating system, Xiaomi peddles software through a dedicated app store, including proven money makers such as mobile games. It has made investments in video content and smart home technology. That Google is largely absent from the Android app store game in China has given Xiaomi room to breathe."[aj]

While some analysts attribute Xiaomi's success to its business model, others laud its different approach to marketing and strategising.[ak] Moreover, according to Kenneth Chew, Head of Communications at TradeGecko[al], "XIaomi's unique, wildly successful business model is one for the history books—they've drastically cut down on the traditional costs associated with marketing and distributing, by relying purely on the internet for sales ... What Xiaomi has done, is to essentially eliminate the large 20 percent to 25 percent cut retailers/distributors typically get, and pair that with the vision of earning profits from accessories and web applications/services within its eco-system (MIUI) instead. That's not to say Xiaomi does not earn from its mobile phones at all, for it still certainly does (albeit at a much lower margin)."[am]

However, by the end of the year 2015, Xiaomi seemed to lose some steam and analysts the world over doubted its high valuation figures.[an]

ARE THE GOOD DAYS OVER FOR XIAOMI?

The third quarter of the year 2015 ushered in interesting facts about Chinese smartphone market. As reported by the research firm Canalys, Huawei had surpassed Xiaomi to become the number one smartphone selling brand.[ao] While Huawei had witnessed a robust 81% year-on-year growth in its sales, Xiaomi was grappling with the possibility that its 2015 target would not be met after all. Xiaomi had set its 2015 target of 100 million phones which was revised to 80 million during the course of the year. According to market reports, there was a strong possibility of the company not able to meet the target of 80 million also. According to Canalys, Xiaomi was 'under tremendous pressure to keep growing as an international player as it is slowing down in its key home market'.[ap] This was in stark contrast to Xiaomi's status in the year 2014[aq], when Xiaomi had raced its way to the top leaving behind Apple, Huawei and Samsung in the Chinese smartphone arena[ar] **(Exhibit 3)**. As analysed

ah   Osawa Juro and Dou Eva, "In China's Smartphone Battle, Huawei Catches Up to Xiaomi", http://www.wsj.com/articles/xiaomi-loses-its-top-spot-in-china-to-huawei-1445534662, October 22nd 2015

ai   Back Aaron, "Xiaomi's Valuation Backed By More Than Buzz", http://www.wsj.com/articles/xiaomis-valuation-backed-by-more-than-buzz-heard-on-the-street-1419241661, December 22nd 2014

aj   ibid.

ak   "Xiaomi Success Story", http://successstory.com/companies/xiaomi

al   TradeGecko is a Singapore based software-as-a-service company that develops online inventory and order management software targeted at SMEs. The company was recognised as one of the most innovative business-tobusiness software providers at the Red Herring Asia 100.

am   Chew Kenneth, "Here's the secret behind Xiaomi's disruptive success—are you ready?", https://www.tradegecko.com/blog/heres-the-secret-behind-xiaomis-disruptive-success, October 31st 2014

an   Culpan Tim, "Xiaomi's $45 Billion Valuation Seen 'Unfeasible' as Growth Cools", http://www.bloomberg.com/news/articles/2015-11-25/xiaomi-s-45-billion-valuation-seen-unfeasible-as-growth-cools, November 25th 2015

ao   Russell Jon, "Huawei Overtakes Xiaomi To Top China's Smartphone Market For First Time: Report", http://techcrunch.com/2015/10/23/huawei-overtakes-xiaomi-to-top-chinas-smartphone-market-for-first-time-report/, October 23rd 2015

ap   "Huawei Overtakes Xiaomi To Top China's Smartphone Market For First Time: Report", op.cit.

aq   Shu Catherine, "Xiaomi Edged Out Samsung As China's Top Smartphone Vendor In 2014, Says IDC", http://techcrunch.com/2015/02/17/xiaomi-beats-samsung-in-china/, February 17th 2015

ar   ibid.

by the research firm IDC[as], Xiaomi had acquired this remarkable success on the basis of 'a combination of its low prices and online flash sales'.[at] Besides, as told by Hugo Barra, Xiaomi's Vice President of International, the company's strategy of keeping the price of smartphones low through a 'combination of a smaller smartphone portfolio coupled with longer average selling time per device' served as a catalyst in making Xiaomi to top the market share list.[au]

EXHIBIT 3
Xiaomi's Scorecard 2014

Table 1
China's Smartphone Shipments by Vendor, 2014Q4 vs 2014Q3 and 2013Q4

Rank	Tenure	2014Q4 Market Share	2014Q3 Market Share	2014Q4 Market Share	Year-on-Year Unit Growth in 2014Q4
1	Xiaomi	13.7%	14.8%	6.5%	150%
2	Apple	12.3%	5.0%	7.4%	99.7%
3	Huawei	11.0%	9.1%	10.2%	28.3%
4	Lenovo	9.5%	12.8%	13.2%	−14.3%
5	Samsung	7.9%	11.0%	18.8%	−49.9%
	Others	45.6%	47.2%	43.9%	23.5%
	Total	100%	100%	100%	19.1%

Source: IDC Asia/Pacific Quarterly Mobile Phone Tracker, February 2015

Table 2
China's Smartphone Shipments by Vendor, 2014 vs 2013

Rank	Vendor	2014 Market Share	2013 Market Share	Year-on-Year Unit Growth in 2014
1	Xiaomi	12.5%	5.3%	186.5%
2	Samsung	12.1%	18.7%	−22.4%
3	Lenovo	11.2%	11.9%	13.7%
4	Huawei	9.8%	9.3%	27.4%
5	Coolpad	9.4%	10.7%	4.6%
	Others	44.2%	44.9%	22.0%
	Total	100%	100%	20.0%

Source: IDC Asia/Pacific Quarterly Mobile Phone Tracker, February 2015

Source: Shu Catherine, "Xiaomi Edged Out Samsung As China's Top Smartphone Vendor In 2014, Says IDC", http://techcrunch.com/2015/02/17/xiaomi-beats-samsung-in-china/, February 17th 2015

---

as   IDC (International Data Corporation) is a global market intelligence and consulting firm. It specializes in providing market intelligence, advisory services, and events for the information technology, telecommunications, and consumer technology markets.
at   "Xiaomi Edged Out Samsung As China's Top Smartphone Vendor In 2014, Says IDC", op.cit.
au   ibid.

By November 2015, it was clear that Xiaomi was heading towards missing its annual sales target.[av] Incidentally, the sales target was to sell nearly 80 million Xiaomi smartphones in the year 2015.[aw] Tim Culpan made a pertinent point when he remarked, "Xiaomi's falter shows the startup's challenge in trying to maintain momentum after a meteoric ascent past Apple Inc. and Samsung Electronics Co. in China. Investors bought into the company's story of youthful disruption and online sales, yet the subsequent lowering of China's growth target and the copying of its sales strategy by rivals have neutralized Xiaomi's first-mover advantage, putting its high price tag in doubt." Xiaomi's damp squib performance in the year 2015 led the market analysts express doubt over the company's high $45 billion valuation. In the view of Alberto Moel, Analyst at Sanford C Bernstein in Hong Kong, "All those expectations of growth aren't being realized, which now makes that $45 billion valuation unfeasible. The argument was that their business is kind of like Apple and they're growing very fast, but they're no longer growing so fast and they're not as good as Apple." As per Canalys' statistics, domestic shipments of the company's smartphones (premium Mi4 and budget Redmi series) plunged by 8% (in comparison to Q3 of the year 2014) in the Q3 of the year 2015. As per the reports of another market research firm-IHS-Xiaomi shipments dropped 3.9% in the year 2015 as this drop had led to Huawei Technologies Company almost closing the gap with Xiaomi.[ax]

Talking of competition and competitors, Canalys reported in November 2015 that Huawei posted a whopping 81% growth in year-on-year sales and pushed Xiaomi behind.[ay] While Huawei rose phenomenally in the maturing Chinese market, Xiaomi seemed to lose the race.[az] In the words of Canalys' analyst Jessie Ding (Ding), "Huawei's ascent to China's smart phone throne is a remarkable feat, especially in the context of an increasingly cutthroat and maturing Chinese smart phone market." While saying so, Ding reminded that Xiaomi was under tremendous pressure to expand overseas as the market in its home ground was cooling off."[ba]

While its market was cooling off on home ground, Xiaomi was setting its eyes on the US market, albeit with no specific time line.[bb] US market was not devoid of challenges either.[bc] Evan Blass, Freelance Editorialist at Venturebeat hit the nail on its head when he stated, "A lot of it comes down to simple economics: whereas Xiaomi has built up a sizable infrastructure and partner network in Asia over the last several years, its assets in the Western hemisphere are restricted to a single South American nation (Brazil) and a few U.S. distribution channels for its Mi Band wearable. In other words, many of the factors that allowed it to drive down costs at home and among neighboring markets abroad are lost when it comes to large-scale ambitions halfway around the world. Of course, much of that can be overcome, if the will to do so is strong enough. It seems, then, that the major impediment is at the same time more subtle but also deeper-seated: a cultural divide that places a higher value on intellectual property in the West, as well as a wariness with regard to Chinese brands, in particular, that entrants like Huawei are all too familiar with. Overcoming these intangibles is no small task, even for a company able to throw a lot of money at its problems."[bd] With much hyped valuation in doubt, shrinking market on home turf and with ambitions to capture the US market, was Xiaomi really on the right track?

av   "Xiaomi's $45 Billion Valuation Seen 'Unfeasible' as Growth Cools", op.cit.
aw   ibid.
ax   "Xiaomi's $45 Billion Valuation Seen 'Unfeasible' as Growth Cools", op.cit.
ay   "Xiaomi's $45-billion valuation 'unfeasible': Report", http://timesofindia.indiatimes.com/tech/tech-news/Xiaomis-45-billion-valuation-unfeasible-Report/articleshow/ 49933097.cms, November 26th 2015
az   Gilbert David, "Xiaomi Loses Title Of China's Top Smartphone Company To Huawei As It Considers US Expansion", http://www.ibtimes.com/xiaomi-loses-title-chinas-top-smartphone-company-huawei-it-considers-us-expansion-2151782, October 22nd 2015
ba   ibid.
bb   ibid.
bc   Blass Evan, "Xiaomi in the U.S.: Challenges and opportunities", http://venturebeat.com/2015/12/11/xiaomi-in-the-u-s-challenges-and-opportunities/, December 11th 2015
bd   ibid.

China's Smartphone Market: An Overview

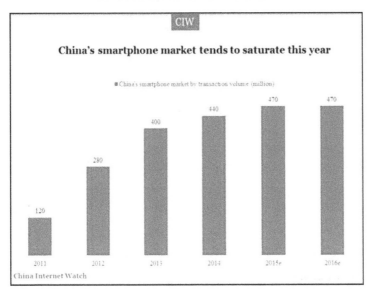

Source: Wang Amy, "Android OS Dominates China Smartphone Market",
http://www.chinainternetwatch.com/16230/smartphone-market-overview-2015/, December 16th 2015

ANNEXURE 2

Dynamics of China's Smartphone Market (Price-wise)

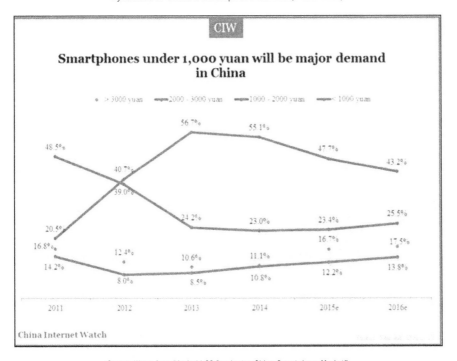

Source: Wang Amy, "Android OS Dominates China Smartphone Market",
http://www.chinainternetwatch.com/16230/smartphone-market-overview-2015/, December 16th 2015

ANNEXURE 3
Dynamics of China's Smartphone Market (Brand-wise)

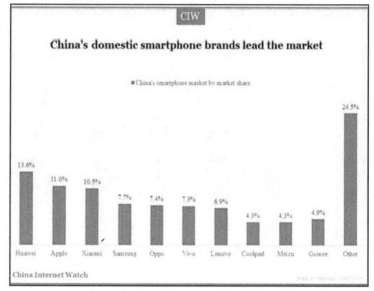

Source: Wang Amy, "Android OS Dominates China Smartphone Market",
http://www.chinainternetwatch.com/16230/smartphone-market-overview-2015/, December 16th 2015

ANNEXURE 4
Dynamics of China's Smartphone Market (Operating System Wise)

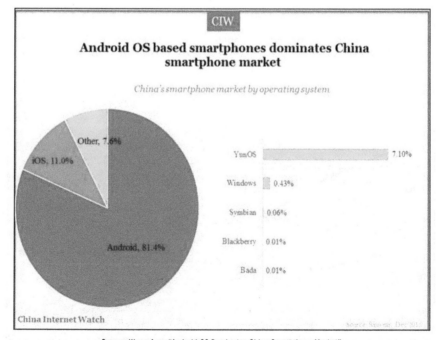

Source: Wang Amy, "Android OS Dominates China Smartphone Market",
http://www.chinainternetwatch.com/16230/smartphone-market-overview-2015/, December 16th 2015

8 AVON'S TURNAROUND PLANS: A MOVE IN THE RIGHT TRACK?

BY NILOSHA SHARMA

"The challenges that Avon faces developed over time, not overnight, and it will take time to implement the solutions as well." [a]

—Sherilyn S. McCoy, Chief Executive Officer, Avon Products Inc.

Avon Products Inc. (Avon) was the leading beauty products manufacturer and direct seller with annual revenue of $9 billion. Avon, one of the world's largest direct sellers sold its products through 6 million active independent sales representatives globally. Avon comprised of brands like ANEW, Avon Color, Skin-So-Soft and Advance Techniques. The product line of Avon comprised skincare, color cosmetics, fashion and home products and fragrance.[b] In order to strengthen the performance of the company and also to increase the revenue growth, Andrea Jung, the then CEO of Avon came up with a multi-year restructuring effort in 2005.[c] Jung worked hard to expand the company internationally and also emphasised on the betterment of women in the society. During the reign of Jung, Avon was saddled with issues like bribery and declining sales in the US.[d] In the wake of such challenges, Jung was replaced by McCoy as the new CEO in 2012. McCoy took various measures to revive the company.[e] As part of that, in 2015, Avon had to spin off its North American business to Cerberus Capital Management which acquired a majority stake in the company.[f] Furthermore in 2016, under the leadership of McCoy, the company came up with a three year turnaround plan which focused on markets like Brazil and Russia, leveraging social media to promote the company[g] and also to increase the number

---

a   Morrissey Janet, "Wall St. Is Pounding on Avon's Door", http://www.nytimes.com/2013/02/03/business/avon-tries-a-new-turnaround-plan-and-wall-st-is-anxious.html, February 2nd 2013

b   "About Avon", http://www.in.avon.com/PRSuite/whoweare_main.page

c   "Avon Embarks on Multi-Year Restructuring Effort", http://media.avoncompany.com/index.php?s=10922&item=23132, November 15th 2005 "© 2016, Amity Research Centers HQ, Bangalore. All rights reserved."

d   Petrecca Laura, "Avon names Sherilyn McCoy CEO, replacing Andrea Jung", http://usatoday30.usatoday.com/money/companies/management/story/2012-04-09/avon-ceo-sherilyn-mccoy/ 54122886/1, April 9th 2012

e   "Avon Board of Directors Announces Appointment of Sherilyn S. (Sheri) McCoy as Chief Executive Officer of Avon", http://media.avoncompany.com/index.php?s=10922&item=126082, April 9th 2012

f   "Avon And Cerberus Announce A $605 Million Strategic Partnership To Drive Avon Shareholder Value", http://www.cerberuscapital.com/avon-and-cerberus-announce-a-605-million-strategic-partnership-to-drive-avonshare-holder-value/, December 17th 2015

g   "Avon to Cut 2,500 Jobs and Move Headquarters to Britain", http://www.nytimes.com/2016/03/16/business/international/avon-move-hq-britain.html?_r=0, March 15th 2016

of sales representative across the world.[h] However, stockholders at Avon were not convinced about the three year turnaround plan. Also they were dissatisfied by the results in the last quarter of 2015.[i] In this scenario, the case study would discuss McCoy's initiatives to turnaround the company and the opportunities and challenges that lie ahead.

AVON PRODUCTS INC.: A BACKGROUND NOTE

Avon Products Inc. was started in 1886 by David H. McConnell (McConnell), who was a salesman selling books door-to-door.[j] McConnell had to make great efforts to entice the customers and as part of that gave free perfumes as perk along with books to his female customers. McConnell witnessed that the female customers were ardent about the perfume and also enjoyed networking with other women.[k] This encouraged McConnell to set up a perfume company named as 'The California Perfume Company' and recruited Albee as its first General Agent. In 1939, the company was renamed as Avon Products Inc. In 1955, the company started 'Avon Foundation for Women' which worked towards the betterment of women. By 1972, the sales of the company were $1 billion and Avon had around 600,000 Beauty & Fashion Advisors worldwide.[l]

In 1988, James E. Preston (Preston) was appointed as the President and CEO, and in 1989 Edward J. Robinson was appointed as the executive vice-president and chief financial officer.[m] By 1998, the top management witnessed several changes as Charles Perrin replaced Preston and was appointed as Vice Chairman and chief operating officer. Preston said, "We wanted someone who had experience as a chief executive of a global company. A lot has been made of the gender issue. But the first responsibility of the Avon board is to place Avon in the hands of someone who can lead it."[n]

Thereafter, in 1999, within two years of leadership Perrin was replaced by Andrea Jung (Jung) as the chief executive of Avon. The company relied on Jung to revamp Avon's business which faced stiff competition from Procter & Gamble's Oil of Olay cosmetics and declining sales in the United States. Jung who took over as chief executive was enthusiastic to revive the brand. Stanley C. Gault, Director, Avon, said, "Ms. Jung has a thorough knowledge of the company and the global beauty industry, as well as the passion to mobilize the organization during this period of significant change. It has been the board's intention that Andrea would become Avon's next C.E.O., and given Charlie's decision to retire, we firmly believe this is the right time."[o]

Given the challenging business scenario, Avon, came up with multi-year restructuring effort in 2005 under the leadership of Jung. With restructuring in place, Avon tried to strengthen its overall performance and increase its revenue growth. Jung commented that, "With this plan, we're taking very aggressive action to address the issues we faced in 2005, and to become a far more streamlined global competitor that is closer to its consumers. By taking a comprehensive approach to our enterprise expense base and global value chain, we are identifying more efficient and effective ways of operating. We will, in turn, reinvest much of the projected savings to fuel topline growth and improve our competitive position." Jung further concluded that, "Avon's strengths remain enviable, and we continue to believe that we have the right overall strategies and a powerful business model.

h "Avon Loss Widens, Revenue Declines", http://www.nasdaq.com/article/avon-loss-widens-revenue-declines-20160211-00714, February 11th 2016

i Swamynathan Yashaswini, "Avon's turnaround plan does not instill confidence: analysts", http://www.reuters.com/article/us-avon-shareholders-idUSKCN0V02OH, January 22nd 2016

j "A Brief History", http://www.in.avon.com/PRSuite/history.page

k "Experience Avon's History", http://www.avoncompany.com/aboutavon/history/index.html

l "Avon Heritage", http://www.in.avon.com/PRSuite/avon_heritage.page

m "Avon Products, Inc. : Developing A Global Perspective", https://www.dsef.org/wp-content/uploads/2012/01/Avon_Products.pdf

n Wayne Leslie and Gilpin N. Kenneth, "Avon Calls On a Man to Lead It; Female Cosmetics Executives Passed Over for Top Post", http://www.nytimes.com/1997/12/12/business/avon-calls-man-lead-it-female-cosmetics-executives-passed-over-fortop-post.html, December 12th 1997

o Candey Dana, "Opportunity Re-Knocks at Avon; Passed Over Before, a Woman Is Named Chief Executive", http://www.nytimes.com/1999/11/05/business/opportunity-re-knocks-avon-passed-over-before-woman-named-chiefexecutive.html, November 5th 1999

The actions we announced today are intended to accelerate our transformation, and return our business to a sustainable growth trajectory in both revenue and earnings per share."[p]

In the same year, realising the strategic importance and long-term growth potential, Avon decided to align its global business operating structure by classifying Central and Eastern Europe and China as stand-alone business units. With such development, Avon's geographical regions were divided as—North America, Latin America, Western Europe, Middle East and Africa, and Asia Pacific. Furthermore, in order to speed up the information flow, Avon planned to unify its brand marketing and supply chain functions under Global Business Units (GBU). All the regional staffs were expected to report directly to functional heads of GBU. Talking on the changes, Jung stated that, "Our rapid growth in recent years requires a new way of operating that improves focus on priority geographies, reduces operating complexity, and allows us to achieve the full benefits and efficiencies that come with increased scale. By flattening the organization, strengthening integration and centrally managing the global brand and supply chain functions, we will significantly increase speed and flexibility in decision-making, become closer to our Representatives and customers, and achieve our goal of delivering world-class products at world-class cost."[q]

Elizabeth Smith (Smith) was appointed as the Executive Vice President and President of North American business and also global marketing. Jung mentioned that, "With these management appointments, we have put in place a very talented team of leaders with the right skills and experience to drive our business going forward. Coupled with the comprehensive structural realignments, we have made significant changes that we believe will position the business for sustainable growth."[r] In 2007 Smith was elevated as the President of Avon and given additional responsibility of Global Supply Chain and Global Information Technology. Jung said, "Liz has played a key leadership role in Avon's turnaround since joining the company three years ago. She has been instrumental in setting the company on the path to sustainable growth and has significantly elevated our analytical and operational rigor." Jung further added that, "Aligning our product-to-market functions under a leader of Liz's caliber will help us accelerate the global integration of our key business processes and technology. This will be an important enabler for two of the company's most critical turnaround initiatives, Product Line Simplification and Strategic Sourcing, which together are projected to deliver total annual benefits of more than $400 million to help us fuel continued growth."[s]

In 2009, Avon continued with its restructuring efforts and focused on improving its cost structure and effectiveness of its global operations. Charles Cramb, Vice Chairman, Chief Finance and Strategy Officer, Avon said, "When fully implemented, the initiatives approved to date reflect almost half the costs to implement the 2009 restructuring program, and are expected to generate approximately 60% of the targeted annualized savings. As a result, we are on track to achieve our stated goal of approximately $200 million in total annualized savings by 2012-2013, with costs to implement all initiatives expected to be in the range of $300-$400 million."[t] Apart from this, Avon also explored business opportunities in UK and as part of that acquired Liz Earle Beauty Co. Limited.[u] Jung said, "We are delighted to welcome Liz Earle Naturally Active Skincare to Avon, and we see this new partnership as a perfect fit for both companies. Liz Earle's tightly edited range of award-winning, naturally active skincare products is highly complementary to Avon's anti-aging skincare and broader beauty portfolio. It also represents a long-term opportunity to develop a stand-alone Liz Earle direct-selling Representative channel."[v]

p   "Avon Embarks on Multi-Year Restructuring Effort", op.cit.
q   "Avon Realigns Operating Structure", http://media.avoncompany.com/index.php?s=10922&item=22944, December 7th 2005
r   ibid.
s   "Elizabeth Smith Appointed President, Avon Products, Inc.", http://media.avoncompany.com/index.php?s=10922&item=23117, September 11th 2007
t   "Avon Highlights Initial Restructuring Actions Under 2009 Program Announced In February", http://media.avoncompany.com/index.php?s=10922&item=22844, July 22nd 2009
u   Liz Earle Beauty Co. Limited, privately-held UK brand of naturally active skincare products sold primarily through direct-to-consumer channels.
v   "Avon Acquires Liz Earle Beauty Co. Limited", http://media.avoncompany.com/index.php?s=10922&item=22848, March 25th 2010

Apart from this, Jung worked hard to expand the company internationally and also emphasised on the betterment of women in the society. Although, Jung strived hard to take to company to newer heights, she faced various financial and legal issues which included 'falling stock value', declining sales in the US and various bribery scandals across the countries.[w] In between, Avon received a letter from Coty Inc. to consider the proposal to acquire the company.[x]

These issues led Avon to look for leadership change in the company. In 2011, the company decided to divide the roles of Chairman and CEO. Jung was appointed as Executive Chairman and began to search for a new CEO. Jung said, "I believe the time is right to separate the Chairman and CEO roles and I look forward to continuing to serve Avon as Chairman as we address the company's growing scale and opportunities. Over the past twelve years we have transformed the business from a decentralized group of local operating entities to a globally-managed business in over 100 countries with global brands and a global operating model. In the process, revenues have more than doubled, and the number of Representatives has doubled as well. As we look to the future, Avon's business model remains advantaged, with both the Beauty and Direct Selling industries growing around the world, and with our broad, geographic footprint. A new CEO will provide a fresh lens and additional operational and executive leadership."[y]

In 2012, the search for new CEO ended with the appointment of Sherilyn S. (Sheri) McCoy (McCoy) as the new Chief Executive Officer of Avon. Fred Hassan, Lead director, Avon's Board, said, "The Board conducted an extensive search among many world-class candidates across the direct selling, retail and consumer sectors, and Sheri emerged as the clear choice to take Avon into the future. Sheri has a unique combination of strategic and finely-honed operational skills, a significant turnaround track record, global experience and people leadership. Given her consistent record of outperforming against new challenges, we have great confidence that under Sheri's leadership Avon can successfully execute against our strong long-term prospects."[z]

CAN CEO SHERI McCOY GIVE A FACELIFT TO AVON?

McCoy, who joined Avon as the new CEO, formerly worked with Johnson & Johnson (J&J) and had successfully completed 30 years of her professional career. McCoy had four US patents and pursued BS in textile chemistry from University of Massachusetts, did her Post graduation in Chemical engineering from Princeton University and completed her MBA from Rutgers University. McCoy joined J&J in 1982 as a scientist and looked after consumer women's health business. McCoy rose to the role of Vice Chairman, Executive Committee, and member of the Office of the Chairman at Johnson & Johnson and left in 2011 to join Avon. Upon joining Avon, Jung mentioned that, "We are thrilled to have someone of Sheri's caliber assuming the leadership of Avon. Throughout her career at J & J, Sheri has had a demonstrated track record of successfully achieving results and driving change across highly diverse operating units with widely varying product lines, customers, distribution channels and business models. She is also known for her ability to identify and empower great talent and motivate and inspire people. I look forward to supporting Sheri as Avon's new CEO"[aa] (**Exhibit 1**).

w   Petrecca Laura, "Avon names Sherilyn McCoy CEO, replacing Andrea Jung", http://usatoday30.usatoday.com/money/companies/management/story/2012-04-09/avon-ceo-sherilynmccoy/54122886/1, April 9th 2012

x   "Avon Receives Letter from Coty", http://media.avoncompany.com/index.php?s=10922&item=126094, May 10th 2012

y   "Avon to Separate Roles of Chairman and CEO", http://media.avoncompany.com/index.php?s=10922&item=96618, December 13th 2011

z   "Avon Board of Directors Announces Appointment of Sherilyn S. (Sheri) McCoy as Chief Executive Officer of Avon", http://media.avoncompany.com/index.php?s=10922&item=126082, April 9th 2012

aa   ibid.

EXHIBIT 1

Sheri McCoy: Avon's CEO

Source: Lublin S. Joann, et al., "Avon Picks a CEO From J&J",
http://www.wsj.com/articles/SB10001424052702303815404577333322094827312, April 9th 2012

Joining Avon, McCoy stated that, "I am extremely honored and excited to join Avon—a great company with an iconic brand and so much clear potential. Avon has an unparalleled global direct selling sales force of over six million Representatives and an enviable geographic footprint. I look forward to working with the team to develop and execute a roadmap to achieve the next phase of growth for the company."[ab] However, many industry observers opined that it would be a tough task for McCoy to recreate the brand Avon. According to Lawrence Hrebiniak (Hrebiniak), Management Professor, Wharton, "She is clearly qualified, but she has no direct sales experience." Hrebiniak further added that, "This lack of familiarity with Avon's business model means McCoy faces an unusually steep learning curve. Her biggest challenge … is to refocus a brand that former CEO Andrea Jung led astray over the past few years in her attempts to recreate Avon as a retail powerhouse that could compete with the likes of L'Oreal. Yet the company never had the manpower or resources to make it to that level." Hrebiniak further opined that, "Even as it was turning away from its tried and true direct sales model. Jung really created strategic uncertainty for the company. It's still in the position of deciding what it wants to be when it grows up."[ac]

Upon joining, McCoy had various immediate issues to be solved like planning a strong strategy, deal with the bribery issues cropped up during Jung's time, revamping the IT structure of Brazil which was one of the most important markets for Avon and improving the performance of the company in the market. According to Denise Cox, a representative at Avon Canada, "It would be pretty hard to predict what's going to happen now with a new CEO. Hopefully things will settle down and get back on track."[ad] In 2011, Avon witnessed a decline in worldwide revenue by 4% in

---

ab   "Avon Board of Directors Announces Appointment of Sherilyn S. (Sheri) McCoy as Chief Executive Officer of Avon", op.cit.

ac   "Changes Needed at Avon Are More Than Cosmetic", http://knowledge.wharton.upenn.edu/article/changes-needed-at-avon-are-more-than-cosmetic/, April 25th 2012

ad   Lublin S. Joann, et al., "Avon Picks a CEO From J&J", http://www.wsj.com/articles/SB10001424052702303815404577333322094827312, April 9th 2012

the fourth quarter. Only the Mexico market recorded an increase in revenue. Beside this, another challenge for McCoy was to enhance the image of 'Avon Lady' among the customers. Apart from this, the sales force across the regions declined by 3% in the fourth quarter of 2011 particularly in Russia and North America. According to Hrebiniak, "McCoy needs to 'shake up the culture' and redefine what it means to sell Avon products, especially if she wants to attract younger women to the sales force." Hrebiniak further added that, "She needs to revitalize it with new incentives and increased pay. She's going to have to play up the brand and [create] a lot of excitement."[ae]

Furthermore, some of the industry observers felt that, McCoy had to generate emotional connection with women in emerging markets. According to Monica McGrath (McGrath), Adjunct Professor of Management at Wharton, said, "As the new CEO, McCoy must also focus more on recruiting sales representatives in emerging markets, where many women still have few employment opportunities outside the home." McGrath further added that, "McCoy should tap into the emotional attachment a significant number of women still have for Avon, while making the Avon connection attractive to a new generation. Many people have a very warm and nostalgic feeling about the brand. For my mother's generation, it was the only way a woman could be a working mother. [McCoy] needs to figure out how to ... leverage those feelings."[af]

In 2012, McCoy proposed to implement various measures and save annual cost of $400 million by 2015 (Exhibit 2). As part of the initial cost saving measures, the company planned to layoff around 1500 positions worldwide and also go away from Vietnam and South Korean markets. McCoy said, "In order to turn around the business, we are focused on driving top-line growth and aggressively managing our cost base. The decisions outlined today are necessary to stabilize the company and begin the process of returning Avon to sustainable growth."[ag]

EXHIBIT 2
McCoy's Strategic Priorities for Avon

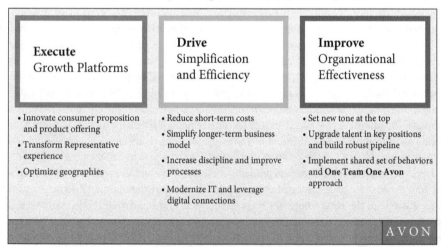

Source: Brodo Robert, "A Business Leadership Lesson from the Beauty Queen", http://www.advantexe.com/blog/business-leadership-lessons-from-the-beauty-queen, November 3rd 2015

---

ae   "Changes Needed at Avon Are More Than Cosmetic", op.cit.
af   ibid.
ag   "Avon Announces Initial Steps of Cost Savings Initiative", http://media.avoncompany.com/index.php?s=10922&item=126192, December 11th 2012

Despite various efforts, Avon's North American sales declined to $1.46 billion in 2013 and by 21% in 2014 (**Exhibit 3**). In 2014, Avon had to further lay off around 600 representatives in the North American market.[ah]

EXHIBIT 3

North American Sales of Avon 2007-2014

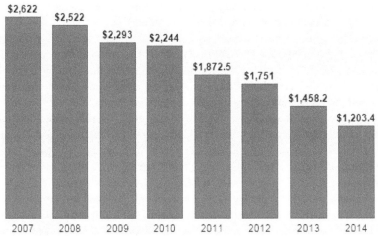

Source: Wahba Phil, "Here Are 5 Reasons Avon Fell Apart in the U.S.", http://fortune.com/2015/12/17/avon-us-decline/, December 17th 2015

Although, McCoy made various attempts to augment the commission structure, targeting the Hispanics community who were ardent Avon customers, bringing new computers to enhance the order management and payment structures for sales representatives, it failed to improve the position of Avon.[ai] Avon was left with no alternative but to spin off its North American business. According to analysts at RBC Capital Markets, "We believe Avon is coming to terms with the reality that cost cuts are not the answer and it needs to recapitalize and finding funding for a massive $500M-$1B reinvestment needed to fix the business. Seeking strategic alternatives is likely Avon's best option, but also a risky one for the partner involved with Avon as a fix is not guaranteed."[aj]

Thereafter in 2015, Avon joined hands with private investment firm Cerberus Capital Management (Cerberus) who pumped $435 million as an investment in Avon Products Inc. in the form of preferred stock. Moreover, Cerberus decided to take 80.1% stake in Avon North American business for a $170 million as a part of equity investment.[ak] The new spun off division would also have $230 million of long term liabilities from Avon. Steven F. Mayer (Mayer), Senior Managing Director and Co-Head of Global Private Equity, Cerberus, said, "By privatising the North American business, we will have the time and ability to improve the company's competitiveness, enable each representative to earn more, help her conduct business more efficiently and increase her customers' satisfaction."[al]

ah   Wahba Phil, "The depths of Avon's U.S. despair", http://fortune.com/2014/07/18/avon/, July 18th 2014

ai   Wahba Phil, "Here Are 5 Reasons Avon Fell Apart in the U.S.", http://fortune.com/2015/12/17/avon-us-decline/, December 17th 2015

aj   "Avon exploring sale of North America business: WSJ", http://www.reuters.com/article/us-avon-prdcts-strategy-idUSKBN0N51Z720150414, April 14th 2015

ak   "Avon And Cerberus Announce A $605 Million Strategic Partnership To Drive Avon Shareholder Value", op.cit.

al   "Cerberus to take Avon North America private", op.cit.

McCoy stated, "After a thorough, thoughtful and deliberate process by both parties, we are creating a strategic partnership that will improve Avon's performance and drive shareholder value. We believe this partnership and structure will also accelerate profitable growth in the remaining Avon portfolio—which represented approximately 86% of consolidated revenues for the nine months ended September 30, 2015—as we focus resources on our top markets, the majority of which are profitable and growing. The capital infusion from Cerberus, alongside the suspension of the dividend, and additional operating efficiencies provide us the needed financial flexibility to implement operational and capital plans that fully support the international business. We look forward to sharing the Avon growth plan at our investor day in January."[am]

Talking on the split off of the North American business, McCoy explained, "There is high potential for the Avon brand and business model in both our international business and Avon North America. However, we believe that the separation of Avon North America is the best way to ensure that both businesses have an unencumbered path to profitability and growth and this was a key principle as we considered alternatives. Importantly, Cerberus has both the conviction and resources to support our Representatives. We are confident that relief from the short-term pressures of a public company reporting cycle, the substantial investment that Cerberus is making to support and reinvigorate the business and the operational excellence and discipline that define Cerberus' reputation, will return Avon North America to health. With our continuing ownership position, we look forward to helping advance the Avon mission in North America, while allowing our shareholders to participate in the upside potential."[an] Talking on the partnership, Mayer mentioned that, "We have long admired the Avon brand, business model and products and see significant potential for Avon both in North America and internationally. We are strong believers in the direct selling model, the principle of empowering Representatives, and the growth that direct selling can generate when Representatives are appropriately supported and incentivized to build their businesses."[ao]

However one of the shareholders of Avon, Barington Capital Group[ap], which owned 3% stake in the company was not convinced about the deal. James A. Mitarotonda, Chairman and Chief Executive, Barington, opined that, "We are astonished that Sheri McCoy remains as C.E.O. We intend to explore all available options."[aq] In the wake of such concerns, Avon under the leadership of McCoy devised a three year plan to restructure its operations in around 70 markets.[ar] McCoy said, "Today, we are taking another important step forward in the execution of Avon's transformation plan. With the recent completion of the sale of the North American business, our commercial operations are now fully outside of the United States, allowing us to dramatically rethink our operating model. The actions we are taking today will bring our corporate and commercial businesses closer together, which will drive efficiencies, improve operational effectiveness and deliver significant cost savings."[as]

As part of the plan, Avon announced to lay off around 2500 positions worldwide and also planned to move its corporate headquarters from New York to UK.[at] McCoy said, "The actions we are taking today will bring our corporate and commercial businesses closer together, which will drive efficiencies, improve operational effectiveness and deliver significant cost savings." Furthermore, the company estimated to accumulate around $50 million by various costing cutting measures related to employment.[au] Avon also planned to retain its New York

am   "Avon And Cerberus Announce A $605 Million Strategic Partnership To Drive Avon Shareholder Value", op.cit.
an   ibid.
ao   ibid.
ap   Barington Capital Group, L.P. is a fundamental, value-oriented activist investment firm that was established by James A. Mitarotonda in January 2000.
aq   Picker Leslie, "Avon in Deal to Split Off North American Business", http://www.nytimes.com/2015/12/18/business/dealbook/avon-in-deal-to-split-off-north-american-business.html?_r=0, December 17th 2015
ar   Dunkley Nicole, "Avon Discloses Plan To Downsize And Move Headquarters To Britain", https://www.businessforhome.org/2016/03/avon-discloses-plan-to-downsize-and-move-headquarters-to-britain/, March 16th 2016
as   "Avon Announces Additional Details in Execution of 3-Year Transformation Plan", http://media.avoncompany.com/2016-03-14-Avon-Announces-Additional-Details-in-Execution-of-3-Year-Transformation-Plan, March 14th 2016
at   "Avon to Cut 2,500 Jobs and Move Headquarters to Britain", http://www.nytimes.com/2016/03/16/business/international/avon-move-hq-britain.html, March 15th 2016
au   "Avon Discloses Plan To Downsize And Move Headquarters To Britain", op.cit.

office. According to the Company Official, "The move of its headquarters to the U.K. wasn't for tax purposes, but rather to move the corporate functions closer to the bulk of company operations."[av] McCoy stated that, "With the recent completion of the sale our commercial operations are now fully outside of the United States, allowing us to dramatically rethink our operating model."[aw]

Furthermore, in 2016, the company planned to reduce costs by $350 million. Also the company planned to leverage the ongoing trend of social media to promote its brand and invest in technology.[ax] Beside this, Avon tried to focus on markets like Brazil and Russia and also increase the number of sales representative worldwide. Despite McCoy's efforts, Avon incurred a loss of $333.4 million in the fourth quarter of 2015, as compared to $330.7 million in 2014. The revenues of the company dropped to 20% to $1.61 billion.[ay]

Furthermore, industry observers felt disappointed by the plan of action revealed by Avon in an investor meeting in 2016. B.Riley, Analyst, Linda Bolton Weiser, opined that, "We came away from Avon's analyst meeting without gaining confidence in a successful turnaround." Chris Ferrera, Analyst, Wells Fargo Securities, said, "These opportunities are not new, and Avon offered little detail to in still confidence that things will be different this time."[az] In the wake of such a scenario, would McCoy be able to revive the fortunes of Avon?

av   Terlep Sharon, "Avon to cut 2,500 jobs, move headquarters to U.K.", http://www.marketwatch.com/story/avon-to-cut-2500-jobs-move-headquarters-to-uk-2016-03-14, March 14th 2016

aw   "Avon to cut 2,500 jobs, move headquarters to Britain", http://economictimes.indiatimes.com/news/international/business/avon-to-cut-2500-jobs-move-headquarters-tobritain/articleshow/51406551.cms, March 15th 2016

ax   "Avon to Cut 2,500 Jobs and Move Headquarters to Britain", op.cit.

ay   "Avon Loss Widens, Revenue Declines", http://www.nasdaq.com/article/avon-loss-widens-revenue-declines-20160211-00714, February 11th 2016

az   "Avon's turnaround plan does not instill confidence: analysts", op.cit.

GLOSSARY

Term	Definition	Chapter
Accounting Equation	(1) Assets = liabilities + Owners Equity; (2) Assets = nonowners claims on assets (liabilities) + owners claims on assets (owners equity); (3) current assets + noncurrent assets = current liabilities + noncurrent liabilities + owners equity	2
Agency Theory	Argues that corporate boards and company managers are appointed by owners of the firm (shareholders) and thus must always act solely as agents of the shareholder—that is, maximize stockholders' wealth (profit).	3
Aggressive or Growth Strategy	A recommended strategy when (1) the firm's product has superior financial resources and strengths; and (2) the external competitive market is highly attractive.	5, 6
Benchmarking	is the continuous process used by a firm to learn about or take advantage of the best industry or organizational practices	5
Best Cost or Value Strategy	A generic strategy where competitive advantage is achieved by offering customers better value at a reasonable price for its products or services (either industry wide or focused) compared to its rivals' products and services.	4
Blue Ocean	Represents uncontested market space where no current rivals exist. Presents an opportunity for a firm to compete in a market where the firm can create greater value opportunities for buyers as well as for the company itself. Firms pursuing a blue ocean strategy define their own industry boundaries and compete on value innovation.	6
Bricolage	The creative rearrangement of resources to generate true novelty. In entrepreneurial settings, bricolage is the "creative organization." The use of social networks and extremely limited resources creates unique products and services that challenge silos or bureaucracies found in larger organizations.	8
Business Economics	in its broadest sense defines how an organization procures, manages, and allocates its resources, and capabilities to make money and gain a competitive advantage	2
Business Ethics	A form of applied ethics or professional ethics that examines ethical principles and moral or ethical problems that arise in a business environment.	3
Business Model	(1) Defines and identifies a firm's value creation activities, or in other words, how strategic managers intends to create customer value and extract value for the firm.	1, 2
Business Risk	Refers to the normal risks of doing business such as poorly crafted strategies, ineffective execution, inability to capitalize on industry opportunities, or failure to adapt to changing market forces and conditions.	8
Business-level Strategy	Focuses on how business-level managers compete in specific industries.	3, 6

Term	Definition	Chapter
Buyer Power	Buyers comprise the market for a firm's output of products and services. Buyer bargaining power is based on the buyer's ability to put the selling firm under pressure.	4
C Corporation	(C Corp) Taxed separately from its owners under United States law	8
Central Problem	A situation or question with no clear/obvious remedy or answer.	2
Centralized Decisions	Made at the highest level of the firm, usually in the firm's home (headquarters), or divisional offices (divisional vice presidents) by a small number of senior strategic managers.	8
Certified B Corporation	Corporations are firms certified by the nonprofit BLab™ to have met rigorous standards of social and environmental performance, accountability, and transparency.	8
Chance Event	Disruptive developments outside the control of firms and governments in a host country that may allow new firms to enter the country. New firms may be better able to exploit opportunities arising from a reshaped industry structure caused by chance events than the existing firms.	8
Change Process	Includes the following steps: (1) Unawareness, people facing change have a feeling of comfort with the way things are normally done; (2) Awakening, individuals become aware that things are changing and that better ways of doing things might exist; (3) Reordering and Chaos, people begin analyzing the existing situation and challenging the status quo becomes commonplace; (4) Transforming, the individual or group creates a vision for change from an analysis of information and the feelings that come from awaking and reordering and chaos; (5) Commitment, people take responsibility for the implementation of a vision; (6) Implementation, the transformation vision becomes included in the daily activities of the individual or group; (7) Integration, an understanding or belief that the changes are real and here to stay.	7
Charisma	A Greek word meaning "a gift." In Biblical times, charisma was associated with leaders and certain religious members.	7
Charismatic Leader	Followers' devotion stems from the leader's attributes, personality, and behaviors.	7
Closed-system	A system that does not exchange energy, matter, or information with its environment (other systems), but is self-contained within its own system boundaries (all variables are known and can be managed efficiently and effectively).	1
Company Vitality	The capacity of a company to explore new options, renew its strategy, and grow sustainably. In a fast-changing world, only companies that can adapt and maintain vitality will survive.	6
Competitive Advantage	When a firm can earn above average profits by providing the same value as its competitors at a lower price, or charge higher prices by offering greater value through differentiation.	1, 2
Competitive Forces School of Strategic Thought	Focuses on the attractiveness of a firm's products and services within the industry(s) in which it competes.	4
Competitive Intensity	The degree of similarities in rivals' strategic actions and conduct that drive customer value creation.	4

Term	Definition	Chapter
Competitive Strategy (**see SPACE**)	Recommended when the business performs favorably on its industry attractiveness and competitive advantage scores, but unfavorably on its financial strengths and environmental stability scores.	5
Complementary Products or Services	A product or service that can increase demand for a focal (another) industry's or focal (another) firm's products or services. Complements share similar demand curves or competitive dynamics.	4
Concentration Strategy	Adopted when a company concentrates all its resources on a particular product, industry, market, or technology.	6
Conglomerate Company	The combination of two or more corporations engaged in entirely different businesses that fall under one corporate group (usually involves a parent company and many subsidiaries). Conglomerates are often large and multinational in scope and scale.	5
Conglomerate Integration	Occurs when a company adds new, but unrelated products to its existing product or service offerings.	6
Conservative or Maintenance Strategy	A recommended strategy when the firm's products are financially strong, but the industry or market is not considered to be attractive.	6
Core Capability	A business activity that a company performs at a consistently high level of competency. Designated by the company as critical to its competitive position in the marketplace.	3, 5
Corporate Social Responsibility	The approach and actions an organization undertakes to balance its responsibilities toward society, stockholders, and other stakeholders when making business decisions.	3
Corporate-level Strategy	Focuses on what industries the firm will compete in and how it will be judged.	3, 6
Cost Leadership Strategy	A generic strategy where competitive advantage is achieved when (1) a firm is able to offer its products or services at a lower price than rivals' products or services; and (2) the customer is willing to pay the lower price.	4
Country Comparative Advantage	Exists when a country specializes in products or services that it can supply more efficiently or at a lower cost compared to other countries' products or services.	8
Country Competitive Advantage	Occurs when the country has a monopoly in specialized resources or expertise or is the sole source of an item, the only producer of an item, or the most efficient producer of an item comared to all other countries.	8
Creative Destruction	The process of industrial change or mutation which entails revolution-izing the economic structure both within and outside an industry. The need to let go of or destroy past paractices or institutions in order to move creatively on to new practices and institutions.	8
Creativity	Any act, idea, or product that changes an existing domain (current state of things, set of symbolic rules or procedures, etc.)	1
Critical Theory (*See also Theory of Knowledge*)	The conceptual foundation for critical thinking. Critical theory or thinking is based on an epistemological approach to learning.	1
Critical Thinking (**Paul and Elder**)	The art of analyzing and evaluating one's thought process with the view toward improving it.	1

Term	Definition	Chapter
Cultural Risk	Encompasses a firm's poor strategic decisions due to a lack in understanding of the values, norms, social customs, and belief systems of the people and social institutions of the host country. Many businesses fail to achieve their international goals not because of business or political risks, but because they neither understand nor adapt to a country's cultural norms.	8
Culture	Encompasses shared explicit and tacit assumptions, beliefs, knowledge, norms, and values, as well as the prevailing attitudes and behaviors in a company. Culture determines what is acceptable or unacceptable behavior for a firm. It is typically lasting, passed down from one set of managers to the next.	3, 7
Customer Knowledge	As a product moves through its life cycle, the amount of knowledge a customer needs to determine a product's value (and the related costs of acquiring the product) decreases as customer experience with the product increases.	4
Customer Value Proposition	The value (benefits) derived by the customer from purchasing a company's products or services.	1, 5
Data	(1) facts about something that can be used in calculating, reasoning, or planning. (2) information expressed as numbers for use especially in a computer; data form the main inputs for preparing reports and financial statements. Data is unorganized, uncategorized and unclassified information	2
Decacorn Company	Term used for those rare start-up companies valued at over $10 billion.	8
Decentralized Decisions	Organizational decisions that are localized and made lower down in the firm by strategic managers in the firm's several domestic and international facilities (sales offices, business offices, research and development centers, field engineering) and operations (manufacturing, warehousing, distribution centers).	8
Decision Coordination	Determines where and how decisions are made for a firm's facilities and operations.	8
Defensive or Exit Strategy	The recommended strategy when (1) a firm's business or product is in an unattractive industry; and (2) future prospects are poor.	5
Deliberate Strategy	Set of carefully formulated actions and steps with well-defined outcomes or endpoints. As opposed to emergent or adaptive strategy.	1
Demand Curve	Aggregate number of customer purchases.	4
Demographics	Statistics that track a region's or country's characteristics such as birth rates; aging populations; and growth in college graduates, advanced degrees (Masters, PhD), and STEM education.	8
Diamond Model of Competitive Advantage of Nations (M. Porter)	Assumes that a firm's ability to achieve competitive advantage stems from value creation in the firm's approximate environment. This is ultimately an act of innovation resulting from four dynamic interdependent factors: (1) factor conditions (natural resources, geographic location); (2) demand conditions (demand requirements of the firm's most sophisticated customers); (3) relating and supporting industries (geographic grouping of industries into clusters); and (4) firm strategy, structure, and rivalry (the systematic differences in how firms compete within and across industries).	8

Term	Definition	Chapter
Differentiation Strategy	A generic strategy where competitive advantage is achieved when (1) a firm creates enough uniqueness (either perceived or actual) in its product or service compared to rivals' products or services; and (2) the customer is willing to pay a premium price.	4
Disparate Control	A type of leadership where the leader's authority, power, or influence is used to exercise greater control over the action of others.	7
Disruptive Technology	An innovation or technology that blocks or replaces the focal firm's product, service and/or position (hinders firm's ability to effectively compete).	4, 6
Distinctive Competence	A core capability that gives the firm a unique advantage over its rivals.	3
Diversified Major Company	A multi-business firm with a diversified (unrelated) portfolio of multiple companies under one operating "roof" or legal structure.	5
Division Organizational Structure	Clusters the firm's functions, tasks, and activities by product groups, customer groups, or geographic regions or countries. The firm is composed of several divisions, with each division overseen by a CEO, president, or general manger. The division leader typically has profit and loss responsibility. The division grouping or units engage in primary (line) and secondary (staff) functions.	7
Domain	State of things or set of symbolic rules or procedures.	1
Driving Forces	Forces (events, innovations, trends, etc.) outside the firm (external factors) that trigger the change of strategy within the firm.	4
Dynamic Capabilities	The firm's ability to renew its capabilities and competencies (constant innovation) to maintain a competitive advantage.	5
Dynamic Model of the Strategy Process	Method of understanding how strategic actions occur. Recognizes that strategic decisions are dynamic—that is, strategy making involves a complex pattern of actions and reactions. This model is both partially planned and partially unplanned.	1
Dynamic Work Design	Dynamic work design maintains the traditional mechanistic work design while empowering workers to override mechanistic approach when things go awry. Dynamic work design enables managers to create work processes in their own organizations that are both more flexible and efficient in comparison to the scientific method work design.	6
Elephant or Dinosaur Company	Slow moving, larger companies that have failed to adapt to disruptive changes in the market.	8
Emergent or Adaptive Strategy	Set of certain consistent actions or behaviors that form a pattern not previously anticipated in the initial planning phase. As opposed to deliberate strategy.	1
Enlightened Self-interest	Asserts that strategic managers will act to further the interests of others because to do so furthers their own self-interest and the self-interest of the firm.	3
Entrepreneur	Creative visionaries who create customer and firm value by mobilizing resources to exploit market opportunities.	8
Entrepreneurship	Individuals who design, launch, and run a new company.	8

Term	Definition	Chapter
Entrepreneurship School of Strategic Thought	Argues that all organizations, no matter size or context, need to be innovative in order to sustain performance and survive. Strategic management is a two-sided coin: one side representing the strategist's business acumen and leadership skills, and the other the innovative and creative talents and mindset of an entrepreneur. A firm's wealth creation comes from human creativity, imagination, intellectual expertise, and fast action. This school is rooted in the mysteries of intuition, improvisation, and imagination.	8
Entry Deterring Price	The price or cost that a prospective entrant into an existing industry is unwilling to pay for entry. That is, if costs are greater than benefits, then potential new entrants will be deterred from entering the industry.	4
Epistemology	Term first used by the Scottish philosopher James Frederick Ferrier to describe the branch of philosophy concerned with the nature and scope of knowledge.	1
Ethics	The study of right from wrong.	3
Evidence	Something that makes plain or clear (e.g., an indication or sign). In law, evidence (testimony of witnesses, records, documents, objects, etc.) is presented in court to determine the guilt or innocence of the defendant. In business, evidence (numbers, words, images, diagrams, videos, etc.) is used to support a recommendation or answer a critical issue or question.	2
Evolutionary Industry Cycles	Incremental change in business practices (e.g., how things are done) within an industry or its subgroups (strategic groups).	4
Expat	An individual who relocates to another country for a job, to learn professional practices, or start a business.	8
Experience or Learning Curve	Builds on the S-curve and is based on the notion that unit labor cost decreases as experience in product production increases.	4
Firm Backward Integration	Occurs when a firm acquires a former supplier (e.g., Yahoo!'s acquisition of Maven Networks, a supplier of Internet video players and video advertising tools).	6
Firm Forward Integration	Occurs when a company acquires a present customer (e.g., Google's acquisition of YouTube).	6
Firm Value Proposition	The value (benefits) derived by the firm from selling its products. If revenues are greater than expenses and all costs of doing business (transactions) then the company's business model is working effectively.	1, 5
Firm Vertical Integration	Aimed at increased control over either one or more of a firm's former suppliers or customers.	6
First-mover Advantage	Similar to the old adage "the early bird gets the worm." Being the first company to sell a new product or service may (but not always) provide long-lasting benefits and competitive advantages. Typically refers to the first company to successfully enter a new market, not necessarily the first company to develop a product (the inventor).	8
Focal Firm	The firm being analyzed for its competitive position, influence, and ability to exploit a focal industry's or subgroup's overall attractiveness (see PIE).	4

Term	Definition	Chapter
Focal Industry	The industry being analyzed for its attractiveness in conducting a competitive forces analysis.	4
Focused Strategy	A generic strategy (can be either cost or differentiation) where competitive advantage is achieved in only one particular market segment (niche).	4
Foreign Direct Investment	Making investments in a host country through mergers and acquisitions, building new facilities (greenfield investments), reinvesting profits earned in the host back into the host country, and intra-company loans (to host country licensees, franchisees, strategic partners, and joint ventures), etc.	8
Functional Organizational Structure	Designed around the firm's activities or tasks performed. The primary and secondary activities in the firm's value chain mirror the professional expertise and skills found in the functional structure.	7
Functional-level Strategy	Focuses on the operational processes, activities, and actions required from each function or operational unit necessary to carry out (implement and execute) corporate- and business-level strategies.	3, 6
Gazelle Company	High growth technology businesses that achieve accelerated market growth.	8
GE/McKinsey's Spotlight Matrix	One of the earliest and most popular analytical tools for assessing industry attractiveness at the corporate level. The grid is depicted as a nine-cell matrix that offers a systematic approach for the multi-business corporation to prioritize its investments among its units based on industry attractiveness scores and assessments.	6
Global Economics	The interdependence of national economies through foreign direct investment (FDI), trade agreements, global institutions (trading of stock on foreign stock exchanges), migration of firms (knowledge transfer), people (immigration), and other resources (off shoring and outsourcing resources across international borders).	8
Global Industries	Firms whose products compete globally and dominate several different industries.	8
Global Institutions	Rise of non-state players such as: World Trade Association (WTA); NGOs (non-governmental organizations like the Red Cross or Greenpeace, and terrorist groups like ISIS and Al-Qaeda); global brands (accelerated growth in the number of firms competing globally); and Trans-Pacific Partnership (TPP), WTO, NAFTA, and other regional trade organizations that have lowered international trade and investment barriers.	8
Global Market	Occurs when a firm's products and services are sold across several markets, with little or no change to the product or service.	8
Global Strategy	A firm that sells in many, if not all, of the countries that have, or potentially have, representative markets for a firm's products and services. Determining global strategy starts with answering the following question: Is your theory of strategy at home (domestic markets) transferable to other countries' markets?	8
Globalization	The increasing interaction of people, states, and countries through the growth of the international flow of money, ideas, and cultures.	8

Term	Definition	Chapter
Goals	The long-term expected or hoped for results that, if achieved, will lead to the firm's overall accomplishment of its mission.	3
Harvest or Exit Strategy	A recommended strategy when a business no longer holds value and is experiencing poor performance. (Both industry and business attractiveness are so unfavorable that management has no choice but to disengage the troubled business.)	6
Hectocorn Company	Term used for those rare start-up companies valued at over $100 billion.	8
Heuristic	Self-guided learning that employs analysis to draw conclusions. Specifically, simple and efficient rules which people often use to form judgments and make decisions. They are mental shortcuts that usually involve focusing on one aspect of a complex problem and ignoring others.	2
Horizontal Integration	Undertaken when a firm acquires or merges with a company (former rival) that sells similar products or services. Horizontal integration is an inorganic growth strategy since this action adds products or markets from former rivals through acquisition. The recent announcement of Charter Communications' intent to merge with Time Warner Cable (TWC) is an example of horizontal integration through merger.	6
Host Country	A country where a firm that is based in another country has business activities.	8
Human Capital	The knowledge, know-how, and capabilities of a firm's individuals. All organizations need human resources, especially people who can think creatively.	5
Incremental Change	Small organizational adjustments that are less threatening to employees and management than large-scale change. Incremental change focuses on continuous improvements via TQM (Total Quality Management), benchmarking, Six Sigma, etc.	7
Industry	A group of competitors that offer similar goods and services, and compete directly with each other. An industry can also be identified through its customers, suppliers, rivals, and the extent to which it is regulated or governed by third parties (governmental or regulatory agencies). Basic unit of analysis in a competitive forces school.	4
Industry Boundaries: Agitation Stage	An industry depicted by increased agitation or the "stirring up" of industry dynamics and relationships. Advances in technology are also starting to "heat up" at a more accelerated pace. Change is no longer incremental, but rather borders on revolutionary. Industry boundaries are fading fast. Firms', rivals', and customers' once stable relationships are no longer clear (become blurred) forcing each player to seek new opportunities to move into another's space.	6
Industry Boundaries: Prospecting Stage	Technology in this stage acts as a catalyst for softening an industry's boundaries (although its boundaries remain relatively fixed and clear), forcing industry players to prospect for new "competitive spaces."	6
Industry Boundaries: Quiescent or Stable Stage	An industry that features stable or steady boundaries between the firm and its rivals, customers, and suppliers. Because boundaries are recognizable and fixed, industry change becomes evolutionary.	6

Term	Definition	Chapter
Industry Boundaries: Turbulent	An industry that reflects a highly chaotic and turbulent environment. Exponential technological growth and accelerated change has stirred up the agitation to such a degree that radical inclusive thinking becomes the predominant environmental paradigm and mental model. The pace of change has also "heated up" to the point where change is no longer discrete and evolutionary, but quantum and revolutionary. Consequentially, the firm's competitive environment remains in constant flux. Industry boundaries are no longer clear. Firms, rivals, and suppliers find it extremely difficult to maintain or erect barriers to prevent entry or defend current positions.	6
Industry Condition	A characteristic or event that must be considered and/or addressed by all rivals (e.g., rapidly falling demand).	2
Industry Entry/Exit Barriers	Entry barriers determine the degree to which a potential new entrant can easily enter a focal industry or one of its subgroups. An exit barrier determines the degree to which a focal firm can easily leave a focal industry or its strategic group.	4
Industry Legacy Effects	An industry where players conform to the existing industry's known competitive rules or standards.	6
Industry or Business Cluster	A geographic concentration of interconnected businesses, suppliers, and associated institutions within a particular industry.	8
Information	(1) processed data turned into some useful classification, form or category; (2) data that is converted into organized and categorized knowledge used to make informed decisions. At a minimum, the general manager (responsible for the profit and loss of an organizational entity)	2
Information Graphics ("Infographics")	Graphic visual representations intended to present complex information quickly and clearly.	2
Information Technologies	Computers, smartphones, satellites, and other devices that make it possible the send information, data, services, and communications virtually via networks.	6
Innovator's Dilemma	A critical strategic choice that requires deciding when to let go of past practices, products and ways of doing business and when to move on new innovative ones.	8
In-sourcing	A firm elects to keep internal control over critical production or competencies.	5
Intangible Resources	Resources that are not easily quantifiable, but can be extremely valuable (e.g., intellectual property, brands, patents, copyrights, trademarks, trade secrets, software, algorithms, customer data-bases, partnerships, and joint ventures).	5
Intensity of Rivals	For most industries, the intensity of competitive rivalry provides the major determinant of the competitiveness of the industry. Rivalry occurs because one or more competitors either feels the pressure or sees the opportunity to improve position within an industry.	4
International Strategy	Involves offering a firm's products and services in more than one nation, but not globally.	8

Term	Definition	Chapter
Internet of Things	Commonly defined as the network of physical devices, vehicles, home appliances, and other items embedded with electronics, software, sensors, actuators, artificial intelligence (AI), virtual network connectivity-enabled devices, and individuals connected to exchange data and information.	6
Intuition	Innate understanding based on knowledge and experience.	1
Investment Priority Screens	Used in conducting a GE/McKinsey Spotlight Matrix for reviewing the performance of each business to determine a corresponding and appropriate investment. Each unit is sometimes referred as a "strategic business unit" or SBU.	6
Joint Venture	When a business elects to work with another business on special projects or investment opportunities.	6
Key Success Factor	Organizational capabilities, actions, and activities that a firm has (or must acquire) that can potentially be used to exploit industry driving forces.	4
Knowledge	The stock of information converted into the know-how employed by managers to make decisions with greater certainty.	1
Kritikos (Greek)	Greek word meaning 'judgment' or 'discernment'; an approach to learning.	1
Learning Community/ Organization	An institution that facilitates the learning of its members and continuously transforms itself. A learning community achieves competitive advantage by having superior information and problem-solving capabilities compared to rivals.	7
Learning School of Strategic Thought	A paradigm built on the premise that competitive advantage is based on continuous learning. Firms are viewed as coalitions of groups whose decisions are based on practice. To create and sustain competitive advantage, strategists must replace the traditional hierarchical structure with structures that foster learning communities and organizations.	6
LEED	Certification for green buildings, Fair Trade certification for produce or products produced in low-wage countries (certified that a "living" wage is being paid); and for certification of organic and all natural products such as 100% organic coffee.	8
Limited Liability Company	(LLC) A business structure that combines the pass-through taxation of a partnership or sole proprietorship with the limited liability of a corporation.	8
Line Organizational Units	In the manufacturing firm, line activities include all functions that are directly engaged in the procurement, value added operations (manufacture), and distribution of the final product to customers. In the service firms, such as legal, professional, and financial services, line function and activities generate fees and profits via the services provided to clients.	7
Liquidation Strategy	A recommended strategy when a business faces poor financial health and has no tangible or intangible valuable assets to attract potential suitors or buyers.	6

Term	Definition	Chapter
Macro Environment	The major external, uncontrollable factors that influence an organization's decision making and affect its performance and strategies (e.g., economic factors; demographics; legal, political, and social conditions; technological changes; and natural forces).	3
Majority Stockholder	An individual or organizational entity that has a controlling interest in a company based on number of shares owned, specifically the proportion of shares owned to the total shares held by all shareholders.	5
Management Audit	Evaluates management's effectiveness, especially with regard to the firm's vision, mission, strategic objectives and strategies, and its overall resource strengths.	3
Market Development	Calls for marketing existing products to new geographic markets or segments (niches) within existing markets.	6
Market Penetration	Aimed at increased market share by means of selling more of the same products to existing customers or taking market share from competitors.	6
Matrix Organizational Structure	Designed around teams of employees to accomplish activities by: (1) taking advantage of the firm's many resource strengths, and (2) limiting the weaknesses or disadvantages found in the functional and divisional structures. The matrix structure is based on two principles: (1) the authority of functional knowledge or expertise, and (2) the authority of knowledge of managing people and teams.	7
Mental Model	An explanation of an individual's thought process regarding how something "works" in the real world.	1
Metcalfe's Law	States that where N is the number of nodes or points of contact on a network, the power of the internet or network is N squared (Nn). If you double the number of nodes, you quadruple the overall value of the network. Thus, the network becomes more valuable to each user as new users join.	6
Mezzo Environment	The transactional level of a firm's external industry environment that consists of market forces (e.g., suppliers, supply and demand, distribution, competitors, customers, and industry associations).	3
M-Form Organization Structure	A corporate federation of semi-independent product or geographic groups plus a headquarters that coordinates such groups and oversees corporate strategy.	7
Micro Environment	The organizational level of the firm that involves the internal environment of the firm (e.g., vision, mission, strategy, resources, processes, products and services).	3
Minority Stockholder	an individual or organizational entity that does not have a controlling interest in a company based on the number of shares own—the proportion of shares owned to the total shares held by all shareholders	5
Mission Statement	A short statement specifying a company's goals, objectives, products, services, markets, customers, and technologies. The mission statement also guides the actions of the organization, exemplifies its overall goal, provides a sense of direction, and influences decision-making.	3, 7
Monopolistic Competition	The firm is the price setter as a result of possessing a unique, differentiated product that is not easily substituted with rivals' products.	4

Term	Definition	Chapter
Moore's Law	Predicted that the performance capacity of the microprocessor (think computer) would double and the cost of manufacturing the micropro- cessor with be cut in half every two years. Moore's prediction has held true since it was first proposed and paralleled the rapid growth of the mini computer and work stations in the late 1960s and 1970s followed by the explosive growth of the mini and personal computer in the 1980s and 1990s, as well as the integrated Internet, cloud technologies, and other digital devices and advances in the 2000s and 2010s. Today Moore's Law has become known as the "law of exponential growth" or the "law of accelerating change."	6
Mouse or Ant Company	Very small companies and medium-sized companies are sometimes referred to as "mice" or "ants." While small in number, their cumula- tive and aggregative effect on a community and society is large.	8
Multi-domestic Strategy	Industries are represented by competition in which one country's institutional environment is independent of another country's cultural institutions.	8
Multiple Sovereign Model of the Firm	Assumes that managers use their discretion and power in a socially acceptable context. Stockholders hold no special status in this model. Rather, management acts as a hub of activity and is entrusted with equitably distributing its energy, corporate rewards, or resources fairly among each of these stakeholders or interest groups.	3
Net Neutrality	An Obama administration regulatory policy that requires broadband providers to treat all internet traffic equally without blocking or slowing content or providing "fast lanes" for favored sites and services.	6
Normative Moral Relativism	The idea that because nobody is right or wrong, we ought to tolerate the behavior of others even when we disagree about its morality.	3
Not-for-profit	An organization that is formed to serve some public purpose or good rather than for financial gain. As long as the not-for-profit's activities are for charitable, religious, educational, scientific, or literary causes, it is exempt from paying income taxes.	8
Objectives	The benchmarks or results that are identifiable and measurable milestones on the path towards achieving a firm's short-term mission and longer-term vision.	3
Off-sourcing	A firm elects to send work, production, or certain competencies to be performed to a different country.	5
Open-system	A system which continuously interacts with its external environment or surroundings. This interaction can take the form of information, energy, or material exchanges into or out of the system boundary (many, many variables operating in a dynamic, interdependent, and interpenetrating manner).	1
Operating Company	A multi-business firm with several related companies under one "roof" or operating structure.	5
Operational Configuration	Determines the firm's physical footprint of its value chain activities, facilities, and operations both within domestic and international markets.	8
Opportunity	A positive industry trend, condition, or factor that provides an open- ing in the external environment that an organization can potentially exploit in order to gain a competitive advantage.	3

Term	Definition	Chapter
Opportunity Cost	The cost of choosing one alternative over another and missing the benefit offered by the forgone opportunity.	5
Organizational Learning	Enhances the firm's collective ability to accept, make sense of, and respond to internal and external change on an organization-wide level. Organizational learning is more than the sum of the information held by employees.	7
Organizational Intangible Resources	Intangible assets such as culture, structure, processes, systems, dynamic learning, problem-solving capabilities, formal and informal working relationships, dynamic work design, and highly effective, high performing teams.	5
Organizational Structure	The design of the organization through which strategy is crafted, implemented, and executed. Design aims to effectively manage organizational diversity and complexity.	7
Out-sourcing	A firm elects to contract work previously done in-house to an external contractor or organization.	5
Paradigms	(1) Offer cognitive models that support strategic decisions and are shaped by the co-influence of practice (real world decision making) and scholarly thought based on what scholars of management assume to be real/what they take to be true; and (2) consist of the intellectual perception, models, and widely held beliefs shared by leading scholars, practitioners, scientists, politicians, etc. and coalesce around a model or pattern of how things "work" in the real world.	1
Parent or Holding Company	A company that manages the unrelated or subsidiary businesses of a conglomerate. The parent or holding company often acts as a bank or investment broker that buys and sells companies based on the continued success (return on investment) of the independently managed and operated subsidiary.	5
Pass Through Income	For tax purposes, income generated by the partners is shared (based on the partnership agreement) and treated as personal income to avoid additional business-related tax.	8
Perfectly Competitive Market	An industry where rivals are price takers (price set in the market's interplay of supply and demand) since products and services are homogeneous (similar) and customers can shop around for the best price in rivals' similar products.	4
PEST	Acronym for **P**olitical, **E**conomic, **S**ocial/Cultural, and **T**echnological environmental factors. The strategist must analyze each PEST factor to determine the difference between a firm's home market competitive dynamics and the competitive dynamics of another country.	8
PESTEL	Acronym for determining political, economic, social, technical, environmental, and legal factors in a firm's external environment.	3
PIE	An acronym relating to attractiveness and industry forces. (**P**osition the firm relative to the overall attractiveness of industry forces at any given time. Assess the firm's ability to **I**nfluence these competitive dynamics in its favor. **E**xploit its position and influence by shifting the balance of power in its favor).	4
Political Risk	Encompasses the stability and challenges that face host governments and institutions. Political risk can harm a firm's business success.	8

Term	Definition	Chapter
Primary Value Chain Activities	All revenue and profit generating activities and functions contained in a firm's value chain (e.g., procurement, manufacturing, selling).	5
Principles	Capture the fundamental norms, rules, or values that represent what is desirable for an organization or company.	3
Process Benchmarking	Used to learn about another firm's method of operations (e.g., how firms employ best practices in one or more points on its value chain, etc.)	5
Product Benchmarking	Undertaken when one company's product or service continuously outperforms its rivals' in terms of total sales, profit margins, performance, quality, customer satisfaction, special features, etc.	5
Product Development	Aims at increasing sales by (1) modifying or improving existing products and services; or (2) by introducing new products or services to the market.	6
Product or Technology Licensing	consists of formal contractual arrangements where a firm transfers the rights to use its products, services or technologies to a another firm	8
Professional Limited Liability Company	A special form of LLC which the state may allow the professional service enterprise to organize under.	8
Pure Case	A detailed narrative or description of a real-life situation. Includes sufficient intriguing decision points and provocative undercurrents to make a student/student group think and argue about it.	2
Quantum Change	The pace of change has "heated up" to the point where change is no longer discrete and evolutionary.	6
Radically Inclusive Strategic Thinking	The type of thinking "where there is no box at all." Driven by radical external change with simultaneous acceleration and interaction between technology, globalization, climate change, etc.	6
Radically Inclusive Criitcal Inquiry	A critical inquiry process that includes as many relevant people, processes, disciplines, organizations, and technologies as possible in crafting and executing strategic decision making.	6
Red Ocean	The known competitive space (represents all the industries in existence today). Red ocean industries have inherent legacy effects, where industry players conform to the existing industry's known competitive rules. In existing industries, competitors try to outperform one another by fighting for greater market share. As the market space gets crowded, prospects for profits and growth are reduced.	6
Relative Market Share	Determined by dividing a firm's market share for its products or services by the market share of its largest competitors (total share of its top three or four industry rivals).	5
Resource Heterogeneity	Assumes the firm's resource strengths (both tangible and tangible) differ from that of its rivals.	5
Resource Immobile Assumption	Assumes that resource strengths are not mobile and thus do not move easily from the firm to its rivals. In takes a long time, if at all, for a rival to copy or imitate the firm's resource strengths, core capabilities, and distinctive competencies.	5

Term	Definition	Chapter
Resource-Based View of the Firm	Assumes the external environment is chaotic, uncertain, and unpredictable which is contrary to Competitive Forces School. Competitive landscapes are fiercely competitive. Dynamic capabilities are essential for creating and sustaining competitive advantage. RBV's focus is on nurturing and developing internal, tangible, and intangible resources. The firm's competitive advantage is determined by the its ability to utilize heterogeneous (tangible and intangible) resources in unique ways that generate revenue and profit. Successful firms are able to implement different strategies to outperform rivals. Therefore, a firm can achieve superior competitive advantage by utilizing its different branches of resources.	5
Resources	Provide the firm with the capacity to carry out formulated strategies.	3, 5
Reverse Engineering	The reproduction of another firm's product and/or processes following a detailed examination of its construction or composition.	5
Revolutionary Industry Cycles	A major shift in the very nature of competition and industry practices. Revolutionary change destroys the old order of things and ushers in a new order.	4
S (Sub) Corporation	An S Corporation is not itself subject to income tax. Rather shareholders of the S Corporation are subject to tax on a prorated share of income based on percent of owned. To qualify to make the S corporation election, the corporation's shares must be held by residents, individuals, or certain qualifying trusts.	8
Scientific Management	Based on the idea that organizations are designed to solve customer problems. When the external environment is relatively stable/predictable, then hierarchical and mechanistic structures work best. Frederick W. Taylor, an early advocate and pioneer of the mechanistic approach to organizational design, maintained that if work is regularly repeated it can be studied and improved through time, motion studies, and observation—a process and theory that eventually became known as "scientific management."	6
S-Curve	A type of curve or pattern that shows the growth of one variable (e.g., sales in dollars) in terms of another variable (e.g., time). Usually takes the shape of the letter 'S.' Extremely useful in conducting a situational analysis.	4
Secondary or Support Value Chain Activities	All revenue and profit supporting activities (e.g., accounting, maintenance, personnel management) that do not generate revenues or profits, but aid revenue and profit activities.	5
Simple Organizational Structure	The most common structure. Centers on the founder(s) or owner-manager personal approach to managing resource dependency (access to limited resources). This structure is usually associated with small- to medium-sized firms in their early stage of growth. The firm typically has one or a limited number of products and minimal staff.	7
Single Sovereign Model of the Firm (M. Friedman)	Assumes that the firm is responsible only to stockholders or owners. Thus the social responsibility of the firm becomes maximizing profits for stockholders as long as it remains within legal boundaries.	3
Skunk-works	A standalone organizational unit designed to foster innovation and creativity without the entrapments of organizational bureaucracies.	8

Term	Definition	Chapter
Social Contract	Maintains that a firm gets its right to exist from society. If the firm abuses these rights, its own right to exist can be forfeited.	3
Social Entrepreneur	An entrepreneur that makes the social mission explicit and central to the purpose of the enterprise.	8
Social Innovation	Defined as "new ideas that work in meeting social goals." Draws distinctions between innovation and improvement, creativity and invention.	8
Socratic-method	(1) one of the oldest methods still used for learning based on the Greek philosopher Socrates and his approach to teaching; (2) a form of cooperative argumentative dialogue between individuals. Based on asking and answering questions to stimulate critical thinking and draw out ideas and underlying presumptions; and (3) an approach to case study based on debate and learning through discovery—that is, asking the right questions and deriving a plausible answer.	2
SPACE	Acronym for Strategic Positioning and Competitive Action Evaluation.	5
SPACE Factors	Depicted as a four cell metric divided into two external factors representing overall industry attractiveness: Industry Attractiveness (IA) and Environmental Stability (ES); and two internal factors representing overall business attractiveness: Financial Strength (FS) and Competitive Advantage (CA).	5
SPACE Matrix	A management tool used to analyze overall resource strengths and industry attractiveness for a firm with multiple businesses. It combines both an internal and external situational analysis in the strategy setting process.	5
Spin-off or Divest Strategy	A recommended strategy when a company's managers decide to sell (or spin-off) an existing business or product because the entity no longer holds any value or does not fit with its current vision, mission, or portfolio of products/services.	6
Staff Organizational Units	Secondary activities that support the primary or line activities, but are not directly engaged in generating profits. These units provide support for line functions, such as engineering, advisory (legal), service (human resources), or control (accounting) groups. Staff groups are the support to the core or primary line functions of the enterprise.	7
Stakeholder	Any group or individual who is affected (negatively or positively) by the decisions of the firm and who, accordingly, can have an impact (positively or negatively) on the firm.	3
Stewardship Theory	Argues that managers, left to their own devices, will indeed act as responsible stewards of the assets they control because it is in the strategic manager's (and the firm's) enlightened self-interest to protect, develop, and grow the assets of the firm within societally determined boundaries.	3
Strategic Action	Distinct from an operational or routine action in that, if a strategic action is not achieved, the overall well-being and health of the organization becomes threatened.	1
Strategic Architecture	The brain (intellectual energy) of a company.	7

Term	Definition	Chapter
Strategic Audit	A useful framework/tool for critically analyzing a company's overall internal strengths and weaknesses, as well as external opportunities and threats.	3
Strategic Benchmarking	Examines the actions other organizations take to improve performance and maintain long-term organizational vitality.	5
Strategic Change	A significant restructuring of an organization's business or strategies on a large scale (e.g., market, product, or business model restructuring/positioning).	7
Strategic Industry Group	Firms that offer comparable strategies and approaches form a strategic group. Homogeneity of strategies is greater in the strategic group than outside the group. Consequentially, competition in a strategic group is usually more intense than competition outside the group.	4
Strategic Intent	A dream that energizes a company. Driven and shaped by capstone strategic architecture that illuminates the future with an ambitious and compelling strategic intent. Strategic intent implies a significant stretch for the organization. With strategic intent and stretch, the strategic leaders' focus on winning becomes a core obsession, capable of sustaining a sense of urgency within the organization and in its strategy execution. The "heart" (emotional energy) of a company.	7
Strategic Partnership	A relationship between two commercial enterprises, usually formalized by one or more business contracts. Also sometimes referred to as a "strategic alliance."	8
Strategic Thinking	Understanding and making sense of the firm's internal and external environments and taking actions that capitalize on this understanding. Strategic thinking is about synthesis or making sense of things based on intuition, knowledge, experience, and creativity.	1
Stratego (Greek verb)	Greek verb that means "to plan the destruction of one's enemies through the effective use of resources." Implies action and forward thinking.	1
Strategos (Greek noun)	Greek noun literally interpreted as "the art of the general."	1
Strategy (Freedman)	(1) Continuous process of improving organizational performance with no end point; different notions, interpretations, and meanings (each of us has our own); and (2) employing whatever resources are available to achieve the best outcome in situations that are both dynamic and contested.	1
Strategy Cases	Pure cases that are comprehensive in scope because they provide (1) detailed descriptions of companies, competitive markets, and administrative and management processes; and (2) intriguing decision points and provocative undercurrents.	2
Strategic Control	A step in the strategic management conceptual model that assesses whether or not formulated and implemented strategies are working and producing the intended or desired outcomes.	3, 7
Strategy Execution	The active, constant, daily management of strategies, resources, systems, people, activities, tasks, etc. required to improve organizational performance.	3, 7

Term	Definition	Chapter
Strategy Formulation or Crafting	Aimed at closing any performance gap between the firm's present situation (existing strategies and performance—what is) and desired strategies and performance (what should be). Moves the organization toward accomplishing its vision, mission, goals, and objectives.	3, 7
Strategy Implementation	A step in the strategic management conceptual model that considers how and what resources are required for formulated and crafted strategies to be carried out (executed). This step also determines who will be responsible for strategy execution and monitoring its effectiveness (strategic control).	3, 7
Strategic Plan	A well-crafted and reasoned document that moves the organization and its decisions in predetermined steps towards a specific desired or planned for conclusion.	1
Strategy Schools	Include the main strategic thinking, prevailing assumptions, theories, principles, frameworks, and analytical tools developed and applied by strategy scholars and experts to create and execute value creating strategies.	1
Strength	Organizational resources and capabilities that facilitate organizational purpose (goal achievement) by exploiting opportunities or negating threats. Strengths turned into core capabilities and distinctive competencies drive a firm's competitive advantage and performance.	3
Success Syndrome	A situation where prior successes are viewed by management as a sufficient proxy for future successes.	2
Supplier Power	Suppliers provide the inputs, such as raw material, parts and components, systems, networks, labor, services, and other factors that go into a firm's products or services. Supplier power is determined by the supplier's ability to influence or control buyer input prices.	4
Supply Chain	A system of organizations, people, technology, activities, information, and resources involved in moving a product or service from supplier to customer.	5
Supply Curve	Aggregate number of firms supplying products or services to customers.	4
Sustainability Business	Meeting the needs of the present without compromising the ability of future generations to meet their own needs. Sustainability is balancing a firm's economic, social, and environmental demands (e.g., profits, people, planet).	3
Sustaining Technology	An innovation or technology that advances a focal firm's existing product, service, and/or industry positioning (facilitates the firm's ability to compete).	4
SWOT	Acronym for determining (1) strengths and weaknesses in the firm's internal environment; and (2) opportunities and threats in a firm's external environment.	3
SWOT Analysis	A structured approach to evaluate the strengths, weaknesses, opportunities, and threats involved in a strategic decision regarding a new business model, product, service, process, project, business, etc.	3
Symptoms	Events or signs that signal something is wrong.	2

Term	Definition	Chapter
System	Set of detailed steps, actions, methods, procedures, and routines created to carry out a specific set of decisions.	1
Tangible Resources	Physical resources that can be quantified either by total number of units or by assigning a market or financial value to each tangible resource (e.g., plant and equipment, materials, inventory, financials, location, technology, distribution, warehouses, transportation, and physical and cyber networks).	5
Task Environment	Any factor or force in a firm's external and internal environment that is relevant or potentially relevant in facilitating or hindering the firm's strategies and goals. Stated in terms of: external opportunities and external threats.	3
Technical Learning	Defines and specifies the main elements, characteristics, and components of a newly crafted strategy (e.g., what it is, what its components are, and what differences and similarities exist among the current strategy(s) and the newly crafted strategy(s)).	7
Technology	Process by which strategic leaders' creatively transform labor, capital, materials, or information into new strategies, business models, products or services, processes, and activities aimed at creating customer value.	1
Telecommunications	Information technologies and telecommunications bridge temporal (time), physical (organizational), and spatial (distance) boundaries while extending the richness (quality) and reach (spread) of information.	6
Theory of Knowledge	A means to gather and analyze information with the end goal of converting information into knowledge.	1
Theory of Strategy	A construct of what actions and activities will improve future performance.	8
Threat	An external trend, condition, or factor that can potentially block or destroy an organization's competitive advantage and its ability to create value for customers.	3
Threat of New Entrants	The entry of new rivals into an existing industry is determined by the market's output profitability. Markets that yield high returns will attract new firms. This results in many new entrants which eventually decreases profitability for all firms in the industry unless existing rivals can block their entry.	4
Threat of Substitute Products	The existence of products or services that offer buyers (customers) a better value proposition outside the competitive markets or common market boundaries.	4
Top-down and Bottom-up Decision Making	A firm's decision process that involves input from all managers, subordinates, and stakeholders.	5
Transaction Costs	The cost associated with exchange of goods or services in the firm's value chain and incurred in overcoming market imperfections. Transaction costs cover a wide range: communication charges, legal fees, informational cost of finding the price, quality, and durability, etc., and may also include transportation costs.	1, see: Exhibit 1.1; and 5

Term	Definition	Chapter
Transactional Leadership	The idea that to be a leader you must have a follower. Leaders and followers approach one another with an eye toward exchanging something valued. The leader (CEO, manager, supervisor) and follower (subordinate, team, or department members) influence one another reciprocally so that each receives something of value. Leadership is contingent upon the leader's ability to satisfactorily meet and respond to the reactions and changing expectations of the followers.	8
Transformational Leadership	A type of leader that acts in accordance with deeply held value systems (e.g., justice and integrity). These values are end values—that is, values that cannot be negotiated. The transformational leader is able to raise the level of performance in the followers and change followers' goals and beliefs. The personal characteristics of the transformational leader include self-confidence, dominance, and a strong conviction in the moral righteousness of one's beliefs.	7
Transformational or Radical Change	Driven by radical technological innovation or shifts in the market and changes the very nature of the organization and business practices. Requires change in underlying strategies, culture, philosophies, values, mindsets, and other ways of doing business.	7
Transnational Strategy	Combines global configuration and coordination of business activities with local responsiveness and continued organizational learning.	8
Turnaround Strategy	A recommended strategy when a firm's business, products, or services still hold value (are profitable), but are experiencing poor performance in its market.	6
Unicorn Company	High growth, non-technology businesses are sometimes referred to as unicorns, because they are so rare in number.	8
Value	The amount a buyer is willing to pay for a firm's product or service.	5
Value Chain	The interlinked value-adding activities that convert a firm's inputs into outputs, which in turn add to the firm's top line (revenues) and bottom line (profitability).	1
Value Chain Infographic	Describes a firm's activities and processes along with trade-offs in costs or effectiveness among the various linkages (e.g., its transaction costs or costs of doing business). A value chain can be depicted as infographic that illustrates how and where a firm can extract value from these activities and processes.	5
Value Chain Analysis	Involves an examination of a firm's cost of doing business.	5
Value Proposition	The mix of goods and services, price and payment terms, and other amenities offered by the firm to its customers.	2
Values	Beliefs that legitimize one's behavior.	3
Vertically Integrated	Firms may be fully or partially vertically integrated backwards (that is, they make all or some of the components that go into the manufacture of a product), or are vertically integrated forward by selling directly to buyers instead of through an intermediary (big box stores, retailers, resellers, etc.).	6
VIRO	Acronym outlining dynamic capabilities that serve as a source for creating a sustaining a firm's competitive advantage: **V**aluable, **I**mitable, **R**are, **O**rganizational.	5

Term	Definition	Chapter
VIRO: Imitable Test	Determined by the question: Is there organizational causal ambiguity that hinders rivals' understanding of how the resources are linked to competitive advantage, thereby making it hard and costly for rivals to copy?	5
VIRO: Organization Test	Determined by the question: Are the resources dynamic and flexible? That is, are they adaptable and lasting with changing market dynamics and conditions?	5
VIRO: Rarity Test	Determined by the question: Is there organizational social complexity that could be related to organizational cultural attributes that facilitate competitive advantage? That is, are they so rare and unique they can not be easily substituted for with other resources?	5
VIRO: Value Test	Determined by the question: Are there special historical conditions or factors that lead to acquisition of tangible and intangible resources that provide unique value customers?	5
Vision Statement	captures the long-term direction and purpose of a company. Also implies a common thread or unifying theme that remains unchanged over time. Outlines long-term end values, core purpose, and customer focus.	3
Weakness	Resource limitations or lack of know-how (capabilities) that can prevent a firm from achieving the organization's purpose as well as creating and sustaining a competitive advantage.	3
Wisdom	The creative use of knowledge; what we know to be true.	1

CPSIA information can be obtained
at www.ICGtesting.com
Printed in the USA
LVHW06s1053110918
589706LV00003B/50/P

9 781516 525669